Psychology and Criminal Justice

Publications of the European Association of Psychology and Law
Series editors: David P. Farrington and Friedrich Lösel

Psychology and Criminal Justice

International Review of Theory and Practice

Edited by

János Boros
Iván Münnich
Márton Szegedi

Walter de Gruyter · Berlin · New York 1998

Prof. *János Boros*, Head of Department of Research and International Relations, Ministry of Justice, Budapest, Hungary

Prof. *Iván Münnich*, Head of Department of Psychology, National Institution of Criminology, Budapest, Hungary

Prof. *Márton Szegedi*, Psychiatric Clinic, Semmelweis Medical University, Budapest, Hungary

With 82 tables and 26 figures

∞ Printed on acid-free paper which falls within the guidelines of the ANSI to ensure permanence and durability.

Library of Congress Cataloging-in-Publication Data

Psychology and criminal justice : international review of theory and practice / edited by János Boros, Iván Münnich, Márton Szegedi

p. cm. – (Publications of the European Association of Psychology and Law)

Papers presented at the 5th Conference of the European Association of Psychology and Law, held in Budapest in 1995.

Includes bibliographical references and index.

ISBN 3-11-016329-2 (alk. paper)

1. Criminal justice. Administration of–Psychological aspects–Congresses. 2. Criminal psychology–Congresses. I. Boros, János. II. Münnich, Iván. III. Szegedi, Márton. IV. European Association of Psychology and Law. Conference (5th : 1995 : Budapest, Hungary) V. Series.

HV7243.P78 1998

364'.01'9–dc21 98-36246

CIP

Die Deutsche Bibliothek – CIP-Einheitsaufnahme

Psychology and criminal justice : international review of theory and practice / ed. by János Boros ... – Berlin ; New York : de Gruyter, 1998

ISBN 3-11-016329-2

Technical Editor and Desktop Publishing: Vince Huszár, Budapest. – Printing and Binding: WB-Druck GmbH, Rieden am Forggensee. – Cover Design: Johannes Rother, Berlin. – Printed in Germany.

Preface

Between 30 August and 2 September 1995 the European Association of Psychology and Law organised its fifth Conference in Budapest with the participation of more than two hundred delegates from 28 countries. We were delighted that the countries of Central and Eastern Europe were impressively represented: 79 delegates from 12 of these countries were active participants in the programmes, and 28 of them presented lectures in their specific sections.

The 50 articles included in this volume are made up of the 5 keynote addresses delivered at the Conference, and a selection from the 129 papers and 8 posters discussed in the 25 workshops.

The members of the Organising Committee (Júlia Benedek, János Boros/Chair, Ferenc Deák, László Huszár, Iván Münnich, Eszter Szalma, Márton Szegedi, Mária Vörös) owe a debt of gratitude to all the people and organisations who gave their support to the Conference and to the preparation of this book.

We wish to thank the Executive Committee of the EAPL for granting Hungary the privilege of hosting the Conference and for their extensive help in its preparation and organisation. Personal thanks go especially to President Friedrich Lösel for presenting the opening and closing addresses. Sincere thanks also and our appreciation to Professor Lösel and the Volkswagen Foundation for making it possible to organise a small but intimate meeting after the Conference where psychologists from Central and Eastern Europe met and were able to make contributions who had not had the opportunity to do so at the Conference itself.

We received significant assistance from the Hungarian Prison Administration of the Ministry of Justice and from the Psychiatric Clinic of the Semmelweis Medical University. Director-General Ferenc Tari of the Hungarian Prison Administration gave indispensable support by making provisions for the accommodation, catering and transportation of the participants, by arranging the welcome reception, by providing facilities for the subsequent seminary, board and lodging for its participants from Germany and Eastern Europe, and by making it possible for the Department of Research and International Relations to take the lion's share of the preparation and organisation. His support to the preparation of this volume was also essential.

We would like to thank Professor László Tringer, who opened the Conference and provided both the premises and the staff necessary for the success of the workshops.

We are also grateful to Judit Csiha, the then State Secretary of the Ministry of Justice for her welcome address and for the farewell reception.

We wish to thank the Patron of the Conference Pál Vastagh, Minister of Justice, the Advisory Board (István Czigler, Kálmán Györgyi, Sándor Pintér, László Pusztai†, Pál Solt, Péter Sótonyi, András Szabó, László Tringer, Ferenc Tari), the Programme Committee (Márton Szegedi/Chair, Iván Münnich, János Boros, Friedrich Lösel, Graham Davies, Vincente Garrido, Dick J. Hessing, Peter van Koppen, Sally Lloyd-Bostock, Santiago Illescas Redondo, Giovanni-Battista Traverso), our invited speakers (Endre Bócz, Graham Davies, Jess Maghan, Márton Szegedi, Richard Tremblay), and all those who have contributed to this volume.

Thanks to Judith Finn for proofreading and to Éva Pásztor for the organisation and liaising with the Publishers. It has been great pleasure for us to co-operate with Bianka Ralle and her colleagues during the editing process. Special appreciation to Vince Huszár, who joined the Editing Committee in the tedious and demanding concluding phase; we are most grateful for his contribution to the translations and for his conscientious and accurate work in bringing the book in line with the high standards of Walter de Gruyter & Co.

The Editors

Contents

Preface V

Introduction
János Boros, Iván Münnich and Márton Szegedi XIII

Contributors XIX

Part 1: Children as Witnesses

Videotechnology and the Child Witness
Graham Davies 3

Explaining Conversation Rules as a Method to Reduce Suggestibility of the Child Witness
Aldert Vrij, Marianne R. Mulder and Julie Cherryman 10

Interviewing Children: The Importance of Omission Errors
Graeme Hutcheson, James S. Baxter, Karen S. Telfer and David Warden ... 20

The Defence Mechanisms and the Deformations of the Testimony Given by Sexually Abused Juveniles
Teresa Jaskiewicz-Obydzinska 33

Part 2: Cognitive Interview and Police Reaction

Further Perspectives in Cognitive Interviewing: New Directions
Elizabeth Noon and Julian Boon 47

The Effects of the Cognitive Interview on Recall, Recognition and the Confidence/Accuracy Relationship
Patrick Gwyer, Brian R. Clifford and Barbara Dritschel 53

Cognitive Interview: When Any Context Reinstatement Instruction is Successful
Laura Campos and Marisa Alonso-Quecuty 61

Cognitive Interview: Confronting True and False Statements
Estefania Hernandez-Fernaud and Marisa Alonso-Quecuty 67

Perceptions of the Credibility and Evidential Value of Victim and Suspect Statements in Interviews
Anna Costanza Baldry and Frans Willem Winkel 74

Police Officers' Inadequate Impression Formation in Confrontations with Offenders as a Result of Physical Effort
Aldert Vrij 82

Police Folklore and Attributions of Guilt: Can Psychology Challenge Long Held Assumptions?
Peter B. Ainsworth 94

Part 3: Judicial Decision-Making

State of Ohio v. X: Science and Strategy in the Criminal Court
Sandra B. McPherson and Jay Milano 103

Impact on Verdict of Gender Homogeneous Juries in a Case of Rape
Ramón Arce, Francisca Fariña, Mercedes Novo and Santiago Real 113

Judicial Decision Making: Information Processing and Judgements Given by Blind Subjects
Emilia I. De la Fuente, Juan García and José A. Belmonte 120

Polygraphs in Criminal Justice Systems: The Effect of Different Legal Cultures on the Use of Scientific Evidence
Petra van Kampen 130

The Jury Decision Rule: An Empirical Study of Four Methods
Ramón Arce, Francisca Fariña, Carlos Vila and Mercedes Novo 152

Juror's Decision in Capital Cases
Vladimir Konečni 160

Parents Fighting for Custody of Children
Alicja Czerederecka 188

Part 4: Characteristics and Therapy of Offenders

Boys' Behavioral Patterns in Kindergarten Predict Male Delinquency, Withdrawal, and School Adjustment
Richard E. Tremblay and Jaana Haapasalo 197

Assessing Loss of Self-Control in Violent Offences Committed by Juveniles
James McGuire 212

Social Competence and Sociomoral Reasoning in Young Offenders
Emma J. Palmer 222

Feminist Group Therapy for Women Who Self-Harm
Helen Liebling and Hazel Chipchase 229

Heterogeneity of Murders as the Fundamental Problem in the Psychological Profiling of a Perpetrator
Józef K. Gierowski, Teresa Jaskiewicz-Obydzinska and Maciej Szaszkiewicz 237

Necrophilia: Love at Last Sight
Philip D. Jaffé 242

Are Causal Theories of Paedophilia Possible? A Reconsideration of Sexual Abuse Cycles
Dennis Howitt 248

Expert Psychological Opinion for the Court in Cases of Homicide under Emotional Strain in Poland
Jan M. Stanik 254

The Problem of Depression's Diagnostic in Forensic and Civil Law in Women
Evgenia V. Korolova 262

Part 5: Prison and Offender Research

Effects of Prison Factors on Recidivism
János Boros 269

Prison Between Values and Efficiency
Dragan Petrovec 278

Symbolic Patterns in Prisoners' Thinking: Imported Values and Indigenous Roles?
László Huszár 287

Allowing Male Convicted Prisoners to Wear Their Own Clothes: The Psychological Effects
Peter Marshall 293

A Harm Reduction Approach to the Depenalization of Drug Crime via Community Based Outpatient Treatment
Brian McKenna and Michael Smith 301

Interplay of Religion, Medicine and Prison: A Preliminary Historical Study
Roberts Girgensons 310

International Benchmarking
Cynthia McDougall and John Powls 315

Training of Prison Officers for Leading Problem-Oriented Groups of Inmates
Bernhard Wydra 319

Riots in the Romanian Penitentiaries after the Revolution of December 1989
Georghe Florian 322

Correctional Treatment in Portugal
Rui Abrunhosa Gonçalves 327

Part 6: Crime and the Public

Terrorist Mentality
Jess Maghan 335

Fear of Crime and Victimization
Helmut Kury 346

The Social and Personal Influence of Positive Beliefs on Coping with Direct and Indirect Victimization
Adriaan Denkers and Frans Willem Winkel 354

Psychological Aspects of the Process of Victimization
Juan Horacio Del Popolo and Stella M. Spezia 366

Victim–Offender Mediation in the Italian Juvenile Justice System:
A First Attempt of Definition
Anna Costanza Baldry, Gaetano De Leo and Gilda Scardaccione 377

The Impact of Professional Roles on Subjective Explanations of
Juvenile Delinquency
Mechthild Averbeck and Friedrich Lösel 385

Turning Heroes into Villains: The Role of Unconscious Transference in
Media Crime Reporting
Peter B. Ainsworth 399

Part 7: History and Perspectives of Law and Psychology

Comparing Legal Cultures: Difficulties in the Cross-Cultural Applicability
of Psychological Research Results
Johannes F. Nijboer 407

Recent Changes of the Hungarian Legal System and Their Psychological
Impact
Endre Bócz 411

The Effects of the Guarantee System of Human Rights and Legality
on the Delinquents
György Vókó 422

Legal Psychology in Europe: Results of a Survey
Helmut Kury 428

Difficulties Experienced in Conducting Research in Forensic Psychology
Janet Clare Wilson and Elizabeth Noon 436

The Development of Hungarian Forensic Psychology
Márton Szegedi 441

Subject Index 457

Introduction

János Boros, Iván Münnich and Márton Szegedi

At the end of the summer of 1995 the European Association of Psychology and Law organised its fifth scientific conference in Budapest, this being the first time a country of the Central-Eastern European region has acted as host.

This decision, which emancipated the region's achievements in legal psychology and effectively integrated psychologists working in Central and Eastern Europe, had been preceded by a long period of development. The Introduction chapters of the Nürnberg and the Oxford conference volumes provide a most expressive description of the period preceding and following the first conference in Maastricht in 1988, and are very important documents both of the development of legal psychology and of the foundation of the Association signifying the institutionalisation of legal psychology.

During this period a number of efforts were made at the national and international level at establishing a forum for the experts working in the field of legal psychology in a wider sense, where they can demonstrate their research results, discuss the theoretical and practical problems encountered, and work out effective ways of putting their research findings into practice. Since 1988 there has been an expressed need for regular international conferences.

At the 1990 Nürnberg Conference the present content and structure of European Law and Psychology Conferences were established. Witness testimony and police interrogation of suspects, decision-making in courts, the role of the court expert, the assessment of offenders, correctional treatment, prison psychology, the development and perspectives of legal psychology became traditional topics of prime concern. The formal structure of the conferences also became institutionalised: in between the opening and the closing ceremony there are comprehensive lectures delivered at plenary sessions which are followed by meetings of 6–8 concurrent workshops. At the Oxford Conference in 1992 the European Association of Psychology and Law was formally inaugurated and started functioning as a scientific association, with a membership, a charter, a general assembly, a president and an executive committee. In Barcelona, 1994, the General Assembly made an important decision: the EAPL Conferences would be organised not bi-annually but annually.

The first conference of the new arrangement was organised in Budapest in 1995. One reason for this choice was the increased activity since 1990 of Hungarian legal psychologists within the Association. Another reason was the organisational and infrastructural capacity offered by the Hungarian Prison Administration and its Department for Research and International Relations, proven in several well-received international conferences in cooperation with the Council of Europe and other organisations.

The Budapest Conference justified the decision. The one-year period proved to be adequate both for the organisers and the participants, it was ample time to make the appropriate arrangements and to prepare stimulating and captivating lectures. The higher representation of Central and Eastern European psychologists was an additional piquancy of the Budapest event: nearly a quarter of the contributions were made by regional experts. This happened in full compliance with the intentions of the Executive Committee which chose Budapest with the expressed aim of promoting and integrating Central and Eastern European psychologists. For more than 30 of these delegates the Organising Committee and the Volkswagen Foundation supported participation and funded an additional German–East European Symposium on Psychology and Law at Pilisszentkereszt. A selection of the papers presented at this satellite meeting is included in the present volume.

The interest invoked by the EAPL Conference highlighted the soundness of the decision of the Executive Committee. 28 countries from 3 continents were represented. It was also important that the Conference inspired experts from most of the countries in Central and Eastern Europe.

About 150 lectures were delivered at the Conference. This volume contains an edited selection of 50 papers. The contributions have been grouped around seven themes. The reader will find 3 types of articles in this volume. The first category includes the somewhat longer and more comprehensive overviews of topics as presented by the invited speakers. The second group comprises some shorter but practical presentations of topical issues (as, for instance, some of the East European contributions) or papers highlighting interrelations and regularities through interesting case analyses. The third group of articles, into which most of the papers belong, incorporate the so-called 'lege artis' studies.

Let us give an overview of the main themes covered in the seven parts of the book, although no attempt is made to summarise all the published papers.

Part 1 bears the title *Children as Witnesses*. The documents of the previous conferences indicate that testimony psychology is one of the best established and most fruitful areas of legal psychology. This is especially true in the case of child witnesses, whose credibility has quite frequently been questioned in traditional court procedures. It is undeniable that due to the stress invoked by police investigation and court hearings the interrogation of the child witness, especially when he is also a suspect, necessitates techniques that lessen the tension in the child without harming the content of the testimony. The first article addresses this problem, and at the same time gives an example of how scientific research can influence legislation, in this specific case the legal acceptance of witness testimony recorded on video tapes, and how jurisdiction uses researchers to test the efficacy of the new method. The findings reveal that the application of video-technology does not diminish the effectiveness of the testimony as compared to personal interviews. Other important issues addressed in Part 1 are open questions, the application of specific questions in general context, and the role of defence mechanisms in the testimony given by sexually abused juveniles.

Part 2 is closely interrelated with the first theme and deals with the *Cognitive Interview and Police Reaction*. Combining the two areas under one title is justified by the role of police apparent in both. The Cognitive Interview is a gift for police interrogators presented by legal psychology. The effectiveness of this approach, introduced by Fisher and Geiselman, is significantly higher than that of the standard interviewing techniques traditionally used by the police. Furthermore, it is easy to learn and easy to integrate into police training programmes. With the help of the Cognitive Interview we may obtain more information from the witnesses, but the amount of inaccurate information and confabulation might also increase. Part 2 also contains convincing research findings with regard to techniques of reducing false statements. In addition, there is an interesting coverage of the cross-cultural approach to the differing police perceptions in different countries, reactions of the police in an emergency and the traditional 'police folklore' which is to be challenged by psychologists if they wish to have their new methods accepted.

Part 3 is devoted to *Judicial Decision-Making*. As in previous conferences, research on the psychological problems related to the functioning of juries remains highly popular. Although formerly this theme had been a traditional research territory of British and American experts (as they represent countries where juries traditionally function), it seems to have become a major area of concern for Spanish experts, who author most of the papers on juries in this volume. There are interesting articles in sub-categories like the role of the gender of jurors in the predictability of biased verdicts in cases of rape, information processing and judgements given by normal and blind subjects. Serious consideration is given to the study of the cost-effectiveness and time-efficiency of smaller juries and majority decision rule as opposed to unanimity. An American study focuses on jury selection and functioning in potential capital cases, and presents an attitude scale to measure scruples to death penalty. There is an article on how the legal culture of a given country determines the application of the polygraph, plus a topic outside the realm of the criminal court on the fight of divorcing parents for custody of their children.

Characteristics and Therapy of Offenders is a highly popular theme of Law and Psychology Conferences, to a great extent due to the diversity in research fields and applied methods. Apart from being interesting, this area, too, demonstrates notable practical assets: exploring the personality traits and motivations of offenders may contribute to the drawing up of successful short-term and long-term crime prevention programmes. Part 4 starts with a less highlighted although important topic: to what extent can behaviour in kindergarten become a predictive factor for adult crime. Two papers address juvenile crime, one of them examines the social competence of juvenile offenders and ways of improving their social reasoning, the other presumes that in some cases the loss of self-control accounts for violent juvenile crime and offers Anger Control Training as a remedy, attaching great importance to the interaction and cooperation between researchers and practitioners. There are two articles on murderers. One of them explores the role of expert psychological opinion for the court in cases of murder committed under emotional strain, the other focuses on the difficulties encountered in the psychological profiling of the perpetrator. The paper on group therapy for women who self-harm and another one on the difficulties in diagnosing depression represent interesting contributions. Part 4 also addresses two special areas of sexual offending: paedophilia and necrophilia.

Part 5 comprises accounts in *Prison and Offender Research.* In view of previous experience and the papers included in this section it is perhaps not an exaggeration to say that prison psychology is one of the most dynamically developing areas of legal psychology. This section contains the biggest number of articles, and we found it especially pleasing that half of the authors are from Eastern Europe. Thus the reader can compare the peculiarities of the prison systems in Hungary, Slovenia, England, Latvia, Romania and Portugal. In addition, one of the papers examines the possibility of alternative measures to replace incarceration for drug related offenders. A German author introduces a system of training volunteers in leading problem-solving groups of inmates in Bavarian prisons. There is also an interesting article on international benchmarking, which is aimed at comparing, analysing and enhancing the prison systems in the particular countries.

Part 6 under the heading *Crime and the Public* is made up of two sub-categories. One set of articles concentrates on the psychological aspect of victimisation, whereas the other group of papers focuses on the public perception of crime and its coverage in the mass media. The first paper in this section gives an analysis of the social, economic, religious, and psychological background of the terrorist mentality. The theme of victimisation embraces both the aspects of the fear of crime and of becoming a victim, the role of the victim's partner in processing the tensions of the victim, and the psychological analysis of the process of victimisation. One paper relates positive experiences in Italy of victim–offender mediation without the setting up of specific organisations. A German paper reveals that professional socialisation is an essential component of the explanation for juvenile crime and criminal attitudes. Finally, an article highlights the influence of the media on witness errors in identifying offenders.

The last section, Part 7, bears the title *History and Perspectives of Law and Psychology*. Again, this section involves two major themes: one is legal psychology and the diversity of the legal environment in the European countries, the other is the history and development of legal psychology in Europe. The articles also help in understanding how history determined the peculiarities of the present system, and also the problem-specific sensitivity, the preferences to certain methods and strategies of the researchers working in the countries of Central and Eastern Europe.

In conclusion, the Budapest Conference was an important milestone in the development of Psychology and Law in Europe and the authors offer valuable contributions to the literature of the discipline.

Contributors

Ainsworth, Peter B., School of Social Policy, University of Manchester, Manchester M13 9PL, England
Alonso-Quecuty, Marisa, Department of Cognitive Psychology, Faculty of Psychology, University of La Laguna, Campus de Guajara, Tenerife, Spain
Arce, Ramón, Faculty of Psychology, University of Santiago de Compostela, 15706 Santiago, Spain
Averbeck, Mechthild, Institut für Psychologie I, Universität Erlangen-Nürnberg, Bismarckstraße 1, 91054 Erlangen, Germany
Baldry, Anna Costanza, Department of Social and Developmental Psychology, Faculty of Psychology, University of Rome La Sapienza, I – via dei Marsi, 78, 00185 Rome, Italy
Baxter, James S., Department of Psychology, Strathclyde University, Glasgow GI 1RD, Scotland
Belmonte, José A., Organización Nacional de Ciegos Españoles, Plaza del Carmen, 18009 Granada, Spain
Bócz, Endre, Office of the Attorney General of Budapest, 1055 Budapest, Markó u. 27, Hungary
Boon, Julian, University of Leicester, University Rd, Leicester, LE1 7RH, England
Boros, János, National Prison Administration, 1054 Budapest, Steindl u. 8, Hungary
Campos, Laura, Department of Cognitive Psychology, Faculty of Psychology, University of La Laguna, Tenerife, Spain
Cherryman, Julie, Department of Human Communication, De Montfort University, Scraptoft Campus, Scraptoft, Leicester, LE7 9SU, England
Chipchase, Hazel, University of Liverpool, Liverpool L69 3BX, England
Clifford, Brian. R., Department of Psychology, University of East London, The Green, Stratford, London E15 4LZ, England
Czerederecka, Alicja, Institute of Forensic Research, ul. Westerplatte 9, 31–033 Krakow, Poland
Davies, Graham, Department of Psychology, University of Leicester, University Rd, Leicester LE1 7RH, England
De Leo, Gaetano, Department of Social and Developmental Psychology, Faculty of Psychology, University of Rome 'La Sapienza', I – via dei Marsi, 78, 00185 Rome, Italy

De la Fuente, Emilia I., Dpto. de Psicología Social y Metología, Facultad de Psicologia, Universidad de Granada, 18071 Granada, Spain

Del Popolo, Juan Horacio, Universidad Aconcagus, 4/10 Mendoza 5500, Argentina

Denkers, Adriaan, Department of Social Psychology, Vrije Universiteit of Amsterdam, De Boelelaan 1081, 1081 HV Amsterdam, The Netherlands

Dritschel, Barbara, Department of Psychology, University of East London, The Green, Stratford, London E15 4LZ, England

Fariña, Francisca, Faculty of Social Sciences, University of Vigo, r/Sierra 40, 36002 Pontevedra, Spain

Florian, Georghe, Ministerul Justitiei, Directia Generalá A Penitencialeror, Str. Maria Ghiculesea 47, 77228 Bucuresti, sector 2, Romania

García, Juan, Dpto de Filosofía Metodología Psicología Social y Pedagogía, Facultad de Humanidades, Universidad de Almería, Almería, Spain

Gierowski, Józef K., Department of Social Pathology, Collegium Medicum, Jagellonian University, ul. Kopernika 21, 31-42 Krakow, Poland

Girgensons, Roberts, Brivibas 215-B-6, Riga, LV –1039, Latvia

Gonçalves, Rui Abrunhosa, University of Minho, Braga, Portugal

Gwyer, Patrick, Department of Psychology, University of East London, The Green, Stratford, London E15 4LZ, England

Haapasalo, Jaana, Department of Psychology, University of Jyväskylä, SF-40351 Jyväskylä, Finland

Hernandez-Fernaud, Estefania, Department of Cognitive Psychology, Faculty of Psychology, University of La Laguna, Campus de Guajara, Tenerife, Spain

Howitt, Dennis, Department of Social Sciences, Loughborough University, Loughborough, Leicestershire, LE11 3TU, England

Huszár, László, National Prison Administration, 1054 Budapest, Steindl u. 8, Hungary

Hutcheson, Graeme, Social Science Methodology Unit, Adam Smith Building, Glasgow University, Glasgow G12 8RT, Scotland

Jaffé, Philip D., Faculty of Psychology and Education Sciences and Institute of Legal Medicine, University of Geneva, Switzerland

Jaskiewicz-Obydzinska, Teresa, Institute of Forensic Research, ul. Westerplatte 9, 31-033 Krakow, Poland

Konečni, Vladimir, Department of Psychology, University of California, San Diego, La Jolla, California 92093, USA

Korolova, Evgenia V., Serbsky National Research Centre for Social and Forensic Psychiatry, ul. Tolstogo 22/2-155, 103001 Moscow, Russia

Kury, Helmut, Max Planck Institute, Günterstalstrasse 73, Freiburg 79100, Germany

Liebling, Helen, Ashworth Hospital, Parkboum, Maghull, Merseyside, L31 1HW, England

Lösel, Friedrich, Institut für Psychologie I, Universität Erlangen-Nürnberg, Bismarckstraße 1, 91054 Erlangen, Germany

Maghan, Jess, Center for Research in Law and Justice, College of Liberal Arts and Sciences, 400 South Peoria Street, Chicago, Illinois 60607-7035, USA

Marshall, Peter, Home Office, Cleland House, Page Street, London SW1P 4LN, England

McDougall, Cynthia, HM Prison Service Headquarters, Cleland House, Page Street, London SW1P 4LN, England

McGuire, James, University of Liverpool, Department of Clinical Psychology, Whelan Building, The Quadrangle, Liverpool L69 3GB, England

McKenna, Brian, ICAAT-Hungary, 1073 Budapest, Erzsébet krt. 39. III/4, Hungary

McPherson, Sandra B., 12434 Cedar Road, Cleveland Heights, Ohio 44106, USA

Milano, Jay, 2639 Wooster Road, Rocky River, Ohio 44 116

Mulder, Marianne R., Free University, Department of Social Psychology, De Boelelaan 1081c, 1081 HV Amsterdam, The Netherlands

Nijboer, Johannes F., Leiden University, Galgewater, Leiden 2311V2, The Netherlands

Noon, Elizabeth, Department of Human Communication, De Montfort University, Scraptoft Campus, Leicester LE7 9SU, England

Novo, Mercedes, Faculty of Psychology, University of Santiago de Compostela, 15706 Santiago, Spain

Palmer, Emma J., School of Psychology, University of Birmingham, Edgbaston, Birmingham, B15 2TT, England

Petrovec, Dragan, Institute of Criminology, Maroltova 10, 61000 Ljubljana, Slovenia

Powls, John, HM Prison Service Headquarters, Cleland House, Page Street, London SW1P 4LN, England

Real, Santiago, Faculty of Psychology, University of Santiago de Compostela, 15706 Santiago, Spain

Scardaccione, Gilda, Department of Psychological Medicine, University of Rome 'La Sapienza', I – via dei Marsi, 78, 00185 Rome, Italy

Smith, Michael, ICAAT-Hungary, 1073 Budapest, Erzsébet krt. 39. III/4, Hungary

Spezia, Stella M., Universidad Aconcagus, 4/10 Mendoza 5500, Argentina

Stanik, Jan M., Department of Clinical Psychology, University of Silesia, ul. Tyszki 53, 40-126 Katowice, Poland

Szaszkiewicz, Maciej, Institute of Forensic Research, u. Westerplatte 9, 31-033 Krakow, Poland

Szegedi, Márton, Psychiatric Clinic, Semmelweis Medical University, 1083 Budapest, Balassa u. 6.

Telfer, Karen S., Department of Psychology, Strathclyde University, Glasgow, England

Tremblay, Richard E., Université de Montréal, GRIP, 3500 Edouard-Montpetit, C.P. 6128, Succ. Centre-Ville, Montréal, Quebec, H3C 3J7, Canada

Van Kampen, Petra, Leiden Institute for Law and Public Policy, Herengracht 48, Leiden 2312LE, The Netherlands

Vila, Carlos, Faculty of Psychology, University of Santiago de Compostela, 15706 Santiago, Spain

Vókó, György, Office of the Attorney General of Hungary, 1055 Budapest, Markó u. 27, Hungary

Vrij, Aldert, University of Portsmouth, Department of Psychology, King Charles Street, Portsmouth PO1 2ER, England

Warden, David, Department of Psychology, Strathclyde University, Glasgow GI 1RD, Scotland

Wilson, Janet Clare, Psychology Department, Leicester University, Leicester LE1 7RH, England

Winkel, Frans Willem, Department of Social Psychology, Vrije Universiteit of Amsterdam, De Boelelaan 1081, 1081 HV Amsterdam, The Netherlands

Wydra, Bernhard, Bayerische Justizvollzugschule, Aussere Passauerstraße 188, Straubing, Germany

Part 1
Children as Witnesses

Videotechnology and the Child Witness

Graham Davies

In England and Wales, the laws governing the treatment of child witnesses and their evidence have changed radically in the last decade. These changes have been dictated partly by the increase in awareness of child's sexual and physical abuse and partly by psychological research which has undermined the traditional legal view of the child witness as unreliable and infinitely gullible (see Davies, 1991; Spencer & Flin, 1993 for reviews). This change in perspective was reflected in Criminal Justice Acts which progressively dismantled the traditional legal obstacles to hearing of children's evidence. The competency test, the corrobation rule and the special caution regarding the evidence of minors have all been swept aside in England and Wales. The 1993 Criminal Justice Act and Public Order Act reiterated the new view that the courts should normally be prepared to listen to the evidence of children but it is up to the jury to decide what weight to attach to it.

These parliamentary acts have also brought in procedural changes designed to make the tendering of evidence less stressful for the child. Research on children's fears at court have consistently demonstrated that fears of giving evidence in front of the accused and the alien nature of courtroom procedures are major concerns among prospective witnesses. The 1988 act introduced the "Live Link" into the United Kingdom; a form of closed circuit television which permits children to be seated in a small room adjacent to the courtroom and to be examined and cross-examined by counsel stationed in the courtroom. An evaluation of the effectiveness of the system was conducted by Davies and Noon (1991). A survey of the opinions of judges and barristers who had practised experience of the system suggested widespread acceptance of its effectiveness in reducing stress among juvenile witnesses, and also in improving the quality of evidence. The idea that increased stress is associated with problems of retrieving information from memory will be a familiar one to all amateur actors (or expert witnesses!) and has received support from experimental research (Saywitz & Nathanson, 1993). As a result of these positive findings, the live link is now available in over half of the Crown Court Centres in England and Wales and will shortly be available in all major Scottish cities (Murray, 1995).

However, the system was not without its critics who were concerned that evidence presented via television would have less impact than live testimony. As one QC claimed, "Even though the child is in the other room, the idea of television removes the reality". It is this negative view of the "Live Link" which seems to have dominated many court centres. According to Plotnikoff and Woolfson (1995), when protection from the accused is offered to the child, the use of screens is still more common than the "Live Link" whose usage in England and Wales is reported to have dropped from 128 cases in 1990 to just 91 in 1992. The use of screens as a device to obscure the accused from the child in court remains haphazard and unregulated and in terms of their impact on children' demeanour and quality of evidence produce results midway between the "Live Link" and testifying in open court.

The 1991 Criminal Justice Act introduced a further extension of the use of videotechnology to assist the courts in hearing children's evidence: the admission of video-recorded interviews as evidence for a range of offences involving physical and sexual assaults. At the discretion of the judge, the prosecution could substitute for live examination at court a videotaped interview conducted by a police officer and for social worker which explored the allegations made by the child. The child would, however, still have to be present live at court for cross-examination by the defence and any re-examination by the prosecution.

The proposal in the Act stemmed from the recommendations of the in 1989 which had endorsed the introduction of tape recorded interviews as a more satisfactory way of gathering and hearing evidence from juveniles. These interviews, it was agreed, would record in the child's own words a vivid and contemporaneous account of the allegations, untarnished by the passage of time. Such interviews would avoid the need for multiple interviews and permit the badly traumatised child to receive some form of therapy between the interview and any trial, obviating any allegation of coaching or contamination. Pigot also suggested that video recording could be extended to the defence cross-examination which might be conducted prior to trial in an informal setting in the presence of the judge and the child's own legal representative, thus avoiding the need to appear in court at all. However, the Home Office rejected this radical extension despite extensive support within the legal and child care professions (Spencer 1991).

The Home Office did, however, recognise the need identified by Pigot for some rules of guidance as to how the recorded interviews were to be conducted. As Pigot noted, such interviews were both investigatory and evidential and it was essential that the form of questioning employed should be in accord with those acceptable to a court of law. In 1992, the Home Office, in conjunction with the Department of Health published the Memorandum of Good Practice, which summarised the findings of an enquiry by a psychologist and lawyer into the best practice and the recommendations of a working party of concerned professionals. The Memorandum advocated that as far as possible, children should tell their own story and that leading questions and other suggestive procedures should only be used as a last resort. The publication also included guidance on legal matters and technical detail designed to ensure that the interview was of a quality suitable for court.

When the legislation came into force in October 1992, the Home Office commissioned an evaluation of the new procedure from a team at Leicester University (Davies, Wilson, Mitchell & Milsom, 1995). The evaluation covered the views of users, which were sampled at the time of the introduction of taped interviews and again some 18 months later when users had had practical experience of legislation. Observation was also undertaken in courts where children gave evidence using both traditional and new procedures, and their performance was evaluated by means of rating scales. In addition, the team received the full co-operation of the police and Lord Chancellor's Department in establishing the frequency and outcome of trials under the new procedures.

The Act was subject to "rolling implementation"; different regions began making recordings at different times, once trained staff and the necessary taping equipment became available. It was evident from the earliest days that some police forces and social work departments embraced the new legislation with enthusiasm, whereas others hung back. Butler (1993) conducted a survey of county police authorities in the first six months of the Act. This revealed that in that period, some 14,912 tape recorded interviews had taken place with children which had results in approximately one in four being referred to the Crown Prosecution Service for further action. However, these figures revealed widespread variation between different forces, both in the number of interviews undertaken and in the proportion of interviews leading to further action.

Such figures suggest considerable ambiguity over what circumstances and when video interviews should be conducted. Some police forces appeared to be routinely interviewing all witnesses falling within the Act, whereas others seemed to be more selective over who was interviewed and when. The decision over the precise moment to interview remains fraught with difficulty. Interviewing too early risks a child minimising an allegation or refusing to disclose any information because trust and rapport are insufficiently established. Leaving an interview to a later stage may provoke an allegation from the defence that the child's testimony has been irredeemably contaminated by the investigative process. This issue has remained a source of concern throughout the lifetime of legislation.

When Butler conducted his survey in June 1993, just 152 applications had been made to show video recordings in court and only 44 had actually been shown. These figures inevitably gave rise to concerns that a massive diversion or recourses had occurred to very little purpose. These figures, however, do not tell the complete story. The number of video applications has shown a steady rise from a rather uncertain beginning. Figures from the Lord Chancellor's Department show that between October 1992 and April 1994, there were some 1199 trials relating to charges under the Act of which 640 or 53% were accompanied by applications to show videotapes. Moreover this average figure conceals a steady increase in the proportion of cases in which video applications were made; by June it had reached 75% of all cases considered in that month.

Nonetheless, critics of the legislation will point to the small number of videos actually shown in court. Throughout the 18 months from October 1992, only 202 were known to have been shown. However, these figures should also be examined carefully. Does this mean judges were refusing applications? No, our best estimate is that only 15% of video recordings were turned down by judges for which poor technical quality was the most frequent cause. The principle reasons for the discrepancy between applications made and videos shown are twofold. Late guilty pleas by the accused which obviate the need to pursue a case further (see below) and last minute changes in courtroom tactics by prosecuting counsel.

The child's barrister may well change between the time of application to show a video being made and a case coming to trial. His or her new representative may decide on the day of the trial to interview the child live at court, because they believe this will have a greater impact on the jury. Such late changes of opinion can have quite disastrous consequences for the child witness involved. The child will have proceeded under the assumption that his or her live testimony will not be required, only to have that decision abruptly reversed in the courtroom. Moreover, as the video is not played at court, the child may have had no opportunity to refresh his evidence. He will be asked to recall events which occurred two or more years ago. In these circumstances it will come as no surprise that in the sample of cases which we attended at court, such tactics were invariably unsuccessful from the point of view of the prosecution.

When a video has shown, what impact did it have on the outcome? In the period surveyed, Lord Chancellor's Department statistics suggest that 47% of cases resulted in a late guilty plea by the accused. When the case went to trial, juries returned guilty verdicts on a further 23% of cases while 27% of defendants were acquitted (the remaining 3% involved re-trials and other outcomes). How does this rate of convictions relate to comparable trials where no videotaped evidence was shown?

Scrutiny of the relevant figures provides no support for the view that juries are reluctant to convict on the basis of taped evidence. When the Crown's evidence was taken by "Live" examination at court, convictions were returned in 43% of cases. When a videotape was submitted the figure was 48%: a somewhat higher figure though not one which is statistically different from the rate for conventional examinations.

A related concern was that when videotapes were submitted by the Crown it would follow that the child's first experience of examination at court would be from the defence barrister. There were fears that in the absence of acclimatization to the courtroom provided by the prosecutor through gentler questioning, the child would then be more vulnerable to robust cross-examination techniques (Spencer, 1991). There was little support for this view in terms of rates of conviction, nor were rating of mood and anxiety during cross examination any different between those who had and had not experienced examination in chief live at court.

One final issue of concern is whether the presence of videotaped evidence as part of the Crown's case would in itself increase the rate of guilty pleas. The view that the very existence of an incriminating videotape might shame an accused into pleading guilty had been expressed by the Pigot Report (1989) on the basis of anecdotal evidence from experiments in the United States. The actual figures for England and Wales are somewhat equivocal on this point. Where the prosecution made an application to show a videotape, 49% of accused tendered a guilty plea, compared to 43% where no application was made: a difference in the expected direction, but not statistically significant.

The bold statistic concealed some differing views and perspectives of the parties to the videotaping legislation. Our survey results suggested that the police officers, social workers, and presiding judges generally welcomed the introduction of this novel form of evidence and their enthusiasm was maintained albeit to a diminished degree throughout the period of our research. Barristers on the other hand took a sceptical view of the proposals, fearing that children would get away more easily with lies when questioned on tape than in the courtroom. Concerns about lying diminished with experience of the system in practice, but this was matched in turn by a growing concern that videotaped evidence would have less impact on a jury. As has been noted, there was no statistical evidence to support this view from trial outcomes.

The primary concern of social workers at the instigation of the Act was that they would be insufficiently trained to produce videotapes of a quality acceptable to a criminal court. Our survey data suggest that these concerns were diminished over time, to be replaced by fresh concerns that their skills and perspective were being undervalued and sidelined by a prosecution-driven process that paid little attention to the real needs of the child. This view was echoed in the Social Services Inspectorate Report (1994) which suggested that police officers normally led the interviewing process in 75% of local authorities. This in part reflected the greater experience and more intensive training undertaken by the police and it seems likely that only when Social Service developed a training regime involving a select cadre of experienced interviewers was parity of leadership (and esteem) achieved.

It is evident from our survey results that some parties to the 1991 legislation harbour serious reservations on its impact in practice. Lawyers fear that their forensic skills have been hijacked by other professionals and that their chances of winning – or defending – cases have been reduced. Social workers fear that they have been marginalised in many areas of child protection work and the question of whether prosecution is always in the child's best interests is insufficiently addressed. The police and the judiciary on the other hand, have fewest reservations on the outcome of the legislation. All parties have welcomed the introduction of the Memorandum of Good Practice, which, despite its inevitable imperfections has had a positive impact both on levels of training and the consequent quality of interviews. Our survey data suggests that of 110 children we observed whose videos were submitted to the court, only 2% were rejected as breaking the rules of evidence and only 27% were edited before being shown to the jury. While serious concerns remain, there seems little likelihood of a return to the conventional interviewing, though clearly there is room for further improvement.

One major consideration highlighted in our Report (Davies et al, 1995) is the need for a new edition of the Memorandum of Good Practice. This might include more explicit directives on when to formally interview a child and the limits on pre-interview contact. The latter would be designed to give the child a clearer idea of the purpose and focus of any interview as well as gauging whether the child had anything to say and was prepared to say it. Such preparation might reduce the inevitably large investment in personnel and plant involved in "Memorandum" procedures which is giving serious concern among Directors of Social Services (Social Services Inspectorate, 1994).

However, it would be a mistake to believe that the problem of the child witness in the English court was solely focused in the investigative phase of an enquiry. Our researchers discovered that many of the difficulties surrounding children's court appearances highlighted in earlier reports from non-technological age were still present today. Children were still waiting far too long to have their cases heard (as long as 40 weeks in some parts of the United Kingdom, Plotnikoff and Woolfson, 1994). When they arrived at court they were kept waiting often in unsatisfactory conditions: the average delay before giving evidence was 2 1/2 weeks with a minority waiting 6 hours or more. Considerable progress has been made in preparing children for the court experience, but still 30% of all children observed were visiting the court for the first time on the day they gave evidence and only 1 child in 4 had had the opportunity to practice communication via Live Link. Just 16% had met the Prosecutor prior to trial and only 1% had been introduced to the judge. As long as the trial process remains so often non-child friendly, video technology will only supply an important but partial answer to the dilemma of the child in court.

References

Butler, A. J. (1993). Spare the Child. *Police Review*, pp.141-151.

Davies, G. M. (1991). Research on Children's Testimony: Implications for Interviewing Practice. In C. R. Hollin, & K. Howells (Eds.). *Clinical Approaches to Sex Offenders and their Victims*. Chichester: Wiley.

Davies, G. M., & Noon, E. (1991). *An Evaluation of the Live Link for Child Witnesses*. London: Home Office.

Davies, G. M., Wilson, J. C., Mitchell, R., & Milsom, J. (1995). *Videotaping of Children's Evidence: An Evaluation*. London: Home Office.

Home Office and Department of Health (1992). *Memorandum on Good Practice on Videorecording of Interviews with Child Witnesses for Criminal Proceedings*. London: Her Majesty's Stationery Office.

Murray, K. (1995). *Live Television Link: An Evaluation of its Use in Scottish Criminal Trials.* Edinburgh: Her Majesty's Stationery Office.

Pigot, T. (1989). *Report of the Advisory Group on Video Evidence.* London: Home Office.

Plotnikoff, J., & Woolfson, R. (1994). *The Pace of Child Abuse Prosecutions: An Evaluation of the Government's Speedy Progress Policy.* A report to the Nuffield Foundation.

Saywitz, K., & Nathanson, R. (1993). Children's Testimony and their Perceptions of Stress in and out of Courtroom. *Child Abuse and Neglect, 17*, 613-621.

Social Services Inspectorate (1994). *The Child, the Court and the Video.* London: Department of Health.

Spencer, J. R. (1991). Reformers' Despair. *New Law Journal, 141*, 787.

Spencer, J. R., & Flin, R. (1993). *The Evidence of Children: The Law and the Psychology* (2nd ed.). London: Blackstone.

Explaining Conversation Rules as a Method to Reduce Suggestibility of the Child Witness

Aldert Vrij, Marianne R. Mulder and Julie Cherryman

Young children who have become the victim of sexual abuse are often the only witnesses of the crime. Consequently, testimonies of these children are necessary to find out exactly what took place, and to detect and charge the perpetrator. There have for a long time been doubts about the competence of children to act as witnesses, with children being thought to be very susceptible to suggestions, making their statements untrustworthy. An often cited example is an experiment conducted by Varendonck in 1911 (see Ross, Miller and Moran, 1987). He asked a group of seven-year old schoolchildren, what colour was the beard of one their teachers. Most children mentioned a colour, while in fact the teacher did not have a beard at all. Varendonck concluded that children are unreliable witnesses.

Recently there has been much research conducted concerning the suggestibility of children (see Ceci & Bruck, 1993, for an overview). This research shows that children are able to resist misleading questions and give reliable information about events. However, there are factors which influence the susceptibility to suggestion and thus threaten the reliability of testimonies. At first it was thought that only cognitive factors (such as memory and knowledge) cause suggestibility. However, various experiments have shown that other factors are involved. Moston (1990) and Spencer and Flin (1990) found that children sometimes give answers to questions which are known to them to be incorrect. King and Yuille (1987) found that children sometimes give incorrect answers, whereas in a 'free recall' situation they remembered the event correctly. When asked, the children explained their inconsistent answers by saying they "just went along" with the questions. This behaviour looks more like a social shortcoming than a cognitive shortcoming. Authors like Ceci and Bruck (1993), Elbers (1991), Dent and Stephenson (1984), Goodman (1984), Moston (1990) and Warnick and Sanders (1980) suggest that, during an interview with a child, misapprehensions occur between interviewer and child which cause the child to give wrong answers. These misapprehensions are caused by social-psychological factors which influence the interaction between the child and the interviewer.

In this experiment the influence of two such social-psychological factors on the suggestibility of children was examined. The first factor is that children are accustomed to receiving help from the adult with whom they are interacting, which explains why they expect help during an interview: (1) Expectation of help.

The second factor is that children are not aware that in some cases it is better not to give an answer than to give the wrong answer: (2) the "I-don't-know"-option. Both factors are discussed by different authors (Bekerian & Dennet, 1992; Bull, 1992; Ceci, 1993; Ceci & Bruck, 1993; Lepore, 1991; Lepore & Sesco, 1994; Moston, 1990; Saywitz, Nathanson, Snyder, & Lamphear, 1993; Vrij & van Wijngaarden, 1994; Zaragoza, Dahlgren, & Muench, 1992) as factors which may influence suggestibility.

Expectation of help

Elbers and colleagues (Elbers, 1991; Elbers & Kelderman, 1991), Ornstein (1991) and Poole and Lindsay (1995) emphasize the fact that children do not know the social conversational rules of an interview. The most important rule in this kind of interaction is that the child has to tell something which is unknown to the adult. But the child is not used to this situation with adults (cf. the 'transfer of control' aspect of the 'enhanced cognitive interview' (Memon, Wark, Bull, & Köhnken, 1994)). Children are accustomed to the conversational rules at school (in interaction with the teacher) and at home (in interactions with their parents). Though there are differences in these situations, there is one important similarity. Both in school and at home adults play a supporting role in conversation: children can count on support and help. Also, these children know that adults often already have the relevant information. During an investigative interview, however, the (adult) interviewer cannot help the child to answer the questions. It is probable that children are not aware of this fact. To eliminate the danger of suggestion as much as possible it is necessary for the interviewer to explain this "new conversational rule". The interviewer should explain to the child that the child may well know things that the interviewer does not know and that the child is the only one who can tell these things. It should be emphasized that the interviewer cannot help the child in answering the questions. Elbers and Kelderman (1991) investigated the influence of expectation of help on task performance in children aged five and six years old. They were given two rows with six blocks and after the child had verified that the amount of blocks in each row was the same (this posed no problem), the experimenter took apart one of the rows. The children were then asked whether both rows still contained the same amount of blocks. There were three experimental conditions. In the first condition ('expectancy of help' condition) an expectancy of help towards the experimenter was created by giving the children a pretask in which they received help from the experimenter. In the second condition ('no help' condition) the experimenter explicitly stated in the pretask that he could not give the child any help and that the child had to do it alone. The children in the control condition did not receive a pretask. The results showed that children in the 'no help' condition gave the best performance. Children in the other two conditions performed the same. Explaining to the child that the experimenter could not give any help resulted in a better performance. In the present experiment the idea whether this manipulation will also make children less susceptible to misleading questions is tested.

I-don't-know option

Dent and Stephenson (1979) and Warnick and Sanders (1980) proposed that incorrect answers emerge from the fact that individuals (adults as well as children) assume that they have to answer every question whether they know the answer or not. According to these researchers the "I-don't-know" answer is never encouraged. Using a task involving the identification of people by adults Warnick and Sanders (1980) investigated the effect of giving an "I-don't-know" option. They explained to one group that an "I-don't-know" option would be acceptable and this group made significantly fewer mistakes in the identification task than did the control group (which had not received this information). This has been replicated by Cutler and Penrod (1995) among others.

Moston (1987) and Vrij and Winkel (1994) have conducted similar experiments with children. The experimental group was told that an "I-don't-know" answer would be acceptable, the control group did not receive this information. The results did not show any effects of this manipulation: both groups gave the same amount of incorrect answers. A possible explanation is that the "I-don't-know" option was not given sufficient emphasis and had not been sufficiently explained thus explaining the lack of effects between the groups of children. The interviewer in the Vrij and Winkel experiment had the impression that not all the children had understood the explanation of an "I-don't-know" answer. Perhaps a more elaborate and, to an adult, seemingly exaggerated explanation of the meaning of an "I-don't-know" answer would lead to more positive results. Recent British government advice to investigative interviewers (Bull, 1992; Home Office, 1992) strongly recommends advising children that 'I-don't-know' is an acceptable reply, but no guidance is given on how best to do this. In the present experiment the effectiveness of an extensive "I-don't-know" explanation has been tested.

In the present experiment the following two hypotheses have been tested: children will be less susceptible to misleading questions when the interviewer states clearly that she was not present during the event and cannot help the child in answering the questions (Hypothesis 1); children will be less susceptible to misleading questions when they receive an instruction explaining at length that an "I-don't-know" answer is also acceptable (Hypothesis 2).

Two age-groups participated in the study, very young children (age 4-6) and somewhat older children (age 8-10). This made it possible to investigate whether the two factors in the different age-groups have the same or different effects.

It's not unthinkable that the two introduced factors have unwanted side-effects. For instance, it might be possible that due to the "I-don't-know" option children answer "I-don't-know" to every question and as a result don't give any other information. To control this an open-ended question and two leading questions were asked besides the three misleading questions about the event.

Method

Subjects

A total of 114 children participated in the experiment, 45 children who attend kindergarten, aged 45 and 69 children who attend the third grade, aged 8-10. There were 57 boys and 57 girls.

Procedure

The subjects attended an elementary school in Amsterdam and participated with their parents' approval. The experiment took place during school hours. The children were confronted with the following staged event:

> At the beginning of class a woman (a confederate) comes into the room with a book in her hand and a handbag over her shoulder. The teacher tells the children that the woman has come to read them a story. The moment she starts to read a man (also a confederate) comes in and claims that the woman has his book. The woman denies and says he is lying. The man tries to snatch the book away and they both start pulling at the book. The woman threatens to hit the man on the head with the book if he does not leave. The man pulls the book out of her hand and informs her that his name is written in the book. He then suggests that her book might be in her bag. This turns out to be true. The woman took the book out of her bag. The man leaves with his book and the woman starts reading.

After the woman had finished the story, the instructor took the children one by one out of the class and brought them to the interviewer explaining that she was bringing the child to someone who wanted to know what happened in the classroom between the man and the woman. The interviewer was not present during the classroom event and didn't have insight into the aims of the experiment.

The interview with the children was taped on video. The children were told not to mind the video and that the interview would be recorded for the interviewer to look at again later on. The children were randomly assigned to the different conditions.

The teachers were aware of the experiment and afterwards they gave the children a debriefing in which they explained that the quarrel between the man and the woman was only play and not real.

Independent Variables

In this experiment three independent variables were used, "Expectation of help", "I-don't-know" and "Age".

The variable "Expectation of help" was manipulated by having the interviewer explain to half of the children (n=61) that she was not present in the classroom and did not see the event, the child is the only one of them who has seen the event and therefore the interviewer will not be able to assist the child in answering the questions. The other half of the children (n=53) were not given any explanation.

The variable "I-don't-know" was manipulated by having the interviewer instruct half of the children (n=62) that in case of doubt they should answer with "I-don't-know". She gave an example by asking the children if they knew her name. When the children answered she told them that they could not know her name because she had not told them her name and that therefore it was correct to answer with "I-don't-know". The other half of the children (n=52) were not given any explanation.

Two age-groups participated in the study, "younger children" (4-6 years old) and "older children" (8-10 years old).

Dependent Variables

The interviewer asked the children six questions, three misleading questions (i.e. leading to an incorrect answer), two leading questions (i.e. leading to the correct answer) and one open question. The *misleading questions* were (the correct answers are between brackets): – Who threw the book across the classroom? (The book wasn't thrown across the classroom.) – What colour were the woman's glasses? (She was not wearing glasses.) – How hard did the woman hit the man on the head? (She did not hit him.)

Afterwards the percentage of incorrect answers were calculated (the total amount of wrong answers divided by three, the number of misleading questions). Following common procedures (Bottoms et al, 1989) we considered "I-don't-know" as a correct answer, because it indicates resistance to suggestion.

The *leading questions* were (the correct answers are between brackets): "Who took the book out of the bag?" (the woman) and "Who came to read the children a story?" (the woman). Afterwards the percentage of incorrect answers were calculated (the total amount of wrong answers divided by two, the number of leading questions). In this case we considered "I-don't-know" as an incorrect answer.

The *open question* was: – "Please describe the man." The amount of features mentioned by the child, (without receiving help from the interviewer) was scored. A distinction was made between correct features and incorrect features.

Results

To examine Hypotheses 1 and 2 the data were analyzed (ANOVA) on the basis of a 2 (Expectation of help: no help vs control) X2 (I-don't-know: don't-know vs control) X2 (Age: 4-6 year olds vs 8-10 year olds) design. The percentage of incorrect answers was the dependent variable. The percentages for the eight cells are provided in Table 1.

Table 1: Percentages of incorrect answers

	No help expectancy	Control
I-don't-know		
– younger children	.17	.24
– older children	.20	.25
Control		
– younger children	.36	.59
– older children	.33	.59

The analysis revealed two main effects, namely for Expectation of help, $F(1,106)=6.52$, $p<.05$ and for "I-don't-know", $F(1,106)=18.22$, $p<.001$. None of the other effects were significant. Supporting Hypothesis 1, the children gave fewer incorrect answers (26% vs 40%) when they were explicitly told that the interviewer could not help them answer the questions. As predicted by Hypothesis 2, children gave fewer incorrect answers (21% vs 46%) when they were told that an "I-don't-know" answer would also be accepted. With these results Hypothesis 2 is also supported.

The percentages in Table 1 are also noteworthy. They show that the results of the younger and the older children are almost identical: the age difference doesn't show a difference in susceptibility to suggestion and the age-groups are influenced by the experimental conditions in the same manner.Although the interaction effects were not significant it is remarkable that the percentage of incorrect answers in the condition with the most information (the "No-expectation of help" and the "I-don't-know" condition) is the lowest (in total 18%, 17 for the younger children and 20 for the older children) while the percentage of incorrect answers in the condition without any information is the highest (in total 59%, 59 for both younger and older children). The difference between 18 and 59 per cent was highly significant, $F(1,47)=24.41$, $p<.001$.

To analyze the data concerning the leading question a further ANOVA was conducted, based on the same design. The analysis did not reveal any significant outcome. Hence, the manipulations did not affect the answers to the leading questions.

To analyze the open-ended question a MANOVA was conducted based again on the same design. The number of correct and incorrect features mentioned was the dependent variable. On the multivariate level the analysis resulted in one significant effect, a main effect for Age, $F(2,105)=26.75$, $p<.001$. All other effects were not significant. Univariate tests revealed a significant effect for the number of correct features mentioned, $F(1,106)=52.53$, $p<.001$. Older children mentioned more correct features (M=2.25) than younger children ($M=.64$). The total number of incorrect features mentioned by the children was small, averaged $M=.28$.

Discussion

The present experiment examined the effects of giving children an "I-don't-know" option and explaining to them that the interviewer is not able to help them answer any questions on children's suggestibility in interviews. In this experiment children were asked three types of questions after witnessing an event. An open-ended question which gave the children the opportunity to give information spontaneously, three misleading questions and two leading questions concerning the event.

The open-ended question was put to the children when the interviewer asked them to describe the man. The older children mentioned more features than the younger children. The information given by the children turned out to be reliable: the younger children as well as the older children gave little to no incorrect information. These results are similar to the findings of Cole and Loftus (1987) and King and Yuille (1987): in response to open-ended questions children give little but reliable information while the amount of information given increases with age. Davies (1991, 1994) gives three reasons why children's ability to recall information improve as they become older. First, there is growth in general knowledge with age which helps children to place the new experience or observation in the context of what they already know. Second, with age, children learn certain "scripts" or routine sequences of action in their everyday living, which facilitate memory processing. Third, as children become older they learn more efficient and effective strategies for encoding information (e.g. the use of rehearsal, visual imagery and associative links).

Nevertheless, the total amount of information given by the children was small. This could be explained by the fact that the question, being very general, didn't give the children much to go on and therefore was difficult to answer. It would be difficult (if not impossible) to trace someone on the basis of less than three features. An interviewer would therefore not be able to abstain from asking more specific questions in order to get more information.

When these specific questions are misleading, the interviewer risks being misinformed by the children. Our results show that the number of incorrect answers given by younger children as well as older children can be substantially reduced by explaining some rules of conversation in advance of the interview. They are an "I-don't-know" answer is acceptable and that the interviewer cannot give the child any help in answering the questions. The explanation of these conversational rules helps the child to understand what is expected and rules out misapprehensions between interviewer and child. This experiment showed that after explanation of the "I-don't-know" option and the "Expectation of help" 18% of the answers were incorrect, while 59% of the answers were incorrect when no explanation was given. A statement containing information of which 59% is incorrect can be found very unreliable, whereas a statement with information of which 18% consists of incorrect answers is much more reliable. Thus, explanation of conversational rules seems to change children from unreliable witnesses into relatively reliable witnesses. In our opinion therefore every interview with child witnesses should begin with this information.

Contrary to earlier experiments our explanation of an "I-don't-know" answer did result in a reduction of incorrect answers. Our explanation of what "I-don't-know" means was more elaborate and simple and therefore more understandable for the children than in other experiments. This shows that it is important to give an explanation which is clear to very young children. Moreover it is important to verify whether the child has really understood the explanation.

The introduction of the "expectation of help" rule in child interviews needs to be done with prudence. Emphasizing that "the adult cannot help the child" can easily lead to a situation in which the child will feel abandoned. Such a situation is ethically inadmissible and, of course, has to be avoided. One possible way of avoiding this is to compensate this rule with conducting the interview in locations which are perceived by children as being safe and supportive (for example by creating nursery rooms in police stations where the interviews can be held).

Interestingly, the manipulations did not affect the answers to the leading questions. Apparently, the manipulations did result in an increased resistance to misleading questions only and did not lead to a "shut up" of the child, that is, resistance to give any information at all.

The small amount of incorrect information given in answer to the open-ended question, the drastic reduction of incorrect answers resulting from explanation of the conversational rules, and the fact that this explanation did not result in providing less correct information sustains the assumption that suggestibility is influenced not so much by (a lack of) cognitive abilities of children, but mostly by wrong conceptions held by the child about how s/he should react during an interview (i.e. a social psychological explanation).A possible draw-back of the present experiment was that the children in the control-condition did not get any explanation at all, which makes it unclear how they interpreted this situation. However the only possible alternative was to tell the children in the control-condition that they could not give an "I-don't-know" answer and that they could expect help from the interviewer, which would have been a very unnatural situation.

The results also showed that younger children are no more suggestible than older children. This corresponds with other research in this field (Ceci & Bruck, 1993). Moreover it turns out that the factors "Expectation of help" and "I-don't-know" have the same effect on older and younger children. The influence of these factors is not subject to age. In short, even the older children don't seem to know the conversational rules of an interview.

The factors "Expectation of help" and "I-don't-know" did influence the suggestibility, but not the answers to the open-ended question. This indicates that the children did not clam up by only answering with "I-don't-know" after hearing this explanation, but that they realized when an "I-don't-know" answer was appropriate and when it was not.

We will conclude with two remarks. First, we acknowledge the fact that our quarrel-scene was very short and that the time lapse between the event and the interviews was also less than it is in real life. Secondly, we are aware that the event with which we confronted the children and the following interview were not very stressful. In sexual abuse cases however, the abuse often takes place for a longer period of time and the time lapse between the event and the interview is also greater. If results such as the ones found in this study can be generalised to such, more stressful cases, then the implications are encouraging. In order to investigate possible generalisations we suggest that this type of experiment should also be done in settings which cause more stress, for example when visiting the doctor or the dentist, and also to vary the time lapse between event and interview.

References

Bekerian, D. A., & Dennett, J. L. (1992). The truth in content analyses of a child's testimony. In F. Lösel, D. Bender, & T. Bliesener (Eds.), *Psychology and Law: International Perspectives*. Berlin, New York: Walter de Gruyter.

Bottoms, B. L., Goodman, G. S., Rudy, L., Port, L., England, P., Aman, C., & Wilson, M. E. (1989). *Children's testimony for a stressful event: improving children's reports.* Paper presented at the 97th American Psychological Association. New Orleans, LA, August.

Bull, R. (1992). Obtaining evidence expertly: the reliability of interviews with child witnesses. *Expert evidence: the international digest of human behaviour science and law, 1*, 3-36.

Ceci, S. J. (1993, August). *Cognitive and social factors in children's testimony.* Paper presented at the American Psychological Association meeting, Toronto.

Ceci, S. J., & Bruck, M. (1993). Suggestibility of the child witness: a historical review and synthesis. *Psychological Bulletin, 113*, 403-439.

Cole, C. B., & Loftus, E. F. (1987). The memory of children. In S. J. Ceci, M. Toglia, & D. Ross (Eds.), Children's eyewitness memory. New York: Springer-Verlag.

Cutler, B., & Penrod, S. (1995). Assessing the accuracy of eyewitness identification. In R. Bull & D. Carson (Eds.), *Handbook of psychology in legal contexts*. Chichester: Wiley.

Davies, G. (1991). research on children's testimony: implications for interviewing practice. In C. R. Hollin & K. Howells (Eds.), Clinical approaches to sex offenders and their victims. Chichester: Wiley & Sons, pp. 93-115.

Davies, G. (1994). Children's testimony: research findings and police implications. *Psychology, Crime, & Law, 1*, 175-180.

Dent, H. R., & Stephenson, G. M. (1979). An experimental study of the effectiveness of different techniques of questioning child witness. *British Journal of Social and Clinical Psychology, 18*, 41-51.

Elbers, E. (1991). Context en suggestie bij het ondervragen van jonge kinderen. *Gezin, 4*, 234-243.

Elbers, E., & Kelderman, A. (1991). Verwachtingen en misverstanden bij het toetsen van kennis. *Pedagogische Studiën, 68*, 176-184.

Goodman, G. S. (1984). The child witness: conclusions and future directions for research and legal practice. *Journal of Social Issues, 40*, 157-175.

Home Office (1992). *Memorandum of good practice for videorecorded interviews with child witnesses in criminal proceedings.* London: Her Majesty's Stationery Office.

King, M. A., & Yuille, J. C. (1987). Suggestibility and the child witness. In S. J. Ceci, M. P. Toglia, & D. F. Ross (Eds.), *Children's eyewitness memory*. New York: Springer-Verlag.

Lepore, S. J. (1991). Child witness: cognitive and social factors related to memory and testimony. *Issues in Child Abuse Accusations, 3*, 65-89.

Lepore, S. J., & Sesco, B. (1994). Distorting children's reports and interpretations of events through suggestion. *Journal of Applied Psychology, 79*, 108-120.

Memon, A., Wark, L., Bull, R., & Köhnken, G. (1994). *Children's event memory*. Paper presented at the Biennial Convention of the American Psychology – Law Society. San Diego.

Moston, S. (1987). The suggestibility of children in interview studies. *First Language, 7*, 67-78.

Moston, S. (1990). How children interpret and respond to questions: situational sources of suggestibility in eyewitness interviews. *Social Behaviour, 5*, 155-167.

Ornstein, P. A. (1991). Putting interviewing in context: commentary on Dent's "Experimental studies of interviewing child witnesses." In J. Doris (Ed.), *The suggestibility of children's memory* (pp. 147-152). Washington, DC: American Psychological Association.

Poole, D. A., & Lindsay, D. S. (1995). Interviewing preschoolers: effects of nonsuggestive techniques, parental coaching and leading questions on reports of nonexperimental events. *Journal of Experimental Child Psychology*, in press.

Ross, D. F., Miller, B. S., & Moran, P. B. (1987). The child in the eyes of the jury: assessing mock jurors' reactions to child witnesses. In S. J. Ceci, M. P. Toglia, & D. F. Ross (Eds.), *Children's eyewitness memory.* New York: Springer-Verlag.

Saywitz, K., Nathanson, R., Snyder, L., Lamphear, V. (1993). *Preparing children for the investigative and judicial process: improving communication, memory and emotional resiliency.* Final report to the national center on child abuse and neglect (grant 90CA1179). Torrance, CA: UCLA School of Medine.

Vrij, A., & Van Wijngaarden, J. J. (1994). Will truth come out? Two studies about the detection of false statements expressed by children. *Expert Evidence: the international digest of human behaviour science and law, 3*, 2, 78-84.

Vrij, A., & Winkel, F. W. (1994). Strategies to detect and reduce false statements in children: a social-psychological approach. *Journal of Police and Criminal Psychology, 10*, 1, 22-29.

Warninck, D. H., & Sanders, G. S. (1980). Why do eyewitnesses make so many mistakes? *Journal of Applied Social Psychology, 10*, 362-367.

Zaragoza, M. S., Dahlgren, D., & Muench, J. (1992). The role of memory impairment in children's suggestibility. In M. L. Howe, C. J. Brainerd, & V. F. Reyna (Eds.), *Development of long-term retention.* New York: Springer-Verlag.

Interviewing Children: The Importance of Omission Errors

Graeme Hutcheson, James S. Baxter, Karen S. Telfer and David Warden

Introduction

Experimental studies have shown that children as young as six can give evidence which is as accurate as that from adults provided that free-recall, or general questions are used to elicit details. The resulting statements are, however, generally less complete than those obtained when interviewer uses more specific questions (Cohen & Harnick 1980; Dent, 1982; Goodman & Reed, 1986; King & Yuille, 1987; see Ceci & Bruck, 1993, for a review) and are said to contain "errors of omission", as all the relevant information the child has, is not given to the interviewer. Although the completeness of a child's statement may be increased by asking specific questions, such a strategy often results in a decrease in accuracy, (King & Yuille 1987; Dent, 1992) suggesting that young children's statements are either relatively complete but inaccurate, or accurate but relatively incomplete. Given the importance of accuracy in legal contexts, interviewers are often encouraged to use general, open-ended questions whenever possible (see, for example, recommendations published by the Home Office, 1992). However, such a strategy can lead to errors of omission thereby seriously affecting the value of the child's testimony in court.

The present study aims to access the quality of statements elicited from children who have witnessed a realistic incident, by professional, experienced interviewers, questioning "as they would normally". The use of experienced, practising interviewers increases the degree to which these results can be generalised to actual interviews increases the degree to which these results can be generalised to actual interviewers as they are carried out normally and also enables an assessment of interviewer skills which have been developed over a number of years. Drawing on previous experimental findings which suggest that the type of question used has a significant effect on the quality of information obtained, the interviewers' use of general and specific questions is assessed. Of particular importance is the identification of interviewing practices which are likely to lead to incomplete responses through omission errors. An assessment of the impact that such errors have, and the identification of where they occur, is a first step devising interviewing procedures to reduce their impact and improve the quality of children's testimonies.

Method

A detailed explanation of the methods used in this study[1] is provided in Hutcheson, Baxter, Telfer, & Warden (1995).

Participants

Eight police officers, four social workers, and four reporters to the Children's Panel[2] acted as interviewers: eleven were females and five were male. The interviewers were the most experienced who were available to participate. Over the course of the study 55 children selected from schools in the greater Glasgow area (5-6 and 8-9 year olds) took part, parental permission having been obtained. The only selection criterion used was that, as far as possible, particularly shy children were not interviewed. The group of children chosen to take part in the study was not therefore a random sample as selection depended on parental consent and teacher selection, and also a subgroup of quiet children was excluded from the analyses (even after the initial selection eight children did not provide any information at all). In total, 47 interviews were analysed; 20 interviews (13 male and 7 female) with 5-6 year olds and 27 interviews (17 male and 10 female) with the 8-9 year olds.

Procedure

Each interviewer questioned two 5-6 year olds and two 8-9 year olds about one of two different incidents. The incidents were staged by actors on the school premises early in the morning and the children were interviewed later same day.

Incidents

The children were not told that the incidents were going to happen or that, afterwards, they were to be questioned about them. The incidents were carefully

---

1 This project was supported by a grant from Economic and Social Research Council (grant number: R000232968). We are indebted to the many schools that supported the project and to the pupils, teachers, police, social workers and reporters to the children's panel who generously gave their time.

2 In Scotland all cases involving children may be referred to a children's panel who decide how a particular case is to proceed. The reporter to the children's panel investigates cases brought to his or her attention and decides which are to be referred to the panel (see Spencer & Flin, 1993: chapter 2).

scripted and rehearsed to ensure a degree of realism and consistency over a number of stagings at different schools. Due to ethical restrictions on the nature of the incidents which could be staged, two incidents were scripted which contained an element of "seriousness". One incident involved an argument between two technicians who were setting up a film projector, and another involved the loss of an electric drill by some workmen.

Instructions given to the interviewers

The interviewers were informed of the general aims of the project and were asked to interview "as they would normally". Printed instructions explained that they were to interview four children during the day about two incidents (two children about Incident One, and two about Incident Two). Although each interviewer interviewed two children about the same event the effect of this additional knowledge did not appear to influence the quality of the second interview (see results). All interviewers were asked to concentrate on eliciting information about what happened and what was said, descriptions and names of anyone involved, and the Child's overall thoughts and impressions about what had happened.

Data transcription and coding

All interviews were videotaped and transcribed. Each incident was broken down into a number of points; 51 points for Incident One and 56 points for Incident Two. Statement quality was assessed through two measures: accuracy and completeness. Accuracy rates were measured by dividing the number of points in the coding scheme about which accurate points reported (see Dent, 1992). For example, if a child gave information about 13 points on the coding scheme and only 11 of these were accurate, the child's statement would be considered to be 84.62% accurate (11/13 x 100).

Completeness was measured by dividing the number of points referred to by the child in each report (accurate and inaccurate) by the number of points in the coding scheme which reflected the amount of relevant information obtained whether it was accurate or not. In a statement taken about Incident One (which had 51% separately coded points of information) a child who mentioned 35 of them would have achieved a statement which was 64.71% complete. (35/51 x 100).

Inter-observer reliability for accuracy and completeness was calculated for two independent coders and a point-by-point reliability score of above 90% was obtained for a random sample of over 10% of the transcripts. Also, to guard against coding errors, all transcripts were coded twice.

Results

Quality of statements

The results from the two incidents were analysed together as there were no significant differences between the incidents in overall completeness or accuracy (t(45)=.22, p=.824; t(42.82)=1.89, p=.066). There was also no significant difference between the completeness and accuracy of the first and second interviews for either group indicating that there was no significant "learning" effect between repeated interviews about the same incident. Table 1 shows the overall accuracy and completeness scores for the two age groups and for the sample as a whole.

Table 1: Quality of Statements: Mean overall scores

	Completeness		Accuracy	
age group	mean	sd	mean	sd
5-6	28.2	11.1	79.2	12.8
8-9	48.2	12.1	85.6	8.3
overall	39.7	15.3	82.9	10.8

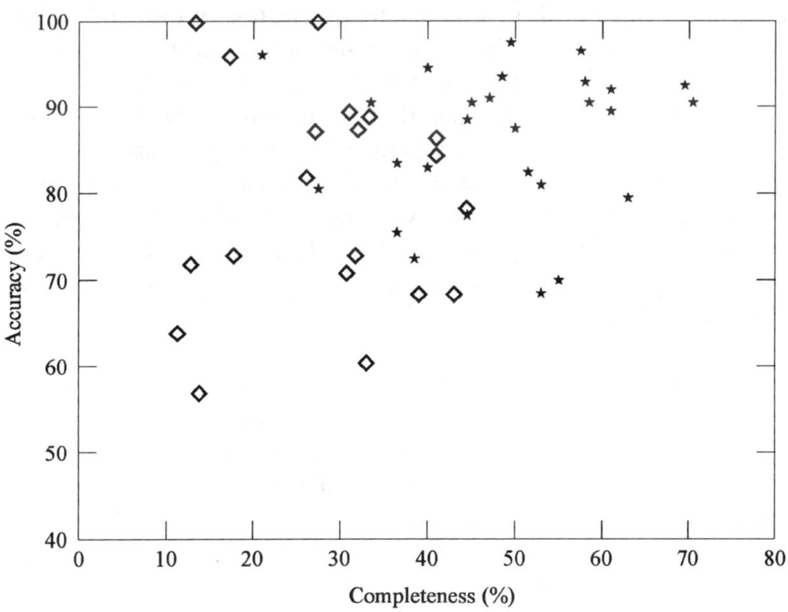

Figure 1: Quality of statements elicited from 5-6 and 8-9 year old children

The age of the child

Comparisons of the two age groups showed that the 8-9 year old children recalled significantly more information than did the 5-6 year olds ($t(45)=-5.8$, $p<.005$). Although there was not a significant difference between the groups in the accuracy of recall ($t(30.6)=-1.95$, $p=.06$) the difference was nearly significant and in the direction which has been found in previous experimental studies. It seems reasonable to assume that a larger sample size might well show a significant difference between the two age groups.

The scatter plot in Figure 1 displays overall completeness and accuracy scores for the two age groups and demonstrates a significant difference between the age groups in statement completeness with a degree of overlap in the distributions. Some 5-6 year old children compare favourably to some 8-9 year olds, at least when compared on overall measures of completeness and accuracy.

Question type in relation to statement quality

As children's ability to respond to certain types of questions has been identified as having an important influence on the amount of information they give in their responses to general and specific questions were analysed. The generality of questions in the present study was based on a functional description of the scope of the question *in relation to the incident.* This type of definition made it possible to divide questions into two groups without the need for an analysis of the linguistic structure of the questions.[3] General and specific questions were identified on the basis of the number of points on the coding scheme which that question addressed. If more than one point was addressed, the question was considered to be general. For example, "Can you tell me what he was wearing?" was classed as a general question as it relates to more than one point on the coding scheme, whereas "Tell me what the lady was doing when you first went into the room?" was classed as a specific question as it only relates to one point in the coding scheme.

A number of questions were excluded from the analysis if, for example, the children had not been given an adequate opportunity to answer (in cases where, for example, a number of questions were asked by the interviewer concurrently without a break), or if the question was not related to the incident ("What does your Mum look like?") and when the question was subjective or involved imagination or guess-work on the part of the child (for example, an answer to the question "What do you think she was planning to do with the drill once she took it outside?" could only involve conjecture as this information was not part of the

3 It is important to note that many of the questions defined as general in the present study would have been similarly defined using a more linguistically-based definition.

incident). Such questions were excluded from all analyses presented in this paper. Only those questions which were directly related to the incident were included.

The relationship between question type and statement quality is shown in Table 2. This table shows the correlation coefficient for each child's overall scores for accuracy and completeness in relation to the number of specific and general questions asked during the interview.

Table 2: Completeness and accuracy in relation to question type

Number of questions	Completeness	Accuracy
5-6 year old		
– Total	.2746	–.4659*
– Specific	.2285	–.5337*
– General	.3152	.2498
8-9 year old		
– Total	.633***	–.0643
– Specific	.644***	–.0309
– General	.1093	–.2299
Overall		
– Total	.4094**	–.2483
– Specific	.4294**	–.2613
– General	.0211	–.0084

Person's Product-Moment correlation coefficient

* $p<.05$
** $p<.01$
*** $p<.000$

The children responded differently to questions depending on their age. Interviewers who asked 5-6 year old children a high proportion of specific questions tended to elicit statement which were no more complete but were significantly less accurate (r=–.5337; p=.015). In contrast to this, those interviewers who asked 8-9 year old children a relatively large number of specific questions elicited significantly more information (r=.664; p<.0005) without significantly affecting accuracy. On the basis of these results it could be argued that interviews should modify the type of question they use according to the age of the child. When interviewing 5-6 year old children it may be best for interviewers to restrict their use of specific questions in order to minimize errors of omission. Such a restriction could perhaps be relaxed with older children as they appear able to provide accurate answers regardless of the type of question used.

General questions and errors of omission

By far the biggest difference in the quality of the statement elicited from 5-6 year children compared with 8-9 year olds is in completeness. This difference could be due to the amount of information actually encoded by the children or could be due to the differences in the amount recalled. If at least some of the difference is due to the latter, then younger children's statements might be significantly affected by errors of omission. Experimental evidence which indicates that the young children have difficulty in answering general questions suggests that the use of these in an interview does not tend to elicit all information a child knows. The extent to which errors of omission in response to general questions may affect young children's' testimonies was the subject of investigation.

The following analyses looked in detail at the answers elicited by general questions and distinguished between negative responses where no information was provided (for example, when a child does not answer a question, indicates that she/he does not know, or provides a straight "No") and positive responses where the child provided information, or at least indicated that they knew more. The results showed that there was no significant difference between the two groups of children in the number of general questions they were asked, however, 5-6 year old children answered a significantly greater proportion of them negatively (51.5% compared to 24.9%; $t(30.61)=3.95$, $p<0.0005$).

Omission errors made in response to general questions were identified by those general questions which had been answered negatively, only for information relevant to this question to be provided later. For example, if a question such as "Was there a man in your classroom?" is answered negatively we cannot be sure whether the child did not know the information or was unable or unwilling to give it to the interviewer. If, later in the interview, the child says that there had been a man in the classroom it is clear that the initial general question did nit elicit relevant information and could have resulted in an error of omission. Table 3 identifies possible omission errors by showing the number of instances where general questions were responded to negatively and those instances where relevant information was elicited later in the interview.

Table 3: Indications of Omissions

Age Group	General questions answered negatively	More information given	Proportion
5-6	54	41	76.0%
8-9	40	29	72.5%
overall	94	70	74.3%

Such an analysis can only indicate the number of times when at least some information was given after a general question had been answered negatively. It does not reveal the amount of additional information which was given nor does it distinguish omission errors in cases where the child only provided limited information in response to a general question, when in fact she/he knew more. For example, if the interviewer asked "What was he wearing?" and the child replied "He had a hat.", this was recorded as a positive response even though the information given is very limited and more may have been available. Even with these limitations, which are likely to underestimate the role played by errors of omission,[4] it is clear that the children in this study did not always give complete answers in response to general questions, at least not initially.

In over 70% of the cases where a general question had been answered negatively, at least some relevant information was given later in the interview. Both age groups have a tendency to answer general questions negatively even when they have relevant information and a negative reply to a question need not therefore indicate a lack of knowledge. It is clear that the children's initial negative answers to general questions are not indicative of their knowledge and that such answers should therefore not be taken at "face value".

The following extract show some examples of interviews where children have provided negative answers to general questions and subsequently provided relevant information. In the following example a child is being questioned about one of the actors who entered her classroom that morning.

Subject # 6, Female 8-9 year old:
INT: Can you tell me what this girl looked like?
CHI: Mmn I can't remember what she looked like.
INT: Mmn?
CHI: I can't remember what she looked like.
INT: You can'... can you maybe tell me about what age she was?
CHI: Em ... she was about twenty I think.
ans: Correct answer.
INT: About twenty and how tall was she?
CHI: She was quite tall.
INT: Quite tall, as tall as me if I stand up?
CHI: Mmn yes.
INT: As tall as me, was she?
CHI: Nearly.
INT: Nearly a wee bit smaller than me?
CHI: A bit.
ans: Correct answer
-----

4 As this total also includes where the interviewer had terminated questioning on a negative answer (cases where the child was not asked for any more information) it is likely that the children could have provided more information on other points as well.

INT: Do you remember what colour of hair she had?
CHI: Em...no.
INT: No think hard try and picture it in your head.
CHI: I think it was sort of brown.
com: Correct answer
INT: Sort of brown...and do you remember what kind of style her hair was?
CHI: (no reply)
INT: Was it long hair or short hair or can you tell me?
CHI: Long.
ans: Correct answer
INT: Long... do you remember what she had on?
CHI: No.
INT: Think hard again try and picture it in your head.
CHI: I think it was something like painting sort of clothes that you use for painting.
INT: Clothes that you use for painting ... What makes you think you would use them for painting what was it about them that made you think?
CHI: Cos they were all old and people would use them for painting when they're old.
ans: Correct answer: Woman had work clothes on – Jeans and boots.

In this short extract three general questions are answered negatively even though the child knew at least part of the answer: this information could have been lost had the interviewer accepted the child's original reply and not pursued more detail. This extract also demonstrates two techniques which can be used to help encourage the child to give more information. The first is to break down the scope of the general question making it more specific, a strategy particularly effective with older children who are more able to answer specific questions. Secondly, the interviewer encouraged the child to focus her memory on the incident and to "picture in her head" what had happened, a technique successfully incorporated into the Cognitive Interview (see Geiselman, Fisher, Mackinnon & Hollan, 1986; Memon, & Köhnken, 1992). The following also shows an example of a child who initially answers a general question negatively and gives some information relevant to this question when the same information is requested later in the interview.

Subject # 36, Male 5-6 year old:
INT: Right em ... Do ... Can you remember what this lady and man looked like?
CHI: No.
INT: No, can you remember anything about them at all?
CHI: No. (Shakes head).

INT: Can you remember what Iain looked like at all?
CHI: No, he had a big white jacket on.
ans: correct answer
INT: He had what on?
CHI: He had a big white jacket on.
INT: A big white jacket, oh right, that's a good help isn't it. Erm ... Do you remember what else he had on?
CHI: No. (Shakes head).

INT: Right do you remember what she was wearing?
CHI: No. (Shakes head).
INT: No.
CHI: I think she was wearing a big white jacket as well.
ans: correct reply

Although we cannot gauge the amount of information lost to errors of omission it is possible to indicate where in an interview these errors are likely to occur. Given that general questions are frequently answered negatively and that in the majority of these cases the children in fact know more information, omission errors are likely when interviewers terminate questioning on a negative (or limited) answer to a general question. In the present study there were numerous examples of this:

Subject # 20, Female 5-6 year old:
INT: What about the man, the man that was in, do you know what he was wearing?
CHI: (No reply. Shakes head)

In the above example the general question about what the man was wearing was the only question used by the interviewer which attempted to access this information. When the child indicated that she didn't know, no more questions were attempted and no information was obtained on this topic. Given the age of this child there is a high probability that she would have answered negatively to this question even if she knew some of the relevant information. Without any further attempt to elicit information it is likely that the poor completeness of information about male appearance (only 7.1% complete) was at least partly due to omission errors. It was not the case that this child was generally a poor witness as she managed a score of 25% complete for the appearance of the female who was seen for a similar amount of time as the man. The following shows another example taken from an interview with a 5-6 year old child.

Subject # 42, Male 5-6 year old:
INT: And did the lady say anything to you?
CHI: (No reply, shrugs shoulders)
INT: Did you hear her say anything?
CHI: No. (Shakes head).
INT: Did she say anything when the metal fell off?
CHI: Yes, she said "What am I going to do?"
ans: correct answer
INT: And did she say anything else?
CHI: No.
com: there was a lot said after this
CHI: That's all.

In the above example, the child relates only 7.1% of the information about what was said compared to an overall completeness score of 41.9%. General questions are all answered negatively and the only information obtained is in responses to the more specific question "Did she say anything when the metal fell off?" In this example it is likely that the child knew more about what had happened, but was unable to give the information in response to general questions. The very poor completeness score for speech information is therefore likely to be due at least in part to errors of omission.

To summarise, both groups of children tend to answer general questions negatively even when they have relevant information. Omission errors were likely to have had a larger effect on the younger age group as they had a stronger tendency to answer these questions negatively ($p<.0005$). As children do not readily volunteer information and questions which received negative responses were not always repeated, the significantly greater number of omission errors. Younger children also do not provide narrative responses as readily as older children (see Poole, 1992), and their answers therefore tend to contain only limited information, a behaviour which also contributes to the overall age difference in statement completeness.

Discussion

The age of children was an important factor in determining the quality of the statements elicited as children aged 5-6 years provided significantly poorer statements than did children aged 8-9 years, particularly in relation to the amount of information. The type of question used by the interviewers also played an important role in determining statement quality as the two groups of children responded to questions differently depending on their age. For 8-9 year old children, the use of specific questions was significantly correlated with statement completeness, but their use did not significantly affect statement accuracy. Whereas with the 5-6 year olds the use of specific questions was not significantly associated with either completeness or accuracy (the association between specific questions and accuracy was, however, bordering on significance with a p value of 0.06). This finding seems to be at variance with those of experimental studies which have found that use of specific questions enhances statement completeness albeit at a cost to accuracy (see Dent, 1992; King, & Yuille, 1987). An explanation for the difference may lie in the differing methodologies used, as in the present study interviewers were given almost no basis for the formulation of specific questions, and were often given little or nothing more to go on by the 5-6 year old interviewees. The interviewers in the present study were often not able to even formulate specific questions and as they were experienced interviewers did not use ill-formed "shots in the dark", answers to which would have been likely to have reduced the children's overall accuracy. Had the interviewers been able to formulate and ask greater numbers of specific questions this may have increased the overall completeness of the younger children's statements and also introduced inaccuracies.

Children, particularly the younger ones, show a tendency to answer general questions negatively, even when they know relevant information, and thereby make errors of omission. One reason for this lack of information in response to general questions may be that they do not provide a five year old with enough support for, or constraint on, retrieval (cf. Ackerman, 1985). Given that over 50% of general questions asked of 5-6 year old children in the present study were answered negatively, and of these, in at least 76 % of cases, it was demonstrated that the child knew relevant information, errors of omission were likely to have played a major role in determining statement quality.

The safest option open to interviewers may be somehow to improve the effectiveness of their general questions. The primary problem experienced interviewers have when dealing with young children is that their answers are either negative or tend to be quite short (the problem of "kiddie conciseness"; Poole, 1992). This limits the amount of information which can be elicited and also limits the variety of questions which can be used by the interviewer using purely verbal means. If statements are to be substantially improved then methods for encouraging accurate narrative responses must be developed. The problem facing interviewers when questioning young children is to assist the children to cope with and answer general questions.

A number of technique have been developed to encourage children to provide more complete statements These include the Cognitive Interview (Fisher, & Geiselman, 1990; Geiselman, Fisher, Mckinnon, & Holland 1986; Memon & Bull, 1991), visual and auditory feedback (Poole, 1992; Steward, Bussey, Goodman, & Saywitz, 1993; Telfer, Baxter, Hutcheson & Warden, 1994) and context cues (see Davies, & Thompson, 1988, for a review). However, the effectiveness of these techniques with children has yet to be fully researched and validated (Poole, 1992; Memon, & Köhnken, 1992). Another possibility is that other variations in the social and cognitive dynamics of the interview may influence children's recall. Baxter, Hutcheson, Telfer, Warden & Stocks (under review) found that interviewers who adopt a formal, "business-like" interviewing style elicit more complete accounts from 5-6 year old children, possibly because such an approach concentrates children's retrieval efforts more effectively than does an informal, conversational approach. Generally, however, significant improvements in the quality of statements elicited from children are unlikely without a better understanding of children's verbal behaviour and more thorough investigations of a broad range of interviewing techniques.

What does seem clear is that omission errors significantly affect the quality of young children's statements At least some of the information which is currently lost using standard interviewing techniques (that is, verbal questioning) may be retrievable from the children if the interviewers understand how these errors arise and understand the problems younger children have with answering general questions. Acquiring such understanding would be a first step towards reducing the amount of information lost to errors of omission, and should ultimately enable higher quality statements to be elicited.

References

Ackerman, B. P. (1985). Constraits on retrieval search for episodic information in children and adults. *Journal of Experimental Child Psychology, 40*, 152-180.

Baxter, J. S., Hutcheson, G. D., Telfer, K. S. Warden, D., & Stocks, R. (in prep.). *The effects of interviewer style on the completeness and accuracy of children's recall.*

Ceci, S. J., & Bruck, M. (1993). Suggestibility of the child witness: a historical review and synthesis. *Psychological Bulletin, 113*, 403-439.

Cohen, R. L., & Harnick, M. A. (1980). The susceptibility of child witness to suggestion. *Law and Human Behaviour, 4*, 201-210.

Davies, G. M., & Thompson, D. M. (1988). Context in context. In G. M. Davies, & D. M. Thomson (Eds.), *Memory in context: Context in memory*. (pp. 335-345) New York: John Wiley & Sons.

Dent, H. R. (1992). The effects of age and intelligence on eyewitness ability. In H. R. Dent, & R. Flin (Eds.). *Children as Witnesses* (pp.1-13). Chichester: John Wiley and Sons.

Fisher, R. P., & Geiselman, R. E. (1990). *Evaluation and field implementation of the cognitive interview.* Final report to the Institution of Justice, Grant # USDJ-85-IJ-CX-0053.

Geiselman, R. E., Fisher, R. P., Mackinnon, D. P., & Holland, H. L. (1986). Enhancement of eyewitness memory with the cognitive interview. *American Journal of Psychology, 99*, 385-401.

Goodman, G. S., & Reed, R. S. (1986). Age differences in eyewitness testimony. *Law and Human Behaviour, 10*, 317-332.

Home Office (1992). *Memorandum of good practice on video recorded interviews with child witnesses for criminal proceedings.* London: HMSO

Hutcheson, G. D., Baxter, J. S., Telfer, K. S., & Warden, D. (1995). Child witness statement quality: Question type and errors of omission. *Law and Human Behaviour, 19(6)*, 631- 648.

King, M. A., & Yuille, J. C. (1987). Suggestibility and the child witness. In P. Toglia, & D. F. Ross (Eds.), *Children's Eyewitness Memory.* (pp 24-35). New York: Springer Verlag.

Memon, A., & Bull, R. (1991). The cognitive interview: its origins, empirical support, evaluation and practical implications. *Journal of Community and Applied Social Psychology, 1*, 291-307.

Memon, A., & Köhnken, G. (1992). Helping the witness to remember more: the cognitive interview. *Expert Evidence, 1*, 39-48.

Poole, D. A. (1992). *Eliciting information from children with non suggestive visual and auditory feedback.* Paper presented at the NATO Advanced Study Institute: The Child Witness in Context, Lucca, Italy.

Spencer, J. R., & Flin, R. (1993). *The evidence of children: The law and the psychology.* 2nd ed. London: Blackstone Press Ltd.

Steward, M., Bussey, K., Goodman, G., & Saywitz, K. (1993). Implications of developmental research for interviewing children. *Child Abuse and Neglect, 17*, 25-37.

Telfer, K. S., Baxter, J. S., Hutcheson, G. D., & Warden, D. (1994). Cueing memory retrieval: implications for interviewing child witnesses. *Police Journal, January*, 46-52.

The Defence Mechanisms and the Deformations of the Testimony Given by Sexually Abused Juveniles

Teresa Jaskiewicz-Obydzinska

Introduction

The research that has been conducted at the Department of Forensic Psychology of the Institute of Forensic Research for several years concerning the psychological conditioning of testimonies made by minor sex crime victims focused on the causes for changes in testimonies, as well as on the influence of victim-perpetrator relationship upon the chosen testimony features. The research showed, among other things, that the following properties of minor witnesses have an essential influence upon stable and reliable testimonies: small intensity of fear reactions, moderate anxiety of social evaluation, small striving for cooperation, lack of symptoms of striving for acceptance, small intensity of openness in the communication with the surroundings, level of aspiration of the examined adequate to ability (Jaskiewicz-Obydzinska, Czerederecka, 1992).

In the course of the research over the influence of victim- perpetrator relationship on a testimony, an essential dependency was found between the emotional relationship towards the perpetrator and such general testimony features as spontaneity and attention to details in the testimony, and related to the motivation in giving testimony self-deprecation and pardoning the perpetrator (Steller, Boychuk, 1992). Full spontaneity of testimony occurred only when the perpetrators were unknown to the victims and the act itself was not drastic. Thus, it was observed only those cases where the victims had a neutral or negative emotional attitude towards the perpetrator and the testimony did not require the necessity of description of drastic elements of the event. Attention to details in testimony occurred most of all in victims who had a negative emotional attitude towards the perpetrator. One can not preclude therefore, that detailed description of the event was a form of emotional discharge of aggression towards the perpetrator in a socially acceptable manner.

Description of psychical states – the victims and that of perpetrator's occurred only with those victims whose attitude toward the perpetrator had a marked emotional colouring – positive or negative. Statements indicating self-deprecation occurred first of all with victims of acts committed by known perpetrators with whom the victims had had many contacts. No relationship was found between the occurrence of this feature of testimony and the manner in which the victim had been treated and the character of the act. The striving for pardoning of the perpetrator occurred exclusively with the victims who had cooperated, which might be seen as a tendency to decrease the meaning of the act in order to maintain positive self-esteem (Jakiewicz-Obydzinska, Czerederecka, 1995).

The results of the above-mentioned research clearly indicate that the evaluation of testimonies of sexual crime victims requires an accurate analysis of the circumstances of the crime and its detection, as well as the determination of those individual psychical features of the witness which might influence the manner in which the crime in which he had participated was perceived. The manner of perception of this situation determines the psychical effects for the victim. What is crucial here, is especially the evaluation of victim's role in the crime of which the indications are the interpretations of victim's own behaviour and that of perpetrators by the witness. One may therefore assume that the situation of a victim of a sexual crime fulfils the conditions of the occurrence of defence mechanisms. These conditions include: the threat to "ego" (real or anticipated), the presence of fear or other negative emotions, e. g. shame or feeling of guilt (real or anticipated), the disturbance of cognitive processes (Grzegołowska-Klarkowska, 1986, p. 266). One should expect therefore, distortions which stem from defence mechanisms of a personality in testimonies of such witnesses.

The subject, aim, and the method of research

In the research the concept of defence mechanisms elaborated by Klarkowska-Grzegołowska has been used. The author differentiates the category of basic defence mechanisms by which she means such distortions in the course of cognitive processes which occur in the situation of protection of ego or its anticipation. These are therefore activities whose aim is to protect ego and to reduce fear. Basic defence mechanisms include: perceptual defence (denial and negation), repression, isolation (simple and intellectualisation), rationalisation, reversal and fantasizing (Klarkowska-Grzegołowska, 1989).

The aim of the research was to determine whether these mechanisms, and to what extent, influence the occurrence of deformations, regarding both the form and the content of the testimonies made by juvenile victims of sexual crimes and as a consequence distort their reliability. The research aimed at the determination of the role the defence mechanisms play in the process of perception, processing and recollection of elements of crime situations in these witnesses.

The research included a group of 30 girls, victims of crimes committed by known and unknown perpetrators. Incest cases were excluded, being regarded as a separate research problem. In all cases the experts participated in, at least, one interrogation of these witnesses. Subsequently the witnesses were psychologically examined and opinions were issued concerning reliability of their testimonies. The following variables were analysed:

I. The perpetrator and the act

1. Category of perpetrator (known, unknown).
2. The character of the act (exposing genitals and showing sexual acts, sexual contacts based on arousing intimate parts of the body, sexual intercourse).
3. The duration of contacts (one time, a month, under 1 year, over 1 year).
4. The manner in which the victim has been treated (brutal, with elements of aggression, gentle).
5. Objective conditions of the first contact situation with the perpetrator (safe, elements of threat, threatening).
6. Revealing of the event (spontaneous, accidental, provoked).
7. Reaction of the environment (adequate, inadequate).

II. The victim

1. Age (3 groups were distinguished – under 7, 7-10, 11-15).
2. Behaviour during the event (cooperation, submission, effective defence).
3. Understanding of the situation (full, not full, lack of).
4. Chosen psychical features (understanding of social situations, ability of perception, fear, anxiety of social evaluation – graded in 3-point scale, defence mechanisms revealed in examinations by means of apperception techniques).
5. The evaluation of psychical effects of the event (lack of, present, serious).

III. Testimony

1. General features of testimony (spontaneity, attention to details – graded in 3-point scale).
2. Specific content of testimony (description of subjective states – those of the victim's and the perpetrator's.
3. Content connected with the motivation to giving testimony (pardoning the perpetrator, deprecating oneself).
4. Deformation of testimony due to defence mechanisms (present, lack of).
5. Character of deformations.
6. Evaluation of the probability of testimony (high, average, low).

The following hypotheses have been put forward:

1. The defence mechanisms occur primarily in those victims who cooperated with the perpetrator or obeyed his orders.

2. These mechanisms influence the content of the testimony concerning the interpretation of the victim's behaviour through repression or rationalisation of the victim's extreme emotions (positive or negative) accompanying sexual impressions.
3. Deformations of testimony may occur as the restriction of information concerning the victim's participation in the event, or providing socially acceptable motives as to the victim's behaviour.

The characterisation of the examined group

All of the examined were under age 15. According to current law they were, regardless of their behaviour, victims of a crime. Three age groups were distinguished: the youngest one – under 7 – 26%, the two others were equal in number – from 7 to 11 and from 11 to 15 – 37%. In 43% of cases the perpetrator was known to the victim – in the remaining 57% – an unknown person. Crimes limited to one contact with the perpetrator constituted 70% of cases, in the remaining 30% the contacts were multiple, encompassing a period ranging from 1 month to 1 year. Gentle treatment of the victim was found in 33% of cases, elements of aggression were found in 40% of cases, in the remaining 27% of cases the treatment of the victim was brutal.

Acts committed with regard to minors were divided into three categories: exposing intimate parts of the body together with touching the victims constituted 26% of cases; physical contacts based on arousing intimate parts of the victim's body occurred in 44% of cases. The behaviour of the victims in 54% of cases was evaluated as submission to the perpetrator's orders with simultaneous defence attempts. In the remaining 46% of cases, half of the victims cooperated with the perpetrator and the other half effectively resisted. The initial circumstances of the contact with the perpetrator were regarded as safe in 54% of cases, with elements of danger in 33% and threatening in 13% of cases. The crime was revealed by the victim in a spontaneous way in 57% of cases and in 26% the revealing was provoked by custodians, upset by physical or psychical symptoms in minors; in 16% of cases it had an accidental character. The reaction of the immediate environment was regarded as adequate in 60% of cases. Good care was taken of the minors, they were helped and mutually supported. In the remaining 40% of cases the reaction was regarded as inadequate and two forms were differentiated. In the first case the custodians had the tendency to put too much meaning into the event, expressed their own emotions and their own conviction about the irrevocable consequences of the event (16%). In the second case the event was taken lightly, the effects were thought of as negligible and the victim was blamed (24%). The testimony of the examined was regarded as highly reliable in 66% of cases, probable in 24% and less probable in 10% of cases.

Psychical effects on the victims were found in 66% of the examined. They were evaluated as serious (i.e. causing changes in selfesteem, deep fear reactions) in 23% of the examined.

Discussion of the results

The presence of defence mechanisms was found in 80% of the examined. The comparison of extremal parameters of a crime situation showed that they were present in the examined regardless of objective threat at the moment of the first contact with the perpetrator. The way in which the victim was treated during the event had a certain influence on their occurrence. The more aggressive the behaviour of the perpetrator was, the more frequent their occurrence was (r_p=0.47, Table 1).

Table 1: Perpetrator's behaviour and the occurrence of defence mechanisms

Perpetrator's behaviour	Defence mechanisms		N
	Occur	Do not occur	
Gentle	6	4	10
With elements of aggression	11	1	12
Brutal	7	1	8
N	24	6	30

r_p=0.47 average relationship power

The high relationship power (r_p=0.65) was found between the behaviour of the victim and the occurrence of defence mechanisms (Table 2). They were found in all victims whose behaviour was evaluated as cooperation, in clear majority of those whose behaviour was evaluated as passive and only in half of those who successfully resisted. Further analysis proved that the occurrence of defence mechanisms was not related to the acquaintance with the perpetrator. A minor relationship power was found between the reaction of the immediate surroundings of the examined to the event and the occurrence of the defence mechanisms. The results indicate that the occurrence of defence mechanisms is primarily conditioned by the particular elements of the relationship between the perpetrator and the victim and especially the character of interaction with the perpetrator.

Table 2: Victims behaviour and the occurrence of defence mechanisms

Victim's behaviour	Defence mechanisms		
	Occur	Do not occur	
Co-operation	7	0	7
Submission	14	2	16
Active defence	3	4	7
N	24	6	30

r_p=0.65 high relationship power

Table 3: Age of victim and defence mechanisms

Age of victim	Defence mechanisms				N
	Occur		Do not occur		
below 7	7		1		8
7 – 10	6		5		11
11 – 15	11		0		11
N	24	(80%)	6	(20%)	30

r_p=0.63 high relationship power

Further analysis showed a high relationship power (r_p=0.64) between the age of the examined and the occurrence of the defence mechanisms (Table 3). They occurred in the oldest age group in all of the examined; in 87% of the cases in the youngest group and only in half of the examined in the age group of 7 to 11 years old.

These results should be connected with two factors whose relationship with the age also proved to be strong (r_p=0.64). The first one is the character of act and the second one is the behaviour of the victim during the event. Both in the oldest and the youngest group the acts in the majority of cases included physical contacts with the perpetrator, such as mutual arousal of genitalia including sexual intercourse. In the middle age group the sexual intercourse was not present at all and the majority of acts (54%) did not involve the physical contact between the victim and the perpetrator (Table 4).

Table 4: Age of victim and the character of the act

Age of victim	Character of act			N
	No physical contact	Manipulation	Sexual intercourse	
below 7	2	4	2	8
7 – 10	6	5	0	11
11 – 15	0	4	7	11
N	8	13	9	30

r_p=0.64 high relationship power

At the same time no behaviour evaluated as cooperation was found in the youngest victims, whereas such behaviour was shown by almost the half of the oldest group. The effective defence which stopped the act was undertaken by only one member of the youngest group, one of the oldest group, and almost by half of the members from the middle age group (Table 5).

A more extensive explanation of the causes for the occurrence of defence mechanisms in the examined from the youngest and the oldest group was achieved by examining their relationship with the understanding of the crime situation by the victims. The lack of understanding or incomplete understanding of the situation was found in all of the examined in the youngest group, full understanding of the situation in 90% of the examined in the oldest group. The comparison of these results with the results concerning the relationship between the understanding of the situation by the victim and her behaviour leads to the conclusion that the causes of the occurrence of defence mechanisms in those victims might be different (Table 6).

Table 5: Age and victim's behaviour

Age of victim	Victim's behaviour			N
	Co-operation	Submission	Active defence	
below 7	0	7	1	8
7 – 10	2	4	5	11
11 – 15	5	5	1	11
N	7	16	7	30

r_p=0.61 high relationship power

Table 6: Understanding of crime situation and behaviour of victim

Understanding of crime situation	Victim's behaviour			N
	Cooperation	Submission	Active defence	
Full	5	5	3	13
Not full	2	9	2	13
Lack of	0	2	2	4
N	7	16	7	30

r_p=0.42 average relationship power

What was decisive in the youngest victims was the fact of finding oneself in an unknown and incomprehensible situation. In the oldest victims, understanding the situation, and often actively participating in the event, the most crucial were the negative emotions e.g. shame or the sense of guilt – real or anticipated.

This conclusion can be justified by the qualitative analysis of the results obtained by means of apperception techniques, on the basis of which the character of defence mechanisms was determined. It turned out that in the youngest group, the most frequently observed defence mechanism was repression and perceptual defence in the form of negation. In the oldest group, together with repression and perceptual defence (both in the form of negation and isolation) there was also rationalisation (Table 7).

It might indicate, that in the youngest group the mechanisms served first of all as a way of getting rid of negative emotions connected with the experience of the incomprehensible crime situation. One can not preclude that such reaction was additionally strengthened by the circumstances of the investigation, the interest shown by the environment, and the necessity to relate the event.

Table 7: Age of victim and character of defence mechanisms

Age of victim	Defence mechanisms				N
	Repression	Perceptual defence	Multiple mechanisms (+rationalisation)	Do not occur	
below 7	3	4	0	1	8
7 – 10	2	4	0	5	11
11 – 15	2	3	6	0	11
N	7	11	6	6	30

r_p=0.70 very high relationship power

The additional assumption leading to such a conclusion might be the results of the analysis of these deformations in the form and content of the testimonies of the examined of which the relationship with the defence mechanisms was evaluated as probable. In this group the occurrence of such deformations was found in half of those examined (Table 8).

Table 8: Age of victims and deformations of their testimony

Age of victim	Deformations of testimony		N
	Occur	Do not occur	
below 7	4	4	8
7 – 10	4	7	11
11 – 15	7	4	11
N	15	15	30

r_p=0.32 average relationship power

They were expressed primarily by the restriction of information concerning the sexual character of the event (in extreme cases the testimony was not obtained at all), and the concentration on secondary details. No statements leading to the justification of one's behaviour was found. In the oldest group the situation was different. The character of the defence mechanisms might indicate that they served rather as the support of the positive self-evaluation through the justification of the victim's behaviour by socially acceptable motives.

At the same time the most serious psychical effects of an event were found in victims from this group. The deformations of testimony of which the causes were referred to defence mechanisms were found in over half of the examined (63%). These deformations were limited to restricting information concerning the victim's active participation in the event, explanation of the sequence of the victim's behaviour by means of socially acceptable motives, the denial of the existence of threat in the initial stage of the event (Table 9).

The connection between the existence of defence mechanisms in the examined and the chosen testimony features essential for the evaluation of its reliability has also been analysed. Among the general features, a strong relationship power has been found between the occurrence of defence mechanisms and the spontaneity of the testimony (r_p=0.50). The defence mechanisms limited it to a large extent (Table 10). The existence of defence mechanisms did not much affect the attention to details (r_p=0.40, Table 11).

Table 9: Age of victim and the character of deformation

Age of victim	Character of deformation			N
	Restriction of information	Giving socially acceptable motives	Do not occur	
below 7	4	0	4	8
7 – 10	3	1	7	11
11 – 15	1	6	4	11
N	8	7	15	30

r_p=0.61 high relationship power

Table 10: The occurrence of defence mechanisms spontaneity of testimony

Defence mechanisms	Spontaneity of testimony			N
	Full	Not full	Lack of	
Occur	4	10	10	24
Do not occur	3	3	0	6
N	7	13	10	30

r_p=0.50 high relationship power

Table 11: The occurrence of defence mechanisms an attention to the details

Defence mechanisms	Attention to the details			N
	High	Average	Lack of	
Occur	8	11	5	24
Do not occur	4	2	0	6
N	12	13	5	30

r_p=0.40 average relationship power

It is, however, significant that the lack of attention to details was found exclusively in the group of the examined where these mechanisms did occur. One may assume then that this phenomenon is related to the repression mechanisms. The relationship between the occurrence of defence mechanisms and such specific content of the testimony such as the description of psychical states both the victim's own and that of a perpetrator has been analysed, such descriptions were found in half of the examined, exclusively in the age group of over 7 years old. This fact is connected first of all with development features. One should note that their number was equal both in those who revealed the defence mechanisms and in those who did not. This testimony feature has a weak relationship with their occurrence.

Among the features connected with the motivation to giving testimony self-deprecating remarks, were scant (4 cases). In all cases, however, they were accompanied by the occurrence of defence mechanisms. A small number of group members preclude the generalisation. It suggests, however, that the verbalised self-deprecation does not prove greater objectivity in the evaluation of the victim's behaviour and the insight into mechanisms that control such behaviour. The analysis of statements pointing at the pardoning of the perpetrator yielded interesting results. Such tendency was shown exclusively by the youngest of the examined with accompanying defence mechanisms (Table 12).

Table 12: Age of victim and pardoning the perpetrator

Age of victim	Pardoning the perpetrator		N
	Occur	Do not occur	
below 7	6	2	8
7 – 10	0	11	11
11 – 15	3	8	11
N	9	21	30

r_p=0.76 very high relationship power

This fact should be connected to these mechanisms which bring about the tendency of denying the threat, deprecating the meaning of the event, and repressing the unpleasant experiences. The relationship between the occurrence of defence mechanisms and the evaluation of the reliability of the testimony turned out to be average. (r_p=0.40, Table 13). It seems to be understandable when we take into consideration the fact that deformations of the testimony, connected with the existence of defence mechanisms concern most of all the interpretation and evaluation of the victim's and the perpetrator's behaviour, and to a lesser extent the descriptions which, in turn, are most essential for the evaluation of the reliability of the testimony.

Table 13: Defence mechanisms and the reliability of the testimony

Defence mechanisms	Reliability of the testimony			N
	High	Average	Low	
Occur	14	7	3	24
Do not occur	6	0	0	6
N	20	7	3	30

r_p=0.40 average relationship power

Conclusions

1. The defence mechanisms were found in 80% of the examined, primarily in the youngest and the oldest age group.
2. It was found that their occurrence was related to such properties of the victim – perpetrator relationship, the character of the act, and the behaviour of the victim during the event.
3. These mechanisms occurred first of all in those examined who had cooperated with the perpetrator or had obeyed his orders, and the character of the act involved a physical contact with the victim.
4. Marked qualitative differences connected with the child's development have been found. In the youngest group the mechanisms connected with perceptual defence and repression were dominant. In the oldest group the rationalisation mechanisms appeared.
5. These mechanisms influence the deformations of testimony in a specific way. Perceptual defence and repression lead to the restriction of information and the tendency to devalue the meaning of the act through the pardoning of the perpetrator and the denial of threat. Rationalisation results in the victim's giving socially acceptable motives of her behaviour in different stages of the event through underlining the lack of assent for contact and her own active defence.
6. These deformations primarily concern the interpretation and the evaluation of the victim's and the perpetrator's behaviour, and to a lesser degree the descriptions. For this reason they do not have an essential influence on the reliability of the testimony.
7. The determination of the character of the defence mechanisms and in a larger context of the ways in which the victim might cope with internal and external stimuli, allows a psychological expert to explain the deformations and the lack of consistency in their testimony.

References

Grzegołowska-Klarkowska, H. (1986). *Mechanizmy obronne osobowoci*. Warszawa: PWN.

Jaskiewicz-Obydzinska, T., & Czerederecka, A. (1995). Psychological Evaluation of Changes in Testimony Given by Sexually Abused Juveniles. In G. Davies, S. Lloyd-Bostock, M. McMurran, & C. Wilson (Eds.), *Psychology, Law, and Criminal Justice: International Development in Research and Practice.* Berlin, New York: Walter de Gruyter.

Jaskiewicz-Obydzinska, T., & Czerederecka, A. (1995). The Influence of Victim–Offender Relationship on Chosen Testimony Features of Minors–Victims of Sexual Abuse. *Acta Sexologica, Vol. 1, No. 1.*

Steller, M., & Boychuk, T. (1992). Children as Witnesses in Sexual Abuse Case. In H. R. Dent, & R. Flin (Eds.). *Children as Witnesses*. Chichester: John Wiley and Sons.

Part 2
Cognitive Interview and Police Reaction

Further Perspectives in Cognitive Interviewing: New Directions

Elizabeth Noon and Julian Boon

Introduction

One of the most attractive aspects of the cognitive interview as it was introduced in the mid 1980's was the promise that, with the minimum of training, police officers or investigative interviewers would be able to increase the amount of information that they could elicit from a witness without significantly effecting the amount of inaccurate information and confabulation elicited.

Early results were promising (for reviews see Geiselman, 1992; Memon and Bull, 1991; and Memon and Köhnken, 1992). However, the research has moved on and the definitive manual (Fisher and Geiselman, 1992) has underlined the metamorphosis of the interview from a simple mnemonic driven device to a more general broad based technique with an emphasis on communication skills. Two of the original mnemonics (change order and change perspective) receive a great deal less attention in the 1992 version of the technique. Indeed, Fisher (1992) suggested that certainly the change perspective mnemonic might usefully be consigned to the interviewers' 'tool box' to be used only where necessary.

Other research also raises questions about the functional utility of the change perspectives mnemonic (Boon and Noon, 1994).

In Britain, the Central Planning and Training Unit (CPTU) adopted the CI, and incorporated it in a national training programme. A guide for investigative interviewing was developed under the direction of a joint Association of Chief Police Officers (ACPO) and Home Office Steering Group. The CI technique has been summarised for the CPTU booklet (1992) which is now available to all police officers. The booklet summarises the interview with the aid of a flow chart diagram. A feature of this summary of the technique is the suggested sequential nature of the CI with the implication that a second recall should be a complete recall based on the change order mnemonic and a third recall should be based on the change perspective mnemonic. The summary may be interpreted as suggesting that it is only after these recalls that a probing phase should begin.

There is the risk that in adopting this summary, the underlying logic of the CI may be overlooked in favour of a rigid interview format. The aim of the current research was to examine the effects of the CI when the mnemonics were used sequentially.

Method

Participants and Design

A total of 42 students participated in the study as part of a course credit scheme. Participants were divided into two groups. Group 1 (experimental group) received CI instructions sequentially. The initial instruction was to 'reinstate context and report all', the second recall instruction was to 'change order', and the third recall instruction was to 'change perspectives'. Group 2 (control group) received standard instructions to write down everything they remembered from the video followed by requests to 'try again'.

Materials

The stimulus video was a professional quality video. It lasted for one minute and depicted an armed robbery in a small bank. The video was shown to participants individually using a 36" colour monitor from a distance of approximately four feet.

Procedure

Participants were recruited to take part in a study concerned with 'cognitive psychology'. On arrival they were shown the stimulus video and then an arrangement was made for them to return two days later.

Upon their return, participants were given a pad of A4 paper and given verbal instructions for their first recall. Participants were given as much time as they wished to complete their recall attempts. Once they had completed their first recall they were given instructions for a second recall. On completion of the second recall participants were given instructions for a third recall.

Scoring

All the participants' responses were coded and scored following the technique originating from a procedure used by Hollin (1980, 1981) and developed by Noon (1987, 1993). Information was divided into three categories; appearance, action and verbal and was coded as correct, inaccurate or confabulation.

Results

Traditionally, CI versus standard interview comparisons have examined the total information elicited from participants. In this study the aim was to compare the responses of participants in each group using the traditional approach to analysis, and also to examine the amount of additional information elicited by each recall attempt.

The amount of information elicited from participants in each group is shown in Figure 1. As can be seen, participants in the cognitive interview condition reported more information in each category than did the participants given standard instructions.

The difference in the amount of information elicited was found to be significant for appearance information ($t=2.90$, $df=40$, $p<0.01$) and for action information ($t=5.41$, $df=40$, $p<0.001$), but not for conversation ($t=1.85$, $df=40$, $p>0.05$).

An examination of the overall amount of accurate information, inaccurate information and errors of commission elicited showed that participants in the CI condition produced significantly more accurate information ($t=5.82$, $df=40$, $p<0.001$), significantly more inaccurate information ($t=2.72$, $df=40$, $p<0.05$) and also significantly more errors of commission ($t=2.56$, $df=40$, $p<0.05$) than did participants in the control condition (see Figure 2 and Table 1).

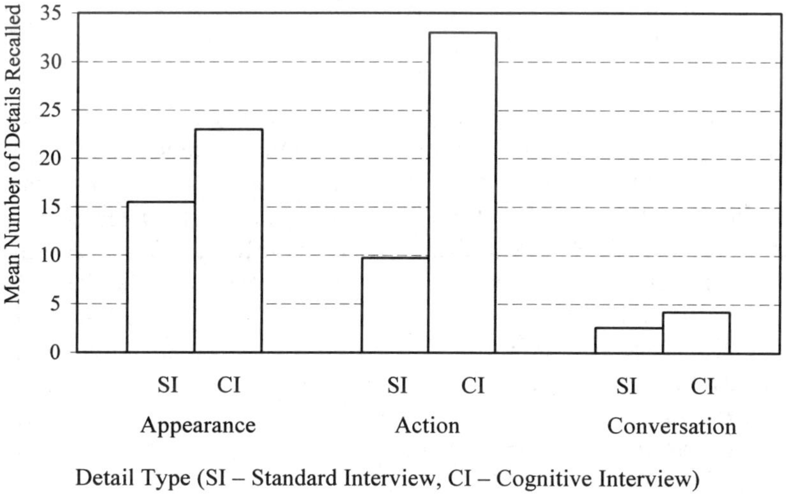

Figure 1: Types of Detail Most Frequently Recalled in Standard and Cognitive Interviews

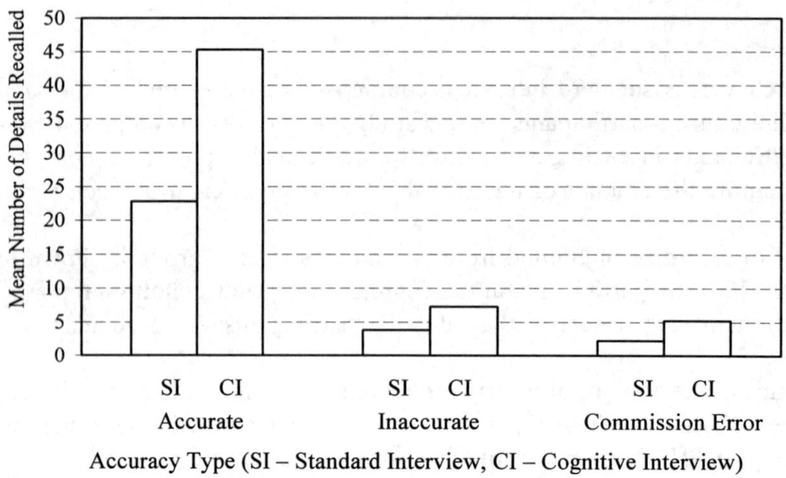

Figure 2: Accurate Recall/Inaccurate Recall/Commission Error in Standard and Cognitive Interviews

Table 1: Total Information: Means

	Cognitive interview	Standard interview	Significance
Accurate	45.52	22.57	0.001
Inaccurate	7.33	3.57	0.05
Errors of commission	5.24	2.19	0.05

A more detailed examination of the information elicited showed that participants in the CI condition gave more accurate information about the appearance of the individuals seen in the film ($t=3.09$, $df=40$, $p<0.01$), and more accurate information about what happened in the film ($t=5.23$, $df=40$, $p<0.001$) than did participants in the control condition. However, there was no significant difference in the amount of accurate information elicited about the verbal content of the film, the conversation ($t=1.91$, $df=40$, $p>0.05$).

No significant difference was found in the amount of inaccurate information elicited from the two groups about appearance ($t=0.81$, $df=40$, $p>0.05$) or what was said ($t=0.28$, $df=40$, $p>0.05$). However, participants in the CI condition reported significantly more inaccurate information about what happened than those in the control condition ($t=4.15$, $df=40$, $p<0.001$).

Similarly, there was no significant difference between the two groups' propensity to confabulate about appearance ($t=1.03$, $df=40$, $p>0.05$) or conversation ($t=0.66$, $df=40$, $p>0.05$), but there was a significant difference in the amount of confabulation about what happened ($t=2.70$, $df=40$, $p<0.05$).

Results

Results indicated that the CI was responsible for significantly more correct descriptive recall, as compared to the SI ($F(1,63)=41.9$, $p<.0001$). However delay ($F(1,63)=1.5$, $p<0.2$) and the delay * interview interaction ($F<1$) proved non significant. Analysis of incorrect descriptive recall (errors), proved non significant for interview technique ($F(1,63)=2.4$, $p<.09$), delay ($F(1,63)=2.3$, $p<0.1$) and the interview * delay interaction ($F<1$). Thus these results for recall, demonstrating the beneficial effects of the CI without a corresponding increase in errors, are consistent with the current literature on the CI.

Analysis of the number of questions asked, indicated that the CI was responsible for significantly more questions being asked ($F(1,65)=39.7$, $p<.0001$) than the SI. Delay was also found to be significant ($F(1,65)=8.8$, $p<.005$), with the number of questions being asked increasing, across both interview techniques, with prolonged delay. The interaction interview * delay proved non significant ($F(1,65)=1.2$, $p<.3$). Worried about a possible confound between the number of questions asked and the obtained beneficial effects of the CI, an ANCOVA analysis was performed using the number of questions asked as the co-variate. Results indicated that interview technique remained significant.

Analyses of the amount of feedback given by the interviewer to encourage the witness, indicated that the CI interviewers were responsible for significantly more feedback ($p<.0001$) as compared to the SI interviewers, delay also proved significant ($p<.01$), with the amount of feedback given increasing with prolonged delay. The interaction interview * delay proved non significant ($F<1$).

Table 1: Means for Recall and Percent Rates of Recognition for both Interview Conditions

	Cognitive Interview Recall	Structured Interview
Recall		
– Correct Recall	36.4	18.8
– Errors Reported	7.8	5.9
– Pre–Post Confidence Difference	+1.4	+0.7
– Number of Questions Asked	18.2	9.8
– Amount of Feedback Given	5.7	1.4
Recognition		
– Correct Blank Rejection	83%	64%
– Correct Filled Identification	58%	52%

Interview Confidence Ratings

In order to gage the magnitude and direction of any changes in subjects' interview confidence ratings, due to either interview technique or delay, a "pre–post interview difference" measure was calculated. This involved subtracting a witness's pre-interview confidence rating from their post-interview confidence rating. This pre–post interview difference was significantly higher in the CI condition as compared to the SI ($F(1,64)=4.6$, $p<.04$). However with delay and the interaction interview * delay proved non significant (both F's<1). This indicates that an individuals confidence ratings are higher after an interview of any type, but only significantly so for the CI.

On the bases of an AAH, it can be hypothesized that a witness draws on a number of different sources before making a confidence judgment. It was hypothesized, therefore, that these differences in pre–post interview confidence ratings may be accounted for by differing amounts of recall, feedback, and the number of questions asked, associated with each interview technique. However multiple regression analysis with these predictors, proved non significant for both interview techniques.

This suggests that higher pre–post interview confidence ratings obtained from the CI may be more intrinsically related to the CI as an overall technique. We suggest that the use of the cognitive mnemonics may accentuate this increase in confidence. For example, the "report all" and "context reinstate" mnemonics may encourage a witness to believe that as they have recalled so much about the event – where they saw it, the feelings they experienced, and even the seemingly unimportant information, – they must have a good memory. Similarly the recalling of information from a variety of perspectives (change order & change perspective), may act to "cement" the event more firmly in the memory, making it more consistent, thus making a final access, from which to asses accuracy, easier, more coherent and vivid, therefore implying accuracy.

The Confidence Accuracy Relationship for Recall

Several Spearman's correlations were conducted between pre-, post- and the pre-post interview difference and correct recall. These r's were conducted as a function of interview technique and delay. However, very few of these analysis proved significant, and those that were can be considered spurious because of (a) the large number conducted, and (b) the unprincipled nature of the significant correlations obtained.

Further analyses of the confidence/accuracy relationship were also conducted for the particular recall domains, person, object, action, location, and temporal, as a function of interview technique. Significant relationships were found only for the recall domains Person in the CI condition, and Object in the SI condition.

Sixty-four within subject correlations, were also conducted. It was intended from these scores to calculate a mean within- subject correlation, as done by those studies which have previously looked at within- subject scores, (for example Smith, Kassin and Ellsworth 1989). However, out of the 64 correlations conducted only 5 proved to be significant, and so further analysis was not undertaken.

It is somewhat surprising that with so many correlations being conducted, so few proved to be significant. A frequent explanation put forward for failures to find significant confidence/accuracy relationships is Deffenbacher's "optimality hypotheses" (1980), in which it is suggested that confidence/accuracy relationships will only be found in optimal conditions. We, however, do not believe that in this instance this is a viable explanation for our non findings. We believe that, because of the optimal viewing condition provided at encoding, and the relatively short delay utilized, conditions were in fact optimal. One suggested reason for our non findings is our use of an active interview, be it a CI or SI, which required witnesses to reconstruct and recall event information in as much detail as possible.

Leippe (1980) notes that more complex memories, such as that needed to recall an event, depend upon our cognitive abilities, past experiences, and expectancies, to reconstruct them. He nicely summarizes the importance of the reconstructional nature of memory, in the finding of confidence/accuracy relationships, with the premise that "as the reconstructive processes become more extensive, the accuracy/confidence relationship should become correspondingly smaller." In addition to this, Leippe also notes the importance of social influences on the confidence/accuracy relationship. "As social influences increase, the correspondence of accuracy and confidence should decrease."

We suggest that by using interviews, recall was not only actively reconstructed, but also socially enriched, therefore giving more scope for the use of an AAH for a witness to draw upon when giving a confidence assessment of their accuracy.

Confidence and Lineup Presentations

One of the most important findings to come out of these analyses on confidence for recognition ability, is that unlike for recall, lineup presentation confidence ratings did not significantly differ as a function of interview technique. This alleviated one of our major fears about the CI's confidence boosting effects on recall following through to the lineup stage of the investigation. The data did suggest however, that differing sources of information may be drawn upon for confidence judgments for recall and recognition.

On the bases of our AAH we next aimed to investigate what factors regressed to the confidence ratings for recognition. However, due to the predominantly non significant of our results, they will be presented only briefly in tabulated format.

As can be seen across confidence ratings, no consistent moderator was found. The person confidence rating, proved significant only for pre- and post-filled confidence ratings. Delay proved non significant for all ratings. Correct person recall proved significant for only the pre-blank confidence rating, with choice from blank proving significant for only pre-filled confidence ratings, and with choice from filled also proving non significant. Total person recall does however appear to be a promising candidate for future research, as it is significant for 3 of the 4 confidence ratings.

Table 2: Moderators of Confidence Ratings (Pre and Post) for Both Blank and Filled Line Up Presentation (Interview Technique Combined)

Moderators	Blank		Filled	
	Pre	Post	Pre	Post
Person Confidence Score	t= 1.3	t=–.2	t=2.2*	t=2.5**
Delay	t=–1.1	t= .7	t= .3	t=–.4
Correct Person Recall	t= 5.8**	t=1.9	t=1.7	t= .9
Total Person Recall	t=–2.9**	t= .4	t=1.9*	t=2.8**
Choice from Blank	–	t=1.7	t=2.2*	t= .4
Choice from Filled	–	–	–	t=1.2
* Significant at p<.05 ** Significant at p<.001	Pre Blank Adjusted R=.31 Sig F<. 001	Post Blank Adjusted R=.06 Sig F<. 05	Pre Filled Adjusted R=.25 Sig F<.001	Post Filled Adjusted R=.15 Sig F<.01

Predictors of Recognition Ability

Our major hypotheses, the effect of interview technique on recognition ability, proved non significant by chi square analyses, and so is in line with the previous findings on the effects of the CI on recognition (i.e., Fisher et al, 1990). As context reinstatement is a key component of the CI, these findings (non effects of the CI on recognition) are inconsistent with those studies which have indicated a beneficial effect of context on recognition (for example, Malpass and Devine 1981).

One of the most commonly cited explanations of the non effects of context manipulations on recognition performance, is that of the outshining hypotheses as suggested by Smith (1988). Our results from this and two follow up studies (Gwyer & Clifford, in preparation), fit nicely into such an explanation, as context effects were found for free recall, a task with weak cues, but not for recognition, a task with powerful cues.

In our follow up studies on the effects of context reinstatement on recognition, we have used varying context reinstatement manipulations, with results indicating that CI type context reinstatement manipulations do not reliably improve recognition. However multiple reinstatement manipulations, as used by those studies which have found a positive effect of context on recognition, are yielding more promising results.

We next used multiple regression analyse to test several predictors of recognition ability for both lineup presentations. These are presented briefly below in Table 3. As can be seen from the table, none of the confidence ratings were significantly related to recognition performance, delay also proved to be non significant. Interview technique did in this instance prove significant, but only for the blank lineup presentation, with the CI being responsible for more correct rejections. The negative effect is purely an artefact of the method of data entry.

Table 3: Predictors of Recognition Accuracy From Both Blank and Filled Line Up Presentations (Interview Technique Combined)

Predictor of Recognition	Blank	Filled
Pre Line Up Confidence	t= .6	t= .7
Post Line Up Confidence	t= 1.5	t= .8
Pre- Post Presentation Confidence	t= −.6	t= .9
Person Confidence	t= −.6	t= 1.9
Interview Technique	t=−2.9**	t= .6
Delay	t= 1.3	t=−.7
Correct Person Recall	t= −.5	t=2.2**
Total Person Recall	t=−2.4*	t=−.5
Choice From Blank	–	t=1.0
* Sig at $p<.05$	Adjusted R=.13	Adjusted R=.04
** Sig at $p<.001$	Sig $F<.001$	Sig $F<.08$

Correct person recall proved significant for correct identification from the filled lineup presentation, such that increases in person recall correlated with correct identification. This is seemingly out of line with the work of Wells (1985), and Pigott and Brigham (1985), who noted that prior verbal descriptions of faces are not related to recognition accuracy. However the low adjusted R value, and the overall non significance of the analyses, indicates the amount of variance accounted for is marginal, and so is not contrary to such research.

The negative value for total person recall, was somewhat perplexing. It suggested that increased total person recall produced an increase in incorrect identification from the blank presentation. This is odd as the CI, which is indicative of an increase in total person recall, was responsible for more correct rejections: the opposite effect! This finding was clarified, however, by further analysis of interview technique, which indicated that this negative value was due to the SI condition. The CI allowed an increase in total person recall, without a detrimental effect upon correct rejection. In the SI, however, increases in total person recall were responsible for increases in the rate of false identification.

Conclusion

Overall, in the recall phase of the experiment, we have found that the CI was responsible for a significant increase in confidence, correct recall, the number of questions asked, and the amount of interviewer feedback utilized relative to the SI. The hypotheses of an AAH being able to account for this increase in confidence was not confirmed, with none of the expected predictors significantly contributing to these increases in confidence ratings. We therefore suggest it may be the cognitive mnemonics of the CI which account for this increase in confidence.

In regard to the confidence/accuracy relationship, despite several attempts to expose such a correlation, no consistent relationship between confidence/accuracy was found. We suggest that this may be due to the interactive nature of the interview techniques used.

As for recognition, we suggest that the use of mental context reinstatement instructions, as found in the CI are sufficient to improve recall but not recognition. Our follow up studies have indicated that for context manipulations to be powerful enough to improve recognition, they may have to be stated multiple times.

One worry we had, that the CI could produce an unwarranted increase in feelings of confidence in wrongful identification was, thankfully dispelled: the CI did not produce unjustified confidence in wrong identifications.

With regard to our hypotheses that a witness draws upon a number of sources when assessing the accuracy of recall or recognition, via the use of an AAH, it can be clearly seen that we are a long way from an answer. However, it does seem clear that witnesses do consider recall and recognition to be two quite different tasks, as shown by the differential effects of the CI on confidence in recall and identification.

References

Deffenbacher, K. A. (1980). Eyewitness accuracy and confidence: Can we infer anything about their relationship? *Law and Human Behaviour, 4*, 242-260.

Fisher, R. P., Geiselman, R. E., Raymond, D. S., Jurkevich, L. M., & Warhaftig, M. L. (1987). Enhancing enhanced eyewitness memory: Refining the cognitive interview. *Journal of Police Science and Administration, 15*, 291-297.

Fisher, R. P., Quigley, K. L., Brock, P., Chin, D., & Cutler, B. L. (1990). The effectiveness of the cognitive interview in description and identification tasks. In D. Ross, J. Read, & M. Toglia (Eds.). *Eyewitness memory: Current trends and developments*. Cambridge University Press 1994.

Geiselman, R. E., Fisher, R. P., Firstenberg, I., Hutton, L. A., Sullivan, S. J., Avetissian, I. V., & Prosk, A. L. (1984). Enhancement of eyewitness memory: An empirical evaluation of the cognitive interview. *Journal of Police Science and Administration, 12*, 74-80.

George, R. (1991). *A field and experimental evaluation of three methods of interviewing witnesses/victims of crime.* Unpublished manuscript. Polytechnic of East London, London.

Krafka, C., & Penrod, S. (1985). Reinstatement of context in a field experiment on eyewitness identification. *Journal of Personality and Social Psychology, 49*, 58-69.

Leippe, M. R. (1980). Effects of integrative memorial and cognitive processes on the correspondence of eyewitness accuracy and confidence. *Law and Human Behaviour, 4*.

Malpass, R. S., & Devine, P. G. (1981). Guided memory in eyewitness identification. *Journal of Applied Psychology, 66*, 343-350

Smith, S. M. (1988). Environmental context-dependent memory. In G. M. Davies., & D. M. Thomson (Eds.), *Memory in Context: Context in Memory*. Chichester: Wiley.

Smith, V. L., Kassin, S. M., & Ellsworth, P. C. (1989). Eyewitness accuracy and confidence: within versus between subject correlations. *Journal of Applied Psychology, 74, (2)*, 356-359.

Wells, G. L. (1985). Verbal descriptions of faces from memory: Are they diagnostic of identification accuracy. *Journal of Applied Psychology, 70*, 619-626.

Wells, G. L., & Murray, D. M. (1984). Eyewitness confidence. In G. l. Wells., & E. F. Loftus (Eds.). *Eyewitness Testimony Psychological Perspectives*. Cambridge University Press.

Cognitive Interview: When Any Context Reinstatement Instruction is Successful

Laura Campos and Marisa Alonso-Quecuty[1]

Since Geiselman and Fisher devised the procedure of interviewing known as Cognitive Interview (CI) under laboratory conditions (Geiselman, Fisher, Firstenberg, Hutton, Sullivan, Avetissian and Prosk, 1984), a great number of studies have been carried out on CI (see Bekerian and Dennett, 1992). Some of these studies show context reinstatement as the most effective technique of CI (e.g.: Memon and Köhnken, 1992). Research into the effects that context reinstatement has on memory is abundant (e.g.: Bower, 1981; Bower and Cohen, 1982; Davies, 1986; Godden and Baddeley, 1975; Godden and Baddeley, 1980; Goodwin, Powell, Bremer, Hoine and Stern, 1969; Smith, Glenberg and Bjork, 1978), and the results obtained frequently show that context reinstatement aids memory, both in recollection as well as in recognition.

The beneficial influence of context reinstatement has its theoretical explanation in the Encoding Specificity Principle developed by Tulving and Thomson (1973). According to Tulving, the memory, or retrieval of a specific event depends on the extent to which environmental cues at the time of retrieval overlap with the initially encoded features (Tulving, 1979). In this way, any aspect of an environment in which a "to be remembered" stimulus is encoded can, in theory, serve as a contextual cue; therefore, a retrieval context, which reconstructs the original environment, should enhance memory (Bekerian and Bowers, 1983).

But the context does not always support the subjects' memory. Sometimes context reinstatement does not affect significantly the subjects' efficiency in recollection tests nor in recognition tests; or it may even have a "negative cueing" effect (Fernández and Alonso, 1994; Fernández and Glenberg, 1985; Loftus, Manber and Keating, 1983; Saufley, Otaka and Bavaresco, 1985). The theoretical explanation for the absence of effects of the context reinstatement is proposed by Smith (1988), who states the Outshining hypothesis. According to this hypothesis, an incidentally encoded context cues memory when better cue sources are absent (i.e. they were not encoded or they were missing from the test information), but context cues can be completely outshone when better cues are present. Outshining emphasizes the rela-

[1] This research was supported by the Spanish Ministerio de Educación y Ciencia (PB93-0566-C03-01) and the Canarian Government (grant 93/171).

tivity of context cueing; a cue's effectiveness depends upon the presence of better cues. Finally, when a correct codification of the "to be remembered" event has not been performed, the additional contextual information will always enhance memory (Smith, 1985a).

The Cognitive Interview has been the object of numerous studies where a variety of context reinstatement instructions has been used. Thus, some researchers give the subjects instructions to remember environmental details of the scene (weather, specified time, the place where he or she was, people who were present), other researchers give the subjects instructions to remember their emotional reactions, feelings and thoughts where the event took place (surprise, fear) and usually both types of context reinstatement instructions are given together (Fisher, Geiselman, Raymond, Jurkevich and Warhaftig, 1987; Fisher and Geiselman, 1992; Geiselman et al., 1984; Geiselman, Fisher, MacKinnon and Holland, 1985; Memon and Bull, 1991).

According to Tulving`s Encoding Specificity Principle where the stimulus to be remembered has been encoded can serve as (Tulving and Thomson, 1973), any aspect of an environment a contextual cue. Therefore, we can hypothesize that the type of context reinstatement instruction given to the subjects will not produce significant differences in their statements. Nevertheless, this hypothesis has not been experimentally tested.

The main aim of this research is the systematic study of different context reinstatement instructions and their possible effects on the statements of the eyewitnesses obtained by means of the CI. Thus, it is expected that the statements obtained by means of CI will not be affected by the type of context reinstatement instruction used (Tulving and Thomson, 1973). Furthermore, it is expected that the Cognitive Interview will always produce richer statements as compared to a Standard Interview (Fisher and Geiselman, 1992).

Method

Subjects

One hundred and two undergraduate students from University of La Laguna volunteered to participate in the experiment. There were 80 females and 22 males. Their ages ranged from 19 to 21 (mean 19.38).

Materials

A video tape with a simulated incident was recorded in the campus parking area of the University of La Laguna. The recording began with two young people approaching a parked car. They tried to open the door in a very suspicious manner.

Then, several people appeared arguing about whether they had the right to open the car or not. Among them appeared the car owner and, later, an accomplice of the suspects. The sequence culminated in physical and verbal threats from the three young men (the two thieves and the accomplice) against the owner of the car (who was threatened with a knife) and a witness. The dispute came to an end with the arrival of the police and the flight of the three suspects.

The tape lasted 15 minutes. The length of the incident and the action-packed event, gave the material a high ecological validity as compared with that traditionally used in the CI research (a three minute event with only two characters: the owner of the Liquor Store and the assailant) (Hernandez-Fernaud and Alonso-Quecuty, 1997). A protocol for analysis of the dependent variables was also created.

Design

A nested design was used. The first factor (type of interview)has two levels: standard/cognitive. A second factor was nested in the cognitive interview (type of context reinstatement). This one had four levels: laboratory/ film/ internal/ physical. The following dependent measures were employed:

1. Accuracy: exact information given by the subjects. Response accuracy was classified into three categories according to whether the exact detail mentioned referred to persons, objects or events.
2. Errors: information given by the subjects which, even though it featured in the recording, was in some way distorted (e.g. if he car's make was "Renault", describing it as "Seat"). Errors were classified into three categories according to whether they referred to persons, objects or events.
3. Confabulation: information given by the subjects that did not appear in the film (e.g. the mention of a motorbike). Once again, confabulation was classified into three categories: persons, objects and events.
4. Contextual Information: information given by the individuals which refers to space and time aspects (where and when details)
5. Semantic Information: explanations and inferences given spontaneously by the subjects.
6. Sensorial Details: information given by the subjects which can be perceived by the senses (colours, textures, sounds...).
7. Internal Information: idiosyncratic information given by the subjects (emotions, thoughts).

Procedure

All the subjects went through two experimental stages. In the first phase, the subjects observed the video tape sequence showing the simulated incident in groups. After having seen the sequence, the subjects carried out a distracting activity for fifteen minutes (a crossword puzzle). When finished, they entered individual cubicles where the second phase of the experiment took place.

In the second phase, separate individual verbal statements were collected. These were audiotaped by trained interviewers. The subjects were distributed randomly among five experimental groups according to the type of interview and type of reinstatement of context to which they had been assigned. Thus, the subjects in group 1 were questioned using a standard interview narrative. It consisted of only asking the question "What happened?", taking down a statement in narrative form. In the groups 2, 3, 4 and 5 subjects were questioned using a Cognitive Interview. These groups were differentiated by the reinstatement of context instruction. The subjects in group 2 had to reinstate mentally the laboratory context where they watched the film (furniture, specified time, temperature of the room...); the subjects in group 3 had to reinstate mentally the physical context in the film where the event took place as if they really had been there (student residence, parked cars...); the subjects in group 4 had to reinstate mentally the internal context they experienced when they watched the film (emotions, feelings, thoughts). Finally, the subjects in group 5 were placed in the real context where the event happened (the campus parking area of the University of La Laguna) and there they were questioned using a Cognitive Interview.

Results and discussion

As a preliminary step towards the analysis of the dependent variables (accuracy, errors and confabulations) a synthesis of the sequence seen by the witnesses was created. This transcription, in the form of a script, listed the most relevant elements of the action.

A group of judges decided when contextual information, semantic information, sensorial details and internal information were present in each statement. The judges were doctoral students trained in this detection task. The agreement between the judges was higher than 0.80.

Several students t-tests were performed on each of the dependent variables comparing accounts from subjects questioned using the SI with those from subjects questioned using the CI:

- SI/CI with laboratory reinstatement instruction
- SI/CI with film reinstatement instruction
- SI/CI with internal reinstatement instruction
- SI/CI with physical reinstatement instruction

Significant differences between SI/CI were found in all of these contrasts. The statements obtained by means of the CI contained more contextual information, more sensorial details, more semantic information, more internal information and were more accurate than those obtained by means of the SI, independently of the type of context reinstatement instruction (laboratory/ film/ internal/ physical) used. Likewise, the CI did not significantly increase the number of confabulations in the statements. These results are consistent with those previously obtained in research on the CI performed both by American (Fisher and Geiselman, 1992), and by European researchers (Köhnken, Schimossek, Aschermann and Höfer, 1991).

A significant increase of number of errors about persons were found in statements obtained by the CI. The results are similar to those obtained in research on the CI performed in Europe.

Several one way analyses of variance (ANOVA) on each one of the dependent variables were performed. No significant differences were obtained for the type of context reinstatement instruction on any dependent variable.

Thus, our first hypothesis has been also confirmed: the type of interview seems to be the critical factor that explains the differences between statements; consistent with the Encoding Specificity Principle (Tulving and Thomson, 1973).

However, in our experiment, all the participants were students from University of La Laguna who had frequently visited the campus parking area, that is, the context where the event took place. Thus, the effects produced by the different types of context reinstatement instructions could have been outshone if the subjects used cues provided by their previous knowledge (Smith, 1988).

When a new experiment was carried out to test the Outshining Hypothesis, results confirmed the importance that the previous knowledge of the "crime context" has in research on the CI (Campos and Alonso-Quecuty, in press).

References

Bekerian, D. A., & Bowers, J. M. (1983). Eyewitness memory: were we mislead? *Journal of Experimental Psychology: Learning, Memory and Cognition, 9*, 139-145.

Bekerian, D. A., & Dennett, J. L. (1993). The Cognitive Interview Technique: Reviving the Issues. *Applied Cognitive Psychology, 7*, 275-297.

Bower, G. H. (1981). Mood and Memory. *American Psychologist, Vol. 36, No. 2*, 129-148.

Bower, G. H., & Cohen, P. R. (1982). Emotional influences in memory and thinking: data and theory. In M. Clark, & S. Fiske (Eds.): Affect and Cognition, IEA, NJ.

Campos, L., & Alonso-Quecuty, M. L. (in press). Memory and knowledge of crime context: Beyond context reinstatement instructions. *Memory.*

Davies, G. M. (1986). Context effects in episodic memory: a review. *Cahiers de Psychologie Cognitive, 6 (2)*, 157-174.

Fernandez, A., & Alonso, M. A. (1994). Contexto ambiental y recuerdo: el efecto nulo de la manipulación de habitaciones. *Revista de Psicologia General y Aplicada, 47 (1)*, 41-44.

Fernandez, A., & Glenberg, A. M. (1985). Changing environmental context does not reliably affect memory. *Memory and Cognition, 13*, 333-345.

Fisher, R. P., & Geiselman, R. E. (1992). *Memory-Enhancing Techniques for Investigative Interview*. Illinois: Charles C. Thomas Publisher.

Fisher, R. P., Geiselman, R. E., Raymond, D. S., Jurkevich, L. M., & Warhaftig, M. L. (1987). Enhancing eyewitness memory: refining the cognitive interview. *Journal of Police Science and Administration, 15*, 291-297.

Geiselman, R. E., Fisher, R. P., Firstenberg, I., Hutton, L. A., Sullivan, S. J., Avetissian, I., & Prosk, A. (1984). Enhancement of eyewitness memory: an empirical evaluation of the cognitive interview. *Journal of Police Science and Administration, 12*, 74-80.

Geiselman, R. E., Fisher, R. P., MacKinnon, D. P., & Holland, H. L. (1985). Eyewitness memory enhancement in the police interview: cognitive retrieval mnemonics versus hypnosis. *Journal of Applied Psychology, 70*, 401-412.

Godden, D. R., & Baddeley, A. D. (1975). Context-dependent memory in two natural environments: on land and underwater. *British Journal of Psychology, 66*, 325-332.

Godden, D. R., & Baddeley, A. D. (1980). When does context influence recognition memory? *British Journal of Psychology, 71*, 99-104.

Goodwin, D. W., Powell, B., Bremer, D., Hoine, H., & Stern, J. (1969). Alcohol and recall: state dependent effects in man. *Science, 163*, 13-58.

Hernandez-Fernaud, E., & Alonso-Quecuty, M. L. (1997). Cognitive Interview and lie detection: A new magnifying glass for Sherlock Holmes? *Applied Cognitive Psychology, 11*, 55-68.

Köhnken, G., Schimossek, E., Aschermann, E., & Höfer, E. (1991). *The cognitive interview and statement validity analysis.* Paper presented at the International Conference on Memory in Lancaster.

Loftus, E. F., Manber, M., & Keating, J. P. (1983). Recollection of naturalistic events: context enhancement versus negative cueing. *Human Learning, 2*, 83-92.

Memon, A., & Bull, R. (1991). The cognitive interview, its origins, empirical support, evaluation and practical implications. *Journal of Community and Applied Social Psychology, 1*, 291-307.

Memon, A., & Köhnken, G. (1992). Helping witnesses to remember more: The cognitive interview. *Expert Evidence*, pp. 39-48.

Saufley, W. H.; Otaka, S. R., & Bavaresco, J. L. (1985). Context effects: classroom tests and context independence. *Memory and Cognition, 13*, 522-528.

Smith, S. M. (1985a). Environmental context and recognition memory reconsidered. *Bulletin of the Psychonomic Society, 23*, 173 176.

Smith, S. M. (1988). Environmental context-dependent memory. In G. M. Davies, & D. M. Thomson (Eds.), *Memory in Context: Context in Memory, 2*, 13-34. Chichester: Wiley.

Smith, S. M., Glenberg, A. M., & Bjork, R. A. (1978). Environmental context and human memory. *Memory and Cognition, 6*, 342-353.

Tulving, E. (1979). Relation Between Encoding specificity and levels of processing. In Cermak, & Craik (Eds.): *Levels of processing in human memory.* Hillsdale, NJ: Lawrence Erlbaum Associates.

Tulving, E., & Thomson, D. M. (1973). Encoding Specificity and Retrieval Processes in episodic memory. *Psychological Review. 80*, 5, 352-373.

Cognitive Interview: Confronting True and False Statements

Estefania Hernandez-Fernaud and Marisa Alonso-Quecuty[1]

Generally, the police interview witnesses and victims asking them for a narrative account of the incident. More specific questions are then formulated based on the witnesses' account. The use of these standard interviewing techniques may interfere with the reliability of information gathered. That has led Geiselman et al. (1984) to develop an alternative method of questioning known as the Cognitive Interview. The cognitive interview (CI) is composed of four techniques: a) cognitive reestablishment of the context, b) emphasis on the recovery of all kinds of details, c) recounting events in a different order, d) change in perspective. After obtaining this final version of what occurred, a series of auxiliary techniques are employed where appropriate for the recollection of details concerning: physical appearance, names, objects, conversations and features of speech.

The Cognitive Interview has been the object of numerous studies undertaken both by American (Fisher and Geiselman, 1992), and by European researchers (Bekerian and Dennett, 1993; Boon and Noon, 1994; Köhnken, Milne, Memon and Bull, 1992). In the majority of cases, it has been observed that the individuals who were interviewed by means of the CI remembered more accurate information concerning persons and the sequence of events and did not generate more inaccurate information than the standard interview (SI). However in a metaanalysis on the effects of the cognitive interview based on several studies (Köhnken, Milne, Memon and Bull, 1992) an overall significant increase in incorrect information was found.

The CI starts from the premise that the witness, victim or suspect wishes to collaborate. But, what happens if this is not the case? More seriously, what happens if he/she is lying? Only on one occasion has the capacity of the CI to obtain information from persons not wishing to collaborate been researched (Stephenson, 1991). The results of this study were still favourable for the CI

[1] This research was supported by the Spanish Ministerio de Educación y Ciencia (DGICYT grants PB89-0170-CO3-01 and PB93-0566-C03-01)) and the Canarian Government (grant 93/171) of the second author and a postgrade grant (DGICYT) of the first author. Special appreciation to Ray Bull and Günter Köhnken for their suggestions.

against the SI. However, the second of our questions remains unanswered: How does the CI work with witnesses who lie?

The main aim of this study is to examine the differences between true and false statements as regarding the interview technique employed (CI/SI).

We have formulated the following hypotheses:

The Cognitive Interview will produce more accurate details, without increasing errors, as compared to a Standard Interview (Fisher and Geiselman, 1992).

The truthful statements will be distinguished from the false ones according to the following criteria:

(i) truthful statements will be more accurate

(ii) false statements will contain more confabulations.

The CI will enable a greater discrimination between true and false accounts of witnesses as compared to SI.

Method

– *Subjects:* The sample was composed by seventy three undergraduate students from the University of La Laguna.

– *Materials:* A video tape with a sequence of a simulated incident: the robbery of a car. The tape lasted 15 minutes. The length of the incident (15 minutes) and the action-packed event (12 characters), gave the material a high ecological value as compared with that traditionally used in CI research.

– *Design:* A 2 (type of interview: standard/cognitive) x 2 (type of statements: true/false) factorial design was used.

The following dependent measures were employed: (1) Accuracy: exact information given by the individuals. (2) Errors: information given by the individuals, which, even though it featured in the recording, was in some way distorted. (3) Confabulation: information given by the individuals that did not appear at any time in the film. The accuracy, errors and confabulations were classified into three categories: persons, objects and events.

– *Procedure:* Subjects passed through two experimental phases:

First phase: the individuals observed in groups the video tape sequence showing the simulated incident.

Second phase: individual verbal statements were collected separately. These were audiotaped by trained interviewers.

Subjects were distributed randomly among four experimental groups according to the type of interview and type of statement to which they had been assigned:

Group 1: Standard Interview + Truthful Version

Group 2: Standard Interview + False Version

Group 3: Cognitive Interview + Truthful Version

Group 4: Cognitive Interview + False Version

Results

Several 2 (type of interview) x 2 (type of statement) analyses of variance (ANOVA) performed on each one of the dependent variables revealed some significant main effects and interactions.

Accuracy

– Persons: In the first place, a significant effect of Type of Interview ($F(1,68)=34.54$; $p<.01$) was obtained. The statements obtained by means of CI contain more accurate information than those obtained by means of SI. Likewise, a significant effect of Type of Statement ($F(1,68)=38.32$; $p<.01$) was obtained. The number of accurate details referring to persons is greater in the true statements than in the false ones. No significant interaction of Type of Interview with Type of Statement was found ($F(1,72)=0.26$; $p>.05$).

– Events: A significant effect of Type of Interview ($F(1,68)=45.23$; $p<.01$) was secured. The statements obtained with CI contained more accurate information on events than those obtained through SI. A significant effect of Type of Statement ($F(1,68)=52.36$; $p<.01$) was also found. The truthful statements presented a greater amount of accurate information on events.

Finally, a significant Type of Interview with Type of Statement interaction ($F(1,72)=5.23$; $p<.05$) was found. The CI enables the extraction of more accurate information in the true testimonies than the SI.

– Objects: a significant effect of Type of Interview ($F(1,68)=11.05$; $p>.01$) was found. More accurate information on objects is obtained with the CI than with the SI. No significant effect of Type of Statement ($F(1,68)=2.79$; $p>.05$), nor any significant interaction of Type of Interview with Type of Statement ($F(1,72)=0.79$; $p>.05$) were found.

The results obtained confirm what was raised in our first two hypotheses for the accuracy variable: the statements obtained by means of the CI provided a greater number of accurate details relating to persons, events and objects than did those obtained by means of the SI, the truthful statements always containing the greater number of accurate details.

Errors

– Persons: In the first place, a significant effect of Type of Interview ($F(1,68)=19.94$; $p<.01$) was obtained. The statements secured with the CI contained more errors on persons than those obtained with the SI. Likewise, a significant effect of Type of Statement ($F(1,68)=4.04$; $p<.05$) was obtained. The number of errors referring to persons is greater in the truthful statements than in the false ones. No significant interaction of Type of Interview with Type of Statement ($F(1,72)=1.07$; $p>.05$) was found.

– Events: A significant effect of Type of Statement ($F(1,68)=6.46$; $p<.05$) was found. The number of errors referring to events is greater in true statements than in false ones. No significant effect of Type of Interview, nor interaction of Type of Interview by Type of Statement ($F(1,72)=0.15$; $p>.05$) were found.

– Objects: No significant effect of Type of Interview ($F(1,68)=2.41$; $p>.05$), nor of Type of Statement ($F(1,68)=1.79$; $p>.05$) were found. Neither was a significant Type of Interview with Type of Statement interaction ($F(1,72)=2.17$; $p>.05$) found.

The results secured almost totally confirm what was raised in our first hypothesis for the error variable: the CI did not produce more errors than the SI, except where persons were concerned.

Confabulations

– Persons: In the first place, a significant effect of Type of Interview ($F(1,68)=59.31$; $p<.01$) was obtained. The statements secured by means of the CI contained more confabulations on persons than those secured in the SI. Likewise, a significant effect of Type of Statement ($F(1,68)=48.38$; $p<.01$) was found. The false statements showed a higher quantity of confabulations than did the truthful ones.

Finally, a significant Type of Interview with Type of Statement interaction ($F(1,72)=51.76$; $p<.01$) was discovered. The CI enabled greater discrimination between the truthful and false accounts than did the SI.

– Events: a significant effect was obtained of Type of Interview ($F(1,68)=18.81$; $p<.01$). The statements secured with the CI contained more confabulations of events than those secured with the SI. A significant effect of Type of Statement ($F(1,68)=59.40$; $p<.01$) was also discovered. The false statements showed a higher quantity of confabulations.

Finally, a significant Type of Interview with Type of Statement ($F(1,72)=9.01$; $p<.01$) was found. Once again, the CI allows far greater discrimination between the truthful and false accounts than does the SI.

– Objects: In the first place, a significant effect of Type of Interview ($F(1,68)=5.97$; $p<.05$) was found. The statements obtained with the CI contained more confabulations on objects than those obtained with the SI. A significant effect of Type of Statement ($F(1,68)=15.26$; $p<.01$) was also found. The false statements showed a higher amount of confabulations than the true ones. No significant Type of Interview by Type of Statement was found ($F(1,72)=3.16$; $p>.05$).

These results confirm our second hypothesis: the false accounts contained more confabulations than the truthful ones. As far as the type of interview is concerned, in the recalling of events, the result was the one foreseen: the CI did not increase the amount of confabulations, but, contrary to our predictions, the CI indeed did so in the case of persons and objects.

By jointly analysing the results obtained in this group of variables: accuracy, errors and confabulations, our fourth hypothesis is confirmed. The CI is seen to be an amplifier of the differences between true and false accounts, concerning both the number of exact details it provides and the confabulation it contains.

Discussion and Conclusions

The study began by emphasising how the questioning method used with a witness is a key factor in obtaining a completely accurate statement. The Cognitive Interview, based on our knowledge of memory, reveals itself as an alternative to traditional systems of interview used until now by the various plaintiffs of legal proceedings. The studies carried out on the CI have shown that it elicits a greater amount of accurate information than the standard interview, without increasing the number of errors (see Fisher and Geiselman, 1992, and Memon and Bull, 1991 for a summary).

Generally speaking, our results confirm those secured in previous research. The statements that we have obtained with this type of interview are more accurate with an insignificant increase in the number of errors. Only in the descriptions of persons did the errors increase with the CI. This result might be explained by taking into consideration the large number of characters who made up the action which came across in the video sequence used in our research. In previous studies, only two characters appear; those involved in the hold up at the Liquor Store. Ours included twelve persons, therefore, the margin of error in the description of them logically increased. Another explanation of these results is that context reinstatement instructions could increase the witnesses confidence in their memory, making them believe that they can describe persons better than they really can.

Another unexpected result of our work is linked with confabulation. Likewise, in this case it is with persons that our results do not coincide with those of previous research. The CI elicits more confabulations on persons than the SI and the same occurs with objects. The objects which appear in our sequence (keys, knife, car, bags) were also far more numerous than in the case of the Liquor Store hold-up (gun).

On the other hand, it is in persons and objects that the Auxiliary Techniques employed in the final stage of the CI take effect. It is here that the witness may find himself forced to answer without being sure of what he is stating. At this moment in time, we are carrying out a more detailed analyses of interview procedure with the aim of detecting the behaviour of the different variables in each one of them (Hernandez-Fernaud and Alonso-Quecuty, in prep.).

This explanation is apparently inconsistent with the fact that confabulation is not increased, when the witness describes the event about which he is giving a statement. In this case, the CI continues to provide more accurate information, but without any risk of error or confabulation. If the action in our video is also far more complex and extensive than that of the Liquor Store why were no more confabulations obtained? In our opinion the answer lies once again in the Auxiliary Techniques that are focused on aspects related to objects and persons but no questions are asked about details of the event, so that the risk of error on this variable is less.

In short, the CI is shown to be a system of interview which enables the securing of accurate statements, in which the witnesses feel especially motivated to give an account of what has happened. It only remains to consider the possibility that the Auxiliary Techniques employed at the end of each procedure may affect the description of persons and objects, thus increasing the number of errors in the statement. On the other hand, the use of more complex sequences in these experiments could bring the results obtained in CI research closer to reality.

In this work, we were interested in the study of the CI, not only when the witness gives a true account of the facts, but also when the statement is intentionally false. We know that the CI leads to more detailed accounts than those achieved with the SI. Therefore, one hopes that the untruthful person will have great difficulty in keeping to his version throughout the CI. Logically, the greatest difficulty for this person is to adapt to each of the four techniques of which the CI is composed, as this should be reflected in a greater difference between these accounts and the true accounts on each of the variables used. These assumptions are confirmed in two of the three variables under study in the CI: accuracy (events) and confabulation (persons and events). Only the errors do not comply with this tendency.

The explanation of our results might be found in the flexibility which this method of questioning demands. The CI is not based on the simple repetition of the account of the event, but demands that the witness change his perspective, that he tells what happened in a different order, etc. That is to say, he is asked to be capable of giving flexible accounts and, with them, maximum information.

But, what happens to the account of a witness who lies? Our results show that the CI amplifies the differences between both types of accounts. Why? When an untruthful witness is interviewed with the SI he must keep two accounts going: the true one and the false one, which he is giving. However, with the CI, he must also introduce constant modifications to the false version. The new versions which he is required to provide make him give away more and more information on what has occurred. This information cannot correspond to reality, since he is being untruthful. All in all, the differences between his false account and what really happened gradually mount up throughout the interview.

Until now, everything that has been mentioned enables us to conclude that the Cognitive Interview is a more successful procedure for obtaining information than the Standard Interview, as it facilitates the securing of more accurate information. A second advantage of the CI lies in its greater capacity to discriminate between true and false accounts of witnesses than the SI, which, in due time, could be beneficial for lie detection.

References

Bekerian, D. A., & Dennett, J. L. (1993). The cognitive interview technique: Reviving the issues. *Applied Cognitive Psychology, 7*, 275-297.

Boon, J., & Noon, E. (1994). Changing perspectives in cognitive interviewing. *Applied and Cognitive Psychology, Vol. 1*, 59-69.

Fisher, R. P., & Geiselman, R. E. (1992). *Memory-Enhancing Techniques for Investigative Interview*. Illinois: Charles C. Thomas Publisher.

Geiselman, R. E., Fisher, R. P., Firstenberg, I., Hutton, L. A., Sullivan, S. J., Avetissian, I., & Prosk, A. (1984). Enhancement of eyewitness memory: an empirical evaluation of the cognitive interview, *Journal of Police Science and Administration, 12*, 74-80.

Hernandez-Fernaud, E., & Alonso-Quecuty, M. L. (in prep.). *La Entrevista cognitiva paso a paso: un estudio pormenorizado de las técnicas que la componen.*

Köhnken, G., Milne, R., Memon, A., & Bull, R. (1992). *A metaanalysis on the effects of the cognitive interview.* Paper presented at the 3rd European Congress on Psychology and Law, Oxford, England.

Memon, A., & Bull, R. (1991). The cognitive interview, its origins, empirical support, evaluation and practical implication. *Journal of Community and Applied Social Psychology, 1*, 291-307.

Stephenson, G. (1991). *Police interrogation*. Paper presented at First Joint Spanish-British Conference on Psychology Crime and the Law, Pamplona, Spain.

Perceptions of the Credibility and Evidential Value of Victim and Suspect Statements in Interviews

Anna Costanza Baldry and Frans Willem Winkel

The likelihood of convicting a suspect is higher if the witness' story is considered to be more convincing, more credible, and to have more evidential value (Crombag, Van Koppen, & Wagenaar, 1992). Convictions are generally of crucial importance in laws on penal evidence. If the available legal evidence does not convince the judge, in principle the acquittal of the suspect will follow. The basis in which such convictions are rooted sometimes is extremely weak, particularly in cases of rape or sexual intimidation. In reviewing the pertinent legal literature Nijboer (1994:228) for example suggests that rape and sexual assault convictions are merely based on a witness statement made by the victim, in which she actually claimed to have been raped by the suspect, supported by the statement of the suspect, in which he is *denying* the charge and which further *merely implied*, that the two parties, at a particular date, were together in his car, or that he invited her to his home.

Statements made by the victim during a police interview can thus have far reaching (and if confidence is not justified, unacceptable) consequences for the suspect. On the other hand, unjustly doubting the integrity of the victim constitutes a secondary victimization: if the credibility and evidential value of her statements is undermined by irrelevant (or extra-legal) factors – which should not play a role in the judgmental process – in a sense the victim reporting to the police is victimized or wounded again (Winkel, 1991; Winkel, Vrij, Koppelaar, & Van der Steen, 1991). Several studies suggest such irrelevant factors to be operative in police interviews of victims (Winkel & Koppelaar, 1991, 1992; Baldry, Enthoven, & Winkel, 1996; Winkel, 1981; Winkel, & De Winter, 1995). Other studies suggest such factors to be operative also in police interviews of suspects (Vrij, 1991; Vrij & Winkel, 1989, 1991, 1991a, b, 1992, 1994; Winkel & Koppelaar, 1986; Koppelaar & Winkel, 1987; Winkel, Koppelaar, & Vrij, 1988; Winkel, 1991, 1991a, 1993). Together, these studies suggest that the credibility of the communicator – either a victim or a suspect – may be undermined by extra-legal factors.

In the present experiment these two lines of research were combined in a design in which Dutch and Italian police officers were exposed to a video interview of a victim, followed by an interview of a suspect. The design is such that the victim is making a 'positive' claim, while the suspect is actually denying. As to extra-legal factors the style of self-presentation of the communicator – a so called 'dynamic' factor – during the interview was manipulated. Following Holmstrom and Burgess (1974), and Burgess (1988) the victim tells her side of the story in an 'emotionally expressive' or in an 'emotionally controlled' or numbed way. Following the suggestions of Erickson, Lind and O'Barr (1978), the suspect moreover tells his side of the story, utilizing a 'powerful' or 'powerless' speech style. Main hypotheses tested were that an emotionally expressive style (unjustly) enhances the credibility of the victim, and the evidential value of her statements, while a powerless speech style (unjustly) reduces the credibility and evidential value of the suspect's statements. Moreover, the interaction- effects due to the police officers' nationality were explored.

Method

– *Subjects.* A sample of two hundred and five police officers participated in the experiment. Of the Italian police officers, 53.5% were male and 46.5% female. Their average age was 31 years. 56.1% of the Dutch police officers were male and 43.9% female. Their average age was 24 years.

– *Procedure.* Subjects were randomly divided into 4 independent groups. The experiment started with the researcher giving a short introduction explaining what subjects were going to see and what they were expected to do. After this oral introduction, they were all exposed to a video. All videos started with a short story explaining the sequence of the events: A girl, named Christina, gave a party for her birthday on Saturday night. She also invited Paul, an acquaintance of her, who lives on the same floor as she does. During the party they spent quite a lot of time together, dancing, and drinking. When all the other guests had left the party, Paul stayed longer to help Christina cleaning up. Both agree that sexual intercourse took place but the woman says it was against her will whereas the man says that she did not show any resistance. Then the testimony of the woman starts. Two groups saw the 'emotional' woman, the other two saw the 'numbed' version. Then they all saw and heard the testimony of the accused. Two groups were exposed to the suspect with a 'powerful' speech style and two to the 'powerless' one. After exposed to the videos, subjects had to fill out a questionnaire measuring the main dependent variables.

Subjects were told, before the experiment started, that the story they were going to see was based on a scenario that actually happened, and was taken from police files. In the post experimental debriefing, they were then informed that the roles of both the victim and the suspect were played by professional actors.

– *Independent variables.* In all experimental conditions and for both languages, the role of the victim and the suspect was played by the same actor and actress. Regarding the style of self-presentation of the woman, the 'emotional' woman tells her story while openly showing emotions, such as a trembling voice and fits of crying. In the 'numbed' version, she tells her story in a cool and detached way.

In the 'powerful' version the suspect uses a 'powerful' style, that according to Erickson et al. (1978) and Lind, Erickson, Conley, O'Barr (1978) is a clear and direct one: straightforward answers are given when questioned. In the 'powerless' version, the actor tells his story in a hesitant way, using language features such as intensifiers (very, definitely, surely), hedges (sort of, kind of), hesitation forms (uh, eh, ah, you know...) and repetitions of questions.

– *Dependent variables.* To measure the perceived credibility of both the alleged victim and the suspect we used the 'Perceived Credibility Scale' (Winkel & Koppelaar, 1991). Reliability was assessed through item analyses and factor analyses.

Sample items of perceived credibility of the woman are: "Does the woman make a credible impression on you?" and "Does she make the impression of hiding the truth?" (Cronbach's alpha=.83, Dutch version; alpha=.85, Italian version).

Sample items of perceived credibility of the suspect: "Does his testimony seem trustable?" and "Does he make the impression to hide the truth?" (Cronbach's alpha=.76, Dutch sample, alpha=.86, Italian sample). Perceived strength of evidence included, inter alia: "How strong is the evidence against the suspect?" and "How strong is the evidence to start a legal procedure?"

All answers could be entered on a seven point-scale ranging from 'certainly not' (1) to 'most certainly' (7).

– *Manipulation checks.* A univariate analysis of variance revealed that the manipulations were successful. Sample items measuring the emotionality of the woman: "Do you think that the woman was emotionally shocked?"; and the powerfulness of the speech-style of the man: "Did the man talk in an hesitant way?"). Answers could be entered on a seven point scale ranging from completely disagree to totally agree.

All items used to assess emotionality of the victim loaded on the same factor and were then computed on a single dimension measuring 'emotionality' (alpha=.78, Italian subjects; alpha=.90, Dutch subjects). For the Italian subjects a main effect emerged ($F(1,128)=89.94$, $p<.001$) as well as for the Dutch one ($F(1, 74)=114.35$, $p<.001$), indicating that the emotional victim was perceived as being more emotional. (See table 1).

All items used to assess the degree of hesitation in the style of self presentation of the suspect were reduced to a single factor dimension (alpha=.70, Italian sample; alpha=.81 Dutch sample).

Results showed that subjects that saw the 'powerless' version actually perceived the man as being more hesitant than the ones who saw the 'powerful' version. For the Italian subjects $F(1, 128)=125.03$, $p<.001$; for the Dutch subjects, $F(1, 74)=30.38$, $p<.001$. (See table 1).

Table 1: Manipulation check on victim's and suspect's style of self presentation

	Manipulation check	
Victim's style of self-presentation	Italian victim	Dutch victim
"emotional"	4.56	4.73
"numbed"	3.22	2.54
F	89.94*	114.35*
Suspect's speech style	Italian suspect	Dutch suspect
"powerful"	5.05	4.87
"powerless"	3.22	3.49
F	125.03*	30.38*

* p<.001
High values indicate high emotions: 1=low emotionality, 7=high emotionality
High values indicate use of a powerful speech style: 1=powerless, 7=powerful

Results

Hypotheses testing

Data were first analysed multivariately with a 2 (style of self presentation of the victim: emotionally expressive versus emotionally controlled) X 2 (speech style of communication of the suspect: powerful versus powerless) X 2 (nationality of police officers: Dutch versus Italian) design.

This multivariate analysis revealed a victim style by nationality-interaction, approaching significance: Fm (11,186)=1.75, p=.06. Main effects emerged for subject nationality (Fm (11, 186)=6.05, p<.001), for suspect style (Fm (11, 186)=2.20, p<.01), and for victim style (Fm (11, 186)=2.05, p<.05).

Although a univariate analysis yielded various significant outcomes, we will generally confine ourselves here to the dependent variables that were more systematically impacted, that is having an impact on a majority of dependent variables relating to a given construct (either perceived credibility of the victim statements, suspect statements, and the perceived evidential value of these statements or perceived strength of legal evidence).

The univariate analysis revealed that only perceived credibility of the suspect was systematically impacted by the victim versus nationality-interaction (see Table 2): significant effects emerged on the impression that he is hiding the truth (F(1,196)=3.71, p<.05), on the idea that his testimony appears trustable (F(1,196)=2.43, p=.06), and on the impression that his testimony is false (F(1,196)=2.47, p=.05).

Table 2: Means on the perceived credibility of the suspect's testimony: victim style of self-presentation (emotional versus controlled) by subject nationality (Italian vs Dutch police officers)

Perceived credibility of suspect	Victim style of self Presentation		
	Expressive	Controlled	F(1,196)
Dutch police officer	2.42	2.90	
He is hiding the truth			3.71*
Italian police officer	3.05	2.72	
Dutch police officer	4.44	4.25	
His testimony seems trustable			2.43*
Italian police officer	3.92	4.35	
Dutch police officer	2.78	2.80	
His testimony is false			2.47*
Italian police officer	2.59	2.42	

* p<.05
Higher scores indicate stronger agreement with the statement

Nationality exerted a systematic impact on all items pertaining to the evidential value of the various statements made (see table 3). Significant differences between Dutch and Italian Police officers emerged on the perceived strength of evidence generally available for further legal procedures ($F(1,196)=23.50$, $p<.001$), on the evidence available against the suspect ($F(1,196)=42.59$, $p<.001$), and on the strength of evidence in favour of the victim ($F(1,196)=20.10$, $p<.001$). On all items Italian Police officers reported more favourable impressions regarding strength of evidence.

Table 3: Means on perceived strength of legal evidence of Dutch and Italian police officers

Perceived strength of evidence	Nationality of police officers		
	Dutch	Italian	F(1,196)
Strength of evidence against suspect	2.57	4.10	23.50*
Strength of evidence favouring victim	2.78	3.72	20.10*
Strength of evidence to start a legal procedure	3.01	4.17	23.50*

* p<.001
Higher scores represent stronger evidence

The suspect's style of denying the charges laid against him – although significant at a multivariate level – did not result in a systematic influence on any of the relevant dependent variables. The factor was thus excluded from further examination. Finally, the victim's style of self presentation significantly affected all items relating to the perceived credibility of the victim (see table 4). Emotional victims made much more favourable impression than emotionally controlled victims. Emotional victims generally made a more credible impression (F(1,196)=6.71, p<.01), less strongly made the impression to hide the truth (F(1,196)=6.71, p<.01), and her testimony was considered less strongly to be false (F(1,196)=4.68, p<.05). Finally, the testimony of victims reporting in an emotionally controlled way did leave a less trustable impression (F(1,196)=14.95, p<.01).

Table 4: Means on the perceived credibility of the victim by victim style of self presentation (emotionally expressive versus emotionally controlled)

Perceived Credibility of the	Victim Style of Self Presentation		
Victim	Controlled	Expressive	F(1,196)
Victim makes a credible impression	3.94	4.21	3.71*
She is hiding the truth	3.28	3.06	6.71*
Her testimony is false	2.93	2.77	4.68*
Her testimony seems trustable	3.87	4.26	14.95*

* p<.01
Higher scores indicate stronger agreement with the statement

Discussion

Emotional victims run less risk of secondary victimization when interviewed by police officers. There seems to be a universal stereotype that rape victims should clearly and openly express to the outside world their feelings of distress and negative emotions. The perceived credibility of the suspect was not affected by his way of presenting the story, though it was weakened by the emotionally expressive victim, particularly for Italian police officers. This outcome once more confirms our first research hypothesis regarding the positive impression left by an emotionally expressive woman. Data thus generally suggest that in the Netherlands an emotionally controlled style posits a handicap, while in Italy it even results in a 'double handicap'. For Italian police officers 'emotionality' thus has a more dramatic, at least stronger effect: reducing her, while enhancing his credibility.

As to perceived strength of legal evidence a nationality main effect emerged. This effect may be due to crosscultural differences in 'legal traditions' betweeen the two countries. In the Netherlands police officers may be more experienced in evaluating the evidential value of a statement because they tend to have more discretionary power ('opportunity' versus 'legality' principles). Future research might profit from focusing explicitly on such legal differences.

References

Baldry, A. C., Enthoven, D. S., & Winkel, F. W. (1996). Paralinguistic and nonverbal triggers of biased credibility assessments of rape victims by police officers. In J. Bajet, & S. Redondo (Eds.), *Handbook of Psychology and Law*. Berlin, New York: Walter de Gruyter.

Burgess, A. W., & Holmstrom, L. L. (1974). *Rape: Victims of crisis*. Bowie: Brady.

Burgess, A. W. (1988). Rape and sexual assault II. N. Y., London: Garland.

Crombag, H. F. M., Van Koppen, P. J., & Wagenaar, W. A. (1992). *Dubieuze Zaken: De Psychologie van Strafrechtelijk Bewijs*. Amsterdam: Contact.

Koppelaar, L., & Winkel, F. W. (1987). Creating Suspects in Police-Citizen Encounters: An attribution experiment. *The Journal of Justice Issues, 2*, 2, 41-55.

Lind, E. A., Erickson, B. E., Conley, J., & O'Barr, W. M. (1978). Social attribution and conversation style in trial testimony. *Journal of Personality and Social Psychology, 36(12)*, 1558-1567.

Nijboer, J. F. (1994). *Strafrechtelijk Bewijsrecht*. Nijmegen: Ars Aequi Libri.

Vrij, A., & Winkel, F. W. (1989). Recognition of own and other-race faces: the effects of quality versus quantity of crosscultural interaction. *Journal of Police and Criminal Psychology, 5*, 2, 24-30.

Vrij, A. (1991). *Misverstanden tussen politie en allochtonen: sociaal-psychologische aspecten van verdacht zijn*. Amsterdam: VU Uitgeverij.

Vrij, A., & Winkel, F. W. (1991). The frequency and scope of differences in nonverbal behavioural patterns: an observation study of Dutchmen and Surinamers. In N. Bleichrodt, & P. Drenth (Eds.), *Contemporary Issues in Crosscultural Psychology*. Amsterdam: Swets en Zeitlinger, 120-137.

Vrij, A., & Winkel, F. W. (1991a) Encounters between the Dutch police and minorities: testing the non-coopertion hypothesis of differential treatment. *Police Studies, 14*, 1, 17-22.

Vrij, A., & Winkel, F. W. (1991b). Cuultural patterns in Dutch and Surinamer nonverbal behaviour: an analysis of a simulated police-citizen encounter. *Journal of Nonverbal Behaviour, 15*, 3, 41-61.

Vrij, A., & Winkel, F. W. (1992). Crosscultural police-citizen interactions: the influence of race, beliefs and nonverbal communication on impression-formation. *Journal of Applied Social Psychology, 22*, 1546-1559.

Vrij, A., & Winkel, F. W. (1994). Perceptual distortions in Crosscultural Interrogations: the Impact of Skin Colour, Accent, Speech Style, and Spoken Fluency on Impression Formation. *Journal of Crosscultural Psychology, 25*, 2, 284-295.

Weir, J. A., & Wrightsman, L. S. (1990). The determinants of mock jurors' verdicts in a rape case. *Journal of Applied Social Psychology, 20*, 11, 901-919.

Winkel, F. W. (1981). Beslissingen: het rechtspsychologisch perspectief. *Delikt en Delinkwent, 11*, 9, 506- 520.

Winkel, F. W., & Koppelaar, L. (1986). Being suspect in Crosscultural Interaction: a psychological analysis. *Police Studies, 9*, 3, 125-134.

Winkel, F. W., & Koppelaar, L. (1987). Slachtoffers van sexueel geweld: zelf-presentatie en hulp van anderen. In G. Bruinsma, E. Leuw, E. Lissenberg, & A. Van Vliet (Eds.), *Vrouw en Criminaliteit: Vrouwen als plegers en slachtoffers van criminaliteit*. Amsterdam: Boom, 153-168.

Winkel, F. W., Koppelaar, L., & Vrij, A. (1988). Creating suspects in police-citizen encounters: two studies on personal space and being suspect. *Social Behaviour, 3*, 4, 307-319.

Winkel, F. W., & Vrij, A. (1990). Interaction and impression formation in a crosscultural dyad: frequency and meaning of culturally determined gaze behaviour in a police interview setting. *Social Behaviour, 5*, 4, 335-350.

Winkel, F. W. (1991). Interaction between the police and minority group members: victimization through the incorrect interpretation of nonverbal behaviour. *International Review of Victimology, 2*, 4, 15- 28.

Winkel, F. W. (1991a). Conclusions and Recommendations of the Task Force on Victims' Rights and the Justice System. In E. C. Viano (Ed.), *Victim's Rights and Legal Reforms: International Perspectives* (pp. 340-347). Onati: OPS.

Winkel, F. W., & Koppelaar, L. (1991). Rape victims' style of self-presentation and secondary victimization by the environment: an experiment. *Journal of Interpersonal Violence, 6*, 1, 29- 41.

Winkel, F. W., Vrij, A., Koppelaar, L., & Van der Steen, J. (1991). Reducing secondary victimization risks and skilled police intervention: enhancing the quality of police-rape victim encounters through training programmes. *Journal of Police and Criminal Psychology, 7* ,2, 2- 11.

Winkel, F. W. & Koppelaar, L. (1992). Perceived credibility of the communicator: studies of perceptual bias in police officers conducting rape interviews. In F. Lösel, D. Bender, & T. Bliesener (Eds.), *Psychology and Law: International Perspectives*. Berlin, New York: Walter de Gruyter.

Winkel, F. W., & De Winter, S. (1992). Opnieuw Slachtoffer: Secundaire victimisatie vanuit een sociaal-psychologisch perspectief. In A. Lammers–Van der Flier, & N. Bokhove (Eds.), *Documentatie Slachtofferhulp*. Utrecht: LOS.

Winkel, F. W. (1993). Police and victimization of foreign born citizens: A Dutch experience. In S. P. Singh Makkar, & P. Friday (Eds.), *Global Perspectives in Victimology*. Lamixpura: ABS Publications, 219-234.

Winkel, F. W., & De Winter, S. (1995) The perceived credibility of rape victims during a police interview: an experiment among victim assistance workers.

Police Officers' Inadequate Impression Formation in Confrontations with Offenders as a Result of Physical Effort

Aldert Vrij

Police officers can arrive on the scene of crime in two different ways: by walking quietly or by rushing. In the latter case, more physical effort is needed than in the first case. In which way does physical effort of police officers prior to the confrontation with an offender influences their perception and shooting behaviour during that confrontation? The present two experiments deal with that question.

On the basis of theoretical perspectives (theories of emotion and attributional processes (Schachter, 1964; Zillmann, 1978, 1983) and Kahneman's (1973) variable-allocation capacity model) it can be predicted that physical effort will lead to an underestimation of the offender's aggression, less aggressive feelings towards the offender and decreased willingness to shoot at the offender. The physical effort – perception – behaviour relationship is graphically outlined in Figure 1.

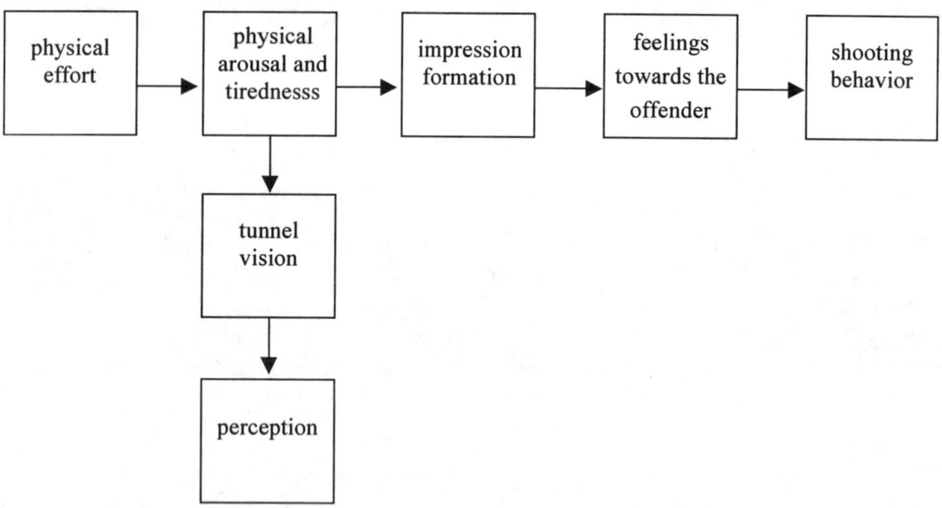

Figure 1: The physical effort – impression formation – behaviour relationship

Physical effort will lead to physical arousal (increased heart rate, increased respiration and so on). The core of the theories of emotions and attributional processes (Schachter, 1964; Zillmann, 1978, 1983) is that individuals, being aware of this state of physiological arousal, will try to explain this arousal. Basically, they can attribute this arousal to two different sources, that is, to internal sources (their own activities) or to external sources (the environment). Thus, in confrontations with offenders, physically aroused police officers can attribute their physical arousal to their physical effort (own activity) or to the offender's aggression (the environment). Obviously, aggressive feelings towards the offender are more likely after attributing the arousal to the offender's aggression. However, it is unlikely that they will attribute their arousal to the offender. The physical effort takes place before the confrontation with the offender, hence, the arousal is already present before the confrontation with the offender. This makes it more likely to attribute the arousal to physical effort than to the offender. Thus, physical arousal will lead to a less aggressive impression of the offender and to less aggressive feelings towards the offender. Finally, less aggressive feelings will decrease the likelihood to shoot at the offender.

The core of Kahneman's model is that a person's physical and mental capabilities are limited. The available physical and mental capacity has to be divided among different physical and mental activities by means of an "allocation policy". A person has to check the relevance of each signal that comes to him. By way of a costs and benefits analysis s/he has to decide whether or not the signal requires (a) further attention and (b) (physical) response. In case of further attention or physical response, physical effort is required. We may assume that individuals will be physically tired after a physical exercise and, therefore, less willing to supply physical effort. As a result, the costs–benefits analysis may have different outcomes when physical tiredness is present or absent, that is, physically tired persons may tend to interpret the situation in such a way that a physical response (i. e. shooting at the offender) is not required. An interpretation that makes a physical response unnecessary (and aggressive feelings towards the offender unlikely), is to deny the offender's aggression.

In brief, we expect that physical effort will result in incorrect judgement of the aggression of aggressive offenders. This incorrect judgement is caused by erroneous information processing. An alternative explanation is that physical effort will lead to impaired perception. However, this alternative explanation is unlikely. Research findings suggest that physical effort improves perception (Tomporowski & Ellis, 1986). This could be explained by Easterbrook's "Cue-Utilization Hypothesis" (Easterbrook, 1959). The core of this hypothesis is that physical arousal (the consequence of physical effort) produces a narrowing of attention (tunnel vision), with the subject concentrating more and more on the central features of the situation and paying less and less attention to more peripheral ones. As a result of physical effort, in a police officer – offender confrontation, police officers will concentrate their attention on the offender, leaving less attention available for viewing other items.

In two experiments the impact of physical effort on police officer's impression formation, shooting behaviour and perception was examined. In both experiments police officers faced an aggressive offender. Their perception of the offender's aggressive intentions, their own aggressive feelings, their shooting behaviour and their description of the offender and a bystander were investigated. In the physical effort condition, subjects had to pedal on a bicycle ergometer before they were confronted with the offender, no physical exercise took place in the control condition. The following four hypotheses have been tested in each experiment:

1. The offender will make a less aggressive impression in the Physical Effort condition than in the control condition
2. The police officers will experience less aggressive feelings in the Physical Effort condition than in the control condition
3. Less police officers will shoot at the offender in the Physical Effort condition than in the control condition
4. Physical Effort will improve the description of main features (i.e. the offender) of the situation and will impair the description of less important features (i.e. a bystander) of the situation.

Experiment 1

Method

Subjects

A total of 40 patrol police officers participated in the experiment, 88% of whom were male and 12% of whom were female. The average age in the sample was M=29 years (SD=4 years). The average experience with police work was M=6 years (SD=4 years).

Procedure

The experiment was conducted among local Dutch police forces during regular shooting exercises. Police officers participated individually and their participation was voluntary. All invited officers were willing to participate. The experimenter introduced the experiment as "an investigation of police officers' conflict handling". After the experimental manipulation (see Independent Variables) subjects were brought to the experimentation room in which the Fire Arms Training System (FATS, an American shooting simulator recently introduced in the Netherlands) was located. The system uses the latest technology to provide scenarios that are as true to life as possible, that is, what officers see and hear is what they would experience in reality. The system uses video and laser disc plays to project scenarios on to a screen. The images are in full colour and are full size. Subjects in the experiment faced a scenario and were asked to act as they would act in reality.

Their behaviour was videotaped and scored afterwards. Following the experiment subjects completed a questionnaire.

Scenario

The following scenario was shown to the subjects. The subject (the camera's point of view) and a female colleague are patrolling in a shopping-centre. Suddenly, a waiter runs to them and asks them to come with him to a Chinese restaurant because a customer is causing trouble. Both police officers join the waiter and walk to the Chinese restaurant. When entering the restaurant they see the back of a man (this man will be referred to as the "offender") who is shouting to a waitress that she has to give him her money. The subjects' colleague walks towards the offender and calls "Hey, what are you doing." The offender turns around, kicks the colleague in her stomach (she runs away to the left, out of sight of the subject), takes his firearm and points at the subject. The waitress runs away (behind the man), and the offender shoots at the subject. The scenario lasted one minute, the period between taking his firearm and shooting at the subject lasted 3.5 seconds.

Independent Variables

Physical Effort of the police officers. The experimental manipulation of this factor was identical to the manipulation of Zillmann, Katcher, & Milavsky (1972). In the experimental condition, prior to the exposure to the scenario, subjects had to cycle fast on an exercise bike for one minute. The distance covered by the police officers during that minute was about 400 meters. The exercise bike was located next to the experimental room with the FATS-simulator. Immediately after the cycle exercise the subjects were brought into the experimental room and the scenario began. No physical effort was required in the control condition. The subjects were randomly assigned to the experimental or control condition (20 subjects to each condition).

Dependent Variables

In order to investigate police officers' *shooting behaviour* the experimenter noted down whether or not the police officer did shoot at the offender. The other variables were measured via a questionnaire.

The *impression of the offender* was measured with three items, namely "To what extent did the man make an aggressive impression?", "To what extent did the man make a dangerous impression?" and "To what extent was the man upset?". Answers could be entered on 7-point scales, ranging from certainly not (1) to most certainly (7). The three items have been clustered in one index 'impression of the offender' (Cronbach's alpha 0.57).

The *aggressive feelings of the police officer* was measured with three items, namely "To what extent did you feel irritated by the man?", "To what extent did you feel annoyed by the man?' and "To what extent did you intend to shoot at the man?". Answers could be entered on 7-point scales, ranging from certainly not (1) to most certainly (7). The three items have been clustered in one index 'aggressive intention of the police officer' (Cronbach's alpha 0.67). In order to *describe the offender* six multiple choice questions were asked (yes or no options), amongst others: "Did the man have a moustache?" Afterwards, the percentage of right answers was calculated. In order to *describe the bystander* five questions were asked about the waitress, amongst others: "Did the waitress carry a tray?" Again, the percentage of right answers was calculated. We considered the items concerning the offender as the dominant (important) features and the items concerning the waitress (bystander) as the less important items.

As a manipulation check of physical effort we asked the subjects about their physical tiredness during the experiment (not tired at all (1) to very tired (7)). The questionnaire concluded with demographic data (gender, age, work experience).

Results

Manipulation Check

A one-way ANOVA was used as a manipulation check for the Physical Effort factor. The results showed that the subjects were more physically tired in the experimental condition than in the control condition ($M=3.95$ versus $M=1.95$, $F(1, 38)=22.29$, $p<.001$). Hence, the manipulation was successful.

Questionnaire

In order to test Hypothesis 1 (The offender will make a less aggressive impression in the experimental condition compared to the control condition), Hypothesis 2 (The police officers will experience less aggressive feelings in the experimental condition compared to the control condition) and Hypothesis 4 (The police officers will give a better description of the offender and a worse description of the bystander in the experimental condition than in the control condition) a MANOVA was conducted with Physical Effort (present or absent) as the independent variable. The dependent variables were "impression of the offender", "aggressive feelings of the police officer", "description of the offender" and "description of the bystander". At a multivariate level the analysis revealed a significant effect, $F(4, 35)=6.12$, $p<.001$. Univariate tests showed significant effects for the impression of the offender, $F(1, 38)=4.52$, $p<.05$, the aggressive feelings of the police officer, $F(1, 38)=6.56$, $p<.05$), and the description of the offender, $F(1,38)=11.93$, $p<.001$. The effect for the description of the bystander was non-significant, $F(1,38)=.73$, ns. The mean scores concerning these univariate tests are provided in Table 1.

Table 1: The impression of the offender, the aggressive feelings of the police officer, and the description of offender and bystander as a function of Physical Effort (present or absent)

	Physical Effort	
	present	absent
Impression of the offender	3.12	3.98
Aggressive feelings of the police officer	5.23	6.00
Description of the offender	0.88	0.73
Description of the bystander	0.49	0.55

Table 1 shows that the offender made a less aggressive impression in the Physical Effort present condition. This supports Hypothesis 1. Moreover, the police officers felt less aggressive in the Physical Effort present condition. This supports Hypothesis 2. Finally, the police officers gave a better description of the offender in the Physical Effort present condition; no difference emerged in the description of the bystander. This partly supports Hypothesis 4.

Behavioural Observations

In order to test Hypothesis 3 (Less police officers will shoot in the experimental condition compared to the control condition) a Chi-square analysis was conducted with Physical Effort (present or absent) as the independent variable and shooting behaviour as the dependent variable. The analysis revealed that less police officers shot at the offender in the Physical Effort condition (80% versus 100% shot at the offender, $X^2(1, N=40)=4.44$, $p<.05$). This supports Hypothesis 3.

Discussion

In this experiment we examined the effects of physical effort on police officers' perception and *behaviour* in confrontations with an (aggressive) offender. The results supported all four hypotheses. The offender made a less aggressive impression as a result of physical effort (Hypothesis 1); physical effort resulted in decreased aggressive feelings of police officers towards the aggressive offender (Hypothesis 2); and, police officers shot less at the offender as a result of physical effort (Hypothesis 3). In this experiment, the police officers were confronted with a very aggressive offender, he even shot at the police officer. Hence, physical effort resulted in an underestimation of the offender's aggression.

In Hypothesis 4 it was stated that physical effort would lead to a narrowed attention: subjects would concentrate on the dominant features, leaving open less opportunities to watch less important items. In agreement with this hypothesis was the finding that physical effort did improve the description of the offender. This finding is interesting. As we mentioned earlier, subjects in this situation did assess the offender less aggressively as a result of physical effort. Since the man shot at the subject, this judgement appeared to be wrong. The results imply that this wrong judgement is not caused by impaired perception but rather by wrong information processing.

No differences emerged in describing the bystander. Looking at the mean scores reveals that in both conditions the percentage of correct answers are approximately 50%, which could be expected by chance only. It suggests that subjects in both conditions did not look carefully at the bystander, probably because they were confronted with a dangerous offender who required all their attention.

We want to address two limitations of this experiment. Firstly, it is likely that the subjects were surprised by the events that took place in the scenario. They were not informed about the aggressive intentions of the offender, and the event went very fast (the whole event lasted only one minute). The results showed that physical effort leads to an underestimation of danger in these unexpected situations. However, will the underestimation also occur in events in which the police officers can anticipate the offender's aggressive intentions? The second experiment dealt with this issue. In this experiment subjects received explicit information about the aggressive intentions of the offender prior to the confrontation. Providing pre-information is consistent with police practice. Police officers are frequently informed about what they could expect at the scene of crime.

Secondly, the physical effort manipulation in the first experiment did not occur within the event. The experimental manipulation took place before the setting was explained to the subjects (as a result, subjects were requested to cycle without knowing the reason for it). In the second experiment the physical effort manipulation was embedded within the event, making the experiment more realistic. The same hypotheses as in the first experiment have been tested in the second experiment.

Experiment 2

Method

Subjects

A total of 44 patrol police officers participated in the experiment, 84% of whom were male and 16% of whom were female. The average age in the sample was M=28 years (SD=6 yrs). The average experience with police work was M=6 years (SD=4 years).

Procedure

The procedure was almost identical to the procedure of experiment 1. The only difference was that the Physical Effort manipulation was embedded in the event. Prior to the manipulation the experimenter told the subject that s/he was requested to go to a certain location because a man is threatening a woman with his knife in their backyard. It was further told that the man got into trouble with the police before and was known as being aggressive. The FATS-scenario started immediately after the experimental manipulation.

Scenario

The subject (the camera's point of view) and a colleague arrive near the backyard. Neighbours run to them (in panic) telling them that the man is upset, aggressive and holding a knife. When they had arrived at the backyard, they see a man (this man will be referred to as the "offender") shouting at a woman and brandishing a knife. The colleague calls the offender to order. Then, the offender turns towards the subject, threatening with his knife. After a few moments he moves forward and stabs the subject. Altogether, the scenario lasted 90 seconds.

Independent Variable

Physical Effort of the police officers was introduced as the independent variable in this experiment. The experimental manipulation was identical to the manipulation in experiment 1. The subjects were randomly assigned to the experimental or control condition (22 to each condition).

Dependent Variables

The *impression of the offender* and the *aggressive feelings of the police officer* were measured in the same way as described in experiment 1 (alpha's of the constructs were 0.63 and 0.60 respectively). In order to *describe the offender* four multiple choice questions were asked (yes or no options), amongst others: "Did the man have a moustache?" Afterwards, the percentage of right answers was calculated. In order to *describe the bystander* four questions were asked about the woman, amongst others: "Did the woman wear leggings?". Again, the percentage of right answers was calculated. We considered the items concerning the offender as the dominant (important) features and the items concerning the woman (bystander) as the less important items.

Observations of the videotapes revealed that three different *behaviours* could be distinguished, namely (1) shooting at the offender, (2) not shooting at the offender but getting out of the way, and (3) neither shooting at the offender nor getting out of the way (this will be referred to as "no reaction").

Results

Questionnaire

In order to test Hypothesis 1 (The offender will make a less aggressive impression in the experimental condition compared to the control condition), Hypothesis 2 (The police officers will experience less aggressive feelings in the experimental condition compared to the control condition) and Hypothesis 4 (The police officers will give a better description of the offender and a worse description of the bystander in the experimental condition than in the control condition) a MANOVA was conducted with Physical Effort (present or absent) as the independent variable.

The dependent variables were "impression of the offender", "aggressive feelings of the police officer", "description of the offender", and "description of the bystander". At a multivariate level the analysis revealed a marginal significant effect, $F(4, 39)=2.20$, $p<.09$. Univariate tests showed significant effects for "impression of the offender", $F(1, 42)=4.36$, $p<.05$ and "aggressive intention of the police officer", $F(1, 42)=6.43$, $p<.05$). The effects concerning descriptions of the offender and bystander were not significant, $F(1,42)=1.28$, ns and $F(1,42)=.34$, ns. Table 2 provides the mean scores concerning these univariate tests.

Table 2: The impression of the offender, the aggressive feelings of the police officer, and the description of offender and bystander as a function of Physical Effort (present or absent)

	Physical Effort	
	present	absent
Impression of the offender	4.08	4.79
Aggressive feelings of the police officer	3.36	4.23
Description of the offender	0.84	0.77
Description of the bystander	0.41	0.47

Table 2 reveals that the offender made the least aggressive impression in the Physical Effort present condition. This supports Hypothesis 1. Moreover, the police officers felt less aggressive in the Physical Effort condition. This supports Hypothesis 2. Physical effort did not have an impact on the description of the offender and bystander. Hence, Hypothesis 4 is not supported.

Behavioural Observations

In order to test Hypothesis 3 (Less police officers will shoot in the experimental condition compared to the control condition) a Chi-square analysis was conducted with Physical Effort (present or absent) as the independent variable and shooting behaviour as the dependent variable. The frequency distributions are given in Table 3.

Table 3: Behavioural patterns as a function of Physical Effort (present or absent)

	Physical Effort	
	present	absent
Shoot at the offender	32%	41%
Get out of the way	36%	41%
No reaction	32%	18%

Table 3 shows that less police officers shot at the offender in the Physical Effort present condition (32%) than in the control condition (41%). This is in line with Hypothesis 4. Moreover, more police officers didn't react in the Physical Effort present condition (32%) than in the control condition (18%). Not reacting implies in this situation that the police officer would have been stabbed by the offender. Hence, it is an incorrect response and an underestimation of danger. The *behavioural* results are in agreement with the expectations, though, the differences are too small to reach significance (X2(2, N=44)=1.14, ns. Hypothesis 3 is thus not supported.

Discussion

In this experiment the effect of physical effort on police officer's perception and shooting behaviour in confrontations with aggressive offenders was investigated. The main difference between this experiment and the first experiment was that in this experiment police officers could anticipate the situation, they were informed twice that they would be confronted with an aggressive offender (one time by the experimenter and one time by the neighbours in the scenario). Results showed that police officers who were engaged in physical exercise before the confrontation with the offender assessed the offender as being less aggressive and held less aggressive feelings towards this offender than police officers who were not engaged in physical exercise before the confrontation. The offender in this situation was aggressive (he tried to stab the police officer), hence, despite the information provided about the aggressive intentions of the offender, the police officers still underestimated the offender's aggression after physical exercise.

No differences emerged in the description of the offender and bystander. The mean scores in Table 2 reveal a very poor description of the bystander in both conditions. The same finding was found in the first experiment. The description of the offender was much more accurate in both conditions. Apparently, subjects concentrated more on him than on the bystander. It is unclear why physical effort did not result in a better description of the offender. However, and probably more important, the findings showed that physical effort did not result in a worse description of the offender. This implies that the underestimation of the offender is not caused by impaired perception but rather by wrong information processing.

The outcomes of both experiments show that physical effort results in an underestimation of danger, which can have obvious serious repercussions for police officers. An underestimation of danger can easily result in a (too) weak response, causing serious problems. We gave two possible explanations for these findings (Kahneman's (1973) variable-allocation capacity model) and theories of emotion and attributional processes (Schachter, 1964; Zillmann, 1978, 1983) without determining which approach mostly accounts for the outcomes. Our data does not give us the opportunity to do this. In future research attention could be paid to this issue.

It is important to stress the context of our experiments, as it has an impact on the results. These experiments dealt with the impact of physical effort on perception and behaviour, *directly after* the physical effort, when the physical consequences of the effort (arousal) are still clearly present. In this situation physical effort leads to an underestimation of danger and a decrease in aggression (i.e. shooting at the offender). However, what will happen if the residual arousal has almost faded away? Our experiments did not deal with this question. The Kahneman explication, for instance, is not applicable to this situation, because it is based on the assumption that there is a state of physical tiredness. Some other experiments dealt with the impact of physical effort in this different situation (Zillmann et al., 1972; Zillmann & Bryant, 1974). The outcomes showed effects contrary to our findings, that is, physical effort resulted in increased aggression. The excitation transfer theory offers an explanation for the different outcomes (Zillmann, 1979, 1983). Immediately after exercise subjects are cognizant of the fact that they are aroused from exercising; consequently they will attribute this arousal to the exercise. After a brief recovery period, the residual arousal still exists but the subjects believe that they are fully recovered. In that case it is likely that they attribute the remaining arousal to the environment, for example to the offender's aggression, an aggressive reaction towards the offender is then likely to occur.

The outcomes have several implications for the police practice. Firstly, in our view the tendency to underestimate danger directly after physical exercise has to be explained to police officers during their shooting exercises. Secondly, the results demonstrate the importance of excellent physical condition; it makes the presence of physical arousal after physical exercise less likely, and the described effects will not occur without physical arousal. Thirdly, it is important to avoid police officers' having physical effort before confrontations with offenders as much as possible. This could be done in two ways, on the one hand by going by car to the scene of crime (which usually happens), and on the other hand, by considering carefully if rapid response of the police to the scene of crime is necessary. This doesn't happen very often. A quick arrival of the police is usually considered an advantage and therefore usually pursued.

References

Easterbrook, J. A. (1959). The effect of emotion on cue utilization and the organization of behaviour. *Psychological Review, 66*, 183-201.

Kahneman, D. (1973). *Attention and effort*. Englewood Cliffs, NJ: Prentice Hall.

Schachter, S. (1964). The interaction of cognitive and physiological determinants of emotional state. In L. Berkowitz (Ed.), *Advances in Experimental Social Psychology, Vol. 1*. New York: Academic Press.

Tomporowski, P. D., & Ellis, N. R. (1986). Effects of exercise on cognitive processes: a review. *Psychological Bulletin, 99*, 338-346.

Zillmann, D. (1978). Attribution and misattribution of excitatory reactions. In J. Harvey, W. Ickes, & R. Kidd (Eds.), *New directions in attributional research, Vol. 2* (pp. 335-368). Hillsdale, NJ: Erlbaum.

Zillmann, D. (1983). Transfer of excitation in emotional behaviour. In J. Cacioppo & R. Petty (Eds.), *Social psychophysiology: a sourcebook* (pp. 215-240). New York: Guilford Press.

Zillmann, D., & Bryant, J. (1974). The effect of residual excitation on the emotional response to provocation and delayed aggressive behaviour. *Journal of Personality and Social Psychology, 30*, 782-791.

Zillmann, D., Katcher, A.H., & Milavsky, B. (1972). Excitation transfer from physical exercise to subsequent aggressive behaviour. *Journal of Experimental Social Psychology, 8*, 247-259.

Police Folklore and Attributions of Guilt: Can Psychology Challenge Long Held Assumptions?

Peter B. Ainsworth

As modern history, recent publications, and indeed this conference have shown, the areas of psychology which are of relevance to policing have increased substantially in recent years. (See Ainsworth, 1995; Brewer & Wilson, 1995) Having said that, the work of psychologists has not always been welcomed or accepted by police organisations. As with any close-knit occupation, there is a tendency for police forces throughout Europe and in the U.S.A. to be suspicious of research carried out by "outsiders".

It is often argued that policing is such a complex and difficult job that only insiders can fully appreciate the intricacies of the work. The work of so called "experts" is often dismissed as being either irrelevant or misguided, and policing maintains its relative insularity. As the literature on attitude change shows, when people are presented with material which challenges long held assumptions, they tend not to simply accept such information. Rather there is a tendency to distort the message so that it appears to be either similar to the listener's own view or to be so extreme as to be unbelievable. Alternatively, the listener may well try to discredit the source so that their views are seen as irrelevant.

This can often be seen in the way in which police officers react to information given by "outsiders". If the outsider's views are consistent with those of police officers, then the information is accepted willingly and added to the officers' self belief. Alternatively if the views are different, especially if they challenge the officers' competence or ability, then they are distorted, ridiculed, or dismissed. Academic conferences are not the best places to rely on anecdotal evidence, but I hope the audience will allow me one brief example to illustrate these points.

When I give talks to police officers in England, there is invariably a tendency for the audience to be initially suspicious of both myself and my motives. If my talk goes on to question tactics which the police officers use, then hostility rises and the inevitable probing questions from some members of the audience begin. The first line of attack is generally along the lines of "Yes, well, this is all very interesting but you obviously don't *really* understand what police work is all about – you need to have done the job before you can give us advice." Unlike many psychologists I am able to respond to this challenge by informing the audience that as a former police officer I do have some idea of what police work is all about. The response to this is equally predictable: in a further attempt to discredit the source, members of the audience will next ask either "So when did you leave?" or "Which force were you with?" Response to the first question is greeted with the predictable response: "Ah, well, that explains it – things are very different now than they were then." Alternatively the force in which I was a serving officer is ridiculed in an attempt to throw doubt on my ability to give advice to these people who are supposedly from "a superior force". Graef (1990) provides some lovely examples of this tendency to see "other" police forces as inferior. (See Ainsworth, 1995, p. 62).

If these tactics fail then the next question from the floor invariably asks "So why did you leave the job?" (It is interesting that serving officers tend to refer to their occupation as "the job" – this indirectly emphasises in-group solidarity.) My response to this question is actually irrelevant as the sceptical have, in their own mind, already found enough reason to dismiss my views. To many police officers, someone who leaves "the job" is viewed with deep suspicion – perhaps even more so than someone who has never been in the force. Each member of the audience, despite having had thoughts of leaving themselves, needs to justify their decision to stay in the force by discrediting a person who chose to leave. (Most of these reactions can be explained persuasively by Festinger's Cognitive Dissonance Theory.) The views of someone who leaves the police voluntarily can be dismissed as they must have had "no commitment to the job". Someone who has been forced to leave is also viewed as some kind of oddball who clearly didn't fit in and thus was "not like us".

The reason for this anecdotal diversion is to draw attention to the fact that police officers, like many cohesive groups, will not simply sit down and take in information which challenges long held assumptions. There is an exquisite example of this provided in Canter's recent book *Criminal Shadows* (1994). In this, Canter describes the reaction of one member of an audience of police officers who were listening to a talk on offender profiling. The old detective sergeant, speaking for most of the audience is reported to have said "Why do we need all this newfangled stuff professor? After all, we've got 150 years of police experience to draw on." (Canter, 1994, p. 12). As has been argued elsewhere (Ainsworth & Pease, 1987), doing the same thing the same way for 150 years is not the same as gaining 150 years worth of different experiences. The question, however, remains the same. Given this degree of suspicion, can psychologists *really* expect to change attitudes and beliefs by disseminating the results of their studies to a police audience? That question will be considered further at the end of this paper. For present purposes I wish to discuss some of the difficulties encountered by taking one particular example, i. e. the assumptions made by some police officers when interviewing suspects.

The subjects of interviewing and interrogation have recently attracted a great deal of interest by psychologists. Much of this work has been extensively reviewed by Gudjonsson (1992). One area addressed in such work is the tendency for many police officers to see the interrogation of a suspect as simply an attempt to persuade the (obviously guilty) suspect to confess. This is, after all, one of the hallmarks of "a good copper". Many senior detectives have dined out on stories of how they were able to get a "cough" from the most unwilling and uncooperative of suspects. Such stories lead to officers being held in great esteem by colleagues and by more junior officers who aspire to such abilities. Such respect has been tainted only slightly by the recent release of prominent prisoners who were said to have made false confessions.

In some cases the elicitation of false confessions has been explained by the pressure which is put on officers to solve high profile cases. However, in other investigations, the difficulties seem to have arisen because of the assumptions made by the officers at the start of the interrogation. As has been noted already, police officers may well enter the interrogation situation with certain assumptions:

1. In many cases the person who they are about to interview is, at least at this stage, the only suspect.
2. He/she would not have been arrested unless he was guilty.
3. He has previous convictions for this type of offence or has previously been a suspect. (Interestingly this in itself may explain points 1 & 2!)
4. The person does not want to go to jail, so he/she will almost certainly lie in order to prevent the officer getting a true picture of events.

The introduction of some of the provisions of The Police and Criminal Evidence Act (PACE) and the use of so-called ethical interviewing techniques have undoubtedly helped to curb some of the worst excesses of enthusiastic officers. However, in themselves these changes have not challenged many of the assumptions and attributions made by investigating officers.

Because police officers enter the interrogation room with certain assumptions, the behaviour of the suspect is invariably interpreted in such a way that it fits the template inside the officer's head. In other words, police officers rarely view the suspect's words and actions objectively, but rather interpret them in such a way that they fit the stereotype. "He's denying the offence and says he's telling me the truth but then he would say that wouldn't he?" What police officers in this scenario are doing is perhaps no different from what all of us do every day in our own lives. Attribution theory has shown how people often use inaccurate attributions to explain the behaviour of others. Stereotypes play a vital role in allowing us to take "cognitive shortcuts" in our dealings with others, but they also mean that we are biassed in the way in which we perceive or interpret the actions of members of the stereotyped group. "Suspects" are seen as a distinct group by most police officers, sharing the 4 attributes outlined earlier. As such, all suspects are assumed to lie and to have a desire to avoid punishment. It is thus rare for police officers to take what the suspect says at face value but rather attributions will be made about *why* the person is saying what he/she is. Police officers may also be inaccurate in assessing the power of the situation to affect the suspect's behaviour.

The *Fundamental Attribution Error* is perhaps the most researched and most widely accepted bias within the Attribution literature. It is concerned with the way in which people underestimate the power of situational influences on behaviour and overestimate the influence of personality. This fundamental error means that a suspect who is nervous is perceived as being nervous because he/she "obviously" has something to hide. The fact that the interrogation situation in itself may make the person nervous is dismissed in favour of an explanation which supports the officer's initial assumption of the suspect's guilt.

Members of this audience might wish to consider the following question. If you were arrested this evening and falsely accused of a crime how would you go about convincing your accusers of your innocence? How could you ensure that your protestations of innocence were not reinterpreted as the pathetic attempts of an "obviously" guilty person to evade imprisonment? Would you have confidence in the interrogating officers' ability to tell the difference between a guilty liar and a genuinely innocent person? I do hope that none of you have the opportunity to answer these questions during your stay in Hungary!

However, to return to a more serious note, it is perhaps appropriate to recall one of the most infamous studies in the psychological literature, i. e. that of Rosenhan (1973). Psychologists may well recall that in this study Rosenhan had a number of normal people gain admission to psychiatric hospitals by claiming that they were hearing voices. All were admitted but immediately afterwards claimed to be no longer suffering any symptoms. On Rosenhan's instructions they were left to their own devices to try to obtain their release from the hospitals. All were eventually released mainly with a diagnosis of "schizophrenia in remission". Space does not permit a more detailed discussion of this study but for present purposes we should bear in mind one of the major findings; the behaviour of the pseudopatients was always *reinterpreted* so that it fitted the original diagnosis. Thus normal, everyday activities were seen with prejudiced eyes as somehow symptomatic of the person's schizophrenia. The most famous example of this was the way in which the pseudo-patients' note taking was recorded in the patients' clinical notes as "patient engages in writing behaviour". In other words people who were doing something which is perfectly normal were assumed to be doing so because of their illness. I would not wish to claim that students who attend my lecture suffer from schizophrenia yet they also "engage in writing behaviour"! What the example does show is that once a person has been given a label of some kind (in this case schizophrenia) all their subsequent behaviour is reinterpreted so that it fits the diagnosis.

Is this not largely similar to the interrogation situation? Is it not likely that all the actions of the innocent as well the guilty will be reinterpreted so that they fit the label, rather than being taken at face value?

I hope that my audience will allow me one further anecdote. Some years ago I was teaching police officers attending an extramural psychology course. The topic was "psychological testing" and the students were filling in and then marking the Eysenck Personality Questionnaire. Somewhat missing the point of the exercise, one officer showed concern over his rather high score on the Psychoticism scale. Seeking to rubbish the test he picked out one of the questions on the scale which was "Do people often tell you lies?" How, he asked, could answering yes to this question imply that he was psychotic? He argued that to a police officer, being told lies was an occupational hazard! His humour may actually conceal a more serious point – that police officers do actually believe that many people, especially suspects, will in most cases tell them lies. With this in mind they are highly unlikely to believe the protestations of innocence from the hapless suspect in the interrogation room.

Of course all this may not be so important if police officers are able to tell accurately when someone is lying and when someone is telling the truth. Most police officers *believe* that they can do so, but some recent psychological research has questioned this. (See Vrij & Winkel, 1993). This research certainly exploded the myth that experienced detectives are actually very good lie-detectors. In total, there accuracy rate was 49%, when chance would have produced 50%. Interestingly, police officers were often found to attend to inappropriate cues (e. g. the person's clothing or their level of social skills) when deciding on a person's truthfulness. Presumably the officers were relying on stereotypes of the physical appearance of "villains" versus innocent people. This research must be a worry to the senior detectives who were discussed earlier. The eventual "cracking" of the suspect often starts with the officer's supposedly uncanny ability to spot when a person is lying. In recounting the way in which the interrogation was conducted the officer may even admit how he knew "for certain" that the person was not telling the truth – a shifting of the eyes, or a nervous cough may be reported as "unmistakable" proof of guilt. But as psychologists and even some polygraphers would admit, telling whether or not a person is lying is never quite so simple. (See Ekman, 1985).

So how and where do police officers learn how to tell whether or not a person is lying? Whilst some knowledge of non verbal communication is taught at Training School, the emphasis is not just on the detection of deception. The police officer is much more likely to pick up tips during their *informal* socialisation on the job. (See Stratton, 1984). Alternatively police officers may learn about such things from articles in publications such as *Police Review*. Police Review is claimed to be the most widely read British police magazine. Articles within it tend be very much job related, and are often written by serving officers. It was in this publication that a rather worrying article appeared (Oxford 1991). In this article, the author (a Cambridgeshire detective) states that: "... powers of lie detection are usually instinctive, based on years of experience, but the techniques can be learned" (Oxford, 1991, p. 328).

The article suggests that the interrogating officer "needs to be able to turn himself into a human polygraph" (p. 328). This statement may be particularly worrying for those psychologists who already have serious doubts about the validity of so-called scientific polygraph tests. (See Gale, 1988).

Oxford goes on to say: "The experienced interrogator ... has an armoury of lie-detecting tactics to spot those who are hiding their guilt."

The article then identifies a large number of ways in which lies can supposedly be detected. It would not be appropriate to list all of these, but a couple of examples will illustrate the potential problem:

> A delayed response can often betray a lie. Especially in long and complex interviews, suspects need time to invent a plausible answer ... The suspect might begin his reply with such phrases as 'If I remember correctly' or 'Now let me think'. Some of these apparently innocent expressions can say more about the suspect than he would wish. (Oxford, 1991, p. 328).

Throughout the article there is an assumption that most suspects are not truthful: "Suspects usually lie to avoid guilt or criminal proceedings" (p. 328).

Any detective reading Oxford's comments may well assume that if their version of events differs from that of the suspect's, there can be only one reason – the suspect is lying. The possibility that the person is not agreeing with the officer because he/she really is innocent, and that the detective is wrong, is hardly considered. A further example will illustrate the point:

> I know what you are saying but ... is another favourite, but an innocent person has no need to show he understands the question before he gives an answer ... When the suspect is normally fluent, but suddenly begins to stutter and stammer, he can be indicating that he is unable to think up lies quickly enough. (Oxford, 1991, p. 328).

The point about all these assertions is that the comments may well apply to a lying suspect, but may equally apply to a perfectly innocent person – especially one who is beginning to realise that a totally false version of events is being taken seriously by the interrogating officer, regardless of the repeated attempts to protest (genuine) innocence. A final example highlights the potential danger:

> Both the innocent and the guilty will be nervous, but the guilty person's nervousness is often more physical, reflected in excessive perspiration, ... nervous laughter, yawns or sighs. Efforts to hide guilt often cause problems with the adrenal system. (Oxford, 1991, p. 329).

All of the symptoms described above are recognised signs of stress. However, there are few psychologists who would support the assertion made by Oxford that the anxiety of a guilty person can be differentiated from the anxiety produced in an innocent person wrongly accused. Perhaps this article reflects the differences of approach between the "science" of policing and the "science" of psychology. Whereas the former may be content to rely on anecdote and experience, the latter would investigate the issue by means of carefully controlled studies, the results of which would be analyzed statistically. Whilst the latter method produces its own difficulties (in particular the problems of external validity), the police method is in danger of merely producing a self-fulfilling prophecy. The police officer may choose not to believe the suspect, apply pressure which leads to a confession, which in turn leads to a conviction. The police officer thus has "proof" that he/she was right all along – otherwise the person would have been acquitted. Of course innocent people never get convicted, do they?

If psychologists wish to have their views taken seriously by cynical police officers, they may well need to do more than simply tell officers that they are wrong. Obtaining confessions from a suspect is one of the cornerstones of the great mythology of the "good detective's uncanny powers". Lined up against such folklore, even the convincing results such as those of Vrij & Winkel (1993) will be unlikely to be accepted willingly. Rather, psychologists will need to use their own knowledge of the attitude change literature to produce a change of thinking. Police officers are practical people. They use techniques which have been developed by other officers and which are claimed to work. Folklore and rumour are often far more powerful persuaders than a chapter in a psychology book. However, if psychologists are aware of the likely reaction to their work, they can produce more persuasive arguments. Of course they must bear in mind and be able to answer a very awkward question which may well follow: "OK, professor, you've convinced me that I'm not as good as I thought at telling when someone is lying – now you show me how it should be done." Do we have our answer ready? If not, our reputation may well decline further in the eyes of the police officer.

References

Ainsworth, P. B. (1995). *Psychology and Policing in a Changing World.* Chichester: Wiley.

Ainsworth, P. B. & Pease, K. (1987). *Police Work.* Leicester: BPS/Routledge.

Brewer, N. & Wilson, C. (1995). *Psychology and Policing.* New Jersey: LEA.

Canter, D. (1994). *Criminal Shadows.* London: Harper Collins.

Ekman, P. (1985). *Telling Lies.* New York: Norton.

Graef, R. (1990). *Talking Blues: The Police in their own Words.* London: Fontana

Gale, A. (1988). *The Polygraph Test: Lies, Truth and Science.* London: Sage.

Gudjonsson, G. (1992). *The Psychology of Interrogations, Confessions, and Testimony.* Chichester: Wiley.

Oxford, T. (1991). Spotting a Liar. *Police Review,* 328-329.

Rosenhan, D. (1973). On being sane in insane places. *Science, 179,* 250-258

Stratton, J. G. (1984). *Police Passages.* Manhattan Beach, CA: Glennon.

Vrij, A. & Winkel, F. W. (1993). Objective and subjective indicators of deception. *Issues in Criminological and Legal Psychology, 20,* 51-57.

Part 3
Judicial Decision-Making

State of Ohio v. X: Science and Strategy in the Criminal Court

Sandra B. McPherson and Jay Milano

Introduction

In the United States, there has been a fair amount of attention recently given to a kind of hysteria that has sometimes played too important a part in the processing of sexual abuse allegations cases. In a return of the pendulum toward the center, that sexual abuse allegations have to be carefully evaluated rather than presumed true, which was the extreme stance of the early 80s (Campbell, 1992; Mikkelsen, et al, 1992).

The U.S. criminal justice system is highly adversarial insofar as the trial process is concerned, but actually and practically, upwards of 80 to 90 per cent of criminal cases are resolved through the process of plea bargaining (U. S. Dept. of Justice, 1984). Sexual abuse allegations are as likely to be handled this way as any other category, but because of the unique nature of these cases and the residual emotional reactivity that exists on the part of some who are involved, the development of the case can reflect much more irrationality than is found in other areas of criminal justice.

It can be noted that the difficulties, as well as to some degree the absurdity of resolution typified in this case, but not uncommon in the system as a whole, would not be likely in countries where criminal cases are handled through a more inquisitorial approach, such as Germany (Volbert, 1990), or where there is a carefully constructed system for investigations as has been developed in Israel (Morag, 1990).

Within this context, the following case is instructive for the way in which the court pre-empted the defense expert, thus that serving the overall case process very well.

Synopsis of the Case

X and his wife were married in 1981. The young people were significantly enmeshed with the wife's family. They lived in the maternal grandparents' basement. Only one year after the marriage the couple separated, after which their first daughter was born (D1). During this period of separation, custody of D1 went to the mother, and for the first year of her life, D1 lived in her maternal grandfather's bedroom. The Domestic Relations Court family unit investigated and reported that the marriage could work if the young people could disengage from the mother's family. An attempt at reconciliation took place with a move to a separate household, but every morning the maternal grandfather came for breakfast, X would have to leave, and D1 spent every weekend with the maternal grandfather.

In 1987, D2 was born, and D1 became significantly ill with gastrointestinal symptoms. D1 was treated at a children's hospital and, subsequently, there was counselling of the family. The treating psychologist indicated maternal problems were contributory to the child's distress. Subsequently, the mother was hospitalized for six weeks during which time D2 stayed with the maternal grandparents. Mother was diagnosed with bulimia. In September of 1991, the mother asked for a divorce. At this point, her behaviour became questionable including activities that suggested infidelity. She also began taking money from a joint account.

Late in September, 1991, the maternal grandfather physically assaulted X and threatened X that he would never be allowed to see the children. The attack took place after D2 allegedly said that she had been sexually abused by her father, but this "disclosure" occurred shortly after the mother arrived home from a late night out, attired in a nightgown, and threatening X with a rape report should he take action against her. Mother then moved back in with her father.

During the ensuing period, allegations of sexual abuse continued to be raised. The younger child, D2, was surprised by the mother, while dancing nude on her bed. In response to mother's questions what she was doing, the child stated, "Daddy does it." She then drew a picture allegedly of the father sticking a pencil and a toe in a vagina. These pictures and allegations, when presented to the Social Services worker during a sex abuse assessment of D1, were denied by the older child as representing reality. The younger child, however, had become the spokesperson and would continue to claim that these events occurred. In a further sexual abuse assessment by a hospital based psychologist specialized in this area, the younger child made allegations relative to herself, and at this point, the older child reversed her original denial.

By the end of 1991, the mother emptied the joint account, and X was taken in for police interrogation. It was alleged, among other things, that there was bed clothing with the children's blood and the father's blood on it. The statements about the blood were subsequently shown to be untrue. X had been interrogated on the basis of false statements.[1]

---

1 In Great Britain, for example, it is not allowed to provide false facts in an attempt to "break down" a suspect. In the United States, however, the use of misleading statements is still explicitly allowed (Gudjonsson, 1992).

X asked to take a lie detector test but was not granted his request. The children were given a physical examination in relationship to the allegations of sexual abuse. Social Services and the Domestic Relations Court family unit were both involved. At this point, assessments of the parents were also conducted. In the course of that evaluation, D1 indicated there had never been any sexual abuse.

X lost his job in early 1992 as a result of actions taken by the mother. He continued, however, to press for contact with his children. In the meantime, the psychologist who was performing the sexual abuse assessment made the statement that X should be "locked away forever"; this psychologist had to be restrained from a physical attack upon the defendant.[2]

Physical examinations allegedly raised some question about sexual abuse of D1, though not of D2. However, this physical evidence was reportedly preserved on slides, but these were misplaced by the physician colleague at the psychologist's hospital based sexual abuse evaluation unit.

After X was indicted on counts involving both girls, the psychologist who did the specialized sex abuse assessment requested no visitation contact until X admitted his guilt. At the time of the indictment, the mother and maternal grandfather were observed laughing and gesturing to the effect that X was defeated. In the meantime, the mother was also requested the eviction of X from the marital home, which remained a material struggle in the divorce case.

Functioning of the Expert

In March of 1994, the psychologist (McPherson) was retained by the attorney (Milano) to provide consultation regarding the case and to prepare testimony if warranted from an evaluation of the data developed by defense. It was also hoped – but not expected – by the attorney to have access to the child witnesses (motions for access are usually denied). However, there was a motion for access to the records on the basis of which professional opinions provided to the prosecution would be tendered, which motion was ultimately granted.

In the meantime, the consultant prepared a psychological report for defense which was submitted to the Court (McPherson, 1994). It summarized the research to date on the nature of memory, developmental factors, suggestibility, and deception. It set out methodological factors of importance in approaching sexual abuse evaluations, including conditions of data collection, appropriate and inappropriate questioning techniques, considerations of developmental factors, preservation of data (referencing especially the importance of audio tape and/or video tape processing), and data interpretation.

2 The psychologist also stated to X during this incident, "You know what they do to child molesters in prison."

The report also described diagnostic factors of importance and implications for evaluating behavioural symptomology referencing especially the literature on Post Traumatic Stress Disorder and the requirement in DSM-IV for an independently verified trauma rather than permitting backwards reasoning from symptom presentation in order to arrive at that diagnostic conclusion. The report also discussed the sexual abuse accommodation syndrome (referencing the purposes for its development and its improper use as a proof of sexual abuse), and the appropriate roles of mental health professionals within the context of this kind of case, focusing especially on the problematic imposition of therapy in a case where sexual abuse has only been alleged and not proven, and the potential for therapy to become a factor in distortion of witness function.

Conclusions from this extensive memo based on a survey of relevant research over the past 60 years, but primarily focused around the data which has been developed since 1980, included the following:

1. The nature of memory is such that the retrieval of information involves construction and is subject to influence and distortion, depending upon the context of the original learning and the means of rehearsal and retrieval which takes place between the time of learning and the time of reporting.
2. Young children are more suggestible than adults, but methods exist for reducing that suggestibility by the way in which data is collected.
3. Young children are capable of deception and are specifically observed to have made deceptive comments with respect to sexual abuse but, depending upon context, are more or less likely to evidence such behaviour.
4. The procedures of data collection can greatly minimize the likelihood of false conclusions in regard to sexual abuse of children, and these procedures must involve the preservation of data in its original form as much as possible, and the non-reliance on the memory and secondary recording processes of an observer.
5. The role of the mental health professional has to be defined and delimited depending upon the needs of the court system and the case, and cross-over between roles must be prevented if the court is to have available information of value that does not distort the process of justice.
6. There are specific contextual factors which must be assessed in developing court worthy information in cases of child sex abuse, especially including initial disclosure conditions, situationally determined motives and communication patterns and content, especially the presence of influence, coercion or intimidation which may arise in the context of psychotherapy or may emanate from the family or social system.

Based on that report and motions by defense for discovery of relevant records, the Court denied access to the children but allowed access to the records in order to assess them for adequacy of procedure. The conditions of the Court were that the psychologist would restrict herself to commentary on procedure rather than providing any opinions as to credibility or implications for the issue of guilt, and that the report of findings would be available to defense, prosecution and the Court.

Evaluation Strategy

In addition to evaluating the notes and looking at the literature to provide a foundation from scientific studies as to variables relevant to an analysis of procedure, there was an inquiry as to whether prosecution reviewed the chronology of the case against litigation related events. That analysis was not in evidence. When the data was organized in that way, there were important co-occurrences between allegations and events representing potential agendas on the part of the mother and her family. Correlation is, of course, not causation, but this type of correlational analysis is a necessary component in developing information as well as in developing the focus of investigation in any situation of this type.

The next step in the analysis consisted of a review of the following materials. After some negotiations to obtain a complete set of records, especially relating to the ongoing therapy, a second memo was provided to defense and tendered to the Court and prosecutor which provided an evaluation of the data collected.

Interviews of the Girls

Original interviews of the girls were evaluated as having a "fair amount of detail as to questions and answers, but in the absence of video or audio recording, it would not be possible to know that the wording in the record was exactly the wording of the inquirer. There could be no analysis point-by-point of the content of the interview and, thus, it would not be possible to effectively apply criteria of detail, consistency and plausibility to statements made. The review also showed the interview was contaminated from the beginning on the basis that the mother was present for a discussion of D1's problems, and she had brought pictures that the mother had used in her original interrogation of the children. The record indicated equivocal data was left to stand on its own and then subsequently interpreted. For example, it was alleged that the child was asked where the father's clothes were, and she indicated "in the dresser". It as then concluded by the professional that the father had no clothes on.

The interview of the other child was reported in summary form with no indication, even retrospectively, of the question and answer sequence or the particular wording of question or response. The interview did indicate different theories of the case in what was apparently an open-minded approach, but there were conclusory statements using a biased form of expression as part of the written record by the worker.

Interviews of Parents

The interview of the mother only focused on the possibility of the father as the alleged perpetrator.[3] When father was interviewed, he denied the allegations and provided a number of facts from his perspective. There were no indications in any of the materials that these facts were systematically evaluated. Interviews of the mother were in summary form and explicitly recorded what would normally be considered hearsay and mother's theories. There was no indication in any of the records surveyed of follow-up of some of the inconsistencies with the presentation of X.

Medical Records

Review of medical records showed a long history of upper and lower gastrointestinal difficulties from birth forward regarding D1. The medical records provided a basis to entertain two theories: that substantial physical problems could have overfocused the child on elimination areas; and, that there could have been an ongoing sexual abuse situation that would have impacted the GI symptomology. There were two instances of blood in the stools noted.

Review of Psychological Treatment Records

The treatment records clearly indicated the presumption of sexual abuse and a presumption of guilt of the father.

Records of the therapy included references to group work. A request was made for the specific content of the group exercises and therapy strategy. The psychologist wished to know whether children in the group were coming from situations of known or proven abuse, as well as children where abuse was simply alleged; however, content and description of techniques were not provided. Based on the notes alone, a content analysis was conducted to look at coherence, consistency, and whether departures were investigated and accounted for. What was found was that no inquiries were made into inconsistent or illogical statements, conclusions relative to diagnosis and to the correlates of abuse were not based in any kind of independently verifiable information, and data consistent with false allegations was not given the same attention that data consistent with sexual abuse was given.

3 From the beginning, X is identified as the "alleged perpetrator" and mother is identified as the "non-offending caretaker". There was thus an established bias in the labels used as well as seen in the content of the procedure. These writers would argue that it would be better procedurally to identify all of these people as witnesses or informants rather than initially placing them in the categories of possible offender versus non-offender.

Legal culture, 130, 149-151, 407, 409
Legal psychology
  research, 186, 430
  survey, 429, 430, 434
Legal systems, 112, 130, 146, 152, 160, 164, 178, 180, 380, 386, 407-409, 411, 429, 436, 438
Lie detection, 66, 73, 98, 105, 130-132, 134-151, 432-433
Lineup identification, 54, 57-59, 404
Live Link, 3, 4, 8, 439

Media, 177, 179, 335, 337, 339, 340, 352, 400, 413, 416, 421
  crime reporting, 399
Medical records/history, 108
Memory
  memory processing, 16
  memory test, 401

Necrophilia, 242-244, 247

Offenders, 82-92, 95, 108, 249-252, 269-271, 275, 302-306, 312, 315, 328-331, 377-384, 394-395, 408, 420, 445, 455
  descriptions, 86, 89
  juvenile crime, 222, 226-227, 293-294, 298-299, 377-382, 397-398, 445-446
  profiling, 95, 237-239, 241, 335, 408
  sex offenders, 18, 248, 251-253, 346-347
  treatment, 315, 318, 327-328, 330-331
  victim/offender mediation, 378, 380, 383
Omission errors, 20, 26-27, 29-31
Organised crime, 154, 308, 408
Overcrowding, 269, 276, 301, 322, 327, 330

Police
  informal socialisation, 98
  police interview, 52, 66-67, 74, 80-81
  training, 98
Polygraphs, 98, 130-132, 134-151
Post Traumatic Stress Disorder, 106
Prison
  clothes, 293-295, 297, 299-300
  deprivation, 270-272, 274-276, 283, 290, 313, 388-390, 392-393
  offender treatment, 315, 331
  overcrowding, 269, 276, 301, 322, 327, 330
  prison culture, 289, 292
  prison factors, 269, 276
  prisonisation, 270, 272, 274, 276
  socialisation, 270-272, 274-276

Profiling, 95, 237-239, 241, 335, 408
Prosecution, 4-7, 105, 107, 111, 115, 150, 155-156, 162, 166, 177, 301, 305, 307, 353, 379, 413, 417-418, 425-426
Prosecutor, 6, 8, 107, 109, 110-112, 145, 150, 166, 181-182, 306, 379, 411, 417-418, 420-421, 425-426
Protection, 4, 34, 112, 147, 191-192, 375-376, 412, 423, 425, 427, 444-445, 447, 451, 454
  of the child witness, 7, 248, 442, 444, 446
Psychological profiling, 237, 241
Psychological therapy, 230, 248
Psychotherapy, 106, 242, 244-246, 251, 455
Public education, 442-443

Rape, 74, 79-81, 104, 113-116, 118-119, 155, 369, 371, 375, 379
Recidivism, 269-276, 280-281, 304, 316, 331, 389, 412, 424
Reconciliation, 104, 378, 380, 382-383
Re-Enactment Theory, 251
Rehabilitation, 270, 278, 280-286, 303, 310-311-316, 321, 328-331, 384, 386, 396
Religion, 310-313, 335-336, 339, 342, 449
Remedial education, 442-443, 446, 451

Scene of crime, 82, 88, 93, 115, 181-182, 238, 240, 399
Self-control, 211-216, 218-221, 258
Self-harm, 229-235
Sentencing, 111, 118-119, 160, 165, 169, 171, 176, 180, 286, 397, 417
Sexual abuse, 10, 18, 103-106, 108-113, 118, 217, 245, 248-253, 440
Sexual crime, 33-34, 248, 251, 253, 330, 371
Sexual offence, 18, 248, 251-253, 346-347
Social competence, 222-227, 319
Social maladjustment, 199, 203, 206
Socialisation, 114, 271-272, 274-275, 377, 386, 395-396, 424
  in prisons, 270-272, 274-276
  informal, 98
Standard Interview, 31, 49, 62, 64, 67-68, 71, 73
Statements, 17, 20, 22, 24-26, 30-32, 64, 66, 68-79, 98, 105, 142-143, 148, 184-185, 232, 307, 313, 316-317, 375, 409, 442
Stress, 3, 18, 92, 99, 198, 249, 252, 255-257, 260, 263, 304, 373, 376
  Post Traumatic Stress Disorder, 106

Suggestibility, 10, 16-19, 105-106, 109, 446

Taped interview, 4-5
Terrorism, 335-340, 342-344
Testimony
defence mechanisms, 34
descriptions, 86, 89
Therapy, 4, 106-108, 190, 193, 229-232, 235, 246, 248-249, 278-279, 304
feminist group therapy, 229
psychological, 230, 248
Training
Anger Control Training, 213
Cognitive Interview, 52
police training, 98
Transference, 399-400, 402-404
Treatment
group treatment, 229, 319, 321
offender treatment, 315, 318, 327-331
outpatient treatment, 302-304, 307

Victim–offender mediation, 378, 380, 383
Victims
crime victims, 34, 36, 53, 60, 347, 352, 354, 356-358, 361, 363, 365-366, 368, 372, 374, 384
rape victims, 79-81, 118-119, 375
victim-offender mediation, 378, 380, 383
Videotaped interview, 4
Videotechnology, 4

Witherspoon standard, 181
Witness
child witness, 3, 6, 8, 17-19, 32, 105, 436, 439
memory processing, 16
witness protection, 7, 248, 442, 444, 446
Witt standard, 181

Young offenders, 222, 226-227, 294, 298, 380, 397

Of significance was the joint treatment of D1 and D2, with the therapist valid. D2 as the person who could speak for the older child and discriminate that whic was real from that which was not. The therapist presumed D1 to have a dissociative disorder and be unable to adequately discriminate reality, thus providing a rationale for believing the statements of D2 whose original allegations had implicated the older girl at the time when the younger one was caught doing something disapproved of by the mother. Furthermore, there was a history of sibling rivalry between the girls that was explicitly noted and even a focus of treatment and clearly would be a foundation for this instruction having particular power. In places where exact wording of the children was explicitly quoted in the record, the use of terminology atypical for a child and stilted in form was not questioned.

Defense Strategy

Cases involving allegations of abuse are different, however, from any other criminal case. They touch beliefs that are at the core of both individuals and politics. No one wants to appear soft on the molestation of children. As a result, more than in other criminal case work, the system balances against the defendant. As an example, in this instance, the Domestic Relations Court determined after investigation that supervised visitation between father and daughters was appropriate. The Criminal Court, with no investigation and with awareness of the Domestic Court order, nonetheless forbade visitation at the request of the prosecutor.

The effect on the trial of such a separation can be substantial. The isolation of young witnesses with their accusing parent may add to the dynamic of suggestibility. As a result, the criminal trial of these cases requires a more thorough and patient education process than normal. Significant time must be spent in opening the court to the possibility of unfounded allegations and the processes which may nurture them.

Thus, this case required all of the usual defense activities that a complex case necessitates, including basic investigation, repeated interviews for factual information, development of data, and the creation of a timeline. Various legal options were evaluated, including the importance of whether to raise the competency issue.

The issue of the competency of children as it relates to allegations of abuse is complex. The general rule has been that children under ten years of age are not competent to testify. However, that convention is routinely ignored in sexual abuse cases. Rather, the court examines the child to determine whether the youngster can accurately receive and relate true impressions. It is at this hearing that questions of suggestibility of children in general and specific factors related to the child in question may be examined. There is a distinction raised between competency, which is a question for the judge, and credibility, which is question for the jury. Thus, while this hearing is limited as to scope, it is an educational opportunity for the defense to enhance the understanding of the trial judge as to important factors that have a bearing on children's statements.

Defense counsel had to balance the gains possible in such a hearing against other available modes of educating the court about the case. The down side of a competency hearing can be the general feeling of sympathy and identification that anyone comes to feel towards appealing youngsters in a difficult situation.
In this case, defense chose instead to ask the court to admit expert witness testimony as an important means of educational input.

Case Outcome

Although the majority of cases involving allegations of child sexual abuse turn out to be substantiated, the consistent exceptions have been those in contested custody suits. Even here, there is a significant proportion of true allegations (Campbell, 1992; Horner & Guyer, 1991; Mikkelson, 1992). Unfortunately, many persons involved in child sex abuse investigations have a "validation" mentality. Many involved in human services, who see large numbers of cases where allegations are true, along with those who serve the courts in a prosecutorial capacity, tend to look at these cases noncontextually and to presume guilt rather than innocence. The result from a defense perspective is a situation which may require the use of expert testimony. Defense is hampered because there is usually no access to the alleged victim, and frequently, the victim is verified or validated by an accredited professional person who may have little scientific or factual basis for the assertions that come to be made in the courtroom. When, in spite of these burdens, the defense presents significant evidence supporting innocence, an offer of a plea which moves dramatically from a life sentence potential to a probational level is not entirely unusual, and it is common in such instances for the defendant to accept the potential stigma of a conviction rather than risk trial at the felony level.

Legal Process

Most plea bargaining lives within what might be called a rational range of possible outcomes. However, the special category of sexual abuse cases has not infrequently been known to involve extreme reductions which reflect more the prosecutor's desire to achieve some conviction and his or her belief that in some way the alleged perpetrator must be guilty since there is still some tendency to believe that children will not lie about sexual abuse on the part of many professional people.

The plea bargaining process in State v. X went as follows. As the date of the trial approached, the prosecutor was more and more aware that the facts would not warrant a first degree felony conviction with its sentence of life in prison. Accordingly, a reduced charge plea was offered. Basically, the prosecutor conveyed the information that the defendant could plead to any felony crime with a sexual component and receive probation. X, however, did not want to be found guilty of a sexually related crime and, therefore, sent back by way of his attorney a willingness to plead to a felony charge of assault while at the same time acknowledging in the course of that plea that he was doing so to avoid prosecution. The advantage to the prosecutor would be a felony conviction; the advantage to the client would be a non-sex related offence on his record, and the same probationary outcome with avoidance of the liabilities associated with a full trial. As a further note to the peculiar nature of these proceedings, in the county of record, the acceptance of a so-called Alford plea[4] is not permitted by prosecution, but the acceptance of the language from Alford is allowed. In the course of these negotiations, it was at one point suggested that a victim rather than the child could be named, but the prosecutor drew the line at this request.

Following the plea, defense counsel joined the domestic relations attorney to request resumption of visitation through the Family Court. Ensuing negotiations involved both courts; ultimately, no contact was ordered until after sentencing, at which time the client was allowed supervised visitation.

Conclusions

The handling of this case supported the use of psychological expertise in the evaluation of data which had a bearing on the issue of guilt. The case also illustrated the functioning of a defense expert as provider of input to the court. Finally, the case was an excellent example of an increasingly well-known pattern involving both the domestic relations and criminal court systems – namely, that allegations of sexual abuse are raised as a part of the complex emotions and involvements of the extended family system. Myriad motives may well have played a part not only in the decisions that were made by the parties, but also in actions of authorities in the course of handling this case. Personal issues were identifiable in professionals as well as in the parties.

While the end result allowed some resolution to the case, the place of logic and rationality took a back seat to ego. Furthermore, professionals, more likely than

---

4 North Carolina v. Alford (1970) involved a murder conviction in which the defendant pled guilty to second degree murder in order to escape the possibility of a first degree conviction with death penalty liability. In so doing, Alford disclaimed guilt but accepted sentencing. He later appealed on the basis of coercion, but the trial Court's acceptance of what was a nolo contendere plea was upheld.

not, created for the children significant harm beyond what may or may not have occurred as a result of their dysfunctional family system. Finally, the possibility of an unidentified perpetrator of abuse remains an issue. The case and its outcomes provided an illustration of the need for scientific/investigative objectivity on the part of those whose primary purpose is that of protecting society – namely, the office of the prosecutor and the experts enlisted to assist it. At the same time, the Court essentially benefited from the activity of the defense expert through its instructions as to the scope of the expert's function. In following the mandate set forth by the court, the defense expert was able to specify on a scientific basis appropriate procedural standards and identify why those standards were not met. This contribution became part of the groundwork which allowed the case to reach its ultimate resolution through the plea bargain process.

References

Campbell, T. (1992). False allegations of sexual abuse and their apparent credibility. *American Journal of Forensic Psychology, 10, 4*, 21-35.

Gudjonsson, G. (1992). *The psychology of interrogations, confessions and testimony*. New York: John Wiley & Sons.

Horner, T. & Guyer, M. (1991). Prediction, prevention and clinical expertise in child custody cases in which allegations of child sexual abuse have been made. 1) Predictable rates of diagnostic error in relation to various clinical decision-making strategies. *Family Law Quarterly, 25, 2*, 217-251.

McPherson, S. B. (1994). *Psychological perspectives as they may have relevance to the court in regard to allegations of child sexual abuse.* Memo prepared as a basis of testimony and submitted to Attorney Milano and the Criminal Court in the State of Ohio v. X.

Mikkelson, E. J.; Gutheil, T. G.; & Emens, M. (1992). False sexual-abuse allegations by children and adolescents: contextual factors and clinical subtypes. *American Journal of Psychotherapy, 26, 4*, 556-570.

Morag, T. (1990). *Children's evidence in child abuse proceedings under the Israeli legal system – the law of evidence revision (protection of children)*, 1955. Paper presented at the Second European Conference on Law and Psychology, Nuremburg, September. North Carolina v. Alford, 400 US 25; 91 S Ct 160, 1970.

Volbert, R. (1990). *Child witnesses and the criminal justice system of the RG.* Paper presented at the Second European Conference on Law and Psychology, Nuremburg, September.

Impact on Verdict of Gender Homogeneous Juries in a Case of Rape

Ramón Arce, Francisca Fariña, Mercedes Novo and Santiago Real

Introduction

The role of gender as a mediator of differences in information processing, capacity to persuade, and as the source of bias in juror judgement making has received considerable attention, specifically since the working assumption has been that gender gives rise to bias, particularly in cases of rape. Several authors have reported differences between men and women in this type of case, i.e., women emit more guilty verdicts than men (Sealy and Cornish 1973; Efran, 1974; Scroggs, 1976; Davis et al., 1977; Rumsey and Rumsey, 1977; Miller and Hewitt, 1978; Arce, 1989; Sáinz and Sáinz, 1989; McNamara, Vattano and Viney, 1993). A further case type which is frequently associated with gender bias is sexual abuse of children; women are more likely to give credibility to the child and emit a guilty verdict than men (Crowley, O'Callaghan and Ball, 1994). The gender of the defendant has also been linked to the jurors' judgement. Angira (1991) observed that in the case of robbery, men received shorter sentences than women, but did not find a relationship between the defendants and the jury's gender. In contrast, other studies report an interaction between the defendant's and the juror's gender since longer sentences are recommended for an accused of the same gender (Stephan, 1974).

For other case types, no evidence of differences between men and women have been observed (Simon, 1967; Griffith and Jackson, 1973; Gray and Ashmore, 1976; Bray and Noble, 1978; Eisen and McArthur, 1979; Hastie et al., 1983; Arce, 1989). Though the tendency of gender to generate bias has been well documented, we cannot disregard studies that have shown no differences between men and women jurors in rape trials (Jones and Aronson, 1973; Sealy and Cornish, 1973). Consequently, the reviews, in accordance with the inconsistency of the most of the research undertaken regarding jury bias, reject the theory that gender and other sociodemographic variables can explain juror decision given their low predictive value and for their lack of consistency from one case type to another (Penrod, 1990).

Another variable that has been evaluated is the persuasive capacity, which is greater in men than in women (Hastie et al., 1983). In addition, the attractiveness of the defendant seems to mediate in judgement making, and seems to be greater in male rather than female juries (Efran, 1974; Hastie et al., 1983). In this sense, Thornton (1977) found that, in cases of rape, though male jurors imposed heftier sentence if the victim was physically attractive, no differences in the conviction rate was observed between both sexes. The guilty threshold probability, that is to say the cut off point at which they vote guilty is also different between men and women in rape cases (Nagel, Neef and Lamm, 1981; Vila, 1993; Arce et al., 1994).

Thus, the data suggest that gender, as a response to differences in socialisation, can influence decision making, particularly in cases of rape. Nevertheless this has to be considered in the light of three modulating variables: case type, the quality and amount of evidence presented, and the management of juror samples or jury composition. In relation to case type, it is not possible to compare predictors in different contexts; gender may be a good predictor of bias in cases of rape but not in other case types. This suggests that the factors that lead to bias must be assessed in the appropriate context, in order to be of predictive value (Bem and Allen, 1968). Studies concerned with jury bias have focused on the search for universal predictors of bias, especially with reference to conviction-proneness and leniency. Furthermore, it is worth highlighting that there are even discrepancies among researchers as to what constitutes rape. Muehlenhard and colleague's (1992) exhaustive review of the literature reveals the wide variety of definitions of rape.

With respect to the evidence, in cases where it is clear the predictive value of bias is nil. In fact, Dane and Wrighstman (1982) found that bias disappears when the evidence is heavily weighted one way or the other. Likewise, Spanos, Dubreuil and Gwynn (1992), demonstrated how an expert testimony on the myths of rape undermined the credibility of the defendants testimony and increased the probability of being found guilty. No differences generated by gender were observed. It was also shown, that an expert's cross-examination had an adverse effect on the probability of the defendant being found guilty. Female jurors tended not to believe the defendant, and significantly higher numbers of female jurors found the accused guilty. In other words, the results obtained with different case types or the amount of evidence cannot be compared, though the reviews of the literature have not taken into account these aspects.

The study of juror sample and jury composition, Aubrey and Ewing (1989) found that students were less inclined to stereotype battered women, and that gender did not influence the results. In comparison, a sample obtained from the voting register was more inclined to stereotype battered women and exhibited significant differences according to gender.

Bearing in mind the results obtained with homogeneous groups, it is plausible to believe that the indicators of bias in the deliberation will have a multiplying effect. Our findings suggest that ideologically or attributionally homogeneous groups multiply the predictive value of bias after group interaction (Arce, Sobral and Farina, 1992). The same tendency has also been reported by Cowan, Thompson and Ellsworth (1984) but with excudable and non-excudable homogeneous juries in relation to the death penalty, the former being more inclined to convict. The aim of the present work is to determine whether gender homogeneous juries differ in a trial of rape, by controlling the decision at the level of the juror and of a homogeneous jury.

Method

Procedure and Subjects. Each jury was shown a video recording of an actual rape trial, in which there were no eyewitnesses. The victim identified the accused in the street and once again in a line up. Though the defendant, who had no previous criminal record, had been identified at the scene of the crime, he claimed it was a case of mistaken identity, and that he could not have committed the crime because he had been in the company of his friends at the time. At the trial both the defence and the prosecution presented various witnesses as well as the testimony of several experts and police officers.

In the light of the literature reviewed, it was reasonable to expect a verdict of guilt or innocence, dependant on the composition of the jury. Before compiling the data for this study, the written script of the trial was given to a sample of jurors who were legally qualified for jury service in Galicia in order to determine if the evidence was counterbalanced. Two hundred ninety-two jurors were selected to create a social representation as close to real life as possible with respect to socio-demographic variables. The variables taken into consideration are: gender, age group, cultural background, social class and geographical location. Though the results revealed a slight tendency towards an innocent verdict (53%), the results also presented that the evidence was perfectly counterbalanced and valid for our purposes i.e., to examine bias in the verdict as a consequence of gender differences and jury composition.

A total of thirty juries were formed with two hundred forty subjects aged between eighteen to sixty-five taken from the electoral register, and consisting of eight randomly selected members. Of these, ten were women only and ten were men only, the remaining ten were composed of five men and five women. The jurors were required to complete a sociodemographic questionnaire before viewing the video of the trial. Thereafter, the jurors filled in a questionnaire to record their verdict, estimated sentence, probability of guilt, recall and evaluation of evidence, and the reconstruction of the events. Afterwards, group deliberation took place, and a unanimous decision was required. The group was instructed to elect a foreman and was allowed to consider the possibility of a hung jury. In the case of a hung jury, they would not receive any instructions designed to bring about a unanimous verdict (dynamite instructions). In the post deliberation, the juror's decisions were once again individually evaluated.

Results

The study assessed whether gender was a good predictor of the juror's verdict in this case of rape. (see Table 1). No differences between women and men were observed (Chi(1)=1.68; NS).

Table 1: Pre-deliberation Verdict. All Sample

	Guilty	Not-guilty
Men	60	60
Women	70	50

As could well be the case, by chance, the jurors that were randomly assigned to homogeneous groups may exhibit differences influenced by gender (see Table 2), but no significant differences were observed (chi(1)=3.05; NS).

Table 2: Pre-deliberation Verdict. Experimental Conditions

	Guilty	Not-guilty
Men	38	42
Women	49	31

In contrast, in the post-deliberation with homogeneous groups, the tendency to convict was significantly higher for women than men (chi(1)=34.3; p<.001, see Table 3), whereas with mixed juries no significant differences were found in relation to gender (chi(1)=.05; NS, see Table 4).

Table 3: Homogeneous Juries. Post-deliberation Verdict

	Guilty	Not-guilty
Men	20	60
Women	51	19

chi(1)=34.30; P<.001.

Table 4: Mixed Juries. Post-deliberation Verdict

	Guilty	Not-guilty
Men	14	26
Women	15	25

chi(1)=0.05; NS.

The probability for changes in verdict was practically the same for men (.35) as for women (.3375). Nevertheless, there was a wide range of reasons that accounted for the change in verdict (see Table 5). Thus, women tended to significantly change their verdict from innocent to guilty rather than vice versa ($Z(80)=3.44$; $p<.01$), whereas as men in the opposite direction i.e., from guilty to innocent ($Z(80)=4.23$; $p<.01$).

Table 5: Change of Verdict

	NG/G	G/NG
Men	.075	.275
Women	.2875	.05

NG/G=change of verdict in the deliberation from innocent to guilty; G/NG=change from guilty to innocent.

Discussion

The literature concerning individual juror bias in decision-making provides numerous examples as well as contradictions when compared to group decision making which does not reveal the existence of bias. In fact, Kaplan and Miller (1986) have shown that individual bias is immediately neutralised in the deliberation. They suggest that the source of this bias was exclusively of an emotional nature. Obviously, if emotional bias were to influence group decision making, the jury would cease to be of any value. However, other types of bias may intervene. If we were to show the same case to various juries, we would observe opposite verdicts. Thus, group decision making is not only the result of the coming together of various perspectives, but also of each individual's bias.

What would occur then if all the jurors share the same bias in the same case? The reply would be predictable, there would be no forces to counterbalance any possible bias which would lead to a biased group decision. A possible explanation is that people resort to epistemic pluralism with different alternative interpretations which are sometimes contradictory. Once one of these options has been adopted, such as anchoring which guides pre-oriented information, the juror is able to reach a verdict.

Another possible alternative is the search for adjustments once the evidence has been heard. In this case, the jury would be inclined to reject the evidence from discredited witnesses. If we take into account that the juror is involved in an epistemic pluralism, the subjects who belong to a high risk bias group would be inclined to reach a pre-oriented opinion if other jurors share the same bias in the pre deliberation. If this were not the case, we would have to resort to a unitary epistemology of the juror, in which case the only possible way to reach a pre-oriented verdict would be through erroneous information processing. This explanation may be suitable for the juror but not for the jury given that in groups the jurors recall more than 90% of the evidence, including the key evidence (Hastie et al., 1983).

We should bear in mind that bias is not synonymous to error. In other studies we have observed that a biased group decision may arise from a partial appraisal of the evidence. In the deliberation jurors do not focus on the evidence or resort to what we have termed second order heuristic devices (see Arce et al., 1994 for an example) which refer to strategies such as the lack of evidence, or credibility, or inadmissible evidence. Clearly, these devices can be interpreted in either way, pro-innocent and pro-guilty are both perfectly feasible verdict since both may be the end product of bias.

References

Angira, K. K. (1991). Effect of sex of transgressor on the juridicial judgement of male and female simulated jurors. *Psycho-Lingua, 21(2),* 79-84.

Arce, R. (1989). *Perfiles Psicosociales, Veredictos y Deliberación en Jurados Legos.* Unpublished Doctoral Thesis. Universidad de Santiago de Compostela.

Arce, R., Fariña, F., & Vila, C. (1994). Sobre la calidad y ubicación de las instrucciones judiciales al jurado. *Revista de Psicología Social Aplicada, 4(3)*, 105-119.

Aubrey, M., & Ewing, Ch. P. (1989). Student and voter subjects: Differences in attitudes toward battered women. *Journal of Interpersonal Violence, 4(3)*, 289-297.

Bem, D. J., & Allen, A. (1974). On predicting some of the people some of the time: The search for cross-situational consistencies in behaviour. *Psychological Review, 81*, 506-520.

Bray R. M., & Noble, A. (1978). Authoritarianism and decision of mock juries: Evidence of jury bias and group polarization. *Journal of Personality and Social Psychology, 36*, 1424-1430.

Cowan, C. L., Thompson, W. C., & Ellsworth, P. C. (1984).The effects of death qualification on jurors' predisposition to convict and on quality of deliberation. *Law and Human Behaviour, 8(1/2)*, 53-79.

Crowley, M. J., O'Callaghan, M. G., & Ball, P. J. (1994).The juridical impact of psychological expert testimony in a simulated child sexual abuse trial. *Law and Human Behaviour, 18(1)*, 89-105.

Dane, F. & Wrighstman, L. (1982). Effects of defendants' and victims' characteristics on jurors' verdicts. In N. L. Kerr, & R. M. Bray (Eds.). *The psychology of the Courtroom.* New York: Academic Press.

Davis, J. H., Kerr, N. L., Stasser, G., Meek, D., & Holt, R. (1977). Victim consequences, sentence severity, and decision process in mock juries. *Organizational Behaviour and Group Performance, 18*, 346-365.

Efran, M. G. (1974). The effect of physical appearance on the judgement of guilt, interpersonal attraction, and severity of recommended punishment in a simulated jury task. *Journal of Research in Personality, 8*, 45-54.

Eisen, S. V., & McArthur, L. Z. (1979). Evaluating and sentencing a defendant as a function of his salience and the perceiver's set. *Personality and Social Psychology Bulletin, 5,* 48-52.

Gray, D. B., & Ashmore, R. D. (1976). Biasing influence of defendants' characteristics on simulated sentencing. *Psychological Reports, 38*, 727-738.

Griffitt, W., & Jackson, T. (1973). Simulated jury decisions: The influence of jury-defendant attitude similarity-dissimilarity. *Social Behaviour and Personality, 1*, 1-7.

Hastie, R., Penrod, S., & Pennington, N. (1983). *Inside the Jury.* Cambridge, MA: Harvard University Press.

Jones, C., & Aronson, E. (1973). Attributions of fault to a rape victim as a function of respectability of the victim. *Journal of Personality and Social Psychology, 26*, 415-419.

McNamara, K., Vattano, F., & Viney, W. (1993).Verdict, sentencing, and certainty as a function of sex of juror and amount of evidence in a simulated rape trial. *Psychological Reports, 72*(2), 575-583.

Miller, M., & Hewitt, J. (1978). Conviction of a defendant as a function of juror-victim racial similarity. *Journal of Social Psychology, 105*, 159-160.

Muehlenhard, Ch. L., Powch, I. G., Phelps, J. L., & Giusti, L. M. (1992). Definitions of rape: Scientific and political implications. *Journal of Social Issues, 48(1)*, 23-44.

Nagel, S., Neef, M., & Lamm, D. (1981). Decision theory and jury decision making. In B. Sales (Ed.). *The Trial Process.* New York: Plenum Press.

Nelligan, P. J. (1988). The effects of the gender of jurors on sexual assault verdicts. *Sociology and Social Research, 72(4)*, 249-251.

Penrod, S. D. (1990). Predictors of jury decision making in criminal and civil cases: A field experiment. *Forensic Reports, 3(3)*, 261-277.

Rumsey, M. G., & Rumsey, J. M. (1977). A case of rape: Sentencing judgements of males and females. *Psychological Reports, 41*, 459-465.

Sáinz, E., & Sáinz, J. (1989). Estratégias de decisión de un jurado bajo condiciones de simulación. *Revista de Psicología General y Aplicada, 42(4)*, 509-523.

Scroggs, J. R. (1976). Penalties of rapes as a function of victim provocativeness, damage and resistance. *Journal of Applied Social Psychology, 6*, 360-368.

Sealy, A. P., & Cornish, W. R. (1973). Juries and the rule of evidence. *Criminal Law Review, April*, 320-322.

Simon, R. J. (1967). *The Jury and the Defense of Insanity.* Boston, MA: Little Brown.

Spanos, N. P., Dubreuil, S. C., & Gwynn, M. I. (1992). The effects of expert testimony concerning rape on the verdicts and belief of mock jurors. *Imagination, Cognition and Personality, 11(1)*, 37-51.

Stephan, C. (1974). Sex prejudice in jury simulation. *Journal of Psychology, 88*, 305-312.

Thornton, B. (1977). Effect of rape victim's attractiveness in a jury simulation. *Personality and Social Psychology Bulletin, 3*, 666-669.

Vila, C. (1993). *Sobre las Instrucciones Judiciales al Jurado. Un Análisis desde el Jurado Individual.* Unpublished Master Doctoral Thesis. Universidad de Santiago de Compostela.

Judicial Decision Making: Information Processing and Judgements Given by Blind Subjects

Emilia I. De la Fuente, Juan García and José A. Belmonte

Introduction

The research on how people make judgments under uncertainty is large, and rife with controversy (Kahneman, Slovic & Tversky, 1982; Kyburg,1983; Einhorn & Hogarth, 1985; De la Fuente, Salinas, Ortega & Martín, 1990). One reason for the controversy is that although there is agreement that uncertainty is a crucial factor in assessment of probabilities.

From our perspective, perceived uncertainty captures an important aspect of how people make inferences from unknown, or only partially known facts. Ambiguity and uncertainty are two subjective variables, but it should be possible to identify "objectively" some situations likely to present high ambiguity, by noting situations where available information is scanty, obviously unrealiable, or highly conflicting.

The task of the jury is to establish a social judgement from the existing evidence. The process is an individual decision by each one of its members. Then, the individual judgements have to be appropiately combined to form a group pespective, under a specific decisive rule, to produce the final verdict in the judicial process.

A juror is not just "economic man", a passive subject who behaves according to the dictates of a formal rule, but an active one, who has a limited capacity to process the information presented to him and possesses an adaptative character. This has four basic consequences: perception of the information is selective and opened to influence; people cannot simultaneously integrate great quantity of information; information processing necessarily depends on the operations which simplify the judgements task and reduce mental effort; memory capacity is limited and has a reconstructive character.

With respect to the situations that will have to be analysed in order to render judgement, not only their structure is considered. Also content, context, and the method of presenting the alternatives or evidence, are variables that the researcher should take into account. Since it has been shown that these may have as much influence in the ultimate choice preferences of individuals as in the strategies used by them in order to arrive at a judgements (Einhort and Hogarth, 1981; Payne, 1982; De la Fuente et al., 1994)

Finally, it is very important to study the person´s attitude toward process circumstances or ambiguity in these circumtances. This is reflected in the persons tendency to give differential attention or weight to some evidence. The differential attention can be motivated by strange elements to the process, by example, the pre-trial publicity.

Model for combining sources

We use a model (De la Fuente et al. 1994) which describes how jurors can make an individual decision regarding the probability of an event in a scale of guilt assignment. The model is constructed in a manner which involves the subjects faced with a situation in which they observe ambiguity. The judgement expressed is based on blocks of evidence of different sources with limited reliability.

This model postulates that the jurors will utilise a strategy of anchorage and adjustment. The way of combining the information is additive, directly related to the credibility of the source of evidence and inversely related to the ambiguity perceived in these sources. In this model it is expected that the subject's attitude is a parameter which may cause the individually expressed judgement to vary.

It is a function of aggregation of information in the case of multiple sources which may be contrasted empirically with experimental series. This model considers the initial evaluation of the probability obtained from different sources, the amount of ambiguity perceived from the different sources, and the personal attitude towards ambiguity in the circumtances.

If a combination of the judgement estimated from each one of the K considered sources of information is established, a final individual verdict or assessment results, which, suitably developed, has the following form:

$$s(f_1c_1,\ldots,f_kc_k)=\frac{\sum_i\theta_i}{k\sum_i n_i}\sum_i\left[\frac{n_ip_{A_i}}{\theta_i}+k-p_{A_i}-p_{A_i}^{\beta}\right]$$

Where f_1, c_1; .....; f_k, c_k, are the reports in favour and against an event of interest proceeding from k sources of information F1, ..., Fk. The total number of observers who report from both sources is called n_1, ... n_k, and, θ_1, ..., θ_k the components of total perceived ambiguity corresponding to F1, ..., Fk, respectively.

The different testimonies provide points of anchorage P_{A1}, ..., P_{Ak}. Finally, β represents the personal attitude towards ambiguity in the circumtances (see, De la Fuente et al., 1994).

Objective

In this paper the adjustment and properties of a model for combined sources are studied. With this model, we hope to predict the decisions of two groups, normal subjects and blind subjects, in a task similar to one that is carried out by a jury. An experimental series is created, in which we manipulate the presentation of the judicial process information. The differences in the accuracy of the adjustment of the model, the processing of information, and the judgments of our two groups are analyzed.

Experiment

Subjects

Two experimental groups are used. The first group comprised 8 students from the University of Granada. They are "normal" subjects (G1). The second group comprised 8 students also from the University of Granada. They are blind subjects (G2). All participation is voluntary.

Stimuli

The material used consisted of two booklet of 25 pages. Each booklet consists of a set of scenarios which involve a robbery/homicide in a bank office, and witnessed by varying numbers of people.

The first group of witnesses is composed of the bank-employees. They are the first source of information (F1). The second group of witnesses is composed of drunk people returning from a party. They are the second source of information (F2). The testimony is information about the recognition of the defendants.

Each scenario consists of the same basic story but varies in the total number of witnesses (n). Moreover, of the n witnesses to the robbery one claimed that the thief is the defendant, whereas another claimed that he was not.

Each scenario was printed on a separate page and contained a 0 – 100 point rating that was used by the subject to judge whether the robbery had been carried by the defendant.

Three independent variables were manipulated, source of information, point of anchorage, and number of testimonies with each subject. The first with two levels, F1, F2, the second with 13 levels, and the third with 25 levels, p=1.00, n=6; p=0.89, n=18; p=0.80, n=5, n=10, n=20; p=0.75, n=4, n=9, n=15; p=0.67, n=3, n=6, n=9, n=18, n=20; p=0.60, n=10; p=0.50, n=12; p=0.40, n=5; p=0.33, n=18; p=0.25, n=4; p=0.20, n=5; p=0.11, n=9, n=10, n=18, n=20; p=0.00, n=20.

Two dependent variables were measured in both group G1 and G2, likelihood of guilt and confidence degree.

Procedure

The experiment, with the first group, was carried out collectively in the University of Granada. The experiment, with the second group was carried out individually in the Organization National of Spanish Blinds (ONCE).

Estimating the model

To estimate the model from the experimental data, we need to rewrite equation (1) and include a random error term to represent judgemental inconsistency. This equation requires a non-linear estimation technique. We used a non-linear regression program (Dixon, 1990) and chose the criterion of minimizing mean absolute deviations for estimating the parameters.

Results

General fit of the model; Global Analysis

Firstly a global analysis of the data obtained is presented. For each of the 25 stimuli in the groups G1 and G2, the judgements from the 16 subjects were averaged to form the mean judged likelihood S(f,c). This was then used as the dependent variable to be fitted by the model. The parameter values obtained from the estimation program were (see Tables 1, 2, 3, 4.):

θ=0.455110	β=0.707798	for source F1 in G1.
θ=0.507466	β=0.282050	for source F1 in G1.
θ=0.249830	β=0.149610	for source F1 in G2.
θ=0.045648	β=94.51021	for source F2 in G2.

There is no significant difference between the observed series of judgments and the judgements predicted by model. All of this indicates that for the type of subjects used in this experiment, the testimony of drunk persons (F2) is less credible than the testimony of bank employees (F1). The global parameter of ambiguity θ is very similar in the first and second group. The blind subjects are a minor perceived ambiguity, compared to the normal subjects. The blind subjects have an attitude parameter higher than the normal subjects (more positive). This results support the accuracy of model.

Table 1: Source 1 – Group 1

Subject	Theta	Beta	F	P
1	0.175284	0.466476	0.46	0.5044
2	0.377359	0.742847	1.28	0.2682
3	0.782335	1.04531	1.94	0.1763
4	2.577460	3.072091	2.79	0.1080
5	–0.022266	2.312920		
6	–1.234006	0.659403		
7	1.511675	0.196021	1.36	0.2545
8	–0.163506	4.323890		
Mean	0.455110	0.707798		

Table 2: Source 2 – Group 1

Subject	Theta	Beta	F	P
1	0.865062	10.007511	1.13	0.2993
2	–0.129665	111.01002		
3	–0.356090	0.026796		
4	1.991406	1.478758	0.09	0.7620
5	0.033181	2.522206	0.21	0.6490
6	–0.656237	0.469428		
7	0.565211	0.309354	0.07	0.8007
8	–0.189534	0.838393		
Mean	0.507466	0.282050		

Table 3: Source 1 – Group 2

Subject	Theta	Beta	F	P
1	0.155383	0.831206	1.19	0.2852
2	–0.500800	1.867733		
3	0.326337	1.179945	1.64	0.2123
4	0.047096	0.558637	0.43	0.5178
5	0.824273	1.247128	0.15	0.7044
6	0.062698	0.536891	0.05	0.8937
7	0.200420	6.031296	0.02	0.8999
8	–0.602427	0.306659		
Mean	0.249830	2.149610		

Table 4: Source 2 – Group 2

Subject	Theta	Beta	F	P
1	–0.067269	82.65799		
2	2.231408	0.144571	3.25	0.0840
3	0.176334	1.617882	1.00	0.3279
4	–0.041366	104.7492		
5	–0.660906	0.705781		
6	0.604932	0.360627	0.02	0.8809
7	–0.599911	1951.382		
8	0.482857	0.767689	0.79	0.3830
Mean	0.045648	94.51021		

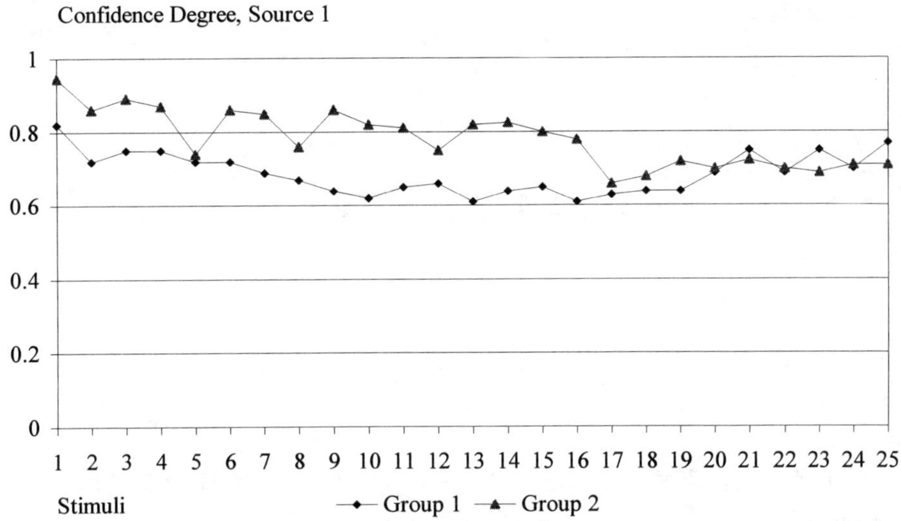

Figure 1: Confidence Degree, Source 1

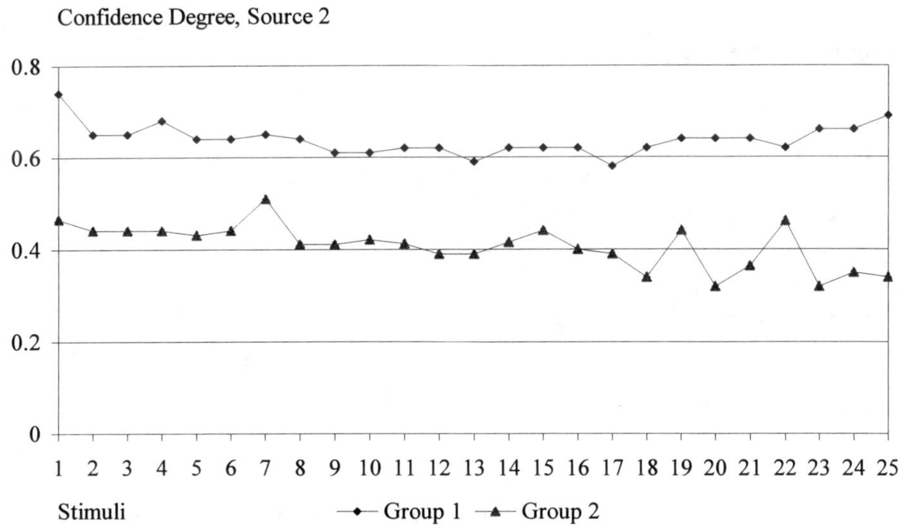

Figure 2: Confidence Degree, Source 2

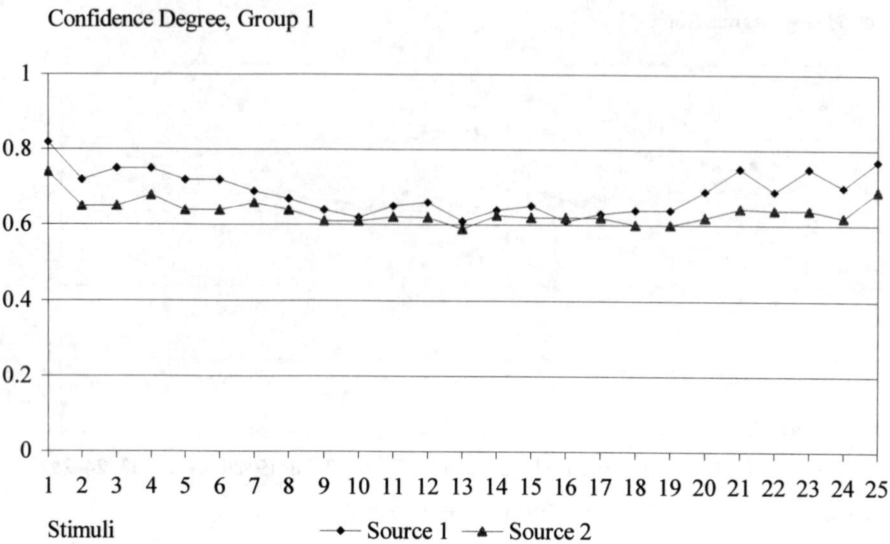

Figure 3: Confidence Degree, Group 1

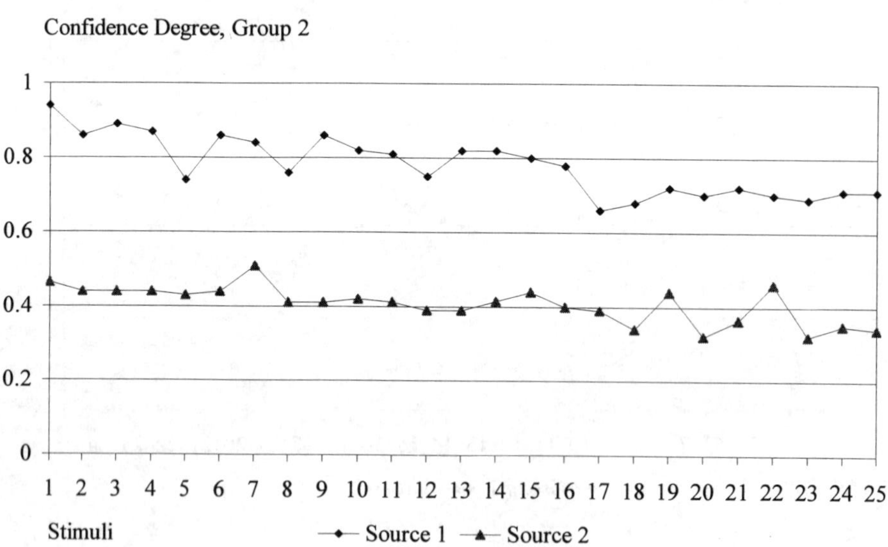

Figure 4: Confidence Degree, Group 2

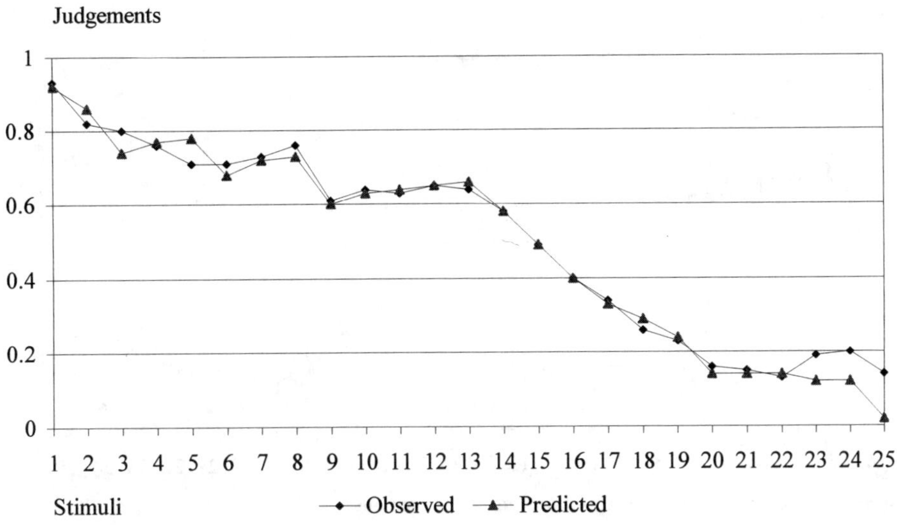

Figure 5: Source 1 – Group 1

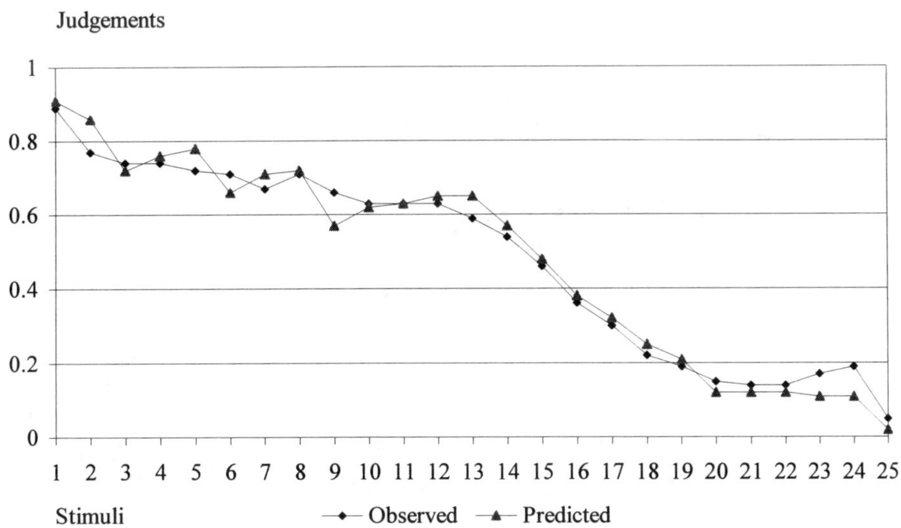

Figure 6: Source 2 – Group 1

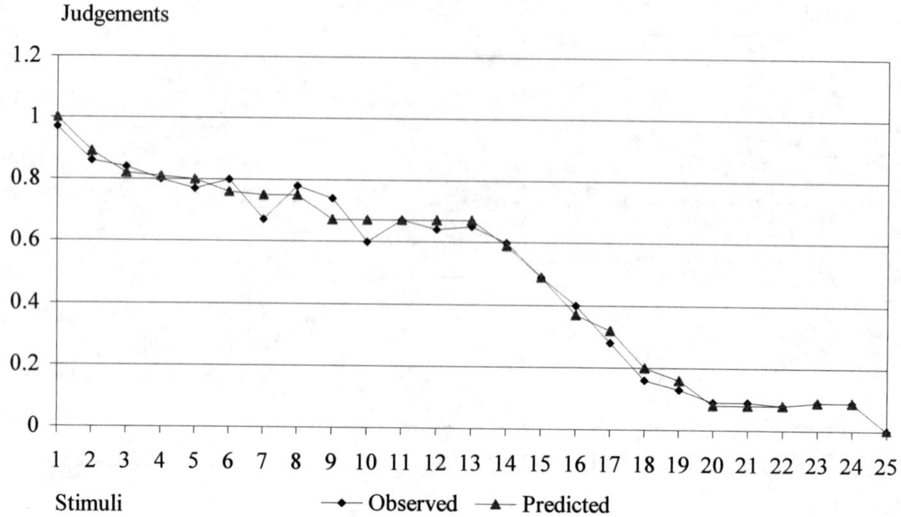

Figure 7: Source 1 – Group 2

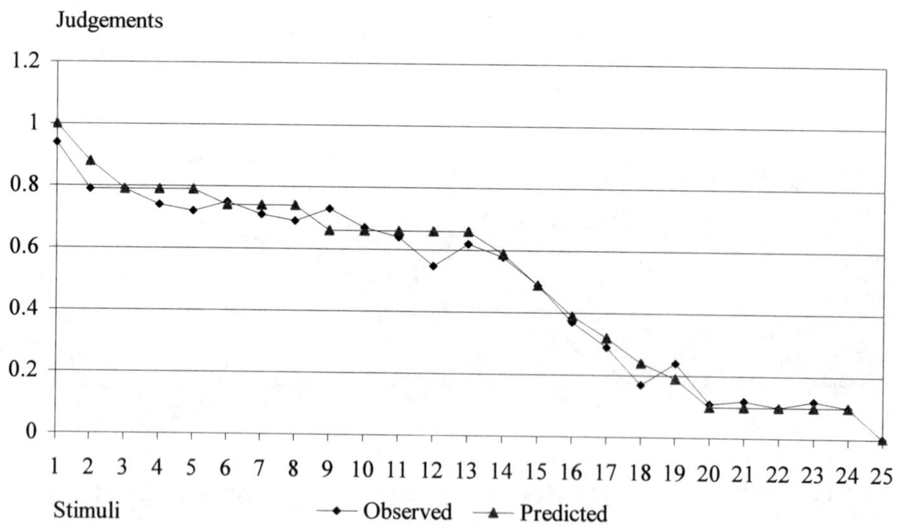

Figure 8: Source 2 – Group 2

Graphics of the predicted and observed judgements series are presented (see Figures 5 to 8).

The predictibility level of the model is smaller in the first group than in the second group. The second group does not have problems of under confidence or oner confidence in the extreme values of the probability ranking. These problems are produced in normal subjects (see Figures 1 to 4).

Subjects in the second group are more cofident when they answer, if the testimony comes from confident source and less confident, if the testimony comes from the less credible source.

Fit of the model; Individual analysis

The model can be adjusted to the data of each individual. We wish to test possible irregularies in the fit, and also subjects who do not fit our theory. Estimates of the parameters of the model for each individual are therefore presented (Tables 1, 2, 3 and 4) and similarly the values of the F-statistics, in order to contrast the judgements made by each subject with those predicted by the model. Similar numbers in both the first and second group do not have a good fit with the model.

Conclusions

The results obtained in the experiment empirically support the model for combine sources that have been proposed in both normal and blind groups. However, more detailed experiments with a larger number of subjects are needed to identify the factors that could influence the judgements as well as the diferences between normal and blind groups.

References

De la Fuente, E. I., Salinas, J. M., Ortega, A. R., & Martín, I. (1990). *Juicios bajo ambigüedad y su modelización.* Seventh National Congress of Psychology. Barcelona.

De la Fuente, E. I., Ortega, A. R., Martín, I., & Trujillo, H. (1994). *Formal Pattern in Jury Decision Making.* Fourth European Conference of Psychology and Law. Barcelona.

Dixon, W. J. (1990). *BMDP Statistical Software.* Berkeley: University of California Press.

Einhorn, H. J., & Hogarth, R. M. (1981). Behavioral decision theory: Processes of judgment and choice. *Annual Review of Psychology, 32*, 53-88.

Einhorn, H. J., & Hogarth, R. M. (1985). Ambiguity and uncertainty in probabilistic inference. *Psychological Review, 92*, 433-461.

Kahneman, D., Slovic, P., & Tversky, A. (1982). *Judgment under uncertainty: Heuristics and biases.* New York: Cambridge University Press.

Kyburg, H. E., Jr.(1983). Rational Belief. *Behavioral and Brain Sciences, 6*, 231- 273.

Payne, J. W. (1982). Contingent decision behavior. *Psychological Bulletin, 92*, 382-402.

Polygraphs in Criminal Justice Systems: The Effect of Different Legal Cultures on the Use of Scientific Evidence

Petra van Kampen

Buzz Fay had no idea how incompletely and inaccurately he understood the way lie detectors work. He shared the popular misconception that polygraphs don't make mistakes, that they are truly objective. He had not thought about the role of the person who interprets the test results: Objectively achieved results gain what meaning they have only from subjective evaluation by the polygraph operator. Nor did he consider the possibility that apparently objective factors can be altered. "I believed the polygraph worked," he stated repeatedly in later years. "But it's ridiculous," he would add ruefully. "Any criminal who knows how to beat a polygraph can beat it.[1]

Introduction

Every legal system engages in a search for truth, at least partly. The certainment of truth, however, is not the exclusive goal of criminal justice systems. Ultimately, we search for justice. But whereas truth is not equal to justice, it nevertheless plays an important role in seeking justice. Truth itself is a dangerous concept, a 'terrible thing'.[2] If anything, our inquisitorial past has taught us that the unparalleled and zealous search for truth can lead to overstepping the boundaries of human liberty and integrity. Despite our experiences with this search, we still do not seem to be able to stay away from it. After all, most of us feel that the only legitimate aim of punishing is the fact that people are truly guilty of the crime with which they have been charged. The problem with the concept of truth is that there is no easy way of finding out whether what one believes or says is indeed objective. In criminal cases, this is nowhere more apparent than in the evaluation of eyewitness testimony. As Kaplan said, mistaken eyewitness testimony is the major cause of conviction of the innocent in the United States,[3] and has been for years. Yet, for most part, the (eye)witnesses truly believed that the accused was indeed the person they saw committing the alleged crime. Few people would

1 Michael L. Radelet, Hugo Adam Bedau and Constance E. Putnam, In Spite of Innocence, The Ordeal of 400 Americans Wrongly Convicted of Crimes Punishable by Death, Northeastern University Press 1992, 221.

2 Robert P. Warren, All the King's Men, Bantam Books 1981, 343.

3 John Kaplan, foreword by Elizabeth F. Loftus, Eyewitness Testimony, Harvard University Press 1979, vii.

blame witnesses who honestly – but mistakenly – identify the defendant as the wrongdoer, or testify to the matter concerned. However, many would blame the witness who identifies the wrong person on purpose. Or for that matter, a defendant who is lying on the spot. The first is a problem of human error, the second of cheating. In that respect, the problem is that we oftentimes have no way of knowing which is which. How do you evaluate the credibility of witnesses and defendants if you have little to go by? And so, as Wigmore once said, "If there is ever devised a psychological test for the evaluation of witnesses, the law would run to meet it."[4]

At the time Wigmore wrote this, a test to detect deception, had indeed been developed. This test, called the systolic blood pressure test, was a precursor of what we nowadays mistakenly call a lie detector test, the more scientific name is the polygraph test. Eighty years later, Wigmore has been proved right. The law did run to meet the polygraph, but the outcome has not been favorable to the polygraph, at least in the United States. The main reasons for the refusal of the American courts to allow introduction of the results of such tests – conducted in the pretrial phase – in court can be found in the still questioned reliability and validity of the test, and considerations regarding the possible influence on the trier of fact. Currently, the question of the usefulness and appropriateness of the polygraph in police investigations is subject to discussion in the Netherlands. In this paper, it is analyzed whether the introduction of the polygraph in such investigations is an option worth considering, taking into account the different judicial setting and culture of the Dutch criminal justice system.

The Polygraph

The Underlying Theory

The basic theory behind the polygraph has only partly been developed. According to the U.S. Office of Technology Assessment, the most commonly accepted theory is that "when a person being examined fears detection, that fear produces a measurable physiological reaction when the person responds deceptively."[5] These physiological responses are changes in blood-pressure, pulse, respiration, and galvanic skin resistance.[6] It is then for the polygraph examiner to interpret these results with regard to the question of whether this particular person is deceiving

4 Wigmore, A Treatise on the Anglo-American System of Evidence in Trials at Common Law's. 875, 237 (2nd ed. 1923).

5 U.S. Congress, Office of Technology Assessment, Scientific Validity of Polygraph Testing: A Review and Evaluation - A Technical Memorandum, 12 Polygraph 201 (1983).

6 Paul C. Giannelli and Edward J. Imwinkelried, Scientific Evidence, The Michie Company (1993), 217.

the examiner. It has been argued that the polygraph test detects neither deception nor fear of deception, but rather provides a recording of changes in physiological responses from with the examiner can infer deception.[7] "The polygraph does not detect lies, but merely records physiological phenomena which are assumed to be related to conscious deception."[8]

There seems to be little question that the polygraph does indeed measure these responses of the body to questions asked. The more difficult question is whether these responses actually do represent deception, or anything like that. Critics have argued that the physiological responses caused by fear of detection have not been shown to be any different from the changes in bodily response caused by other emotions such as the emotions associated with being falsely accused of a crime, anxiety, or answering sensitive topics,[9]. Based on the testimony of preeminent polygraphists, psychiatrists, psychologists, psychophysiologists and others, the U.S. Committee on Government Representatives argued that

> [T]here is no 'lie' detector. The polygraph machine is not a 'lie detector', nor does the operator who interprets the graphs detect 'lies'. The machine records physical responses which may or may not be connected with an emotional reaction – and that reaction may or may not be related to guilt or innocence. Many, many physical and psychological factors make it possible for an individual to 'beat' the polygraph without detection by the machine or its operator.[10]

The proponents, however, argue that deception can be inferred by the examiner from the response to certain, carefully structured, questions.[11]

The Questions

Currently, there are three main types of examinations used in relation to the polygraph. The original test is the so-called relevant-irrelevant question. Relevant questions are questions that are related to the specific crime under investigation, whereas irrelevant questions concern neutral questions. The assumption underlying this type of examination is that innocent persons will not react to

---

7 Ibid, at 216.

8 United States v. Alexander, 526 F.2d 161, 163 (8th Cir. 1975).

9 See Kleinmuntz & Szucko, On the Fallibility of Lie Detection, 17 Law & Society Review (1982) 87. See also J. A. Matte, Defense Access to Police Polygraph Tests, 65 N.Y. State Bar Journal (1993), 36, in which the author mentions that the physiological reaction on the polygraph chart caused by 'fear of error' cannot be distinguished from the physiological reaction caused by 'fear of detection'. The same is true for the emotion of anger.

10 The Committee on Government Operations of the House of Representatives, House Representatives Rep. No. 198, 89th Cong. 1st Sess, 13 (1965). The rationale behind the reasoning of the Committee was based on the fact that there are too many uncontrollable factors which may affect the conclusion as to the veracity or falsity of the responses.

11 See Matte, supra note 9.

relevant questions concerning the crime. That assumption, however, is dubious. Even the proponents of the polygraph test agree on that. Raskin stated that "there is no clear and systematic way to interpret the outcome of a relevant-irrelevant test, and the result is subject to a great deal of error."[12] The second type of examination is the control question technique. The person being tested is being asked questions which can only be answered by yes or no. The subject is familiar with the questions asked, as he/she has reviewed the question together with the examiner during the pretest interview. What the subject does not know is the sequence of questions asked. The questions are either neutral questions, relevant questions, or control questions. Control questions concern acts of wrongdoing of the same general nature as the main incident under investigation. It is assumed that the subject will probably lie to those questions, and are, according to Imwinkelried and Giannelli, "designed as a stimulus for the truthful subject."[13] By comparing the response of the control questions to the relevant questions, it is said that the examiner can detect deceptive persons, as these persons, in all probability, will respond more to the relevant questions than the control ones, whereas the situation is the other way around for the truthful person.[14] Nevertheless, whether caused by asking the wrong questions or caused by a flaw in the assumption, the control question technique suffers from the fact that there are more false positives than false negatives when this type of questioning is used.[15]

The third and most recently developed type of examination – the guilty knowledge test – differs significantly from the two aforementioned. The relevant-irrelevant and control question techniques are deception tests, the guilty knowledge – or peak of tension – technique is not. The purpose of the test is to test the subject with regard to details of a crime that have not been disclosed to the public. The subject is tested on concealed knowledge that only the perpetrator will possess. The facts that only the guilty suspect can recognize are presented to the examinee in the form of multiple choice items, embedded in a set with more than two alternatives that would seem equally plausible to an innocent subject without guilty knowledge.[16] The underlying assumption is that the guilty subject will show a greater response to the significant alternative than an innocent subject will. The presence of alternatives functions as a device of control with regard to the innocent subject, who may deem the other items shown equally plausible. Due to the fact that there has to be concealed knowledge of which the public is not aware,

---

12 Raskin, The Polygraph in 1986: Scientific, Professional and Legal Issues Surrounding the Application and Acceptance of Polygraph Evidence, 1986 Utah Law Review 29, 33.

13 Giannelli & Imwinkelried, supra note 7, at 221.

14 See also Recherche Advies Commissie, De "Leugendetector" Een verkennend onderzoek naar de mogelijkheden van de polygraaf. Den Haag 1994, 10.

15 Giannelli & Imwinkelried, supra note 7, at 222.

16 Kleinmuntz and Szucko, supra note 9, at 98.

the test is of limited use,[17] but, at the same time, even the critics of the more commonly used lie detection techniques deem this test to be a more accurate detector of guilt.[18] The reason for this is that "the discrimination of guilty from innocent suspects can be increased by increasing the number of items."[19]

The Examiner

The outcome of the polygraph test depends heavily on the interaction between the examiner and the person being tested. The examiner has multiple tasks to fulfil. He has to determine the suitability of the subject,[20] formulate testing questions, control the circumstances in such a way, that no other factors influences the test other than the fear of detection, ensure that the subject understands the meaning of the questions asked, and ensure that the subject cooperates.[21] For the effectiveness of the test, the cooperation and confidence of the examinee in the effectiveness of the polygraph test is deemed to be crucial. If the examinee is not convinced that the polygraph is able to detect deception, the examinee will not fear that detection either. As Skolnick said, the myth of infallibility is essential to the polygraph: "As in the trial by ordeal, the subject must believe in the efficacy of the diagnostic instrument in order for it to achieve maximum response."[22]

After the actual test has been conducted,[23] the examiner has to interpret the charts. And although the physiological responses to questions can be objectively

17 Skolnick lists the conditions that have to be met in order for the test to be workable. First, some recognized article connected with the crime must be involved, secondly, the item must not have gone unnoticed by the guilty party, thirdly, only the examiner and the guilty party must know the identity of the stolen objects, and fourth, the information of the examiner must be accurate. Jerome H. Skolnick, Scientific Theory and Scientific Evidence: An Analysis of Lie-Detection, 70 Yale Law Journal (1961), 694-728 (710-711).

18 See Kleinmuntz and Szucko, supra note 9, at 98-101. Skolnick does not agree. He fears the "ease with which an innocent man might be inculpated by its results." See Skolnick, supra note 18, at 711.

19 Kleinmuntz and Szucko, supra note 9, at 100.

20 The polygraph test cannot be used on pathological liars, children, mentally handicapped persons, and persons who are not able to distinguish between truth and false. See however People v. Barbara, in which an expert witness testified that "individuals who would lie about anything and everything also pose no problem," and that there were no illnesses or diseases that caused him a problem. 255 N.W.2d 171, 176 (1977).

21 See for example United States v. Ridling, 350 F. Supp. 90, 93 (1972).

22 Skolnick, supra note 17, at 705.

23 The test procedure is roughly as follows: First, there is a pretest interview, conducted without the aid of the polygraph, which is used to obtain biographical data and evaluate the subject's attitudes towards dishonesty. The second stage is the actual polygraph test. The test is usually repeated three or four times, with a stimulation test conducted during the intervals. The stimulation test is used to convince the subject that the polygraph is infallible. During this test, the subject is presented with a set of cards, and is asked to select one of the

registered, the final outcome of the test cannot, that is, depending on the actual evaluation method used. According to Kleinmuntz and Szucko, most interpreters tended to use a "global evaluation method without specific measurement on scoring."[24] The examiner interpreted the charts in light of other factors, such as the demeanor of the subject before, while and after testing. They looked for signs of differential autonomic disturbances. As a result, the examiner's judgment became highly subjective and possibly speculative. Nowadays, evaluation of the test usually takes place by using the Backster Zone Comparison Method, in which the subjective influence of the examiner is absent.[25] The final outcome of the test can be one of three possibilities: the subject is deceptive (i.e. not telling what the subject believes to be truth), the subject is truthful (i.e. telling what he believes is truth), or the test is inconclusive (i.e., the examiner cannot tell if the subject is or is not telling the truth).

But even leaving aside the involvement of the examiner's judgment with regard to interpreting the charts, it is clear that the examiner is the 'linchpin' of the procedure.[26] Even the proponents agree, that there are serious problems in this respect. In 1981, Kleinmuntz and Szucko conducted a study which focused on the fallibility of polygraph examiner. The results showed that the polygraph examiners were highly fallible.[27] Raskin has stated that "a substantial proportion of those who conduct tests in the public and private sectors lack adequate training and competence."[28]

Validity

Many tests have been done over the years to establish the validity of the polygraph test, mainly with regard to the control question technique. These tests are either

---

cards. The examiner then tries to identify the selected card by means of the polygraph. The third stage is the after-test discussion, in which the results of the test are being discussed with the subject under examination. See Kleinmuntz & Szucko, supra note 9, at 88-89. As for the card test, the problem with this test is, as Skolnick indicated, that the examiner is always in the advantageous position of knowing that the subject has lied on one of the questions. This is not true with regard to the actual polygraph test. Skolnick, supra note 17, at 708.

24 Kleinmuntz & Szucko, supra note 9, at 89.

25 In that score, only the recorded responses are being taken into account. See Report of the Recherche Advies Commissie, supra note 14, at 13.

26 See United States v. DeBentham, 348 F. Supp. 1377 (S.D. Cal.), aff'd 470 F.2d 1367 (9th Cir. 1972), in which the court noted that "the most important factor involved in the use of any [polygraph] is the ability, experience, education and integrity of the examiner himself." Id., at 1385. See also Note, Pinocchio's New Nose, 48 New York University Law Review (1973), 399-368 (358).

27 Kleinmuntz & Szucko, supra note 9, at 94.

28 Raskin, supra note 13, at 66-67.

field studies of actual cases or mock crime experiences, i.e. laboratory simulations. The problem with the first study is that there is no independent criterion the results of the polygraph test can be measured against.[29] Although a subsequent confession by the subject is assumed to be the best criterion, this in no way establishes the validity of the test, as confessions can occur for several reasons, only one of which is that the subject is actually guilty.[30] The problem with laboratory simulations is that the laboratory environment is significantly different from the actual forensic environment. After all these years of study, the validity of the polygraph, particularly in relation to the control question technique, remains controversial.[31] In 1989, Raskin concluded that "the voluminous scientific literature indicates that they can be highly accurate when properly employed in appropriate circumstances, but they are also subject to abuse and misinterpretation."[32]

Legally, one of the highly relevant issues concerning the validity is the occurrence of false positives or false negatives. From a legal point of view – based on the presumption of that we would rather let go of ten guilty persons than convict an innocent one, there are good grounds to argue that false negatives are more acceptable than false positives. False negatives are on the safe side, meaning that the test has not detected the deceiving subject. From a scientific point of view,

---

29 See Skolnick, supra note 17, at 699. See also United States v. Alexander, 526 F.2d 161, 166 (8th Cir. 1975).

30 As for jury verdicts as independent criterion for determining the validity of the polygraph test, such a verdict, "although legally conclusive is not a scientifically controlled means of verification." See People v. Barbara, 255 N.W.2d 171, 190 (1977), footnote 26. See also Skolnick, supra note 17, at 699.

31 John Reid estimated that there is a 9% rate of error under optimal testing conditions. See United States v. Zeiger, 350 F. Supp 685, 689 (1972). Others estimated the rate of error closer to 25%. See United States v. Alexander, 526 F.2d 161, 165 (8th Cir. 1975). In his dissenting opinion in United States v. Piccinonna, 885 F.2d 1529 (9th Cir. 1989) Judge Johnson listed the results of 10 field studies and fourteen individual analog studies, all using the control question technique. The results were as follows:
individual field studies:
– correct guilty detections ranged from 70,6 to 98,6%; averaged 86,3%
– correct innocent detections ranged from 12,5 to 94,1%, averaged 76%
– false positive rate ranged from 0 to 75%; averaged 19,1%
– false negative rate ranged from 0 to 29,4%; averaged 10,2%
Individual analog studies:
– correct guilty detections ranged from 35,4 to 100%; averaged 63,7%
– correct innocent detections ranged from 32 to 91%; averaged 57,9%
– false positive rate ranged from 2 to 50,7%; averaged 14,1%
– false negative rate ranged from 0 to 28,7%; averaged 10,4%
Note that there is a 50% chance that one who answers the question, 'is this person lying' is correct.

32 Raskin, Polygraph Techniques for the Detection of Deception, in Psychological Methods in Criminal Investigations and Evidence, 290 (D. Raskin ed. 1989).

however, both a high rate of false positives and false negatives undermine the validity of the technique. In 1983, the Office of Technology Assessment compiled the results of ten field studies and fourteen analog studies regarding the control question technique. These results show that in both types of studies, the average of false positives is higher than the rate of false negatives.[33] Thus, more persons are wrongly concluded to be lying than lying persons wrongly are concluded truthful, and it has therefore been argued that the polygraph seems to be a better indicator of innocence than of guilt, because the rate of false positives is higher than the rate of false negatives.[34]

Admissibility of the Polygraph: the United States

In the United States, where police departments and government agencies utilize polygraph test results in their day to day operations,[35] the courts have struggled with the admissibility of polygraph tests administered by the police for some 80 years.

The admissibility of this evidence was first considered in Frye v. United States by the District of Columbia Circuit Court in 1923. In 1921, James Frye was first arrested for robbery and then questioned about the death of a wealthy physician. Frye confessed and was charged with second degree murder. At his trial, he sought to introduce the results of a systolic blood pressure test, which were favorable to Frye. Frye claimed that the confession was occasioned by Sergeant Jones, who told him that he would squash the robbery charge if Frye would plead guilty to the murder. The trial court ruled the results of the tests – which were favorable to Frye – inadmissible. The Court of Appeals stated:

> Just when a scientific principle or discovery crosses the line between the experimental and demonstrable stage is difficult to define. Somewhere in this twilight zone the evidential fore of the principle must be recognized, and while courts will go a long way in admitting expert testimony deduced from a well-recognized scientific principle or discovery, the thing from which the deduction is made must be sufficiently established to have gained general acceptance in the particular field in which it belongs.[36]

Frye was subsequently convicted of murder in the second degree. Throughout the years following the decision of Judge Van Orsel, the decision – generally known

---

33 See note 32.

34 See Note, supra note 26, at 365. This is also due to the legal assumption that one is innocent until proven guilty. Whereas the state has to prove beyond a reasonable doubt that the defendant is guilty, the defendant merely has to raise doubt about his guilt to escape conviction.

35 United States v. Ridling, 350 F. Supp. 90, 93 (1972).

36 Frye v. United States, 292 F. 1013, 1014 (D.C. Cir. 1923).

as the Frye test or the general acceptance standard – became the standard for deciding the admissibility of scientific evidence. It developed into "the almost universal view, with the overwhelming majority of federal and state courts following it,"[37] though not without an ever growing amount of criticism.

Whereas the proponents of the test argued that the strength of Frye – among others – lies in the conservative nature of the test, the critics argue that Frye is too conservative, and that it shields the fact finder too much from evidence that is possibly reliable. A favorite argument of the opponents has been that Frye was in fact innocent, just as the test results showed, and was acquitted after another man confessed to the crime.[38] James Starrs, who reviewed the documentary material of the Frye case, concluded that this is a serious distortion of the actual facts. The murder of which Frye was convicted was not confessed to by anyone else, and Frye was not released because of that. The record shows that Frye was paroled in 1939, two months short of serving 18 years in jail.[39]

Based on the Frye test *and* the presence of countervailing considerations that would outweigh its probative value,[40] the polygraph has – overwhelmingly – been held to be inadmissible by the American courts, until the 1970s.[41] In the 70s, some courts started to admit the results of polygraph examinations. In United States v. Ridling, a federal district court argued that the theory of the polygraph was sound and directly relevant to the issue of the case in question, a perjury case.[42] The court held that the evidence of polygraph experts pertaining to the polygraph examination of the defendant and their opinions would be admitted under certain

---

37 Edward J. Imwinkelried, The Standard for Admitting Scientific Evidence: A Critique from the Perspective of Juror Psychology, 28 Villanova Law Review (1982-1983) 554, 556-557.

38 See for example Barry Tarlow, Admissibility of Polygraph Evidence in 1975: An Aid in Determining Credibility in a Perjury-Plagued System, 26 The Hastings Law Journal (1975), 971- 974 (923), and State v. Sims, 369 N.E.2d 24, 33 (1977).

39 James E. Starrs, "A Still-Life Watercolor": Frye v. United States, 27 Journal of Forensic Sciences (1982) 684, 690.

40 McCormick on Evidence, St. Paul 1992, 375. Note that even when polygraph evidence would have been admissible under the general acceptance rule, the judge then has to determine whether the polygraph evidence proffered will help the trier of fact, i.e. the probative value of the testimony, and whether the value is outweighed by countervailing considerations such as unfair prejudice with regard to the defendant, confusion of the jury, waste of time and such. Currently, this is laid down in Federal Rule of Evidence 403, and similar provisions in state statutes.

41 See for example State v. Kolander, 52 N.W.2d 458 (1952): "We have not doubt that the lie detector is valuable in investigative work of law enforcement agencies and may frequently lead to confessions or the discovery of facts which may ultimately lead to the solution of many crimes; but we are in accord with the rule that the lie detector has not yet attained such scientific and psychological accuracy, nor its operators such sureness of interpretation of results shown therefrom, as to justify submission thereof to a jury as evidence of the guilt or innocence of a person accused of a crime." Id. at 465.

42 350 F. Supp. 90, 95 (1972).

conditions when administered by a court-appointed expert. In that same year, another federal district court held the results of a polygraph test admissible in United States v. Zeiger.[43]

Although the decisions in Ridling and Zeiger were seen as a forecast of the more general admissibility of the polygraph, the prediction did not come true. In general, the courts have not decided upon the admissibility of polygraph evidence favorably to the proponents. A number of courts exclude polygraph evidence per se, for example the Court of Appeals for the eight circuit.

In United States v. Alexander, this court held that "while the polygraphic science and its instruments have advanced significantly since the Frye case, we are still unable to conclude that there is sufficient scientific acceptability and reliability to warrant the admission of the results of such tests into evidence."[44]

A substantial minority of courts admit polygraph evidence only upon stipulation of the parties,[45] and a few courts recognize the trial court's discretion to admit polygraph evidence. In most cases, also due to the prejudicial impact on

---

43 350 F. Supp. 685 (1972). "Today, polygraph has emerged from that twilight zone into an established field of science and technology. Id., at 688. Zeiger was reversed per curiam. See 475 F.2d 1280 (D.C. Cir. 1972). See also United States v. Sims, 369 N.E.2d 124 (1977), in which the Court of Common Pleas of Ohio held that the polygraph, conducted by trained and experienced examiners of integrity, is highly reliable in disclosing deception or lack of it. The scientific basis for proper use of the polygraph test in detecting deception was deemed to be so well established in 1977 as to meet the standards for its reliable use as stated in Frye.

44 United States v. Alexander, 526 F.2d 161, 166 (1975). See also United States v. Wilson, 361 F. Supp. 510 (1973), People v. Barbara, 255 N.W.2d 171 (1977), People v. Melock, 599 N.E.2d 941, 957 (Ill. 1992). In Melock, it was decided that the results of a polygraph examination might be admissible on the issue of whether the confession was voluntary, as the jury then must consider the totality of the circumstances surrounding the confession.

45 See United States v. Piccinonna, 885 F.2d 1529 (11th Cir. 1989). Apart from stipulation, the court in Piccinonna argued that another situation in which polygraph evidence may be admitted is when used to impeach or corroborate the testimony of a witness at trial. Id., at 1536. See also State v. Dean, 307 N.W.2d 628 (Wis. 1981) (polygraph evidence is not to be admitted in any criminal proceeding in the State of Wisconsin unless the parties have stipulated its use). The admissibility of polygraph evidence on stipulation of the parties is suspect, as the stipulation itself does not enhance the validity and reliability of the technique itself. The reason why it is nevertheless admitted upon stipulation is because the stipulation functions as a waiver of objections to the use of such evidence at trial. See Dean, at 637. However, by stipulating, the parties are not held to have waived their objection to the reliability of the particular test, as this reliability cannot be assessed fully prior to stipulation. See Dean, at 643. Thus, notwithstanding the stipulation, the trial court has the discretion to admit or reject the evidence. In Dean, the Supreme Court of Wisconsin decided to hold polygraph evidence inadmissible per se, as the court felt that the conditions of stipulations, established by the court in State v. Stanislawski, 216 N.W.2d 8 (1974) did "not function in a manner which enhanced the reliability of polygraph evidence" and did not protect "the integrity of the trial to the degree necessary to justify its continuance." See Dean, at 653.

the jury[46], trial courts exercise this discretion by ruling against polygraph evidence.[47]

In 1993, the Frye decision was finally held to have been overruled by Federal Rule of Evidence 702, in the landmark case of Daubert v. Merrell Dow Pharmaceuticals Inc.[48] Rule 702 establishes that:

> if scientific, technical, or other specialized knowledge will assist the trier of fact to understand the evidence or to determine a fact in issue, a witness qualified as an expert by knowledge, skill, experience, training, or education, my testify thereto in the form of an opinion or otherwise.

According to the Daubert court, the trial judge – in his gatekeeping role – must determine whether the expert is proposing to testify to (1) scientific evidence that (2) will assist the trier of fact to understand or determine a fact in issue.[49] Several factors bear on the inquiry whether the evidence offered is indeed scientific evidence: whether the theory or technique has been tested; whether the theory or technique has been subject to peer review or publication; the technique's known or potential rate of error; the existence and maintenance of standards controlling the technique's operation; and general acceptance.[50]

As polygraph evidence is evidence derived from psychology – it is a psychological test designed to obtain a measure of a sample of psychological behavior[51] – such evidence, in order to be admissible, must pass the test set forth by the Daubert court. And although it has been asserted that the Daubert standard for admissibility is more flexible than the Frye ruling, it remains to be seen whether polygraph evidence would be admissible under this rule. To name but one concern, it might well be argued that the potential rate of error is too significant for the evidence to be admissible as scientific evidence. Apart from that, even if it

---

46 Note that when polygraph evidence is proffered by the defendant, the court might need to admit the results of a polygraph test into evidence due to the compulsory process clause of the 6th Amendment to the American Constitution - i.e. the right to present evidence -, but only of the court considers the evidence sufficiently reliable. See Chambers v. Mississippi, 410 US 284 (1972). See for cases in which this right affected the admissibility of polygraph evidence State v. Dorsey, 532 P.2d 912, (N.M. App.), affirmed on other grounds 539 P.2d 204 (1975), Jackson v. Garrison, 495 F. Supp. 9 (W.D.N.C. 1979), rev'd 677 F.2d 371 (4th Cir. 1981), State v. Sims, 369 N.E.2d 24, 46 (C.P. 1977).

47 See United States v. Benveniste, 564 F.2d 335 (9th Cir. 1977): "With the polygraph's misleading reputation as a 'truthteller,' the widespread debate concerning its reliability, the critical requirement of a competent examiner and the judicial problems of self-incrimination and hearsay, a trial court will rarely abuse its discretion by refusing to admit the evidence, even for a limited purpose and under limited conditions." Id., at 339.

48 113 S.Ct. 2786 (1993).

49 Daubert, at 2796.

50 Daubert, at 2797.

51 Kleinmuntz & Szucko, supra note 9, at 86.

could be established that the polygraph evidence is indeed sound scientific evidence, it has been argued that the evidence will not assist the jury in determining the facts at issue, as the polygraph can only predict whether a person is lying slightly better than chance.[52] Even a determination that polygraph evidence is scientifically reliable and helpful, however, does not necessarily mean that it should be admitted. Even if it is admissible under Federal Rule of Evidence 702, the judge has to take into account Federal Rule of Evidence 403, in which it is stated that:

although relevant, evidence might be excluded if its probative value is substantially outweighed by the danger of unfair prejudice, confusion of the issues, misleading the jury, or by considerations of undue delay, waste of time, or needless presentation of cumulative evidence.

Many courts have listed the fear of unfair prejudice as an additional barrier against admissibility. In United States v. Alexander, the court noted that "when polygraph evidence is offered in evidence at trial, it is likely to be shrouded with an aura of near infallibility, akin to the ancient oracle of Delphi."[53] The court feared that despite the sophistication and increased intellectual capacities the jury was likely to give significant weight to the opinion of the examiner.[54]

Other courts have argued that the polygraph examiner will only testify as to the veracity or falsity of the defendant's responses and does not testify as to the guilt or innocence of the defendant. As the Alexander court noted, however, the distinction is illusory.

If a properly phrased question or series of questions are asked which encompass all relevant elements of the crime and the polygraphist testifies that the defendant's exculpatory responses were fabricated, the import of the testimony is clear. The implicit conclusion is that the defendant was a participant in the crime.[55]

---

52 See the dissenting opinion of Judge Johnson, United States v. Piccinonna, 885 F.2d 1529, 1541 (9th Cir. 1989).

53 United States v. Alexander, 526 F.2d 161, 168 (8th Cir. 1975).

54 For an opinion to the contrary, see United States v. Sims, 369 N.E.2d 24, 42 (1977): "Juries will not slavishly follow the polygraph as though it were the last word in every question of credibility.[..] Polygraphy would be nothing more than another aid to their determination as to what the facts are." See for a recent (tax)case in which the results of a polygraph test were excluded on the sole basis of prejudicial effect Conti v. Commissioner of Internal Revenue, 39 F.2d 658, 663 (6th Cir. 1994).

55 Id., at 168. Note that under the Federal Rules of Evidence (1975), it is not forbidden to give an opinion with regard to the ultimate issue. In FRE 704 (a) it is stated that "testimony in the form of an opinion or inference otherwise admissible is not objectionable because it embraces an ultimate issue to be decided by the trier of fact." The exception to this rule is mentioned in 704 (b) (expert witness is not allowed to give an opinion or inference as to whether the defendant "did or did not have the mental state or condition constituting an element of the crime charged or of a defense thereto").

Assuming that the outcome of a polygraph examination does not bear on the guilt or innocence of the defendant, the result is still the same: the slight probative value of polygraph evidence, bearing on the credibility of the defendant, might be outweighed by the possible prejudicial effect on the trier of fact.

Privilege against Self-Incrimination

Both in the United States and on the Continent, every defendant enjoys the – testimonial – privilege against self-incrimination. In Schermber v. California, the Supreme Court of the United States indicated that a compelled submission to a polygraph test would violate the defendant's fifth Amendment right, as lie detectors – despite their apparent focus on physical evidence – might be viewed as directed at eliciting testimonial responses.[56] Thus, it cannot be used as a coercive measure against suspects. However, the privilege against self-incrimination can waived by the defendant by voluntarily submitting to a polygraph examination. American courts have held that the privilege against self-incrimination is not at issue with regard to a voluntary the polygraph test, as long as adequate warnings are given as to the possible use of the tests.[57] "The taking of the test itself is a waiver of the privilege."[58] Indeed, it appears that the voluntary polygraph test does not violate the privilege against self-incrimination.[59] The remaining question with regard to the waiver is whether the defendant actually does have a choice in refusing to submit to such a test. As Justice Coleman said in People v. Barbara:
"it is no answer to say the tests are voluntary. Those refusing the tests will be suspect. Their testimony could be discredited before it is even heard."[60]

---

56 384 US 757, 764 (1966).

57 See United States v. Ridling, 350 F. Supp. 90, 97 (1972). Depending on the jurisdiction, the person who submits to a polygraph test also has to be cautioned about his right to remain silent. See Recherche Advies Commissie, id., at 20. In the United States, the Miranda warnings, stating that the defendant has a right to remain silent, are required only if the defendant is in custody and is being interrogated.

58 See United States v. Ridling, 350 F. Supp. 90, 97 (1972).

59 In considering the right to remain silent, one has to distinguish between the actual statements made by the defendant during the examination, and the statements made after the defendant has been told the results of the examination. Most commentators direct their comments to the first problem. In the Netherlands, Melai has argued that statements made during a polygraph examination cannot be said to be voluntarily, as the defendant does not control his physiological reactions. A. Melai, Het Wetboek van Strafvordering, aantekening 11 bij Art. 29 Sv. Lensing, on the other hand, argues that the right to remain silent is not affected, as the polygraph does only register physiological reactions of the subject under investigation; his freedom to make a statement is not at issue. J.A.W. Lensing, Het verhoor van de verdachte in strafzaken, Nijmegen 1988, 173.

60 People v. Barbara, 255 N.W.2d 171, 203 (1977). See also J.M. van Bemmelen, Onderzoekingsmethoden in strafzaken, Nederlands Juristenblad 1956, 501.

It should be noted that other arguments related to the privilege, seem to be based on the false assumption that the polygraph tests the unconscience of the defendant. It does not, it tests the physiological reactions of a person to questions asked. It can only detect whether the person actually does not believe what he responds. The unconscience is not involved.[61]

Legally seen, one of the most important collateral issues related to the polygraph test is the question of the voluntariness of a confession obtained after the test has been administered. Indeed, it has been argued that the use of a polygraph is actually to obtain a confession.[62] In the United States, a confession has to be made voluntarily to be admissible at trial, and the situation is no different on the Continent. Is a confession, obtained after a polygraph test has been administered, voluntarily, or is the confession contaminated by the outcome of the test?

The answer to the question is difficult.[63] One could argue that a confession made after the test results have been made known to the subject, is not contaminated by the results, as only a guilty person will actually confess. Based on that assumption, there is no relation between the confession and the test. However, the assumption is false. We know that there are many more reasons why persons actually confess to a crime, only one of which is the fact that they are indeed guilty. In this respect then, the problem is that using the polygraph test to obtain confessions will not affect a guilty defendant, but it will most definitely affect a innocent person, as this person might be induced to a confession that is unreliable because it is not in accordance with the actual facts. As Lykken has said:

> the polygraph testing situation is a powerful inducer of confessions or at least of damaging admissions. When told they have failed the polygraph, many suspects, feeling that all hope is gone, confess.[64]

---

61 See Skolnick, supra note 17, at 725.

62 See Skolnick, supra note 17, at 722.

63 With regard to the statements made after the polygraph examination has taken place, Timmenga seems to argue that the statement of a defendant during interrogation is the consequence of inducement, as a result of which the right to remain silent is violated. S.J. Timmenga, Is de toepassing van de narco-analyse en de leugenverklikker (lie-detector) in het strafproces geoorloofd? Tijdschrift voor Strafrecht 1951, 33. At the same time, Meyjes has argued that the right to remain silent is not really a right, but more a recognition of the moral obligation on the part of judges and police officers not to force a defendant to a confession. For that reason, he argues that confessions obtained through polygraph examination do not interfere with the right to remain silence. P. Meyjes, In hoeverre behoren onderzoekingsmethoden in strafzaken ten aanzien van de persoon van de verdachte aan beperkende voorschriften te worden onderworpen? Preadvies Nederlandse Juristen Vereniging 1956, 158-159.

64 David T. Lykken, The Validity of Tests: Caveat Emptor, Jurimetrics Journal 1987, 262-282 (270).

A related question is whether a confession that has been made after the examiner has mislead the defendant concerning the outcome of the test. There are cases that testify to the fact that defendants are actually mislead by the examiner. In People v. Melock for example, the defendant, who offered to submit to a polygraph examination, was told by the examiner that he was '150% sure' that the defendant had killed his grandmother, although no responses from his polygraph examination could be read. Defendant then confessed to the murder.[65] On appeal, he argued that the examiner's deception concerning the results of the exam rendered his confession involuntary.[66] The Supreme Court of Illinois stated the believe that the deception of the examiner largely contributed to defendant's decision to inculpate himself.[67] However, according to the court, the fact that a confession is procured by deception does not invalidate the confession as a matter of law.[68] Due to the fact that defendant was not threatened or mistreated during the questioning, and was not subject to continuous questioning, the court found that defendant's will was not so overborne as to render his confession incompetent.[69] Nevertheless, the court also decided that the exclusion of the polygraph evidence deprived defendant of his fundamental right to a fair opportunity to present a defense. The polygraph evidence should have been admitted for the limited purpose of determining the credibility and reliability of the confession.[70]

Thus, depending on the actual circumstances of the case, a confession resulting from misleading information about the test may be admissible. The assumption is that innocent suspects will not be induced by the test results, although it can be questioned whether the assumption is correct. Again, the problem is that there is no objective criterion for judging the accuracy of the confession obtained. The only possible safeguard against introducing unreliable confessions is to ensure that the confession contains enough verifiable new information, which information is then subsequently verified by the investigators.[71]

Use of Polygraph evidence in the Netherlands: An Analysis of Possible Problems

From the foregoing, it is apparent that despite the progress claimed by its proponents, the polygraph test is still largely inadmissible in the United States. The refusal to admit the results of such tests are held not to have gained general

65 599 N.E.2d 941, 952 (Ill. 1992).
66 Id., at 949.
67 Id.
68 Id., at 953.
69 Id., at 954.
70 Id., at 960.
71 See Lykken, supra note 64, at 270.

acceptance in the scientific community and to have a prejudicial effect on the jury. In the Alexander case, the court expressed this by saying that polygraphy is an art rather than a science.[72] Despite the inadmissibility of the evidence at trial, the polygraph is widely used as an investigative tool by the government and the police.[73] From a legal point of view, such practice can be condoned on the ground that, as the court said in Barbara, "damage done by false results may be more easily correctable in an investigative situation."[74] In the investigative phase of a criminal process, the polygraph can be used as a screening device to fetter out untruthful witnesses or defendants, if one believes that the polygraph is capable of doing that. In that way, it can contribute to the conduct and outcome of the investigation. But even if it is conceded that it cannot really fetter out untruthfulness, the use of the polygraph in the investigative stage is not destructive. After all, it is at the trial itself that it has to be established that the defendant is guilty as charged. By ruling polygraph evidence and any reference to a polygraph evidence inadmissible, the jury is prevented from hearing any evidence related to the use of polygraph tests, and thus cannot be influenced by it.[75]

The story is completely different in most of the Continental countries. Particularly in the Netherlands and France, the investigative phase and the trial phase are less clearly separated when it comes to evidentiary sources. This is due to the fact that the criminal justice systems in these countries rely heavily on the dossier, the case file, when it comes to proving the charges. Although pretrial findings and conclusions are regarded as tentative, the actual fact is that interim decisions and findings tend to become 'fixated'.[76]

> The typical pattern that emerges is that courts, during the course of the proceedings in a case, repeatedly regard previously determined facts as known and established. As a consequence, the final verdict is a type of culmination of all decisions made during the course of the proceedings."[77]

---

72 United States v. Alexander, 526 F.2d 161, 167 (1975).

73 See United States v. Ridling, 350 F. Supp. 90, 94 (1972) and United States v. Zeiger, 350 F. Supp. 685, 688 (1972).

74 People v. Barbara, 255 N.W.2d 171, 193 (1977). See also Skolnick, supra note 17, at 722.

75 See Morris v. State, 1995 WL 15403 (Ga.). Morris was charged with malice murder and felony murder. In two (inconsistent) statements to the police, defendant conceded that he had helped dispose of the body, but that Hicks had committed the murder. In her opening statements, the prosecutor said that Hicks had submitted to a polygraph test that 'checked out'. The Supreme Court of Georgia reversed the judgment, stating that 'merely asking a witness about whether he has taken a polygraph exam raises an inference that the witness took and passed a test." The Court considered this a harmful error, as the reference to Hicks' test served only to bolster the credibility of the witness. This credibility was vital, because Morris' statements implicated Hicks as the perpetrator.

76 See Enschede, Bewijzen in het Strafrecht, 468-518 (1966) and J. F. Nijboer, Forensic Expertise in Dutch Criminal Procedure, 14 Cardozo Law Review (1992), 165-191 (174).

77 Nijboer, supra note 76, ibid.

Nevertheless, although these countries do not have admissibility rules, they do have decision rules, which have a function similar to the admissibility rules in the United States.[78] In the Netherlands, the decision rules are such, that a verdict can only be based on legal means of proof. If the verdict rests on evidence which is not defined as a legal means of proof, the conviction will be squashed. At this moment, polygraph evidence is still not admissible as a means of proof, presumably due to the unreliability of the evidence.[79] Apart from the unreliability of the polygraph however, there is no legal barrier to the use of such evidence as a basis for a conviction. As we have seen, polygraph evidence is scientific evidence, offered by means of an expert witness. In general, the report and oral testimony of an expert witness is a legal means of proof. Thus, if the report or oral testimony of an expert witness satisfies the definition of those means of proof, polygraph evidence could indeed be used as a means of evidence, as long as the court deems the evidence sufficiently reliable, without actually changing the rules of evidence.[80]

Slightly more than a year ago, the Dutch Recherche Advies Commissie produced a report, which analysed the use of polygraph evidence, particularly in the United States. In the report, the question of whether or not polygraph evidence should be used either during police investigations or at trial is not asked. Although it is not clear whether the authors indeed favor the introduction of polygraph evidence into the Dutch legal system, they indicate its possible use during the investigative stage.[81]

The question is whether this use is appropriate and worth considering. First of all, viewed from the fact that polygraph tests seem to be conducted with the idea of obtaining confessions, the predominant question related to the use of polygraph evidence during police investigation is how far the state may go to induce confessions.[82] But even if it is asserted that the state can conduct polygraph examinations to obtain confessions, or that the goal is not to obtain confessions but to screen the credibility of suspects, there are several problems with regard to this proposition.

---

78 See J. F. Nijboer, Common Law Tradition in Evidence Scholarship Observed from a Continental Perspective, 2 American Journal of Comparative Law (1993) 299-338 (314).

79 See G. J. M. Corstens, Het Nederlandse strafprocesrecht, Gouda Quint 1993, 263. The Report of the Recherche Advies Commissie mentions a case in which a polygraph test was conducted on the request of the defense. Based on the results of this test, the defendant was deemed to be truthful in his responses to the questions asked. The Court of Appeals stated that it deemed the reliability of the results of the test not beyond dispute, and felt the examination had not taken place under ideal conditions. Therefore, the court decided not to use the results of the tests in its decision. Report, supra note 14, at 41.

80 See the Report of the Recherche Advies Commissie, supra note 14, at 22.

81 Report Recherche Advies Commissie, supra note 14, at 18.

82 See Skolnick, supra note 17, at 727.

One of these problems is that if and when the polygraph evidence would be used as a screening device by the police, there is the barrier of the privilege of self-incrimination. In order not to infringe the defendant's right to abstain from self incrimination, he has to waive this right and be informed of the right to remain silent during the polygraph examination, even if he consents to its use. To ensure that the defendant understands what he gets himself into, the most appropriate safeguard for the defendant would be the presence of a lawyer before and during the examination, to ensure protection of the defendant's rights during the test.[83]

However, in the Netherlands, the defendant has no right to a lawyer during a normal police interrogation. The question then is whether there is such a crucial difference between police interrogation and a polygraph examination that different procedural safeguards are necessary. Indeed, there is.

First of all, polygraph evidence is and will be presented to the subject under examination as infallible evidence. Secondly, it is presented at trial as scientific evidence, with the aura of credibility attached to it. Related to the issue of credibility is the fact that scientific evidence is much harder to disprove than other, nonscientific, evidence. Thirdly and lastly, and, maybe most important, polygraph evidence is evidence that goes right to the heart of the facts at issue:

> the polygraph is unlike other scientific evidence, since the quantity it attempts to measure [..] is so directly related to the essence of the trial process.[84]

In that respect then, polygraph examinations seems to warrant a different treatment than normal interrogations by the police do.

The core of the problem with regard to the use of the polygraph in police investigations on the Continent in general and the Netherlands in particular, however, is related to the structure of the judicial system under review. First of all, there is the presence of the case file. If the polygraph is used during police investigations, the case file will have to contain the results of the test administered, or the refusal of the defendant to voluntarily submit to such a test.[85] Thus, different from the United States, the trier of fact, in this case the judge, will then know about this from the case file. And even though the trier of fact might not be able to use the results as a means of proof, he will nevertheless be aware of it. The

83 See for the United States the article of Matte, supra note 9.

84 See Note, supra note 26, at 1141. See also Lykken, supra note 64, at 269.

85 Of course, it could be argued that the police may use the polygraph as a screening device, and, to shield the trier of fact, will not mention this in the case file. That, however, creates other, significant problems, as in that case, the police works with a hidden agenda. In that respect, the defense is seriously hindered in actually arguing the case, as the actual investigation is not contained in the case file. To mention only one, but serious problem, the defense is not able to attack the confession obtained after a polygraph examination has been conducted.

prejudicial effect of this should not be underestimated, as the evidence might possibly contaminate all the other evidence available in the case file. This is particularly problematic in case the results are incriminating to the defendant or when the defendant refused to submit to a polygraph test. In case of refusal, the judge will know that an actual offer was made. The inference can easily be made that obviously, the defendant has something to hide. If he is 'clean' he will pass. Thus, the only reason to refuse is because he is guilty. And to say that a judge might consider the defendant's silence or presumably lying statement when considering the issue of guilt is not far off from actual Dutch criminal practice. Although the defendant has a right to remain silent, it has been established by the Supreme Court of the Netherlands that a partial refusal of a defendant to make a statement or a presumably lying declaration can be used in evidence.[86]

On the basis of the case file, the judge might also become aware of the fact that the defendant has failed the test. A logical inference on face of this fact could be that the defendant is lying. The fixating tendency of Dutch trials in relation to the use of polygraphs in the pretrial phase is thus much more detrimental for the defendant than it is in common law courts, or courts that more strictly adhere to the principle of immediacy.

But deception does not prove the truth of the opposite assertion. That a suspect has been lying when he answered particular questions about the crime, does not establish that he is guilty of that crime. However, it comes dangerously close to that, because the – scientific – evidence goes right to the heart of the issue at stake. The inference behind the polygraph is that lying has a reason, a particular reason related to the crime under investigation. As a result of the assumption behind lying, every expert witness who testifies as to the truthfulness of the examinee in effect answers the question the trier of fact alone is legally allowed to answer: "is the defendant guilty as charged?"

The reason why the fact that the expert witness is testifying to the very essence of the trial is problematic, is also due to the fact that in Dutch courts, usually only one – court appointed – expert will testify (in written rather than in oral form).
The Dutch Code of Criminal Procedure is structured in such a way, that the expert witness is – or should be – appointed by the court only, either by the trial judge or the investigative judge. If and when the expert witness is appointed as such by a judge, the defendant has the right to be present during the expert's investigation and may request that the expert being appointed is one recommended by him. In practice, however, expert witnesses, in the case of polygraph tests psychologists, are almost always consulted by the police. In that stage of the process, the

86 See HR 27 June 1972, NJ 1972, 492. See generally, Corstens, supra note 79, at 599-601, J. F. Nijboer, Strafrechtelijk bewijsrecht, Ars Aequi Libri 1994, 216-219, and J. M Reijntjes, Strafrechtelijk bewijs in wet en praktijk, Gouda Quint 1980, 167-170 and 200-201. Only when the defendant refuses to make a statement at all, it is not allowed to use this refusal in evidence. Corstens, at 600.

defendant has no right whatsoever to request presence of a second expert, nor does he have the opportunity to gain insight into the actual method employed. In this respect, it is questionable whether the presence of his lawyer will do much to alleviate that problem. At some point, the defense does have access to the case file, but at that time, it will usually be too late to base his defense on the problems related to the polygraph test, in addition to the fact that his lawyer will usually lack insight in the method itself. Of course, the defense can consult an expert, but that will depend on the amount of money available. As a result, the report of the expert witness consulted by the police will almost always be the only expert evidence available to the court.

This brings us to another problem with regard to the use of polygraphs in police investigations; a problem related to the structure of the Dutch criminal justice system, but basically a problem of legal culture. As a consequence of the longstanding practice of court-appointed experts – the appointment of one expert witness who then – on paper – testifies to the nature of the expertise in question – is that judges seem to have considerable faith in the qualifications of such experts; their expertise is hardly ever doubted. In that sense, the expert witness indeed seems to be much like the oracle of Delphi. Once it has been established by the proponents that polygraph tests are reliable and valid, and institutionalized in actual police practice, there is a likely change that judges will not question the technique much any more, even if the defense attacks the method.

The current situation is such, that the defense, in order to compel the court to reason why the results can still be used as a means of evidence despite the arguments put forward by the defense, has make a compelling argument that the test is controversial and that significant errors have indeed been made in the particular case.[87] It is not enough to state the opinion that the method is flawed nor to outline that possibly errors have been made by the expert witness. The defense has to make a showing that something has gone wrong, not that things might go wrong.[88] Without such a showing, the court is not obliged even to motivate why it nevertheless decides to use the results of scientific evidence as a means of proof. And in any event, the fact that the defense did not have access to a second opinion does not mean that the results of the polygraph evidence cannot be used in evidence. This is different from the situation in the United States, where scientific evidence is much more criticized in court and the defence has much more opportunity to attack such evidence. But precisely because the defense in the Netherlands has little opportunity to gain insight into the method used in the actual case, it will be very difficult to make a showing of a lack of evidentiary reliability in the instant case at all.

---

87 See HR 28 February 1989, NJ 1989, 748.

88 See for example HR 18 February 1992, NJ 1993, 28.

Both the legal rules with respect to expert evidence and prevailing Dutch legal culture, have consequences for the weight given to the testimony of polygraph examiners. In that respect, even the most preferred polygraphic questioning method, the guilty knowledge test, seems to be problematic in the Dutch context. This test, as has been argued, is designed to test the suspect with regard to information about the crime that only the perpetrator will possess; an investigative technique that is already used by the police in complex criminal cases (but at present without the help of a polygraph). But even when the test is conducted by experienced and trained examiners, and the defendant is safeguarded by the presence of his lawyer either before or also during the interview, the faith in scientific knowledge and the structure of the system will mean that there are enormous barriers for the defendant to attack such evidence, despite the fact that such an attack could be based on extensive scientific literature on the subject and the ongoing controversy between the critics and proponents of the polygraph.

As for the introduction of polygraph evidence by the defense, it should be noted that the faith in court-appointed experts also works the other way around. A consequence of the fact that Dutch judges are used and have faith in court-appointed experts seems to be that courts are much more skeptical of expert evidence that is introduced by the defense, even if that evidence casts doubt on the evidence introduced by the prosecutor. One Dutch case in which the results of a polygraph test were actually introduced seems to indicate this. In that particular case,[89] the results – which were favorable to the defendant – were introduced by the defense. The Court of Appeals did not take the results of the test into account, stating that the examination had not taken place under ideal circumstances, although the examiner disputed that conclusion. As a result of the skeptical attitude of judges towards other than court-appointed experts, the defense is placed on an unequal footing with the prosecution.

Due to the prevailing structure of the Dutch criminal justice system and the current view of scientific evidence by the courts, it seems unwise to allow the use of any kind of polygraph examination in police investigations at all.

Summary and Conclusions

Although widely used in the United States during police investigations, the theory and technique of the polygraph is still heavily debated. The theory that lying is reflected in physiological responses might be true, but it has been asserted that other factors show similar responses of the body. The polygraph evidence itself cannot distinguish which is which. The crucial factor in any polygraph examination is the examiner. As a result, the outcome of the test to some extent

---

89 See supra note 79.

will always rely on the interaction between the examiner and the subject under investigation, and is basically of a subjective nature. The validity of the test results remains controversial, but the tendency seems to be that the test results show a higher rate of false positives than false negatives. Due to the unreliability of the test and countervailing considerations with regard to its probative value, polygraph evidence is still largely inadmissible in the United States, even if a defendant has consented to the test itself. Such consent is necessary, as a involuntary test violates the defendant's right to abstain from self-incrimination. Despite the fact that the defendant cannot be forced to take such a test, it remains open to doubt whether confessions obtained after a polygraph test has been conducted can indeed be said to be voluntarily. The very nature of the test is said to incorporate coercion.

In the United States, the dividing line between investigation and trial, and the fact that all evidence has to be admissible before the jury may even be aware of it, means that the use of polygraph evidence might not be destructive, although it is problematic. In the Netherlands, and possibly in other Continental countries, however, the problems related to the use of polygraph evidence in police investigations as experienced in the United States will be heightened by the structure of the criminal process and the prevailing legal culture. The existence of a case file means that even when the polygraph is used as a screening device by the police, similar to its use in the United States, the trier of fact will be aware of the results of the polygraph test, or the absence of it. Such awareness might have a detrimental effect on the state of mind of the trier of fact. This is even more so, as Dutch courts are used to court-appointed experts, as a result of which there is usually only one expert reporting to the scientific nature of the test. As result of this longstanding practice, courts seem to have an as of yet unquestioned faith in scientific knowledge. On top of that, the defense will only have very limited possibilities to counter the results of polygraph evidence, and even fewer – if any – possibilities if the expert is being called to assistance by the police. The ongoing controversy relating to the reliability and validity of the polygraph does not warrant unconditioned faith in this particular psychological test or one particular court-appointed expert testifying to its use in a particular case. Therefore, it is argued that polygraph evidence should not be used as such in police investigations in the Netherlands under the prevalent circumstances.

The Jury Decision Rule: An Empirical Study of Four Methods

Ramón Arce, Francisca Fariña, Carlos Vila and Mercedes Novo

Introduction

Though the jury is conceived of as a group of lay people who decide on the verdict in a trial, many variations of this common principle may be found in terms of either the number of jurors and/or the decision rule. These two apparently minor differences have a major impact on the quality of the decision rule (Hastie et al., 1983; Sobral and Arce, 1990). The absence of any uniformity in jury size can be seen from the wide range of options which have been adopted. In the USA, 12 member juries are the most predominant composition though in certain states, the figure may be 8, 6 or even 5 jurors. Similarly, in the UK a jury of 12 jurors is the norm but in Scotland 15 jurors is the legal requirement. Without a doubt there seems to be no magical number which is universally acceptable to the different legal systems. Those who favour large juries argue that as the jury becomes larger so does its social representation. Thus, Zeisel (1971) points out that if a population were composed of 90% from one social grouping and a 10% from another, a jury composed of 12 jurors would contain at least one juror who represents the minority in 72% of trials. However, if the jury were smaller, composed only of 6 jurors, the percentage would fall to 47%. Nevertheless, it has been argued that the size of the jury is not very significant since there are few ethnic minorities. This view is floored given that the term minority does not exclusively refer to ethnicity but also to sociodemographic variables such as sex, social class, age, profession, and education, which have a direct impact on decision making. Greater social representation is not only a question of reflecting the social fabric of society but also improves the quality of the decision rule. In contrast to 6 member juries, 12 member juries are more likely to reach the same decision in the same case (Hans and Vidmar, 1986). This implies that small juries may exhibit considerable disparities in the conviction rate as opposed to large juries.

On the other hand, others have argued that in large juries some jurors could be eliminated on the grounds that they do not intervene in the deliberation. This view seems to hold some weight since it has been observed that, after hearing the pro-innocence and pro-guilty arguments, silent jurors modify their judgements and thus sway a verdict one way or the other (Arce, Sobral and Fariña, 1991). In reply to the above criticism, others have suggested that silent jurors are no obstacle in the deliberation since limited involvement in the deliberation allows them to be more objective.

A key issue in judicial decision making by jurors is the decision rule (Saks, 1982). Initially, unanimity was the legal requirement but gradually this has given way to majority decision rules (see Hans and Vidmar 1986, for a critical review). The consequences of manipulating the decision rule seem to be greater than those attributed to the size of the jury. Controlled laboratory experiments have shown that, when majority decision rules are introduced, the quality of the discussion diminishes, the deliberation becomes shorter, there is less of a tendency to feel that justice has been done, the deliberation stops once the minimum quorum has been reached, the decision is oriented towards the verdict and not towards the evidence etc. (Nemeth, 1977; Saks and Hastie, 1978; Hastie et al, 1983; Nemeth, 1986). A further argument in favour of unanimous decisions refers to the loss of the individual juror's recall of the evidence, estimated to be around 30% of the evidence and leads to important errors of judgement. However, 90 to 100% of the evidence is remembered by the jury when there is a stimulating debate and non deliberating decisions brought about by majority decision rules are avoided (Hastie et al, 1983).

The most comprehensive study concerning the impact of the decision rule on the deliberation has been undertaken by Hastie, Penrod and Pennington (1983), who found that, in comparison to unanimous decisions, majority decisions led to shorter deliberations. Nevertheless, this is not just a mere question of longer or shorter deliberations since unanimity led to the greater participation of minorities, greater juror satisfaction with the final verdict and a more detailed appraisal of both the law and the evidence. Majority juries, however, apply a criterion of exclusion of testimonies i.e., they classify witnesses as either credible or not credible. This contrast with unanimous juries who apply a criterion of integration i.e., they compare and unite the different occasions. These findings are in agreement with the results reported in other studies (Kerr et al., 1976; Nemeth, 1977; Nemeth, 1986). Nonetheless, other studies suggest that different decision rules do not lead to variations in the verdict (Hastie et al., 1983; Kameda, 1991; De Paul, 1994), the discrepancy in the results may be due to the fact that only unanimous and 2/3 majority decision rules were evaluated. It is also worth noting that quite often juries implicitly adopt a unanimous decision rule (Davis et al., 1976), this may be due to the nature of the task demands and/or social desirability. Thus, we should reject these juries in order to assess the direct impact of the decision rule on the verdict. Simple majority decision rules, however, have been found to have a direct incidence on the verdict, in comparison to a unanimous decision, a simple majority decision rule tends to give rise to not guilty verdicts (Sáinz and Sáinz, 1990).

Overview

We have already mentioned that there is no universal decision rule, the most widespread formula being unanimity as is the case in most of the USA, and which was already in force in feudal times (Sobral and Arce, 1990). The majority decision rule introduced under the Jury Selection and Service Act (1968) has been the subject of considerable controversy. Those in favour, have argued that similar verdicts are obtained with either decision rule, moreover, they point out that jurors may come under pressure by defendants who belong to organised crime, drug dealers, and the like. In the UK the judge is empowered to vary the decision rule from unanimity to majority of 10 to 12 after a given period of time in the deliberation. This combination of decision rule is designed to avoid hung juries and increase the possibility of convicting this type of criminal. Similarly, in Spain, a new type of decision rule known as the "qualified majority", which consists of different criteria for decisions of innocence (simple majority) and guilt (from 5 to 7 or from 7 to 9), is to be introduced on the grounds that it will avoid hung juries and that the certainty to convict or absolve should be differently weighed. Evidently, this rule substitutes the judges instructions concerning the Standard of Proof. Theoretically, however, since this rule does not guarantee the quality of the decision, the judge is therefore empowered to ask the jury to reconsider its verdict.

Method

Subjects

The sample consisted of 260 subjects aged between 18 to 65 who were selected from the electoral register. Care was taken to ensure a balanced selection in terms of gender, age and socio-economic status.

Definition of Experimental Groups

The experimental design consisted of manipulating the decision rule (unanimity, 2/3 majority, combined and qualified majority). From this the following combinations of randomly assigned jurors were drawn:

a) Jury of six members and a unanimous decision.
b) Jury of six members and a 2/3 majority.
c) Jury of seven members and a unanimous decision followed by a majority of 5 to 7 after a 20 minute deliberation. From here onwards referred to as a combined rule.
d) Jury of seven members and a qualified majority rule (4 for innocence and six for guilty).

Procedure and Design

The juries were shown on video a real life trial of rape and murder or a trial of grievous bodily harm (GBH). Both cases included the defence and prosecution's plea, the testimony of eyewitnesses and legal experts, the closing arguments of both the defence and prosecution and the judge's summing up. In the case of rape and murder the defendant was a young man and the victim a young girl. There were no direct eyewitnesses though there were eyewitnesses who testified that he had been the last person to be seen accompanying the young girl. The defendant tried to coax a witness into backing his alibi but he refused. A forensic expert reported the existence of haematomas around the genital organs of the defendant, though he also stressed that the lesions could not be directly attributed to rape. The defence council pleaded not guilty and alleged the prosecution's case rested entirely on conjecture. The prosecution accused the defendant of both crimes and that he should be sentenced accordingly.

In the second case i.e., (GBH) occurred in a fight between two people at a public bar. The issue was to determine if the aggression was in self-defence or not. After the closing remarks, the judge instructed the jury on the legal definition of self-defence.

Each subjects had to fill in three questionnaires. The first covered sociodemographic data. After viewing the videos and prior to the deliberation, a questionnaire was completed, referring to individual juror decision, verdict, estimated sentence, as well as deciding the probability of guilt using a percentage scale with guilty, innocence polarity. In the third, a post deliberation questionnaire containing the same variables as the pre deliberation was administered as well as a self-report 5 point Likert type scale measuring seriousness of the deliberation, satisfaction with the verdict, in depth analysis of the evidence, persuasive capacity, impartiality and a feeling of loneliness.

Results

A statistical analysis was undertaken to determine if the subjects assigned to the experimental conditions exhibited differences in the pre deliberation verdict. No differences in the individual decisions were observed [chi(3)=4.34; NS]. After the group decision was taken, again no differences were found in the individual post deliberation verdicts [chi(3)=2.22; NS]; that is, the decision rule does not influence the group verdict. Moreover, the post deliberation juror self-reports reveal that the probability of guilt does not lead to difference among the groups ($F(3,246)=1.54$; NS).

Consequently, it is plausible to believe that the decisions are the same; however, the differences rest on the jurors excluded from the final decision. Thus, a quarter of the jurors in the 2/3 majority decision rule, and 24.85% of the qualified majority were excluded from the final decision whereas 12.85% of jurors in the combined decision rule were excluded from the final decision. Obviously in the unanimous decision no juror was excluded from the final decision. In fact, 3.33% of the jurors impede decisions to be taken by provoking hung juries.

The post deliberation juror self-reports exhibit differences mediated by the decision rule. Thus, the justice perceived from the verdict derived from the group decision is influenced by the decision rule ($F(3,246)=3.37$ $p=.01$). A contrasting analysis shows that the qualified majority have less of a feeling that justice has been done in comparison to jurors from the combined decision rule [$t(138)=2.72$; $p=.00$] or the unanimous decision [$t(129)=2.04$; $p=.04$]. The majority decision condition also has lesser feeling that justice has been done in comparison to the combined decision condition [$t(128)=2.34$; $p=.02$] or the unanimous condition [1(119)=1.71; $p=.07$, marginally significant]. However, neither the qualified and the simple majority exhibit differences between them, nor do the unanimous and the combined decisions.

Furthermore, differences can be observed regarding the satisfaction with the verdict ($F(3,246)=2.61$; $p=.05$). The contrast analysis highlights that the unanimous condition have greater satisfaction than the simple majority [$t(119)=2.37$; $p=.02$] or the qualified majority [$t(129)=2.53$; $p=.01$]. The combined majority showed greater satisfaction than either the simple majority condition [$t(128)=2.03$; $p=.04$] or the qualified majority [$t(138)=2.16$; $p=.03$].

The key seems to lie with those jurors that change their decisions or those that are excluded from the group decision. As was expected the intransigent jurors who are excluded from the group decision are less satisfied with the verdict [$t(92)=3.68$; $p=.00$] and are in less of a belief that they have reached a just verdict [$t(92)=2.57$; $p=.01$].

Discussion

Saks (1982) has pointed out that the reduction in both the number of jurors and the decision rule is designed to fulfil three objectives: a) to increase cost effectiveness and reduce time; b) to provide greater advantages to the prosecution in the belief that non unanimous verdicts would increase the conviction rate; c) and finally, small juries with a non unanimous decision rule would eventually lead to the eradication of the jury system itself. It is true to say that non unanimous decision are cost effective in terms of both time and money. Hence, we should bear in mind that hung juries, though theoretically possible, are in fact practically non-existent, particularly with qualified decision rules. The answer to the second question remains unclear, since there appears to be no increase in the innocence or conviction rate with non unanimous decisions. Though individually jurors tend to exhibit a higher conviction rate than when in groups, this tendency does not correspond with an expected higher conviction rate for non unanimous decisions. The third hypothesis, that the reduction in the number of jurors and the decision rule would eventually lead to the eradication of the jury system seems to be well founded. Our results show how, with majority or qualified majority decisions, a quarter of the population is excluded from the final decision and they feel less satisfied that justice has been done with the group decision.

Obviously, there is no doubt, that the experience of these subjects will change their views regarding justice and the jury system, which will in all probability lead to its rejection. Moreover, the possibility of taking irrational decisions in specific juries increases, since they have not been deliberated. In other words, bias in judgement making, errors in information processing, the influence of emotional states, the inability to assess all of the evidence, etc. are much more likely to occur with non unanimous juries.

Our results leave little room for non unanimous decisions. To exclude 25% of the population does not seem to be a suitable principle on which to base a decision rule, as occurs with both the 2/3 and qualified majority decisions. Moreover, if we take into account that non unanimous decisions lead to poorer deliberations (Hastie et al., 1983), the famous saying that a jury is nothing but the result of the sum of the individual ignorances in which minorities do not count. In the light of our results, one cannot argue in favour of a group decision which excludes a quarter of the population. Justice cannot be reduced to a mere question of the number of individual or group votes.

Experimental Conditions

a) Jury of six members and a unanimous decision.
b) Jury of six members and a 2/3 majority.
c) Jury of seven members and a unanimous decision followed by a majority of 5 to 7 after a 20 minute deliberation. From here onwards referred to as a combined rule.
d) Jury of seven members and a qualified majority rule (4 for innocence and six for guilty).

Results on the Decision

a) No differences in the individual decisions were observed [chi(3)=4.34; NS].
b) After the group decision was taken, again no differences were found in the individual post deliberation verdicts [chi(3)=2.22; NS].
c) The post deliberation juror self-reports reveal that the probability of guilt does not lead to difference among the groups (F(3,246)=1.54; NS).

Perceptions of the Quality of the Deliberation

The justice perceived from the verdict derived from the group decision is influenced by the decision rule (F(3,246)=3.37 p=.01). A contrast analysis shows that the qualified majority have less of a feeling that justice has been done in comparison to jurors from the combined decision rule (t(138)=2.72; p=.00) or the unanimous decision (t(129)=2.04; p=.04). The majority decision condition also has less of a feeling that justice has been done in comparison to the combined decision group (t(128)=2.34; p=.02) or the unanimous group (1(119)=1.71; p=.07, marginally significant). However, the qualified and the simple majority do not exhibit any differences between them, neither do the unanimous and the combined decisions.

Furthermore, differences can be observed regarding the satisfaction with the verdict (F(3,246)=2.61; p=.05). The contrast analysis highlights that the unanimous group have greater satisfaction than the simple majority (t(119)=2.37; p=.02) or the qualified majority (t(129)=2.53; p=.01). The combined majority are showed greater satisfaction than the simple majority group (t(128)=2.03; p=.04) or the qualified majority (t(138)=2.16; p=.03).

Effects on Social Participation

A quarter of the jurors in the 2/3 majority decision rule, and 24.85% of the qualified majority were excluded from the final decision whereas 12.85% of jurors in the combined decision rule were excluded from the final decision. Obviously in the unanimous decision no juror was excluded from the final decision. In fact, 3.33% of the jurors impede decisions to be taken by provoking hung juries.

Thus, the intransigent jurors who are excluded from the group decision are less satisfied with the verdict (t(92)=3.68; p=.00) and are in less of a belief that they have reached a just verdict (t(92)=2.57; p=.01) in comparison with those jurors that change their decision.

References

Arce, R., Sobral, J., & Farina, F. (1991). Acerca de la partición de los jurados en las deliberaciones y sus implicaciones legales. *Análisis y Modificación de Conducta, 17(51)*, 71-83

Davis, J. H., Stasser, G., Spitzer, C. E., & Holt, R. W. (1976). Changes in group members' decision preferences during discussion: An illustration with mock juries. *Journal of Personality and Social Psychology, 34*, 1177-1187.

De Paul, P. (1994). Análisis de la deliberación de jurados que varían en tamano y regla de decisión. *Revista de Psicología Social, 9(1)*, 19-29.

Hans, V. P., & Vidmar, N. (1986). *Judging the jury.* New York: Plenum Press.

Hastie, R., Penrod, S., & Pennington (1983). *Inside the jury.* Cambridge, MA: Harvard University Press.

Kameda, T. (1991). Procedural influence in small-group decision making: Deliberation style and assigned decision rule. *Journal of Personality and Social Psychology, 61*(2), 245-256.

Nemeth, Ch. J. (1977): Interactions between juror as a function of majority vs. unanimity decision rules. *Journal of Applied Psychology, 7*, 38-56.

Nemeth, Ch. J. (1986). Procesos de Grupo y Jurados: Los Estados Unidos y Francia. In S. Moscovici (Ed.), *Psicología Social. I.* Buenos Aires: Paidós.

Sáinz, E., & Sáinz, J. (1989). Estrategias de decisión de un jurado bajo condiciones de simulación. *Revista de Psicología General y Aplicada, 42(4)*, 509-523.

Saks, M. J. (1982). Innovation and change in the courtroom. In N. L. Kerr, & R. M. Bray (Eds.). *The Psychology of the Courtroom.* New York: Academic Press.

Saks, M. J., & Hastie, R. (1978). *Social Psychology in court.* New York: Van Nostrand Reinhold.

Sobral, J., & Arce, R. (1990). La psicología social en la sala de justicia. *El jurado y el testimonio.* Barcelona: Paidós.

Zeisel, H. (1971). ... And then there was none: The diminution of federal jury. *University of Chicago Law Review, 35*, 228-241.

Juror's Decision in Capital Cases

Vladimir Konečni

Factors Affecting Simulated Jurors' Decision In Capital Cases[1]

In the legal systems of the United States, veniremen in capital cases can be excluded from serving on a jury if a judge decides that they hold strong beliefs opposed to the death penalty. The rationale for this exclusionary rule has been that these citizens, if empaneled, may prevent the legal imposition of the death penalty either by refusing to find a defendant guilty or by refusing to vote for capital punishment in the sentencing phase of the trial, regardless of the merits of the case. All cases, therefore, in which the possibility of capital punishment existed, have been decided by "death-qualified" juries. In *Witherspoon v. Illinois* (1968), the death penalty imposed on the defendant was challenged on the grounds that the systematic exclusion of jurors opposed to the death penalty had created a jury biased toward bringing in the verdict of "guilty". It was argued that the exclusive use of death-qualified jurors violated Witherspoon's constitutional rights to a fair trial as guaranteed by the 6th an 14th Amendments.

The few, then unpublished, social-science studies presented to the U.S. Supreme Court when it heard the case (Wilson, 1964; Zeisel, 1968; Goldberg, 1970) failed to convince the Court that Witherspoon had been convicted by a biased jury. In a split decision, the Court found the evidence supporting this contention to be of a "tentative and fragmentary" nature and that Witherspoon had not met the burden of proof that jurors who are not opposed to capital punishment are more prone to convict. This precedent-setting decision confirmed the constitutionality of the use of death-qualified juries and opened the door for subsequent research on the issue of systematic bias of juries thus empaneled.[2]

---

1 The authors wish to thank Lynda Tyll for her valuable participation on this project.

2 Our data were collected before it became clear that the case of *Wainright v. Witt* (1985) would set the new standard for the qualification of juries in capital-crime cases. We feel that the value of the research presented here is by no means diminished by the fact that *Witt* replaced *Witherspoon* as the standard for the selection of juries in capital cases. Rather, one can view the implications of the present body of data and the methodological criticism as indicative of the type of skepticism that the Court may have covertly expressed in the *Witt* opinion regarding the merit and applicability of the tendentious social-science reasearch that followed *Witherspoon*. See also the Conclusions section of this article with regard to *Witt*.

All veniremen are questioned about their attitudes and feelings regarding case-related issues prior to being empaneled (*voir dire*). Those who in the opinion of the judge would for any reason unable to render an impartial verdict are excused from serving. Juries in capital cases are unique in that they have the potential dual responsibility of deciding both the guilt of the defendant and the sentence. Figure 1 is an authentic representation of the chart used in the Superior Courts of San Diego to explain to prospective jurors in capital cases the extent of their decision-making responsibilities should they be empaneled. Therefore, the *voir dire* of such prospective jurors includes the additional process of "death qualification."

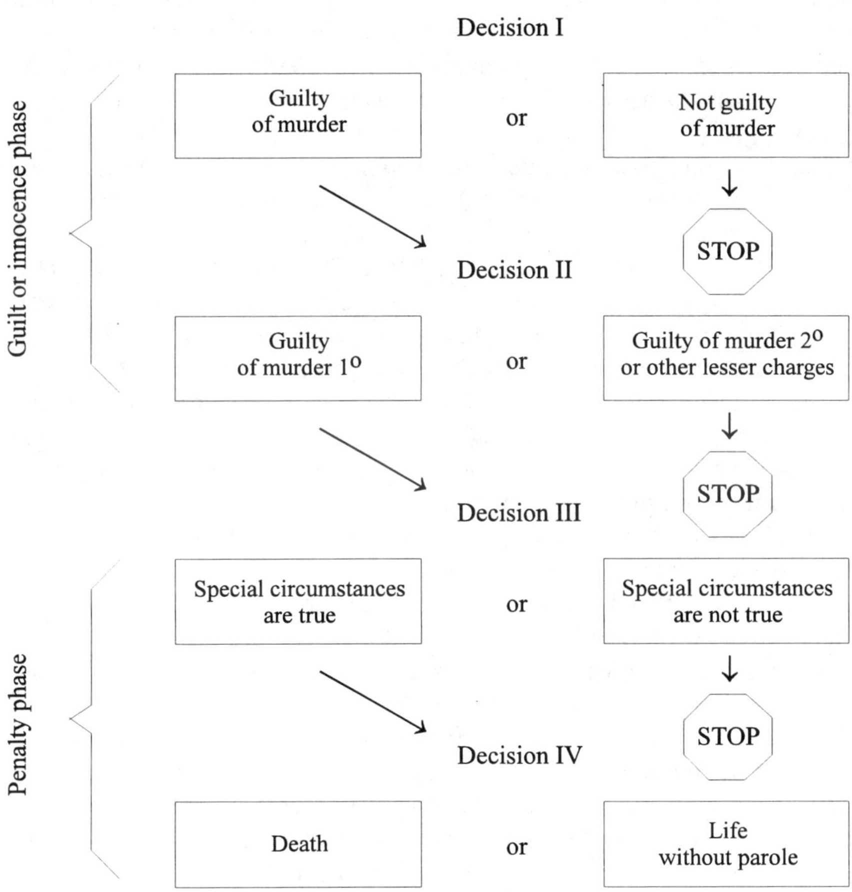

Used by permission: Office of the District Attorney, San Diego, California

Figure 1: Juror Decisions from Guilt Phase to Penalty Phase

In capital cases following *Witherspóon*, the goal of the death-qualification portion of *voir dire* is to identify three groups of veniremen: *Nullifiers*, who would be unable to render an impartial verdict due to their beliefs about the death penalty and are therefore excused from serving; the so-called *Witherspoon* excludables, who would refuse to vote for the death penalty regardless of the evidence presented (even though they could render an impartial verdict), and are thus also excused; and the so-called *death-qualified* veniremen who fall into neither of the above categories and are deemed qualified to sit on the jury in a capital case.

It is the systematic exclusion of veniremen who oppose the legally available death-penalty option regardless of the merits of the case, their verdict-reaching impartiality notwithstanding, that has given rise to allegations that the composition of the juries in capital cases is skewed toward conviction-proneness. Since "nullifiers" would be excluded from serving regardless of the *Witherspoon* decision, the key research comparison has been between *Witherspoon* excludables and death-qualified jurors.

Early research on the issue of death-qualification and jury bias focused on the relationship between death-penalty attitudes and other attitudes toward crime and punishment (Bronson, 1970; Goldberg, 1970; Zeisel, 1970; Jurow, 1971). These studies have been reviewed elsewhere (e.g., , 1984; Thompson, Cowan, Ellsworth and Harrington, 1984) and need not be discussed again here. The study by Moran and Comfort (1986) is the only one to date which found a positive relationship between pro-capital-punishment views and conviction-proneness in people who had previously, in fact, been impaneled on a felony jury. however, not only was a very low percentage of mailed questionnaires returned (22,7%), but the failure to provide a breakdown by type of felony raises the distinct possibility that the results are irrelevant for verdicts in capital cases.

Other research has focused on the specific question of whether death-qualified simulated jurors as a group are biased toward conviction in comparison to the group of potential jurors who are excluded under the *Witherspoon* decision. Cowan, Thompson and Ellsworth (1984) divided subjects into nullifiers, Witherspoon excludables, and those who were considered death-qualified. This was done by asking one question about the subjects' ability to render an impartial verdict, given their attitude toward the death penalty (to identify the *Witherspoon* excludables). After eliminating the nullifiers from the sample, the remaining 30 excludable and 258 death qualified subjects were shown a videotaped reenactment of a synopsized murder trial. On several measures, the death-.qualified group was significantly more likely to convict than the *Witherspoon* excludables.

Thompson et al. (1984) presented death-qualified and *Witherspoon* excludable subjects with a videotapes simulation of an assault trial so as to assess the possible differences in the way the two groups interpret the evidence presented. Death-qualified subjects interpreted testimonial evidence as more favourable to the prosecution than did the excludable group. The authors concluded that the alleged difference between the two groups in conviction-proneness may be due, in part, to differential perceptions of the strength of the evidence against the defendant.

A related line of research examined the possibility that the death-qualifying *voir dire* procedure itself could have a biasing effect on the subsequent decisions of jurors. Haney (1984) asked a group of subjects (from which nullifiers and excludables had been removed) to watch a videotape of a *voir dire* procedure in a capital case being performed on other simulated jurors. For half of these observer-subjects, the tape included the death-qualifying process, while for the other half this part this part of the tape was edited out. All subjects then completed a questionnaire. Findings indicated that subjects who had watched the death-qualifying questions and answers were more likely to (a) believe that the defendant would be found guilty, (b) believe that the judge and both attorneys assumed the defendant to be guilty, and (c) choose the death penalty than the subjects who had watched the jury selection without the death-qualifying segment.

Although no case of any kind was presented and no verdicts were rendered, this single study (at that time unpublished) was cited as the key factor in a California Supreme Court decision to require individual sequestration of prospective jurors for the death qualifying portion of *voir dire*. The opinion, written by then Chief Justice, Rose Bird[3], stated:

> In order to minimize the potentially prejudicial effects identified by the Haney study, this court declares, pursuant to its supervisory authority over California criminal procedure, that in future capital cases that portion of the *voir dire* of each prospective juror which deals with issues which involve death-qualifying the jury should be done individually and in sequestration. *(Hovey v. California, 1980).*

This opinion demonstrates the potential of social-science research to influence in important ways the fundamental workings of the criminal justice system. The Hovey decision changes the way capital juries are selected in California, adding, at minimum, cost and time loss to process. While this kind of direct impact has been rare, a considerable problem is demonstrated here in applying findings from simulation research, the external validity of which had yet to be established. Although the various studies described here support the notion that the death-penalty attitudes may affect verdict decisions, and therefore allow the inference that conviction-biased juries are being created through the use of Witherspoon exclusions, we find this argument far from convicting, given the nature of the research that has been conducted in this area. [See the complementary criticism by Elliot

---

3 Chief Justice Rose Bird and two other California Supreme Court Justices, J. Grodin and C. Reynoso, failed to be re-elected (under confirmation law) by people of California in 1986. It is generally agreed that this occured because of the Court's frequent reversal of death-penalty verdicts in a State where 80% of the electorate favors capital punishment. Fifty-two of 55 death-penalty decisions heard by the Court during the tenure of these Justices were reversed (Lacayo, 1986).

(1991a) of the brief the American Psychological Association filed in *Lockhart v. McCree* (1986)].

Most of the above research (and all of the recent studies) has relied on simulation methodologies. The difficulty of achieving external validity with the exclusive use of this method is well-known (see Konecni and Ebbesen, 1979, 1982). There is little reason for assuming a priori that survey questions, written case-summaries, audio- or video tapes can produce attitudes in subjects that activate or reflect the same underlying decision mechanism that control the behaviour of real juries.

Furthermore, these studies are inferentially weak for an even stronger reason, namely, their exclusion of other presumably important influences on real jurors' verdicts. The criminal justice system predicates that verdicts be based solely upon the facts of the case as presented during the trial – the evidence. Even if prior research has consistently shown the effects of death-penalty views on verdicts, it should have been self-evident to those researchers that the relative importance of their effects could not be known until the percent of variance these effects accounted for was compared to that accounted for by the evidence. If inferences about the legal system are to be drawn from simulation research, it is crucial to simulate other important factors in the real-world system that can be plausibly believed to influence the behaviour of interest. The influence of pre-trial attitudes may, for example, be eliminated when the evidence and the jurors' motivation to follow the judge's instructions to base their verdict solely on that evidence are both strong.

We therefore carried out two simulation that examined the relationship of death-penalty attitudes to verdicts in the context of an experimental manipulation of the strength of two key trial factors: evidence and heinousness. Although two of the present authors have written extensively on the potential dangers of generalizing from simulation methodology in psycho-.legal research (e.g., Ebbesen and Konecni, 1980, 1985; Konecni and Ebbesen, 1979, 1981, 1984, 1992), we intentionally chose this methodology in the present research to allow for comparisons (conceptually, at least) between our findings and the existing body of literature. It might seem strange that a study designed to explore the external validity of previous simulations would continue to use simulation methodology. One might rightly argue that a better test of generalizability would employ methods very different from those already used. However, in the present case, because we were on various grounds predicting results different from those previously found, we felt that a stronger argument could be made about the inferential errors made by the authors of prior studies if our procedures were methodologically similar to those they utilized. Were our methods completely different from those used in past research, critics could point to these differences as explanations for failure to replicate.

The following factors were combined in a single experimental design:

Evidence. The evidence presented in open court during a trial ought to be primary and central factor in a jury verdict. In order to examine this factor in comparison with others that are functioning concurrently in a legal setting, the strength of the case against the defendant was varied systematically.

Heinousness. This a factor present in all capital cases, but its effect in simulated jurors' verdicts has not before been studied. It was included in order to determine what influence, if any, it may exert on verdicts in the context of a simulation-research approach. Heinousness was also used to provide a test of discriminal validity in that, while heinousness might not affect verdicts, it should (if our procedures and methods are adequately sensitive) influence sentencing decisions.

Voir dire. Claims have been made (Haney, 1984) and accepted by the California Supreme Court in *Hovey* that the very process of questioning veniremen about death penalty prior to being empaneled may bias them toward guilty verdicts. However, due to serious questions about the adequacy and completeness of the prior research, this contention was re-examined using a different approach than had been employed in previous work.

Death-penalty attitudes. The connection between death penalty attitudes and verdicts in capital cases is the central issue in the death-qualification controversy. Until now, however, this connection has not been tested in the presence of variation of the other key factors listed above. it can be argued from reasoning about stimulus-person interactions (Mischel, 1976), for example, that death penalty attitudes will only exert their effects in cases in which the evidence against the defendant is weak.

Since evidence was found to be the overwhelmingly dominant factor in subjects' verdicts in the first study, a second experiment was designed to replicate Experiment 1 conceptually and to explore the influence of evidence in greater detail.

Experiment 1

Method

Subjects, Design and Materials. Undergraduate students (N=198) at the University of California, San Diego who indicated that they either had a valid California driver's licence or were registered to vote in California were randomly assigned to groups exposed to simulated murder cases involving varying amounts of evidence (three levels), differing degrees of heinousness (two levels), and differing death-qualifying *voir dire* conditions (two levels), in a between-subjects design. The subjects' assessed levels of scruples regarding the death penalty was treated as a co-variate.

Six written case summaries of capital crimes were developed. They varied systematically in terms of evidence and heinousness. All case summaries were variations of the same basic crime: A murder committed with a handgun during the commission of a robbery in a convenience store. Both the prosecutor's and the defense attorney's cases were summarized.

Evidence. In the weak evidence condition, there was one witness who was hiding in the store and heard, but did not see, what took place. She was able to make a voice identification and offer testimony as to the defendant' attire. Other relatively weak circumstantial evidence was presented. In the moderate evidence condition, the witness hiding in the store had a better view of the robbery and shooting and was able to make a positive identification of the defendant and offer more detailed information about his attire. Additional evidence regarding cash found in the defendant's possession was also included. In the strong evidence condition, there were two eyewitness hiding in the store. Their accounts of the events if the murder agreed, including their identification of the defendant and his attire on the night of the crime. Additionally, in the strong evidence condition, the murder weapon, wrapped in a jacket possibly belonging to the defendant, was found in a trash dumpster near the place where the defendant was captured. A pilot study determined that these three levels of evidence were at approximately equal intervals of discriminability.

Heinousness. In the low heinousness condition, the gunman entered the store and demanded money. The store attendant, while complying, triggered the store alarm at which time the robber shot the attendant, grabbed the money and ran out of the store. In the high heinousness condition, the gunman entered the store, pistol-whipped the attendant repeatedly, tied him up, forced him to kneel, and shot him. He then shot the body of the attendant five more times before grabbing the money and running out of the store. A pilot study determined that subjects clearly discriminated between these levels of heinousness.

The various levels of evidence and heinousness were combined to create six different case summaries (see Appendix 1 for a sample case summary).

Voir dire and Death-Penalty Scruples. A 10-item questionnaire was developed to assess the subjects' scruples about the death penalty. In an attempt to insure that this simulated *voir dire* asked legally appropriate questions about death penalty beliefs, the first five items were stated exactly as they are in the preliminary screening of jurors in the San Diego Superior Court system in cases where the death penalty is being sought by the prosecution. The final five items were designed to be similar to some of the follow-up questions which the attorneys or the judge might ask prospective jurors during *voir dire* in order to assess further their position on the death penalty (see Appendix 2 for the complete questionnaire).This questionnaire was given to all subjects in the study. However, half of the subjects responded to the questionnaire prior to reading the case summary (pre-*voir dire* condition), while the other half answered the questionnaire after they have had been exposed to the case summary and reached the decision about the verdict and the sentence (post-*voir dire* condition).

This death penalty questionnaire was also used to measure the subjects' scruples regarding the death penalty (the fourth factor in the design). Thus a single instrument was employed both to assess the death-penalty scruples and, by varying when the subjects completed the questionnaire, to examine the effect of pretrial exposure to a simulated death-qualifying procedure.

Procedure

Subjects were treated in groups of 12 to 15. Each subject was randomly assigned to one of 12 conditions combining evidence, heinousness, and pre- versus post-*voir dire*. Each subject received a packet which contained the following: 1)case summary; 2) verdict measure; 3) special circumstances measure; 4) sentence measure; 5) death penalty questionnaire; and 6) demographic items. As mentioned above, the death penalty questionnaire came first in the packet for half of the subjects and after the sentence measure for the other half.

After being instructed about their role as jurors, subjects were given simulated California Jury Instructions Criminal (CALJIC) instructions that emphasized the need to base their decisions solely on the evidence. Subjects were then told to proceed through their packets slowly and carefully, one page at a time, and not to look ahead in the packet at any time. Once they had responded to an item, they were not allowed to change their answers.

The verdict measure required subjects to find the defendant guilty or not guilty of first degree murder and to indicate the level of confidence in the verdict decision. The special circumstances page explained the meaning of this concept and required the subject to decide if these circumstances were true for the case presented. For the sentence measure, subjects were required to decide between the death penalty and life imprisonment without the possibility of parole. Only those who found the defendant guilty were required to make a decision regarding special circumstances and sentence. Demographic items were: Gender, age, whether the subject had a California driver's license, whether the subject was registered to vote in California, and the subject's political party affiliation. Voter registration and driver's license lists are commonly used for selecting individuals for jury duty in California.

Results

Scores on the death-penalty attitude measure were coded so that higher scores indicated increasingly pro-capital punishment attitudes. One of the original ten items was dropped from the total since it was designed to assess impartiality and therefore did not directly relate to the attitude score. The death-penalty measure was found to have a fair degree of internal consistency when tested overall (Alpha=.73). On the other hand, when the five items taken from the San Diego Superior Court were analyzed independently from the five new follow-up items, the Court's items were found to contain poor internal consistency (Alpha=.04), probably due to the confusing wording of the questions. The new follow-up items fared considerably better (Alpha=.76).

To enhance the external validity of the scruples measure, responses to all nine questions were used to compute total scruples scores, despite the lack of internal consistency in the five questions used by the San Diego Court. These total scores on the questionnaire were divided into equal thirds to produce three groups of subjects – holding pro-, moderate, or anti-death-penalty attitude.[4] This trichotomized-scruples variable was used in some of the subsequent data analyses.

Table 1: Chi-square and Log-linear Analyses of Evidence (E), Heinousness (H), Pre- vs. Post-Voir Dire (P/P), and Death-Penalty Scruples (DP) in relation to Sentence (S)

	x^2 main effect analyses on sentence		
Factor	*df*	x^2	*p*
Evidence	2	1.80	>.10
Heinousness	1	4.12	.05
Pre/Post Voir Dire	1	2.8	<.10
Death Penalty Scruples	2	24.03	<.001
	Model 1*		
Marginals+(SxDP)**	21	17.87	.66
Marginals+(SxDP)+(SxE)	19	16.07	.65
Residual from dropping (SxE)	2	1.87	>.10
Marginals+(SxDP)+(SxH)	20	13.68	.85
Residual from dropping (SxH)	1	4.19	<.05
	Model of best fit		
Marginals+(SxDP)+(SxH)	20	13.68	.85

* Model analyses were collapsed across Pre/Post Voir Dire for log-linear analysis to avoid excessive zero-cells. Results were unchanged when analyses were performed on a data table across evidence and the contribution of Pre/Post Voir Dire was examined.

** The (Sx Factor) parameters in the log-linear models are the equivalent of main effects in analysis of variance models in which sentence is the dependant variable.

In order to assess the efficacy of the death-penalty scruples measure, analyses were performed treating sentence as the dependent variable, and using the trichotomized scruples variable, heinousness, pre/post *voir dire* and evidence as predictors. To the extent that our scruples-measurement and case-simulation procedures tapped attitudes and decision processes similar to those active in real jury decisions, it was logical to expect scruples and heinousness to predict sentence as

4 This procedure is, of course, far removed from the manner in which attorneys and judges detect veniremen who are *Witherspoon* excludables. Questionnaires, whether consisting of one or two questions (as in the studies reported by Ellsworth and her colleagues, or by Haney) or consisting of nine items, as in the present research, may well not capture the decision rules used by the actual participants in the system to qualify jurors.

nature of the evidence in the case were constructed to increase the range of stimulus conditions used.

Method

Subjects, Design and Materials. Subjects for the second study were 179 undergraduate students at the University of California, San Diego who had valid California Driver's license or were to vote in California. Participation in research projects was part of their course requirements.

Summaries of murder cases were written exactly as is Experiment 1 except that evidence was factored into three levels of eyewitness evidence and three levels of physical evidence (weak, moderate, and strong) on the assumption that a scruples x evidence interaction may depend on the nature as well as strength of evidence. The eyewitness conditions involved increasing visibility and number of eyewitnesses as in Experiment 1. Strength of physical evidence was varied by increasing the quantity and decreasing the circumstantial nature of the evidence (See Appendix 1 for a sample case summary). This created a 3 x 3 between-subjects design. In view of the results of Experiment 1, heinousness was not varied in Experiment 2.

Since the five items on the death-penalty questionnaire that were taken from the San Diego Superior Court were internally inconsistent and, we concluded, difficult to understand, these were eliminated from the questionnaire in this second study. Instead, five new questions were developed and combined with the five "follow-up" questions from our first study to create the second questionnaire (see Appendix 2 for the complete questionnaire).

Procedure

Subjects were again tested in groups of 12 to 15. Each subject was randomly assigned to one of the nine conditions and presented with a packet containing the death penalty questionnaire, the case summary, a verdict measure, and several demographic items as in Experiment 1. Since the murder described in the case summaries was committed during a serious felony (armed robbery), the presence of special circumstances was assumed and the subjects were not asked to decide this issue. Another reason for this was that nearly all subjects in Experiment 1 who found the defendant guilty also found the special circumstances to be true due to the nature of the crime.

Results

As expected, the death-penalty attitude questionnaire developed for this second study was found to have a higher degree of internal item-consistency (Alpha=.85) than the original questionnaire. Scores on the questionnaire were trichotomized as in Experiment 1 and analyzed along with eyewitness and physical evidence in relation to sentence and verdict. In a manner identical to the first experiment, the revised measure of scruples was significantly related to sentence ($x^2(2)=33.10$, p.<.001). As would be expected if the scruples measure were valid, only one of the 33 subjects chose this sentence. The revised scruples measure thus received strong support. Also analogously to Experiment 1, neither of the two evidence factors (nor their interaction) had a significant effect on sentence.

Whereas the scruples measure predicted the sentences the subjects imposed, only the eyewitness-evidence and the physical-evidence factors predicted the verdicts, as can be seen in Table 4.

Table 4: Chi-square and log-linear analyses of Eyewitness Evidence (E), Physical (P) and Death-Penalty Scruples (DP) in relation to Verdict (V)

	x^2 main effect analyses on verdict		
Factor	*df*	x^2	*p*
Eyewitness evidence	2	7.57	.02
Physical evidence	2	11.02	.004
Death Penalty Scruples	2	.08	.96
	Model		
Marginals+(VxP)	44	37.01	.76
Marginals+(VxP)+(VxE)	42	29.19	.93
Residual from dropping (VxE)	2	7.82	>.025
Marginals+(VxP)+(VxE)+(VxDP)	40	29.12	.90
Residual from dropping (VxDP)	2	0.8	.96
	Model of best fit		
Marginals+(VxP)+(VxE)	42	29.19	.93

Both evidence factors were necessary in a log-linear odds analysis to describe the data. However, the scruples was again unnecessary and did not improve the fit of the model. The interaction between the two types of evidence did not approach significance. Table 5 reflects the arrangement of the data for the model of best fit. Replacing the results of Experiment 1, additional analyses found no significant interactive effect on verdicts between scruples and either of the evidence factors. As in the first study, subjects were again divided into death-qualified and *Witherspoon*-excludable groups according to the pattern of their answers to the questionnaire and compared on verdicts. And again no differences in verdict choices were found between these two groups ($x^2(1)=.089$, p=.96).

Table 5: Percent guilty verdicts reflecting log-linear model of best fit from Table 4

	Physical evidence		
Eyewitness evidence	Weak	Moderate	Strong
Weak	45.0%	68.4%*	84.0%*
Moderate	50.0%	50.0%	70.0%
Strong	70.0%	75.0%	95.0%

* For these cells, n=19. For others, n=20.

Experiment 2 succesfully replicated the subjects' utter reliance on the strength of evidence (both eyewitness and physical) in reaching their verdicts. Also, the lack of relationship between death-penalty scruples and verdicts found in Experiment 1 was replicated with the new measure of scruples, as were the weak relationships found in Experiment 1 between death-penalty scruples and the subjects' gender ($x^2(2)=7.84$, $p<.025$) and political party ($x^2(4)=8.48$, $p=.075$). Again as in Experiment 1, neither the subjects' gender ($x^2(1)=.04$) nor their political party affiliations ($x^2(2)=3.20$, $p=.20$) was related to their verdict decisions.

General Discussion

Taken together, these findings question the soundness of the conclusions reached by Haney (1984), Cowan, et al., (1984) and Thompson et al., (1984) regarding the potential of the *Witherspoon* selection procedures to bias juries against defendants.

In examining the relationship between death-penalty attitudes (death-qualified versus Witherspoon-excludable jurors) and verdicts, the present experiments did not find any support whatsoever for these past studies, nor for the California Supreme Court opinion in Hovey. And whereas death-penalty scruples appeared to be related to the subjects' gender and political party, neither scruples nor gender nor political party predicted verdicts. Instead, we found that our subjects' verdict decisions were determined, virtually exclusively, by the strength of the evidence presented in the case, exactly as is legally prescribed. Furthermore, we did not find that death-penalty attitudes were more likely to predict verdicts in cases with weak evidence. On the other hand, the sentences the subjects chose to impose could be predicted by the degree of heinousness of the crime and, even more so, by the subjects' death-penalty attitudes as measured by the simulated *voir dire*.

These findings can be viewed from at least two different perspectives. One addresses the potential explanations for the different patterns of results produced by our procedures compared to those from previous studies. The second explores the implications of our findings, in the light of previous studies and consequent judicial decisions, for the legal issues surrounding the death-qualification procedures.

Explanations for Discrepancies Across Studies

Measurement Issues. One explanation for the differences between the past and present results is the possibility that our attitude measures failed adequately to assess the death-penalty scruples (or some related construct) and, therefore, their inability to predict verdicts was simply a result of a poorly constructed questionnaire. This explanation is untenable: Our measure of the death-penalty attitudes was highly predictive of sentencing decisions in both studies (only one of the 45 subjects that our procedures classified as being strongly against the death penalty chose the death penalty after deciding the defendant was guilty of first degree murder). Not only does this finding indicate a high degree of validity of the scruples measure, but it makes intuitive sense in terms of how sentencing decisions are made in actual capital trials. Most significantly, this finding strongly supports the rationale for and practice of the removal of strongly anti-death-penalty veniremen from capital juries.

One might still argue that our procedures for measuring scruples, despite their ability to predict sentencing decisions, were somehow less "meaningful" than those used in prior research. Scruples may only predict verdicts, this tortuous argument goes, when "correctly" measured. However the argument can be abruptly halted by a simple (methodo)logical observation: If the relationship between scruples and verdicts is that hypersensitive to the instrument and procedures used to assess scruples, then the true *legal* relevance of any social-science finding concerning verdicts can by definition be achieved only by measuring scruples in experiments exactly as they are determined by actual court-room *voir dire* procedures. As far we know, this step has never been taken in a research study and it is unlikely that the extensive questioning of veniremen during the Witherspoon *voir dire* can be adequately simulated. For example, one questionnaire used to help select jurors in a recent capital case in California (People v. Davis, 1995) included 23 different questions about death-penalty attitudes. Furthermore, returning to the argument critical of our scruples-measuring instrument, it would seem that our measurement procedures more closely approximate those used in real court cases than do those used in prior research. Unlike past studies, one of our scruples criteria was based on aggregating responses to a number of different, though related, death-penalty attitude items.

A different methodological line of thought would focus on the measurement of verdict decisions across different experiments. In Cowas, et al. (1984), for example, subjects were asked to indicate whether they thought the defendant was guilty of 1st degree murder, 2nd degree murder, manslaughter, or not guilty. There were no difference in the rate at which death-qualified and excludable subjects chose either 1st (7.8% and 3.3%, respectively) or 2nd degree murder (21.3% and 23.3%, respectively) in predeliberation decisions (the same was true for post-deliberation decisions). The differences between death-qualified and excludable subjects emerged in the rates at which they chose the manslaughter and not guilty alternatives. in our studies, subjects simply indicated whether they felt the defendant was guilty of 1st degree murder or not. It is possible that scruples have no effect on the rate at which more severe verdicts are chosen. If so, it could be said that our results actually replicate a part of the Cowan, et al. findings, namely the failure of scruples to affect the rate of 1st degree murder decisions. This view of the data leads to the intriguing conclusion that attitudes toward the death penalty affect only the rate at which subjects pick verdicts that cannot possibly result in the death penalty. Are the subjects sophists? Are the jurors?

Case Differences. Another line of reasoning would pursue the idea that the differential presentation of the defendant's behaviour across experiments, rather than the strength of the evidence against the defendant, is what matters. In Cowan, et al., the issue that the simulated jurors had to decide was whether the defendant intended to harm the victim or did so actually, in as escalating sequence of aggressive encounters. In the present studies, the intention of the criminal to cause harm was clear. Simulated jurors had to decide whether the evidence was strong enough to tie the accused to the crime. Scruples may play part only when the motives of the defendant are at issue, but not when the evidence is strong enough to convince the simulated jurors that the person being tried really committed the crime. from this viewpoint, one would hope that future studies vary even more features of the cases than the strength of evidence and heinousness. It seems especially important to investigate the various features of the type of cases in which the prosecution modally seeks a 1st degree murder conviction Scruples may effect verdict choices, but only in cases in which the prosecution would not seek the death-penalty (such as cases used by Cowan, wet al., in which the link between the defendant's intention and the crime is so weak that even a charge of 1st degree murder would be unlikely). In other words, scruples may predict verdicts only in cases in which the question of juror death-qualification would be immaterial. More juror sophistry?

Theoretical (Social-Psychological) Issues. A still different approach to explaining our findings might focus on factors that have been shown to affect the attitude-behaviour consistency, for example, the amount of direct experience on which the attitude is based (Fazio & Zanna, 1978) or the degree of presence of factors that might constrain behaviours that would otherwise reflect attitudes (Warner & DeFleur, 1969).

In the former case, one might argue that our college-age subjects were less likely than other registered voters to have had a direct experience with verdict and death-penalty decisions and therefore the relationship between the verdicts (behaviour) and attitudes was not as strong as in previous research. But it is entirely unclear why college students who are taking philosophy, political science, economics, and sociology classes should not have more experience with death-penalty issue than do the average registered voters, especially those (as in the Moran-Comfort 1986 study) whose exposure to the local news media coverage of various felonies is so minimal that they manage to get impaneled (i.e. are not excused during *voir dire* for having already formed an opinion about the guilt of the defendant).

In the latter case, if the stimulus-constraint explanation were correct, one might have expected to find a stronger effect of scruples on verdicts in the weaker evidence conditions of both experiments. This was not the case. The scruples were equally unable to predict verdicts at all evidence (and heinousness) levels. On the other hand, evidence by itself may not be the crucial constraining factor that prevents prior attitudes from affecting behaviour in jury trials. Strong (and authoritatively delivered) judicial instructions to base a decision only on the evidence presented in court may be sufficient to cause jurors to set aside their opinions about the death penalty when contemplating the defendant's guilt. In the present research, we made a special point of emphasizing to all subjects the need to reach decisions solely on the basis of the evidence. It is unclear whether other researchers did the same. If this explanation is correct, it is imperative that future research make every effort to simulate, as closely as possible, not only the content, but the aura of authority and motivational force of CALJIC (or its equivalent) jury instructions. Our observation of *voir dire* in several capital cases suggests that judges and attorneys spend a considerable amount of time before, during, and after *voir dire* explaining that the law requires the verdict and sentence decisions to be independent.

Implications for the Legal System

The second perspective from which the present research can be viewed is the challenge it poses to the persistent attempts by social scientists (a relatively small group of interested researchers, actually) to influence legal thinking and judicial policy on death-qualification issues by reference to the previous simulating studies, the findings of which the present results directly contradict. We believe that their efforts are, and have been even prior to our studies, grossly misguided and misleading.

Regardless of the reasons for the differences in the results between the present and previous studies, the key question that plagues simulation research concerns external validity. As was mentioned in the introduction, we undertook this research within the simulation paradigm in order to make a point about the external validity of the bulk of the past findings. In particular, although some previous studies have used broader subject sampling, they have been manifestly narrow in their sampling of case facts. Researchers who rely exclusively on this methodology (we certainly have not, in our other work on legal decision-making) usually defend their simulation as "more realistic" or as being more externally/ecologically valid than other simulations that produce conflicting findings. Such defensive claims, however, are often logically groundless.

For example, some of the recent studies cited here used videotaped materials, rather than written summaries or questionnaires (Cowan, et al, 1984; Thompson, et al., 1984; Haney, 1984). We assume that this was done because of the authors' intuition that a videotaped presentation of events is somehow better at simulating reality than something written (or, more cynically, a part of a more convincing persuasion package for the courts). Without an empirical substantiation of this claim, it is equally reasonable to argue that in the age of television the subjects are totally desensitised to videotaped presentations of any kind and therefore give make-believe responses to them. Until evidence is painstakingly obtained that speaks directly to the external validity of findings across divergent media of stimulus presentations for specific populations, one is left not knowing which method best simulates the domain to which one wishes to generalize.

As researchers in personality have known for some time, the weakest form of validity is face validity. To infer that a procedure simulates basic processes because the procedure has some distant surface similarity to generalization domain is simply incorrect. To infer that a conclusion has general value because several different methods yield similar results is certainly better logic, but its correctness depends on just how different the various methods really are and on the minute details of the requirement that the results be "consistent" across methods. Our results suggest that the method-specific variance may limit the generality of the relationship between the death-penalty attitudes and verdict decisions.

Besides, what is the significance of increased experimental realism for the issue of death-qualified juries? Trial procedures in a real court of-law create a complex, intimidating, and powerful environment. It is a basic social psychological principle that as situational influences increase, individual behavioural differences decrease (Mischel, 1976). It follows that the more realistic simulations would *suppress* the effects of individual attitudes on verdict decisions and increase the role of situational (i.e., case) factors, such as evidence, to an even greater extent than the present – not very realistic – studies showed.

An additional point about external validity concerns the fact that the death-qualification portion of *voir dire* in capital cases comprises only a very small part of the entire pre-trial selection procedure. The majority of the questions normally asked of veniremen has been ignored in the entire body of research on death-penalty scruples. Not only may prosecuting and defense attorneys use peremptory challenges to excuse veniremen for many reasons other than scruples, but judges typically eliminate a very large portion of veniremen for cause and hardship. It is conceivable that in real trials, the small percentage of veniremen who would be excused on Witherspoon grounds (only 10-15% in our and prior studies), would be eliminated anyway on issues peripheral to the death-penalty attitudes (e.g., pre-trial knowledge of the case, attitudes about crime and criminals, past personal experience with violent crime, etc.)

For example, even though the O.J. Simpson trial is not a capital case, the questionnaire filled out by the potential jurors *prior* to *voir dire* consisted of 61 pages and contained 297 items, many of which had numerous parts with probing "Why do you believe that?" and "If yes, please explain" questions. Nor is this atypical. A questionnaire for veniremen in a recent, virtually unpublicized capital case in

California contained over 140 different multi-part questions. Clearly, the problem of jury bias that is addressed by the death-qualification research may be too circumscribed to warrant the attention it has received.

Judging from face value (an intellectual stance we normally do not recommend, but must now adopt in view of other authors' inferences from their research), the present experiments fully support the current use of death-qualified juries in capital cases. This is because our research, within its framework, unambiguously demonstrates (a) the overriding effect of the strength of evidence on verdict decisions, and (b) the virtually non-existent effect of the Witherspoon-exclusion part of *voir dire* on the subjects' verdicts. To critics who might argue that such conclusions follow from "null" results, we respond that the very use of different scruples measures (an almost unprecedented feat in this area of research), the fact that our different scruples measures all successfully predicted sentencing behaviour, and the fact that the effects of other variables were captured with the same measures, accumulate to a very substantial and consistent pattern of findings. The pattern becomes more significant when it is considered together with the conceptual and methodological critique of prior work.

In our view, there is no logical way to circumvent the paramount importance of thoroughly testing the external validity of research findings before applying them to legal – or any other – system. The high-quality research evidence (in terms of methodological sophistication, data-collection thoroughness, ideologically impartiality, etc.) simply does not exist to warrant a fundamental change in an established procedure, such as a shift to a dual-jury system for the two phases of capital crime trials. We similarly deplore the dearth of evidence (i.e., Haney, 1984) on the basis of which the California Supreme Court mandated the costly and time-consuming sequestration of jurors during the death-qualification *voir dire*.

Monahan and Walker (1985, 1986) have observed that the U.S. legal system is gradually becoming more receptive to social science data. This is objectively an unfortunate development, unless the researchers seriously strive to design studies that may acquire "probative value" (Walker & Monahan, 1988). A social-science finding, by definition, cannot and should not have probative value without possessing a high degree of external validity. And it is extremely difficult for vociferous traditions in social science research – that rely almost exclusively on simulation methods that are often applied in a facile manner, and seem oblivious to their pitfalls – to acquire overnight the discipline and rigor that for example, the archival methodology requires.

Conclusions and Witt

Since *Witherspoon*, the Supreme Court has consistently resisted social scientists' attempts to use the results from simulations to influence the process by which death-qualified juries are selected. The fifteen studies introduced in *Lockart v.*

McCree (1986) were individually criticized by the Court and the brief filed by the American Psychological association on that occasion (Bersoff & Ogden, 1987) fared no better. In fact, even before deciding *McCree*, the Court considerably modified the *Witherspoon* standard in *Wainwright v. Witt* (1985). By citing the language from *Adams v. Texas* (1980), that a potential juror may be excused for cause if his views would "prevent or substantially impair the performance of his duties as a juror in accordance with his instructions and oath" the *Witt* decision – the current death-qualification standard – dispensed with the restrictive terminology of *Witherspoon* and essentially gave judges far broader discretion to exclude potential jurors.

Witt was predictably attacked on legal grounds (e.g., Callans, 1985; Meltzer, 1985; Rosenson, 1986; Thompson, 1989), as was the Court's related reasoning in and interpretation of *Adams, McCree, and Witherspoon* (e.g., Ellsworth, 1991; Faigman, 1991; Thompson, 1989). In some cases, the protests came from barely concealed ideological-*cum*-high-moral positions; occasionally they bordered on discourtesy to the Court, seemingly borne out of impotence to influence its decisions.

With Elliot (1991a, 1991b; 1992; Elliot & Robinson, 1991), we feel – and the data and methodological review presented here support us – that the social scientists' frustration has been well-earned through the inappropriateness of much research regarding death qualification. The Supreme Court has simply continued to indicate its disapproval of the quality of social-science advice it has received since *Witherspoon* invited it.

Appendix 1: Case Summaries

Case Summary, Experiment 1

High Evidence – High Heinousness Condition

At 11:45 p.m. on November 2, 1985, a man entered a convenience store on El Cajon Boulevard, pistol whipped the attendant repeatedly about the head and face, tied him up, forced him to kneel, and shot him through the head, killing him instantly. The gunman then shot the body of the store attendant five more times, took the money from the cash register and ran from the store. Approximately 5 minutes later, a patrol car on its way to the scene, captured a man – the defendant, Robert Green – running down an alley 4 blocks from the scene of the crime.

The Prosecutor's case is as follows:

There were two customers, a man and a woman, in the rear of the store during the entire episode. Both crouched down behind some shelves and were not seen by the gunman. Although they were afraid to move and risk drawing attention to themselves, they could catch glimpses of the crime through cracks between the products on the shelves and were able to hear everything that happened. Their reports of the events of the crime were substantially in agreement: A man entered the store with a gun, beat the attendant brutally and repeatedly with the gun, tied him up, forced him to kneel, and shot him through the head. The gunman then fired five more bullets into the body of the attendant, opened the cash register, filled a bag with money, and ran out of the store. Both witnesses positively identified the defendant, Robert Green, as the man they saw commit the crime. Both agree that the perpetrator was wearing light blue sweat pants, a blue levis denim jacket, and running shoes. When the defendant was taken into custody, de was wearing a t-shirt, light blue sweat pants, and running shoes. Additionally, when captured, he was in possession of $280.000 and could not account for where he obtained the money. Finally, the murder weapon, wrapped in a blue levis jacket was found in a trash dumpster in the alley where the defendant was captured. The jacket fit the defendant.

Case Summary, Experiment 2

Low Eyewitness Evidence – Low Physical Evidence Condition

At 11:45 p.m. on November 2, 1985, a man entcred a convenience store on El Cajon Boulevard, robbed the store, and shot the attendant to death. Approximately 5 minutes later, a police patrol car on its way to the scene, captured a man – the defendant, Robert green – running down an alley near the scene of the crime. The police report stated that the store attendant was shot once through the chest and was dead at the scene. The cash register drawer was open and contained only pennies, nickles, dimes and checks. The store owner estimated that there would have been approximately $250 to 300 in the register at the time of the robbery. The following is a summary of the main points in the case of the People versus Robert Green. The defendant is charged with first degree murder and has pleaded not guilty.

The Prosecutor's case is as follows:

Eyewitness Testimony – A customer in the store who hid behind some shelves and was not seen by the gunman, heard the entire episode. She claimed that the robber entered the store and demanded money. The store attendant, while complying, triggered the store alarm. When the alarm sounded, the robber shouted "Hey, no alarm!" and shot the attendant. The robber then put the money in a bag and ran out of the store. The witness further testified that as the gunman ran out of the store she was able to see that he was wearing faded blue levis and running shoes.

Later, when the police brought the defendant back to the scene and asked him to speak, the witness said that the voice of the man in custody was the same as the voice of the gunman.

Physical Evidence – A bag from the convenience store containing $283.00 was found in a trash dumpster about one block from where the defendant was apprehended. When the defendant was taken into custody he was wearing faded blue levis and running shoes.

The Defense Attorney's case is as follows:

Rebuttal to Eyewitness Testimony – In cross-examination it was pointed out that because the witness in the store was hiding and afraid to be seen by the gunman, she never actually saw anything and cannot identify the defendant as the robber except by the sound of his voice, which is subject to a great deal of human error. it was made clear that she is only speculating about what happened based on what she heard. From her position, crouched down behind the shelves, she was only able to catch a glimpse of the robber's clothes.

Rebuttal to Physical Evidence – The defense argued that the levis and the running shoes prove nothing since it is a very common attire. The defendant testified that he was innocently jogging through the alley when he was taken into custody by police. He said that he had not been in the convenience store at all day and had no knowledge of a murder or any money in a trash dumpster.

The Judge's charge to the Jury is as follows:

As jurors, it is very important to remember that the defendant is presumed to be innocent and the fact of being charged with a crime is not to be taken as evidence against him. You must find guilt beyond a reasonable doubt in order to convict. It is rarely possible to prove anything to an absolute certainty, but the evidence must be such that you, the jury, are willing to rely and act upon it.

Appendix 2: Death Penalty Questionnaire

Death Penalty Questionnaire (Experiment 1)

Please respond to the statements below by indicating after each whether you agree, are not sure, or disagree with the statement.

1. I entertain a conscientious opinion regarding the death penalty such that I could not make an impartial decision as to the defendant's guilt or innocence regardless of the evidence presented.
   _____________*agree*_______________ *not sure* ______________ *disagree*
2. I entertain such conscientious opinions regarding death penalty that I would automatically and without regard to the evidence refuse to find an alleged special circumstances to be true.
   _____________*agree*_______________ *not sure* ______________ *disagree*
3. I entertain conscientious opinions regarding the death penalty such that if I found the defendant guilty of murder in the first degree, I would automatically and without regard for the evidence find the special circumstances to be true.
   _____________*agree*_______________ *not sure* ______________ *disagree*
4. If I found the defendant guilty of murder in the first degree, and further found on of the special circumstances to be true, I would then feel compelled to automatically vote for the death penalty.
   _____________*agree*_______________ *not sure* ______________ *disagree*
5. If I found the special circumstances allegation to be true, I would automatically and without regard for the evidence, vote for life imprisonment without the possibility of parole.
   _____________*agree*_______________ *not sure* ______________ *disagree*
6. I am opposed to the use of the death penalty no matter what the crime.
   _____________*agree*_______________ *not sure* ______________ *disagree*
7. When someone is found guilty of first degree murder, I believe the death penalty should always be the punishment used.
   _____________*agree*_______________ *not sure* ______________ *disagree*
8. When someone is found guilty of first degree murder, there might still be certain circumstances which would make the death penalty *not* appropriate.
   _____________*agree*_______________ *not sure* ______________ *disagree*
9. Sometimes a crime is so brutal and terrible that the death penalty is the only appropriate punishment.
   _____________*agree*_______________ *not sure* ______________ *disagree*
10. I believe the death penalty should be used more often than it is now.
   _____________*agree*_______________ *not sure* ______________ *disagree*

Death Penalty Questionnaire (Experiment 2)

Please respond to the statements below by indicating after each whether you agree, are not sure, or disagree with the statement.

1. When someone is found guilty of first degree murder, I believe the death penalty should *always* be the punishment used.
   _____________ *agree* _______________ *not sure* _______________ *disagree*
2. When someone is found guilty of first degree murder, there might still be certain circumstances which could make the death penalty *not* appropriate.
   _____________ *agree* _______________ *not sure* _______________ *disagree*
3. Sometimes a crime is so brutal and terrible that the death penalty is the *only* appropriate punishment.
   _____________ *agree* _______________ *not sure* _______________ *disagree*
4. I am opposed to the use of the death penalty no matter what the crime.
   _____________ *agree* _______________ *not sure* _______________ *disagree*
5. The death penalty should be used more often than it is now.
   _____________ *agree* _______________ *not sure* _______________ *disagree*
6. If I were a juror in an actual murder trial and the defendant were found guilty of first degree murder, I would *not* be able to vote for the death penalty.
   _____________ *agree* _______________ *not sure* _______________ *disagree*
7. If, on the next election ballot, a measure appears to make the death penalty illegal, I will vote against it (vote to keep the death penalty legal).
   _____________ *agree* _______________ *not sure* _______________ *disagree*
8. The state does *not* have the right to take someone's life no matter what the reason.
   _____________ *agree* _______________ *not sure* _______________ *disagree*
9. Life imprisonment without the possibility of parole is preferable to the death penalty as the maximum penalty allowed by law for capital crimes.
   _____________ *agree* _______________ *not sure* _______________ *disagree*
10. Anyone who intentionally kills another person deserves the same fate.
   _____________ *agree* _______________ *not sure* _______________ *disagree*

References

Adams v Texas 448 U. S. 38 (1980).

Bersoff, D. N., & Ogden, D. W. (1987). In the Supreme Court of the United States: Lockart v. McCree. *American Psychologist*, *42*, 59-68.

Bronson, E. (1970). On the conviction proneness and representativeness of the death qualified jury: An empirical study of Colorado veniremen. *University of Colorado Law Review, 42*, 1-32.

Callans, P. J. (1985). Sixth Amendment. Assembling a jury willing to impose the death penalty: A new disregard for a capital defendant's rights. *Journal of Criminal Law & Criminology, 76*, 1027-1050.

Cowan, C., Thompson, W. & Ellsworth, P. (1984). The effects of death qualification on juror's predisposition to convict and on the quality of deliberation. *Law and Human Behaviour, 8*, 53-60.

Ebbesen, E. B., & Konecni, V. J. (1980). On the external validity of decision-making research: What do we know about decisions in the real world? In T. S. Wallsten (Ed.), *Cognitive processes in choice and decision behaviour*. Hillsdale, NJ: Lawrence Earlbaum Associates.

Ebbesen, E. B., & Konecni, V. J. (1985). Criticism of the criminal justice system: A decision-making analysis. *Behavioural Sciences and the Law, 3*, 177-194.

Elliot, R. (1991a). Social science data and the APA: The Lockart brief as a case in point. *Law and Human Behaviour, 15*, 59-76.

Elliot, R. (1991b). Response to Ellsworth. *Law and Human Behaviour, 15*, 91-94.

Elliot, R. (1992). On the alleged prosecution-proneness of death qualified jurors and juries. In P. Suedfeld & P. Tetlock (Eds.), *Psychology and social policy.* Washington, DC: Hemisphere.

Elliot, R., & Robinson, R. J. (1991). Death penalty attitudes and the tendency to convict or acquit: Some data. *Law and Human Behaviour, 15*, 77-90.

Faigman, D. L. (1991). "Normative Constitutional fact-finding". Exploring the empirical component of Constitutional interpretation. *University of Pennsylvania Law Review, 139*, 541-613.

Fazio, R. H., & Zanna, M. P. (1978). Attitudinal qualities relating to the strength of the attitude-behaviour relationship. *Journal of Experimental Social Psychology, 14*, 398-408.

Goldberg, F. (1970). Toward expansion of Witherspoon: Capital scruples jury bias, and the use of psychological data to raise presumptions in the law. *Harvard Civil Rights-Civil Liberties law Review, 5*, 53-69.

Haney, C. (1984). On selection of capital juries: The biasing effects of the death qualifying process. *Law and Human Behaviour, 8,* 121-132.

Hovey v. California 28 Cal.3d 1 (1980).

Jurow, G. L. (1971). New data on the effects of a death qualified jury on the guilt determination process. *Harvard Law Review, 84*, 567-611.

Konecni, V. J., & Ebbesen E. B. (1979). External validity of research in legal psychology. *Law and Human Behaviour, 3,* 39-70.

Konecni, V. J., & Ebbesen, E. B. (1981). A critique of theory and method in social psychological approaches to legal issues. In B. D. Sales (Ed.), *Perspectives in law and psychology, Volume II: The trial process*. New York: Plenum.

Konecni, V. J., & Ebbesen, E. B. (1982). Social psychology and the law: The choice of research problems, settings and methodology. In V. J. Konecni & E. B. Ebbesen (Eds.), *The criminal justice system: A social psychological analysis*. San Francisco: W. H. Freeman & Co.

Konecni, V. J., & Ebbesen, E. B. (1984). Methodological issues in research on legal decision-making, with special reference to experimental simulations. In F. Lösel, D. Bender, & T. Bliesener (Eds.), *Psychology and Law: International Perspectives*. Berlin, New York: Walter de Gruyter.

Lacayo, R. (1986). Shaking the judicial perch. *Time, 128*, September 15, 76.

Lockart v. McCree, 106 S. Ct 1758 (1986).

Meltzer, C. L. (1985). The battle over standards for death-qualifying juries: Defendants lose another round. *Chicago Kent Law Review, 61*, 611-628.

Mischel, W. (1976). The interaction of personality and the situation. In D. Magnusson & N. S. Miller (Eds.), *Personality at the crossroads: Current issues in interactional psychology.* Hillsdale, NJ: Earlbaum.

Monahan, J., & Walker, L. (1985). *Social science in law: Cases and materials*. Mineola, NY: Foundation Press.

Monahan, J., & Walker, L. (1986). Social authority: Obtaining, evaluating, and establishing social science in law, *University of Pennsylvania Law Review, 134*, 477-517.

Moran, G., & Comfort, J. (1986). Neither "tentative" nor "fragmentary". Verdict preference of impaneled felony jurors as a function of attitude toward capital punishment, *Journal of Applied Psychology, 71*, 146-155.

People v Richard Allen Davis, Sonoma County, California (1985). Unpublished jury questionnaire.

Rosenson, V. T. (1986). Wainwright v Witt: The Court casts a false light backward. *Boston University Law Review, 66*, 311-343.

Tesser, A. (1978). Self-generated attitude change. *Advances in Experimental Social Psychology, 11*, 289-338.

Thompson, W. C. (1989). Death qualification after *Wainwright v. Witt* and *Lockart v. McCree*. *Law and Human Behaviour, 13,* 185-215.

Thompson, W. C., Cowan, C., Ellsworth, P., & Harrington, J. (19849 Death penalty attitudes and conviction proneness: The translation of attitudes into verdicts. *Law and Human Behaviour*, *8*, 95-100.

Wainwright v. Witt 105 S. Ct. 844 (1985).

Walker, L., & Monahan, J. (1985). Social facts: Scientific methodology as legal precedent. *California Law Review, 76*, 877-896.

Wilson, W. (1964). *Belief in capital punishment and jury performance*. Unpublished manuscript, University of Texas.

Witherspoon v. Illinois 391 U.S. 510 (1968).

Zeisel, H. (1968). *Some data on juror attitudes toward capital punishment*. University of Chicago law school: Center for studies in criminal justice.

Parents Fighting for Custody of Children

Alicja Czerederecka

This report summarizes the research carried out so far at the Psychology Department of Institute of Forensic Research on broken-up families, in which both parents fight for custody of their children. These families were investigated at the Institute in connection with the formulating psychological expertise concerning parental competence.

The group differed from other broken families as the conflict between custodians was especially acute and prolonged, both parents sought contact with the children and did not accept solutions proposed by the opposite side, experts psychologists and the court ruling, including a series of appeals and not respecting the court decisions.

The studies referred to a few main questions connected with parental competence of custodians:

1. psychical features deciding about a social adaptation (3),
2. emotional ties with children (2),
3. involving children into the conflict (1),
4. an influence of custodians gender on education of the child (4).

Selection of the group and used methods

Some modifications were made in the selection of group depending on investigated problem, especially from the point of view of methods used when preparing expertise. According to that, while studying social adaptation of custodians, only these causes were taken into consideration, in which both parents were investigated using Rorschach test; the population counted 60 people. When studying emotional ties, the families, whose children were investigated using CAT or TAT, were taken into consideration; the number of examined parents was 84. The problem of involving children into the conflict was measured on the basis of interviews and judicial acts; the criterion of lower limit of child's age of 4,5 was also included and not fewer than one projective test used in their investigation. In this case the number of examined parents was 78. The basis of selection in exploring the influence of custodial gender on development disorders in children were the same criteria as exploring emotional ties, but the care was taken to select two equal groups of children – those under the mother's custody and those under the father's custody. There were 72 custodians in the population.

The acute conflict between parents had lasted for at least for one year, but in most cases, more than three years, and in the time of investigation it concentrated on the problem of how to determine the primary custodian. The psychological expertise was at least second in concern.

The acute conflict between parents had lasted for at least one year, but in most cases, more than three years, and in the time of investigation it concentrated on the problem of how to determine the primary custodians. The psychological expertise was at least second in concern.

Characterisation of the examined group

The age of parents varied from 23 to 49, but the majority of examined people were between 30 and 40. Subjects generally lived in big cities (about 70%), more rarely in villages (13-15%). The examined families had a high standard of living, which, one may assume, is not accidental – the long duration of a divorce case is usually connected with a considerable financial strain, which people having a lower standard of living cannot afford to bear.

The majority of parents had at least secondary education (above 80%) and there was a low percentage of people with only primary school education. At the same time, results of investigations suggested that the intelligence level of the subjects remained within the limits of the norm. Parents were generally physically fit and only 5-6% of population had been treated psychiatrically. A social pathology was found in about 10% of the group (twice more frequent in fathers).

Discussion of the results

Difficulties in social adaptations of people experiencing material failures.

This problem was researched by Alicja Czerederecka and Ewa Wach. The research led to the following conclusions:

A. A person experiencing serious material failure most often:

– is not able to, or does not want to, react to reality according to social expectation and behave conventionally (X+%<70, P<4),

– is prone to avoiding responsibility and to depending on other people's decisions (a+1<p),

– is not able to show emotions in a natural way: reveals them seldom (low Sum C), but in an impulsive (FC<CF+C) or even uncontrolled way (Pure C>0),

– easily gives up expressing his individuality or, on the contrary, reacts in a negative way (S=0 or>2),

– has a lower level of sensitivity to the surrounding and experiences of other people (Blends<4),
– shows a lower sense of self-esteem, or excessive concentration on his own problems, (Ego I<0.33) and a heightened sense of narcissism (Fr>0),
– manifests little interest in other people (low Sum H), or, on the contrary, concentrates on social life in an excessive way (high Sum H),
– in relation with other people he often bases his convictions on his own fantasies (high /H/), is distrustful and suspicious (Hd>H), shows a sense of damage and humiliation (MOR>2), suppresses aggression (AG=0) and is unable to co-operate (COP=0),
– undergoes a deep psychical crisis usually in the form of depression (DEPI I) and a deficiency of defence mechanism (CDI).

B. Putting together results in couples, indicates that particularly unfavourable for the functioning of the union were:
– inability to co-operate within surroundings,
– inadequacy in the evaluation of the situation,
– lack of flexibility of thought,
– difficulties in the modulation of emotion,
– disorder of self-image.

One may assume, that these variables are instrumental in marital failures and cause inability to compromise during and after the divorce. One should underline the disquietingly high results suggesting psychical pathology. The survey showed, that as many as 11 mothers and 9 fathers wanted specialist intervention, while actually only 3 people had been treated. Taking up the therapy on time could have possibly kept the marriage intact or could have led to a separation with less psychical cost.

Emotional ties between parents and children

This problem was researched by Alicja Czerederecka and Teresa Jaskievicz-Obydzinska with the aim of determining the influence of the established mutual emotional bond between parents and children on the conclusion of psychological expertise. This report will be limited to presenting the results concerning emotional attitude of parents.

The research showed, that the mutual emotional ties were stronger between custodians and children of the same gender. Fathers were not as closely attached to children as mothers. Mothers showed stronger ties with children of early school age, and mutual negative relations were found only between parents and older children. A large discrepancy between the declarations and the genuine relationship was found:
– established relationships were usually weaker than declarative ones, especially given by custodians,

– children were usually more closely attached to parents not having direct custody than they declared in the beginning, which shows that they were prejudiced by main custodians,

– recurrently the established attitude towards a child was decidedly worse when the mother was not the main custodian. A suggestion might be put forward that endeavours of these mothers to gain custody were the result of public pressure and did not come from emotional needs (this result is quite significant because such a discrepancy was not found in fathers).

The research of the relation between mutual emotional ties between custodians and children and the satisfaction of psychical needs has also given interesting results:

– satisfaction of needs was found if the emotional ties between fathers and children were strong, but in relations with mother – there occurred slight and inappreciable problems; one may suppose, that the observed difference is the result of greater expectation of children towards the mother than the father, especially those concerning care and the time devoted to them and, at the same time, attributing less authority to her, even treating her as a weak person requiring assistance and protection,

– even of the emotional attitude of children was weaker, the strong bond on the part of parents protected children from the lack of satisfaction of their basic needs,

– when mutual ties decreased, a much greater lack of satisfaction of needs as well as disorders in child's development were found,

– parents weakly connected with children showed a neglecting or excessively demanding attitude towards them; parents whose attitude towards a child was negative usually presented personality disorders in a form of: emotional frigidity, inflexibility, a heightened level of aggression, complete lack of understanding of the children's feelings and also helplessness in dealing with them.

Involving children into the conflict

This problem was examined by Alicja Czerederecka and Teresa Jaskiewicz-Obydzinska in the work concerning factors neutralising development disorders in children from broken-up families.

There were 9 forms of conflicts which had been observed between parents: verbal and physical aggression, manipulation of the child, refusing to consider the solution proposed by the partner (negative attitude), presentation of inadequate and pathological forms of behaviour by one of the parents, inflicting corporeal punishment on children as the transfer of aggression towards the partner, isolation of one of the parents from the conflict (complete separation, lack of contact), involving a wider circle of people, being subject to other court cases (often of criminal nature).

The results showed that simultaneous occurrence of many forms of conflict between parents correlates significantly with developmental disorders shown by the child.

Among discussed forms of conflicts between parents the most important one is child manipulation. As long as the child is not forced to take sides and remains merely a passive observer, despite an acute conflict between parents, he has a chance of a correct development. As the child's involvement into the conflict increases, developmental disorders deepen.

A considerable influence of inadequate patterns of behaviour on the part of the parents and of involving a greater number of people into the conflict on the psychic well-being of the child was also found.

It was observed that isolation of one parent from the conflict led to a diminishing of disorders in the child. One could not, however, exclude that the effect is only temporary, and in the future such a situation may have a disturbing influence on the process of formation of self-image, psycho-sexual attitude patterns, models of family, etc. in the child.

The symptoms of physical and verbal aggression between parents – forms of behaviour so often thought to be, especially by custodians, the main factors disturbing the correct development of the child – had a negligible influence on the formation of disorders in children.

The results of the research proved beyond any doubt (a high correlation) that the isolation of the child from the conflict gives advantageous effects for his development. Practical advice for the main custodian is to concentrate on the protection of the child: do not seek support in them or understanding of one's own negative emotions regarding former partner and, if possible, show him in a positive light.

Custodians' gender and the development disorders in a child

Investigation of this problem was conducted by Alicja Czerederecka and Teresa Jaskiewicz-Obydzinska. The results proved significant differences between children remaining under the custody of parents of different gender:

– fathers' custody much more often was a cause of disorders in each spheres of development: forming self-image, social development, but first of all in emotional development,

– mothers' custody more often warranted correct social development,

– children remaining in father's custody more frequently have shown a fluctuation in self-esteem, unfulfilling of the emotional support and love need or even the safety need, lack of self-depending or inadequacy in coping, isolation from the social life or seeking for help,

– children, whose main custodian was mother more frequently have shown intensive tendency to the denial of conflicts,

– in father's custody much more frequently than in mothers' the educational progress has been found, especially if they have taken care of girls; however this progress has not often created the satisfying state of the child,
– lack of considerable disorders was found only in these cases of father's custody, in which they had taken a custody over children after the pre-school age and whose contact with mother as the second custodian was correct.

The results lead to the conclusion that in the cases of breaking-up of a family fathers can be the main custodian as well as mothers. However, they should incorporate a striving for the establishment of better mutual contacts between a child and a mother into their educational activities much more than they do and not to concentrate on a conflict with former spouse and seeking social support for such forms of behaviour.

The results of the research of the broken-up families gathered up to the present give a picture of strongly "toxic", unfavourable educational environment but, at the same time, they give some advice how to avoid the greatest dangers, even in the circumstances of the strong conflict. It turns out, that in this situation fathers as well as mothers can secure conditions of correct development for the children, if they present loving attitude to them, take care not to involve them into the conflict with the former partner, and try hard to establish correct relations between the second custodian and a child. The last postulate refers especially to fathers as the research confirms the basic importance of mother's participation in a custody, especially of boys and children younger than three.

The above mentioned conditions could be satisfied only when the parents themselves are able to present a mature attitude and a distance to his or her problems with the former partner. As the research of parents' social adaptation shows, disorders and problems presented by parents make it impossible for them to show mature attitudes. The majority of the examined need or even require help of intervention of specialists. Such help should be proposed in the early stage of the court process, and the therapy should be given for the whole family.

The authors plan to lead the research of personality of parents fighting for a custody on the child in the future. Their results could help in working out the program of prophylaxis and therapy of broken-up families.

References

Czerederecka, A., & Jaskiewicz-Obydzinska, T. (1994). Emotional Ties Between Parents and Children and their Influence on the Experts' Opinion Concerning Parental Custody. *Problems of Forensic Sciences.*

Czerederecka, A., & Jaskiewicz-Obydzinska, T. (1996). The Factors Neutralizing Development Disorders in Children from Broken Families. In G. Davies, S. Lloyd-Bostock, M. McMurran, & C. Wilson (Eds.), *Psychology, Law, and Criminal Justice: International Development in Research and Practice.* Berlin, New York: Walter de Gruyter.

Czerederecka, A., & Jaskiewicz-Obydzinska, T. (in print). Custodians Gender and Disorders in Psychical Development of a Child. *Proceedings of The Fourth European Conference of Law and Psychology*, Barcelona.

Czerederecka, A., & Wach, E. (1994). Difficulties in Social Adaptation of Persons Experiencing Marital Failures. *Problems of Forensic Sciences.*

Part 4
Characteristics and Therapy of Offenders

Boys' Behavioral Patterns in Kindergarten Predict Male Delinquency, Withdrawal, and School Adjustment

Richard E. Tremblay and Jaana Haapasalo[1]

In trying to predict later problem behaviors from early behavioral markers, most investigators have relied upon the "variable approach", where one variable assessed at one point in time is correlated with another variable measured at a later point in time. For example, childhood aggression has been showandn to be a good predictor of subsequent antisocial behavior (Farrington, 1994; Loeber & Dishion, 1983; McCord, 1983; Pulkkinen, 1983; Stattin & Magnusson, 1989; Tremblay, Masse, Perron, LeBlanc, Schwartzman, & Ledingham, 1992). Yet, it has been suggested that the variable approach is limited for the study of behavioral development, especially in the field of developmental psychopathology (Cairns, Cairns, Neckerman, Ferguson, & Gariépy, 1989; Hinde & Dennis, 1986; Magnusson & Bergman, 1990). Using aggression and antisocial behavior as an example, it has been shown that other behavioral dimensions, such as anxiety and hyperactivity, can modulate the predictive value of this variable (e.g., Ensminger, Kellam, & Rubin, 1983; Farrington, Loeber, Elliott, Hawkins, Kandel, Klein, McCord, Rowe, & Tremblay, 1990). It is also clear that childhood aggression may lead to other future adjustment problems, besides antisocial behavior (e.g., Dobkin, Tremblay, Mâsse, & Vitaro, 1995; Kellam, Brown, Rubin, & Ensminger, 1983; Robins, 1986; Serbin, Peters, McAffer, & Schwartzman, 1991).

A person-oriented approach has been suggested as an alternative to the variable-oriented approach (e.g., Cattell, 1965; Magnusson, 1988). The full importance of using a person-oriented approach can best be understood in relation to the concept of comorbidity, (i.e., the co-occurrence of different adjustment problems at the same or at different points in time). A configural strategy of research should help to identify groups of children who share a certain set of behaviors and who may follow different developmental pathways. This approach may assist in detecting different

[1] This work was made possible by grants from the Conseil Québécois de la Recherche Sociale, the FCAR fund of the province of Québec, and the Social Sciences and Humanities Research Council of Canada. We are grateful to Héléne Beauchesne and Lucille David for data collection, to Lyse Desmarais-Gervais for data management, to Héléne Boileau for data analyses, to Minh Trinh and Marie-Claude Dumont for documentation, to Chantal Bruneau for manuscript typing, and to Patricia Dobkin for revising the manuscript. We also wish to thank Dr. Rolf Loeber for his helpful comments on the manuscript.

comorbidities as they develop over time and to predict joint occurrences of later behaviors from early behavior patterns (e.g., Loeber, 1990, 1991).

When using the person-oriented approach, for grouping children on the basis of their similarity on behavior problem profiles, a distinction between externalizing and internalizing behavior patterns has been made (e.g., Achenbach, 1989; Cairns & Cairns, 1992). The externalizing behavior pattern has been shown to act as a stepping stone on the developmental path towards delinquency and antisocial behavior (Farrington et al., 1990; Haapasalo & Tremblay, 1994; Stattin & Magnusson, 1989; Tremblay, Boulerice, Arseneault, & Junger, 1995; Tremblay, Mâsse, Vitaro & Dobkin, 1995). Poor school adjustment and educational problems may also be preceded by early externalizing behaviors (e.g., Kupersmidt & Coie, 1990; Loeber, 1988; Parker & Asher, 1987; Slavin, 1989; Tremblay et al., 1992). In a similar vein, anxiety and withdrawal in childhood have been associated with later internalizing disorders (Bowlby, 1988; Kellam, 1990; Kellam et al., 1983). Using dimensions of externalizing and internalizing social behaviors to classify children's behavior problems may prove useful in determining risks for future manifestations of maladjustment (Cicchetti & Toth, 1991). However, there are a number of individuals who show both internalizing and externalizing behavior problems (Achenbach, 1989; Kellam et al., 1983; Toth, Manly, & Cicchetti, 1992). Pulkkinen and Tremblay (1992) identified eight comparable behavior patterns across two cultures, French Canada and Finland. Some of the clusters showed internalizing (e.g., Anxious), some showed externalizing behavior patterns (e.g., Bully), and some evidenced both internalizing and externalizing problems (e.g., Multiproblem). This chapter reports on the links between those childhood behavior patterns and early adolescence adjustment problems, while focusing on the modulating effect of family adversity.

An extensive body of literature has noted family factors which are associated with later externalizing and internalizing behaviors. Bowlby (1988), for example, has suggested that developmental pathways toward internalizing (e.g., depression) and externalizing (e.g., aggression and delinquency) behavior problems are due, in part, to different types of family adversity. A number of researchers have studied family contextual variables, such as socioeconomic position, family size, family structure, and their implications for a child's later adjustment. Pagani, Boulerice & Tremblay (1997) as well as Duncan, Brooks- Gunn & Klebanov (1994) have shown that family income affects cognitive and school performance more than externalizing and internalizing behavior problems. However, Pagani, Boulerice, Tremblay, & Vitaro (1997) showed that divorce, especially during early childhood had an impact on both internalizing and externalizing behavior problems. Also, Blanz, Schmidt, and Esser (1991) found that family adversity was predictive of conduct disorders in particular, while Renken, Egeland, Marvinney, Sroufe, and Mangelsdorf (1989) concluded that the level of life stress in the family increased the prediction of aggressive behavior.

Yet, to date, there have been no predictive studies taking into account the interaction between early behavior patterns and family adversity. Living in a disadvantaged family environment could have differential effects on future adjustment among children who differ from each other in terms of behavioral patterns. Adverse conditions may increase the risk for externalizing behaviors, such as delinquency, for the children who are characterized by early aggressive behavioral patterns, but not for the children with non-aggressive patterns. Conversely, family adversity may increase the risk for internalizing behavioral outcomes, such as withdrawal, for children with non-aggressive patterns but not for those with aggressive patterns.

The purpose of the present study was, first, to examine the relationships between family background and the patterns of social behavior identified by Pulkkinen and Tremblay (1992) for kindergarten boys.

Second, we attempted to predict later social maladjustment (delinquency, school adjustment, and social withdrawal) from an index of family socioeconomic adversity and the different behavior patterns. It was expected that high family adversity would predict differential outcomes in the externalizing and internalizing clusters. Specifically, it was expected that family adversity might increase the risk for delinquency for the externalizing clusters and withdrawal for the internalizing clusters.

Third, the extent to which family adversity and the patterns of behavior predicted comorbidity was explored, i.e., the joint occurrence of delinquency, withdrawal, and school adjustment problems.

Method

Subjects

The sample was comprised of subjects living in low socioeconomic areas of a French schoolboard in Montréal, Canada (Tremblay, Pihl, Dobkin, & Vitaro, 1994). At the end of the 1983-84 school year every teacher of each kindergarten classroom in each school of the low socioeconomic status areas rated the behavior of all his male students. To control for culture, boys were included in the study only if both parents were born in Canada and the parents' mother-tongue was French.

The final sample totaled 1034 boys, who were homogeneous in terms of cultural background (white, French speaking, not immigrant) and represented a somewhat restricted range of socioeconomic status (low to lower middle class). The follow-up data (delinquency, social withdrawal, and school adjustment) was obtained for at least 827 boys at ages 10, 11, 12, and 13.

Measures and procedure

Family background

To investigate the family background, six variables were selected for the analysis. All variables were encoded for age 6. The variables were as follows: mother's and father's occupational status, mother's and father's education (number of years in school), mother's and father's age at the birth of the first child. These variables together with a variable of family structure were combined into an index of family socioeconomic adversity in the way described in more detail by Tremblay, Loeber, Gagnon, Charlebois, Larivée, and LeBlanc (1991). All variables, except the family structure variable, were given a score of one, if a parent was in the lowest 30th percentile of the sample. As for family structure, a score of one was given to all boys who did not live with his two biological parents. The maximum adversity score for a boy living with a biological parent and a step- parent was seven. The maximum score for a boy living with only one parent was four: one point for living in a broken home and three points for the parent being in the lowest 30th percentile on age, years in school, and socioeconomic level. In order to form one scale for all boys, scores for those living with two parents were divided by seven and scores for those living with a single parent were divided by four. This index of familial adversity was used in the analyses in order to give a simple composite measure of the degree of adversity in family. The family adversity score ranged from 0 to 1. For logistic regression statistical analyses, the score was converted into five categories from a score of 0.00–0.19 indicating low adversity to a score of 0.80–1.00 indicating high adversity.

Behavior patterns

The behavior patterns were based on teacher ratings at the end of the kindergarten year when the children were about six years of age (in 1984). The Preschool Behaviour Questionnaire (Behar & Stringfield, 1974) and the Prosocial Behaviour Questionnaire (Weir & Duveen, 1981) were completed by the teachers. The ratings were made on a 3 point scale: doesn't apply, applies sometimes, and certainly applies. Five scales formed from teacher ratings were as follows: *physical aggression* (fights with other children; kicks, bites or hits other children; bullies other children; Cronbach's alpha=0.87), *anxiety* (tends to be fearful or afraid of new things or new situations; cries easily; appears miserable, unhappy, fearful, or distressed; alpha=0.72), *inattention* (has poor concentration or short attention span; inattentive; alpha=0.73), *hyperactivity* (restless, runs about or jumps up and down; doesn't keep still; squirmy, fidgety child; alpha=0.69), and *prosocial behavior* (comforts upset child; helps sick child; helps hurt child; praises other; helps task difficulty; helps clear up mess; shows sympathy; invites bystander; stops quarrels; helps pick up objects; alpha=0.92).

After having been recoded on a four-point scale (0=no characteristic in question, 1=characteristic is not strong, 2=characteristic is clear, 3=a pronounced characteristic), the scales were used as cluster variables. For the cluster analysis, the scale of prosocial behavior was reversed to a scale of nonprosocial behavior. The same procedure was used with teacher ratings from the Jyvaskyla sample. Eight comparable clusters were obtained across the two cultures. Means for the cluster variables are given in Table 1.

Table 1: Cluster Means in the Clustering Variables at Age 6

		Clustering variables				
Clusters	N	Aggression	Anxiety	Inattention	Hyperactivity	Non-prosociality
1. Normal	265	0.29	0.33	0.23	0.32	0.35
2. Anxious	63	0.24	2.37	0.44	0.35	1.13
3. Passive	120	0.19	0.63	1.13	0.55	2.50
4. Inattentive	145	1.15	0.85	2.19	2.23	0.71
5. Nervous	157	0.32	1.31	1.81	0.50	0.59
6. Bully	46	2.07	0.46	0.57	1.98	2.35
7. Uncontrolled	73	2.36	2.11	1.99	2.47	0.55
8. Multiproblem	74	2.19	1.17	2.54	2.52	2.51

The clusters can be described as follows: (1) *Normals* who scored low on all deviant behaviors; (2) *Anxious* who scored high on anxiety but low on all other deviant behaviors.; (3) *Passives* who were characterized by a low score on all variables and a high score on non-prosocialíty, indicating low levels of activity; (4) *Inattentives* who scored high only on inattention and hyperactivity, as would children with the attention deficit hyperactivity disorder; (5) *Nervous* who had high scores only on anxiety and inattention; (6) *Bullies* who were aggressive, non-prosocial, and hyperactive but scored low on anxiety and inattention; (7) *Uncontrolled* who were high on hyperactivity, anxiety, inattention, and aggression but did not indicate a lack of prosociality; and (8) *Multiproblem* who scored high on all variables.

Delinquency

At age 10, 11, 12, and 13 years the boys answered a 27-item self-reported delinquency scale (LeBlanc & Tremblay, 1988) which included four subscales (physical aggression, stealing, vandalism, alcohol and drug use). The scale includes items such as "destroy school material", "steal in store", "force others by threatening to beat-up", "take part in group fights", "drink alcohol", "vandalise car", "trespassing", etc. The responses for each item were given on a 4-point scale (never to very often). Thus, the total delinquency scale comprised both the frequency and the range of behaviors. The internal reliabilities (alpha coefficient) for the total delinquency scale were 0.87, 0.88, 0.86 and 0.89 at ages 10, 11, 12, and 13, respectively.

The boys who were above the 20th percentile on the total delinquency scale, for three years out of four, were considered delinquent. This criteria led to the identification of a group of 77 boys (9.3% of the total sample) who were thus labeled.

Social withdrawal

Peer nominations at age 10, 11, and 12 years were used to generate a measure of social withdrawal. The nominations were made by using the Pupil Evaluation Inventory (Pekarik, Prinz, Liebert, Weintraub, & Neale, 1976) containing 34 short behavior descriptors and yielding three factors: disruptive behavior (20 items), withdrawal (9 items), and likability (5 items). Each child in the class was asked to identify four children in his class who were best described by each of the items. Assessments of withdrawal were based on the following items: those who are too shy to make friends easily; those whose feelings are too easily hurt; those who never seem to be having a good time; those who are upset when called on to answer questions in class; those who are usually chosen last to join group activities; those who have very few friends; those who are unhappy or sad; those who often *don't* want to play, and those who aren't noticed much. The internal reliabilities (alpha coefficient) of the withdrawal scale were 0.84, 0.85, and 0.93 at ages 10, 11, and 12 years, respectively. The boys who scored above the 20th percentile on withdrawal in two years out of three were designated as withdrawn. This criteria led to the identification of 80 boys (10.2% of the total sample) as the withdrawn group.

School adjustment

Those subjects who were held back more than one year and/or who were placed in a special environment (special class, special school or residential institution) at age 13 years were classified as having difficulties in school adjustment. Using this criteria, 195 boys (22.0% of the total sample) were regarded as having difficulties in school adjustment. Being in a regular classroom appropriate for the boy's age was regarded as a better measure of school adjustment than grade point averages, since a boy who was held back could have relatively high grade point average compared to another at his age- appropriate level.

Data analysis

Comparisons between the clusters in the family background variables were computed with one-way analyses of variance and post hoc comparisons for pairwise differences. Prediction of later social adjustment from the family adversity index and early behavioral patterns (eight clusters) was completed by using logistic regression analysis with delinquency, social withdrawal, and school adjustment as dependent variables.

Results

Boys' behavior patterns and family background

The differences between the clusters for the family background variables are illustrated in Table 2. The eight clusters having been composed at the age of six years differed from each other in all background variables, apart from the father's age at birth of first-born child. Post hoc analyses indicated (Newman-Keuls, $p=0.05$) that there were pairwise significant differences between the clusters in all variables, except for father's age. In particular, a number of pairwise differences between the groups emerged with the index of family adversity. The Normals and the Nervous boys had significantly less family adversity compared to five clusters: Passive, Inattentive, Bully, Uncontrolled, and Multiproblem. In addition, the Anxious boys had significantly less family adversity compared to the Bullies and the Multiproblem boys.

Family adversity, behavior patterns, and later social adjustment To predict social maladjustment in early adolescence from family adversity and early patterns of social behavior in the Montreal sample, a stepwise logistic regression analysis was used with family adversity and clusters as the categorical independent predictor variables and delinquency, withdrawal, and school adjustment as the dependent outcome variables. Family adversity was entered first into the prediction equation, followed by clusters, since family adversity presumably precedes behavioral patterns. Beta coefficients and odds ratios for predicting delinquency, withdrawal, and school adjustment from family adversity are indicated in Table 3. Family adversity failed to significantly predict withdrawal, while it was successful in predicting delinquency and school adjustment.

Table 4 summarizes the chi square goodness-of-fit of the model with family adversity and kindergarten behavior patterns (clusters) as predictors for all the outcome variables. Improvement chi squares were used to test whether the cluster variable entered into the equation after family adversity significantly improved prediction. Adding the clusters into the equation significantly improved the prediction for each outcome variable. There were no significant interactions between the clusters and family adversity.

Table 2: Family Background Differences for Clusters at Age 6

		Occupational Status		Education		Age at birth of 1st child		FAI[2]
		Mothers	Fathers	Mothers	Fathers	Mothers	Fathers	
Clusters	N[1]	M (SD)	M (SD)	M (SD)	M (SD)	M (SD)	M (SD)	M (SD)
1.Normal	259	41.36 (11.8)	42.42 (13.9)	11.11 (2.6)	11.27 (3.2)	23.61 (3.8)	26.08 (4.3)	0.24 (0.21)
2.Anxious	61	40.65 (14.1)	41.13 (14.8)	10.65 (3.2)	11.00 (3.5)	24.41 (4.3)	27.42 (5.5)	0.29 (0.24)
3.Passive	114	36.19 (12.0)	39.16 (12.3)	10.10 (2.8)	10.07 (3.3)	23.03 (4.1)	26.08 (4.5)	0.34 (0.26)
4.Inattentive	142	37.17 (12.4)	40.11 (13.4)	10.21 (3.2)	9.90 (3.5)	23.05 (4.4)	25.47 (4.8)	0.37 (0.24)
5.Nervous	150	36.52 (10.7)	37.25 (11.1)	10.50 (2.6)	10.34 (2.9)	23.25 (3.6)	26.36 (4.9)	0.27 (0.22)
6.Bully	41	32.87 (9.3)	32.56 (6.6)	9.80 (2.0)	9.71 (2.4)	21.57 (3.7)	25.60 (5.6)	0.45 (0.25)
7.Uncontrolled	72	36.37 (11.1)	36.30 (11.5)	10.22 (2.3)	10.36 (2.6)	22.05 (4.0)	25.19 (4.6)	0.37 (0.24)
8.Multiproblem	69	37.05 (11.4)	35.30 (10.4)	9.79 (2.8)	9.83 (3.5)	22.14 (3.8)	25.60 (6.3)	0.43 (0.25)
F		4.91***	5.51***	3.41***	3.85***	3.64***	1.16	10.12***
Newman-Keuls p=0.05		3,4,5,6,7<1	5,6,7,8<1 6<2,4	3,4,8<1	3,4,5,8<1	6,7,8<2 6,7<1	—	1,5<3,4,6,7,8 2<6,8

[1] Ns vary due to missing data
[2] FAI=Family Adversity Index
** p<0.01; *** p<0.001

Odds ratios were calculated from the logistic regression coefficients to show the odds of each cluster becoming delinquent, withdrawn or having school adjustment problems, using the Normal group as the base rate. It should be recalled that family adversity was controlled for by entering it first in the equation. Odds ratios for all outcomes are shown in Table 5. With regard to delinquency, the odds of the Inattentives, Bullies, and Multiproblem boys to be classified delinquent were higher (about 3 to 5 times) than those of the Normals. The odds of the Anxious, Nervous, and Multiproblem boys to be classified as withdrawn in early adolescence were approximately 2.3 to 3.5 times greater than the odds of the Normals. For school adjustment, all clusters, except the Anxious boys cluster, had higher odds of being classified maladjusted than the Normals. The Multiproblem boys were 12.3 times more at risk for school adjustment problems compared to the Normal cluster.

As expected, in comparison with the cluster of "normal" boys the kindergarten externalizing behavioral patterns more likely lead to delinquency, while the kindergarten internalizing behaviors resulted more often in withdrawal. Poor school adjustment was a high probability outcome for all forms of kindergarten deviant patterns, but particularly for the Inattentive, Uncontrolled, and Multiproblem boys as compared to the Normals.

Table 3: Prediction of Delinquency, Withdrawal, and School Adjustment from Family Adversity

Outcome	Beta Coefficient	Wald	p	Odds ratio
Delinquency	0.25	6.61	0.01	1.30
Withdrawal	0.06	0.37	0.54	1.06
School Adjustment	0.53	56.29	0.00	1.71

Table 4: Stepwise Logistic Regression Model for Delinquency, Withdrawal and School Adjustment with Family Adversity and Clusters as Predictors

Outcome variable	Improvement		Goodness-of-fit	
and steps in the model	x^2	p	x^2	p
Delinquency				
1. Adversity	6.45	0.011	820.10	0.541
2. Clusters	27.77	0.000	822.29	0.441
Withdrawal				
1. Adversity	0.37	0.544	782.00	0.473
2. Clusters	26.59	0.000	786.58	0.350
School adjustment				
1. Adversity	58.99	0.000	875.54	0.592
2. Clusters	73.53	0.000	882.35	0.452

Table 5: Risk (Odds Ratios) of Being Delinquent, Withdrawn and Poorly Adjusted in School for Seven Clusters Compared to the Normals (Controlling for Family Adversity)

Clusters	Delinquency	Withdrawal	School Adjustment
Anxious	1.36	3.52**	1.74
Passive	1.05	1.63	2.73**
Inattentive	3.12**	1.12	5.31***
Nervous	0.79	2.32*	2.82**
Bullies	5.06**	0.40	3.18**
Uncontrolled	2.61	1.67	4.02***
Multiproblem	5.13***	3.21**	12.32***

* $p<0.05$; ** $p<0.01$; *** $p<0.001$

The odds of the Multiproblem boys to develop all negative outcomes were high. This appears to imply comorbidity of delinquency, withdrawal, and poor school adjustment in early adolescence for the boys who show multiple behavior problems in kindergarten. To investigate whether these results for groups in effect reflected comorbidity for individuals, all the combinations of outcomes were cross-tabulated with the clusters, as presented in Table 6. The majority of subjects with some form of kindergarten maladjustment had only one problem (27.9%), 5.6% had two problems, and only one subject had three problems. The Multiproblem kindergarten group had the highest percentage of subjects with comorbidity in early adolescence (20.9%). Comorbidity of delinquency and poor school adjustment was relatively high among the boys who showed Inattentive (6.2%), Bully (6.5%), and Multiproblem (10.4%) patterns in kindergarten. Comorbidity of withdrawal and poor school adjustment was also relatively high for the Multiproblem kindergarten boys (6.3%). It should be noted that comorbidity of delinquency and withdrawal was observed for only three subjects.

Table 6: Comorbidity of Delinquency, Withdrawal, and School Maladjustment in Early Adolescence for the Eight Kindergarten Behavior Clusters

		No problems	One problem			Two problems			Three problems
Kindergarten Clusters	Total N		W	D	S	D+W	W+S	D+S	D+W+S
1. Normal	213	84.0	5.2	3.8	4.2	0.5	0.9	1.4	0.0
2. Anxious	47	57.4	23.4	4.3	10.6	0.0	2.1	2.1	0.0
3. Passive	90	66.7	7.8	3.3	17.8	0.0	2.2	2.2	0.0
4. Inattentive	113	54.9	3.5	8.0	23.0	0.9	3.5	6.2	0.0
5. Nervous	121	62.0	12.4	4.1	17.4	0.0	2.5	1.7	0.0
6. Bully	31	61.3	0.0	16.1	12.9	0.0	3.2	6.5	0.0
7. Uncontrolled	60	56.7	8.3	10.0	18.3	0.0	3.3	3.3	0.0
8. Multiproblem	48	31.3	10.4	8.3	29.2	2.1	6.3	10.4	2.1
Total (%)	723	65.1	8.0	5.8	14.7	0.4	2.5	3.3	0.1

Note: N=723 due to missing data, W=Withdrawal, D=Delinquency, S=School maladjustment

Discussion

The power of family adversity and early patterns of social behavior to predict later social maladjustment was investigated in the present study. It was proposed that unfavorable family conditions, reflected in an index of family adversity, might have differential effects when different early behavioral clusters are considered. Specifically, it was hypothesized that family adversity would increase the risk of delinquency for the externalizing clusters but not for the internalizing cluster, while the reverse would be true for social withdrawal. Further, comorbidity of behavior problems in early adolescence as predicted from family adversity and the eight patterns of kindergarten behavior was examined.

First, it can be inferred from the results that the kindergarten boys with behavior problems, particularly the Bullies and Multiproblem boys, tended to come from more disadvantaged family environments, i.e., parents with low levels of education, who had their first child when they were young, who had a low SES job, and who did not live together. The findings supported the assumption that, even within low SES environments, family adversity predicts delinquency and poor school adjustment. The hypothesis that boys in the externalizing clusters are at high risk for delinquency and those in the internalizing clusters at high risk for withdrawal in early adolescence, after family adversity has been controlled for, was also confirmed by the results. The Inattentives, Bullies, and Multiproblem boys were at higher risk for delinquency than the Normals. Risk for withdrawal was higher for the Anxious, Nervous, and Multiproblem boys as compared to the Normals. Poor school adjustment was a higher risk for all clusters compared to the Normals, except for the Anxious boys; but the Multiproblem boys had by far the highest risk. By contrast, the results failed to substantiate the presumed interactions between family adversity and early behavioral patterns. High adversity did increase the risk for delinquency in the externalizing clusters, but it failed to increase the risk for withdrawal in the internalizing clusters. The risk for the Multiproblem boys, who had both externalizing and internalizing behavior problems in kindergarten, of having all the negative outcomes (delinquency, withdrawal, and poor school adjustment) in early adolescence was considerable as compared to the group of Normal boys. Comorbidity of delinquency and school problems was present to some extent for the Inattentive, Bullies and Multiproblem boys. However, it was obvious that most of the boys with problems had only one problem. A small proportion of the sample had comorbidity of problems (5.9olo).

Risk for poor school adjustment was high for all groups of boys in comparison with the Normals, but the effect was most flagrant for the Multiproblem, Inattentive, and Uncontrolled boys. It should be noted that inattention and hyperactivity were the common denominators of these three clusters (see Table 1). These behaviors are known to be related to school problems (e.g. Barkley, 1990; Farrington et al., 1990). Hence, they may well contribute to low performance and adjustment difficulties at school for these three groups of boys. Hyperactivity and attention problems of the Uncontrolled boys may place them at higher risk for poor school adjustment, while their relatively high anxiety score (see Table 1) may protect them more than other aggressive clusters against delinquency. There is good evidence that internalizing tendencies, such as shyness, anxiety or neuroticism, serve as protective factors against later delinquency and antisocial behavior (Farrington, Gallagher, Morley, Ledger, & West, 1988; Kerr, Tremblay, Pagani, & Vitaro, 1997; McCord, 1987). This was clearly the case for the Anxious cluster in this sample.

Family adversity proved to be an important predictor for delinquency and school adjustment but not for later withdrawal. This result requires an explanation. First, there is evidence that the two most important components of social withdrawal (behavioral inhibition, and lack of social reward dependence or psychotism) are under relatively high genetic control (Cloninger, 1987; Kagan, Anidman, & Arcus,1992; Kagan, Reznick, & Snidman,1988). If they were under more genetic control than delinquency and school adjustment, environmental effects on

social withdrawal would be more limited than on delinquency and school adjustment. Second, failure to predict withdrawal from family adversity might be explained by the composition of the adversity index. It included variables that were related to parents' social adjustment (schooling, early parenting, job SES, divorce). Using family functioning variables could perhaps help to predict withdrawal from family conditions. This explanation is supported
by the finding that parental conflict and maternal depression predict children's internalizing problems (Shaw & Emery, 1989). However, the later study did not take into account co-morbidity, and it did not look for differential gender effects, our study included only males.

The person-oriented approach employed in this study is congruent with the conceptualization of different developmental pathways from childhood to adult life (Loeber et al., 1993; Rutter, 1989). Grouping individuals by means of their behavioral patterns at two points in time renders it possible to describe developmental pathways. Our results indicated five probabilistic pathways from kindergarten to early adolescence. First, the "Normal pathway" for boys who are within the normal range at both points in time. Second, the "Anxiety pathway" where kindergarten anxiety leads to social withdrawal. Third, the "Nervous pathway" where kindergarten nervousness leads to social withdrawal and school adjustment problems. Fourth, the "Inattentive-Bully pathway" where kindergarten inattentiveness or bullying lead to delinquency and school problems. Finally, the multiproblem pathway, where multiproblems in kindergarten lead to delinquency, social withdrawal and school problems. Some of these pathways have been reported in previous studies (e.g., Ensminger et al.,1983; Farrington, Loeber, & Van Kammen,1990; Kellam et al.,1983; McCord,1987; Moffitt,1990). However, no study had previously related as many predictors and outcomes. This was made possible by the large sample of homogeneous subjects who were available and on whom a variety of dimensions were measured. It should be noted also that the outcome was based on repeated measures for 3 or 4 years during early adolescence. Despite this effort to obtain the largest sample possible with a large set of data, Table 6 shows that we still ran short of subjects to obtain adequate samples of boys in each of the outcome categories, considering the 8 predictor and 4 outcome categories. This is obviously a limitation of the person oriented approach. However, if we are to better understand the development of adjustment problems we will have to use the appropriate samples. Clearly we need large samples of subjects who are followed for long periods of time with repeated measures.

References

Achenbach, T. M. (1989). Empirically based assessment of child and adolescent disorders: Implications for diagnosis, classification, epidemiology, and longitudinal research. In M. Brambring, F. Lösel, & H. Skowronek (Eds.), *Children at Risk: Assessment, Research, and Intervention* (pp. 24-45). Berlin, New York: Walter de Gruyter.

Barkley, R. A. (1990). Attention deficit disorders: History, definition, and diagnosis. In M. Lewis & S. M. Miller (Eds.), *Handbook of Developmental Psychopathology* (pp. 65-75). New York: Plenum.

Behar, L. B., & Stringfield, S. (1974). A behavior rating scale for the preschool child. *Developmental Psychology, 10*, 601-610.

Blanz, B., Schmidt, M. H., & Esser, G. (1991). Familial adversities and child psychiatric disorders. *Journal of Children Psychology and Psychiatry, 32*, 939-950.

Bowlby, J. (1988). Developmental psychiatry comes of age. *American Journal of Psychiatry, 145*, 1-10.

Cairns, B. R., Cairns, B. D., Neckerman, H. J., Ferguson, L. L., & Gariépy, J. L. (1989). Growth and aggression: 1. Childhood to early adolescence. *Developmental Psychology, 25*, 320-330.

Cairns, R. B. & Cairns, B. D. (1992). The sociogenesis of aggressive and antisocial behaviors. In J. McCord (Ed.), Facts, frameworks, and forecasts: *Advances in Criminological Theory* (pp. 157-191). New-Brunswick: Transaction.

Cattell, R. B. (1965). *The Scientific Analysis of Personality*. Chicago: Aldine.

Cicchetti, D., & Toth, S. L. (1991). *International and externalizing expressions of dysfunction: Rochester symposium on developmental psychopathology 2*. Hillsdale, NJ: Erlbaum.

Cloninger, R. C. (1987). A systematic method for clinical description and classification of personality variants. *Archives of General Psychiatry, 44*, 573-588.

Dobkin, P. L., Tremblay, R. E., Mâsse, L. C., & Vitaro, F. (1995). Individual and peer characteristics in predicting boys' early onset of substance abuse: A seven-year longitudinal study. *Child Development. 66*, 1198-1214.

Ensminger, M. E., Kellam, S. G., & Rubin, B. R. (1983). School and family origins of delinquency: Comparisons by sex. In K. T. Van Dusen & S. A. Mednick (Eds.), *Prospective Studies of Crime and Delinquency* (pp. 73-97). Boston, MA: Kluwer-Nifhoff.

Farrington, D. P. (1994). Childhood, adolescent, and adult features of violent males. In L. R. Huesmann (Ed.), *Aggressive behavior: Current perspectives*, (pp. 215-240). New York: Plenum Press.

Farrington, D. P. (1991). Childhood aggression and adult violence: Early precursors and life outcomes. In D. J. Pepler & K. H. Rubin (Eds.), *Development and treatment of childhood aggression.* (pp. 5-29). Toronto: Lawrence Erlbaum.

Farrington, D. P., Gallagher, B., Morley, L., Ledger, R. J., & West, D. J. (1988). Are there any successful men from criminogenic backgrounds? *Psychiatry, 51*, 116-130.

Farrington, D. P., Loeber, R., Elliott, D. S., Hawkins, J. D., Kandel, D. B., Klein, M. W., McCord, J., Rowe, D. C., & Tremblay, R. E. (1990). Advancing knowledge about the onset of delinquency and crime. In B. B. Lahey & A. E. Kazdin (Eds.), *Advances in clinical child psychology* (pp. 283-342). New York: Plenum.

Farrington, D. P., Loeber, R., & Van Kammen, W. B. (1990). The long term criminal outcomes of conduct problem boys with or without impulsive – Inattentive behavior. In L. Robins & M. Rutter (Eds.), *Straight and devious pathways from childhood to adulthood* (pp. 62-81). New York: Cambridge University Press.

Haapasalo, J., & Tremblay, R. E. (1994). Physically aggressive boys from ages 6 to 12: Family background, parenting behavior, and prediction of delinquency. *Journal of Consulting and Clinical Psychology. 62 (5)*, 1044-1052.

Hinde, R. A., & Dennis, A. (1986). Categorizing individuals: An alternative to linear analysis. *International Journal of Behavioral Development, 9*, 105-119.

Kagan, J., Anidman, N., & Arcus, D. M. (1992). Initial reactions to unfamiliarity. *Current Directions in Psychological Science, 6*, 171-174.

Kagan, J., Reznick, J. S., & Snidman, N. (1988). Biological bases of childhood shyness. *Science, 240*, 167-171.

Kellam, S. G. (1990). Developmental epidemiologic framework for family research on depression and aggression. In G. R. Patterson (Ed.), *Depression and aggression in family interaction* (pp. 11-48). Englewood Cliffs, NJ: Erlbaum.

Kellam, S. G., Brown, C. H., Rubin, B. R., & Ensminger, M. E. (1983). Paths leading to teenage psychiatric symptoms and substance use: Developmental epidemiological studies in Woodlawn. In S. B. Guze, F. J. Earls, & J. E. Barrett (Eds.), *Childhood psychopathology and development.* New York: Ravan Press.

Kerr, M., Tremblay, R. E., Pagani-Kurtz, L., & Vitaro, F. (in press). Boys' behavioral inhibition and the risk of later delinquency. *Archives of General Psychiatry.*

Kupersmidt, J. B., & Coie, J. D. (1990). Preadolescent peer status, aggression, and school adjustment as predictors of externalizing problems in adolescence. *Child Development, 61*, 1350-1362.

LeBlanc, M., & Tremblay, R. E. (1988). A study of factors associated with the stability of hidden delinquency. *International Journal of Adolescence and Youth, 1*, 269-291.

Loeber, R. (1988). Natural histories of conduct problems, delinquency, and associated substance use: Evidence for developmental progressions. In B. B. Lahey & A. E. Kazdin (Eds.), *Advances in clinical child psychology* (pp·73-124). New York: Plenum.

Loeber, R. (1990). Development and risk factors of juvenile antisocial behavior and delinquency. *Clinical Psychology Review*, 10, 1-41.

Loeber, R. (1991). Questions and advances in the study of developmental pathways. In D. Cicchetti & S. Toth (Eds.), *Models and integrations. Rochester symposium on developmental psychopathology* (pp.·97-115). Rochester: University of Rochester Press.

Loeber, R., & Dishion, T. J. (1983). Early predictors of male delinquency: A review. *Psychological Bulletin, 94*, 68-99.

Loeber, R., Wung, P., Keenan, K., Giroux, B., Southamer-Loeber, M., Van Kammen, W. B., & Maughan, B. (1993). Developmental pathways in disruptive child behavior. *Development and Psychopathology, 5*, 103-133.

Magnusson, D. (1988). *Individual development from an interactional perspective: A lonqitudinal study.* Hillsdale, NJ: Erlbaum.

Magnusson, D., & Bergman, L. R. (1990). A pattern approach to the study of pathways from childhood to adulthood. In L. N. Robins & M. Rutter (Eds.), *Straight and devious pathways from childhood to adulthood* (pp. 101-116). New York: Cambridge University Press.

McCord, J. (1983). A longitudinal study of aggression and antisocial behavior. In K. T. Van Dusen & S. A. Mednick (Eds.), *Prospective studies of crime and delinquency* (pp. 269-275). Boston: Kluwer-Nijhoff.

McCord, J. (1987). Aggression and shyness as predictors of problems: Another view. In *Biennial meeting of the Society for Research in Child Development*. Baltimore.

Moffitt, T. E. (1990a). Juvenile delinquency and attention deficit disorder: Developmental trajectories from age 3 to age 15. *Child Development, 61*, 893-910.

Pagani, L., Boulerice, B., & Tremblay, R. E. (1997). The influence of poverty on children's classroom placement and behavior problems. In G. Duncan & J. Brooks-Gunn (Eds.), *Consequences of growing up poor*, (pp. 311-339). New York: Russel Sage Foundation.

Pagani, L., Boulerice, B., Tremblay, R. E., & Vitaro, F. (in press). Behavioural development in children of divorce and remarriage. *Journal of Child Psychology and Psychiatry.*

Parker, J. G., & Asher, S. R. (1987). Peer relations and later personal adjustment: Are low accepted children "at risk"? *Psychological Bulletin, 102*, 357-389.

Pekarik, E. G., Prinz, R. J., Liebert, D. E., Weintraub, S., & Neale, J. N. (1976). The Pupil Evaluation Inventory. *Journal of Abnormal Child Psychology, 4* (1), 83-97.

Pulkkinen, L. (1983). The search for alternatives to aggression. In A. P. Goldstein & M. H. Segal (Eds.), *Aggression in global perspective* (pp. 104-144). New-York: Pergarnon Press.

Pulkkinen, L., & Tremblay, R. E. (1992). Patterns of boys' social adjustment in two cultures and at different ages: A longitudinal perspective. *International Journal of Behavioural Development, 15*, 527-553.

Renken, B., Egeland, B., Marvinney, D., Sroufe, L. A., & Mangelsdorf, S. (1989). Early childhood antecedents of aggression and passive-withdrawal in early elementary school. *Journal of Personality, 57*, 257-281.

Robins, L. (1986). Changes in conduct disorder overtime. In D. C. Farran & J. D. McKinney (Eds.), *Risk in intellectual and psychosocial development* (pp. 227-259). Orlando, FL: Academic Press.

Rubin, K. H., & Mills, R. S. L. (1991). Conceptualizing developmental pathways to internalizing disorders in childhood. *Canadian Journal of Behavioral Science, 23*, 300-317.

Rutter, M. (1989). Pathways from childhood to adult life. *Journal of Child Psychology and Psychiatry, 30*, 23-51.

Serbin, R. E., Peters, P. L., McAffer, V. J., & Schwartzman, A. E. (1991). Childhood aggression and withdrawal as predictors of adolescent pregnancy, early parenthood, and environmental risk for the next generation. *Canadian Journal of Behavioural Science, 23*, 318-331.

Shaw, D. S., & Emery, R. E. (1989). Chronic family adversity and school-age children's adjustment. *Journal of the American Academy of Child and Adolescent Psychiatry, 27*, 200-206.

Slavin, R. E. (1989). Students at risk of school failure. The problem and its dimensions. In R. E. Slavin, N. L. Karweit, & N. A. Madden (Eds.), *Effective programs for students at risk* (pp. 3-19). Boston: Allyn and Bacon.

Stattin, H., & Magnusson, D. (1989). The role of early aggressive behavior in the frequency, seriousness and types of later crime. *Journal of Consulting and Clinical Psychology, 57*, 710-718.

Toth, S. L., Manly, J. T., & Cicchetti, D. (1992). Child maltreatment and vulnerability to depression. *Development and Psychopathology, 4*, 97-112.

Tremblay, R. E., Boulerice, B., Junger, M., & Arseneault, L. (1995). Does low self-control during childhood explain the association between delinquency and accidents in early adolescence? *Journal of Criminal Behavior and Mental Health. 5*, 330-345.

Tremblay, R. E., Loeber, R., Gagnon, C., Charlebois, P., Larivée, S., & LeBlanc, M. (1991). Disruptive boys with stable and unstable high fighting behavior patterns during junior elementary school. *Journal of Abnormal Child Psychology, 19* (3), 285-300.

Tremblay, R. E., Masse, B., Perron, D., LeBlanc, M., Schwartzman, A. E., & Ledingham, J. E. (1992). Early disruptive behavior, poor school achievement, delinquent behavior and delinquent personality: Longitudinal analyses. *Journal of Consulting and Clinical Psychology, 60*, 64-72.

Tremblay, R. E., Mâsse, L. C., Vitaro, F., & Dobkin, P. L. (1995). The impact of friends' deviant behavior on early onset of delinquency: Longitudinal data from 6 to 13 years of age. *Development and Psychopathology, 7* (4), 649-668.

Tremblay, R. E., Pihl, R. O., Vitaro, F., & Dobkin, P. L. (1994). Predicting early onset of male antisocial behavior from preschool behavior. *Archives of General Psychiatry, 51*, 732-738.

Weir, K., & Duveen, G. (1981). Further development and validation of the prosocial behaviour questionnaire for use by teachers. *Journal of Child Psychology and Psychiatry, 22*, 357-374.

Assessing Loss of Self-Control in Violent Offences Committed by Juveniles

James McGuire

A majority of researchers and writers on human aggression have endorsed the usefulness of a fundamental distinction between instrumental and affective aggression. This is a widely accepted conceptual division within psychological approaches to the understanding of such behaviour and has been reiterated and clarified in recent overviews of aggression and of criminal violence (see for example Berkowitz, 1993; Blackburn, 1993; Green, 1990).

Instrumental aggression is defined as a form of behaviour in which injury facilitates attainment of non-aggressive goals, such as might occur in the offence of robbery. By contrast, in *affective* or *expressive aggression*, harm or injury to the victim reduces an aversive emotional state in the aggressor.

The usefulness of this distinction could be illustrated with reference to laboratory studies, to criminological surveys, or to theory-construction. Its relevance to the study to be described here, however, is in respect of different approaches to 'treatment'. While it must be recognised that many violent acts are situation-specific, the focus in much research is upon the individual who repeatedly behaves in an aggressive manner and who is also then likely to resort to physical violence. Such an individual may be fairly easily provoked; may perceive threat and insult where others would not; or may react in what appears to others to be an unjustified or disproportionate manner.

The consequences of such acts may be disadvantageous to the actor him- or herself, and the individual concerned may have other adjustment difficulties associated with a generally high levels of tension. At the same time, such individuals may not be readily distinguishable from others by means of any uni-dimensional personality construct like neuroticism or impulsiveness alone. There is evidence, however, that people do differ in respect of their emotional expressiveness and readiness to resort to physical assault when aroused, and that despite situational variations there are some trans-situational consistencies in aggression-proneness. Longitudinal studies reviewed by Olweus (1988) suggest that aggressiveness may be a relatively stable feature of individuals over periods spanning several years.

Affective Aggression and Anger Control Training

The majority of psychological studies of aggression and of violent criminal acts have thus focused on the second of the two categories delineated above: affective or emotional aggression. In particular, clinical studies on treatment designed to reduce the propensity to act violently have dealt with the role of *anger* in instigating aggression. A number of clinical research studies in the 1970s and 1980s suggested that individuals who have poor self-control of anger could be helped to achieve greater control by means of a specific form of intervention called *Anger Control Training*. The initial studies of this were undertaken by Novaco (1975).

Since Novaco's work, a number of authors have extended his basic model to other groups, including: abusive parents (Denicola & Sandler, 1980; Nomellini & Katz, 1983); psychiatric patients (Feindler, Ecton, Kingsley, & Dubey 1986); aggressive adolescents (Feindler, Marriott & Iwata 1984); adult prisoners (McDougall, Barnett, Adhurst, & Willis 1987); teenage drug abusers (Schrader, Long, Panzer, Gillet, & Kornblath 1977); and secure hospital patients (Stermac, 1987). While very few well-controlled comparative outcome studies have been undertaken in this area, preliminary findings from a range of studies using different methodologies have suggestion that this form of aggression-proneness can be reduced by systematic intervention (Tafrate, 1996).

Differences between individuals in capacity for self-control have been recognised in approaches to criminal behaviour from both psychologically-based and sociologically-based perspectives. In sociology the principal proponents of this view of some forms of criminality have been Gottfredson and Hirschi (1990). In formulating their *General Theory of Crime* these authors have incorporated the concept of loss of self-control as the principal, indeed the only reliably-recurring, difference between criminals and non-criminals: "Our perspective asserts that many of the traditional causes of crime are in fact consequences of low self-control – that is, people with low self-control sort themselves and are sorted into a variety of circumstances that are *as a result* correlated with crime." (1990, p. 119, italics in original).

In psychology, the concept of self-control has been considered most extensively within a cognitive-behavioural framework. This presents a model of inter-relationships between three domains or systems of activity; cognition, emotion and behaviour. Individuals may be depicted as possessing self-control when variables within the three domains work in a coordinated manner towards the individual's self-designated goals. In some circumstances this process may break down and become dysfunctional for the individual and/or for others. One cause of this may be loss of control particularly in the interaction between cognitive and emotional processes. The model of anger control forwarded by Novaco (1975) draws upon these conceptual foundations (Novaco & Welsh, 1989). It has of course been argued, most notably by Averill (1993) that such an 'intrapsychic' conception of anger is highly misleading, and that anger is a socially defined and constructed phenomenon used to explain and even excuse aggression. While this perspective is valid to some extent, clinical observations support the view that there are nevertheless some individuals in whom aggressive behaviour and violent acts appear to be emotionally driven and in whom attempts consciously to restrain such acts meet with little success.

Though this line of reasoning is compatible with findings from a sizeable quantity of clinical and criminological research, a significant number of questions remain unanswered. It has not yet been clearly established that some individuals commit violent offences as a direct result of the kind of difficulty envisaged: loss or lack of self-control, conceptualised as a dysfunctional relationship between their thoughts, feelings and behaviour. But if this were the case and if such individuals were identifiable, there are promising and potentially effective interventions available which could assist them in the reduction of their violence-proneness. Research is required to examine more closely the possible links between violent offences and self-control loss; perhaps then also leading to the development of assessment and selection procedures which could facilitate the identification of these problems when they are presented to practitioners in the criminal justice system.

In the United Kingdom, the method of anger control training has been enthusiastically taken up by many professional groups involved in direct, face-to-face work with offenders including prison psychologists, probation officers, juvenile justice staff, residential social workers, and psychologists and nurses in secure psychiatric units. Examining, on an anecdotal basis, some of the reported failures of this work, it is evident that there are potential dangers of allocating to such programmes individuals whose violent offences cannot accurately be stated to be a result of a loss of control over affective aggression. If their violent behaviour was not due to anger and inability to control it, they are probably unlikely to benefit from training in anger management. Simultaneously, their presence in anger-control training groups might even detract from the ability of other participants to gain from the experience.

For these reasons a study was embarked upon with the following aim: *To provide an estimate of the extent to which loss of self-control plays a part in the committing of violent offences, and of the degree to which this can potentially be remedied by direct training.*

Research designed to investigate this question has been conducted in several settings, and to date two inter-related projects have been undertaken.

(a) A survey of assaults committed by offenders (n=39) placed on probation, which entailed completion of a descriptive questionnaire by probation staff (McGuire & Broomfield, 1994).

(b) A study of mentally disordered offenders (n=40) from two groups: those classed as mentally ill and those classed as suffering from psychopathic disorder in terms of the Mental Health Act (1983). These groups were compared with two non-clinical samples, students and Royal Marines respectively (Kilcoyne, 1996).

The study to be reported upon here, which is still at an early stage, is concerned with juveniles charged with and subsequently convicted of offences of personal violence.

Present Study

The young people to be described in the present study were seen for the purpose of assessment and preparation of psychological reports prior to court hearings. Reports were requested either by their defence solicitors, or by juvenile justice departments whose staff had prepared their own Pre-Sentence Reports and were considering possible options for work should the young people be placed on Supervision Orders. Each assessment took a total of three hours usually in three sessions of one hour each. The assessment methods used were as follows.

(1) *Assessment interview*. Each young person was first interviewed, using a pre-arranged semi-structured format concerning his or her personal background, history, development and current circumstances and lifestyle. The interview also included a detailed analysis of offence behaviour and questions concerning attitudes to aggression and violence.

(2) *Structured self-report scales*. A series of five self-report questionnaires was employed in the assessments, as follows.

(a) *Problem Checklist* (Porteous, 1985). A 68-item checklist for self-report of personal difficulties experienced by young people, which yields a screening score, indicating potential needs for counselling; and nine sub-scale scores in key areas of interpersonal functioning.

(b) *State-Trait Anger Expression Scale* (*STAXI*; Spielberger, 1988). A widely used and well-validated scale for assessment of the experience and expression of anger. The *STAXI* contains 44 items rated on a four-point scale, and yield seven sub-scores, with norms for adult, adolescent, and specialised standardisation samples.

(c) *Hostility Inventory* (*BDHI*; Buss & Durkee, 1957). A 66-item 'Yes/No' inventory for examination of feelings and attitudes of interpersonal mistrust and hostility, yielding a total score and seven sub-scale scores indicating levels of negativism, resentment, indirect expression of hostility, assaultiveness, suspiciousness, irritability, and verbal hostility.

(d) *Dissipation-Rumination Scale* (Caprara, 1986). A 20-item rating scale for the self-report of engagement in ruminative cognitions related to seeking retaliation and revenge.

(e) *Schedule of Self-Control Behaviours* (Rosenbaum, 1980). A 36-item self-report rating scale requiring individuals to specify the degree of control they perceive themselves to have over a range of everyday activities such as being able to avoid distraction whilst working on a task.

(3) *Staff questionnaire*. The member of juvenile justice or social work staff best acquainted with the young person was asked to complete a descriptive questionnaire concerning him or her. In almost all cases, this work was undertaken by the members of staff assigned to prepare a Pre-Sentence Reports and in most cases expected to carry out supervision with the young person following his or her court disposal. This instrument was specially designed for this purpose and covered four areas. (a) Basic background information; (b) details of the present offence and up to two previous offences; (c) perceptions of the young person's abilities in self-control; (d) information concerning the respondent. Some questions were open-ended and requested basic data concerning the young person, or narrative accounts of offences. There were also rating scales concerning separate offences, and concerning overall aspects of the young person. In addition there was a checklist of possible causal factors influencing the young person's behaviour.

In a majority of cases, police depositions or sets of statements made by witnesses were also available and were employed in compiling reports. This information was indispensable for forensic purposes but its content will not be reported upon here. In the present paper, preliminary findings will be presented from the study concerning the offence patterns and test scores of the sample, and the potential implications of inter-relations between these for intervention will be illustrated in brief case vignettes.

Results

Basic background information. The following are some basic data concerning this sample. It should be noted that no claim can be made that the sample is directly representative of juveniles who commit offences of violence, as the individuals involved were seen as clinical referrals and not selected on any specified grounds. There were 15 boys and four girls. Their mean age was 15.84 years (15 years 10 months; SD=0.99 yr).

Offence types and descriptions. The principal law governing offences of personal violence in England and Wales is the *Offences Against the Person Act* of 1861. In terms of this law, an assault is committed when an individual carries out a deliberate act intending that it should cause another to fear immediate and unlawful violence to his or her person, or is reckless as to that effect (Carter & Harrison, 1991). A number of different types of assault are defined under this Act. For example, there are separate sections of the act which deal with offences of attempting to choke a victim, attempting to drown someone while at sea, causing bodily harm by gunpowder, or assault on a police officer. However, all of the offences committed by young persons in the present sample can be subsumed under three types, of different levels of severity and covered in different sections of the Act, as follows. Section 47 defines 'assault occasioning actual bodily harm'; Section 20 covers more serious assaults causing 'grievous bodily harm', and

Section 18 assaults where such serious harm was caused pre-meditatively. Amongst the current offences of the present sample, nine were charged with Section 47 assaults, five with Section 20 and six with Section 18 assaults. These legal sections can roughly be employed to constitute a scale of assault seriousness and this procedure was adopted in the study.

Offence patterns. The offence histories of the young people in this sample were as follows. This sample of 19 young people was cumulatively responsible for a total of 35 officially recorded assaults. In a number of instances there were histories or interview self-reports of considerably greater involvement in violence. The mean number of previous convictions for the group was 5.00 (SD=4.32); four of the sample had no previous convictions; two members had more than ten each. The mean number of previous convictions for offences of violence was 0.79 (SD=0.95); ten of the sample had no previous criminal record of violence, while one individual had three previous violence convictions, the maximum number for the sample.

Table 1: Factors listed as contributing to offences

Personal Factors	
Affective states including anger, rage, annoyance (5), frustration (4), anxiety and tension, feelings of rejection, boredom, humiliation, jealousy	13
Alcohol, drinking, drugs	6
Lack of control/loss of control, short temper, processing of emotions	5
Reputation, 'street cred', self-image enhancement, status	5
Being threatened, provocation, name-calling, victim attitude	5
Family violence during development, poor/inconsistent parenting	3
Failure to consider consequences/lack of foresight	3
Poor self-image, lack of confidence, disability	3
'Personality': Lack of maturity, Impulsiveness	2
Feelings of protectiveness towards sister/history of sexual abuse	1
Physical size	1
Attitude to police	1
Poor social-cognitive skills (interpretation)	1
Seeking revenge/retribution	1
Situational Factors	
History of conflict in a relationship, including bullying (2)	7
Peer group expectations / pressure / relationships / peer influence	4
Breakdown of relationship with girlfriend	1
Poor staff management in residential setting	1
Acceptance of behaviour in local area	1
Unsettled future	1
Need for money	1

As part of the questionnaire distributed to criminal justice staff, an open-ended item sought information concerning the perceived likely causes of the young person's offences. A total of 66 contributory causes was given for the violence committed by these young people. This material was classified under the headings shown in Table 1, broadly arranged into two separate categories of 'personal' and 'situational' factors respectively. As can be seen from the Table, aspects of affective aggression, and loss of self-control were nominated as the most frequent categories of causal factors in the offending behaviour of these young people.

Structured self-report instruments. Means, standard deviations and ranges of scores on the principal variables from the five self-report instruments administered are given in Table 2.

Table 2: Means, standard deviations and ranges on self-report instruments

Measure	Mean	Standard Deviation	Range
Problem Checklist	10.00	7.11	0 – 24
STAXI:			
– T-Ang	24.72	7.11	11 – 36
– Ax-Con	16.94	4.06	11 – 28
– Ax-Ex	35.78	9.25	19 – 54
BDHI	38.72	10.57	15 – 53
Caprara DRS	39.00	14.65	14 – 72
Self-Control Schedule	11.43	25.41	-26 to +73

A number of the above scores can be set alongside norms available for several of the measures used. On the *Problem Checklist*, the sample mean score of 10 places this group, on average, at the 76th centile relative to other young people this age, in terms of the numbers of personal difficulties they report. On the *STAXI*, the mean scores for *Trait Anger*, *Anger Control* and *Anger Expression* place the sample at the 60th, 34th and 78th centiles respectively as compared with the normative adolescent group. The mean *BDHI* score corresponds almost exactly to the recommended clinical cut-off score of 38 for the scale. On the *Dissipation-Rumination* scale, for which there are no test norms, the mean score OF 39 is very high by comparison with that reported by Caprara (1986) for research samples. Finally, the mean score of 11.43 on the *Schedule of Self-Control* behaviours is below that given by Rosenbaum (1980) for students samples (score range 23-27) and older subjects (mean score 31) respectively.

The general pattern of self-report scores suggests that the assaults committed by these young people might not, overall, be attributable to marked interpersonal hostility, or notably high levels of trait anger, though these scores do depart somewhat from normative group means. There is a trend towards lower-than-average anger control, and higher than average anger expression, across the sample, who also exhibit high rumination scores and low levels of everyday behavioural self-control.

The discovery of inter-group mean differences, however, was not the objective of this research. Rather, it was to assess the differential role of emotional aggressiveness in the occurrence of assaults. A wide range of scores was found amongst the self-report scales utilised here, yet correlations between the variables were for the most part non-significant. However, a sub-group of the sample as a whole appears to experience particular difficulty in anger management, and it is these individuals who may be appropriate candidates for anger control training or allied clinical interventions.

Staff ratings. On the questionnaire sent to staff, in addition to the open-ended items outlined above, respondents were asked to rate the young people on a number of scales concerning the role of self-control in their violent behaviour and the prospects of change through direct training. Thus, on a six-point scale on which they were requested to rate the young person's *Capacity for self-control of anger*, the distribution of ratings was: 'None' – 0; 'Minimal' – 2; 'Occasional' – 2; 'Achieves control more than 50% of the time' – 7; 'Good' – 2; 'High' – 0. Four individuals, or approximately 20% of the sample, therefore, were perceived as having low or very low levels of self-control. Five Ss were seen as having very little ability to avoid potentially violent situations; while overall, a total of nine individuals was thought susceptible to the possibility of benefit from self-control training.

Case studies

To illustrate the possible implications of the above sample-based findings for direct work with these young people, three brief case studies will be presented.

Case #2. Carl, aged 15, was convicted of a Section 18 assault. He had eight previous convictions though none was for violence. His *Problem Checklist* score showed him to be a very troubled young person, at the 99th centile for his age-group. On the *STAXI*, he obtained a *Trait-Anger* score placing him on the 93rd centile, and an *Anger-Control* score on the 8th centile. His *BDHI* score was 53, well above the cut-off for hostility as a serious problem; his *Rumination* score was 59 and score on the *Self-Control Schedule* was –16. The pattern of scores together with analysis of Carl's offence suggests he both needed and would benefit from training in anger management. Despite the seriousness of his offence, Carl was placed on community supervision and provided with individual counselling and anger-control training. He benefited considerably from this work and when followed up after an interval of 18 months, there was no subsequent history of violence nor of other delinquency.

Case #5. Robert, age 17, was also convicted of a Section 18 assault. He had four previous convictions, two for violence. Robert's score on the *Problem Checklist* placed him at the 47th centile for his age-group; his Trait Anger and Anger Control scores were at the 47th and 57th centile respectively. This profile, combined with a *BDHI* score of 42, *Rumination* score of 35 and *Self-Control Schedule* score of +29 together indicated no pattern which would locate Robert's aggressiveness in anger-related phenomena. However in interview, he emerged as experiencing family problems of long standing, and his outline of a number of offences and other incidents suggested very poor problem-solving skills. His self-esteem was very low and he appeared vigilant for and sensitive to interpersonal threats. The character of Robert's offence and its overall context suggested other explanations for his violence than affective aggression, and he was considered an unsuitable candidate for anger control training.

Case #12. Marie, age 16, was convicted of a Section 47 assault. She had two previous convictions, though neither of them for assault. She too had a *Problem Checklist* score at the 47th centile, and her *Trait-Anger* score placing her at the 66th centile was not notably above the mean for her normative group. Her other scores too were close to their corresponding population means; Anger Control, 34th centile; *BDHI* score 40, *Rumination* score 32. On the other hand her score on the Anger-Out subscale of the *STAXI* was at the 95th centile, and that on the *Self-Control Schedule* was the lowest in the entire sample at –26. In discussion, she showed considerable suspiciousness of others, had distorted perceptions of the motives of others, and attitudes supportive of violence. Once again, this pattern suggested that she had little to gain from anger control training and she rejected the need for any such type of intervention.

Conclusion

In the present paper, it has been possible to report only a portion of the findings from this study, and as the research is ongoing, a fuller report is to be prepared in due course. Obviously, it will be advantageous to have a larger sample and in addition to statistical analysis of whether the patterns observed so far are sustained, this will also allow for the testing of subsidiary hypotheses. The present research is envisaged as adopting the tradition of the 'scientist-practitioner' model in which there is an interchange between applied clinical and research objectives (Barlow, Hayes, & Hersen 1984). This affords many advantages in terms of the links between practice and research, but its limitations must also be kept in mind. Nevertheless in some respects the present study and this approach may produce findings which, though of limited generalisability, are nevertheless crucial in helping to bridge the gap between findings of controlled experiments and the meaningful application of psychology in criminal justice settings.

References

Averill, J. R. (1993). Illusions of anger. In R. B. Felson & J. T. Tedeschi (Eds.) *Aggression and Violence: Social Interactionist Perspectives.* Washington, DC: American Psychological Association.

Barlow, D. H., Hayes, S. C., & Nelson, R. O. (1984). *The Scientist Practitioner: Research and Accountability in Clinical and Educational Settings.* New York: Pergamon.

Berkowitz, L. (1993). *Aggression: Its Causes, Consequences and Control.* New York: McGraw-Hill.

Blackburn, R. (1993). *The Psychology of Criminal Conduct.* Chichester: John Wiley & Sons.

Buss, A. H. & Durkee, A. (1957). An inventory for assessing different kinds of hostility. *Journal of Consulting Psychology, 21*, 343-349.

Caprara, G. V. (1986). Indicators of aggression: the Dissipation-Rumination Scale. *Personality and Individual Differences, 7*, 763-769.

Carter, P. & Harrison, R. (1991). *Offences of Violence.* London: Waterlow Publishers.

Denicola, J. & Sandler, J. (1980). Training abusive parents in child management and self-control skills. *Behavior Therapy, 11*, 263-270.

Feindler, E. L., Ecaton, R. B., Kingsley, D., & Dubey, D. R. (1986). Group anger-control training for institutionalized psychiatric male adolescents. *Behavior Therapy, 17*, 109-123.

Feindler, E. L., Marriott, S. A., & Iwata, M. (1984). Group anger control training for junior high school delinquents. *Cognitive Therapy and Research, 8*, 299-311.

Geen, R. G. (1990). *Human Aggression.* Buckingham: Open University Press.

Gottfredson, M. R. & Hirschi, T. (1990). *A General Theory of Crime.* Stanford, CA: Stanford University Press.

Kilcoyne, J. (1996). *A study to investigate the role of personality and cognitive factors in violent behaviour.* Unpublished dissertation, Doctorate in Clinical Psychology, University of Liverpool.

McDougall, C., Barnett, R. M., Ashurst, B., & Willis, B. (1987). Cognitive control of anger. In B. J. McGurk, D. M. Thornton, & M. Williams (Eds.), *Applying Psychology to Imprisonment: Theory and Practice.* London: Her Majesty's Stationery Office.

McGuire, J. & Broomfield, D. (1994). Violent offences and capacity for self-control. *Psychology, Crime and Law, 1*, 117-123.

Nomellini, S. & Katz, R. C. (1983). Effects of anger control training on abusive parents. *Cognitive Research and Therapy, 7*, 57-68.

Novaco, R. W. (1975). *Anger Control: The Development and Evaluation of an Experimental Treatment.* Lexington: D. C. Heath.

Novaco, R. W. & Welsh, W. N. (1989). Anger disturbances: cognitive mediation and clinical prescriptions. In K. Howells & C. R. Hollin (Eds.), *Clinical Approaches to Violence.* Chichester: John Wiley & Sons.

Olweus, D. (1988). Environmental and Biological factors in the development of aggressive behaviour. In W. Buikhuisen & S. A. Mednick (Eds.), *Explaining Criminal Behaviour.* Leiden: E. J. Brill.

Porteous, M. A. (1985). *Porteous Checklist: An Inventory of Adolescent Problems. Manual.* Windsor: NFER-Nelson.

Rosenbaum, M. (1980). A schedule for assessing self-control behaviours: preliminary findings. *Behavior Therapy, 11*, 109-121.

Schrader, C., Long, J., Panzer, C., Gillet, D., & Kornblath, R. (1977). *An anger-control package for adolescent drug abusers.* Long Island Jewish-Hillside Medical Center, Glen Oaks, New York.

Spielberger, C. D. (1988). *Manual for the State-Trait Anger Expression Inventory (STAXI).* Odessa, Florida: Psychological Assessment Resources.

Stermac, L. (1987). Anger control treatment for forensic patients. *Journal of Interpersonal Violence, 1*, 446-457.

Tafrate, R. C. (1995). Evaluation of treatment strategies for adult anger disorders. In H. Kassinove (Ed.), *Anger Disorders: Definition, Diagnosis and Treatment.* Washington: Taylor & Francis.

Social Competence and Sociomoral Reasoning in Young Offenders

Emma J. Palmer

Introduction

An important area in adolescent delinquency research is that of social functioning and its relation to the development of offending behaviour. In particular various facets of social cognition have received much attention, exploring the way in which the reasoning patterns and subsequent behaviour of delinquents are related. The term "social cognition" is a broad one under which a number of things fall, something that is reflected in the research literature.

Examples of studies in the last 25 years include social competence (Freedman, Rosenthal, Donahoe, Schlundt, & McFall, 1978; Gaffney & McFall, 1981), moral reasoning (Lee & Prentice, 1988; Nelson, Smith, & Dodd, 1990), empathy/role-taking (Chandler, 1973; Kaplan & Arbuthnot, 1985), locus of control (Kumchy & Sayer, 1980), and impulsivity (Rotenberg & Nachshon, 1979; Saunders, Repucci, & Sarata, 1973). The general conclusion from previous research is that offenders, both young and adult, tend to perform more poorly on measures of social cognition than non-offenders.

This study looks at two aspects of social cognition, the social competence and sociomoral reasoning of young offenders, with two main aims. Firstly to explore the relationship between social competence and style and level of moral reasoning in young-offenders. Secondly to look at how these two aspects of social cognition are related to offending behaviour.

Method

Participants

The participants were 22 convicted young offenders, 17 males and 5 females, aged between 14 and 17 years (mean=15.89 years, SD=1.11), drawn from the Milton Keynes area of England. Access was obtained through Buckinghamshire Social Services, and contact made at Milton Keynes Magistrates' Court. Socio-economic status was ascertained by asking about their father's and mother's occupation, and education, using the Standard Occupational Classification (Office of Population

Censuses and Surveys, 1991). The majority of the respondents were of low socio-economic status, mainly being of manual classes.

Measures

Social Competence. This was measured using the Adolescent Problems Inventory (API: Freedman et al., 1978). This consists of vignettes where a social problem situation is outlined, and respondents are asked to say what they would say or do next. Originally having 44 items, 5 were removed for this study due to their inapplicability to England, following the example of Hollin & Swaffer (1993).

The respondents are scored from 0 (very incompetent), 2 (incompetent), 4 (neither competent, nor incompetent), 6 (competent), to 8 (very competent). These may be summed to give a total score (range 0-312), or averaged to give a mean competency score ranging from 0-8. The mean score is more useful due to the inventory nature of the measure. The modal score was also recorded, indicating the most commonly utilised level of competency. Validity and reliability analyses show good levels, and this shortened version has been shown to produce results in line with the 44 item version (Hollin & Swaffer, 1993).

Sociomoral reasoning. This was measured using the Sociomoral Reflection Measure-Short Form (SRM-SF: Gibbs, Basinger, & Fuller, 1992). This is a production, rather than a recognition, measure of moral reasoning, and involves 11 questions probing respondents' reasoning values pertaining to the importance of 5 norms: contract and truth, affiliation, life, property and law, and legal justice. Unlike most other moral judgement assessment it involves no moral dilemmas. Ratings of the highest level evinced are made of the respondents' justifications for each question. The SRM-SF was designed as a shorter, more practical and efficient alternative to the Sociomoral Reflection Measure (Gibbs & Widaman, 1982), and is therefore comparable to the Moral Judgement Inventory (MJI; Colby & Kohlberg, 1987). Previous studies (cited in Gibbs et al., 1992) have established acceptable levels of reliability (all r's=0.88 and above) and validity (SRMS and MJI r=0.69, p=0.0001).

Overall protocol ratings are computed from the scores on the 11 questions, and at least 7 respondents are needed for a valid score: 19 participants gave valid scores. The main summary score is the Sociomoral Reflection Maturity Score (SRMS), which is the arithmetic mean of the item ratings (range 1.00-4.00). For data analysis this can be multiplied by 100, giving a range of 100-400. From this score the Global Score may be assigned; this represents the developmental vicinity of the SRMS scores as follows: 1.00-1.24=Stage 1; 1.26-1.49=Transition Stage 1(2); 1.49-1.74=Transition Stage 2(1); 1.75-2.25=Stage 2 and so on. Again the modal score was recorded to indicate the most commonly utilised level of moral reasoning.

Self-Reported Delinquency (SRD). This was measured using the self-report scale developed by Elliot & Ageton (1980) to try and obtain a clearer picture of actual levels of delinquent behaviour. This measure relates to various offences committed in the past year, with the respondents asked to indicate which offences they had committed, and also to give a tough estimate of how often using the following categories: Once a year; 2-3 times a year; Once a month; 2-3 times a month; Once a week; 2-3 times a week; Once a day; 2-3 times a day. These were used to generate a frequency of offending count, which it was felt would distinguish different levels of offending that the simple count of acts would not allow.

The measure had 46 items, giving the total acts committed variable a range of 0 (low delinquency) to 46 (high delinquency), while the frequency count could range from 0 upwards. Due to non-completion, 21 responses were generated from this measure. The measure shows high reliability (test-retest r=0.70-0.95), and Huizinga & Elliot (1986) conclude that while it is not error free, it is as good as, or better than comparable measures.

Procedure

All participants completed a questionnaire containing the three measures in the following order: API, SRM-SF, SRD. Pilot studies had shown this order to facilitate the best response quality, putting the longer written response questions at the beginning with the easier tasks towards the end. The participants were seen individually, as most required help in completing the questionnaire, and the study was explained to them All questionnaire were anonymous and the participants were assured of the confidentiality of their responses.

Results

Preliminary Analyses

On all three of the API measures, the scores were towards the lower end of the scale, indicating poor social competence. The API mean score had an average of 2.40, falling in the "incompetent" category, while the modal API score showed that the majority of the participants were functioning at a very low level of social competence. These figures are slightly lower than those found by Hollin & Swaffer (1993) using this 39 item version, although their sample was older (15-20 years old). Pearson correlations showed, as expected, that all correlations between the three scores were highly significant with $p<0.001$: API total/API mean r (22)=0.99; API TOTAL/API modal (22)=0.67; API mean//API modal r(22)=0.67.

Table 1: The mean scores for the measures

	Mean	Standard Deviation
Social Competence (22)*		
API Total Score	92.82	(45.24)
API mean score	2.40	(1.16)
API modal score	1.10	(2.12)
Moral Reasoning (19)*		
SRMS	238.11	(49.08)
Global stage	5.05	(1.51)
Modal stage	3.89	(1.41)
SRD (21)*		
Number of offences	23.86	(5.90)
Frequency score	3746.71	(2744.30)

* The number of participants giving scores.

The scores on the moral measures were also low; the SRMS mean of 238.11 corresponds to a global stage of 2(3). This was reflected in the distribution of global stage scores, where stage 2 reasoning predominated. Similarly, the majority of participants' modal stage was 2 or 2/3. These figures are similar to norms quoted by Gibbs et al. (1992) for 11 year old children, emphasising the immaturity of the participants' responses. The three scores were all significantly correlated, with $p<0.001$: SRMS/ global stage $r(19)=0.96$; SRMS/modal stage $r(19)=0.87$; global stage/modal stage $r(19)=0.78$.

Of the two self-reported delinquency scores, the basic count of offences had a narrow range of scores of 11-34. As expected this was not particularly useful as most of the participants had committed a large amount of crime, which was not reflected by this measure. However the frequency score was far more descriptive of delinquency levels, with a range of 284-9885 allowing for greater differentiation among participants The two scores correlated significantly, $r(21)=0.68$, $p<0.001$.

Relationships between variables

Demographic variables. There were no significant relationships for any of the variables with age, sex, or socioeconomic group.

Inter-variable relationships. The moral reasoning measures showed no significant relationships with the social competence scores of self-reported delinquency.

A number of relationships were found between the API scores and self-reported delinquency, both the basic count of acts and the frequency measure. The SRD basic count was significantly negatively correlated to two of the API scores: API total score $r(21)=-0.50$, $p<0.01$, and the API mean score $r(21)=-0.49$, $p<0.05$.

In addition, the correlation with the API modal score approached significance: $r(21)=-0.34$, $p=0.06$. The relationships were stronger for the SRD frequency score: with API total $r(21)=-0.65$, $p<0.001$; with API mean score $r(21)=-0.001$; and with API modal score $r(21)=-0.40$, $p<0.05$.

Predictors of Self-Reported Delinquency

Stepwise multiple regressions were performed to determine which variables best predicted SRD scores on both measures. For the basic count of offences, the only significant variable was API total score with an adjusted R2=0.26, $F\ (1,17)=7.25$, $p<0.05$. Two significant variables were revealed for the STD frequency score: API mean score and sex with an adjusted R2=0.56, $F\ (2.19)=12.43$, $p<0.001$.

Discussion

These results replicate previous findings of young offenders showing low levels of social cognition (Freedman et al., 1978; Blasi, 1980): on both the social competence and moral reasoning measures they performed poorly. Although there was no control group of this study against which to make a comparison, their scores on the API were lower than those found in another sample of young offenders in England (Hollin & Swaffer, 1993), and their moral reasoning was of the level expected from 11 year olds.

Social competence was related to self-reported delinquency, especially the frequency score. This finding suggest that, as expected, the frequency score allowed for greater differentiation among the sample in terms of offending behaviour. Again this replicates previous findings showing that the API discriminates between levels of self-reported delinquency (e.g. Dishion, Loeber, Stouthamer-Loeber, & Patterson, 1984; Leeman, Gibbs, & Fuller, 1993; Simonian, Tarnowski, & Gibbs, 1991).

Moral reasoning was not found to be related to self-reported delinquency, which was not expected. Previous research documents well the link between delinquency (both official and self-reported) and lower levels of moral reasoning (for example, Blasi, 1980; Nelson, Smith, & Dodd, 1990). The lack of any relationship here is likely to be due to the narrow range of scores on the moral reasoning variable.

Furthermore, this reason probably also accounts for the similar lack of relationship with the scores on the API. Theoretically it might be expected that in a more diverse population, level of functioning on one measure of social cognition would be related to that on another, and these to some index of behaviour.

Practical implications

These results show that there is a need to improve both the social competence and moral reasoning levels of young offenders. However, to merely initiate treatment programmes on this basis may be oversimplifying matters. Young offenders are not a homogenous group; as mentioned above they commit crimes for various different motivations. Also the situations they commonly find themselves in may play a role in what crimes they commit, and their reasons for doing so, as may their ability to deal with these situations in a competent matter. Thus, there is a need to look at what sort of incompetencies are most commonly exhibited by young offenders, and in which type of situations these pose the greatest problem. This will enable programmes that address young offenders' social needs and problems more directly to be formulated.

As this study has shown, the links between various facets of social cognition are unknown and problematic. Therefore programmes directed at one cannot be assumed to make an impact in another. Furthermore, it may not be how an individual reasons about something that is most important, but the content of their cognitions (i.e. attitudes, moral values, social norms, etc.) that need to be changed.

Although the moral level being used was predominately stage 2, there was evidence of higher stages (up to stage 3). An interesting question is why were these higher levels used so infrequently? The fact that the ability to reason at higher levels is present in many young offenders is often overlooked, resulting in programmes that merely attempt to improve offenders' reasoning levels. Instead a programme placing a greater emphasis on encouraging individuals to use the reasoning levels they already possess may be more productive, acknowledging what the offenders are capable of achieving.

There is also a need to address the issue of why and how the incompetencies and deficits noted in this area of research arise. Although this knowledge is unlikely to be useful when designing effective treatment programmes for young offenders, it is needed for preventative measures. In the long-term, it is through these that the crime problem is more likely to be reduced.

References

Blasi, A. (1980). Bridging moral cognition and moral action: A critical review of the literature. *Psychological Bulletin, 88*, 1-45.

Chandler, M. J. (1973). Egocentrism and antisocial behaviour: The assessment and training of social perspective-taking skills. *Developmental Psychology, 9*, 326-332.

Colby, A, & Kohlberg, L. (1987). *The measurement of moral judgement: Theoretical foundations and research validation, Vol. 1.* Cambridge: Cambridge University Press.

Dishion, T. J., Loeber, R, O., Stouthamer-Loeber, M., & Patterson, G. R. (1984). Skill deficits and male adolescent delinquency. *Journal of Abnormal Child Psychology, 12*, 37-54.

Elliot, D. S., & Ageton, S. S. (1980). Reconciling race and class differences in self-reported and official estimates of delinquency. *American Sociological Review, 45*, 95-110.

Freedman, B. J., Rosenthal, L. Donahoe, C.P., Schlundt, D. G. & McFall, R. M. (1978). A social-behavioural analysis of skill deficits in delinquents and nondelinquent adolescent boys. *Journal of Consulting and Clinical Psychology, 46*, 1448-1462.

Gaffney, L. R., & McFall, R. M. (1981). A comparison of social skills in delinquent and nondelinquent adolescent girls using a behavioural role-playing inventory. *Journal of Consulting and Clinical Psychology, 49*, 959-967.

Gibbs, J. C., Basinger, K. S., & Fuller, D. (1992). *Moral maturity: Measuring the development of sociomoral reflection.* Hillsdale, NJ: Erlbaum.

Gibbs, J. C. & Widaman, K. F. (1982). *Social intelligence: Measuring the development of sociomoral reflection.* Englewood Cliffs, NJ: Prentice Hall.

Hollin, C. R, & Swaffer, T. (1993). Social functioning and delinquency: A return to basics. *Journal of Adolescence, 16*, 205-210.

Huizinga, D., & Elliot, D. S. (1986). Reassuring the reliability and validity of self-report delinquency measures. *Journal of Quantitative Criminology, 2*, 293-327.

Kaplan, P. J., & Arbuthnot, J. (1985). Affective empathy and cognitive role-taking in delinquent and nondelinquent youth. *Adolescence, 20*, 323-333.

Kunchy, C. I. G., & Sayer, L. A. (1980). Locus of control in a delinquent adolescent population. *Psychological Bulletin, 46*, 1307-1310.

Lee, M., & Prentice, N. M. (1988) Interrelations of empathy, cognition, and moral reasoning with dimensions of juvenile delinquency. *Journal of Abnormal Child Psychology, 16*, 127-139.

Leeman, L. W., Gibbs, J. C., & Fuller, D. (1993). Evaluation of a multicomponent group treatment program for juvenile delinquents. *Aggressive Behaviour, 19*, 281-292.

Nelson, J. R., Smith, D. J., & Dodd, J. (1990). The moral reasoning of juvenile delinquents: A meta-analysis. *Journal of Abnormal Child Psychology, 18*, 231-239.

Office of Population Censuses and Surveys (1991). *Standard Occupational Classification.* London: HMSO.

Rotenberg, M., & Nachschon, I. (1979). Impulsiveness and aggression among Israeli delinquents. *British Journal of Social and Clinical Psychology, 18*, 59-63.

Saunders, J. T., Repucci, N. D., & Sarata, B. P. V. (1973). An examination of impulsivity as a trait delinquent youth. *American Journal of Orthopsychiatry, 43*, 789-795.

Simonian, S. J., Tarnowski, K. J., & Gibbs, J. C. (1991). Social skills and antisocial conduct of delinquents. *Child Psychiatry and Human Development, 22*, 17-27.

Feminist Group Therapy for Women Who Self-Harm

Helen Liebling and Hazel Chipchase

Introduction

Ashworth Hospital is one of the four Special Hospitals in Britain. it is a Maximum Security Hospital which provides care and treatment for male and female patients detained under the Mental Health Act (1983). The current population of women patients is 56.

The research on self-harm has been ongoing since 1992 and has included semi-structured interviews with 40 women patients and interviews with 84 staff who care for them. Initial research findings indicate that the therapeutic needs of women who self-harm at Ashworth Hospital are currently not being adequately met. (Liebling & Chipchase, 1995). Areas found to be significant antecedents to self-harm include severe depression, poor internal locus of control, anxiety, anger, poor communication skills and difficulty solving problems.

Brief Literature Review

There is little research data on the effectiveness of therapy groups for women who self-harm. This is particularly lacking for women detained within maximum security environment.

However, previous research supports the provisions of group therapy in this area. Lovaas & Simmons (1969) cited the need for supportive interpersonal therapy for women who self-harm.

More recently, cognitive-behavioural approaches have been favoured. Linehan (1993) greatly supports the skills training approach for women with a diagnosis of Borderline Personality Disorder. Linehan et al (in press) have shown the effectiveness of cognitive-behavioural approaches with women who self-harm by enhancing behavioural skills.

This approach is also supported by Leibenluft et al (1987) who concludes that therapeutic approaches should involve cognitive interventions and also the development of alternative behaviours.

Research has also shown that therapies which draw on feminist principles demonstrate success (Burstow, 1992). Brown (1985a) cited that emotional empowerment in women is essential as it may lessen the shame women feel about the power they use.

Walsh & Rosen (1988) state that there are advantages to running therapy groups for women who self-harm. Within a group, individual women may learn to identify and practice more adaptive means of meeting their needs than self-harm. They may learn more effective skills, particularly communication skills, and they may find greater self-understanding through sharing common experiences and common fears.

Assistance & Therapy Women Said They Needed

When available research and literature was combined with the initial research findings (Liebling & Chipcase, 1995), there were good grounds for attempting to develop a therapy group for women who self-harm.

From the 40 women interviewed as part of our original research, 88 % stated they wanted involvement in planning their future, 85% wanted positive goals in treatment, 83% wanted help to express feelings and solve problems, and 80% wanted a regular listener.

When we asked what specific therapy women wanted, 85% wanted someone to listen to them, 68% wanted to talk to others who self-harm, 63% wanted anger control, and 63% asked for psychological therapy. Women also said they wanted:
"A place where I can talk to people."
"A nice relaxing hospital, no people shouting and swearing and clean good food."
"Trusting you more."
"Just a normal environment."

Women's Involvement in Planning the Group in Initial Evaluation

A therapy group for women who self-harm was planned and sessions were arranged in which patients were fully involved in making decisions about the structure and composition of the group. Women were invited to attend and they chose to come to the sessions. It was discussed what women would want from the group, the format of the sessions, confidentiality issues, and group agreements. We fed back information from the research with 40 women at Ashworth Hospital and discussed the relevant issues. Women were also involved in interviewing and selecting nursing staff to attend the group.

The main themes which emerged from the planning sessions were that women wanted the first part of each session to be allocated to discussing issues that concerned them in the present. Women consistently wanted to be listened to and taken seriously and this supported the initial research findings (Liebling & Chipchase, 1995). Control was viewed as important, and women wished to be able to exert their control within the group. They partly achieved this by having the option to leave the therapy group room when necessary.

With respect to staff qualities required, women said staff in the group should be emphatic and show understanding of women and self-harm. They stated that any staff involved in the group would have to give a full commitment to it and keep the confidentiality and group agreements. Women felt staff would need to be open to new approaches to dealing with women who self-harm. It was important that staff in the group did not hold grudges against any of the women within it, and previous therapeutic experience was considered helpful for nursing staff to have. Women also asked the staff about their reasons for wanting to join the group.

Initial Evaluation

The group therapy programme originally utilised psychometric assessment of issues shown to be related to women who self-harm. These included assessment of depression using Back Depression Inventory, assessment of anger using the Novaco Anger Scale, and Assessment of Control Using the Levenson Locus of Control Scale. We also involved women with their consent in monitoring their weekly thoughts and feelings in relation to their self-harming. This was assessed using the Personal Questionnaire Rapid Scaling Technique.

Sessions of the group included: reasons why women self-harm, positive and negative staff response, guidelines for implementing care plans for women who self-harm, and common myths about self-harm. Barriers to communicating distress were explored and we addressed some positive solutions to these.

The group utilised discussions, educational information produced by Bristol Crisis Service for women, small group discussions, and role-plays.

Initially within the group sessions, women were quite but all contributed good ideas. Women had the space to talk or not as they chose which enhanced their feelings of control. It was noted by group facilitators, that the mood of the women in the group dramatically dropped at times when self-harm was discussed directly.

Women were well able to communicate their current and previous distress and at times disclosed very painful memories. At these times and throughout the group women supported and empathised with each others' experiences. They were equally sensitive to each others' moods.

Psychometric assessments were mainly unpopular and women made negative statements about them. The facilitators perceptions were that these increased the facilitators sense of control over the women which completely went against the philosophy and theoretical basis of the group. These were therefore discontinued early on in the group and qualitative evaluation measures were utilised instead.

Major issues related to security and transport were identified. Women expressed reluctance to use the hospital transport due to the length of time taken in travelling and the other patients on the bus, who were mainly male. Women often complained of harassment on the transport and efforts have been made to try and provide a more gender sensitive service. These have so far been unsuccessful. Security problems were varied and included escort staff interrupting group sessions, women being taken to group session even though they had been cancelled and women being sent to other areas of the hospital despite their requests to attend the group.

It was noted by facilitators that within each session, the women's mood lifted toward the end. Women often came to the group withdrawn, anxious, or angry but generally left in a brighter frame of mind.

During the fourteen weeks as the group was progressing, women became noticeably more relaxed, communicated more within sessions as trust developed. For the women, one of the main themes was being listened to and taken seriously.

There were several organisational issues which often conflicted with the running and philosophy of the therapy group. Despite the aims of the group being well distributed, pressure was still placed on women not to self-harm. Incidents of self-harm were often viewed as a failure of the group despite clear statement that the group's aims were not to stop self-harming but to provide a forum where women could safely communicate their distress.

Women's Views of the Group and Changes Based on These

As part of the evaluation of the first 14 weeks of the group, all women apart from one were interviewed using a semi-structured interview schedule. Their responses were recorded as follows:

a. Did you enjoy attending the group?
   All of the women stated they enjoyed attending the group. They said:
   "You can say things and they don't go further."
   "You can relax."
   "I liked the discussions and attitudes of staff."
b. What was useful/not useful about discussing here and now issues?
   "It helped to settled into the rest of the group."
   "It is a change to talk about what's going on."
   "Makes me feel better."
   "Helps to have someone to listen."
c. What was useful/not useful about information about women and self-harm?
   "Learn about other people's experiences."
   "Clearer understanding of why women self-harm."
   "It helps to share thoughts, ideas and feelings with others who self-harm."

d. What was useful/not useful about the relaxed part?
"Seemed to go well together with the rest of the group."
"Self-harm is a very emotional subject and the relaxed part of the sessions were good as everyone was able to relax."
e. What was useful/not useful about the assessments?
"Long assessments but feel they are important to see progress."
"Did not like being assessed. Felt like a wind up.
f. What was useful/not useful about the role-plays?
"Helps you understand why people harm themselves."
"Don't like watching them."
"Don't like doing them."
g. Staff
"Just enough staff."
h. What other things did you like about the group?
"Really relaxed, good and beneficial."
"Smoothness of the running of the group. If anyone needed to go out there were always enough staff to go with them and enough to stays in and continue the group."
i. Other things you did not like about the group?
"None."
"I did not like when people got upset."
j. Would you like to carry on with the group?
All responded "yes."
k. Is there anything you would like in future sessions?
"More talking about self-harm."
"To invite people in from around the country who are interested in self-harm."
l. Anything else about the group you would like to say?
"I enjoyed it immensely."
"The group has helped me a lot and taught me different ways of approaching other woman who cut up and stopped me from doing it completely."

However, stopping self-harm was not the short-term aim of the group. The group aimed to provide a forum where women could safely communicate their distress and develop positive ways of coping.

Changes Made to the Group

From the initial evaluation data, it is clear that women valued a forum where they are listened to. The exploration of difficult issues helped women to take things forward themselves.

Due to the distress the psychometric assessment produced in women, the group has been changed to accommodate less intrusive and qualitative methods of evaluation. The group is closed to the original five members and a group process analysis of change is being utilised.

A format for each session has been developed which the women have consistently found helpful. Each session is about two hours and is as follows:

Session Format

1. Here and now issues.
2. Self-harm, underlying distress and coping.
3. Relaxed part of the session.
4. Evaluation:
   What did women like?
   What did women not like?
   What would women like in future sessions?
5. Current Group for Women Who Self-harm

A fourteen week module has now commenced with the original five members of the group. The aims of this group are as follows:

1. To evaluate by Qualitative Methodology Supportive Group work for Women who self-harm.
2. To determine from women themselves the main themes in relation to their self-harming. To extend an understanding of this by taped interviews.
3. To determine what issues arise during a group therapy programme for women who self-harm within a Special Hospital.
4. To produce formulations from each women with respect to how self-harming is linked to other problems.
5. To evaluate the effectiveness of coping strategies at different stages during the group.
6. To determine the women's perceptions of their experiences of the group.

Evaluation measures which are being utilised include:

1. Pre- and post-taped interviews with each women using a semi-structured interview schedule. This is repeated at intervals during the group.
2. All sessions are taped, transcribed and analysed by qualitative methodology.
3. Group facilitators make their own notes about their experiences of the group and organisational factors which impinge on it.
4. At the end of each sessions we brainstorm what women have liked and not liked about the group and what they would like in the future sessions.
6. Evaluation of the Therapeutic Effects of Nurse Training on Patient Care

Part of the ongoing research has involved interviews with staff who work with women who self-harm. As a consequence of this, a pilot staff training group is planned to commence later this year. The effectiveness of this group will be evaluated by research methodology. It will evaluate the outcome of a 14 week research-based training group consisting of 4 volunteer nursing staff, one from each of the women's wards. The group will disseminate information on communication training and give opportunities for staff to feed back and contribute to the development of the programme. The eventual aim is to produce a research-based training manual for trained nursing staff to continue their own training. This is based on staff's expressed desire for training and support for working with women who self-harm.

Summary

It is clear that a feminist therapy group for women who self-harm at Ashworth Hospital is valued and responded to positively by the women themselves and the facilitators of the group. This is supported by the initial evaluation which is encouraging. In contrast, the use of psychometric assessments and cognitive-behavioural approaches are construed by the women as control. As lack of internal control has been highlighted by the authors as a significant factor leading to women's self-harm (Liebling & Chipchase, 1995), this needs to be seriously considered. it is the authors' view that cognitive-behavioural approaches go against the needs of this group of women patients and the theoretical basis of the group. Feminist therapeutic methods and qualitative methods of evaluation are therefore being utilised.

The difficulties of running a therapeutic group for women within a Special Hospital should not be underestimated and several organisational issues conflicted with the smooth running of the group and interfered with its therapeutic value. it is therefore important that these issues are explicitly recognised and addressed.

The therapy group is continuing and has been improved based on the initial results of the evaluation from the women themselves. The proposed staff training group is envisaged to commence later this year and will look at improving therapeutic approaches for women who self-harm. The eventual aim is to produce a research-based training manual for trained staff to continue their own training. This is based on the nursing staff's own expressed desire for support and training in this area.

References

Brown, L. (1985a). Women, Weight and Power: Feminist Theoretical and Therapeutic Issues. *Women and Therapy, 3. 1*, 73-80.

Burstow, B. (1992). *Radical Feminist Therapy.* Newbury Park: Sage.

Cookson, H. M. (1977). A Study of Self-injury in a Closed Prison for Women. *British Journal of Criminology, 17*, 332-347.

Leibenluft, E., Gardener, D. L., & Cowdry, R. W. (1987). The Inner Experience of the Borderline Self-Mutilator, *Journal of Personality Disorders, 1, 4*, 317-324.

Liebling, H. & Chipchase, H. (1995). Research with Women Who Self-harm and Training Needs of Staff Who Work with Them. *Special Hospitals Research Bulletin, Vol. 4.*

Linehan, M. M. (1993). *Cognitive-Behavioural Treatment of Borderline Personality Disorder*. New York: Guildford Press.

Linehan, M. M., Heard, H. E. & Armstrong, H. E. (in press). *Naturalistic Follow-up of a Behavioural Treatment for Chronically Suicidal Borderline Patients.* Archives of General Psychiatry.

Lovaas, O. I. & Simmons, J. (1969). Manipulation of Self-Destruction in Three Retarded Children, *Journal of Applied Behaviour Analysis. 2*, 143-157.

Sellars, C. & Liebling, H. (1988). *Section 3 Patients: The "non-offenders?"*. Division of Clinical and Legal Psychology, Newsletter.

Walsh, B.W. & Rosen, P.M. (1988). *Self-Mutilation: Theory, Research and Treatment.* New York: Guilford Press.

Heterogeneity of Murders as the Fundamental Problem in the Psychological Profiling of a Perpetrator

Józef K. Gierowski, Teresa Jaskiewicz-Obydzinska and Maciej Szaszkiewicz

The research on murder perpetrators has concentrated so far on the determining of the factors conditioning their criminal behaviour. The literature dealing with various circumstances of a murder, psychological and psychopathological analysis of personality of perpetrators, and the processes which govern their criminal behaviour showed a huge variety of internal and external variables which might lead to murder. This variety suggests, quite unequivocally, the lack of any sort of homogeneity in the population of murderers from the psychological and psychopathological point of view. The fundamental reason which precludes treating murder perpetrators as a homogenous group due to personality features, basic parameters of criminogenic situation or the course of motivation processes leading directly to the break of the legal order is the lack of adequacy of legal criteria to the psychological ones. They do not overlap due to obvious reasons. The criteria of legal qualification of an act are primarily based on the evaluation of the criminal act (killing). Basic laws of psychology claim, on the other hand, that a given effect may be the result of occurrence of different variables and psychological processes (Gierowski, 1992). Killing of another man is, from the psychological point of view, a kind of behaviour in which psychopathological personality or situational variables may play a different role.

As in any kind of behaviour, in a criminal behaviour a man shows his individual features. One may, therefore, on the basis of the analysis of mode of operating and left traces, risk an assumption as to the individual, psychopathological features of a perpetrator, especially those concerning his personality and motivation processes. Neither psychiatrists, nor psychologists, nor sexologists deal with the problem in a sufficient way in this country (Gierowski, Jaskiewicz-Obydzinska, & Szaszkiewicz, 1995).

There has been a rise in violent crime recently. At the same time the perpetrators of certain kinds of murders create ever-growing detection problems. Law-enforcement agencies frequently turn to experts to determine psychological silhouette of a perpetrator (i.e. profiling). Expert's opinions have been, so far, based primarily on the individual clinical experience of experts and their actions have had, to a large extent, an intuitive character. For a psychologist, an integral part of profiling is assumptions concerning stable personality mechanisms of the perpetrator, the reconstruction of the psychical state tempre criminis, and the hypothetical course of his motivation processes which are the basis for the analyzed actions. The determination of all of the above mentioned variables will only be possible after a very accurate and chronological reconstruction of the perpetrator's behaviour in its external, behavioural dimension. The personality and motivation variables do not always determine in a direct way the feature or the personality mechanism in such a manner that will allow differentiation of the perpetrator from other people. So, for example, deeply suppressed enmity or the sensitive attitude of a perpetrator to other people is not the kind of information which the law-enforcement agencies could use. Such variables may, however, be useful to recreate the psychological version of an event, its verification, or can be helpful in determining the course of motivation processes.

The above considerations suggest that the variety of the analyzed variables both external and internal has a decisive influence on the evaluation of traces of the event, their interpretation and the creation of the basis to assume different versions of the course of the event. From the methodological point of view profiling must take into account the uniqueness, complexity, and ethiological multi-factor nature of murder.

The development of detection psychology in the world has made it possible to formulate a number of methodological principles helping, to a large extent in creating a reliable profiling of a perpetrator (Geberth, 1990; Ressler et al., 1992, 1995 – with the use of special computer programs). They seem especially useful in profiling the murder perpetrators. Profiling is a process consisting of several stages; it provides a possibility to verify the hypothesis in view of the current state of investigation and the influx of new information. The model used at the Department of Forensic Psychology of the Institute of Forensic Research may be cited as an example. It has been elaborated on the basis of a formula used by specialist of the Behavioural Unit of the FBI in Quantico. The model consists of four basic stages of profiling.

The first encompasses the initial data analysis such as crime scene, victim's personal data, the results of medical forensic examination, and initial assumptions of the investigation. The next stage is the typological analysis of data which includes such issues as: the classification of the type and manner of violence, the evaluation of risk both on the part of the victim and the perpetrator, hypothetical reconstruction of the event, escalation of the perpetrator's actions, the evaluation of time frame of the event, the location of the crime and death, the determination of motivation (Gierowski et al., 1995).

The third stage is the analysis of the criminal act itself which includes legal classification, reconstruction of the event, classification of the type of the crime in view of the choice of the victim, manipulating strategies, sequence of events, and a more precise reconstruction of the course of motivation processes of the perpetrator. The last, key stage of profiling is the characterization of the perpetrator. It includes demographical data, physical features, psychical features, description of association level and assumptions as to the future behaviour of the perpetrator.

The profiling of the perpetrator is, in its essence, a short, dynamic description of characteristic features of the perpetrator. Its aim is to provide a possibility to verify these elements of the version of the event which concern the probability of committing a crime act by a specific person, known to the law-enforcement agencies (Gierowski et al., 1995).

The examples cited below exemplify the methodological difficulties which are inherent in profiling of a murder perpetrator and those methodological difficulties which are derived from the lack of homogeneity of variables which are fundamental in the mechanisms leading to murder.

Between 23 March 1992 and 6 September 1993 in the centre of Warsaw, an unknown perpetrator made 29 assaults on women. He attacked them in arcades or passages coming up to them from behind. He hit them on the head with a hard, heavy object until they lost consciousness and ran away with their handbags in his possession. As a result of these attacks five women died, some became crippled for life – all of them were seriously wounded.

Before attempting a psychological profile of the perpetrator we analysed carefully all the information that was available. The most important one was that the attacks were so numerous. The essential part of our work was to compare the behaviour of the perpetrator in all the events. The obtained similarities allowed us to determine solid aspects of his behaviour whereas the differences allowed us to determine variable and transient behaviour and to determine the dynamics of the perpetrator's behaviour.

From the analysis of the data it was established that the victims were most frequently retired women, thus not having large amounts of money. We put forward a hypothesis that such selection of victims was not accidental for the perpetrator. The psychological analysis of the perpetrator's actions led to the conclusion that the intensity of aggression in his actions exceeded considerably the motivation for robbery. So, we assumed another hypothesis that the perpetrator was not solely driven by economical motivation but also by additional emotional motivation; an urge to defuse aggression in regard to older women. While analysing further information from the testimonies of a few witnesses of the attacks, we found that they described the assailant as a young man. Putting together the above facts and partial hypotheses we formulated an assumption that the perpetrator in attacking his victims vented his pent up aggression which stemmed from his incorrect relationship with his mother. This assumption was included – together with other hypotheses describing the perpetrator – in the final conclusions of our opinion. Later, we were able to verify our hypotheses, as the investigation led to the arrest of the suspect, who had been convicted several times before of assaults to women. We conducted a psychological examination of him. It revealed that the suspect experienced a deep, suppressed grudge towards his mother and he blamed her for his numerous failures in his life. His mother, assuming an excessively protective attitude towards him defended him against the effects of criminal activities, justified him, and did not pose any demands, idealizing him. Driven by unconscious motivation and enmity, he attacked women in a similar age to his mother with strong aggression.

The other case had an entirely different character. In a small village in southern Poland on May 26th 1994, the bodies of an elderly couple were found. The murder took place in their house. The bodies were lying on the sofa, side by side with their legs touching the floor. They were dressed in their pyjamas. The cause of death for both victims was numerous facial and head injuries together with broken bones and brain damage inflicted probably by an axe. On the couch, next to the bodies, three empty alcohol bottles were found. The presence of alcohol (1,4%) was found in the blood of the man, with no alcohol in his urine. His head was bandaged. Blood traces and symptoms of penetrations were found, (no money was found). The perpetrator (or perpetrators) entered the house through the basement by sawing the lock of the grill which secured the window.

Before preparing the profile we carefully analysed (similarly to the above mentioned case) the collected data. But the method of our work had to be, in this case, entirely different.

The most important source of information for us was the traces found at the crime scene. The essential part of our work was to carefully ascertain which of the traces are connected with the perpetrators' behaviour and which ones belong to the victims' behaviour. Blood traces and traces on cotton gloves in the basement indicated that the perpetrator was in the basement together with one of the victims. This fact, together with the number of bottles near the bodies, prompted us to assume the hypothesis that there were more than one perpetrator. During the event which lasted several hours somebody ate food in kitchen and in the basement. We assumed that it was one of the perpetrators. The number and the strength of the blows, and especially their concentration on face suggests that the perpetrator know his victims. Thus, we accepted the hypothesis that at least one of the perpetrators knew at least one of the victims. From the information concerning the victims, it turned out that they did not drink alcohol. So, the presence of alcohol in blood of one of the victims and its absence in urine could be hypothetically interpreted as the result of the perpetrators' actions: they either forced him to drink it just before he died, or poured it into his mouth after he died. The fact of eating – a rare behaviour in such a situation – suggested that one of the perpetrators tended to defuse his emotional tension by eating. The main motivation of the perpetrators was obviously an economical one. However, numerous acts of aggression, especially in the last phase of the event in which the victims were placed on the couch and killed, point to the conclusion that the behaviour of the perpetrators also had a markedly emotional character. Their emotional behaviour might have, its source in a manifold and compiling during the event influence of the group members on one another (there were probably three of them) and in alcohol. The dynamics of perpetrators' actions in a group might be entirely different than that of its members individually. The motivational background for such actions might also have been different. In this case we haven't been able to verify our hypotheses yet.

We have presented two different examples of profiling. Their ultimate effect is similar: our opinions include a short, concise characteristics of perpetrators. The way in which they were achieved, however, was different. The difficulties we have encountered while analysing the cases arose from the fact that each murder is a unique, complex event, which ethiologically has many factors. Heterogeneity of the murderer population is therefore the fundamental methodological problem in psychological profiling of perpetrators.

References

NCAVC FBI Academy (1990). *Criminal investigative analysis of sexual homicide*. Quantico.

Geberth, V. J. (1990). Practical Homicide Investigation. Tactics procedures and forensic techniques.

Gierowski, J. K. (1992). Untersuchungen zur Motivation bei Toetungsdelikten. In T. R. Payk (Ed.), *Dissozialitaet. Psychiatrische und forensische Aspekte* (pp. 64-76). Stuttgart, New York: Schattauer.

Gierowski, J. K., Jaskiewicz-Obydzinska, T., & Szaszkiewicz, M. (1995). Nie wykorzystane możliwoci psychologii ledczej – rola psychologa w typowaniu sprawców przestępstw z użyciem przemocy. *Prokuratura i Prawo, 5*, 30-36.

Ressler R. K. et. al. (1995). *Crime Classification Manual*.

Ressler R. K. et. al. (1995). *Sexual Homicide. Patterns and Motives*.

Necrophilia: Love at Last Sight

Philip D. Jaffé

Introduction

Necrophilia is one of the oldest and most rare perversions. Thus, any original case, especially if it involves murder, deserves attention. This is the case of Mr. S., a 50+ year old man, held in a maximum security psychiatric hospital in North America. He is convicted of murdering a fellow detainee for which he is serving a life sentence. He is also suspected of killing several women as well as a second fellow detainee. For these suspicions, however, and for complex reasons, Mr. S., will never go on trial and will remain psychiatrically hospitalized in a maximum security forensic facility, as he has been for over a decade, on the basis of an Incompetent to Stand Trial statute. Portions of his psychotherapy that took place over several years are examined. Attention is also centred on familial elements and how the nechrophilic interest was displaced from his grandmother to female dates. Scant literature on the subject of necrophilia is also reviewed.

Historical aspects

Necrophilia or love of the dead is on record as far back as funeral and burial rites exist and, like most perversions, it is probably as old as mankind itself. Already in Ancient Egypt, embalming, i.e., the preservation of lifelike features after death, seems to have generated a fear of indecent acts. Herodotus mentions that precautions were taken against necrophilia: "the wives of men of rank, or of great beauty of considerable reputation are not immediately upon their decease delivered to the embalmers: they are usually kept for three of four days, which is done to prevent any indecency being offered to their persons. For one of them was caught while he was abusing the body of a woman just deceased and was turned in by his colleague".

Herodotus visited Egypt around 450 B.C. and it has been suggested by some that his observations amount to nothing more than a Greek caught in cultural rivalry trying to portray Egyptians in a bad light (Tridon, Crobez, Vidailhet, Paugain, & Boissenin, 1994). Nonetheless, observations made by others at a later date mention that women embalmers were trained to deal exclusively with female bodies, thus suggesting that he had perhaps made realistic observations.

According to legend, King Herod, engaged in sexual rapports with his wife for seven years after he killed her (Jones, 1931). Similar legends reportedly apply to King Waldemar and to King Charlemagne. It should be recalled that, in the early middle ages, cannibalism was still practised by some Christian groups who believed in literal transubstantiation. In fact, Charlemagne legislated against this in 785. In those days, the Catholic Church also held official views on necrophilia an considered it as neither whoring, that is "fornicatio", nor bestiality. Precisely, necrophilia was coined as "pollution with a tendency to whoring (Brill, 1941).

Necrophilic activities are contained in a number of folklore and myths. By far the most famous is the vampire myth which involves a person who previously died leaving his tomb at night, attacking his victims, often friends and relatives, sucking their blood to retain his own immortality, and returning to his coffin before sunrise or risking paralysis and total helplessness. Interestingly, remnants of vampirism have also been described in the psychiatric literature (see e.g., Jaffé & DiCataldo, 1994; Jaffé, Tschopp, & DiCataldo, 1994). Finally, the classical "Sleeping Beauty" myth most certainly contains a necrophilic fantasy: the corpse of a young woman is returned to life by sexual contact with Prince Charming.

Definitions

Krafft-Ebing (1886) proposed one of the first psychiatric definitions. He distinguished between necrophiles seeking only sexual contact with the dead, as sex objects that can be subjugated absolutely, and necrophilia accompanied by murder and mutilation. This early categorization finds an echo in later nosologies almost up to the present. What is remarkable is that Krafft-Ebing made his nosological proposals based only on two cases of necrophilia!

At the turn of the century, Havelock-Ellis coined the contraction "necrosadism" to describe necrophilia accompanied by murder and mutilation. As for Magnus Hirschfeld, a major investigator if human sexuality in the 1930's, he proposed a three part classification scheme for sexual activities performed on the dead. He retained the term "necrosadism" as a manifestation in which the sexual impulse is gratified only with corpses. This includes lust murder and any sexual violation on the corpse. He called the second category "necro-stuprum" which refers to merely violating bodies. Finally, "necrophagy" includes both mutilation and consuming parts of cadavers.

These early classifications of necrophilia are rather strictly anchored in behavioural reality. However, this changed considerably following the advent of psychoanalysis. What had been seen as a behavioural manifestation of very disturbed persons gradually attracted the interest of psychoanalysts interested in their clients' fantasy world involving necrophilia and how such fantasies originated. from this theoretical perspective, whether or not these fantasies were acted on in reality is almost beside the point. A tenant of these views, Brill (1941) wrote two articles which to this day stand out among the most authoritative publications on the subject of necrophilia.

Smith and Braun (1978) proposed another enduring distinction. Their scheme distinguishes between two types: 1) "sexual necrophilia", a man's desire to have sexual intercourse or any other kind of sexual contact with a female corpse, and 2) "nonsexual necrophilia", the desire to handle, to gaze at corpses and to be in their proximity, and particularly the desire to dismember them.

Rosman and Resnick (1989) propose differentiating between: 1) "necrophilic homicide", which entails murder to obtain a corpse for sexual purposes, 2) "regular necrophilia", which refers to the use of already dead bodies for sexual pleasure (this group frequently involves persons who find a way to work in contact with deceased), and 3) "necrophilic fantasy" which is fantasizing about sexual activity with a corpse, without carrying out any necrophilic acts. Rosman and Resnick also mention 4) "the pseudonecrophile" as a distinct category having a transient attraction to a corpse, but the corpse is not the object of sexual fantasies. Indeed, in this view, the pseudonecrophile prefers sexual contact with living partners.

Synopsis of an original case

Mr. S. is a 53 year old man the author saw in psychotherapy for several years in a maximum security forensic hospital in North America. Mr. S. was referred for individual psychotherapy for "security" reasons. At the time, Mr. S. was considered so dangerous that the director of the facility hoped that a therapist could detect any minute change in his adjustment and put the rest of staff on alert.

Mr. S. presents as a very lightly coloured African American. His genogram reveals that one set of grandparents were Irish and African American and the other set were native American and Italian. He was in extremely good physical condition, the result of many years of weight lifting in various prisons and of an ascetic and obsessional lifestyle whereby he controlled almost every gram of food he ingested and scheduled his activities down to the minute. He led an organized and isolated life as the only permanent patient on the admissions and medical ward where he single-handedly managed the clothing and laundry of a high turnover patient population.

Mr. S. was born in 1942. His biological parents never married and separated when he was one year old. He has one older sister. His father had a long-standing alcohol problem which he overcame to ultimately become a minister of a small congregation. the record indicates that his mother was a "Negro woman of low morality", because she was unwed with children. She married when her children were well into their teens. Mr. S.'s stepfather was a quiet, low key, but likeable man who was unable to stand up to his energetic and at times overbearing wife. In time, the patient's mother also became a minister of a fundamentalist Protestant congregation. For many years, an all important maternal grandmother lived with the family, and as Mr. S. points out he was the only male confronted with three generations of strong-minded women all older than himself.

Mr. S. grew up in African American neighbourhood in Boston. He attended public school where he did quite poorly, repeating 5th, 6th and 7th grade before leaving school at age 16. A psychometric test of an unknown type was conducted at age 13 and produced a misleading IQ of 93. A WAIS conducted in the early 1990's showed that Mr. S. had an overall IQ in the high average range and a verbal IQ well into the superior range. Indeed, over the years, he more than made up for his initial poor educational environment. During psychotherapy sessions, Mr. S. sometimes shared views on Kierkegaard and Saint Augustin. Later on, he prompted the therapist into discussions on Tolstoy, Umberto Eco, James Joyce and Freud.

After leaving school, Mr. S. engaged in a series of low skill menial jobs. At age 16, he was sent to reform school for 10 months. This began an almost unbroken string of incarcerations. During a 12 year period from 1958 to 1970, Mr. S. was charged with a crime on 27 occasions. Convictions covered Larceny, Destroying Property, Assault and battery by means of a dangerous weapon, Breaking and Entering, Using an Automobile without permission, Drunkenness, Conspiracy, Assault with intent to rob while being armed, Robbery, and Murder.

During a brief period in the streets, Mr. S. married a young woman he had known since childhood. Their marriage was extremely stormy, indeed physically abusive, and it ended in divorce during one of his subsequent prison sentences. He recalls being enraged at his wife and also depressed. When out of prison, Mr. S. also engaged in some alcohol bingeing episodes.

Various psychiatric reports indicate that Mr. S. presented an extremely labile, indeed explosive way. There also seems to have been genuine depressive episodes that do not appear wholly reactive. Yet, several suicidal gestures seem rather superficial and performed in prison for secondary gain. Paranoia, guardedness, hypervigilance are also constants is his presentation. These features also seem to go far beyond the healthy dose of paranoia a prison environment requires for survival.

Mr. S. denied any history of sexual abuse, but recalled being a target and the witness of considerable physical and psychological abuse in his family. He briefly shared some incestuous sexual exploration with his sister when they were both young adolescents. He also shared some sexually seductive activity by his mother when she bathed him. He was involved in a few other short-lived heterosexual relationships. He also experimented early on as a child with homosexual relationships and continued in prison.

The latest arrest had initially been for murder of a woman. While awaiting trial, he committed two more murders in jail. He was serving a life sentence for one of these latter murders and was committed to the maximum security hospital under an Incompetent to Stand Trial statute. In his case it was probably an abusive use of the statute, but it did not allow him to stay in a less threatening and supportive environment where, in fact, he no longer acted out violently.

Retrospectively, one of the first clues that Mr. S. presented an unusual pathology came from a dream he discussed in therapy. He dreamt of being cornered in a surreal world of pipes and unpredictably shifting floor areas of intense heat. In his dream he was in an environment reminiscent of the movie "Brazil" caught in a type of learned helplessness experiment, unable to escape a negative stimulus. The dream evolved into a fantastic escape and Mr. S. described how he was able to peel off layers of his skin on his hands and wrists. He peeled and he peeled until holes appeared and he could look up at the light through the holes in his hands. He could also look horizontally into his hand towards the tip of his fingers and look the source of light filtering through his flesh.

His necrophilic interest emerged slowly thereafter. He shared that he liked older women, women of his grandmother's age. He explained rationally that he had very much liked his grandmother and that she had been protective of him, a source of affection. He also shared a curious relationship he had with an elderly lady in his neighbourhood for whom he would go grocery shopping and with whom he would spend long periods of free time. On one occasion, she discovered that he had cheated her out of some change. From there on he fantasized about killing her and even devised a strategy to use a gun that she owned. In fact, not long afterwards, he discovered her dead body. He adamantly protested in therapy that he had not killed her and that she had died from natural causes. However, he also described being intrigues by this dead body.

Shortly afterwards, his grandmother passed away. This was a traumatic event and Mr. S. recalls feeling abandoned and very lonely. He also shared a highly specific memory of his grandmother's wake which he links to his necrophilic début. He remembers looking at the dead body of his grandmother, at uncovered skin areas and at the region of her covered breasts. This seems to have been his only clear necrophilic fantasy until actually acting on his urge.

In summary, Mr. S. was arrested at age 28 following the disappearance of a young woman he had been dating. He had known her for several years and he was well-liked by her family. He had strangled her in a park and performed cunnilingus, full intercourse and sodomy on her dead body. Over the three years spent in psychotherapy, Mr. S. further admitted to murdering four other young women and performing various sexual acts on their lifeless bodies.

After his arrest, while in detention, he murdered a young cell mate with whom he had become briefly sexually intimate. The murder was extremely brutal and involved facial mutilation and post mortem sodomy. This was followed by a second murder under the same circumstances not too long afterwards after, by mistake, another inmate was made to share his cell. Here again he committed sodomy on his dead victim's body. In psychotherapy, he explained that he derived increased sexual pleasure from this act.

Discussion

It should be noted that Mr. S. loosely fits the pattern of the typical "necrophilic homicide" described by Rosman and Resnick (1989). As the cases they reviewed suggest, the typical necrophile is usually not a highly pathological person, at least not overtly. In the literature, only a minority of necrophiles present psychotic features and a minority are intellectually impaired. Why do they engage in these acts? Commonly mentioned reasons by necrophiles themselves are: 1) to possess an unresisting and unrejecting partner, 2) to reunite with an unavailable romantic partner, 3) conscious sexual attraction to corpses, 4) attempts to gain comfort or to overcome feelings of isolation, and 5) attempts to gain self esteem by the expression of power.

While in Mr. S's case there are undoubtedly multiple factors involved: alcohol, childhood trauma, perhaps constitutional elements, for once I feel quite uncomfortable with a more psychoanalytic explanation that emphasizes pathological mourning. Mr. S.'s feeling of object loss at the death of his supportive maternal grandmother lends some credence to an early thesis of LeBoeuf and Lefebre (1966) that the love instinct must be all powerful in necrophiles to overcome the resistance of shame, horror and disgust.

References

Brill, A. A. (1941). Necrophilia. *Journal of Criminal Psychopathology, 2*, 433-453.

Brill, A. A. (1941). Necrophilia (Part II). *Journal of Criminal Psychopathology, 3*, 51-73.

Burg, B. R. (1982). The sick and the dead: The development of psychological theory on necrophilia from Krafft-Ebing to the present. *Journal of the History of Behavioral Sciences, 18*, 242-254.

Herodotus (translated in 1972 by H. Cary). *Historiae*. Freeport, NY: Books for Libraries Press.

Jaffé, P. D., & DiCataldo, F. (1994). Clinical vampirism: Blending myth and reality. *Bulletin of the American Academy of Psychiatry and Law, 22. (4)*, 533-544.

Jaffé, P. D., Tschopp, C., & DiCataldo, F. (1994). Expertise d'un vampire: Mythe et psychopathologie. *Bulletin de Psychologie, 47 (415)*, 349-356.

Jones, E. (1931). *On the nightmare*. London, Hogarth Press.

Krafft-Ebing, R. von (1886, translated 1990). *Psychopathia sexualis*. Castelnau-le-Lez, Paris: Climats.

LeBoeuf, J., & Lefebre, P. (1966). Contribution â l'étude de la sado-nécrophilie. *Canadian Psychological Association Journal, 11*, 123-131.

Rosman, J. P., & Resnick, P. J. (1989). Sexual attraction to corpses: A psychiatric review of necrophilia. *Bulletin of the American Academy of Psychiatry and Law, 17 (2)*, 153-163.

Smith, S. M., & Braun, C. (1978). Necrophilia and lust murder: Report of a rare occurrence. *Bulletin of the American Academy of Psychiatry and Law, 6 (3)*, 259-268.

Tridon, P., Crombez, Y., Vidailhet, C., Paugain, M., & Boissenin, J. M. (1984). A propos d'un cas de nécrophilie: Approche structurale et psychopathologique. *Annales Médico-Psychologique, 142 (7)*, 1017-1024.

Are Causal Theories of Paedophilia Possible? A Reconsideration of Sexual Abuse Cycles

Dennis Howitt

The factors leading to paedophilia are incompletely understood (Howitt, 1995). Nevertheless, the enormous psychological, social and economic costs of such offending underline the need to minimize sexual crimes against children. Current strategies range from child protection intervention in families, through community based therapy, to medical castration. Recently, psychological therapy for sex offenders within prisons has become increasingly common although far from universal. Some doubt the efficacy of therapeutic programmes for adult offenders (Marques et al., 1989) despite the enthusiasm of some practitioners. This paper reconsiders the possibility that there are cycles of sexual abuse whereby some child victims are more likely to become victimisers. Currently the cycles-of-abuse thesis is disfavoured for the following reasons among others:

1. Some studies of offenders have found relatively low levels of sexual abuse in their childhoods.
2. Most sexually abused children do not grow up to be abusers.
3. Males form the bulk of offenders in most studies. Since being sexually victimized is more common in the histories of females (Howitt, 1992), how can this be explained in terms of cycles of abuse?

Nevertheless, we should not prematurely abandon the cycles-of-abuse hypothesis despite the arguments of some reviewers (e.g. Finkelhor, 1984). For example, increasingly it is claimed that sexual abuse by females may have been drastically under reported (Howitt, 1992). There are also signs that abuse by females may be more criminogenic than previous reviewers have allowed (Carlson, 1991). In other words, abusing by females may be a hidden but especially influential aspect of the abusing cycle of males. Classifying all abusive acts identically might ignore the possibility that certain forms of abuse are more likely to initiate abusive cycles.

Theories of Abuse Cycles

One of the difficulties for cycle-of-abuse theories is the frequent claim that much sexual abuse is the consequence of pathogenic family dynamics. This argument is particularly applied to comparisons between incestuous offenders and extra-familial offenders. However, there is no formal evidence that incestuous families show any particular pattern of pathologies (Conte, 1985). Furthermore, rather than being driven to offending through stress or pathological family structures, it has been shown that many of these offenders show clear patterns of sexual preference for children (Freund et al., 1991) and many have a history of also sexually abusing outside of the family (Becker and Coleman, 1988). That is, they are commonly erotically fixated on children just as extra-familial offenders are. The regression argument may underestimate the difficulties which these men can have relating to adult women psychosexually. Such 'mature' sexual orientations, for example, may rely on paedophile fantasy during intercourse (Howitt, 1995).

Self-awareness of having a paedophile psychosexuality is usually present by early adulthood. Three quarters of paedophiles claim to be aware that they were paedophile by the age of twenty (Bernard, 1985). One implication of this is that paedophilia is well-established by young adulthood – possibly as a consequence of early experiences. There are a number of theoretical accounts of why sexual abuse in childhood may lead to offending against children. Most of these have little systematic research in support or otherwise and rarely are they articulated as formal theories. This aside, the main explanations include: a) Identification with the Aggressor, loosely based on Freudian psychodynamic theory, argues that a child copes psychologically with the experience of being abused by incorporation of aspects of the personality of their abuser – including the abusive behaviours themselves; b) Acting Out Anger: Anger generated by the experience of abuse is acted out by hurting children through abuse; c) Abusive Careers: This suggests that being a victim of abuse may involve a longer term involvement with offender groups which progresses through contact with paedophiles to the stage of victimiser. There are certainly examples of such progressions reported in the literature but these appear to be very much the minority; d) Childhood Fixation Due to Abuse: Basically this suggests that the trauma of the abuse leads to a psycho-sexual developmental blockage which fixes the person's psycho-sexual orientation at a particular stage. This is best exemplified in the notion of fixated paedophiles (Groth and Birnbaum, 1978).

Whatever the validity of these theoretical linkages, each implies a strong relationship between being an abuser and having experienced sexual abuse in childhood. Studies which suggest that abuse in childhood is hardly more common in the childhoods of abusers than non-abusers (e.g. Waterhouse et al., 1994) are an embarrassment to any of these proposed mechanisms. These studies would limit the cycles of abuse thesis quite significantly to, at best, a minority of offenders. But this evidence may not be totally convincing. Since the recognition and disclosure of one's own childhood abuse may involve a slow unveiling process through counselling and therapy, it has to be questioned whether a simple self-completion questionnaire, for example, is an appropriate way of eliciting disclosure. Furthermore, the institutional setting in which the research is being conducted may influence disclosure. The interests of paedophile offenders may be best served by denying their own childhood victimization. The incestuous perpetrator may avoid disclosing, for example, because he or she fears that this would reveal a long-term problem rather than a temporary work-stress or family crisis for which the prognosis is good.

Significant reviews such as those by Finkelhor (1984) and Hansen and Slater (1988) suggest that there are relatively low levels of sexual abuse in the childhoods of offenders compared with non-offenders. However, evidence from other researchers is less hostile to the cycles of abuse thesis. For example, Freund et al. (1990) found that 29% of heterosexual paedophiles, 26% of homosexual paedophiles, 20% and 20% of child molesters had experienced abuse compared with 11% of heterosexual controls and 12% of homosexual controls. Gaffney et al. (1984) noted that 27% of paedophiles in their sample were on record as experiencing abuse in childhood compared with 14% of the other paraphiliacs but this did not reach statistical significance. These are weak support for the cycles-of-abuse thesis but give it some credibility.

Some studies suggest a far stronger cycle of abuse. One study found that 56% of non-violent child molestation offenders were been sexually abused as a child (Tingle et al., 1986). Another showed that approximately 50% of paedophiles (heterosexual and homosexual) and incest offenders reported sexual abuse in childhood compared with 0% of a community control group (Lang and Langevin, 1991). It seems that abuse is common in the early experience of sexually abusive adolescents. Breer (1987) classified some of these as likely to become adult paedophiles and virtually all of these youngsters had been sexually molested by men. In contrast, incestuous and female-oriented adolescent abusers were far less likely to admit abuse – only about a quarter admitted being abused and half of these had been victimised by females.

The Social Construction of Abuse

Given that self-reported retrospective evidence of abuse is impossible to corroborate, factors which might influence recollection and disclosure may be crucial in testing the cycles-of-abuse thesis. Some child abuse victims require counselling and guidance before becoming able to construe their childhood experiences as abusive. Perceptions of the term 'child sexual abuse' vary in different sectors of society just as it varies within professional groups (Howitt, 1992). The most direct evidence in favour of this comes from a study of serial rapists of adult women. Burgess et al. (1988) found that they overwhelmingly denied being sexually abused in childhood when asked directly. The researchers also gathered the men's reports of their earliest sexual experiences and classified three-quarters of them as being sexually abusive using a reasonably standard definition of abuse! Interestingly, the remainder of the offenders seemed to have witnessed at least one sexually disturbing event in childhood. The majority of the men had been abused in a forced or exploitative way.

In an attempt to extend this research, young sexual offenders against children and young non-sexual offenders were interviewed and questioned about their early sexual involvements with different categories of people (Howitt and Glover, unpublished). The term abuse was not used. In keeping with Burgess et al.'s findings on serial rapists, it was found that sexual involvements which were classified by the researchers as abusive were far commoner in the young sexual offenders (81%) than in non-sexual offender controls (25%). Furthermore, there were indications that the sexual acts perpetrated against the future sex offenders in childhood were more serious.

Psycho-Sexual Effects of Abuse

Although there is an extensive literature on the effects of sexual abuse on the psycho-sexual development of females, less is known about males. The cycles of abuse hypothesis would be more convincing if abuse in childhood influences of the psychosexual development of male victims in general. There is some consensus as to effects of sexual abuse on boys. Involvement in sexual crimes is more common in youths who were sexually abused in childhood (Fehrenbach et al, 1986; Groth, 1979; Longo, 1982). Severe sexual abuse may disinhibit sexual behaviour in its victims (Friedrich and Luecke, 1988; McCauley et al., 1983). Inappropriate sexual behaviours such as confusion about sexual matters, compulsive sexual behaviours and sexual acting out including offending may be the more immediate consequences of abuse (Urquiza and Capra, 1991). Finkelhor (1979) and Johnson and Shrier (1985) suggest that victimization by adult men (but not by young males) increased the likelihood of adult homosexuality. The adult psychosexual difficulties encountered by male victims of abuse included sexual adjustment, poor sexual self-esteem and sexual identity problems (Urquiza and Capra, 1991). Olson (1991) compared sexually abused and non-sexually abused men undergoing psychotherapy. Male or female parents were the most common abusers. Victims and non-victims differed the most in terms of problems such as rage, compulsive spending and, significantly in this context, compulsive sexual behaviour.

One implication of this is that childhood sexual involvement with adults can result in a sexualized pattern of behaviour in the victims.

Re-Enactment Theory

One recent important theoretical development in terms of the effects of abuse is re-enactment theory (Burgess et al., 1988). Re-enactment is the process by which the victim offends using either a direct behavioural replication or a symbolic equivalent of their own earlier abuse. Burgess et al. found that over half of their rapist offenders had demonstrated re-enactment in their childhoods. That is, if one compares their own abuse with their first self-initiated sexual activity then there is a close match between the two. It is important to note that the abuse experienced by these men tended to be extreme and somewhat violent with female perpetrators not being uncommon. The confusion and stress generated by the sexual aspects of abuse motivate the re-enactment. Unable to control his own arousal, the child becomes preoccupied with sexual matters and sexually arousing thoughts. Others have noted a close thematic correspondence between early abuse and later abusing. For example, Greenberg et al. (1993) showed that there is a close correspondence between the age at which the offender was first offended against and later the age of his own victims. Howitt (1995) demonstrated a pattern in which the characteristics of the offenders early abuse and their later offending overlap quite distinctively. However, Howitt argues that childhood sexual involvements do not have to be abusive to have an effect. Sexual involvements with peers may be responsible for later paedophilia in some cases.

Conclusion

There seems sufficient theoretical and empirical justification to suggest that the case against the cycles-of-abuse explanation of paedophilia is not proven. Methods of obtaining data on childhood abuse need to be sensitive to subcultural variations in understanding of the term abuse and motivations for disclosure. If the cycles-of-abuse hypothesis is supported in the long term, there are implications for the ways in which offending may be prevented. Therapy and intervention might be far more effective if resources were allocated primarily to young victims with the goal of breaking the cycle of abuse early on. This task would be enhanced if it was clearer which types of abuse are likely to initiate a cycle.

References

Becker, J V., & Coleman, E. M. (1988). Incest. In V. B. Hasselt, R. L. Morrison, A. S. Bellack, & M. Hersen (Eds.), *Handbook of Family Violence.* New York: Plenum.

Bernard, F. (1985). *Paedophilia: A Factual Report.* Enclave: Rotterdam.

Breer, W. (1987). *The Adolescent Molester*. Springfield, IL: Charles C. Thomas.

Burgess, A. W., Hazelwood, R. R., Rokous, F. E., Hartman, C. R., & Burgess, A. G. (1988). Serial rapists and their victims: reenactment and repetition. *Human Sexual Aggression: Current Perspectives, 528, August 12,* 277-95.

Carlson (1991). The Victim/Perpetrator. In M. Hunger (Ed.), *The Sexually Abused Male: Prevalence, Impact, and Treatment, Volume 2.* Lexington: Lexington Books.

Conte, J. R., (1985). Clinical dimensions of adult sexual abuse of children. *Behavioural Sciences and the Law, 3(4),* 341-4.

Fehrenbach, P. A., Smith, W., Monstersky, C., and Deisher, R. W. (1986). Adolescent sexual offenders: offenders and offense characteristics. *American Journal of Orthopsychiatry, 56,* 255-63.

Finkelhor, D. (1979). *Sexually Victimised Children.* New York: Free Press.

Finkelhor, D. (1984). *Child Sexual Abuse: New Theory and Research.* New York: Free Press.

Freund, K., Watson, R., and Dickey, R. (1990). Does sexual abuse in childhood cause pedophilia: an exploratory study. *Archives of Sexual Behaviour, 19(6)*, 557-68.

Gaffney, G. R., Lurie, S. F., and Berlin, F. S. (1984). Is there familial transmission of pedophilia? *The Journal of Nervous and Mental Disease, 172(9)*, 546-8.

Greenberg, D. M., Bradford, J. M. W., and Curry, C. (1993). A comparison of sexual victimization in the chidhoods of pedophiles and hebephiles. *Journal of Forensic Sciences, 38(2)*, 432-36.

Groth, A. N. (1979). Sexual trauma in the lives of rapists and child molesters. *Victimology, 4*, 10-16.

Groth, A. N., & Birnbaum, H. J. (1978). Adult sexual orientation and attraction to underage persons. *Archives of Sexual Behaviour, 7(3)*, 175-181.

Hansen, R. K., & Slater, S. (1988). Sexual victimization in the history of sexual abusers: a review. *Annals of Sex Research, 1*, 485-99.

Howitt, D. (1992). *Child Abuse Errors.* Hemel Hempstead: Harvester-Wheatsheaf.

Howitt, D. (1995). *Paedophiles and Sexual Offences Against Children.* Chichester: John Wiley.

Johnson, R., & Shrier, D. K. (1985). Sexual victimization of boys. *Journal of Adolescent Health Care, 6(5)*, 372-76.

Lang, R. A., & Langevin, R. (1991). Parent-child relations in offenders who commit violent sexual crimes against children. *Behavioural Sciences and the Law, 9*, 61-71.

Marques, J. C., Day, D. M., Nelson, C., & Miner, M. H. (1989). The sex offender treatment and evaluation project: California's relapse prevention program. In D. R. Laws (Ed.), *Relapse Prevention with Sex Offenders.* New York: The Guilford Press, 247-67.

McCauley, N., Burke, P. M., Furukawa, J., & Urquiza, A. J. (1983). *Sexual behaviour problems in pre-pubertal children.* University of Washington, unpublished manuscript.

Olson, P. E. (1991). The sexual abuse of boys: a study of the long-term psychological effects. In M. Hunter (Ed.), *The Sexually Abused Male: Prevalence, Impact, and Treatment, Volume 1.* Lexington Books, 137-52.

Tingle, D., Barnard, G. W., Robbins, L., Newman, Gustave, & Hutchinson, D. (1986). Childhood and adolescent characteristics of pedophiles and rapists. *International Journal of Law and Psychiatry, 9*, 103-16.

Urquiza, A. J., and Capra, M. (1991). The impact of sexual abuse: initial and long-term effects. In M. Hunter (Ed.), *The Sexually Abused Male: Prevalence, Impact, and Treatment, Volume 1.* Lexington Books, 105-35.

Waterhouse, L., Dobash, R. P., Carnie, J. (1994). *Child Sexual Abusers.* The Scottish Office Central Research Unit.

Expert Psychological Opinion for the Court in Cases of Homicide under Emotional Strain in Poland

Jan M. Stanik

Homicide is the gravest crime, for which the Polish Penal Code demands a penalty of at least eight years imprisonment or capital punishment (Art. 148 par. 1. of the Polish Penal Code). However, if a person commits homicide *"under heavy emotional strain justified by circumstances"* the punishment stipulated is between 1 and 10 years of imprisonment (Art. 148 par. 2 of Polish penal code).

This circumstance – *"under heavy emotional strain"* or *"committing homicide under severe provocation"* (cf. German "die heftige Erregung", Russian: "silnoye volnieniye", French: "agitation extreme") – is considered in almost all systems of criminal law in civilized countries, always having the effect of considerable reduction of punishment in case such homicide has been committed. Therefore, discernment of the nature of the act being "under heavy emotional strain justified by circumstances", is of substantial importance as regards the punishment, as such offence is treated less severly than the corresponding standard offence.

The concept of heavy emotional strain in law

The literature of the subject (cf. e.g. Cora, 1973; Tarnawski, 1975; Gierowski, 1991; Pobocha, 1994) in principle agrees that the term heavy emotional strain is a jurisprudential construction – a penal code term, whereas the theory of law and judicial decisions taken by the Supreme Court have to a large extent made its use precise, that is, they clearly determined the scope of its content, which – however – still raises some objections as to both legal-dogmatic aspect of it, and to the practical judicial decisions.

The commentary to the Penal Code (Bafia, Mioduski, & Siewierski, 1987, p. 346) has it that the essence of emotional strain lies in the irritation and excitement, leading to giving vent to the strong emotion by action "in which the emotional content (feelings) prevail over the intellectual (rational) one." This action appears as reaction to the external facts which, due to their content or character, resulted in violent opposition in the psyche of the person which undertook the action in question. Thus the concept of emotional strain stands close to that of indignation expressed in anger, as opposition against facts which touch the given person (ibid.). That is why for the concept of emotional strain (in its legal aspect) the reason and reaction to it are of primary importance.

Art. 148, par. 2. states that it is necessary for that strain to be justified by circumstances, that is by fact which caused it. The justification of such strain is determined on the basis of ethical criteria on the one hand, and rules governing community life on the other hand. The latter, as authors of the commentary mentioned stress, "demand to observe the rights regarding property and interests of others, while also justify the defence of those, keeping in mind its admissible limits – the defence has to be dependent upon what has happened to the person in question. There should be a certain balance between emotional strain and the reason for it. In our sense of law we judge an act less severely if it had been committed under justified emotional strain, if the circumstances which led to that strain deserve a negative social appraisal." (ibid., p. 347).

Another necessary condition for accepting the state of heavy emotional stress under which a given crime of homicide has been committed (in line with the intention of art. 148, par. 2. of the Penal Code) is determining that the degree and character of the strain the perpetrator was under, and his/her attitude to the homicide committed were of such kind that they influenced the perpetrator in a decisive way, thus the perpetrator would not have committed that homicide act had it been not because of that strain (cf. OSNKW 1967, No. 1, p. 14 – sentence of May 06, 1966; IIKR 50/66).

The essence of that privileged state of emotional strain, according to the "Commentary to the Penal Code..." we discuss here is a state of mind in which the emotional processes have advantage over the intellect, because of which the perpetrator acts under the influence of dominating emotions, whilst the controlling activity of reason is severely restricted. The condition stating that the emotional stress must be heavy should be considered a tip that the code gives to a judge, "so that – in every single case the and conspicuous advantage of emotions over the possibility of logical reasoning by the perpetrator be established" (ibid., p. 347). Thesis 17 of the commentary to the Penal Code in force, which being discussed here has it that, as the authors state, heavy emotional strain, meant by Art. 148, par. 2. of the Penal Code, is a mental process experienced. In the psychological sense, this affect is a violent and generally short-lived emotional outbreak, accompanied by a series of noticeable physiological changes in the organism of a given person (blood flow, movements, etc.). However, as the authors stress, this heavy emotional strain is not solely a psychological concept, being also a specific legal one, based on the criteria established in the course of judicial decisions and doctrinal achievements, which consider prerequisites of ethical, criminological, social nature, among others.

In Polish court and penal law procedure, when considering a case of homicide under heavy emotional strain (art. 148, par. 2. of the Penal Code), the establishment of whether the perpetrator in tempore criminis acted under heavy emotional strain is most often entrusted to an expert psychologist or psychologist and pschiatrist who, through specialist investigation and diagnosis determine whereby that state of emotional strain was really justified by circumstances is the domain of the court which, on the basis of evidence (depositions of witnesses and other facts) decide whether the external circumstances in which the homicide took place were of such kind that the victim (the deceased in the murder) violated the rules of community life and rules of ethics, which resulted in evoking that heavy emotional strain in the perpetrator.

The above leads to a conclusion that in order to be able to qualify an act of homicide as an offence – according to art. 148, par. 2 of the Penal Code – it is not enough to prove that the perpetrator acted under heavy emotional stress – affect (the psychological aspect regarding the perpetrator) – yet it is also necessary to prove, in a conjunctive way, that this emotional strain was caused by stimuli justifying its appearance (the legal segment being a feature of that criminal offence). This can be schematically presented in the following way (Figure 1.):

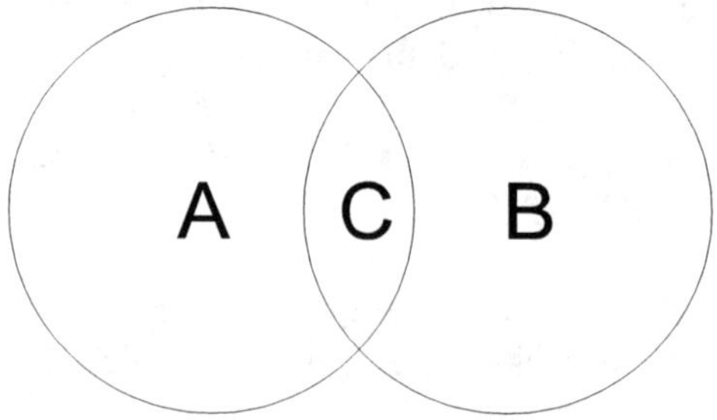

C – heavy emotional strain justified by circumstances
A – psychological affect (the psychological segment)
B – the axiological – legal – segment: "justification by circumstances"

Figure 1: Criteria for the qualification of an act of homicide committed under heavy emotional strain, justified by circumstances (art. 148, par. 2 of the Penal Code)

Psychological definition of the condition of heavy emotional strain

As has been stressed before, the concept of heavy emotional strain is a legal construction with a dogmatically determined interpretation included in the commentary to the Penal Code. For an expert psychologist or psychiatrist pointed by the court, in turn, the diagnosis of that condition of heavy emotional strain must be done using psychological terms, according to the accepted empirical model, determining the internal mechanism of that phenomenon, as well as its operation which, would give the basis for its measurement and psychological diagnosis to be expressed in the expert opinion for the court.

As one lawyer rightly stresses (Cora, 1973, p. 1035) to rely, when qualifying the condition of heavy emotional strain legally, only on the criterion of emotional reaction is erroneous and deceptive, not being satisfactorily psychologically justified. The very way the emotional reaction develops – as a violent outbreak – does not say much about the psychological condition under which this reaction took place. The external character of human reaction depends not only on the kind and specificity of the emotional stimulus, which is generally preferred in legal terminology, but also upon the characteristic features of psychical processes and the structure of the personality of the perpetrator.

To avoid going into too detailed deliberations, it should be stated that forensic psychology in Poland treats the condition of heavy emotional strain or effect as an instance of personality functioning under extreme psychological stress, in line with the two laws of Yerkes–Dodson. As one can read in the Encyclopedia of Psychology (Eysenek et al., 1975) the concept of affect (emotional strain) has not been fully and unequivocally specified: "In general it is used to characterize a feeling of particular intensity. Sometimes an 'affect' is characterized as a state brought about by actions almost wholly devoid of intentional control in accordance with moral and objective viewpoints. The term is also found in the literature as practically synonymous with 'emotion' in certain senses."

Analyzing the psychic condition of the perpetrator being under heavy emotional strain (physiologically) usually the following are determined: direct and distant (remote) motives for action, the emotional state before committing the act, a comprehensive diagnosis of the personality of the perpetrator is carried out, paying special attention to the functioning of emotional processes and self-observation, the other vital psychic mechanisms in tempore criminis. The presentation of such diagnosis markedly enriches the knowledge of the court and makes it easier to determine, in the course of court proceedings, the whole truth about the psychic condition of the perpetrator when committing the act.

The diagnostic criteria of emotional strain (affect) have been determined by numerous authors (cf. Stanik, 1991). In the majority of cases the main criterion was the short duration of the emotional outbreak, and the existence of three phases within it.

According to Pobocha (1994), phase one is unspecific, similar to that during pathological affect, consists of very quick increase of the emotional strain, the tempo of which depends mainly on the personality structure of the perpetrator and (or) the degree of its abnormality, e.g. weakened self-observation, hyper-aggression, neurosis, and the like. The conditions necessary for producing such reaction are: aggravation of conflicts with the future victim, existence of a physical or psychical obstacle make it impossible for the perpetrator to realize his/her plans or desires, strong and prolonged sensation of threat, etc. Generally speaking, the perpetrator experiences a trauma, resulting from the fact that the stimuli are: strong, exceptional, irritating (morally and psychically), unexpected and of subjective importance for the perpetrator. Such trauma may be the result of prolonged persecution, humiliation, threatening to kill, extreme block of fulfilling emotional needs, etc. that is situations, which are legally, culturally, and morally considered "unbearable". All this results in generating a subjective need to act immediately against the person or persons that provoked such condition. Those actions are undertaken without any plan, spontaneously and involuntarily, while the situation is not assessed in the rational way – it slips out of the control of the intellect – as the above quoted definition by Eysenek has it.

The second phase is the emotional outbreak with strong psychomotoric excitation and pronounced changes in the functioning of cognitive processes (the field of visual perception is narrower, the attention stiffens, audio perception loses its edge), but not of pathological or psychotic nature. The behaviour of the perpetrator is usually of the unexpected, unusual, surprising nature, both for him/her and for the surroundings, being alien to his/her personality. Both the perpetrator and, sometimes, the witnesses asses this as: "exceptional reaction to exceptional circumstances." The perpetrator of an act committed under emotional strain (affect), as well as witnesses tend to describe this as experience and manifestation of anger, fury, horrors, harm or humiliation. As has been stressed before, such a perpetrator has his/her stream of consciousness narrowed and enveloped in mist, directed at the person causing the psychosomatic effects in him/her (the future victim of homicide) or at such situation, which results in fragmentary perception and later in partial remembrance of the incident.

Such emotional states in the perpetrator are accompanied by visible changes in appearance and dynamics of behaviour. Besides that, there are often endocrine, vegetative and cardio-vascular reactions. That is why such a person may reveal the following manifestations: clenching teeth and lips, dry mouth, grinding teeth, clenching fists, hoarse voice, partial or complete loss of voice. Sometimes, however, verbal communication is possible, which allows to find orientation partly reserved; whereas other perpetrators utter inarticulate cries or shout. Their movements tend to be trembling and may lack coordination, while the eyelids are wide open, as are the pupils. In some exceptional cases passing water and evacuating one's bowels accompany the above. The range and type of symptoms of heavy physiological strain (affect) depend on the personality structure of the perpetrator, the type of psychotraumatic situation, local conditions (site, circumstances of the act), etc.

The objects used by the criminal as implements of crime – aggression may be accidental. In general, those implements just happened to be "at hand". The acts committed by people under extreme emotional strain usually are of conventional nature and impulsive character, showing symptoms of impaired self-control and ability to anticipate the outcome of such acts. The behaviour of such a perpetrator is a-typical for himself/herself, inconsistent with his/her line of conduct and principles, as well as the hierarchy of values. The a-typicality of the motives of action of such perpetrators results from the unusual situation in which they found themselves and the extremely strong emotional stimulation, being the dominating mechanism for behaviour.

During the third phase of physiological affect, the descending one, labelled exhaustion, the psychical functioning of the individual gets decreased. The emotional stimulation quickly collapses; symptoms of fatigue, apathy, asthenia and weariness. In this phase perpetrators begin to assess their previous behaviour critically. Therefore it often happens that they undertake actions directed at helping the victim, express their grief, apologize, etc. Some of them inform their family about the incident, get in touch with the police or other officials entitled to prosecute, call an ambulance, etc.

It still remains disputable who among the perpetrators acting under strong physiological affect (emotional strain) attempts self-mutilation or suicide. The opinion prevails that persons with irregular personality structure or having contacts with criminal sub-cultures more often engage in self-destructive activities.

It is believed that among additonal factors stimulating the occurrence of physiological affect (emotional strain), besides those listed above, are the following: over-exertion of such person, overwork, physical weakness, elevated temperature, asthenia following a somatic disease, etc.

From the psychological point of view the affect may be of different intensity and may be showed as *continuum* between extremely strong intensity, through various stages of milder intensity, as far as the turning point where this abnormal condition becomes normal emotional activation (Figure 2):

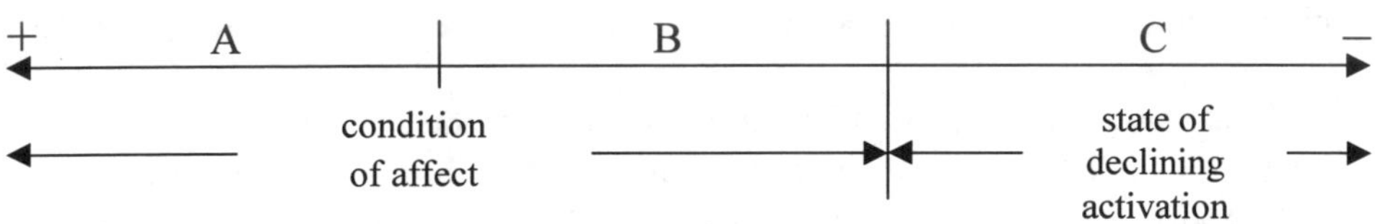

A – extremely strong affect
B – milder affect
C – normal emotional activation

Figure 2: Phases of physiological affect

Therefore, among the tasks of an expert psychologist appointed by the court, besides identifying the occurrence of the affect, is also the establishment and qualification – by means of psychological examinations – of its intensity. This is vital for the court, being one of the fundamental criteria when deciding whether to qualify the act for the 1 to 8 years of imprisonment as suitable punishment for it. The qualification scheme applied by the court, together with the establishment of facts by the expert psychologist appointed by the court are shown in Figure 3.

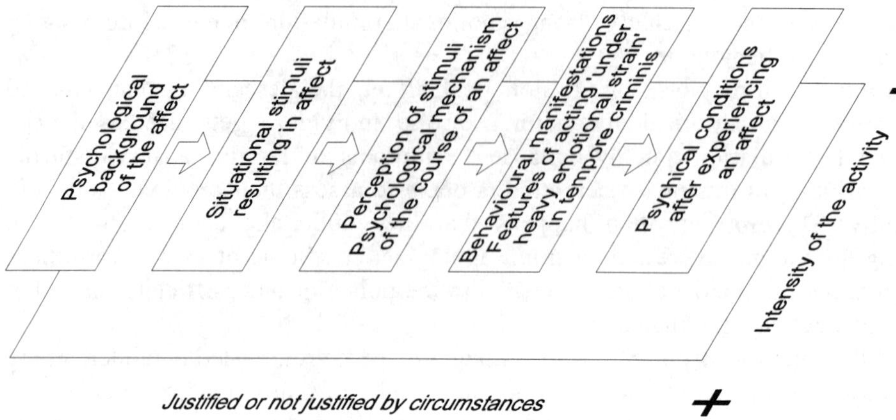

Figure 3: Scheme of the qualification by court of homicide committed under heavy emotional strain strain, justified by circumstances (art. 148. par. of the Polish Penal Code)

The practice of judicial decisions in Poland for cases of homicide committed under heavy emotional stress (art. 148, par. 2. of the Penal Code) still has – languishing in lawyers' decisions – the tradition of overrating the so-called objective circumstances, that is putting stress on facts that are external in relation to the perpetrator and inciting him/her to act, as well as looking for such facts to wholly justify *in tempore criminis hic et nunc* the homicide.

The results of psychological examinations, however, indicate the necessity to extend the conditions determining acting under emotional strain (affect). Here are 3 theses resulting from these examinations (cf. Gierowski, 1991; Pobocha, 1994):

1. "...from the point of view of modern psychology the view represented in the decisions of the Supreme Court and in the specialist legal literature, that – supposedly – to determine the existence of the condition of heavy emotional strain, the external features of the physiological affect should suffice, is erroneous."
2. "...in numerous practical situations the justification of heavy emotional strain need to be sought not in external reasons, but in the psychical peculiarities of the perpetrator."
3. "... the demand to have the reason for the specific emotional situation immediately precede the act, is incorrect. The direct reason may be just the final impulse, the proverbial 'last straw that broke the camel's back', resulting in discharging the emotional energy in the perpetrator."

Unfortunately, the limits of this paper do not allow for introducing the diagnostic methods applied by a psychologist analyzing the condition of heavy emotional strain *in tempore criminis*. I hope to be able to present them some other time.

References

Bafia, J., Mioduski, K., & Siewierski, M. (1987). *Kodeks Karny z komentarzem* (Polish Penal Code with Commentary). Warsaw.

Cora, S. (1973). Zabojstwo pod wplywem silnego wzburzenia w swietle prawa i psychologii (Homicide under Heavy Emotional Strain in the Light of Law and Psychology). *Nowe Prawo, No. 7-8.*

Eysenek, H. J., Arnold, W. J., & Meili, R. (Eds.) (1975). *Encyclopedia of Psychology*. Fonatana, Collins.

Gierowski, J. K. (1991). Afekt fizjologiczny jako przedmiot sadowej ekspertyzy psychologicznej (Physiological Affect as Subject Matter of Psychological Expertise for Court). In Z. Majchrzyk, T. Gordon, & E. Milewskin (Eds.), *Stany afektywne w oponiowaniu sadowym – psychiatryczno-psychologicznym* (Affect Condition in Psychiatric and Psychological Expert Opinion for Courts). Warsaw.

Orzecznoctwo Sadu Najwyzszego, Izba Karna i Wojskowa (Judicial Decisions of the Polish Supreme Court, Criminal Law Division and Division for the Military) (1994). *Palestra, No. 5-6.*

Pobocha, J. (1994). Aspekty psychiatryczne, psychologiczne i prawne stanu silegno wzburzenia (Psychiatric, Psychological and Legal Aspects of Heavy Emotional Strain). *Palestra, No. 5-6.*

Stanik, J. M. (1991). Stan silegno wzburzenia – kompetencje psychologa w opiniodawstwie sadowym (Heavy Emotional Strain – Competence of a Psychologist in Giving Expert Opinions for Courts). In Z. Majchrzyk, T. Gordon, & E. Milewskin (Eds.), *Stany afektywne w oponiowaniu sadowym – psychiatryczno-psychologicznym* (Affect Condition in Psychiatric and Psychological Expert Opinion for Courts). Warsaw.

Tarnawski, M. (1975). Silne wzburzenia jako 'inne zaklocanie czynnosci psychicznych' (Heavy Emotional Strain as 'Specific Mental Disorder'). *Wojskowy Przeglad Prawniczy, No. 2.*

The Problem of Depression's Diagnostic in Forensic and Civil Law in Women

Evgenia V. Korolova

Depression is the most widespread nosology, meeting in Forensic psychiatry, so the assessment of depression is very important. According to Russian Forensic and Civil Law, there are different directions in diagnosis of depression.

As stated in Criminal Code, the person with mental disorders who committed delinquent act had to pass a forensic psychiatric examination involving questions of responsibility-irresponsibility, at the period of the alleged crime, and for evaluation of his capacity to stand the trail. In case of irresponsibility, the person was admitted to coercive treatment in a special psychiatric hospital and also in case of the outbreak of depression at period of imprisonment with a predisposition for emotional traumas. So, the diagnosis of depression is connected to responsibility-irresponsibility and competency evaluation

As per Civil Code the depression diagnostic is connected with assessment of general capacity, accompanied by the order of guardianship. More often patients could litigate civil processes involving different kinds of bargains. The most common bargain was selling or buying of property/flats, houses, etc. The person, suffering with depression could stand as plaintiff in the civil process and the bargain could be made against his interest. Also patients, suffering from depression were civil defendants or could make a civil action or claim. According civil code, it is necessary to estimate the person's state at the moment when the bargain occurs, and directly, his ability to stand in civil trail.

The traditional approach to depression diagnosis in Russian psychiatry last years was nosological, but based mostly on ISD–9,10 and DSM-111-R classifications. Also, used were such measures as psychotic and nonpsychotic or borderline levels of depression. It is mostly spread in forensic psychiatry. The content of this conception is based on criteria of a so-called vital component of depression that includes precardial sadness, somatic symptoms, weight loss, insomnia, and delusions of depressive themes. The condition of psychotic depression made the person irresponsible for alleged crimes and incapacitated in the civil process.

Thus, the main problem of our investigation was attempt to adopt the worldwide classification to be used in Russian forensic psychiatry, and to describe the symptoms of psychotic and nonpsychotic depressions with its features, specified for women.

In this investigation we studied 49 women. In line with international classifications we described patients' current state as Episode of Major Depression and Dysthimia. These women were inpatients at the Center of Social and Psychiatry during 1990-1994. Our method of investigation were clinical-psychopathological and neurochemical, using a biopsychosocial approach. We examined the current stage of depression and background of illness. Each patient was examined by different physicians – internist, neuropathologist, ophtamologist, gynaecologist and so on. In all cases paraclinical and laboratory methods were used. Patients with organic mental disorders, and those with any kind of severe somatic diseases and disturbance of the menstrual cycle were excluded. The age rate at the moment of examination was 22-42 years, so post-adolescent and preclimacteric women only. They had passed forensic examination because of committed crimes (violence and property offence) and because of the civil process, especially bargains, that led to a great loss for the women, suffering with depression.

The results revealed that the course of depression in women was connected with different circumstances that modified the clinical picture.

Firstly, each patient had different stress factors, which, according to DSM-11-R could be classified into enduring circumstances of moderate, severe and extreme levels. As it is known, a specific stress may have greater impact on a person, who is especially vulnerable to them. Typical for women was reaction to conjugal marital and nonmarital psycho-social stress factors as separation, divorce, death of spouse or child. A health history examination revealed that most of patients had previously experienced depression from such emotional traumas. At a current state in the initial stage of depression there was a great influence of acute events that predisposed the onset of depression. So, the clinical symptoms that characterized depression were hidden by psychogenic features. The content of mental disorder was connected with the theme of stress factors that made diagnostic peculiarities. The influence of psycho-social stress could lead to reoccurrence of prior depression in a more severe form, and, more often – to exacerbate an already existing depression, so nonpsychotic level changed into psychotic. The traumatic events caused increasing hetero-aggressive and auto-aggressive motivation in patient's behaviour which led to violent crimes against members of the family. For example, the mental state of women with nonpsychotic form of depression could be aggravated by cruel behaviour of a spouse, it became a psychotic depression. Such patients often committed murders of their children by pathologic motivation to save them from suffering and then tried to commit suicide. In civil law the severe course of depression caused by divorce made women leave all their property to the divorced spouse for the reason of a decision to commit suicide.

The other trait, common to studied women, was combination of depression and personality disorders of a histrionic (hysteric) type and with different forms of anxiety states. All these patients had personality traits such as excessive emotionality, attention-seeking and the rapidly shifting and shallow expression of emotions. Personality disorders which were code on Axis 11 did not play great role in problem of responsibility, but they have covered the mood depressive symptoms, that made a great diagnosis peculiarities. In the clinical picture of examined women the personal features and hysterical stigmas could stand on the first plan. Such symptoms as sadness with sensations of pain in the heart, hardness in the body, immobility often were coved and moderate with "hysterical globus", different sensation in the body, symptoms of astasia-abasia.

The result of investigation revealed that in more than half of the studied patients, the current state of depression was complicated by anxiety states. The clinical history data showed that in this group primary depressions were not observed. All patient had before different forms of mood and anxiety disorders as panic attacks and general anxiety states, and also, depression, caused by psycho-social stressors. These patients had a great number of hereditary disturbances in first-degree relatives – mood disorders (mostly depressions), anxiety disorders, and histrionic personality disorders. All these patients passed forensic psychiatric examination because of criminal behaviour, they committed violent crimes. The diagnostic criteria of the anxiety states, that accompanied depression were the same as described in DSM-11-R. The panic disorders were characterized as disturbances which one of more panic attacks, defined as discrete periods of intense fear of discomfort were observed, The main symptoms were the fear of dying, shortness of breath, dizziness, unsteady feeling and faintness, In all patients their state was considered as panic disorder with agoraphobia. The most common situation in which panic disorders occurred was travelling underground by metro, or, by bus, or car, and being outside the home alone. In half of the patients state could be considered as a mild form, in other half – as a moderate form. But specifically for women, in all cases the early maladaptation firstly in marital and parental functions was observed.

In generalized anxiety disorder, accompanied by depression in women, the main feature was unrealistic or excessive worry about two or more life circumstances and worry about the possibility of setbacks in the future. While the generalized anxiety disorder lasted, most patients were seriously worried about the well-being and health of their children.

The course of depression and anxiety states was closely connected. Sometimes depression was superimposed on anxiety state: sometimes the depression state was an antecedent disorder for anxiety. From the moment when depression and anxiety state began their course together, the clinical picture of both disorders became more severe. Seriousness of depression psychopathology depended on the heaviness of anxiety state symptoms, and degree of anxiety state, in its turn, increased with aggravation of depression. After development of an anxiety state such depressive symptoms, as insomnia, psychomotor agitation, feeling of worthless increased. On the other hand, enforcing of depression's symptoms caused an increase in anxiety, motor tension, and frequency of panic attacks. In case of depression followed by an anxiety state, the manifestation of anxiety had provoked the appearance of mood congruent psychotic features of depression, leading to psychotic level and chronic course of depression.

Depression with general anxiety conducted to affect of anger, affectability, agitation, irritation, explosiveness, that increased aggression of the patients, their suicide and homicide tendencies. The increasing of anxiety led to suicidal and heteroaggressive behaviour. Admission to forensic examination in this group of patients was mostly connected with aggressive crimes, as murder or attempts of murder. Specifically in women, the heteroaggressive crimes that were committed against members of their family and children were cruel. One of the mood symptoms of such state was maladaptation, firstly in marital problem. So, the accompany of depression with anxiety state indicated a severe course of disease, and led to development of psychotic level and chronic course of depression.

The next trait of studied women was frequent development of alcohol abuse during depression, without forming symptoms of chronic alcoholism. The periods of problem drinking coincided with depression and led to the deterioration of the patients' clinical state. Alcohol abuse involved aggravation of symptoms, such as depressed mood, psychomotor agitation and feeling of worthlessness, and suicidal preoccupation. Depressive symptoms increased in hangover, especially the feeling of sadness, ideas of guilt. On the other hand the features of excessive drinking could mask the clinical symptoms of depression. Alcohol abuse occurs in new psychosocial stressors as divorce, separation, physical deseases, which, in their turn, provoked excessive drinking, led to early and quick maladaptation, which also had an influence on the duration of depressions. The severe course of depression in this period was accompanied by impairment of occupational functioning and usual social activities, especially in marital problems and relationship with children, and were factors, that provoked aggressive crimes.

The last trait, characterizing the depression of women in forensic practice was closely related to endocrine factors, modified by age. The clinical picture of depression was modified by endocrine alteration during pre-menstrual tension, pregnancy and post-partumal periods. The patients had periodic mental disturbances, connected with pre-menstrual tension, that were characterized by increasing of irritability, insomnia, hysterical somatoform disorders.

So, the results of investigation revealed that depression in women who were subjects of forensic psychiatric examination in case of criminal and civil process had developed on pathological ground of historical personality disorders, changed with psychosocial and endocrine factors and often were accompanied by anxiety disorders, that made the clinical picture of their state rather atypical. So, there were some problems in the diagnosis of depression, which were the main conditions in patients state, and in the estimate of depressions level, psychotic and nonpsychotic. The clinical picture of depression in women in forensic practice was modernized by many factors, and made some problems in carrying out forensic evaluation.

But, though there were mixed symptoms of different states in all cases it was possible to discern symptoms, characterized Major Depressive Episode and Disthimia. As mentioned, in depression diagnostic we used mainly DSM-111-R approach, adopted to Russian depression scales. And also, in our investigation we did not use nosological approach, but syndromal only. According to DSM-111-R, the current state of patient could be approximately classified as Major Depressive Episode and Dysthimia. There were several of such symptoms as depressed or irritated mood, worse in the morning, retardation, diminished ability to think or focus attention, diminished activities and so in. So it was necessary to do an analysis of different components of the patients' state. We needed to elicit all forms of psychiatric disorders: mood, anxiety and personality and to discriminate them. So it was necessary to put different Codes of diagnosis according described in DSM-11-R.

After evaluating depressive symptoms it was possible to estimate the depressive level: psychotic or neurotic, or nonpsychotic, borderline. The nature of psychotic depression was common with severe and moderate level of Major Depressive Episode, including those of Melancholic type. As per our opinion, this presented, the so-called vital component that contained precardialis sadness, accompanied with sensation of cardiac pain, or pain in the chest, somatic symptoms, such as loss of appetite, stomach disturbance, weight loss and so n, delusion of depressive theme, insomnia, and menstrual cycle disturbance. Presence of several of these symptoms made it possible to diagnosis psychotic level of depression. This diagnosis made patient irresponsible for alleged crime: she had to be admitted to the hospital for coercive treatment. Sometimes depression aggravated and reached the psychotic level after patient was committed to prison. In that case patient is responsible for the delinquent act, but can't stand trail and also needs coercive treatment. After improving her state, the patient can stand the trail and be punished. The estimate of depression in civil law was rather more difficult, it was necessary to review different social factors such as professional occupation and marital state and critical functions of patients. Patients with neurotic depressions needed treatment in time for the penal process.

The different nature of psychotic and neurotic depressions was confirmed by data of neurochemical examination. We studied three comparable groups of patients with psychotic depressions, neurotic depressions and a control group that consisted of women of the same age without depression, who have been in the same conditions. As a consequence of neurochemical examination we got results that confirmed our point of view regarding the division of depression of a psychotic and neurotic origin. In both those groups the level of cathecholamines was higher than in the control group. In group with psychotic depression the level of cathecholamines was suggestively higher than in group with neurotic depressions. So, the receiving of neurochemical data could be used as additional method of diagnostic of depression level.

Part 5
Prison and Offender Research

Effects of Prison Factors on Recidivism

János Boros

Introduction

As early as the 1920s there was research conducted in the United States in which the effect of incarceration on the offender was used as a stand-alone indicator in the prediction of recidivism. Taking into account that incarceration for an undefined period of time played an important role in the American penal system, the behavioural prognostication drawn up by correctional officers played a decisive role in considering the feasibility of a conditional release on parole. Quite understandably this sparked interest in more extensive prognosis research.

From methodological point of view we can divide these research projects into two groups. The first group is represented by the methods of Burgess and Glueck. This approach tries to find objective factors from the individual's previous record to be used in prognostic tables. The other group places emphasis on dynamic factors ascertained from the actual behaviour and reactions of the examined individual using psychological tests. The two methods are often applied in a combined form as well (Warner, 1923; Bruce, Harno, Burgess, & Landesco, 1928; Glueck & Glueck, 1930; Rohden, 1933; Laune, 1936; Ohlin, Meywerk, 1938; Duncan, 1949; Barnes & Teeters, 1951; Morris, 1951; Glaser & Stratton, 1961; Wheeler, 1958; Ward, 1968; Dean & Duggan, 1969; Hassin, 1986; Baumer, 1997).

Independent of the findings, these research projects highlighted the importance of the incarceration period in recidivism. In the very beginning, however, only "rough-and-ready" indicators were used, such as disciplinary problems while in custody or the number of criminal offences committed. In this light, it was hardly surprising that the results were often contradictory. Later, research applied methods relying on more dynamic factors affecting behaviour, such as the psycho-emotive factor, negative disposition against court rulings and treatment programmes, value orientation, etc. This approach offered far more refined and precise measuring systems for the environmental and social effects of penal establishments.

Farrington and Nuttal (1985) ascertained that the size of the prison did not, whereas overcrowding in prisons did have an effect on recidivism; there was negative correlation between overcrowding and effectiveness.

do not think there are any prison practitioners who have not read, or prison researchers who have not referred to the two classical authors: Clemmer (1940) and Sykes (1958). They concluded that the deprivations of prison life, through a peculiar process of counter-socialisation, tend to bring about informal groups of inmates arranged into hierarchy according to their particular principles. They called this hierarchy the subculture of the inmates.

Clemmer assumed that the rehabilitation of offenders who had been well integrated into the prison subculture was far from promising after their release. Clemmer's theory, widely known as the deprivation model, was extremely popular for a time, yet not many researchers ventured to verify it in a framework of an empirical research project (Clemmer, 1940; McKorkle & Korn, 1954; Thomas & Foster, 1972).

Hypothesis

In our research project we focused on the effects on recidivist behaviour of three factors of prison life: deprivation, prison socialisation (prisonisation) and informal status. Our hypothesis was that upon entering the penal establishment, in fact a totalitarian institution, the offender is put into an environment where he has limited possibilities to satisfy his needs. It is not only the physical environment which is different from the outside but also the social environment, the social setting in which he has to live and that regulates his life and behaviour, whether parallel or contrary to the rules set by the prison staff.

We assumed a process of conditioning during which the offenders learn to adapt to official and non-official rules and norms. This takes place in the peculiar social setting described above, and after a time the offender, having "integrated", obtains some sort of place in the hierarchy, commensurate with his behaviour and views.

Our assumption was that these factors – deprivation, prison socialisation and informal status – either independently or cumulatively determine the behaviour of offenders not only within prison establishments but also after release. In other words these interrelated factors have an important role in recidivism, inasmuch as they can either make it easier or make it more difficult to commit new crimes depending on the level of criminal or prosocial value orientation.

Subjects

To verify the validity of our hypothesis 100 male offenders were subjected to scrutiny in 3 penal establishments. Two were maximum security prisons and the third one was a more relaxed agricultural prison. The average age of subjects was 31 years, 75 percent with 8th year elementary school qualifications, 47 percent were violent offenders, 53 percent were non-violent offenders. 39 of them had committed 2–3 crimes, 37 had committed 4–5 crimes, and 24 had committed 6–9 criminal offences in their criminal carriers.

Method

As a method for the survey we compiled a questionnaire to measure the level of deprivation and prison socialisation. Additionally we used a scoring chart to grade the offenders' informal status. The same scoring chart were filled in by the prison officer, the employer and two mates of the offender in question. To grade deprivation we employed the five-scale questionnaire of 5 deprivation factors (freedom, comfort, heterosexuality, autonomy, security) as described by Sykes (1958).

When designing the prison socialisation section of the questionnaire our prime objective was to learn what the subject would do in a specific situation. Obviously, he may have got into similar situations on a number of occasions: consequently the questions we outlined were not imaginary ones. In fact the questions aimed at offender reactions that are rather life-like in prison environment. The situations correlated with the following values: solidarity, power, masculinity and loyalty.

Quite obviously, we couldn't comprise the whole range of prison socialisation and conditioning process, so we used the level of acceptance of informal prison values and norms to describe prison socialisation.

Later on we kept track of the subjects of our survey for a period of three years and registered whether they committed new crimes or not.

We made systematic statistical comparisons of the average scores and the standard deviation of violent and non-violent groups based on their different level of criminality using the t-test. Where there were significant differences in the values contained in the tables below, we made special references under the tables.

The Findings of Research 1

As to deprivation, we assumed that for multiple recidivists it was easier to put up with hardships than for recidivists with 2 to 3 crimes. Our reasoning was that the repeated and longer term imprisonment gave them more opportunity to get conditioned and work out methods to reduce the detrimental effects of deprivation, whereas 2–3-time offenders might find deprivation relatively more unbearable due to the contrast between life within and outside.

The results of the survey did not, or only partially support our hypothesis. In the case of general deprivation (DEP) the results we registered were contradictory to our hypothesis: multiple recidivists scored more points than second and third offenders. When analysing the specific deprivation factors we found only 3 cases out of 10 when the number of sentences was in direct proportion to the number of points.

The analysis of the specific deprivation factors – if we compare only the two extreme groups (with 2–3 and 6–9 sentences) – seems to partially support our assumption: here in 6 cases out of 10 multiple recidivists scored lower than 2–3-time offenders. In 3 fifths of the cases they felt less deprived than their fellow prisoners with fewer sentences.

Table 1: Deprivation

			Number of sentences			
			2–3	4–5	6–9	Σ avg
D1	Violent crimes	Mean	4.46	4.04	4.46	4.26
		SD	0.78	0.92	0.52	0.82
	Non-violent crimes	Mean	4.53	4.86	4.46	4.60
		SD	0.65	0.36	0.78	0.63
D2	Violent crimes	Mean	3.61	3.73	4.46	3.87
		SD	1.12	1.01	0.69	1.01
	Non-violent crimes	Mean	4.07	3.64	4.00	3.94
		SD	0.74	1.33	1.00	0.99
D3	Violent crimes	Mean	4.15	4.09	4.09	4.10
		SD	1.87	1.04	1.22	1.07
	Non-violent crimes	Mean	4.30	4.29	4.15	4.26
		SD	0.79	0.99	1.07	0.90
D4	Violent crimes	Mean	3.30	3.39	3.64	3.42
		SD	1.18	1.08	0.81	1.04
	Non-violent crimes	Mean	3.23	3.71	4.15	3.59
		SD	1.03	0.99	0.90	1.05
D5	Violent crimes	Mean	3.39	2.52	2.46	2.75
		SD	1.50	1.16	1.12	1.29
	Non-violent crimes	Mean	2.54	2.36	2.92	2.56
		SD	1.25	1.08	1.26	1.20
DEP	Violent crimes	Mean	18.92	17.78	19.09	18.40
		SD	3.28	3.19	1.81	2.96
	Non-violent crimes	Mean	18.69	18.86	19.68	18.97
		SD	3.35	3.26	1.90	2.84

As to the prison socialisation questionnaire we expected multiple recidivists to score higher than subjects with fewer sentences; in other words, we assumed that a higher number of prison sentences would generate a higher level of prison socialisation.

Our hypothesis was, again, only partially verified: we found direct relation between recidivism and prison socialisation only in the case of violent offenders (where offenders with a low level of criminality scored significantly lower values than the two other groups with higher levels of criminality). The tendency was similar in the non-violent groups but the difference was not significant. If we analyse the differences between the 4–5 and the 6–9 groups the values are pretty similar, the values for the latter group even tend to be somewhat lower. It seems that prison socialisation comes to end after the fourth or fifth imprisonment, i.e. the process of prisonisation terminates. After that the level of prison socialisation either stagnates or it might even drop back to some extent.

Table 2: Prison Socialisation

		Number of sentences			
		2–3	4–5	6–9	Σ avg
Violent crimes*	Mean	34.85	43.78	43.73	41.30
	SD	6.22	10.98	10.00	10.283
Non-violent crimes	Mean	44.35	47.93	47.85	46.71
	SD	9.61	9.68	8.01	9.1

* 2–3 v. 4–5 t=2.93 p<0.05 2–3 v. 6–9 t=2.91 p<0.05

Our original assumption with regard to categorisation of the offenders according to their informal status was that multiple recidivists would get into higher informal status than second or third offenders, in other words, they would score more points on our social status questionnaire than subjects with fewer prison sentences.

Table 3: Informal Status

		Number of sentences			
		2–3	4–5	6–9	Σ avg
Authority					
– Violent crimes*	Mean	4.61	5.12	5.40	5.04
	SD	0.54	0.83	0.91	0.81
– Non-violent crimes	Mean	4.93	5.21	4.68	4.94
	SD	0.61	0.82	0.60	0.77
Esteem					
– Violent crimes**	Mean	4.75	5.32	5.33	5.17
	SD	0.58	0.74	0.75	0.62
– Non-violent crimes	Mean	5.17	5.16	5.49	5.25
	SD	0.42	0.61	0.68	0.57
Respect					
– Violent crimes***	Mean	4.77	5.15	5.24	5.06
	SD	0.42	0.57	0.68	0.76
– Non-violent crimes	Mean	5.07	4.90	5.13	5.05
	SD	0.62	0.58	0.61	0.62
Popularity					
– Violent crimes****	Mean	4.34	5.00	4.89	4.79
	SD	0.41	0.53	0.48	0.42
– Non-violent crimes	Mean	4.95	4.97	4.82	4.92
	SD	0.46	0.52	0.63	0.67

* 2–3 v. 4–5 t=6.74 p<0.001 2–3 v. 6–9 t=5.96 p<0.001
** 2–3 v. 4–5 t=2.52 p<0.05 2–3 v. 6–9 t=2.39 p<0.05
*** 2–3 v. 4–5 t=2.23 p<0.05 2–3 v. 6–9 t=2.27 p<0.05
**** 2–3 v. 4–5 t=6.74 p<0.001 2–3 v. 6–9 t=5.96 p<0.001

In the case of violent offenders our hypothesis was verified: multiple recidivists got into higher informal status than second or third offenders. With non-violent offenders this interrelation wasn't to be observed. Although the quoted differences were not significant violent offenders seemed to have authority but were not too popular.

The Findings of Research 2

In view of the fact that our research had a follow-up phase as well, in which we registered whether the subjects of our survey committed new crimes after their release, it seemed obvious to compare the results of repeated recidivists with non-recidivists. (Of the 100-person sample 54 became recidivists.)

Table 4: Follow–up reconviction by number of sentences/Deprivation

		Number of sentences			
		2–3	4–5	6–9	Σ avg
Reconviction	Mean	18.27	18.26	18.86	18.65
	SD	3.18	3.19	2.22	2.92
Non–Reconviction	Mean	18.75	18.54	18.75	18.75
	SD	3.24	3.43	2.34	3.04

Table 5: Follow–up reconviction by number of sentences/Prison Socialisation

		Number of sentences			
		2–3*	4–5**	6–9	Σ avg***
Reconviction	Mean	41.33	48.40	47.63	45.38
	SD	6.22	9.16	10.54	7.64
Non–Reconviction	Mean	38.33	42.86	44.12	41.45
	SD	6.87	9.45	9.07	8.12

* $t=2.27$ $p<0.05$
** $t=2.96$ $p<0.05$
*** $t=2.13$ $p<0.05$

An analysis of the obtained data revealed no significant differences as far as deprivation is concerned, in the majority of cases, however, multiple recidivists demonstrated a higher level of prisonisation and informal status than those who did not commit new crimes in the three-year period after their release. This highlights direct interrelation between prison socialisation and recidivism on the one hand, and informal status and recidivism on the other. Interestingly enough, in the case of multiple recidivists (6–9 time offenders) the level of prison socialisation did not have a determining effect on recidivism, the explanation for which might be that prison socialisation practically concludes by the fourth/fifth imprisonment, as shown in Table 2.

The data that we have thus far accumulated do not substantiate a convincing explanation for the lack of significance in the level of informal status and recidivism in the case of offenders with 2 or 3 convictions (see Table 6).

Table 6: Follow–up reconviction by number of sentences / Informal Status

		Number of sentences			
		2–3	4–5*	6–9**	Σ avg***
Reconviction	Mean	4.68	5.46	5.45	5.20
	SD	0.52	0.72	0.83	0.78
Non–Reconviction	Mean	4.73	5.02	5.13	4.89
	SD	0.69	0.63	0.74	0.67

* $t=3.26$ $p<0.01$
** $t=2.03$ $p<0.05$
*** $t=2.47$ $p<0.05$

Conclusion

Recidivism is a rather complex problem of criminology. It is influenced by a large number of components, just to mention a few: the specific situation in which the behaviour becomes manifest, the social and financial background of the individual, his system of personal links, his reference groups or his biological-physical conditioning.

Apart from these, psychological factors also have an important role, let me just refer to the role of the experience that one accumulates during the course of a lifetime and that gets integrated into one's behaviour.

Research findings show that experience gained while staying at totalitarian institutions play a part in shaping later behaviour. Goffmann (1961) observed that in totalitarian institutions individuals are deprived of a vast number of possibilities that they normally possess in everyday life. In prisons there are a number of special deprivations that negate the offender's ego and diminish their self-respect. Informal group-integration, (admission into prison subculture) is a very frequent and effective way of ego-restoration.

Informal groups possess a particular system of values/norms and are arranged into a special social hierarchy, integration into which is only through the acceptance of prison values and norms, that is through prison socialisation. Getting into an informal group, especially higher status positions, reduces the number of deprivations and their side-effects. So we assumed that multiple recidivists, who upon entry carry with them a system of values similar to prison values, tend to get socialised in prison within a pretty short period of time. Due to this – and due to other factors – we expected them to obtain higher positions in prison hierarchy and, as a result, their level of deprivation to be lower. We presumed that second and third offenders enter prisons with somewhat more prosocial values, consequently their prison socialisation is slower, they do not get high positions in the social structure and perceive a higher level of deprivation.

Our hypothesis was not fully verified: it proved to be valid only in the case of violent offenders, and with regard to prisonisation and informal status; the surveys failed to justify our assumption relative to deprivation. True enough, the tendencies in the data series on the non-violent groups were similar to those of the violent groups, nevertheless, the differences found among the non-violent groups were not significant. The follow-up survey, however, did reveal correlation between the level prison socialisation/the position in the informal hierarchy and committing new crimes. This correlation was valid for the whole population, irrespective of the violence of crimes committed.

The results of our research suggest therefore, that we need not modify our initial assumption concerning the effects of prison factors on recidivism. Nevertheless, the feeling of deprivation appears to be more complex than we expected, and apparently necessitates different methods of investigation. We can conclude that increased prison socialisation and informal group integration evoke changes in the individual's system of values and norms that makes it easier for him to commit new crimes.

References

Barnes, H. E., & Teeters, N. K. (1951). *New Horizons in Criminology*. New York.

Baumer, E. (1997). Levels and Predictors of Recidivism: The Malta Experience. *Criminology, 4*, 601-627.

Boros, J. (1979). *Agresszivitás a börtönben*. Budapest: Ministry of Justice.

Boros, J. (1995). Az erőszak és a szociális státusz összefüggése a börtönbüntetésüket töltő visszaeső elítéltek esetében. *Magyar Börtönügyi Szemle (Hungarian Prison Review), 2*, 16-20.

Boros, J. (1996). Visszaeső elítéltek komplex vizsgálata. *Magyar Börtönügyi Szemle (Hungarian Prison Review), 4*, 18-27.

Bruce, A., Harno, A., Burgess, E., & Landesco, J. (1928). *Parole and the indeterminate sentence.* Springfield, IL.

Clemmer, D. (1940). *The Prison Community*. New York: Rinehart.

Dean, C. W., & Duggan, T. J. (1969). Interaction and Parole Prediction. *British Journal of Criminology, 9*, 366-376.

Farrington, D., & Nuttal, C. (1985). Prison size, overcrowding, prison violence and recidivism. In M. Braswell, S. Dillingham, & R. Montgomery (Eds.) *Prison violence in America*. Cincinnati, OH: Anderson Publishing Co.

Glaser, D., & Stratton, J. (1961). Measuring Inmate Change in Prison. In D. Cressey (Ed.), *The Prison*. New York: Holt, Rinehart, Winston.

Glaser, D. (1964). *Effectiveness of a Prison and Parole System.* New York: Bobbs Merrill.

Glueck, S., & Glueck, E. (1930). *500 Criminal Careers*. New York: Alfred A. Knopf.

Goffmann, E. (1961). On the Characteristics of Total Institutions: The Inmate World. In D. Cressey (Ed.), *The Prison*. New York: Holt, Rinehart, Winston.

Hassin, Y. (1986). Two Models for Predicting Recidivism. *British Journal of Criminology, 3*, 270-286.

Laune, F. (1936). *Predicting Criminality*. Evanston, IL: Northwestern University Press.

McKorkle, L., & Korn, R. (1954). Resocialization within Walls. *The Annals of the American Academy of Political and Social Science. Vol. 293*, 88-98.

Meywerk, W. (1938). Beitrang zur Bestimmung der Sozialen Prognose an Rückfallverbrechern. *Monatschrift für Kriminologie, 8,* 422-444.

Morris, T. (1951). *The Habitual Criminal*. London.

Ohlin, L., & Duncan, O. (1949). The Efficiency of Prediction in Criminology. *American Journal of Sociology* 54, 441-451.

Rohden (1933). Gibt es unverbesserliche Verbrecher? *Monatschrift für Kriminologie, 87.*

Sykes, G. (1958). *The Society of Captives*. Princeton University Press.

Thomas, C., & Foster, S. (1972). Prisonisation in an Inmate Contraculture. *Social Problems, 20,* 229.

Ward (1968). The comparative efficiency of differing techniques of prediction scaling. *Australian and New Zealand Journal of Criminology, 2.*

Warner, S. B. (1923). Factors Determining Parole from the Massachusetts Reformatory. *Journal of Criminal Law and Criminology, 14,* 127-207.

Wheeler, S. (1958). *Social Organization in Correctional Communities*. Washington University Press.

Prison Between Values and Efficiency

Dragan Petrovec

Rehabilitation Ideology, its Decline, and Neo-classicism

One can hardly speak about prisons without casting a thought back to the early 1970s, when rehabilitation ideology was flourishing. The development of a host of sciences, from social to predominantly technical, provided this ideology with the momentum and the energy to seek answers to the question of what to do with delinquents. The discovery of man was no less exciting than the discovery of the universe. from the standpoint of authorities, it held a special attraction by promising the possibility of leading disobedient people, and directing, controlling, and bringing them into conformity.

Treatment ideology drew strength from the idea that man, including delinquents, is a valuable part of society. Therefore, mere punishment devoid of content and meaning has no moral justification. man must be helped to become a useful member of society again.

However, like any ideology, treatment ideology is also prone to abuse. As an illustration, it would suffice, perhaps, to look at contemporary developments in America, a country well-known for its openness to innovation in all areas, where freedom of mind is so overwhelming that an overly frequent emphasis on it may blur the distinction between acceptable and unacceptable interventions in human personality.

In 1965, the fifth international criminology congress was held in Montreal on the subject of the "Treatment of Delinquents". A range of crime prevention methods was presented: among the treatment methods, particular value was attached to the medical or surgical method. Fontanesi drew attention to the importance of psychosurgery which, while not reducing criminogenic factors, should nevertheless be used when other therapeutic actions fail. Similarly, we should not renounce experiments, since the development of that kind of therapy, and progress in general, would otherwise be hampered. (Fontanesi, 1969).

Psychological methods of treatment were also dealt with (Pacheco e Silva, 1969). In the therapeutic process, special value is attached to hypnosis, with which it is possible to achieve changes in emotional experience, character, and will. it is to be regretted, however, that the renaissance of hypnosis has not resulted in its wider and more systematic use in the treatment of delinquents, notes Pacheco e

Silva. Psychoanalysis has a special power, and the judicial system would have to change radically for crime to be fought by using knowledge of the delinquent's subconscious (ibid., p. 373.)

Narcoanalysis also represents an indispensable method of treatment, in which censorship of the freedom of expression of thoughts and feelings is removed by the application of different medications. despite objections concerning criminal proceedings, there is no reason why these treatment methods should not be applied to delinquents if it is for their benefit (ibid., p. 376).

The latter thought testifies to society's special concern for the delinquent. The power we wield over delinquents and we are granted legally entitles us to judge what is good for them.

The 1970s also saw entirely opposite ideas being developed by authors who today are still considered the pioneers of humanistic psychology. Carls Rogers, in 1961, wrote the book "On Becoming a Person". Using a new vocabulary, he introduced a significant distinction in the conservative classification into the normal and the abnormal, the honest and the criminal, the healthy and the sick. He calls the person he "treats" a "client", not a patient, without pretending to be an omniscient doctor, but only a therapist who creates adequate interpersonal communication from which both client and therapist will be able to benefit (Rogers, 1961, pp. 34-38).

In the domain of penology, the closest to Rogers is Fenton. Fenton's work "A handbook on the Use of Group Counselling in Correctional Institutions" was published in the mid-60s (Fenton, 1965). In this work, Fenton emphasises the importance of constructive group interaction, which must be characterised by:

a) the creation of a free discussion and the acceptance of the delinquent as he is;

b) enabling delinquents to realise the significance of emotional conflicts from which criminal activity may emerge;

c) improvement of the emotional climate in the institution;

d) treatment by means of constructive interpersonal relationships.

Fenton's model of treatment is free of medical interventions, Clockwork Orange aversion therapies, hypnosis or electroshock therapy, although the model was developed in an era full of such inventions "for the benefit of man".

Maslow opposed the traditional psychiatric categories and viewed the problem in a different way: "The psychology of deviance should not confine itself to the study of schizophrenia. It should include cynicism, authoritarianism, hedonism, the loss of values, prejudices, hatred greed, selfishness, and similar phenomena and characteristics. From the point of view of the value system, these, precisely, are the most serious diseases" (Maslow, 1876, p. 315).

In the same era, treatment ideology came under heavy criticism in Martinson's research (Martinson, 1974). The importance of his work can be judged by the fact that he is still quoted today in almost every work or paper dealing with penology. The fundamental question asked by Martinson was what of all we offer to delinquents with a view to rehabilitating them is effective ("What Works?"). With the crime rate and recidivism growing as they were, his answer was quick and simple – "Nothing Works". Certain changes in his subsequent research (Martinson, 1979) aside, Martinson launched a devastating critique of rehabilitation ideology which was joined later by a number of criminologists and penologists. The criticism suited politics best, especially conservative politics.

I find it necessary to draw attention to certain postulation which strike me as inadequate, not only in Martinson's treatise, but in the majority of those dealing with the problem of efficiency of prisons.

It is probably not by pure accident that more varied philosophical and psychological tendencies have been developed in America than in Europe, which sometimes just picks up inventions made on the other side of the ocean. Free of the burden of medieval philosophical heritage, the United States has for a long time emphasised the importance of human freedom and unrestrained creation. Maybe it is this insistence on the freedom of creation that made consumer philosophy flourish in America, more than anywhere else. The previously mentioned efficiency has become a trademark of all activities. And since it is easier and more convenient to judge something by sort-term results, it is not surprising that many sciences have embraced that principle. Technological sciences are trying to persuade us of the value of the fast-food system, and social sciences of the power of putting human behaviour under control and adjusting it to the system. The principle of efficiency suits politics best, since politicians are always forced to promise citizens – voters – quick results.

It is virtually impossible to discuss prison without referring to the efficiency of these marginal social institutions, which become closer to the focus of our attention the moment a scape-goat for the growing crime rate is to be sought and identified.

One of the arguments against pondering efficiency was proposed by Heather (1978) in connection with the criticism of theories of the criminal type. These theories make life easy for all experts in the field: they are free from obligation to warn, or try to influence a change in social conditions; they need not change their stance; their concept is not the concept of interaction and communication on an equal footing, but a meeting between sublime science on the one side and a deviant person without status and rights on the other.

If we demand efficiency from prisons, such efficiency as will (at least with a high degree of probability) put the delinquent on the right path after he has served his sentence, we would have to ask the same institution to change all the social conditions which generate crime far removed from prisons. This is not to say, of course, that where crime is concerned, prisons as they generally are today do not carry their share of responsibility. But it is unfair to blame the prison for a lost battle while outside it, in society as a whole, we are losing the war for a more just and better world. In a world marked by hostility, fear and aggressiveness towards everything that is different from us, the honest, healthy and obedient citizens, in a world which is becoming indifferent to the pains of others, we criticise prisons for inefficiency and blame them for crime.

We seem to be trying to solve the errors in the system by focusing on only one of its numerous constituent parts. Similarly, we tend to ascribe recidivism to unsuccessful rehabilitation or the inefficiency of prisons in general. But doing so, we close our eyes to the fact that the world to which we are returning the delinquents may be unpleasant and repulsive, hostile and full of violence – briefly, a world which itself generates delinquency. A bad experience in prison may reinforce the unfavourable effect, and a good experience may soon be swamped by the prevailing malign influence.

No wonder, then, that discussions of the efficiency of prisons revolve around a vicious circle which starts with rehabilitation inventions of all kinds and ends in a growing rate of crime. Between these extremes stands a range of ideas on punishment, from justice models to deterrence, all for the good of the individual and the system.

It is perhaps this that offers some answers to why humanistic philosophy, psychology and penology have so readily lost the battle with neo-classicist ideology and just-desert models. Martinson brought some relief by relieving as the agent of political power or of the legally granted power over others – the delinquents in prison – of the obligation of self-evaluation. The majority found the creation of Rogers' communication on an equal footing too difficult, and above all too unpleasant, a task. Furthermore, it is difficult to espouse the idea of the humanistic approach that we, the honest and normal citizens, may learn something from an appropriately established relationship with delinquents. Such an approach puts limits on the abuse of legally granted power over others, who in this case are stripped of certain rights. However, what is more tempting than to have power over others? At this point, one should recall Maslow's words that healthy people do not like to wield power over others (Maslow, 1976, p. 317). Whoever shapes criminal policy from a position of social power should constantly concern himself about his health, and should do something about it, too.

The New Age of Justice has abolished the obvious abuses of treatment ideology, from interventions into human personality to formal legal abuses manifested, for example, in indeterminate sentences. Still, one cannot ignore certain research studies dealing with conditions in prisons in the period between 1970-1973. She found that, in the majority of prisons, there was complete censorship; letters she wrote to prisoners were rejected; breaches of discipline resulted in exemplary penalties, and denouncing was rewarded; punishment for criminal offences committed in prison was pronounced without judicial procedure, and prisoners could not sue anyone for damage inflicted on them in prison (Mitford, 1974).

Conklin cites two research studies (Karagianis, 1978, and research in California in 1971) which showed that only 6% of total resources were used for treatment purposes, with the remainder being spent on security systems and maintenance (Conklin, 1986). For this reason, Weigend's observation that there was little earnest intention to implement the idea that treatment should be taken quite seriously (Weigend, 1983). Riots in prisons during the 1970s were not protests against treatment, but against inhuman conditions, overpopulation, and torture (e.g. the 1971 riot in Attica).

In granting the new age credit for a legitimate showdown with the misconceptions of treatment ideology, one must nevertheless admit that ideological clashes proceeded at the academic level and had less influence on concrete conditions in prisons. it should be emphasised, however, that the time of just deserts had indirectly influenced prisons, too. By invoking justice models, neo-classicism filled prisons to capacity all over the world. In the United States, the number of prisoners doubled in the period between 1980-1990 (Harris, 1993). European conditions are not as drastic, but the number of prisoners is not declining here either. Some countries, the Netherlands for one, are planning to build new prisons for twice the number of convicts.

When speaking about the political dimensions of punishment, we must not forget to mention politicians who reiterate the view that the answer to crime lies in stricter laws, harsher sentences, and a larger number of prisons (ibid.).

The efficiency of crime prevention is increasingly manifesting itself as violence upon delinquents, in line with Hamurabi's "an eye for an eye" law. Obsessed by efficiency as the governing idea of modern consumer society, we forget to ask a question which seems crucial to me: "Is what we are doing with delinquents in the name of criminal policy fair, acceptable, and morally justifiable?".

If we could just for a moment forget about lofty rehabilitation goals, and the methods dedicated to them, and ask instead about the moral justifiability of criminal policy measures, these goals may, perhaps, become easier to attain. By introducing erroneous correlations and unverifiable effects, we are ignoring the fundamental moral questions. To obtain answers to these questions, we must look into ourselves and not only into delinquents. Looking into the mirror is an unpleasant procedure which we, as moral and normal citizens, "by definition" would rather avoid.

Prison as a (Non)Treatment Institution

Continental law seems to exhibit more self-complacency than Anglo-Saxon law. With the development of the philosophy of law, it turned its back on certain scientific disciplines from which, in the domain of punishment, something could be learnt.

An important question that has been asked for decades in connection with prisons is: is treatment being introduced in prisons, or is it being abandoned? It is with this question that the actual division of prisons into treatment and non-treatment prisons is linked.

Why do I think this question is asked in a wrong way? Such a division is justified on the assumption that there are institutions where we do not apply different methods of influencing the convicts. They are the institutions where a convict merely serves his sentence and there is no intention of rehabilitating him, of changing the man, or influencing his future behaviour.

Sensory deprivation experiments, in which subjects are placed in total isolation from any sensual stimulation are known in psychology. The human body, accustomed to receiving various stimuli, could not endure sudden deprivation of those stimuli (Pecjak, 1977, pp. 9-14).

According to Watzlawick, the first principle of communication theory is: "It is impossible not to communicate" (quoted according to Brajsa, 1983, p. 41). This means that there is no human interpersonal relationship that does not contain communication. Communication may be verbal or non-verbal. The latter often contains messages which we do not want to utter, but which are crucial for the person with whom we have a relationship.

Although a simple illustration would suffice to make the notions of sensory deprivation and non-verbal communication clear, these notions are too complicated for legal science to grasp, let alone apply them in its system of tangible norms and sanctions.

Where an understanding of the principles of interpersonal communication exists, the notion of treatment appears in a somewhat different light. Treatment then becomes all we do with a human being, and all we omit but ought to do. Both acts exert an unmistakable influence on man and his behaviour. If we strive for a "non-treatment" prison, we will ultimately create a correct, cold, and impersonal institution where fundamental rights will not be violated but where the lack of human contact between staff and inmates will have a definite (negative) effect on delinquents. Such institutions are not few, but they are largely outnumbered by those in which the violation of rights is obvious, in which communication is aggressive and tantamount to the abuse of power over the convicts.

Decades after the collapse of rehabilitation ideology, authors are writing about its renaissance, about rehabilitation revisited. The problem which in my opinion needs re-examining, concerns the correct asking of questions. If due consideration is given to the theory of communication, then it is impossible to ask "What works?" Firstly, because delinquents are liable to be influenced by everything: secondly, there are no programmes that could be said to be likely to prevent crime as the only goal of punishment policy today. It would perhaps be more appropriate to ask – what, of all that we do with regard to prisoners, is morally justified.

There are no uniform criteria today for the morality of procedures. If we ask who is to define the rules of moral behaviour, the least we can conclude is that politicians are not the right people. The second part of the answer is not easy to find. In matters which affect public feeling as much as crime, it is difficult to rely on public opinion, which ought normally to be the critical instance of political power (Habermas, 1969). Were we not acquainted with totally different ideas on crime prevention in the work of criminologists, it would be easier to rely on the so-called independent expert public. As it is, we come across ideas which range from biological perspectives (Jeffrey, 1993), according to which delinquents should be put in hospitals and potential delinquents should be monitored by biomedical methods from pregnancy onwards, to the construction of a deterrent system in which punishment would be understood as a special value and an aspect of culture (Logan, Gaes, 1993).

It could be interpreted that, in referring frequently to the lack of social values, the authors have in mind the values which we have forgotten or replaced with other values, These new values speak of punishment-oriented social systems (Hood, 1993), in which there is no room of contemplating the attitude of ourselves, the architects of criminal policy. The substance of new values is the persecution of differences, hostility towards all those who are not, like us, obedient and honest citizens.

Therefore, it is perhaps more appropriate to speak not about the renaissance of treatment or deterrence, but of the renaissance of values which we know but found too difficult to follow.

Our Moral Attitudes Revisited

Authors often write about the need to re-examine treatment and rehabilitation ideology (Mair, 1991; Coyle, 1992; Pitts, 1992), but they seldom refer to the need to re-examine their own standards and moral norms.

Looking at the world we live in, we must admit that it is a world of growing hostility towards foreigners, towards other religions and races, and towards delinquents. Given such circumstances, it becomes clear how our value judgements, our views, and especially our prejudices, as stances which contain a powerful emotional component, are being formed. We are sometimes erroneously led to believe that criminal policy measures are based on rational arguments. That may be true of technical sciences, but it hardly applies to social sciences. Those who believe that scientists gather the pros and cons of capital punishment and then decide on balance are wrong. We should recall Clare (Klare, 1973), who wrote that views on capital punishment ring with the essential traits of character and temperament. And these are the traits we receive at such an early stage of life that the views in which they are reflected change only slightly under the influence of the rational. The same applies to the treatment of delinquents.

It is not surprising that so few things in the world are turning out for the better. Prejudices are the most and the resistant of all personality components, especially those prejudices generated by negative feelings.

As for the prisons of the year 2000, it seems that we have already neglected to make the majority of important decisions. It can hardly be expected that the situation will radically improve five years from now if the conditions today are as unstimulating as they are.

Is there any historical memory left of the romantic era of that rehabilitation ideology, which was free of abuse, which sought to treat delinquents seriously and not from a position of superiority, which created equitable communication and agreed to the control of its own methods, and which was ready to look at itself in the mirror? The reference to historical memory is not as naive as one might rashly judge. History, including the history of penology and criminology, has always been a network of cyclical movements in which times of hostility were succeeded by times of tolerance and understanding. The important question is what we can do to encourage this replacement. I think we must first look into our own eyes, and I mean our own, not delinquents' eyes. Then we must declare which values we are striving for – is it fear and aggressiveness that prevail, or tolerance and understanding of crime as a legitimate social phenomenon which we cannot influence by prisons to any significant degree? The next question is whether we are prepared to confront political power, which well demand of us fast-food recipes for crime prevention. Are we prepared to take the risk of perpetual confrontation and conflict which the upright scientific mind is doomed to? Should social science and politics shake hands, this question will, of course, become irrelevant.

Only after these answers are given will it become clearer if the "Prison 200" project will make progress towards becoming institutions in which the consumer philosophy of efficiency and crime prevention will give way to another value system in which there will be above all a moral justification for the treatment applied to delinquents. These fundamental questions do not concern delinquents, but those among us who (co)shape crime policy. And since nothing particular worthy of praise has taken place in prisons for decades now, it may be legitimate to ask if it is the wrong people that are subject to rehabilitation.

References

Brajsa, P. (1983). *Vodenje kot medosebni proces* (p. 242). Ljubljana: DDU Univerzum.

Conklin, J. (1986). *Criminology* (1986). New York: MacMillan Publishing Company.

Coyle, A. (1992). The Responsible Prisoner: Rehabilitation Revisited. *The Howard Journal of Criminal Justice, 1*, 1-7.

Fenton, N. (1965). *A Handbook on the Use of Group Counselling in Correctional Institutions.* Sacramento, CA.

Fontanesi, M. (1969). Methodes medicales et chirurgicales. 5. Congres International de Criminologie, Montreal, 1965. *Annales Internationales de Criminologie, 2*, 359-363.

Habermas, J. (1969). *Javno mnenje* (p. 340). Beograd: Kultura.

Harris, D. A. (1994). The Realities of Punishment. *The Journal of Criminal Law and Criminology, 4*, 1098-1113.

Heather, N. (1987). *Radikalne perspektive u psihologiji* (p. 142). Beograd: Nolit.

Hood, R. (1993). *Psychosocial Interventions in the Criminal Justice System – Draft Conclusions and Recommendations.* 20. Criminological Research Conference, Council of Europe, Strasbourg.

Jeffrey, C. R. (1993). Biological Perspectives. *Journal of Criminal Justice Education, 2*, 291-306.

Klare, H. (1973). Issues in the Treatment of Offenders. *The Howard Journal of Penology, 4*, 330-339.

Logan, C. H., & Gaes, G. G. (1993). Meta-Analysis and the Rehabilitation of Punishment. *Justice Quarterly, 2*, 245-263.
Mair, G. (1991). What Works – Nothing or Everything? *Research Bulletin, 30*, 3-8.
Martinson, R. (1979). New Findings – New Views: A Note of Caution Regarding Sentencing Reform. *Hofstra Law Review, 2*, 243-258.
Maslow, A. H. (1982). *Motivacija i licnost* (p. 376). Beograd: Nolit.
Mitford, J. (1974). *The American Prison Business* (p. 339). London: George Allen and Unwin.
Pacheco e Silva (1969). Les methodes psychologiques. 5. Congres International de Criminologie, Montreal, 1965. *Annales Internationales de Criminologie, 2*, 359, 371.
Pecjak, V. (1977). *Psyhologija spoznavanja* (p. 512). Ljubljana: DZS.
Pitts, J. (1992). The End of an Era. *The Howard Journal*, 2, 133-149.
Rogers, C. (1961). *Kako postati licnost* (On Becoming a Person). Beograd: Nolit.
Weigend, T. (1983). *Neoklacizem – transatlantski nesporazum. Revija za kriminalistiko in kriminilogijo* (pp. 151-161). Ljubljana.

Symbolic Patterns in Prisoners' Thinking: Imported Values and Indigenous Roles?

László Huszár

Mainstream concept of former studies

It has been quite a long-lasting tradition in sociologically-oriented prison literature to approach the prison community as a well-structured social arrangement of different argot roles. Clemmer, Sykes, Wheeler, Giallombardo and others provided quite a convincing description of those crystallised and linguistically objectivated behavioural elements mostly referred to as "Convict Code". This is seen as a normative system, unwritten with strictly normative and coercive feature. The different roles are defined by and related to this Code. The individual's behaviour is judged as deviant or conformable under this system. What is important from our current concern is the direct relation between the two. The Code describes the rule and the individual is supposed to act accordingly, namely take the role of conformist "right guy" or the non-conformist "rat", "punk", "merchant", and so forth. Although it has been admitted that the system is not totally exclusive, does not cover the whole population, it still operates as a fundamental guideline for the prison community.

More current works on the important theory express doubts regarding the exclusive effect of internal articulation of the prison society claiming that other non-prison effects have an immense role in the formulation of behaviour. However, by and large, the direct relation between the norms and the behavioural output was not questioned.

Attempts of replication

The basic idea in our research was a simple replication of this concept in order to explore the existing role and norm structures in Hungarian prisons. The first study was carried out in a female prison on a sample of 50 women by an in-depth interview method and practically no roles were found. The researcher suspects that the surprising result is due to the special characteristics of the women's prison, namely less articulated social frameworks. This explanation was supported by many observations except Giallombardo's.

The following stage of research was done in maximum and medium security male prisons. The research method combined 50 in-depth interviews with "lifers" in the prison as well as participant observation (the researcher worked as an officer for six month). In comparison with female prison there were some roles detected but the system was far less sophisticated than expected on the basis of former studies. What seemed to be quite striking was the observation, that even the existing roles were not "enacted" by individuals. The roles are virtual ones, so to speak, rather than something that can be regarded as social fact. By using different terminology we can say that positions existed in the status hierarchy, but practically no actor had this status in his or her personal role-set.

For instance the role of "csicska" (the person who does the housewife" jobs for more powerful inmates) was well-known. It is clear, that somebody does these jobs for others, either for money or free. Consequently it could be expected that there are inmates who are called "csicska", but there are not. The people doing these jobs would not necessarily be regarded as servants and definitely not categorised as "csicska". They may do "csicska"-jobs (it is a verb in Hungarian) but not labelled as "csicska" (the noun).

I must mention one exception. The role of "rat" or snitch (informer) found to be present in all institution. Although no one dares to question the crucial role of "rats" in a correctional environment, nor the heavy emotional charge related to this honourable job, we believe that this role exists because of the guards not the prisoners. Thus it might be the part of the prisoner community but it is – per definitionem – an external agent in the group. Its existence is up to the authorities and not the prisoners.

Symbolic approach

At this point in the research it became clear, that a simple concept of role structure can not be developed. Moreover a new problem emerged: how to explain these strange virtual roles and if the notion of role can be used in this context at all. it seemed to be beneficial to develop a theoretical model by which we can provide a better coverage of the observed phenomena.

The theory is that we started at the wrong end. We dealt with role enactment, which is an outcome of deeper processes. Even if we take a look at the original deprivational model, the deprivations generate specialised norms and sanctions, and one of the sanctions is the negative categorisation (the role itself). From this viewpoint the role structure is rather a superficial phenomenon. It seemed to be more important to clarify the elements of the actual inmate code, what is obviously a more abstract and symbolic stratum. We hoped that it could then explain the weakness of cohesion in the community as well.

In analysing the content of the interview quite a few repetitive elements were found. These fragments – words, group of words or whole sentences – appeared in the texts regularly. The respondents repeated them in different parts of their speech seemingly totally out of the context of actual communication. Furthermore, I had the impression that they were waiting for the opportunity to mention these expressions.

As these elements – even the longer ones – were pronounced almost exactly the same way by different respondents, we concluded that these are parts of a shared and frequently communicated body of knowledge of inmates. Seeking an adequate label for these fixed expressions we thought that the most sufficient notion would be "topos". This term comes from the literature sciences and the Greek word "place" refers to the repetitive mental elements, clichés in the texts.

Another important feature of this connotative topos is that they express positive or negative judgements concerning certain elements of the prison life or other prisoners.

By the collection, systematic analysis, and categorisation of these topos we formed a set of sentences which is definitely integral part of the prison culture, either rooted in non-prison environment or generated by the prison itself.

Unfortunately these topos are quite meaningless in translation because they are mixture of criminal slang, gypsy language, official-legal terms. Moreover there is no room here to go into the details of this language use. It is important to emphasise that this is not a simple argot language. 80% of its elements can and may be used in other contexts, too. The difference is the frequency and the fixed form of the usage.

We presumed that this set of fixed topos refer to those crucial problems of the prison life every inmate supposed to reflect upon or adapt to. We called these "junction points" adaptational fields – the first level of our model. In other words these are the relevant problematized segments of prison life. These segments might be modified versions of the non-prison field or also overwhelmingly prison-specific ones. In many respects the adaptational fields reflect the deprivations or "pains" of imprisonment.

We distinguished different adaptational patterns in the field as a second level of the model. The notion of patterns is close to the concept of Convict Code. But since the Convict Code is understood as a clear-cut normative system which directly represent prisoner behaviour, our patterns refer to the more symbolic structures of values, beliefs, attitudes, and self-presentations. If we were not so afraid to define the word "culture" we would say that the structure of these patterns generate the prison culture.

These patterns (if we handle them as variables) may take positive, neutral, and negative values. Some of them can be accepted, admitted or punished in the different fields. We supposed, that the respondents presented themselves in the interview situation in a positive way, thus the accepted or admitted values can be revealed by the self-presentations. The negative values emerged in connection with others only, or they were linked to heavy rationalisational ideologies.

From this respect the set of patterns works as the normative code with according sanctions, but it may leave room, in certain cases, to chose among the values or individual interpretation. We believe that the issue of indigenous versus imported theories can be approached in this level, as we will discuss it below.

The third level consists the topos themselves. These can be regarded as the operationalised or objectivated outcomes of the patterns. From the research viewpoint these can be observed empirically. The topos are somehow similar to the elements of mythologies, folktales, clichés that exist in the collective representations. They signify positive and negative heroes, ways of thinking, behaviour, especially problem-solving strategies. These are not roles, and can not be attached to actors or even social types as such roles could be in the classic literature.

To summarise our model we divided the explanation of prison adaptation into two domains. The first domain, focused on the behaviour – let say the "traditional" explanation – differentiated on three levels: (1) deprivations, frustrations, pains, (2) a Convict Code: a set of clear and strict rules, that is supposed to compensate the deprivations by normatively distinguishing good and bad in order to maintain solidarity, and thus satisfy the different needs, (3) roles, as behavioural outcomes of the Code, imposing conformable or different deviant roles on the actors.

The sectors domain focuses on the rather symbolical structures. Its three levels are: (1) adaptational fields, (2) adaptational patterns, (3) topos.

As we mentioned the model of the first domain seemed to be difficult to interpret. Hereby I would like to provide a brief summary of the findings based on the symbolic domain, with special emphasis on one of the field the gender or sexual integrity. To discuss the level of topos would be extremely long and difficult because of the different languages; I will concentrate on the level of field and patterns.

The first field is autonomy. In an institutional environment the opportunity for free and independent movement and activity is severely limited. The most obvious manifestation is the lack of space. It means that the very basic and physical freedom is restricted by the proxemical arrangement. In this situation the only way to gain proper space is to hurt others. because of the physical nature of deprivation, the pattern to satisfy this need is also a physical one: instrumental and partially emotionally motivated aggression. No negative or neutral value is admitted in this case: the predatory attitude must be maintained, or at least expressed verbally, in the self-presentation, otherwise autonomy is lost. Considering the import /indigenous issue, it seems, that this is an exclusively indigenous one. The struggle for space must be fought by all prisoners although they might use power they possess from other fields (especially the socio-economic field).

The second is the socio-economic field. It seems that wealth, which is closely correlated with status in prison hierarchy, is the most important field affecting all other fields. Economic and social statuses are interchangeable, The patterns are exclusively instrumental aggression and sociability. The former is necessary for maintaining the status, the latter is required for upward mobility. The positive values of this pattern require strong self-respect, belief in intellectual capacity and a positive attitude toward manipulating others. In many cases these characteristics are attributed to non-gypsy inmates who can easily control the poorly educated gypsies. From this respect the pattern of instrumental violence is linked to the young gypsy inmates while sociability to the older, better educated non-gypsies. Despite the fact, that the economic and social powers are convertible into each other, the economic wealth is concentrated to some extent in the hands of non-gypsy inmates. The neutral value – withdrawal from the prison economy and politics – is attributed to those who can afford to be separated socially. As it is almost impossible to do, it appears to be a degree of rationalisation of a lower status. The negative value is admitted too – the acceptance of low status. In the economic segment: the well-to do inmates have strong family ties, or external supporters; therefore, the achievement is not up to the person's abilities. At this point a strong import effect can be found.

The third field is status-rationalisation. This field is based on beliefs regarding the committed crime, the criminal procedure, the sentence, the criminal identity and the prisoner status in society. The relevance of this field depends on the length of a sentence or reconviction. The positive value is denial of the crime itself, or recognition of the negative nature of the committed act. Relativity towards social norms also appears: politicians and other successful heroes of the open society commit more serious crimes than the imprisoned people, and, thus the prisoners are victims of the political system. The fixed criminal identity is also a possible pattern. The status rationalisation field is indigenous in a sense that it affects prisoners only, but as it defines the relation between the prisoner and the outer society, all the arguments located in an imported dimension.

The field of mental integrity is problematized in the case of long term prisoners. Although fear of and struggle against madness is an intimate or at least not frequently communicated matter, it still does generate patterns. Nervousness is not a merit nor a shame. We can positively claim, that "to be cool" is not an expectation in the observed population as it was in other studies. One of the possible explanation could be that a nervous state is linked to abrupt behaviour, and that reflects dangerousness which might be positive (indigenous) pattern.

Another positive pattern in this field is the self-improvement by reading, learning and so on. This pattern is given for the better educated inmates mostly. It works as a tool against mental deterioration. It is interesting to note, that philosophical problems attract the prisoners especially.

We believe that the impulsive pattern of the nervousness is basically rooted in the criminal (not necessarily prison) culture, and self improvement expresses a sort of mental separatism from the circumstances through the attachment to intellectual (definitely non-prison) values. In this field an ethnic issue also emerges. it is part of the pattern, that the simple-minded primitive atmosphere of prisons is due to the gypsies. Thus the mental separation, the "intellectual supremacy", is also attached to ethnic prejudices.

The fifth field which we call authority is about the attitude toward the regime. We were convinced that there must be both positive and negative patterns in this field, but what we were able to detect with our methods was a quasi-neutral lack of opinion and extreme conformity. It is quite obvious that these cover hidden non-conformist patterns. I must admit that this field would be better understood by participant observation of a fellow inmate.

The last, maybe the most important and sensitive field is the maintenance of sexual integrity. This is the field in which the male and female population are divided strikingly, and also indigenous and popular cultures indicate different patterns.

In the case of male prisoners, both in the general and in the prison culture, the expectation is to be independent and masculine. It is congruent with the male role of the gypsy community as well. The consequence is an extremely strong fear of homosexuality "bull" role. From indigenous perspective it is not regarded as effeminate thing especially if it includes violence. On the other hand both the general and the gypsy culture do not make distinction between active and passive roles: all types of homoerotic activity is labelled as homosexual, and severely sanctioned. Our observation shows that – at least in the symbolic domain – the external patterns suppress the indigenous ones.

In female populations the prison-rooted patterns forbid any kind of homoeroticism, in addition to the according taboo in the gypsy culture. On the other hand our research confirmed the observation, that the real meaning of homosexual relations in female institutions are rather about the substitution of family relations, in order to maintain the outer wife role. In this way homosexuality means betrayal and maintenance of the outer patterns at the same time. The psychological effect of this incongruency is not our concern here, but we are convinced that it contributes to the damage caused by imprisonment. We found that on the level of patterns the strong taboos of the outer world totally overwhelms the more indulgent prison patterns.

To summarise our results we found that in the symbolic strata of values and attitudes, opinions are arranged into patterns and they remain almost intact during the sentence, In other words an import process works in this domain. The current study was not able to clearly show the domain of behaviour and enacted roles, but it was successful in arranging the symbolic representations into a structured model. Further studies may prove that enacted behaviour may be governed by indigenous rules, but the thoughts, values, attitudes rooted in outer community remain almost intact for a long time.

Allowing Male Convicted Prisoners to Wear Their Own Clothes: The Psychological Effects

Peter Marshall

Introduction

There has been pressure for some time to allow male convicted prisoners to wear their own clothes. Unconvicted prisoners in England and Wales have always had this right and female convicted prisoners were granted it following an experiment in 1970.

One of the many recommendations of the Woolf Report was that "there should be a phased programme to permit male convicted prisoners the choice of wearing their own clothes" and the 1991 White Paper "Custody, Care and Justice, the Way Ahead for the Prison Service in England and Wales" announced that the government intends progressively to allow male convicted prisoners to wear their own clothes if they so wish. However, the intention more recently is that this should be introduced as one of a number of earned privileges, rather than as a right.

Following the White Paper announcement experimental trials were arranged at five prisons holding male convicted prisoners:

– two newly-built "local" prisons (which generally take a mix of remand, recently sentenced and short sentence prisoners);

– one closed young offender institution (YOI) and its geographically separate open campus (which take only sentenced prisoners aged under 21);

– a closed adult training prison (Category C, which held medium security sentenced adult prisoners, including a substantial proportion serving life sentences).

The Home Office Research & Planning Unit was asked to evaluate these trials, covering in particular:

– take-up rates of own clothes,

– security implications,

– practical arrangements,

– costs and savings,

– staff, inmate and visitor reactions.

This paper covers mainly the last element.

No clothing grant was provided for prisoners – instead they had to rely on the clothing they had in stored property and whatever their visitors could provide. All the prisons in the trial were supplied with brand new prison kit to offer to prisoners who did not have enough of their own clothing.

The amount of clothing allowed at the prisons varied, although the average allowance was three pairs of trousers (or jeans), eight tops (shirts, T-shirts and/or sweatshirts), seven pairs of underpants and socks and three pairs of shoes. There were also variations in the length of time clothing had to be retained before it could be replaced. Some prisons allowed exchanges to take place on each visit while others insisted that clothes were held for at least three months.

Clothes were washed in central laundries at one local prison and the open YOI and in wing-based launderettes at the other three locations. Only the category C prison allowed prisoners to wash their own clothing in the launderette – the other prisons had orderlies who performed this task. This is relevant, as one of the aims of allowing prisoners to wear their own clothes had been to increase the amount of responsibility they had for themselves.

Take-up rates

The rate of take-up of own clothes varied from 30% to 80% across the trial prisons and seemed to depend largely on the overall clothing limits set by each establishment and the age of the inmate population (with adult take-up rates higher than those for young offenders).

As a rule, the less generous the clothing allowance (and the more strictly the allowance was adhered to), the lower the take-up rate. For example, at the open YOI where prisoners were not allowed to wear their own clothes for the first 28 days (because young prisoners new to open conditions often abscond, and prison-issue clothing is quite easily recognisable), over half the population had none of their own clothing and a further quarter only had one set of own clothes; on the other hand, at on local prison (where a much more relaxed approach was adopted) take-up rates were around 70-80%.

The proportion of prisoners who had little or none of their own clothing was significantly larger in the YOIs than in adult establishments.

Attitudinal and psychological assessment

Before and after comparisons were not entirely possible in the two local prisons, as they entered the experiment immediately they opened – they had no "before" phase. However in the other three locations such an approach was possible, and in the local prisons staff attitudes could be canvassed before opening (though many were entirely new to the job).

Staff attitudes

Questionnaires were issued to staff before the introduction of the initiative and some months afterwards, when it was hoped that teething problems would have been overcome and valid and fair opinions would have been formed. Some staff has previously worked in prisons where prisoners wore their own clothes (particularly women's prisons – although remand prisoners are permitted to by law, many do not wear their own clothes because of the practical difficulties of washing them, preventing them from being damaged and/or stolen).

Response rates varied before and after, and it was difficult to put a precise figure on them, though tended to be low.

At the "before" stage, staff were asked their opinion on a number of potential problems or benefits associated with the trial. These had been expressed to the researchers before the study as possible consequences of the initiative. At the "after" stage, they were asked again about the hypothetical situation of the initiative being introduced in a prison, rather than about their specific experiences in their own prison. Any changes in opinion were assumed to have been a result of their experiences.

The overall opinion of staff towards the initiative (i.e. either "for" or "against") remained largely unchanged, (at about 35% for and 50% against, with the balance expressing no opinion). However, there was a slight tendency for a reduction in those expressing "no opinion" and corresponding increases in those "against" and "strongly against". While this change was statistically significant (p lt 0.01) there had also been an increase in the proportion "strongly for" the initiative, so the direction of the change was not uniform.

Of the other 20 questions only four showed statistically significant changes in staff opinions after the initiative. Thus, more staff felt that poorer hygiene would result from allowing prisoners to wear their own clothes (p lt 0.05), more expected there to be a decrease in "parcels" (p lt 0.01), fewer expected disputes about ownership of clothing and fewer expected an increase in thefts of clothing (both p lt 0.0001).

It is hoped that these last three result from positive experiences of the initiative. It must be stated however, that the majority (64%) of staff still expected more clothing thefts to result from an initiative such as this one.

When analysis was confined to uniformed staff, whose opinions may be of most interest, while the same trends were observed, there was no statistically significant change in their overall opinion, nor in their opinions about hygiene.

When analysed for each prison, results were more variable. In one local prison, all significant changes in opinion were towards the positive, with fewer staff expecting more disputes over or thefts of clothing (both p lt 0.01), and their overall opinion veering more towards the positive (p lt 0.05). At the other local prison only one significant change was found, and this was that fewer staff expected "barriers" between staff and prisoners to be reduced (p lt 0.01) –

however many staff felt such barriers to be a positive thing, and thus it is difficult to say whether this is a positive or negative change.

Fewer staff in the category C prison expected more disputes (p lt 0.01) and in the closed YOI fewer staff expected more thefts of clothing (p lt 0.05) or more compensation claims for damaged or stolen clothing (p lt 0.01). Fewer staff in the closed YOI expected an increase in their workload (p lt 0.05). There were so few staff in the open YOI that significant results were unlikely to emerge, and the reduction in N caused by analysing for each establishment probably resulted in the loss of significant for other issues.

Apart from changes in opinion, some static opinions are worth reporting. Though 66% of staff (with 12% having "no opinion") felt that the breaking down of barriers between staff and prisoners would be a good thing, only 54% (14% no opinion) did not think that this initiative would achieve such a goal.

64% of staff felt that prisoners' self-esteem would be increased by allowing them to wear their own clothes, and over 70% felt that prisoners would gain "individuality" (though open-ended responses allowed some staff to suggest that this was not necessarily a "good thing"). 60% of staff felt that prisoners would take more responsibility for themselves as a result – it seems unlikely that this would be viewed as anything but an advance.

In general staff remained pessimistic about the effects of the initiative on security (i.e. escapes, absconds, confusion of prisoners with civilian staff and smuggling of contraband into the prisons). On some control issues staff remained pessimistic (though see results on thefts and disputes above) such as 63% expecting more damage to prisoners' clothing, over 70% expecting no reduction in complaints about clothing, and 80% expecting increased claims for compensation for damage to or loss of clothing. Over 70% of staff, before and after, expected pressure on prisoners' families to provide good quality (i.e. expensive) clothing, and their were concerns expressed about the resultant inequalities visible as a result of the initiative.

Over 80% of staff expected their workload to increase as a result of the initiative. Staff with prior experience of working with prisoners wearing their own clothes were much less pessimistic than those with no such experience, both before and after, suggesting that longer experience of the initiative might have further moderated opinions.

Prisoners' attitudes

Questionnaires were not issued to prisoners in the two local prisons, as there was no "before" stage. Different methodologies were adopted in each prison, because of initial problems with response rates, and these may have affected the results.

After the introduction of the initiative, 39% of prisoners said that new clothing had been bought for them, though before the trial 93% said they owned clothing which could be brought in for them. Thus, some financial pressures were clearly being brought to bear on their partners, families or other visitors.

Prisoners' initial pessimism about "control" issues also appeared to be misplaced. Before the initiative, 38% of prisoners felt that there would be an increase in thefts of clothing as a result of the initiative, but afterwards only 8% said there had been such an increase (p lt 0.001). Similarly, before the trial 39% felt there would be more damage to clothing, but afterwards only 29% agreed that this had occurred (p lt 0.001). Before the initiative 53% of prisoners felt there would be more disputes over clothing, but only 13% felt this afterwards (p lt 0.001).

Prisoners' psychological changes

Though prisoners were asked to complete questionnaires assessing their locus of control and their self-esteem, many chose not to do so, and the validity of any findings would therefore have been suspect. For those who did there were in any case no significant changes in their scores.

Young prisoners

A "custodial adjustment questionnaire" (Thornton etc...) was also administered to the prisoners in the two YOIs. It consisted of four scales, titled "inmate", "staff", "distress" and "deviance". These attempt to measure objectively, respectively, prisoners' attitudes to other inmates, to staff, their delinquent behaviour in the prison, and the degree of emotional distress felt.

Of course, being general questionnaires, and not specifically concerned with clothing, any changes found could have resulted from a number of factors, as it was impossible to keep all other factors unchanged when the initiative was introduced. Other regime changes, or simply the passage of time, could have caused or ameliorated (and therefore hidden) any changes. Nevertheless, allowing prisoners to wear their own clothes was probably the most important change in regime that could have occurred in the period of months between the before and after stages of the study, and it may be reasonable to attribute to it any changes found.

After the initiative, young prisoners were found to have a more positive attitude towards staff (p lt 0.05), though only after controlling for response rates in each establishment, which varied.

However, there was apparently a more negative attitude towards other prisoners (p lt 0.05 after controlling for response rates). Prisoners also scored higher on the deviancy subscale after the initiative (p lt 0.05, whether or not controlled for response rates) suggesting that their behaviour had deteriorated slightly.

The "distress" subscale showed no significant change after the initiative, though there was a tendency for scores to be reduced.

Before the experiment, some concern had been expressed about the potential for inequalities to be emphasised, with well-off prisoners having access to good quality clothing, while prisoners with lesser financial resources wearing less prestigious clothing, or prison issue clothing. An attempt was therefore made to test whether there were any differences on the psychological measures, at the "after" stage only, between prisoners wearing their own clothes and those wearing only prison issue clothing or a mixture of the two.

On controlling for response rate in the two establishments, there was only one difference that even approached statistical significance – young prisoners who were wearing only their own clothes were more positive in their attitudes to staff than those who were wearing prison issue clothing ($p=0.056$). However, the low level of statistical significance, and the fact that in one establishment the prisoners had to undergo a period of probation before they were allowed to wear their own clothing, both suggest that this finding should be treated very tentatively.

Adult prisoners

Like young offenders, adult prisoners (in the category C prison) mostly said at the before stage that they owned clothing which could be brought to them – only 20% said they owned none. However, afterwards 70% said that new clothes had been bought for them by their family, partner or others. There was a slight increase in the proportion of prisoners saying that it would be difficult for their families to afford clothes for them, from 56% before to 64% after (p lt 0.1).

It seemed that prisoners anticipation of increased thefts had been borne out, as before the initiative, 29% of prisoners anticipated increases in thefts of clothing, while afterwards 24% agreed this had occurred.

Before the trial, 42% of prisoners felt there would be less damage to clothing as a result of being allowed to wear their own clothes, while afterwards 58% agreed this was the case (p lt 0.01). Their initial pessimism about disputes over clothing appeared to be misplaced, with 25% expecting an increase in problems of this nature in advance, but afterwards only 6% reported that it had been more of a problem than before.

As for psychological assessment, on locus of control and self-esteem there were no significant differences at the before and after stages, nor on the "institutional adjustment" scale (an adult version of the CAQ, but with only two subscales on relationships with other inmates and staff).

Nor were any differences found between prisoners who were wearing their own clothes and those who wore prison issue clothing.

Visitors

A number of different methods were used to canvass the opinions of prisoners' families or other visitors. Some visitors reported having to replace items of the prisoner's clothing which had been damaged or stolen. Many also reported having bought new clothing for the prisoner. While visitors at the local prisons and young offender institutions did not suggest that this was causing any financial difficulties, those at the category C prison did say this. The category C prison probably holds prisoners serving substantially longer sentences. Also, different administrative procedures probably prevented excessive demands in the other prisons.

A few visitors were bothered by the extra security surrounding the scheme, but only at an establishment where a video-imaging system was used to distinguish prisoners from visitors.

The vast majority of visitors favoured the initiative, with the few objectors suggesting that uniformity should be part of the punishment, or that some prisoners might be disadvantaged because of a lack of financial resources. However, no visitor said this last of themselves or the prisoner they were visiting.

Conclusions

The conclusions are fairly clear. Staff retained a broadly negative attitude towards the initiative, though their opinions about some aspects did seem to soften with experience. There was also evidence that staff with prior experience of prisoners wearing their own clothes had less negative attitudes about the idea. This in turn suggests that more experience by staff with no prior experience of it might lead to a further softening of attitudes.

There was little evidence that the widespread increases in theft and vandalism, predicted by staff and by some prisoners, had actually taken place. There was evidence that prisoners had put their families or other visitors under financial pressure by expecting them to provide clothing – many had new clothing bought for them. However, they and their visitors tended not to see this as a particular problem, with visitors tending to see it as a problem for other people and not for themselves.

Though there was some evidence of possible changes in prisoners behaviour and attitudes towards staff and other prisoners, some changes were positive and some negative. In all, it cannot be said that the trial had an overall positive or negative effect.

In fact this is probably the best overall conclusion. Despite prior opinions ranging from apocalyptic to overoptimistic, allowing prisoners to wear their own clothes does not seem to have had any major positive or negative effects. Clearly the decision whether or not to allow convicted male prisoners in the whole prison estate to wear their own clothes will be guided more by practical issues, which have not been discussed in this paper, and more general political and legal concerns.

The current policy is that convicted male prisoners may be allowed to do so as an earned privilege, and that this is most likely to be practicable in parts of prisons where all prisoners have earned the privilege. In practice, there is not expected to be a significant increase in the number of prisoners wearing their own clothes.

References

Home Office (1991). *Custody, Care and Justice: The way ahead for the Prison Service in England and Wales.* London.

Woolf, H., & Tumin, S. (1991). *Prison disturbances April 1990: report of an inquiry.* London: HMSO.

Harries, R. (1994). Allowing male convicted prisoners to wear their own clothes. *Home Office Research Bulletin, 36*, 49-53.

Thornton, D. (1987). Assessing custodial adjustment. In B. McGurk, D. Thornton, & M. Williams (Eds.), *Applying Psychology to Imprisonment: Theory and Practice.* London: HMSO.

A Harm Reduction Approach to the Depenalization of Drug Crime via Community Based Outpatient Treatment

Brian McKenna and Michael Smith[1]

The use of addictive opiates and cocaine continues to increase globally despite intense international efforts to reduce drug supply through interdiction and enforcement. Raymond Kendall, the chief of Interpol, stated publicly in 1994 that repressive measures had failed to reduce trafficking and consumption of illicit substances. He cited the social and economic conditions in producer countries and increasing demand in countries where consumption is already high. His recommendation was to increase efforts to reduce the demand for illicit substances by increasing efforts aimed at prevention, education and treatment. Mr. Kendall supported a policy of depenalization which diverted individuals from the criminal justice system and increased the resources available for treatment.[2]

Recent research supporting Mr. Kendall's position has shown that treatment is more effective than repressive measures in reducing drug use. A study published by the Rand Drug Policy Research Center showed that $34 million invested in treatment in the United States reduced drug use as much as $336 million spent on interdiction or $246 million for enforcement.[3]

The United States and Europe are facing the limits of their respective policies to either repress or tolerate drug use. European countries have generally begun to experience the overcrowding of prisons, which has characterized the United States since the 1980's. The increasing prevalence of drug tourism and the growth of violence in many open drug scenes have led to their closure. Criminal justice professionals on both sides of the Atlantic are increasingly looking for the means to respond to drug using offenders as victims of a psychosocial and medical illness, rather than as criminals.

Reflecting these social realities, innovative programs have been developed in the United States which divert offenders from prosecution and provide humane and effective care that recognizes the rights and responsibilities of drug using

---

1 The authors wish to thank Judge Herbert Klein and the staffs of the Dade County Courthouse and the Metro Dade Office of Substance Abuse Control for their assistance in the preparation of this report.

2 Le Nouvel Observateur. 30 Decembre 1993 - 5 Janvier 1994. Vincent Jauvert. Pps. 41-43.

3 Keeping Score; What We Are Getting For Our Federal Controll Dollars. 1995 Report available from Drug Strategies, 2445 M Street NW, Suite 480, Washington D.C. 20037.

offenders. Based on a model developed in Miami, close to 100 specialized Drug Court Diversion and Treatment Programs have been instituted or are in developmental stages in American cities. These programs utilize a system of comprehensive services based on a foundation of community oriented outpatient treatment, and a unique drug court which determines the eligibility of clients and monitors their progress in treatment. In the drug court model, all participants from the judge to prosecuting and defense attorneys, work in a non-adversarial manner with treatment providers to help the offender become free from addictive drugs and provide the services necessary to assist the offender in achieving social reintegration.

The Miami Drug Court Diversion and Treatment Program was developed in 1989 by Associate Chief Judge Herbert Klein. The Miami Supreme Court appointed Judge Klein to undertake a comprehensive study of drug issues in Dade County, Florida in 1988. Due to the rapid emergence of inexpensive "crack"-cocaine in the 1980's, the numbers of felony offenders incarcerated in Dade County had increased to the point where the criminal justice system itself was severely strained. Judge Klein reported that 80% of the 45.000 felony offenders arrested in Dade County were under the influence of a drug other than alcohol at the time of their arrest. 60% of those individuals had one or two prior arrests and the annual cost for their incarceration was $17.000.[4]

The public health care system was similarly strained, due to the large numbers of babies born addicted to cocaine and requiring intensive care for the first weeks of their lives. The number of cocaine babies born in the State of Florida had grown from 200 in 1986 to over 10.000 in 1988.[5] The cost of intensive care in the United States for a low birth weight and prematurely born cocaine addicted baby can range anywhere from $40.000 to $200.000.

After an in-depth study of treatment options which involved comparing existing treatment systems it was determined that traditional hospital-based private treatment or long term residential treatment was prohibitively expensive. The cost of private, hospital-based treatment for a 28-day residential program ranges from $1800 to $15.000. Long term residential drug treatment costs a minimum of $1800 per month. At the time of the report in Dade County there were less than 1500 treatment slots available for those patients who could not afford private treatment, yet the majority of the individuals who had been arrested fell in that category.[6]

In this report to the Miami Supreme Court, Judge Klein recommended the development of a treatment program utilizing predominantly outpatient services which could effectively and affordably provide care for large numbers of people.

4 Strategies for Action: Combating Drug and Alcohol Abuse in Dade Country. Presented to the Florida Supreme Court, 1989. Herbert M. Klein Associate Chief Judge. Dade County Courthouse, 73 West Flahler Street, Miami, Florida 33130.

5 Ibid.

6 Ibid.

Central to this effort is the participation of the judiciary, the prosecutor and the public defender operating as a team under the leadership role of a judge, who reviews a client's progress, provides personal encouragement, or reminds a client that poor performance may cause the resumption of prosecution. The use of frequent urine testing allows the client and Court to communicate directly. A client becomes responsible for his/her own performance and statement. This demonstrates a healthy system of authority in which people will grow to a higher standard. If the judge understands the relapsing nature of the illness then the judge's actions can reflect realistic expectations for a client's progress at a certain stage of treatment. A person overcoming addiction is in a process of internalizing discipline. Sufficient independence to learn responsible behaviour is essential to developing maturity and self discipline. Urine testing and Court hearings provide the structure necessary to internalize discipline.

Developing trust is essential to all parties involved. The client learns to trust the Court sufficiently to follow the treatment schedule and turn in a positive urine test rather than avoid an appointment with a counsellor. The Court must trust sufficiently in the human capacity for learning in order to provide the conditions for the client to mature The independence of community based outpatient treatment provides an appropriate structure for all parties to develop their relationships.

Acupuncture is seen as strong support in this process because it generally reduces many of the painful obstacles to overcoming addiction. Clients themselves Desiree acupuncture as very helpful in their daily struggle. For treatment providers acupuncture offers a means of assisting clients to overcome their anguish without the use of psychoactive substances. Clients receiving acupuncture learn that they have the capacity within their bodies to feel good without taking drugs. This recognition opens up many new possibilities and will frequently help clients to remain in a therapeutic relationship during the early stages of detoxification before they can utilize verbally oriented therapies. The calming, centering, and empowering effects of acupuncture allow clients to be more introspective and communicative which improves progress in individual and group therapies. Acupuncture is used as a non verbal therapeutic progress which allows the client to have a positive drug free experience with peers. Clients in the early stage of treatment who are unable to utilize verbal therapies can sit quietly and benefit from the process taking place around them.

The Drug Court is patterned after a therapeutic process as well. The dynamics of group process allow newer participants to benefit from the experiences of those further along in treatment. In the Drug Court all cases scheduled on a given day are seen together in an open Court. The Court hearing functions much like a public meeting and is used to educate all incoming offenders and, as well as clients already in treatment, on the results of their behaviour.

In open court all participants are able to observe each other's progress and results. Clients therefore grow to understand the intend of the Court and witness the rewards associated with improved behaviour as well as the possible negative consequence of program failure. Progress in treatment leading to graduation, is openly rewarded by the judge and provides encouragement to everyone in the courtroom. In addition, program failure can be admonished in the context of the judge's expressing his/her belief in the ability of the client to succeed. Sanctions meted out for repeated failure, are naturally seen by clients in a more balanced and fair way. If this progress is guided by an understanding of the principles of human growth and change, then a Drug Court judge can communicate with clients in a personal way which encourages their success. This is arguably the highest use of authority to which any public servant can aspire.

Commentary

The Drug Court movement has grown rapidly in the United States in response to the success of the Miami Model Drug Court and the ongoing increase in the use of illicit and addictive substances. It represents an effort to effectively care for drug users in a socially balanced manner which avoids repressive extremes at the same time neither trivialising drug use, minimizing its consequences, or encouraging consumption. It perhaps can serve as a new model of effective depenalization which retains the right of a society to limit the destructive social behaviour of its members.

In the Drug Court the historical tendency to view drug as a moral and legal problem rather than a medical problem is pragmatically overcome. In Europe and America proponents of harm reduction policies suggest that drug addiction is best approached pragmatically rather than on moral or legal grounds. Proponents of harm reduction tend to promote the use of needle exchange programs and the liberal dispensing of methadone as ways of reducing negative public health and criminal behaviours associated with drug use. While needle exchange and methadone programs are legitimate means of reducing drug related harm, their utility is frequently compromised by polydrug consumption, violence, and sexual behaviours associated with crack addiction. This is well established in methadone program in the U.S. and Europe. Intravenous injection of cocaine is associated with significantly increased risk for HIV transmission in addition to practices involving sexual favours given in exchange for crack.

Harm reduction arguments rest on the presumption that the criminalization and subsequent marginalization of people using drugs cause more destructive social outcomes than drug itself. They point to the ineffectiveness of repressive approaches and frequently argue in favour of legalization from practical and human rights perspectives. While it is true that institutional control and dispensation of addictive drugs would reduce profiting by organized crime, it will not necessarily eliminate the misuse of psychoactive substances. it is clear that certain psychoactive substances impair human capacity and responsible social functioning inviting the loss of individual rights and opening the doors to external forms of control or manipulation, be it by the Courts, drug dealers, medical doctors, or legal suppliers.

History offers us cases of alcohol which was prohibited in the United States and then legalized again in response to overwhelming demand and inability of the federal government to effectively control sales. The 7th Special Report to Congress on Alcohol and Health of 1990 estimated that the revenue for the production and sale of alcohol was $63.1 billion in 1985 while the social costs for the same year were estimated at $116.7 billion.[10] These costs relate to decreased productivity, motor vehicle crashes, unintentional accidents, comorbidities, fetal alcohol syndrome, and alcohol related crimes. These facts indicate that legalization of a psychoactive substance is a process with complex social implications not all of which involve the reduction of drug related harm.

Motor vehicle accidents and violent crimes related to alcohol are examples requiring the intervention of the criminal justice system. In the case of these social circumstances the role of the substance in producing negative behaviours cannot be ignored. To do so not only implies that the person is inherently bad but it undervalues the need for appropriate treatment. Drug Courts serve as a model of effective depenalization while retaining legitimate and pragmatic social limits on potentially destructive behaviours. They may have a significant preventive and educational role to play in the increasingly complex evolution of the human use of psychoactive substances.

---

[10] National Institute on Alcohol Abuse and Alcoholism. 7th Special Report to Congress on Alcohol and Health. Washington D.C. 1990. U.S. Government Printing Office.

Interplay of Religion, Medicine and Prison: A Preliminary Historical Study

Roberts Girgensons

Medicine originates its most fundamental prohibitive rules from the ancient times when Religion and Medicine was not yet two separate realms (Markow, 1988). Subsequent history reveals that transgression of these rules leads to failure of the realisation of the declared objectives not only in Medicine, but by other human institutions where Medicine is used directly or as an analogy.

The most famous ancient Rule of Medicine is the *noli nocere* principle which states not to inflict pain but to relieve it and help man to come to a state of constructive and even better creative activity. This is rehabilitation, the integral part of the Mission of Medicine. The misapplication of medical model, the transgression of the *noli nocere*, began when Penance was called "heavenly medicine". In considering that "Penance" had been designated as Punishment which inflicts pain, the transgression of the fundamental rule becomes evident.

Penance is a fundamental Christian concept: a voluntary harsh treatment which one imposes upon oneself to show repentance after wrongdoing. The true sense of repentance is the returning to God. Penance followed repentance and is a sign of purification and resolve not to sin again, a sign of readiness to receive Force from God, a sign of Force. The Church's approach to repentance is based on the belief that penance is effective only when the sinner has voluntarily repented. Penance may be misinterpreted as punishment only in the unprepared profane mind.

Regarding the trials, which Man returning to God voluntarily meets, as punishments is the reversing of the true sense of Repentance, and becomes an ironical interpretation of the concept of Penance. Application of the punishment analogy to Penance reflects a derisive transgression of the fundamental spiritual rules and by this the attainment of the declared goals of the applicants of such an approach to Penance was doomed to failure.

After this fundamental error was made early in the Christian history, during the times of Tertullian (AD 160-220), the Medicine analogy has been misapplied to the concept of Penance. Penance has been explained as the "heavenly medicine" that heals the wounds inflicted by sin. later Christian public accepted penance imposed by the Church on the grounds that it is better to endure punishment in this world than in the next. So after the erroneous regarding the Penance as punishment, this punishment with pain affliction was designated as Medicine.

The fundamental prohibitive *noli nocere* rule of Medicine was transgressed with inevitably detrimental results for the attainment of the declared goals.

Prison appears on the historical scene of this interplay only after these fatal mistakes have been made and accepted. Prison is the most remarkable of all human institutions which developed obscurely, empirically, almost accidentally, and although it has been in a state of continuous change it remains one of the few institutions that exist in an almost identical form in all modern cultures.

Prison in Ancient World, for example by Biblical prisons, though traumatic and dangerous, initially was not employed as a punishment, and certainly never as a condition for rehabilitation or as the true road to the salvation. Only afterwards, gradually this institution inflicting mental and physical pain has come to be regarded as the place of punishment.

Saint Pachomius (died in AD 346) as a pagan youth of twenty, had been imprisoned in Luxor, Egypt for deserting the army. Christians came to relieve the hunger and thirst of the prisoners. he was so influenced by their ministry to his physical needs that he was converted to Christianity. Saint Pachomius made use of his experience as prisoner to introduce the prison model for the place where penitence is performed. After his release Pachomius established not less than nine monasteries for men and two for women, the first institutions of this kind. he has thus come to be recognized as the founder of "cenotobic" monasticism, a style of religious life in which Christians devote themselves to a common life governed by a Rule. Monastic communities gradually replaced the "eremitic" Christian life-style in which solitary hermits lived an unregulated life alone in the desert.

Subsequent history reveals that despite the good aspirations of the men taking part in the "cenotobic" monasticism the doom and failures of the goals declared by the medieval cenotobic monasticism was determined by the transgression of the fundamental rules of Religion and Medicine.

Religious penitentiaries degenerated, becoming not the sign of Force but rather a sign of weakness. In their likeness to prisons they became indeed used as prisons. The 17th century Benedictine monk Dom Jean Mabillon described the adverse affect which the monastic prisons had on those incarcerated in them imposing thinking upon the sad state into which they have precipitated themselves. The excess of sadness overwhelmed them and caused them to sigh under the burden of their past sins.

This was why Mabillon saw so little fruit from the prison and penance and why the inmates of such institutions so often lost their mind or all sensitiveness becoming insane, hardened or desperate and depressed or becoming adapted only to live in institutions that were more retreats than prisons since there were heated rooms and workshops, This was certainly the sort of "penitentiary" the prison reformers envisioned (James, 1990).

The Church had largely dispensed with religious penitentiaries by the time secular penologists "discovered" the idea in the vain hope of reforming or rather correcting criminals. What did not work for monks was no more likely to succeed with inmates in secular penitentiaries.

With the Reformation of Church began the series of vain hopes and efforts to transform criminals through Prison into non criminals. In secular justice, the principal goal is to preserve and restore the public order by inspiring terror in the offender. When the declarations were issued that the principal goal or even essence of imprisonment must be the transformation of criminals into non criminals (Krumins, 1992), secular justice, whose executive instrument was Prison, nourished hopes from the misconceptions of public mind. No wonder that these "concepts" turned to become failures. Prison reforms may well have honesty misinterpreted the Christian concept of Penitence because of their own ecclesiastic backgrounds. Most of them were members of denominations which resulted from the Reformation's repudiation of contemporary Roman Catholicism's practice of the sale of indulgences as a condition of present or future absolution. If Protestants were in opposition against abuses in the practice of the Sacrament of Penance, it is no wonder that they misapplied its principles. despite its religious justification the reformer's model of punishment and penitence, with medical model implicated, was, in fact, significantly different from that of the Church.

The power of human freedom made it possible to compel someone to feel truly repentant for sin. repentance must be a free act of the will; otherwise, it would not be the result of sorrow or remorse, but of fear or self-interest. The penitential reformers failed to recognize the power of the human will, and the absurdity of trying to force offenders into true repentance by denying them liberty. So the penitentiary prison turned to be absurd.

Ironically, while the penitentiary denied prisoner's physical freedom and had deleterious psychological effects, it failed to eradicate their most important freedom – freedom to resist spiritual coercion. For those in the beginning the penitentiary was a radical change of direction from the nightmare of violence that characterized their society's response to criminals. The penitentiary model is gone except to criminals continues, the nightmare continues.

When the sequence of the misapplication which turned Penance into Punishment and Punishment into Medicine and vice versa inevitably failed to reform criminals into non criminals, penologists applied another misconception in the public mind which turned from Religion to Science, to justification of Punishment by Medicine. They declared that in the treatment of criminals ought to be used the medical model or in certain cases the Medicine directly, especially psychiatry or even surgery. Transgression of the fundamental prohibitive *noli nocere* rule in these extreme cases is the most evident. But even in the cases when sophisticated behavioural control techniques are used transgression still remains because they are employed under coercion.

May be the origin of behaviourism or learning theory needs not to be sought in Pavlovian experiments. Similar behaviour control techniques have been employed in prison from the time of its obscure origins and are theorized by penology in so called progressive system of imprisonment. But considering the essential statement of the European Prison Rules, that the suffering inherent in imprisonment is sufficient for punishment, no aggravation of the conditions of imprisonment is needed. Under such terms any aggravation of the conditions of imprisonment and prison regimes may be regarded as torture. And one may conclude that degrees of liberty implied in progressive system represent various degrees of torture. Moczydlowsky (1992) in his system study of the Polish prisons stated that deprivation of liberty causes pain. This pain in itself is sufficient for punishment. And here answering the question: how to treat human beings who are suffering such a pain Religion and Medicine meet again in one joint position: to help the prisoners to meet the trial of deprivation of liberty so that they can emerge from Prison to a state of constructive and even creative activity. This is the true sense of the Rehabilitation in Prison – positive Prison concept which may be proposed by religion and Medicine.

Medicine through its Psychiatric branch using the new humanistic approach represented by Maslow (1967) and the logotherapy of Frankl (1962) who himself experienced the imprisonment in nazi camp may take the active part in such Prison Renewal.

The first step in this direction must be to stop programming prisoners as criminals. The psychotechnique or rather spiritual device "stop calling them criminals" must be applied. In order to become successful Penology or rather prison Science ought to be separated from Criminology. In this endeavour Prison ought to remember its origins. Maybe Prison is coeval with Religion and Medicine, coeval with Temple. In many respects they seem similar. Isolated, sacred area, almost impenetrable, especially for information and research, inspiring awe rather than fear, immune personal.

To this challenge Society will answer with due respect and rise of the fallen prestige and authority of Prison. Otherwise when Religion and Medicine should be able to take ownership for their history and their impact on the origin, maintenance, transformation and ultimately abolition of penal institutions.

Summary

Failures of the declared positive prison goals are explained by transgression of the fundamental prohibitive rules, particularly by misapplication of medical model. Joint position of Religion and Medicine is to help the prisoners to meet trial of the deprivation of liberty so that they can emerge from Prison in a state of constructive and even creative activity. This is the true sense of the Rehabilitation in Prison.

References

Markow, V. A. (1988). *Fenomen sluchaynosty: Metodologicheskiy analiz*. Riga: Zinatne.
James, J. T. L., (1990). *A Living Tradition. Penitentiaery Chaplaincy.* Ottawa: Chaplaincy Division. Correctional Service of Canada.
Krumins, E. (1992). *Leskats soda izpildes teorija un praksé.* Riga: Latvijas Policijas Akademija.
Moczydlowsky, P. (1992). *The Hidden Life of Polish Prisons.* Bloomington and Indianapolis: Indian University Press.
Maslow, A. (1967). Self-actualization and Beyond. In *Challenges of Humanistic Psychology*. NY.
Frankl, V. (1962). *Man's search for meaning. An Introduction to Logotherapy*. Boston.

International Benchmarking

Cynthia McDougall and John Powls

Introduction

The development of meta-analysis has helped address the problem of gaining an overview of research areas in which many different methodologies and means of evaluation have been used (Lösel & Koferi, 1989; Andrews, Zinger, Hoge, Bonta, Gendreau, & Cullen, 1990; Lipsey, 1992). This approach has been extremely valuable in identifying critical factors in offender treatment related to reducing offences, and has been an important step forward in guiding practice (Hollin, 1993).

A complementary approach, being developed in the Prison Service of England and Wales, is that of attempting to standardize procedures and measure prior to evaluation by means of benchmarking. This process has already begun in co-operation with Prison Services in the USA, Canada and France. We hope to extend the process to include Services in Europe, both custodial and non-custodial.

Benchmarking is a technique derived from the world of business which offers a way of comparing our performance with other providers and analysing the comparisons with the aim to improve performance. It is a systematic approach to the search for good practices and collaborative improvements between organisations. In that regard, it has much in common with the aims of associations such as the European Association of Psychology and Law.

Benchmarking Environment

Although most common in private sector companies, many organisations with a wide range of backgrounds have taken on benchmarking. As it is often the case, after 3 years many are starting to reject the process, and articles are appearing in business journals which question its validity. The tenor of these studies suggests that, where benchmarking has been treated as a "ritual dance" it has raised more dust and grit than enlightenment. The main stumbling blocks have been:
– failure to integrate significant measures of performance and as a consequence, settling for meaningless benchmarks,

– where the whole industry was mediocre, benchmarking produced well defined mediocracy or more shapely chaos,
– methodology difficulties in comparing results derived from different systems for different purposes.

HM Prison Service is trying to learn from the better organisations which have continued to try to define appropriate measures comparing whole organisations. However, they have refined the process by seeking other relevant benchmarkings, and comparing significant areas of work with organisations who are regarded as being the best in a particular approach or area regardless of industry background.

Strategic Approach

The Vision Statement of the Prison Service of England and Wales directs us to a provision of service which will be regarded as a standard of excellence around the world.

As a means of working to achieve this, HM Prison Service is developing a coordinated twin approach.
– The first is pursuing the benchmarking process with the correctional service of USA, Canada and France, beginning with a wide range of measures and jointly managing programme of refinement. Our colleagues in Scotland, Northern Ireland, Sweden, and Romania have asked to be kept advised of progress and wish to discuss joining the group in the near future. The areas to be measured include institutional safety, security and control, healthcare, the content and effectiveness of regimes, personnel issues and cost effectiveness. A joint initiative has already begun to try to produce a common measure of effectiveness for the contribution of imprisonment to reducing recidivism.
– The second is identifying, describing, and developing benchmarks in individual key strategic areas with the best in their field. We have not restricted ourselves to other prison systems only. As an example, Personnel Services plan to develop benchmarks with private sector companies. Information Technology Services are doing likewise with our opposite numbers from a range of public and private sector organisations. Early discussions are also underway with healthcare providers, special hospitals, educators, researchers and providers of equivalent services in the community amongst others.

Our new process of project management includes the generation of a suitable benchmark amongst the outputs required of all future strategic projects. This will ensure that in prioritised areas of development, we benchmark against international market leaders. This process will commence with the current Incentive Based Regimes project, where a visit to the Catalonian Prison and Rehabilitation Service by the project team has taken place, and the initiative on countering drug abuse which is part of a national Government strategy.

Principles and Framework for International Benchmarking

Although the national correctional services already committed to this process have differing jurisdictional and demographic backgrounds, the key elements of our Purpose Statement are common to all. These elements are, serving the public, holding prisoners safely and securely, and reducing criminal behaviour in custody and after release. It is agreed that the process of benchmarking is designed to enable and assist joint and individual performance improvement, and for that reason is entered into co-operatively.

A statement of principles has been drawn up jointly by the three Services to guide this work. A copy of this is available from the second author for anyone wishing to become more involved or have further details.

Part of this statement is a framework for handling comparisons and research processes to manage the outcome from analysis. It is recognised that there are still significant methodological problems in analysing and comparing results across national and/or organisational boundaries. Work on meta-analysis comparing psychological research data is of significant relevance here.

The Role of International Organisations

The culture of internationalism is growing, even in sometimes insular, pragmatic and operationally driven organisations. The prison services already involved, hope that this work will attract the attention of the United Nations and the Council of Europe. We are actively working towards this, but their and our bureaucracy makes progress slow. There are many parallels between the strategy and principles outlined above and those which EAPL and other similar organisations espouse. Links are already established through EAPL with the Forum of International Psychological Associations in Europe (FIPAE).

We believe that there are several areas where EAPL and other similar organisations could contribute. This is not an exclusive list.

- Advising on areas of significance with sufficient existing commonality to be benchmarked.
- Advising on and formulating common methodologies for international comparison.
- Research leading to common international performance standards.
- Influencing opinion formers in various member jurisdictions to become part of a benchmarking network.
- Modelling good practice by devising benchmarks with colleague organisations in the FIPAE and other collaboration bodies.

We would be delighted to act (contact through the second author) as recipients of expressions of interest in this process.

References

Andrews, D. A., Zinger, I., Hoge, R. D., Bonta, J., Genreau, P., & Cullen, F. T. (1990). Does correctional treatment work? A clinically relevant and psychological informed meta-analysis. *Criminology, 28*, 369-404.

Hollin, C. R. (1993). Advances in the psychological treatment of delinquent Behaviour. *Criminal Behaviour and Mental Health, 3*, 142-157.

Lipsey, M. W. (1992). Juvenile delinquency treatment: a mate-analytic inquiry into the variability of effects. In T. D. Cook, H. Cooper, D. S. Cordray, H. Hartmann, L. V. Hedges, R. J. Light, R. T. A. Louis, & F. Mosteller (Eds.), *Meta-analysis for Explanation: A Casebook* (pp. 83-127). New York: Russel Sage Foundation.

Lösel, F., & Koferl, P. (1989). Evaluation research in correctional treatment in West Germany: a meta-analysis. In H. Wegner, F. Lösel, & J. Haisch (Eds.), *Behaviour and the Justice System: Psychological Perspectives,* 334-335. New York: Springer.

Training of Prison Officers for Leading Problem-Oriented Groups of Inmates

Bernhard Wydra

Organisation development in prison is mainly based on the training of staff. So, we in Bavaria place emphasis on selection and training of officers-to-be. We have observed, however, that during the basic training of the future officers – which lasts about 20 months – we reach limits in exploiting the capacities of the trainees. Capacities rely on social competence rather than on intellectual and cognitive abilities. These limits may have to do with one of the goals of the trainees, which is to pass the exam and start work as a civil servant (Beamter). These limits may also have something to do with the fact that in basic training we teach higher level skills. Special social competence for growing needs require special setting which includes voluntary participation.

We have realized that many officers-to-be have social competence. They have developed it as an apprentice in a practical profession, and practised it for a while. This is one of the prerequisites for entering the profession of an officer. Thus, we have decided to invite them to further voluntary training. One kind of training is in leading problem-oriented groups of inmates.

I want to describe briefly the goals, the contents and the process, of this training, and summarize some experiences with the training and the trained people.

The goals in training officers to lead problem-oriented groups of inmates are on two levels, First, the training should enable the officer to lead problem-oriented groups of inmates. These are voluntary groups or groups within a so-called living-unit of a prison (Wohngruppe), where willingness for group work is the necessity condition for the acceptance into the unit. The problems to focus on are multifaceted, they range from coping within the prison conditions, to recognizing behaviours leading to criminal actions, to anticipating their release. They are found out and agreed to with the group of inmates. In talking about the problems. the capacity of the inmates to think differently, to communicate their thoughts, and to tolerate other's opinions is sometimes newly learned.

The group leader, knowing the basics of the group dynamics and getting experienced with them, facilitates the exchange of thoughts, and some emotional contact between the inmates. Ideally there is an open exchange with emotional impact between inmates. There is no psycho-therapeutic goal intended which would aim at a systematic change in the personality of the inmate, though some changes in different areas might occur. Any interchanges which give rise to social behaviours between inmates instead of the destructive clusters of the subculture prison milieu, count as a success.

A second goal of our training aims at the personal development of the officer. It touches upon his attitude towards others, especially towards the inmates and his work. He is invited to broaden his own self-awareness during the training. Positive self-awareness reduces his prejudices against inmates and opens stage for new, fresh encounters, which in turn bring crisp motivation for the work. (I remember a situation where the wife of one of the trained officers met me in the street and exclaimed enthusiastically "I am so grateful that you took my husband into your program. He changed even at home.")

The training lasts about one and a half years. It starts with a week of intensive self-experience at our training centre. Observing and perceiving, giving and receiving feed-back within changing group-constellations are the main ways to self-experience. Thus, the trainee is smoothly and safely confronted with other's reactions to his behaviour and his idiosyncrasies. Group dynamic processes are supported by structures exercises, such that trust and openness can develop. We take care to protect each individual in the group.

Some weeks later the training continues with a basic course in group dynamics. In this one-week-long series of lectures at our training centre, the participants receive some basic information about group dynamics. It is demonstrated and explained mostly in relation to the current processes within the group of participants.

At the end of this week, the participants are encouraged to select a group of inmates in their prisons which they lead in weekly meetings. This leadership is supported by the supervision the trainees get from superiors in their prisons. These officers are trained and supervised by our training centre.

Approximately one year after the basic course, there is another one week seminar in which the experiences of the group leaders are exchanged. They are explained with additional information about group dynamics and demonstrated within the group of participants. The week ends with a final colloqium, in which the participants simulate a group situation and demonstrate what they have learned. They get feed-back from the trainers.

It is always surprising to observe the changes in the reactions and the behaviour of the participants in the course of this training. The changes are not dramatic, but noticeable. The first time they are allowed to lead a group seems to be very important. The trainees feel encouraged to find their own ways in handling the leadership task. The visible result is at it best a self-confident person showing differential reactions in his or her communications with others, and particularly with inmates.

We have trained approximately 300 officers in leading problem-oriented groups in Bavaria. Only about 40 of them are still actively involved. There are a few probable reasons for this fact: some of the trained officers have qualified for a higher level of career and their new responsibilities do not leave time for group leading. Others have taken further training courses which we offer and for which this training is a prerequisite. These workshops include leading a therapeutic workshop, and a social training leadership. In this social training, the inmates are prepared for release. They are given information about experiences in some important matters of daily life after release such as presenting themselves to potential employers or to authorities, organizing their budget, and gaining awareness about their style of communication. Some of the trained officers do not show any respective activity, however. Looking at this high percentage of loss of the targeted activity, we have questioned the worth of training officers, if later they will not be active group leaders. However, we have decided that it is worthwhile to do even in this case.

For certainly all of the trained officers have gained insights and experiences which are useful for the hard tasks they have to perform. We get positive feedback from them, sometimes years later. We hear positively about many of them. We think that this training lays a good ground for attitudes and skills necessary for the rehabilitation we are obliged to attempt to attain by Correctional Law.

In conclusion I want to summarize some of the thoughts about our training: Personnel Development as a central part of Organization Development aims for "professional further training, from the psychological standpoint in particular in training groups. They should contribute for the members of the organization to cope with the (new) tasks by acquiring information, skills and attitudes, adequate to the goals" (P. Braune et al. (1983). In F. Lösel (Ed.), *Kriminalpsychologie*. Weinheim, Basel: Beltz Verlag).

I think the outlined training of officers in leading problem-oriented groups of inmates fulfils this demand. We have observed that training of this kind must be carried out over a relatively long time, even if the participants meet relatively seldom. For example the outlined training met only three times for one week within during a year and a half training period.

It seems to be the emotional company of the participants during a relatively long period which brings positive results. We also emphasize personal relationships, and encourage the trainees to be aware of their needs and anxieties, while we support them in finding personal solutions for their problems. We do not discount cognitive information in further training. We have experienced, however, that cognitive information alone is not sufficient, sometimes even an impediment. It is the emotional relationship within the training group, and personal support which allows new, broadening experiences. Such experiences in turn are helpful, affirming, and motivating. They contribute to changes necessary for Organisation Development in prison.

Riots in the Romanian Penitentiaries after the Revolution of December 1989

Georghe Florian

General Considerations

A changing society implies to a certain extent, disorganisation and a sense of crisis at certain levels of some systems. With the development of new conditions, traditions fail to produce appropriate models of conduct: the resulting confusion and doubt troubles the every day lives of people and existing instructions thus further undermining the political and economical values which used to regulate that conduct.

Because of this confused background, changes in perceptions and inter-personal relations can appear, and the lack of a new longer-term perspective leads most people to concentrate on their immediate needs. If those needs cannot be satisfied within the system, the situation acquire the potential for a catastrophe. Additionally too great an importance given to these immediate aims, also seriously limits the negotiation possibilities of the legal authorities.

The causes of the prisoners' riots in some state penitentiaries must be understood in this general context, but also as an effect of long-term problems which affected after the revolution of December 1989 both prisoners and staff. We must take into account that in the last one and a half decade the Romanian penitentiary system regressed as not fulfilling its social function. This began in 1977 when over 70% of the newly constructed penitentiary units were full. According to the rationalisation the socialist society "does not generate" crimes". Information presented by the General Directorate of Penitentiaries was, however, in conflict with such a conclusion: overcrowding continued year by year. The issuance of some pardoning decrees counterbalanced a bit the increased number of criminal offences.

That is why the prisoners' hostility at the riot's beginning was more directed against the penitentiary system as a whole and less against an individual administration or unit.

In the first days of the revolution, the prisoners' riots were linked with the events developing in the country. In some penitentiaries, aggression moved towards the specific fundamental problems of that unit. Some problems were common to all units: insufficiently trained staff, staff's poor provisional settlement of certain interventions, insufficient rights for the prisoners and so on.

The evaluation made by the prisoners of the new social situation, reflected an attitude as prisoners suddenly considered themselves not criminals but victims of the former dictatorship. As a result they asked to be released. To all of this, they added their concern for the fate of their families in the context of the alarming news about the violence in the capital.

Later on, when some were freed as a result of Article 10 from the 4th of January 1990 Decree, prisoners who did not benefit added a feeling of having been defrauded.

The Revolution brought about some direct changes in the prison population. Once an amorphous mass of individuals they started to organise themselves. Driven by their enthusiasm and by events on free press – radio and TV – they reached the point of asking to be released, and contribute to the actions against the "terrorists".

The refusal by the authorities to grant release and the lack of wider social reaction towards their disobedient actions then brought on demands for the overall improvement of detention regimes.

One alarming fact to consider is that penitentiaries, because of low staff numbers, a great number of prisoners performed vital activities for the necessary functioning of the units. Some prisoners were even guards for certain offence categories. They also performed tasks such as food preparation for the staff and prisoners, bookkeeping, manning thermo-electric power stations, water management, animal husbandry, farming, etc. This independent responsibilities represented a permanent risk factor within the units.

When the hostilities started, the prisoners were waiting credible explanations from the staff concerning the events within the country, and especially regarding their ultimate demands. This became an important event because staff din not provide a satisfactory response.

The development of the riots

In the first days of the Revolution, the factor which created tension among prisoners was the order regarding the suspending of radio and broadcasts and also not delivering the written press. The prisoners new from their past experience that measures like this were hiding important events from them. This led to the proliferation of rumours in some units; the strongest being about the existence of a decree in accordance with which prisoners from all over the country were to be released, and that this was not directed by the Home Affairs Ministry. The anxiety of the prisoners became even greater upon noticing some suspicious movements within the penitentiaries' yards: vehicle movements, control and restraint trainings, etc.

Staff morale within the units was greatly affected by the unrest because they knew they did not have the necessary training required to face mass actions by the prisoners. Lacking the necessary support, the managers of units improvised intervention measures in accordance with the legislation in force. From case to case, any weakness of the planning and decision-making became conspicuous, a situation that negatively influenced the dynamics of the events.

The disorder developed similarly in all the involved penitentiaries. There seems to be 7 identifiable phases:

Phase I – All prisoners become vociferous, asking to be released, not recognising the official authority, the worst prisoners from the units using force and aggressiveness to express their point of view;

Phase II – Chaotic violence, prisoners get out by force from their cells, destroy things, threaten the staff, force the gates of the detention unit; there are revenge actions between prisoners; the great majority of prisoners enjoy the success of this violence;

Phase III – Information gathering. A quiet period, when prisoners find out by means of radio and TV about the events from all over the country. Some prisoners make a "covenant" with the new administration. Members of the staff become nervous;

Phase IV – Organisation for the mass of prisoners: opinion leaders emerge and terrorise those prisoners who want to break with them, leaders voice demands, they ask for new external representatives from the authorities and the army, they organise watch pickets, the doors of the cells remain open, the dialogue with the staff of the unit is reduced to a minimum, there is still a lot of aggression and homosexual rapes;

Phase V – Reorientation towards the staff of the unit, this phase is dominated by two elements: prisoners are disappointed of the different local representatives of the new authorities, who could not solve their demands, and the second appearance of the pardon decree of January 1990, Article 10, which opened the possibility for many prisoners to be released;

Phase VI – Psychological exhaustion of the prisoners and of the staff: the prisoners realise that they cannot force the decisive factors, and the staff that negotiations had lasted too long, their patience was unjustified and taken advantage of;

Phase VII – Intervention forces are in their positions, the prisoners are given an ultimatum which was frequently followed by their return to their cells, the unit is returned to order.

These phases try to reflect the dynamics of the prisoners' actions, the elements of each phase and the possible most appropriate points for the staff interventions. There are some further aspects which appeared during the riots and which must be considered in planning for the future:

– after every major feature of a riot of the prisoners within the detention unit – shouting and noise, forces regrouping, occupation of some new areas, trying to take hostages from the staff, beginning preliminary actions in order to escape, having altercations with prisoners who do not take part in their actions, etc. There is usually a quiet period in which prisoners wait to see the response of the administration, or to regroup their forces for another attempt. Discussions are reduced, they intensify their activity or trying intimidate the staff, the leaders remove themselves to another place in order to analyse the situation;

– External representatives not invited to a second dialogue because initially they could not fulfil prisoners' demands. The prisoners come to believe that only the staff of the unit can solve their problems;

– As the first major riot was coming to an end, in some penitentiaries there were additional outbreaks at varying periods of time. This can be explained by the fact that the unit administration did not continue the dialogue with the prisoners, and they eliminated the perceived shortcomings very slowly or not at all.

– Sometimes new acts of disobedience were a manifestation of solidarity within a group of prisoners, as a reaction to recent and arbitrary punishment (in the prisoners' opinion.)

Conclusions

1. The recent riots had as their objectives dramatising prisoners' complaints and to obtain concessions from decision makers. There will always be premises for such events in the new social conditions and to this we may add ethnic and other social factors.

The riots illustrated the fact that the problem with legitimacy within penitentiaries must be seriously analysed. We must not forget that in the days immediately after the revolution, the staff and the activity of the Home Affairs Ministry were discredited, including in this situation prison institutions. This became an important moral pillar for the action of the prisoners.

2. The penitentiary system equilibrium is a fragile one. It is very vulnerable to external influence. In considering existing experiences of prisoners we must expect more and more organised actions from them. Preventing and dealing with these actions must be part of a repertoire of flexible responses of well trained staff.

3. The situations created in the penitentiaries put into sharp focus the central role played by the governor of the unit. The prisoners considered governors to be objective while regarding the events, and during the discussions governors usually proved to have a vast understanding of issues which increased the prisoners' trust in them. As a consequence they were able eventually to subordinate the prisoners to their control once more. They always must be able to create for the prisoners and the staff the feeling that things will be able to quickly move towards peace and stability;

4. Beyond physical destruction, the prisoners' riots had serious consequences on interpersonal relationships in the penitentiaries and, significantly the riots reorganised the attitudes and the roles played by prisoners capable of extreme misconduct. Reasonable appeals for ceasing disobedient actions are only of

limited worth to the unit taking into account the different phase in the evolution of a riot; the staff certainly noticed when prisoners perceived weakness and the concessions made to their demands would not be forgotten, would be exploited and was expensive to resolve.

5. In accordance with catastrophe theory, the appearance of some disorder within penitentiaries is determined by two linked elements: the tensions created by the feelings of being defrauded, isolated and alienated, and by the intensity of the collective feelings of alienation, by the lack of communication and by the polarisation of the mass of prisoners.

A slow increase of tension is usually followed by controllable disorder for a unit, but, in contrast, a suddenly increased level of alienation leads to a sudden and violent lack of respect for the official order. The response to the latter situation cannot therefore be a continuous process.

The system makes a step change (in our case towards disobedient conduct) when there is no other possibility. Disorder among prisoners quickly reaches its maximum level, and communications with the staff become very difficult. The response required must therefore be flexible.

During the Revolution all the necessary and sufficient factors suddenly came together. The administration of the units and of the service as a whole were not prepared for the situation.

Reference

Poston, T., & Stewart, I. (1985). *The Theory of Catastrophe and its Applications* (pp. 387-389). Bucuresti: Editura technica.

Correctional Treatment in Portugal

Rui Abrunhosa Gonçalves

Introduction

With a population of nearly eleven millions, Portugal has a considerable rate of imprisonment (97 in 1992 and 114 in 1993) which has been growing in the past and is documented by the SPACE statistics (1993). This, in turn, has a considerable impact in the rates of prison's occupation, which tend to be chronically crowded.

At the end of 1993 there was a total 11 252 inmates (92.2% males; 7.8% females) distributed for 11 central prisons (n=6 547), 33 local prisons (n=3 585) and 3 special prisons (930). The remaining 190 prisoners were assigned to psychiatric units outside the prison system. The capacity of the system could only hold for 7267 places, so the rate of overcrowding was particularly high (55%), namely in the local prisons (capacity: 1571; rate of overcrowding=105%).

Reasons for this phenomenon are the facts that alternative measures to imprisonment are rarely used and preventive prison is still very common (nearly 1/3 of the Portuguese prisoners are preventive).

These considerations are important to understand the present state of correctional treatment in our country.

In fact, when prisons are very crowded it is difficult to provide jobs and adequate training in schools or professions- Consequently, prisoners are being left open and, without any significant tasks to fulfil, they tend to involve themselves in disturbances or antisocial behaviours, which naturally leads to an amount of tension in the prison system.

At the end of 1993 the rate of professional occupation of the prisoners was 42.7%, and 17.7% had taken school training or professional training. The remaining 40% were only serving their time. Again the local prisons are the most sacrificed due to their overcrowding rates and their reduced space.

Another important consideration is the fact that in the past thirty years only one prison was built in Portugal, on the island of Madeira, although some improvements have been made to turn the old buildings, most of them aged of forty years, greater and, into better places to hold prisoners. The north of the country, which has the highest population density, is the most problematic because it has only three central prisons.

In the middle of 1994 a pardon was given by the government, sending to freedom a great amount of offenders (1433), while others saw their sentences reduced, allowing them to be presented to the parole board sooner than expected and consequently released under supervision. However, the flux of incarceration soon returned to the former overcrowded situation and in a matter of months (no longer than the end of this year), the situation will stand as in the end of 1993.

Given this picture, what can be said about correctional treatment in Portugal? A little bit of history seems necessary.

Correctional Treatment in Portugal

From our point of view it is possible to distinguish three periods in the Portuguese correctional treatment.

The First Phase

The first phase, from the early 19th century was extended by various means and modifications to the seventies, more precisely to the year of 1974, after which time a revolution occurred putting an end to a period of nearly 50 years of dictatorship. This period was initially characterized by the anthropological ideas that flourished from all over Europe. Portugal embraced the theories of Lombroso, Ferri, and others, producing a considerable amount of work. In the meantime, three Institutes of Criminology were created and an effort was made to evaluate properly the offender population (see Gonçalves, in press a).

The forms of correctional treatment assigned to prisoners were isolation and meditation, hoping that individuals would experience guilt and remorse, and reconsider their crimes, their lives, and make an actual effort to change.

In 1936 an important legislation was produced concerning the penal reform. A particular emphasis was made upon work in prisons as the means of rehabilitation. It must be stressed that this line of force is still remaining in our correctional system. Isolation and deterrence were no longer accepted unless special measures of security were assigned. In this period, several buildings – such as courts and prisons – of the Judicial and Penal Administration were initiated and completed under auspices of prison labour.

In the sixties, when Portugal started the war in the African colonies, all efforts seemed to be made to preserve possessions and the economy began to collapse. Prisons were no exception, and the Institutes of Criminology began their agonizing process.

The Second Phase

In April 1974, Portugal was able to liberate himself from an asphyxiating political system. Whereas previously no official courses of psychology were allowed, Portugal started to join with modern western societies. In 1982 a new Penal Code was produced which due to its particular emphasis on offenders' rehabilitation and resocialization was considered one of the most progressive at the time. Several alternative measures to incarceration were created in addition to flexibility in securing prison sentences. These included short leaves after serving 1/4 of the sentence, and parole relief in the middle of the sentence, and were not related to the crime committed.

In the meantime a new institution was formed – the Social Reinsertion Institute – the purpose of which was to supervise probationers, or other offenders serving alternative punishments. It's aim was to provide material support for the offender and his/her family, as well as see to that he/she could get a job and stay out of trouble while on parole. In this second period, a considerable effort was made to provide prisons with finances to allow academic and professional training for the offenders. Several professional courses were initiated at the end of the seventies, providing the offenders with the opportunity to become skilled professionals such as electricians, civil construction painters, woodcrafters and computers' experts.

Academic training was also emphasized during these 15 years and many inmates finished their secondary courses in prison, while some of them continued to university education.

In the middle of the eighties, psychologists began to work as educators in the prisons but had little time to perform true psychological work. Those professionals were required to fulfil the needs of a system that had previously functioned without any input from the social sciences. So, in a word, they soon became "jacks-of-all-trades and were unable to perform as psychologists.

The Third Phase

At the end of the eighties several events occurred forcing the correctional system to make considerable changes. The major problem was the continuous growth of prison population. By 1987, the rate of prison's suicide increased dramatically and, culminated in a spectacular escape from a central prison resulting in the death of three prison guards.

Finally, a serious crime occurred in a town in the middle of Portugal. A man murdered six people including his wife. This created the notion that something ought to be done not only to judge and punish that kind of criminal, but also treat them within the prison system. This was the beginning of the contemporary period in which considerable effort is being made to give proper assistance to mentally disordered offenders, demonstrated by the establishment of two psychiatric clinics for inmates.

Using a global approach, two programmes were implemented. One designed to help and treat drug-dependent inmates under a community based approach, is located in a building inside a central prison in Lisbon (the Ala-G Project). The other, intends to promote awareness among the prison population of the transmission and the prevention of viral diseases (the Prisons Project).

However no effort has been made to produce an adequate framework for remaining population based on a global model of correctional treatment which considers the characteristics of the offender, of the prison, of the sentence, and of the penal regimen (Gonçalves, in press b; Rentzman, 1992).

Starting in October 1995, a Revised Penal Code is going to be applied. The main differences from the last one in 1982, concern an aggravation of some penalties (sexual crimes) and a more difficult process for gaining parole. This point must be stressed for its future implications in the development of correctional treatment in Portugal.

The Future

While Portugal has a Penal Code that facilitates the application of penalties other than imprisonment, much work has yet to be done in the field of correctional treatment.

As Rutherford (1991) showed, the problem of the prisons requires basically a three side analysis: the prisons' population, the prisons' conditions, and the prisons' capacity.

In Portugal, over the last ten years, offender's population has been changing, specifically with an increase of drug related offences (more than 40% of our prisoners are incarcerated for committing crimes where drugs are the principal cause).

In the meantime few things have been done to make effective changes in the prison conditions, such as providing adequate programmes of rehabilitation which focus on learning prosocial abilities.

Finally, the increasing rates of overcrowding suggest that more prisons must be built, and politicians and judges should find other means of punishing drug consumption, and avoid unnecessary preventive arrest.

As far as prison psychologists are concerned, an effort should be made to produce more accurate interventions, based on serious research. Some of them are now prison's governors so they do not have any excuses at this level.

In 1994 in Barcelona, Vicente Garrido pointed out that we, psychologists have to prove our effectiveness since we have already shown that we are useful. Many meta-analysis (e.g., Lösel, 1994, Gendreau & Andrews 1990) can account for both of these assumptions. The next step is convincing the politicians about it. It seems that this is going to take a longer time.

Some years ago, in article with a colleague, we wrote that psychological work in prison can be viewed as a Sysiphe's work (Gonçalves & Vieira, 1992). Surely you are familiar with the general features of this myth but I will recall them briefly: the punishment of Sysiphe was to push up a mountain a large rock that continuously fell down, thus forcing Sysiphe to repeat the task endlessly. When we see that in spite of the effort being made, the rates of recidivism do not seem to drop as much as expected and society continues to produce new delinquents, we can compare ourselves to Sysiphe.

In Portugal, the last two years of prisons' central administration showed a gradual response to the problems of the conditions and capacity of our confinement institutions. We hope that soon more effective programmes of rehabilitation, based on a psychological and social framework, will reflect our efforts and contributions. Sysiphe would appreciate that very much.

References

Statistique pénale annuelle du Conseil de l'Europe (SPACE) (1993). *Bulletin d'Information Pénologique, 18*, 4-37.

Gendreau, P., & Andrews, D. A. (1990). Tertiary prevention: What meta-analyses of the offender treatment literature tell us about "What works". *Canadian Journal of Criminology, 32*, 173-184.

Garrido Génoves, V. (1994). Paper presented at the Fourth European Conference on Psychology and Law, Barcelona.

Gonçalves, R. A. (in press a). *Criminological and Legal Psychology in Portugal: Past, present and future.* Proceedings of the Fourth European Conference on Law and Psychology. Barcelona.

Gonçalves, R. A. (in press b). Tratamento penitencário: Mitos e realidades, ilusoes e desilusoes (Correctional treatment: Myth and realities, illusions and delusions). *Temas Penitencários.*

Gonçalves, R. A., & Vieira, H. (1992). A psicologia na Prisário: O trabalho de Sísifo (Psychology in prisons: The work of Sysiphe). In R. A. Gonçalves, & J. Barroso (Eds.), *Psicologia e intervençao social de justiça* (53-68). Porto: APPORT.

Lösel, F. (1994). *Reviewing correctional evaluations: Problems and results.* Paper presented at the Fourth European Conference on Psychology and Law, Barcelona.

Rentzmann, W. (1992). Pierres angulaires d'une philosohie moderne de traitment: Normalisation ouverture et responsibilité. *Bulletin d'Information Pénitaire, 16*, 7-14.

Rutherford, A. (1991).. Introduction. In D. Whitfield (Ed.), *The state of prisons – 200 years on* (1-12). London: Routledge.

Part 6
Crime and the Public

Terrorist Mentality

Jess Maghan

When I now read descriptions of troubled parts of the world, in which violence appears primordial and inevitable, a fate to which masses of people are largely resigned, I find myself asking: Is that all there was to it? Or is it possible that the authors of these descriptions failed to find a form – or a style or a voice or a plot – that could accommodate both violence and the civilized willed response to it? (Ghosh, 1965).

Prefatory Note

This paper does not profess to define "the terrorist mentality." Rather, it is a discussion of the varied and multiple psycho-social forces influencing the terrorist mentality. I have chosen a contextual approach to examining these influences relative to recent episodes of terrorism in the United States and globally.

Terrorists personify the full range of every character type from the self-doubting wretch, the cunning and the brilliant, the suicidal, the political zealot, the religious fanatic, as well as those individuals haunted by demons indescribable. These individuals, whether wrapped in some cloak of perceived destiny, ultimate truth, or final nihilistic ecstasy, suddenly choose to seize and inflict the moment of terrorism on us all.

Cybernetic-Journalist Jon Katz, writing in the September 1995 issue of *Wired* magazine, cites the unprecedented rate of changing social, territorial, and cultural reproduction of group identity worldwide, including the emergence of what anthropologist Arjun Appadurai calls new community ethnoscapes. The ecology of these new ethnoscapes is having a far reaching impact: with mobility, diversity, and media exposure profoundly altering group expectations, generating instability, cementing differences, and exacerbating conflict. These forces predominate in the profiling of the 21st century terrorist mentality.

Modern day terrorists, equipped as never before with the technology and capabilities for mass destruction, can now bask in the immediate and world wide media attention given to their terroristic violence. This phenomenon alone is provoking a spiraling drive to constantly exceed the scale and magnitude of terror. Terrorism will be "the crime" of the Third Millennium.

Current research generally view terrorism as either a social product or more directly as a consequence of the actions and the actors involved in committing social violence and terrorist acts. From these perspectives, terrorism is seen as a social product. Therefore, terrorism constitutes "an image," a psychological representation, or social conception (Crenshaw, 1995).

This approach concentrates on contextual studies made of the social, cultural, economic, religious, and intellectual factors related to violence. The effects of terrorism are seen as "perverse" and unforeseeable because of the distance separating the social perception, image, or representation of the terrorist threat from its social reality. From an etiological and behavioral analysis of terrorists, the processes that lead people to violent groups and actions emerge. Crenshaw (1995) cautions that ethnocentric or ideological blinders should not keep us from seeing both aspects.

Equally significant but rarely noted is the response to terrorist acts. It is all too easy to present terrorist violence as apocalyptic, while the responses to it may easily be viewed as absurd or apathetic. As Ghosh, (1995) points out: It is worth asking if the very obviousness of this subject arises out of modern conventions of representation within the dominant aesthetic of our times, the aesthetic of indifference. This limiting perspective eliminates any consideration of wider dimensions to the responses to terrorism. Terrorist insurgencies are rarely isolated phenomena. They tend to reflect diffuse sympathies, desires and aspirations of larger segments of society. And, rather than the primary or sole means of political protest, this terrorism emerges in a milieu or political culture of aggrieved communities.

Terrorism is always a tool wielded for some purpose, but it can also be as an end in itself. A terrorist who willfully dies in an attempt to blow up a government building, for instance, sees his role as one aspect of a group's destiny toward achieving some long-range goal. The enemy is seen as an evil thing, a devil, savage, or beast, that prevents a person or group from consummating its mission, and provides another component for analysis in understanding the complexities of "pure terrorism" in which ends and means are mixed-up, where violence has no limits and the reference to a people, class, or nation is factitious (Crenshaw, 1995).

Freud's thesis about how the culpability of violence applies to an entire society suggests that not even members of a mob will be permitted to escape into a collective anonymity. They simply regress together. Freud writes concerning the First World War. "Think of the colossal brutality, cruelty and mendacity which is now allowed to spread itself over the civilized world. Do you really believe that a handful of unprincipled place hunters and corrupters of men would have succeeded in letting loose all this latent evil, if the millions of their followers were not also guilty?" (Freud, 1960).

Inherent Bias and Values

The lack of a clear-cut definition as to what is and what is not terrorism is an ongoing problem as evidenced by the language employed by the media, the public, and political analysts. The emphasis, nonetheless, is on the "message of the terrorism" and not semantic understanding. The recent poisonous gas attacks in the Tokyo subway, the bombings in Paris, and most recently in Israel, Egypt, and Algeria demonstrate dramatically how a "technology of terrorism" is shaping public life at the cusp of the 21st century. Current strategies toward warding off future terrorism attacks include: government and private sector buildings designed with built-in security and access control barriers; transportation security and communication controls, surveillance systems incorporated at airports, railroad and bus stations, and network points of highway systems.

Terrorism frequently mixes-up so many different meanings, issues and causes that the mixture is necessarily explosive. Terrorism that results from strategic contradictions is likely to be the most dangerous. Additionally, although it is naive to reduce terrorism to the manipulation of violent actors by foreign powers or secret services, it would be shortsighted to refuse to investigate this sort of hypothesis when there is plausible evidence of external involvement in terrorism. How are personal or psychological problems related to political tensions or crises within a group?

Psychological/Motivational Factors

Bassiouni (1975) developed a normative notion of terrorism to carve out of political violence specific behaviors and acts which he believed should be labeled as terroristic. This normative approach suggests that terrorism is a means of communication. Its utility is found in the mentality of "the spectacular." In this context, the copy-cat syndrome of the terrorist pathology finds fertile turf for developing "terrorist deterministic acts" of historical destiny. If heroes are made and not born, so be it with the demons of terrorism .

The dominant emphasis of these perspectives is on the psychological states of those who are attracted to and participate in anti-social movements, although macro social factors (e.g., rapid social change, structural discontinuities, culture conflict) often are considered crucial as the cause of an individual's discontents (Gurr, 1971; Jenkins, 1980; Kelly, 1986; Kittrie, 1975). The growing trend towards demonization labeling of dissident groups as disgruntled persons is viewed to be not only undemocratic but indirectly contributing to terrorists activities (Talhami, 1995).

Albert Bandura (1990) explores this notion relative to understanding a terrorist mind set and finds that social discontent and alienation significantly influences why persons become members of a terrorist group. He states that "the conversion of socialized people into dedicated combatants is not achieved by altering their personality structures, aggressive drives, or moral standards. Rather it is accomplished by cognitive restructuring the moral values of killing, so that the killing can be done free from self-censuring restraints (Bandura, 1990). The motivational approach focuses on recruitment and its psycho-functional appeal and predispositions.

Kelly (1995) describes the motivational model of terrorism as a communication method suggesting a three stage sequence in any social movement affiliation: (1) pre-disposing conditions, such as needs and motives, of the individuals (sometimes supplemented with discussion of societal conditions); (2) an exposure to the new beliefs which appeal to those pre-disposing needs or motives, and occasionally its relation to broader social contexts; and, (3) resulting behavior as a committed member of a group.

Terrorist organizations constitute structures through which discontent can be reflected and expressed. Some of these organizational structures are that:

1. Individuals' motivations remain constant throughout their careers in social movements thus ignoring the requisites of the social movement organization. Individuals' alienation or discontent may be created or intensified by participation in the movement.
2. Individuals in terrorist groups exhibit high levels of alienation, discontent, or tensions. It is at this point that it becomes relatively easy to gravitate toward a pathology orientation to the terroristic modus operandi.
3. Correspondingly, terrorist groups work to mobilize whatever discontents do exist to ensure group survival even, if need be, at the expense of individual members.
4. Social movements are formed to produce social change and yet there is little emphasis on how this is accomplished organizationally when a motivational model is adopted.
5. Interaction between the terrorist group and the larger society is de-emphasized.

The Role of Ideology

Ideologically inspired political violence programs are inherent in movements that have been labeled "terrorist." A major feature of ideology is the historical consciousness it breeds among those who embrace it. Even if the reference to a cause is fictitious, terrorist actors always act in the name of the people, or for the sake of a historical project. The future, the nature of change, and the limits and possibilities of control become ideological questions of overwhelming importance.

A method of interpretation of ideologies must possess some logic – it cannot violate the basic canons of common sense. The establishment of a common sense frame of reference qualifies documents and writings as legitimate sources that forecast significant social change. The key "sacred" texts of so many terrorist

globe" syndrome are manifest in all societies. All over the planet, definitions of what nations are and mean are changing. We live in a world of crisscrossed economies, intersecting systems of meaning and fragmented identities. We have moved into a new kind of social space.

Third Millennium Terrorist Mentality

The next century may well be the age of superterrorism with nuclear, biological, and chemical weapons. Before the 1990s are over, we will be forced to recognize that it is the method, not the motive that makes a terrorist. Predictions of improvised nuclear, biological, or chemical attacks on the United States as increasingly probable are now commonplace. These weapons will be used because the public pays attention only to the spectacular. For instance, a year after the World Trade Center bombing, the blast was little more than a dim memory. Future terrorists will find that they need ever more spectacular horrors to overcome people's capacity to absorb and forget what previously would have seemed intolerable.

The lesson to be learned is the developing responses to these unpredictable acts. Within the context of the ongoing concerns for developing predictive profiles of the "terrorist mentality," these responses can only be promulgated in tactical and proactive modes. However, in a constitutional democracy, they must also be juxtaposed with the responsibility of protecting the civil liberties of citizens and with the fiat of maintaining an open society. In the United States several such actions are being developed (see Addendum).

Conclusion

There are as many terrorist mentalities as there are terrorists (Jenkins 1983, Maghan and Kelly 1989). Again, we are caught in the web of personal, psychological, political and other meanings. Is it the innocuous residue of a broken and split personality, berated by the phantoms of psychic-pain beyond normal being, that defines and drives the mind of the modern terrorist? The highly complex nature of this phenomenon will continue to haunt and confound us.

Criminologists can easily construct character profiles. Religious fundamentalism, nationalism, ethno-violence, and racism continue to percolate as necessary ingredients of terrorism. These forces, coupled with migration and demographic pressures and the widening socio-economic separation of peoples bring a deeper complexity to the characterization of a terrorist mentality. Perhaps psycho-historical theory and the 21st century development of contextual psychology may bring us closer to an answer to this phenomenon.

The British historian, Eric Hobsbawm, in his prize winning work, The Age of Extremes (1994), describes 20th century wars as "total wars against combatants and civilians alike," with casualties measured in the tens of millions. All previous wars were alley fights in comparison. As Hobsbawm concludes: "Since the middle of the century...the old civilization has begun to crack and break. The old maps and charts which guided human beings singly and collectively through life no longer represent the landscape through which we move, the sea on which we sail. We do not know where our journey is taking us, or even ought to take us...Let us hope it will be a better, more just, and more viable world." Regrettably, a terrorist Zeitgeist is informing our mutual global journey. Life in the Third Millennium unfortunately will be defined significantly by terrorist mentalities and by a collective means to prevent and avoid their mastery over our own fate.

Addendum

Current American Response Strategies

Kime (1995) cites additional counter-terrorism measures sought by President Clinton in the aftermath of the Oklahoma City bombing; inter alia:
– hire approximately 1,000 new FBI agents, prosecutors and other federal law enforcement and support personnel;
– require that, within a year, microscopic particles or taggants be placed in the standard explosive device raw materials to permit tracking of the materials post-explosion;
– have the Bureau of Alcohol, Tobacco and Firearms study whether common chemicals can be rendered inert for use in explosives and whether controls can be imposed on certain precursor chemicals used to manufacture explosives;
– allow the armed forces to be involved in crime fighting where chemical or biological weapons are used;
– allow court approval to authorize wiretapping or other electronic surveillance to fight terrorism;
– make it a federal crime to use any chemical weapons (under existing law, gaseous chemical weapons are covered, but those in either liquid or solid form are not);
– extend the statute of limitations on National Firearms Act from three to five years; and,
– provide a mandatory 10-year penalty for anyone convicted of transferring a firearm or explosive, knowing that it will be used to commit a crime of violence or drug trafficking.

References

Bassiouni, M. C. (1975). *International Terrorism and Political Crimes.* New York, NY: Charles Thomas Publishers.

Crenshaw, M. (1995). *Terrorism in Context.* University Park, PA: The Pennsylvania State University Press.

Fanon, F. (1963). *The Wretched of the Earth.* New York, NY: Grove Press.

Freud, E. (1960). *The Letters of Sigmund Freud.* New York, NY: Basic Books.

Ghosh, A. (1995). The Ghosts of Mrs. Ghandi. *The New Yorker*, July 17, 1995.

Gurr, T. R. (1971). *Why Men Rebel.* Princeton, NJ: Princeton University Press.

Hobsbawm, E. (1994). *The Age of Extremes: A History of the World, 1914-1991.* New York, NY: Pantheon Books.

Jacobs, J. B. (1983). The Prisoner Rights Movement and Its Impact, In *New Perspectives on Prisons and Imprisonment.* Ithaca, NY: Cornell University Press.

Jenkins, B (1980). The Terrorist Mindset and Terrorist Decision Making: Two Areas of Ignorance. *Terrorism: An International Journal, 3/4.*

Katz, J (1995). Guilty of Making it Possible to Resolve the Most Important Issues Facing Our Society. *Wired* (September).

Kelly, R. J. (1985). *Implications of the Concept of Terrorism: Terrorism as a Means of Communication.* Unpublished Paper presented at the 37th Annual Meeting of the American Society of Criminology, San Diego, California, November 15, 1985.

Kittrie, N. N. (1975). In Search of Political Crime and Political Criminals. *New York University Law Review, 1.*

Kime, R. C. (1995). Terrorism Legislation in Congress: Both Before and After the Oklahoma City Bombing, In *The Police Chief.* Washington, DC, June 1995.

Maghan, J., & Robert, J. K. (1985). Terrorism and Corrections: The Incarcerated Radical, In J. R. Buckwalter (Ed.), *International Terrorism: The Decade Ahead.* Chicago, IL: Office of International Criminal Justice, University of Illinois at Chicago.

Mannheim, K. (1940). *Man and Society in an Age of Reconstruction.* New York, NY: Harcourt Brace Jovanovich.

Russakoff, D., & Kovaleski, S. F. (1995). Two Angry Young Men. *The Washington Post National Weekly Edition*, July 24-30.

Strauss, W., & Howe, N. (1991). *Generations: The History of America's Future, 1584 to 2069.* New York, NY: William Morrow and Company, Inc.

Talhami, G. (1995). The Homeless Palestinians in Israel and the Arab World. In R. J. Kelly, & J. Maghan (Eds.), *Hate Crime: Global Politics of Polarization.* Chicago, IL: Office of International Criminal Justice.

Fear of Crime and Victimization

Helmut Kury

Introduction

Since the rapid development of social-scientific victim studies, surveys regarding fear of crime have constituted one of the most essential features of these investigations. Triggered by social-scientific victimological research's discovery of fear of crime, an intense debate on this phenomenon has been carried on in the US since the 1960's, which in turn has entailed a nearly immeasurable wealth of scientific publications. The question whether victims of (more serious) crimes exhibit more fear of crime than non-victims, i.e. whether a (serious) victimization leads to an increase in fear of crime is still quite controversial. Meanwhile, US-American investigations and also an increasing number of German studies (cf. e.g. Kury et al., 1992; Kury and Würger, 1993; Kury, 1995) have shown the emergence of fear of crime as a consequence of victimization to be centrally dependent on the seriousness of the victimization concerned and, moreover, on the victim's living conditions and his/her personality variables. In our opinion, assertions such as the one put forward by Boers (1991, p. 344 et seq.), according to which the victimization perspective is to be rejected, as victimization "with the exception of indirect victimization by sexual offenses" does not effect an increase in e.g. avoidance behavior and fear of crime, are no longer tenable. His findings are based on a Hamburg victim study from 1984, they are not necessarily representative of the Federal Republic of Germany as a whole. His assertion that "the central hypothesis of a victim perspective (1991, p. 344 et seq.) has been disproved once again" by the study loses considerable importance in the light of the problem regarding the representativeness of the sample.

Own investigations

On the basis of the data obtained from the International Crime Survey (ICS, 1989) – conducted by an international research team in 17 countries of Europe and on other continents (cf. van Dijk et al., 1990) – and from the first German-German victim study – conducted by the criminological research group of the Max Planck Institute of Foreign and International Criminal Law (cf. Kury et al., 1992) – we have been able to show in earlier publications (cf. Kury and Würger, 1993; Kury 1995) that a differentiated analysis which takes into account the seriousness of the offense concerned and the frequency of victimization reveals a clear, but moderate, connection between victimization and fear of crime variables (e.g. avoidance of certain places in the dark, the estimated probability of being burglarized within the next 12 months) to the effect that victims of (more serious) crimes and also persons repeatedly victimized exhibit more fear of crime than non-victims. This applies to all countries incorporated in the investigation with the exception of Poland (Warsaw). In order to operationalize the seriousness of the screened offenses we combined the recorded victimizations within 11 offense categories to form the following three groups: non-contact crimes (car theft, theft of property from cars, car vandalism, theft of motorized two-wheelers, bicycle theft, theft in general if the victim did not carry the stolen object with her/him at the time of the offense), burglary (including attempted burglary) and contact crimes (robbery, theft if the victim carried the stolen object with her/him at the time of the offense, sexual offenses/sexual harassment, bodily assault and threat). The respondents were asked to report victimizations experienced within the five-year period preceding the investigation. Persons who did not report any victimizations for the period of reference were defined as "non-victims".

In most countries fear of crime increases quite uniformly with the seriousness of the offense (non-victim, non-contact crimes, burglary crimes, contact crimes). In grouping the offense categories according to their seriousness we proceeded on the presumption that burglary and contact crimes are similarly serious. The most important results yielded by these earlier analyses are summed up in Figure 1 and Figure 2. Additionally, they reveal that the differences between non-victims and particularly victims of contact crimes are statistically significant for most countries. In order to determine the significance we conducted multifactorial analyses of variance in consideration of the variables sex, age, size of place of residence and income. With the exception of Warsaw the countries for which no statistical significance was ascertained, due to small case numbers, also exhibit comparable disparities according to tendency. This homogeneousness of results speaks for the victimization perspective, i.e. the assumption that victims of crimes are more afraid as a consequence of their victimization experience than non-victims.

Following the completion of the ICS 92 (a repeat investigation of the ICS 89), which was conducted in 30 countries and capital cities, we examined the victimization perspective once again on the basis of these data. For economical reasons, however, information on fear of crime were collected in merely 6 countries (Australia, Belgium, England/Wales, Finland, Canada and the Netherlands). Among other things we employed the so-called "standard item" (avoidance of certain places in the dark) again in order to operationalize fear of crime.

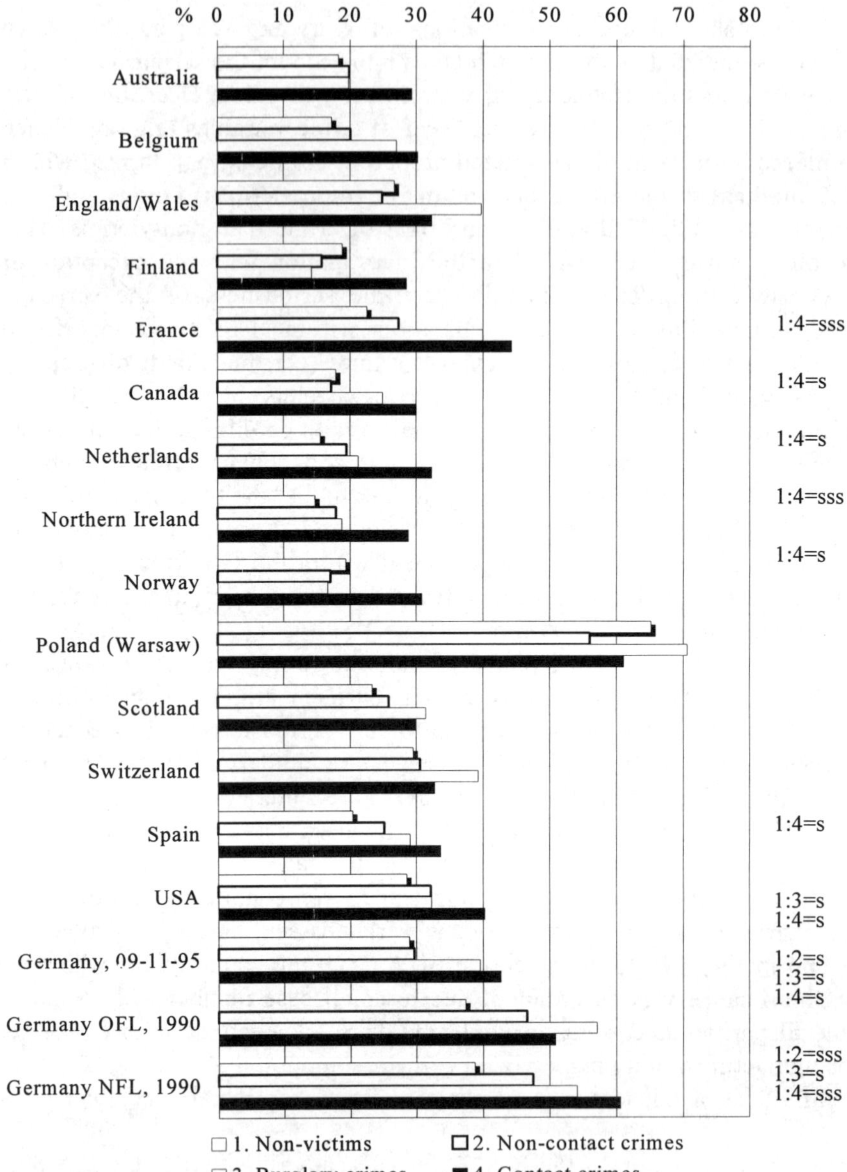

Significance: We conducted multifactorial analyses of variance in consideration of the variables sex, age, size of place of residence, and income. The individual figures indicate the comparisons conducted and the level of significance. The levels of significance are as follows: s – 5% level; ss 1% level; sss – 0.1% level. E.g. France 1:4 sss indicates that the differences between non-victims (category 1) and victims of contact crimes (category 4) are significant on the level of 0.1% (sss).

Figure 1: Results on "Avoidance of certain places in the dark" in relation to different victim categories (ICS 1989, German–German Study, 1990)

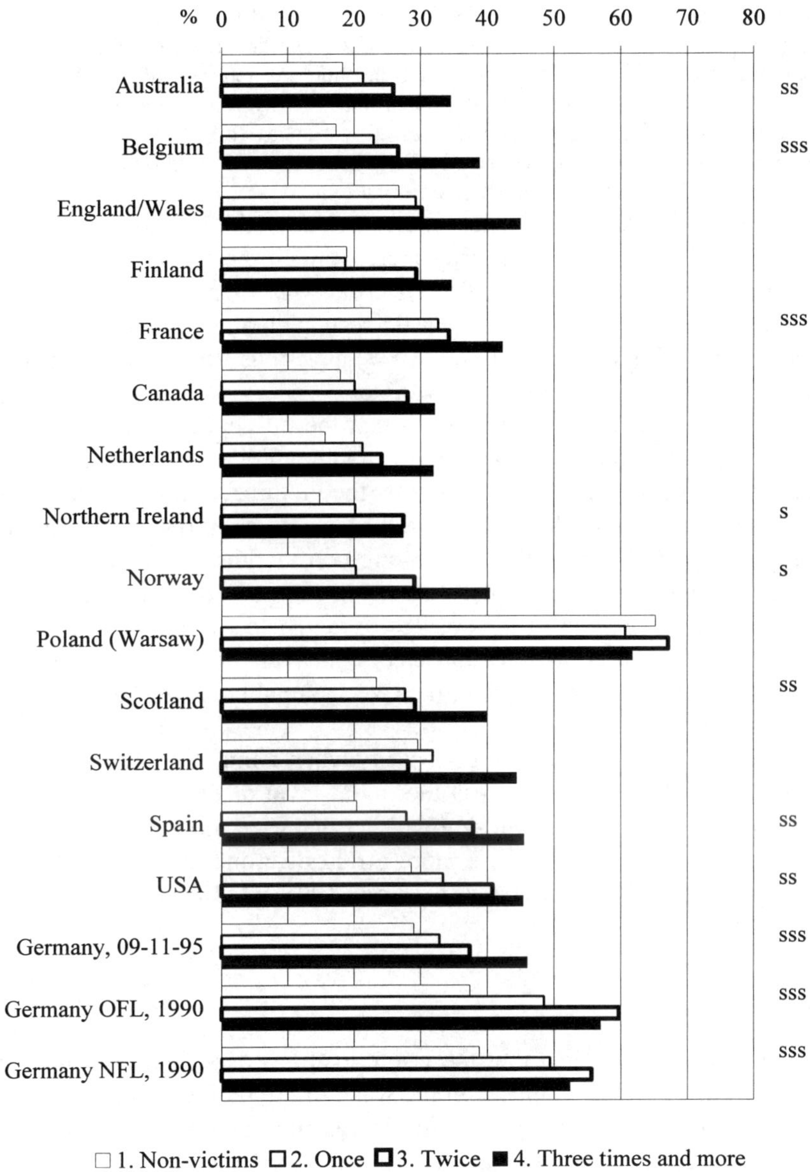

Significance: We conducted multifactorial analyses of variance in consideration of the variables sex, age, size of place of residence, and income. The levels of significance are as follows: s – 5% level; ss 1% level; sss – 0.1% level.

Figure 2: Results on "Avoidance of certain places in the dark" in relation to the number of victimizations (ICS 1989, German–German Study, 1990)

Throughout the world this item has recurrently been employed to screen fear of crime. Although this operationalization is not undisputed (for a summary cf. Kury and Würger, 1993, p. 420 et seq.), we have reason to believe that the standard item records a substantial part of the fear of crime phenomenon. The statistical analyses were conducted in analogy to the earlier calculations (multifactorial analyses of variance) (cf. Kury and Würger, 1993). Figures 3 and 4 depict the results derived on the item for the 6 countries, subdivided according to victim category and frequency of victimization.

The findings wholly confirm the earlier results. In the victim category we found that fear of crime and feelings of insecurity increase with the seriousness of victimization. At the same time, however, fear of crime was found to increase with the number of victimizations as well. The earlier results obtained from the ICS 89 (for a detailed account cf. Kury and Würger, 1993) have thus been corroborated, a fact also speaking for the victimization perspective.

In this context, however, we must point out that the influence of victimization on fear of crime ought not to be overestimated. An increased level of fear of crime among the citizens cannot be explained solely by the victimization perspective, as only comparatively few people (fortunately) fall victim to a serious crime and as fear of crime has increased especially also among non-victims in the last years – particularly since the breakdown of the Eastern European communist-socialist states and the increasing opening of the borders. As expected, relatively high fear of crime values were derived for the "countries of upheaval" of the former Eastern Bloc, i.e. particularly for Hungary, Poland, the Czech Republic, Slovakia and Russia (cf. Boers et al., 1994).

The derived increase in fear of crime (insecurity when going out alone at night) applies to both men and women. Whereas the initial level of fear of crime is dependent on a person's sex – it is a well-known fact that men report less fear than women – both men and women become more afraid of crime after having been victimized irrespective of this initial level (cf. Kury, 1995, p. 148).

Discussion

There is little doubt about the fact that the crime load has experienced a distinct rise in the former Eastern Bloc countries in the wake of the political turning point, the changes in the political-social system, the increasing opening of the borders and the decrease in state control. On the whole the occurrence of crime in the former Eastern Bloc states is approaching or has in fact already reached the Western level. Victim surveys and in particular the two ICS have shown that fear of crime has also experienced a distinct increase, but not solely on account of the increase in crime. The rise in fear of crime is not solely dependent on the increased crime load, but also on social changes in general.

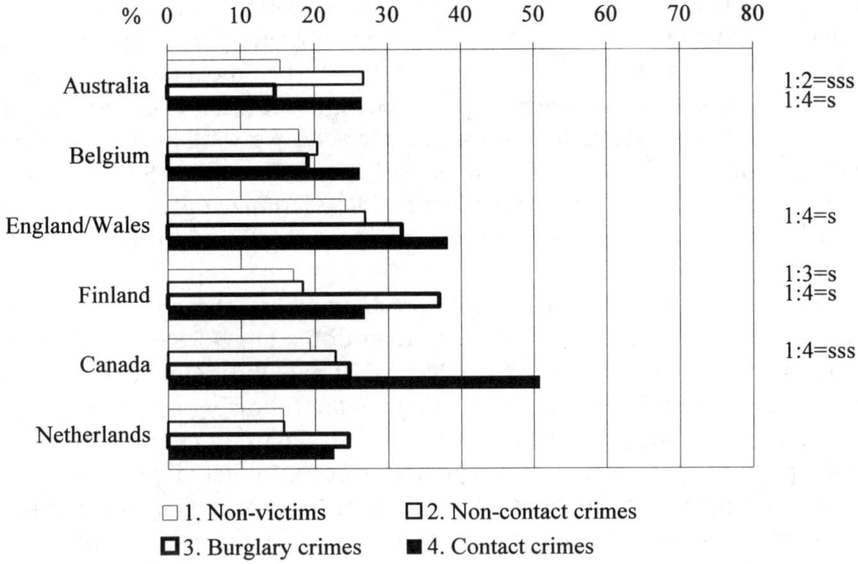

Figure 3: Results on "Avoidance of certain places in the dark" in relation to different victim categories (ICS 1992)

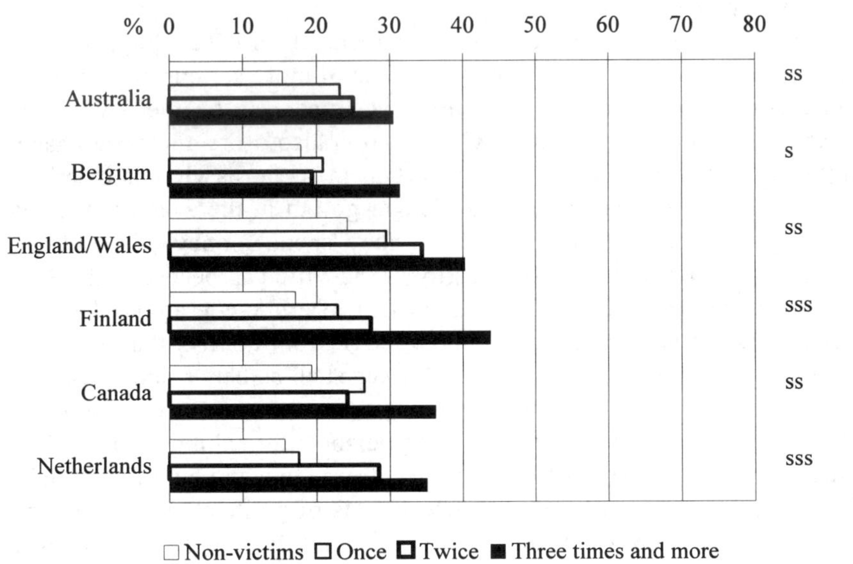

Figure 4: Results on "Avoidance of certain places in the dark" in relation to the number of victimizations (ICS 1992)

The changes which have taken place have evoked feelings of insecurity and anxiety especially among the citizens of the former Eastern Bloc states such as e.g. the former German Democratic Republic GDR (i.e. the present-day new federal Länder). Regarding victimization perspective, i.e. to what extent an earlier victimization experience affects fear of crime adversely, we were able to confirm earlier findings with the aid of more recent data obtained from the ICS 92. Victims of more serious crimes as well as persons repeatedly victimized generally exhibit more fear of crime. On the whole, however, an incident of victimization affects fear of crime only moderately.

Our findings have in the meantime been corroborated by other victim surveys. Greve and Wetzels (1995, p. 24 et seq.), e.g., report on a large-scale victim study which focused particularly on elderly people in East and West Germany. Within the framework of their analyses the authors come to the following conclusion with respect to the victimization perspective (1995, p. 30): "Contrary to the recurrently voiced assumption the present survey has proved once again that victimization experience increases the probability that fear will develop. This applies in particular to elderly people. However, the assumption that the development of fear of crime does not presuppose victimization experience is confirmed as well: the number of people exhibiting fear without having been personally victimized still exceeds the number of victims." This wholly corresponds with and corroborates our findings. Victimization experience is not a prerequisite of fear of crime; however, it does promote its development.

With this background we ought to support the demand for psychological victim support for victims of more serious crimes. Victims of more serious crimes suffer from the effects of their victimization for many years or even for the rest of their lives. Proper digestion of the trauma of victimization also offers the great chance of combating fear of crime. This is also important in so far as victims of crimes frequently change their habits e.g., they no longer go out in the evening, they always ask someone else to accompany them, they spend money on additional safety devices for their homes etc. The quality of their life can become considerably restricted. The above-described increase in fear of crime e.g. among the German people during the last years can also be inferred from the fact that in 1994 5 billion German Marks were spent on safety devices such as better door locks and window bolts, alarm systems etc. for private homes in comparison to a mere 500 million German Marks in 1990. The fact that a person who exhibits more fear of crime evidently shows a tendency toward more conservative and punitive attitudes with respect to the treatment of criminal offenders is of political relevance. As a rule, an increase in fear entails an increase in demands for more severe punishment and legislation, for more police etc., a fact taken advantage of by conservative right-wing political parties in order to enforce their legal-political objectives.

In the last years fear of crime has been a much-discussed issue. As a rule, moreover, press coverage of crime development and fear of crime is without factual basis. The fact that coverage by the media is frequently rather one-sided adds additional fuel to the problems connected with crime and fear of crime. This applies in particular to the former Eastern Bloc states, where the increase in press freedom has prompted the media to try to increase their circulation on the basis of the principle of "sex and crime". As a result of this one-sided coverage the crime problem cannot be dealt with rationally. Attention is directed to the aspect of criminal prosecution and in particular to an intensification of punitive measures at the expense of aspects of crime prevention and deliberations on the social background of and the factors lying behind the rise in crime, even though we have learned from criminological research that severe sanctions are little effective against crime. Primary preventive measures directed against the underlying causes of the rise in crime appear much more promising, although they are difficult to enforce politically. In Germany, by way of contrast, the current discussion will most likely lead to a stiffening of criminal prosecution. At first, this solution might serve to reassure the people. It is to be assumed, however, that this course of action and the introduction of more rigorous legislation alone will significantly reduce the crime load of fear of crime.

References

Boers, K. (1991). *Kriminalitätsfurcht. Über den Entstehungszusammenhang und die Folgen eines sozialen Problems.* Pfaffenweiler: Centaurus.

Boers, K., Kerner, H.-J., & Kurz, P. (1994). *Rückgang der Kriminalitätsfurcht. Weitere Angleichung zwischen Ost und West bei leichter Zunahme der Eigentumskriminalität.* Pressemitteilung 28.9.1995.

van Dijk, J. J. M., Mayhew, P., & Killias, M. (1990). *Experiences of crime across the world. Key findings from the 1989 international crime survey.* Deventer, Boston: Kluwer.

Greve, W., & Wetzels P. (1995). Opfererfahrung und Kriminalitätsfurcht älterer Menschen. *Report Psychologie, 20,* 24-35.

Kury, H. (1995). Zur Bedeutung von Kriminalitätsentwicklung und Viktimisierung für die Verbrechensfurcht. In G. Kaiser & J.-M. Jehle (Eds.), Kriminologische Opferforschung. Neue Perspektiven und Erkenntnisse. Verbrechensfurcht und Opferwerdung – Individualopfer und Verarbeitung von Opfererfahrungen (pp. 127-158). *Neue Kriminologische Schriftenreihe Vol. 102/II.* Heidelberg: Kriminalistik Verlag.

Kury, H., & Würger, M. (1993). Opfererfahrung und Kriminalitätsfurcht. Ein Beitrag zur Viktimisierungsperspektive. In G. Kaiser & H. Kury (Eds.), *Kriminologische Forschung in den 90er Jahren* (pp. 411-462). Freiburg.

Kury, H., Dörmann, U., Richter, H., & Würger, M. (1992). Opfererfahrungen und Meinungen zur Inneren Sicherheit in Deutschland. *BKA-Forschungsreihe Bd. 25.* Wiesbaden: BKA.

The Social and Personal Influence of Positive Beliefs on Coping with Direct and Indirect Victimization

Adriaan Denkers and Frans Willem Winkel

Partners of victims of crime may play two different roles: Indirect victim or important support provider. The positive beliefs of the victim were hypothesised to reduce the negative effects of the incident on both their own and their partners well-being. Likewise, the positive beliefs of the partners of victims were hypothesised to mitigate the negative influence of the incident on their own and their victimized partners well-being. The results of a survey among 1806 respondents, of whom 204 had been victimized during the past year, generally support these hypotheses. However, the positive influence of both the victims and their partners' beliefs on each others well-being appear to outweigh the positive influence of their positive beliefs on their own well-being.

The negative influence of criminal victimization on the individual's well-being is well documented (Frieze, Hymer & Greenberg, 1987). However, not only victims may suffer negative consequences of their situation (Denkers & Winkel, 1994). By communicating about the incident, victims may contaminate others too (Denkers & Winkel, 1993). It is especially plausible that the victim's partner (e.g. husband or wife) is to experience negative consequences, since they are most likely to be in close contact with the victim. On the other hand, besides being a potential indirect victim of crime, partners may be considered one of the most important providers of support (Burman & Margolin, 1992; Denkers, 1996; O'Leary & Smith, 1991). Peculiarly, few studies have attempted to portray the roles of the spouse of the victim. In the present study we will examine both possible roles that the partner of the victim may play: indirect victim of crime and important support-provider for their unfortunate spouse.

Partners influence each other. When one is negatively affected, this may also negatively influence the other. For instance, Coyne, Kessler, Tal, Turnbull, Wortman and Greden (1987) found that 40% of their respondents, who were living with a depressed partner in the midst of an episode, were themselves sufficiently distressed to meet the criterion for receiving psychological intervention. This implies that the degree to which the partner of the victim suffers negative consequences is likely to be a function of the degree to which the victim is affected.

Not all victims suffer an equal deterioration of their well-being as a consequence of the event (Agnew, 1985). Taylor & Brown (1988) argue that one's mental health or well-being depends on one's capacity to create or foster positive beliefs. People make errors when processing information (Fiske & Taylor, 1991). The biases that occur do not seem to be randomly distributed, but are most generally in favour of the individual. Positive beliefs are those self serving biases that occur in a pervasive, enduring, and systematic manner. Three beliefs are considered to be essential for ones well-being: a positive view of self, the perception of personal control, and optimism. Normal, mentally healthy people are supposed to be characterized by such beliefs, while those who are susceptible to psychological maladies and syndromes are not. The bolstering influence of beliefs is expected to be especially advantageous for the individual under threatening circumstances, or when one has to cope with negative information. Victims of crime have been found to suffer less detrimental psychological consequences if they were characterized by positive views of the self, perceptions of personal control, and optimism. Those who lacked such beliefs were not only characterized by a low well-being, but also experienced a further deterioration of their well-being as a consequence of the incident.

The degree to which the partner of a victim suffers psychological consequences, may be partially determined by the extent that the victim suffers psychological maladies. Therefore, partners of victims, whose unfortunate spouse is characterized by a lack of positive beliefs, might also suffer a worse deterioration of their well-being as a consequence of their indirect victimization. Victims that are capable of creating or fostering positive beliefs are themselves unlikely to suffer extreme negative consequences, and will therefore hardly affect their partners.

Additionally, the negative influence of their indirect victimization may also be bolstered by the positive beliefs of the partner of the victim. People who are characterized by positive beliefs are presumed to be capable of effectively coping with threatening events and negative information (Taylor & Brown, 1988). Therefore, one might expect that partners of victims who themselves are characterized by positive beliefs are less likely to be affected, than those with insufficient positive beliefs. Thus, the extent to which partners of victims suffer a deterioration of their well-being may be a function of both their own and their victimized partners positive beliefs.

The degree to which the partner of a victim provides adequate support to their ill-fated counterpart may also be a function of positive beliefs. Taylor & Brown (1988) suggest a social influence of beliefs: positive views of self, perceptions of personal control, and optimism may be associated with the capacity to give beneficial social support. Beliefs may affect the ability to care for and about others, by their capacity to create positive mood. A positive mood is associated with an increased tendency to help others (Cialdini, Kenrick & Baumann, 1982), to initiate conversations with others (Batson, Coke, Chard, Smith & Taliaferro, 1979), and to express liking for others (Diener, 1984; Isen, 1984; Veitch & Grifit, 1976). Therefore, victims are expected to receive more beneficial support if their partner is capable of creating or fostering positive beliefs. Victims who live with someone lacking this capacity, are likely to encounter a partner inept to give the care that is needed to cope with the event, consequently leading to a possible further deterioration of well-being.

This study, explores the adaptive influence of positive beliefs on well-being. Individuals with positive views of self, perceptions of personal control, and optimism are expected to exhibit higher levels of well-being, than those who lack these beliefs. The beneficial influence of beliefs is expected to manifest itself more dominantly among those who themselves have been victimized, and among those who are living with a victim of crime, than among those without (direct or indirect) crime experiences. Those who lack positive beliefs are expected to suffer the worst consequences of the incident. Moreover, besides the beneficial influence on their own well-being, positive beliefs of victims and their partners are also expected to bolster each others well-being. Both victims and their partners are hypothesized to suffer less negative consequences if the other is characterized by positive beliefs, rather then when the other lacks positive beliefs. Thus, positive beliefs are expected to have both a personal and social buffering influence between crime and psychological well-being.

Method

Sample and Sampling procedures. The respondents in this study were members of the panel of the "Stichting Telepanel". The nationwide sample of the panel was generated using random digit dialing procedures. The "Stichting Telepanel" operates with a computerized method of data-gathering. Participating households get the use of a personal computer and modem. With the aid of these devices the central computer of the "Stichting Telepanel" sends questionnaires to the connected households on a weekly basis. Participants may respond at any time during the weekend that suits them. When the respondents have filled out the questionnaire, their answers are automatically returned to the central computer.

Initially 1806 respondents connected to the panel in June 1992 filled out a selection questionnaire consisting of a list of crimes (household burglary, contact-robbery, threat, assault, sex-related crime, or another crime type). The participants were asked if they had been a victim of one or more of these crimes during the previous year. Four months after the initial questionnaire, in September 1992, the 1460 respondents who were still connected to the panel were presented with a second questionnaire, consisting of a well-being, a fear, and three positive belief measures.

Out of the initial sample, in June 1992, 204 respondents had assigned themselves to one of the crimes: 45 reported a burglary, 62 a robbery, 27 threat, 16 assault, 7 a sexual oriented crime, and 68 an other type of crime. Of the respondents in the initial sample, 54.1% were male and 45.9% were female; 51.7% described themselves as being head of the household, 33.7% as being partner of the head of the household 13.0% as kids and 0.7% other (grandparents, roommate, etc.). The median household consisted of three persons. Differences between victims and non-victims were found in relation to age and cohabitation with a partner. On average, victims (38 years) were younger than non-victims (43 years), $F(1,1804)=17.93$; $p<.001$; and non-victims were more often living with a partner (85.6%) than victims (78.4%), $Chi^2(1806)=7.31$; $p<.01$.

Of the 204 victims, 160 were living with a partner. Of these partners, 57 had also indicated to be victimized during the past year. Most of the households in which both partners were victimized, both were victimized by the same type of crime (84%), mainly burglary (50%). The remainder of the partners of victims had not indicated to have been victimized during the past year. 1285 Respondents had not been victimized directly, nor indirectly via their partner. However, 28 of these non-victims had another member of the household who had been victimized. Because these 28 respondents may also be indirectly victimized, they were omitted from further analyses.

In September 1992, 1225 respondents, who lived with a partner, subsequently filled out the second questionnaire. This sample consisted of 128 who had indicated in the initial questionnaire that they were victims of crime, and 126 who were partners of victims. Of these partners 55 had also indicated to have been victimized. The sample included 1026 respondents of whom no one in the household had indicated to have been victimized. These respondents will subsequently be labelled *non-victims*.

In some of the participating households one of the partners had not filled out both questionnaires. Data of both partners was available for 119 households of which one or both were victims, and 468 households of which neither of the partners were victims.

Measures. The second questionnaire consisted of scales measuring well-being, fear, and positive beliefs.

Well-being was assessed by the Dutch translation (Heesink, 1989) of the 5 item "Satisfaction With Life" Scale of Diener, Emmons, Larsen, Griffin (1985; e.g. In most ways my life is ideal").

The scale assessing fear was more crime specific: Fear of Crime (Winkel, 1989), consisting of 3 items about the degree to which respondents feel tense, afraid and aggravated while thinking of the possibility of becoming a crime victim ($\alpha=.82$). All items were all scored on 7-point rating scales.

To assess the three positive beliefs suggested by Taylor and Brown (1988), 3 scales were used. Control was operationalized by a Dutch translation of the E/I-18 for Locus of Control (Den Hertog, 1992; Rotter, 1966) consisting of 18 items (e.g. "I determine what happens to me") which form a reliable scale ($\alpha=.74$); Style of Evaluation was operationalized by 4 items (e.g. "To what degree did you enjoy the past year") in which the respondents could indicate how negative or positive they had experienced the past year financially, socially, healthwise, and in general ($\alpha=.65$; Winkel, 1989). The degree to which the respondents were optimistic (Perlof, 1983) was operationalized by three items about perceptions of relative vulnerability (e.g. “Compared to others in your street, do you expect to have a greater, equal or smaller chance of becoming a victim of crime”), that form a reliable scale (α=.78).

Taylor and Brown (1988) suggest that people are generally characterized by positive beliefs. This is expected to result in positively skewed ratings of belief measures (Denkers, 1996). To explore whether the three positive belief-measures were indeed positively skewed, the scores of each belief-measure was split on the middle of the scale (4).

Table 1 presents beliefs of non-victims, and three groups of victims: (1) Self Victims: those who themselves have been victimized, and whose partner has not been victimized; (2) Partner Victims: those who self have not been victimized, but whose partner has; and (3) Both Victimized: both themselves and their partners have been victimized.

Table 1: Distributions of style of evaluation, control and relative vulnerability among non-victims and victims (those who themselves have been victimized, those whose partner has been victimized, and those who themselves and their partner has been victimized)

	Victimization			
Beliefs (>4 is positive)	Self Victim N=73	Partner Victim N=71	Both self and partner N=55	Non-Victims N=1026
Style of Evaluation				
≤4	16.4%	14.1%	18.2%	12.7%
>4	83.6%	85.9%	81.8%	87.3%
Control				
≤4	19.2%	21.1%	20.0%	23.2%
>4	80.2%	78.9%	80.0%	76.8%
Relative Vulnerability				
<4	21.9%	12.7%	16.4%	7.9%
=4	46.6%	50.7%	49.1%	44.2%
>4	31.5%	36.6%	34.5%	48.0%

Table 1 indicates that the scores on three belief measures were positively skewed. In general, respondents are inclined to evaluate their situation positively, think that they are in control rather than others, and seldom belief that they are more vulnerable than others. Style of Evaluation was scored on, or below the midpoint of the scale (4) by only 13.2% of the respondents, and only 22.7% scored on or below the midpoint (4) on control. Of the total sample, 45.7% indicated that their chances of future victimization were smaller than the chances of others, 44.9% expected equal chances and only 9.4% felt more vulnerable than others. No differences between victims, non-victims, and partners of victims emerged on evaluations of the self or control. However, both victims and partners of victims appeared to regard themselves more vulnerable for future victimization than non-victims; only 33.5% of the victims, 36.6% of their partners, and 34.5% of the doubly victimized partners, compared to 48.0% of the non-victims reported to be less vulnerable than others, $Chi^2(1225)=22.75$; $p<.001$.

Next, the total number of positively scored beliefs was computed for each participant, by adding the number of belief-scales scored above the midpoint (4). This resulted in a 4-point scale: a "3" indicating that evaluations of the self, control, and optimism, were all scored above the midpoint, and a "0" indicating that all three beliefs were scored below the midpoint. Of the total sample, 32.8% scored above the midpoint on all three beliefs, 47.7% on two, 17.0% on one, and 2.5% scored all three beliefs below the midpoint. Non-victims (34.4%) more often reported all three beliefs above midpoint, than respondents of whom either or both of the partners were victims (24.9%), $Chi^2(1225)=6.44$; $p=.01$.

Results

To assess the influence of the number of positive beliefs on coping with direct (Self Victim) and indirect victimization (Partner Victim), a regression analysis was conducted. In the first step of this analysis the background variables; gender, age and age of the partner were entered. In the second step the respondent's and the respondent's partner's victimization status were entered using dummy variables (1=non-victim; 2=victim). Next, in step 3 the number of positive beliefs of the respondent was entered, followed by the number of positive beliefs of their partner. The results of this analysis are presented in Table 2.

Table 2: The influence of direct and indirect victimization and one's own and one's partner's positive beliefs on satisfaction with life and fear of crime.

	Satisfaction with Life				Fear of Crime			
	r	β	t	r^2	r	β	t	r^2
Step 1				.7%				6.1%
Gender	.07	.08	2.80**		.22	.22	7.60**	
Own age	.03	.04	1.04		.09	.12	3.34**	
Partner's age	.01	.01	-.26		.04	-.03	-.79	
Step 2				1.0%				6.2%
Victim								
Self	-.05	-.01	-.34		-.00	.03	.80	
Partner	-.05	-.02	-.67		-.01	-.04	-1.14	
Step 3				6.9%				7.7%
Positive Beliefs								
Self	.24	.20	6.84**		-.13	-.12	-4.12**	
Step 4				9.2%				7.7%
Positive Beliefs								
Partner	.22	.16	5.32**		-.01	.02	.50	

* $p<.05$; ** $p<.01$

Direct effects. Table 2 shows that, of the background variables, gender has a contrary influence on satisfaction with life and fear of crime; women are more satisfied with life, but also more afraid than men. Older respondents report more fear of crime than the younger respondents. Neither one's own nor one's partner's victimization status directly influences satisfaction with life or fear of crime. Apparently, in this study, being a victim or living with a victimized partner does not automatically lead to lower levels of well-being or higher levels of fear. One's own number of positive beliefs are beneficial for both satisfaction with life and fear of crime; more positive beliefs are related to more satisfaction with life and less fear of crime. The number of positive beliefs of the partner has an additional positive influence on one's satisfaction with live. However, fear of crime seems unrelated to the number of positive beliefs of the partner.

Interaction effects. Of special interest to this study is whether one's own and one's partner's positive beliefs buffer the negative consequences of (direct and indirect) victimization on satisfaction with life and fear of crime. Therefore, a series of hierarchical regression analyses was performed. Like the analysis presented in Table 2, background variables (gender, age and age of the partner), victimization status of both the respondents and their partners, and one's own and one's partner's positive beliefs were entered into the first step of the analysis. Then 4 interaction terms were separately entered into the equation: Positive Beliefs of Self X Self victim, Positive Beliefs of Self X Partner Victim, Positive Beliefs of Partner X Partner Victim, and Positive Beliefs of Partner X Partner Victim. To avoid multicollinearity between the predictors and the interaction terms, the multiplicative functions were computed as the product of the standardized scores on the component variables. The interactions were graphed by showing the standardized regression coefficients between the dependent variable and the own and partner's Positive Beliefs within the sample of victims, the sample of partners of victims, and the sample of non-victims. Figure 1 shows the influence of own and partner's Positive Beliefs on satisfaction with life within the samples of victims, partners of victims and non-victims, and Figure 2 their influence on fear of crime.

Positive Beliefs of Self X Self Victim. The interaction between the number of positive beliefs of the respondents and their own victimization status displays the degree to which the influence of positive beliefs on the dependent measures (Satisfaction with Life or Fear of Crime) differ between victims and non-victims. A marginally significant effect emerged when the Own Positive Beliefs X Own Victimization interaction term was entered into the equation on Satisfaction with Life, $\beta=.20$; $t=1.88$; $p=.06$; indicating that the number of positive beliefs of self more strongly influence the satisfaction with life of victims, than the satisfaction with life of non-victims. Positive beliefs thus appear to (somewhat) buffer the negative influence of crime (see Figure 1). The influence of this interaction-term on fear of crime runs in the expected direction but remains insignificant, $\beta=-.17$; $t=-1.52$; $p>1$ (see Figure 2).

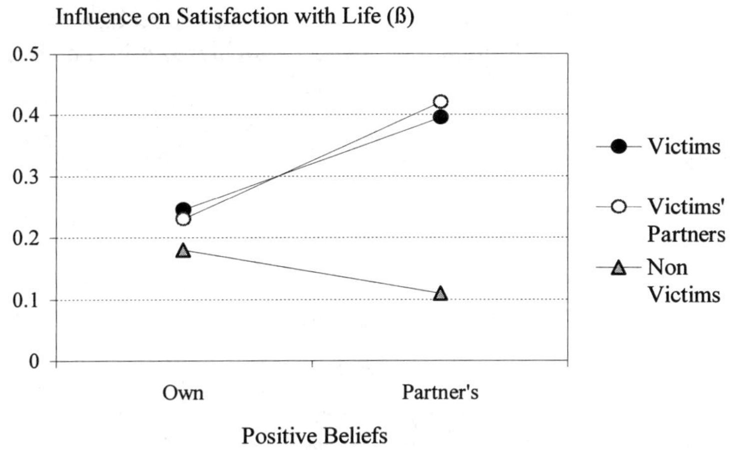

Note. Presented regression coefficients are corrected for the influence of background variables (gender, age and age of the partner). Df in the victim sample (5,113); in the partner of victim sample (5,106), and in the non-victim sample (5,922).

Figure 1: Standardized regression coefficients of the influence of ones own and ones partners Positive Beliefs on Satisfaction with life, among victims, partners of victims and non-victims

Positive Beliefs of Self X Partner Victim. This interaction forms an indication of the moderating influence of the respondent's own positive beliefs on the relationship between their partner's victimization and the respondent's own Satisfaction with Life or Fear of Crime. Although the influence of the interaction between one's own number of beliefs and the victimization status of the partner run in the expected direction for both dependent measures, partners of victims do not significantly bolster their Satisfaction with Life and Fear of Crime with the aid of their own beliefs, resp. β=.18; t=1.62; p>.1; and β=–.14; t=–1.23; p>.1.

Positive Beliefs of Partner X Self Victim. This interaction displays the degree to which respondents are protected from the negative consequences of crime (depreciated Satisfaction with life or inflated fear of crime) through the positive beliefs of their partner. The beliefs of the partner appear to bolster the influence of being a victims of crime on the respondent's satisfaction with life, β=.38; t=3.49; p<.001. The influence of this interaction term on fear of crime was in the expected direction, but insignificant, β=–.16; t=–1.43; p>1.

Positive Beliefs of Partner X Partner Victim. This interaction term exhibits the degree to which the consequences of living with a partner that is a victim of crime on satisfaction with life and fear of crime are buffered by the positive beliefs of this victimized partner. The positive beliefs of the partner significantly interacted with the victimization status of the partner on both satisfaction with life and fear of crime, resp. β=.35; t=3.14; p<.005; and β=–.23; t=–2.01; p<.05. The degree to which the victimization of a partner has negative psychological consequences depends on the extent to which this unfortunate partner is characterized by positive beliefs.

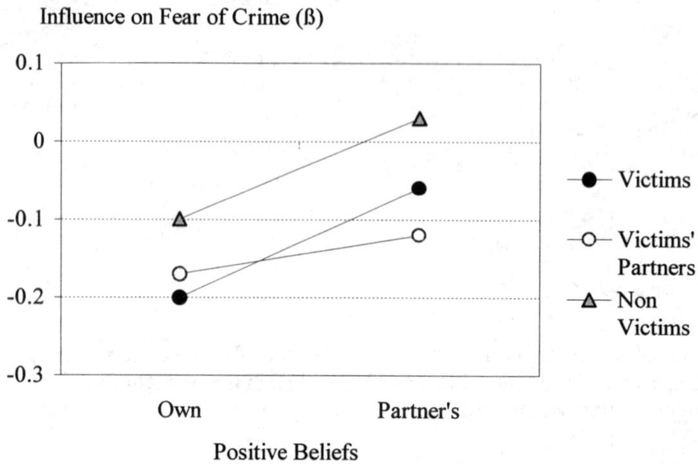

Note. Presented regression coefficients are corrected for the influence of background variables (gender, age and age of the partner). Df in the victim sample (5,113); in the partner of victim sample (5,106), and in the non-victim sample (5,922).

Figure 2: Standardized regression coefficients of the influence of ones own and ones partners Positive Beliefs on Fear of Crime, among victims, partners of victims and non-victims

These results indicate that beliefs are a social, rather than a personal moderator of the relationship between victimization and well-being. Although all interaction terms run in the expected direction, the only three that are significant are between victimization (of self or partner) and the number of beliefs of the partner. The influence of one's own victimisation on satisfaction with life is moderated by the number of beliefs of the partner. The number of beliefs of the victim buffered their partner's satisfaction with life and fear of crime.

Moreover, positive beliefs of victims and partners of victims appear to have more influence on each others satisfaction with life than on their own satisfaction with life. As Figure 1 clearly presents, among those who have been victimized or live with a victimized partner, the influence of the positive beliefs of the partner seems to outweigh the influence of one's own positive beliefs on satisfaction with life. The extent to which the respondents are characterized by positive beliefs has a marginally significant effect on the relationship between one's own victimization and Satisfaction with Life. This result forms the only indication of positive beliefs functioning as a personal moderator of the relationship between victimization and well-being.

Discussion

The aim of this study was to describe the two roles that the partners of victims of crime may play, employing the ideas of Taylor & Brown (1988). In general, both victims and their partners do not suffer from a deteriorated satisfaction with life or an elevated fear of crime. However, evidence was found that partners of victims may be considered both indirect victims and important support providers. The degree to which the well-being of partners of victims is affected, depends on the positive beliefs available to themselves, but more so, on the positive beliefs available to the victim. Those, who live with a victim lacking sufficient positive beliefs, seem to suffer a deterioration of their well-being, while those who live with a victimized partner with sufficient positive beliefs appear to even experience an increased well-being as a consequence of the incident. The degree to which the well-being of the victim is affected, depends on their own positive beliefs, and even stronger on the positive beliefs available to their partner. Victims who live with a partner who is characterized by sufficient beliefs report a higher level of well-being, and those who live with a partner with insufficient beliefs report a lower level of well-being than non-victims.

There are several possible explanations for the strong influence of the partner in coping with victimization. First, people in stressful situations, in general, might be less certain of themselves. This may make them more susceptible to external influences. Second, partners may be aware of each others capacity to cope with stressful situations. Having a partner with insufficient resources might inhibit people from sharing threatening facts or emotions with their counterparts. Sharing facts and emotions is related to better coping (Pennebaker, 1989). Finally, people who are more susceptible to the influence of others, might also objectively be more vulnerable for victimization. This means that those who, even before the incident took place, were more dependent on their partner's beliefs, are possibly more likely to become a victim of crime.

Whatever the precise mechanisms underlying their strong social influence, the finding that the beliefs of support-givers play an important role in coping, may have important theoretical and practical implications. From a theoretical point of view, the mixed empirical findings in the literature, concerning the buffering influence of objective and subjective measures of social support on coping with stressful situations, might be explained by the support-givers personal resources. People differ in their beliefs. One's position in society, for instance, economic class, type of job, education level, or living area, might bc associated with one's ability to create and foster positive beliefs. The average number of beliefs may therefore differ between samples of support-givers. This average level in a sample may be responsible for either a detrimental or a beneficial influence of social support.

From a practical point of view, partners appear to play an important role in how the other copes with criminal victimization. Therefore, intervention programmes, at, for instance, victim assistance bureaux, aimed at helping victims to cope, could be more effective with the partner, or other important support suppliers, of the victim participating. Such programmes should integrate a focus on the capacity to create or foster positive beliefs.

Moreover, because of the strong social influence of beliefs, the ability of professional support-givers to create or foster positive beliefs might be of crucial importance to the effect of such support. This could have important implications for both the selection and training of such support-suppliers.

The results suggest that people (both victims and non-victims) can be characterized by positive views of self, perceptions of personal control, and optimism. The number of available positive beliefs have a strong (personal) influence on both satisfaction with life and fear of crime. Additionally, one's satisfaction with life is also influenced by the number of positive beliefs available to the partner. The extent to which these positive beliefs are truly "illusionary" (Taylor & Brown, 1988), remains a puzzle. The only evidence contradicting the illusionary nature of these biases, are the differences between (direct and indirect) victims and non-victims optimism. Non-victims are much more optimistic, while victims and members of their household are more realistic or pessimistic about their risk of future victimization. This indicates that people are either quite capable of estimating their chances of future victimization, or this bias is not as pervasive, enduring, and systematic as Taylor & Brown (1988) expected it to be.

A few caveats can not remain unnoted. This survey suffers some methodological imperfections. For instance, victimizations occurred between four and sixteen months before the assessment of positive beliefs, well-being, and fear. Therefore, the influence of the incident might have diminished substantially. Furthermore, with only post-victimization measurements available, it seems impossible to determine the illusionary character of the biases, and the causality of relations. People might be accurate when assessing their chances of future victimization, and certain people, for instance those who are more dependent on their partners beliefs, might objectively be more vulnerable for victimization than others. Still, the results of this study are based on a normal sample of the population, dealing with a real-life situation. As Colvin & Block (1994, pp. 17) put it: a "leap of faith ... from laboratory findings".

References

Agnew, R. S. (1985). Neutralizing the impact of crime. *Criminal Justice and Behaviour, 12*, 221-239.

Batson, C. D., Coke, J. S. Chard, F., Smith, D., & Taliaferro, A. (1979). Generality of "glow of good will": Effects of mood on helping and information acquisition. *Social Psychology Quarterly, 42*, 176-179.

Burman, B., & Margolin, G. (1992). Analysis of the association between marital relationships and health problems: an interactional perspective. *Psychological Bulletin, 112*, 39-63.

Cialdini, R. B., Kenrick, D. T. & Baumann, D. J. (1982). Effects of mood on prosocial behaviour in children and adults. In N. Eisenberg (Ed.), *The Development of Prosocial Behavior* (pp. 339-359). New York: Academic Press.

Colvin, C. R., & Block, J. (1994). Do positive illusions foster mental health? An examination of the Taylor and Brown formulation. *Psychological Bulletin, 116*, 3-20.

Coyne, J. C., Kessler, R. C., Tal Turnbull, M., Wortman, C. B. & Greden, J. F. (1987). Living with a depressed person. *Journal of Consulting and Clinical Psychology, 55*, 347-352.

Frieze, I. H., Hymer, S., & Greenberg, M. S. (1987). Describing the crime victim: Psychological reactions to victimization. *Professional Psychology: Research and Practice, 18*, 299-315.

Denkers, A. J. M. (1996). *Psychological reactions of victims of crime: the influence of pre-crime, crime and post-crime factors* (in press).

Denkers, A. J. M., & Winkel, F. W. (1993). De invloed van attributionele reacties uit de naaste omgeving op het welzijn van slachtoffers van misdrijven: een veldonderzoek naar de cognitieve effecten van direct en indirect slachtofferschap. B. Verplanken, P. A. M. van Lange, R. W. Meertens, & F. W. Siero (Eds.), *Sociale Psychologie en haar toepassingen, 7*, Eburon, Delft.

Denkers, A. J. M., & Winkel, F. W. (1994). De invloed van persoonseigenschappen op de verwerking van slachtofferschap van criminaliteit: Een prospectief onderzoek. P. A. M. van Lange, F. W. Siero, B. Verplanken, & E. C. M van Schie (Eds.), *Sociale Psychologie en haar toepassingen, 8*, Eburon, Delft.

Diener, E. (1984). Subjective Well-being. *Psychological Bulletin, 95*, 542-575.

Diener, E., Emmons, R. A., Larsen, R. J., & Griffin, S. (1985). The satisfaction with life scale. *Journal of Personality Assessment, 49*, 71-75.

Isen, A. M. (1984). Toward understanding the role of affect in cognition. In R. Wyer, & T. Srull (Eds.), *Handbook of Social Cognition* (pp. 174-236). Hillsdale, NJ: Erlbaum.

O'Leary, K. D., & Smith, D. A. (1991). Marital interactions. *Annual Review of Psychology, 42*, 191-212.

Pennebaker, J. W. (1989). Confessions, inhibition, and desease. In L. Berkowitz (Ed.). *Advances in Experimental Social Psychology, 22*, 211-245. New York: Academic Press.

Perlof, L. S. (1983). Perceptions of vulnerability to victimization. *Journal of Social Issues, 39*, 41-61.

Taylor, S. E., & Brown, J. D. (1988). Illusion and well-being: A social psychological perspective on mental health. *Psychological Bulletin, 103*, 193-210.

Veitch, R. & Grifit, W. (1976) Good news-bad news: Affective and interpersonal effects. *Journal of Applied Psychology, 6*, 69-75.

Winkel, F. W. (1989). Responses to criminal victimization: Evaluating the impact of a police assistance program and some social psychological characteristics. *Police Studies: The International Review of Police Development, 12*, 59-72.

Psychological Aspects of the Process of Victimization

Juan Horacio Del Popolo and Stella M. Spezia

Introduction

In order to investigate the psychological aspects of the process of victimization, two surveys were carried out in the Province of Mendoza, Republic of Argentina, during the years of 1993 and 1995. These were the first investigations of this type in the Province. Both surveys support each other on investigating the psychological aspects of victimization. The first survey was applied to the victims of crimes who participated as witnesses in the penal process of the First Judicial Circumscription of the Province which has a population of 958,456 inhabitants (1994 census).

The second victimization survey involved 653 respondents. The survey was carried out in the Belgrano neighborhood, which belongs to the Department of Guaymallen, Mendoza.

To gather all the information in this second survey, we used a questionnaire. The questionnaire consisted of three parts: the first part concentrated on the victims' personal information such as sex, age, education, occupation, marital status, nationality, and if he or she rented or owned property.

The second part made allusions to the different types of crimes having as a reference the Argentine Penal Code, even though they were not excluded from other criminal situations. An open question was included in the questionnaire to further explore crimes not listed in the penal code.

The third part of the questionnaire made references to the characteristics of the incidents and the aggression, which included the existence of a police report, the police reaction to the report, the location of the crime, the date of the crime, the criminal's characteristics, and the quantity of criminals.

The construction of the questionnaire was multiple choice and the information obtained was put on an answer sheet. The use of this method started in October of 1993. The haphazard method or the internary method was used in the survey, even though the probability of each one to be included in the survey is unknown. Towards the end of the investigation this method turned out to be the most susceptible. To establish this the Department of Guaymallen was divided into 10 sectors. In each one of these sectors there were two surveyors, one for the east and west, and the other for the north and south. The surveyors covered the zones from the starting point until they completed the coverage of 20 households each.

Due to financial constraints, both investigation tasks were done without economic support by either the State or private entities, only with volunteers. We have currently obtained some of the results, and it is necessary to continue the practice of ulterior analysis. We would like to offer an approach on the results obtained from the first survey (survey done on the victims in the court).

Survey done on the victims in the court

Objectives of the investigation

We were interested in verifying whether the behavioural response patterns differed according to different types of victimization . For example, we asked ourselves if the victims of armed robbery experienced different symptoms from those that were assaulted or raped. The results of the investigation can be used to implement such differential psycho-victimization treatments as coordinated criminal political measurements with the purpose of decreasing the effects of victimization related to each type of crime.

Description of sample

The survey covered a sample of 430 people in the city of Mendoza who were victims of diverse crimes. The First Judicial Circumscription was selected because it is reasonably representative in the Provinces population. Out of the 20 existing Trial Courts, 15 Courts participated voluntarily. The Department of Criminology and Victimology of the Supreme Court of Justice authorized this survey. The survey was applied to all the people that attended court once a week. The days were picked randomly by each court. Table 1 and Table 2 represent the sampling composition according to age and gender.

Data collection technique

The interviewers were members of the Judicial Power and they worked voluntarily. The surveying team received specific training before they started their work. The training included the definition of basic concepts, techniques of interviewing, as well as role playing. This was done to make sure that interviewers became familiar with the contents of the questionnaire.

The interviews were administered in the offices of the courts. Data was collected using the face to face technique and with an administered questionnaire. All the victims were invited to answer questions and they were advised that they had the opportunity to refuse answering questions that they disliked.

Table 1: Composition of sample according to age

Age	Number of victims	Percent
Up to 5	0	0.00
Up to 10	2	0.47
Up to 15	13	3.02
Up to 20	22	5.12
Up to 25	57	13.26
Up to 30	63	14.65
Up to 35	51	11.86
Up to 40	59	13.72
Up to 45	53	12.33
Up to 50	39	9.07
Up to 55	24	5.58
Up to 60	9	2.09
Up to 65	18	4.19
Up to 70	8	1.86
Up to 75	5	1.16
Up to 80	1	0.23
Up to 85	1	0.23
Up to 90	0	0.00
Up to 95	0	0.00
21 to 55	346	80.46
R. with responses	425	98.84
W R	5	1.16

The questionnaire contained 44 questions in order to evaluate different aspects related to the victimization process such as personal characteristic of the victim, characteristic of the incidents, and symptoms experienced by the victims after their victimization. In the following we will present a summary of some of the results obtained.

Table 2: Composition of sample according to gender

Gender	Number	Percent
Male	258	60
Female	172	40

Cases of victimization according to different types of crimes

Table 3 shows the quantity of people victimized according to the type of crime. It is clear from the chart that 35 people were victims of armed robbery. This quantity represents 8.60% percent of the total sample. People who were victims of crime against property represent a 36.27% of the total sample, victims of sexual incidents represent 4.65%, and victims of physical injuries represent 14.18%.

Table 3: Composition of sample according to crime

Crime	N=430
Sexual incidents (rape, sexual contact)	4.65%
Against property (robbery, theft, fraud)	36.27%
Armed robbery	8.60%
Assault (physical injury)	14.18%
Crime against Life (attempted homicide)	1.16%
Crime against freedom	2.79%
Others	29.06%

Table 4: Symptoms and their frequency

	N	%
Fear of recurrence	210	48.84
Fear	136	31.63
Anguish	129	30.00
Feeling of emptiness	112	26.05
Irritability	89	20.70
Sleep disturbances	80	18.60
Flashbacks	79	18.37
Depression	65	15.12
Headaches	59	13.72
Shame	51	11.86
Anxiety	51	11.86
Decline in job performance	50	11.63
Loss of appetite	48	11.16
Heart palpitations	47	10.93
Nightmares	46	10.70
Difficulty in concentration	41	9.53
Gastrointestinal problems	36	8.37
Low self– esteem	34	7.91
Pericardial oppression	33	7.67
Loneliness isolation	33	7.67
Difficulties in breathing	33	7.67
Loss in previous interests	25	5.81
Poor memory	23	5.35
Difficulty to study	22	5.12
Suicidal thoughts	19	4.42
Sexual disturbances	18	4.19
Gain of appetite	15	3.49
Paleness	14	3.26
Excessive sweat	14	3.26
Choking sensation	13	3.02
Rumination	12	2.79
Dizziness	11	2.56
Chest pains	9	2.09
Photophobia	5	1.16

Psychological symptoms

Table 4 shows different psychological symptoms suffered by victims from the highest to lowest amount of occurrences. The left column displays the symptoms that were investigated. The middle column shows the quantity of victims which appeared with each kind of symptom and the right column shows the percentage of subjects related to the total sampling in which each symptom appears. For example, the symptom: “fear of reoccurrence”, appeared in 210 victims out of 430 victims that were interviewed pertaining to a 48.84% percent of the total sample.

The most frequent symptoms were: fear of reoccurrence, feeling of an undescribed fear, anguish, nightmares, feeling of abandonment, irritability, and intruded memories in the percentages that are indicated on the chart. A total of 34 symptoms were investigated. As you can see, the main fear is related to the feeling of fear which provokes the criminal act and also the fear that a new victimization can occur.

Quantity of symptoms presented by the subjects of the sample

Table 5 shows the quantity of subjects in the total of the sample which presents one symptom, two symptoms, three symptoms and so on until reaching eight symptoms. The first column on the left shows the quantity of symptoms, the second column shows the quantity of subjects who suffered from the symptoms, the third column shows the percentage of the quantity of subjects related to the total number of samples and the last column on the right shows the percentage of the accumulated symptoms.

It clear that 77% of the subjects have presented at least one of the symptoms evaluated in the investigation after the crime was committed.

Table 5: Number of symptoms

	N	%
W R	98	22.79
1 symptom	70	16.28
2 symptoms	54	12.56
3 symptoms	40	9.30
4 symptoms	37	8.60
5 symptoms	22	5.12
6 symptoms	22	5.12
7 symptoms	18	4.19
8 or more symptoms	69	16.05
Total	430	100.00

Fear of reoccurrence

In the cases of sexual assaults (such as rape and sexual contact) as well as in the cases of attempted homicides, 100% of the victims said "they experienced fear that new victimization might occur". A total of 20 subjects were interviewed.

In the cases where the subjects suffered physical injuries as a consequence of crime (N=61 subjects) 34 suffered this particular symptom, which represents 55.37% of the subjects.

In the cases of crime against property (theft, robbery, larceny and fraud) out of 152 subjects that were victims of these kind of crimes, 55 experienced this symptom which represents 35.89%.

If the crime was armed robbery, where 37 subjects were involved, 23 subjects presented this symptom, which is 62% of the sample.

These results suggest that this symptom appears when the life or sexual intimacy of the victim is threatened. The fear of revictimization is much less apparent in the case of crimes against property.

From the political criminal point of view it would be necessary to implement, at least in the cases where the victim suffers a sexual crime or assault against their life, specific programs related to this symptom, designed to offer supportive approaches and security such as: hotlines, empathetic soothing, and cognitive control strategies.

Revictimization and average of symptoms

Table 6 shows the quantity of subjects that experienced a new victimization (2 or more) of the same type crime and Table 7 the average of the symptoms experienced for each group. Obviously, the people that were victimized more than once present a higher average of symptoms than the ones victimized in only one incident, of course always referring to the same crime.

Table 6: New victimization

Yes	No	W R	Total
132	287	11	430

Table 7: Number of symptoms

	Yes	No	W R
Number of symptoms	613	1022	41
Average	4.64	3.56	3.73

Symptoms according to crime

Tables 8 and 9 show the appearance of the symptoms on victims of different crimes. These tables show the amounts obtained from the samples corresponding to different types of crimes. The left column contains the symptoms. Each box shows the frequency of each symptom in an average percentage term for each group of crime victims.

Table 8: Symptoms according to type of crime (1)

Symptoms	Assault (physical injury)	Crime against property	Armed robbery
Pericardial oppression	24%	0%	2.70%
Headaches	29.50%	6.41%	2.70%
Difficulties in breathing	18%	3.20%	0%
Heart palpitations	18%	4.48%	8%
Gastrointestinal problems	14.70%	7%	0%
Paleness	6.55%	0.64%	0%
Choking sensations	0%	1.92%	2.70%
Photophobia	3.20%	0.64%	0%
Dizziness	3.27%	0%	2.70%
Pericardial pain	3.27%	0.64%	0%
Excessive sweat	4.90%	0.64%	2.70%
Loss of appetite	4.90%	1.92%	2.70%
Gain of appetite	0%	1.92%	0%

Table 9: Symptoms according to type of crime (2)

Symptoms	Assault (physical injury)	Crime against property	Armed robbery	Sexual incidents
Anguish	44%	21.15%	21%	55%
Anxiety	13.11%	7.69%	8.10%	15%
Fear	37%	17.30%	48%	55%
Poor memory	8%	0.64%	8.10%	20%
Difficulty in concentration	15%	2.56%	8.00%	30%
Decline in job performance	28%	5.12%	13.50%	10%
Flashbacks	21%	6.41%	4%	50%
Isolation	13%	1.92%	0%	35%
Rumination	3%	2.56%	0.00%	10%
Suicidal thoughts	6.50%	1.92%	2.70%	15%
Irritability	18%	21.15%	3%	35%
Isolation	22.95%	11.53%	8.10%	25%
Shame	16%	5.12%	3%	55%
Low self-esteem	10%	6.40%	5.40%	35%
Depression	23%	7.05%	8.10%	50%
Loss in previous interests	8%	1.28%	0.00%	15%
Sexual disturbances	7%	0.64%	0%	10%

Table 10: Symptoms according to duration

Symptoms	Duration		
	Days	Months	Years
Poor memory	52.8	1.76	0.15
Nightmares	130	4.33	0.36
Sleep disturbances	54	1.80	0.15
Headaches	92	3.07	0.26
Dizziness	65	2.17	0.18
Pericardial oppression	109	3.63	0.30
Difficulties in breathing	86	2.87	0.24
Heart palpitations	28.5	0.95	0.08
Gastrointestinal problems	128	4.27	0.36
Paleness	83	2.77	0.23
Choking sensations	10.4	0.35	0.03
Pericardial oppression	1	0.03	0.00
Photophobia	0	0.00	0.00
Excessive sweat	100	3.33	0.28
Loss of appetite	60.5	2.02	0.17
Gain of appetite	90	3.00	0.25
Fear of recurrence	117.8	3.93	0.33
Anguish	98.6	3.29	0.27
Anxiety	41.25	1.38	0.11
Loneliness– isolation	2.75	0.09	0.01
Loss in previous interests	182	6.07	0.51
Difficulty in concentration	300	10.00	0.83
Flashbacks	180	6.00	0.50
Difficulty to study	202	6.73	0.56
Irritability	68	2.27	0.19
Feeling of emptiness	83.45	2.78	0.23
Shame	60	2.00	0.17
Low self– esteem	58.3	1.94	0.16
Depression	162	5.40	0.45
Sexual Disturbances	40	1.33	0.11
Fear	98.7	3.29	0.27
Decline in job performance	48.2	1.61	0.13
Rumination	15	0.50	0.04
Suicidal thoughts	75	2.50	0.21

It is known, that a person's reaction towards any stress factor is highly characteristic and idiosyncratic. It depends on an important number of variables associated with the context, structure of personal history and self organization.

However, it can be seen from these tables, that the victims of sexual incidents present an important number of symptoms which are related to somatic disturbances such as headaches, heart palpitations, gastrointestinal problems, dizziness, sweating, choking sensation, excessive loss and gain of appetite. This group of victims therefore, perceived after the victimization a higher symptomatological in the referred areas.

Table 11: Symptoms according to intensity

Symptoms	Intensity							
	L		M		S		WR	
	N	%	N	%	N	%	N	%
Poor memory	6	37.50	2	14.29	5	35.71	10	7.14
Nightmares	6	26.09	8	34.78	7	30.43	25	8.70
Sleep disturbances	11	13.75	16	20.00	9	11.25	44	55.00
Headaches	6	10.17	11	18.64	20	33.90	22	37.29
Dizziness	2	18.18	4	36.36	1	9.09	4	36.36
Pericardial oppression	6	18.18	6	18.18	5	15.15	16	48.48
Difficulties in breathing	5	15.15	6	18.18	3	9.09	19	57.58
Heart palpitations	2	4.35	9	19.57	6	13.04	29	63.04
Gastrointestinal problems	7	19.44	7	19.44	1	2.78	21	58.33
Paleness	1	7.14	3	21.43	0	0.00	10	71.43
Choking sensations	4	30.77	3	23.08	0	0.00	6	46.15
Pericardial oppression	1	11.11	0	0.00	0	0.00	8	88.89
Photophobia	1	20.00	2	40.00	0	0.00	2	40.00
Excessive sweat	0	0.00	2	14.29	3	21.43	9	64.29
Loss of appetite	5	10.42	7	14.58	4	8.33	32	66.67
Gain of appetite	0	0.00	2	13.33	4	26.67	9	60.00
Fear of recurrence	22	20.37	38	35.19	37	34.26	11	10.19
Anguish	10	7.75	17	13.18	25	19.38	77	59.69
Anxiety	5	9.80	5	9.80	12	23.53	29	56.86
Loneliness– isolation	2	6.06	8	24.24	5	15.15	18	54.55
Loss in previous interests	2	8.00	5	20.00	6	24.00	12	48.00
Difficulty in concentration	2	4.88	9	21.95	5	12.20	25	60.98
Flashbacks	5	6.33	12	15.19	11	13.92	51	64.56
Difficulty to study	3	13.64	4	18.18	3	13.64	12	54.55
Irritability	12	13.48	27	30.34	6	6.74	44	49.44
Feeling of emptiness	14	12.61	29	26.13	15	13.51	53	47.75
Shame	5	9.80	12	23.53	11	21.57	23	45.10
Low self– esteem	2	5.88	11	32.35	5	14.71	16	47.06
Depression	5	7.46	14	20.90	13	19.40	35	52.24
Sexual Disturbances	2	10.53	2	10.53	6	31.58	9	47.37
Fear	17	12.14	24	17.14	22	15.71	77	55.00
Decline in job performance	3	6.00	12	24.00	2	4.00	33	66.00
Rumination	2	16.67	3	25.00	2	16.67	5	41.67
Suicidal thoughts	0	0.00	3	15.79	4	21.05	12	63.16

If related to the groups of victims of crimes against property or armed robbery, injured victims also present an important average percentage of the symptoms associated with somatic disturbances. It presents the highest average percentage related to the following symptoms: pericardial oppression and difficulties in breathing.

The group that presents the lowest average of symptoms associated mainly with the somatic disturbances, includes the victims of crime against property and the victims of armed robbery.

Probably, the post traumatic responses are correlated with increased autonomic nervous system arousal.

The group of sexual assault victims as well as the group of injured victims in a large average number perceived anguished feelings of post victimization. It is possible to hypothesize the existence of a probable correlation between perceived anguish and the appearance of somatic disturbances.

Up to here, you can conclude that the group of sexual assault victims are the most affected by post victimization symptoms. Many researchers have verified that the trauma in this type of crime can have serious disorganizing effects.

Symptoms: duration and intensity

Tables 10 and 11 show the symptoms investigated and their duration and intensity on the total sample.

Some Proposals

Taking into consideration that we have found different symptomatologies in each one of the criminal groups that we have examined, we suggest the following measures in cases of rape victims, sexual assaults victims and attempted murder:

a) When a person is victimized he or she should receive immediate care in the police department as well as in the courts by personnel who are specially trained for the situation in order

– to control the feelings of anguish;

– to be aware of the memory problems that appear associated in the stages of intense anguish, with the objective of implementing an adequate method to receive the victims statement and taking into consideration the presence of this symptom;

– to control the feelings of fear and to correctly advise the victim about protection programs that exist in each community;

– to prepare an adequate surrounding where the victim is going to give his or her statement, respecting and avoiding feelings of shame, humiliation, and low self-esteem.

The interviews with the trained personnel can be done in rooms with double vision glass, which has already been proposed by other researchers throughout the procedures of technical registrations.

b) Also, it is necessary to structuralize a perfectly connected and coordinated service in-between the police force and the courts, so the victim can receive immediate psycho-therapeutic care in order to alleviate

– severe feelings of distress and their correlations that appear in the somatic field;

– the ulterior severeness of the symptoms and fragmentations of the self which probably happens if you take into account the high appearance of stress factors;

– the feelings of shame, humiliation, and low self-esteem.

c) We also propose the intervention with the family with the intention of decreasing anguish and encouraging the family of the victim to be supportive and by trying to minimize feelings of anguish, guilt and detachment which also appear in the survey.

d) To implement effective protection programs in the police and criminal force with the aim of avoiding new victimizations, by offering feelings of security during the most critical periods, according to the time where the symptoms are present and for the minimal duration of 90 days.

In the cases of crimes against property, we believe that it is not justified for the moment to include the trained interrogator due to the frequency of different symptomatologies. It seems to be sufficient to access these programs, only in the major or severe cases like the victims of armed robbery.

However, post victimization fear and the fear of reoccurrence should be taken into consideration for the implementation of community programs that increase the perception of security and trust.

Victim–Offender Mediation in the Italian Juvenile Justice System: A First Attempt of Definition

Anna Costanza Baldry, Gaetano De Leo and Gilda Scardaccione

Introduction

In the penal justice system, the possible ways of responding to the commission of a crime have changed substantially in the last decades. In some countries, Great Britain for example, during the XIII, early XIX century, it was the victim, that had to bring the offender into court to get him convicted. From this perspective the way of dealing with justice has changed, and in most countries, the State has the duty of initiating a legal procedure when a crime is known. In these cases we refer to punitive actions against the offender (in the case of imprisonment or other legal responses where the focus of attention is on restitution and punishment). Another aim of justice is to re-educate prisoners through a socialisation process. On the other hand, when the legal action aims at repairing the damage caused by the offender as well as reducing conflicts, we can fully understand the importance of the role of the victim (Saponaro, 1994).

Although offences are perpetrated against a person, the restitution has to be done through the State which represents the rights of the victim. Another possible way of responding to the commission of a crime from the side of the offender is to take into account only the parties that were involved in the conflict. There are different moments, from the legal point of view, in which conciliation can be implemented. By looking at the law in this regard, 'conciliation' can be part of a probation order imposed by the judge. After the young offender has been convicted the judge can decide that a mediation between the victim and the offender can take place.

It is possible therefore to understand the importance of taking into account the victim. For the Italian penal code, the victim has never played a central role, often treated as a 'piece of evidence', an element just as the others, an important witness. With the new penal procedure code (1989) it has been possible to introduce some rules that pay special attention on the victim such as the right of the victim to oppose the decision of a judge to dismiss his/her case. The victim can sit in court as a civil party and ask for restitution. In the Juvenile Justice System the procedure is different and the victim is further pushed to one side. There is a special rule regarding probation for the suspension of the trail (art.28 D.P.R 448/89, Decree of the President of Republic). With this probation order, the judge charges social workers of the Minister of Justice to develop a special project, for a suitable amount of time, during which the minor has to take part in certain activities, such as a voluntary work or other activities of social utility. Additionally, the judge can recommend a victim/offender reconciliation to repair the damage caused. This is the so called Model of Restorative Justice. (Walgrave, 1994). The focus of attention is also on reducing the conflict that emerges between the two parties. Based on these assumptions, victims have a central and active role in the resolution of the conflict. Most research points out that victims often feel revictimised by the community and the justice system because it is not taken into consideration that they have suffered from the commission of the crime.

National and international publications suggest that there are different victim/ offender mediation schemes that enable the victim to play an active part in the decision making process. (i.e. Gatti & Marugo, 1994; Messmer & Otto, 1992; Wright & Galaway, 1989). The outcome of mediation can be resolution of the conflicts through restitution (material or a symbolic one) or reconciliation (shaking hands, a hug or verbal excuses; Bouchard, 1992). The mediator should not be a representative of any Institution of the justice system, or of any Association for victims. The mediator has to enhance and facilitate the communication: the mediator does not have to find a solution on the behalf of the two parties; he/she has to facilitate the two parties involved, letting them search for conflict resolution. The mediator has to encourage questions, facilitate answers with a blameless approach.

As Italian law stands, it is not clear what is meant by 'reconciliation', which means that it is not clear what should be actually done. As things stand now, the social workers of the Minister of Justice are the ones responsible for mediation.

This poses two limitations: the victim might get the impression that the reconciliation has advantages only for the young offender (i.e. reducing the length of the probation period). It is important to make clear and explain to the victim the meaning of mediation. Otherwise the victim may feel responsible for the success of the mediation. These are the main reasons why the mediator should be a neutral and third party (Giulini, 1994). For the same reason, it is not wise to have somebody as mediator who is working on the behalf of victims. The approach in this case would be biased, and the consequences could lead to the criminalisation of the offender.

Victim-offender reconciliation in the Italian Juvenile Justice System – The survey

In the present study, we wanted to learn more about what is actually done in Italy in terms of mediation and victim-offender reconciliation programmes and try to draw a picture of the Italian situation regarding the restorative justice approach to crime. Literature indicates two different approaches: Hughes & Schneider, (1989), believe that mediation is possible for all kinds of crimes; those against property (thefts), but also the more serious ones perpetrated against the person (attempted murder, rape). Other authors find out from their research that mediation is more successful and can take place only for 'petty crimes', mainly crimes committed against property (Wemmers & Zeilstra, 1991). In some countries of common law, it is possible to develop mediation programmes as a diversion disposition, before the offender is found guilty and sentenced. In Italy because prosecution is mandatory when a crime is known, then mediation is possible only with probation.

In this first part of the survey we wanted to know more about different ways in which mediation took place and learn more about the different models used as well as evaluating the importance and consequences of using mediation in some cases rather than in others. A total of 90 cases was analysed, These are the cases for which the judge stated in the probation order, that the victim and the offender should mediate, but in almost half of these cases mediation actually never took place. As we will see in more specific detail later on, the reasons are manifold. On one side, the victim was not willing to meet the offender or the offender did not show adequate interest and sense of responsibility to follow such a programme. Next to this, social workers themselves say that they do not have adequate skills to promote mediation, although they believe in the possible positive effects and outcomes of mediation. The amount of work social workers have to do is very demanding and time seeking. It is thus not possible for them to think about, and actually promote, mediation.

From the official records of the Ministry of Justice, we found out how many cases were referred to for mediation. A questionnaire was then mailed to the members of these cases. Several questions were included regarding socio-demographic characteristic of the young offender; the type of crime committed; the family and the environment; length of the probation order and the final decision given by the court. The second part of the questionnaire consisted of questions directly related to the mediation session that should have taken place in that specific case. Some items measured the role played by the ones responsible for mediation. Another set of questions referred to the actual mediation: the amount of time during which victim and offender met and the way in which this happened. The aim was to find out what was done in those cases in which mediation took place and if there was a specific way of dealing the case. (As we will emphasize later on the answer is negative.) The only place where there is a specific office for mediation is in Turin. This office is part of the Tribunal for Minors that has developed, on an experimental basis, a mediation programme (AA.VV., 1994). It is possible to send a young offender in a mediation programme at different stages of the legal procedure. During investigation, the public prosecutor in order to have some information about the young offender and his/her personality, the level of his/her maturity, sends the case to the mediation office to evaluate whether there are opportunities for mediation, as long as the victim agrees. If the outcome of the mediation session is positive then the judge dismisses the case with a double advantage: the young offender had the chance to face the consequences of his/her actions and to apologise to the victim, and the victim had, for the first time, a central role in the justice system because he or she was given the opportunity to express the feeling of victimisation and gain some answers regarding doubts she/he always had (Umbreit, 1994). The young offender can be sent to the mediation session also after the conviction as a probation order. During this period the offender has to follow a special programme developed during which he/she has to do some useful social activities as well as voluntary work and in these cases also mediate with the victim. Although things are gradually changing in Italy, regarding mediation, thanks also to the new established Centre for the Promotion of Mediation (C.I.P.M., Giulini, 1994), an association for peaceful conflicts' resolution, although there is a positive attitude from the side of people working in the justice system, there is still a lot to do especially in terms of training programmes.

Main results

Ninety case studies might not be representative of the whole phenomenon, but they can give us an idea of what is actually done in terms of victim/offender mediation. These represent the cases for which the judge indicated reconciliation as part of the probation order programme. The following table shows the distribution of all cases within the country.

Table 1: Distribution of mediation within the country

City	Number of mediation in the project
Ancona	14
Bari	16
Bologna	2
Campobasso	35
Cagliari	1
Caltanisetta	3
Milano	1
Palermo	10
Torino	6
Trieste	2
Total	90

The average age of the young offenders, male in 94.9% of the cases, is 16.9 years; they had an average period of probation of 8.9 months. In 76.26% of the time, the final decision of the judge at the end of the probation, was the dismissal of the case. In the Italian legal system at the end of the probation period the judge can declare that the case is closed with no further legal action.

The following figure refers to different crimes that were committed in the different cases in which mediation took place.

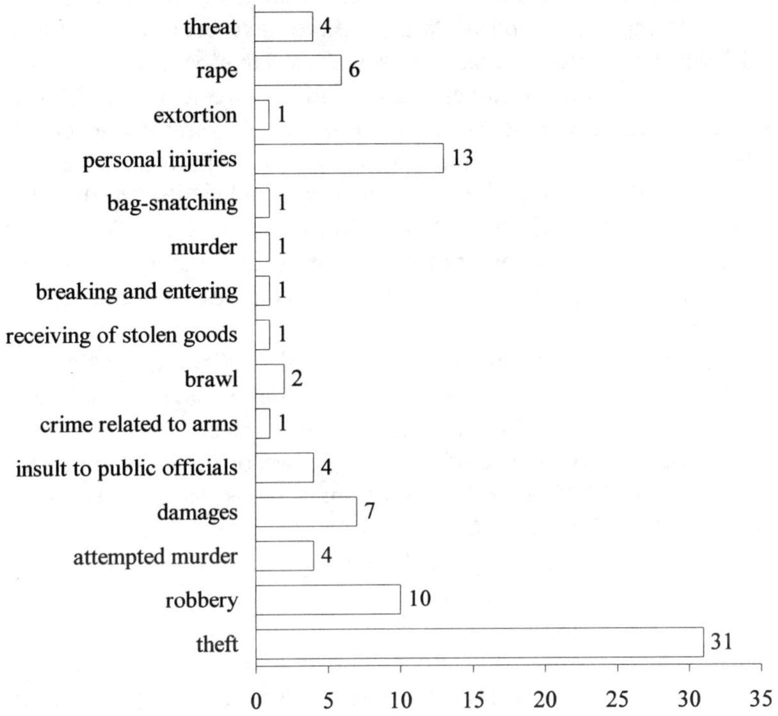

Figure 1: Type of crimes committed in case of mediation

In the next table we take into consideration the ones who took part in the mediation session.

Table 2: Percentage of different people present in the mediation session

Who was present in the mediation session	Percentage of presence ('yes' answers)
Victim	40.5%
Offender	97.5%
Parents of the offender	59.0%
Parents of the victim	26.9%
Other outside members	24.6%
Judge	7.5%
Social worker	98.8%
Educator	3.8%
Psychologist	7.5%
Volunteer	6.3%

N.B. The values refer to the percentage of cases in which the respective person is present.

The figures we presented so far refer to the period January '91 – June '93. Table 1 shows that in Campobasso and in Ancona there have been quite a lot of mediation cases. If we have a closer look at possible explanation why there is a higher concentration in some places rather than in others, we learn that this is partly due to the peculiar environment and characteristics of the town concerned: i.e. Campobasso is a very small town where almost everybody knows each other. It is in the interest of both the offender and of the victim to reduce the conflict that has emerged as a consequence of the offence. Moreover is one of the first concerns of the judge and of social workers to try to bring the young offender, as soon as possible, out of the penal circuit which means giving alternative sanctions to imprisonment.

If we have a closer look at what was done in terms of mediation, we find out that in some cases voluntary work or reparation of the damage caused was ordered. In most cases the kind of mediation that took place required actual meeting of the two parties involved. The offender in 75.9% of the cases made his apologies to the victim, in 47.21% of the cases they shook hands. Mediation usually takes place in quite an informal way.

In some cases, in Bari for example, the mediation consisted of a letter that the offender wrote to the victim apologising for what he/she had done. It is clear, in the assumption of the writer, that this kind of reconciliation is not very useful also because the offender is not able to fully understand its meaning. Moreover, the victim might react negatively when receiving this letter that he/she didn't ask for. With the kind of information we have so far it is impossible to learn about the importance and the role that mediation had for the victim and the offender since the questionnaire was completed by the social workers that took part in the programme. Unfortunately, we do not have any follow-up records that check, for example, that the victim and the offender are all right.

If we now have a look at the people that actually took part in the mediation session, results show that the offender or his parents were always present but not the victim or his/her parents or anybody else representing her/him; this occurred only 40.5% of the times. Social workers are always present during the mediation session; other professionals such as psychologists and judges are not. Regarding the role played by social workers, in 22.2% of all the cases it was explained to the two parties what was meant with the term mediation; 17.4% of the times, social workers prepared the two parties for the actual mediation session; in 13% of the cases they provided some kind of educational role. Most of the sessions took place either in the Social Service Office itself or in some neutral place.

In the last part of the questionnaire, social workers had to rate their perceived satisfaction and usefulness of the mediation as well as the one of the parties involved. Sample items were: "Do you think the victim was satisfied with the meeting?", or "Do you think mediation was useful for the offender?". Answers could be entered on a seven point-scale ranging from 1-not at all satisfied, to 7-completely satisfied. Items revealed a two factor structure (explained variance

60%): namely 'degree of satisfaction' (alpha=.83), and 'perceived utility for the offender and the victim' (alpha=.78). To test whether there were any difference between those cases in which mediation was carried out in an informal way and those that was not, we conducted a Univariate analysis of variance (ANOVA) that revealed two main effects. 'Perceived satisfaction' was higher in those cases in which mediation was carried out in an informal way than when it wasn't (m=5.86 vs. m=4.01, $F(1,41)=28.27$, $p<.0001$). 'Perceived usefulness' was also higher in the former case than in the latter (m=5.81 vs. m=3.92, $F(1,41)=31.06$, $p<.001$). This suggests that is preferred to have informal meetings, shaking hands, apologising rather than formal ones, where the main topics are restitution or reparation of the damage without any sharing of emotion.

General conclusion

This survey showed that a victim-offender reconciliation programme within the probation programme should be strongly encouraged. More attention and investment of resources should be given for specific training programmes for potential mediators. It is therefore important to look at specific training models that already exist (e.g. Bonafè-Schmitt, 1989).

Next to this first point, it is important to notice that the ones responsible for mediation are social workers for the Department of the Ministry of Justice. On the basis of these results we can say that in Italy, victim/offender mediation doesn't have a specific structure. There is a strong positive attitude towards this way of dealing with justice which may promote future intervention. It is our strong conviction that if one of the main aims of reconciliation is to give the victim the opportunity to speak for herself/himself, then there are the two parties having to decide for themselves. Studies that took place in other countries (see Umbreit, 1994; Wright & Galaway, 1989), have shown that satisfaction of the victim was positively related to the opportunity given for restitution. The other positive outcome of mediation is to give the victim the opportunity to meet directly with the offenders, to express feelings and ask them unsolved questions.

References

AA.VV. (1994). Mediazione e riparazione del danno. Proposte per una risposta penale "riparatoria" (Mediation and restore of the damage. Proposal for a restorative justice). *Minorigiustizia, 4*, 26-33.

Bonafé-Schmitt, J. (1989). Alternatives to the Judicial Model. In M. Wright & B. Galaway. *Mediation and Criminal Justice. Victims, Offenders and Community* (pp. 178-194). London: Sage Publications.

Bouchard, M. (1992). Mediazione: dalla repressione alla rielaborazione del conflitto (Mediation: from repression to the analysis of the conflict). *Dei Delitti e delle Pene, 2*, 191-202.

Gatti, U., & Marugo, M. I. (1994). La vittima e la giustizia riparativa. (The victim and restorative justice). *Marginalità e Società, 4*, 12-32.

Giulini, P. (1994). Il Mediatore: Un "terzo uomo" (The mediator. A 'third man'). *Marginalità e Società, 4*, 54-62.

Hughes, S. P., & Schneider, A. L. (1989). Victim-Offender mediation: A survey of program characteristics and perception of effectiveness. *Crime & Delinquency, 35/2*, 217-233.

Messmer, H., & Otto, H. U. (1992). (Eds.). *Restorative Justice on trial: pitfalls and potentials of victim-offender mediation – international research perspectives.* Nato ASI Series: Dordrecht, Kluver Academic Publishers.

Saponaro, A. (1991). The victim of crime in the New Italian Code of Criminal Procedure. In E. A. Fattah, *Towards a Critical Victimology* (pp. 257-266). St. Martin's Press, Onati Proceedings.

Umbreit, M. S. (1994). *Victim meets offender. The impact of Restorative Justice and Mediation.* NY: Criminal Justice Press.

Walgrave, L. (1994). Beyond rehabilitation. In search of a constructive alternative in the judicial response to juvenile crime. *European Journal on Criminal Policy and Research. Juvenile Justice System, 2/2*, 56-75.

Wemmers, J., & Zeilstra, M. I. (1991). Victim policy and restitution in the Netherlands. In G. Kaiser, H. Kury, & H. J. Albrecht, *Victim and Criminal Justice, Vol. I* (pp. 409-422). Criminological Research Reports, Institute for Foreign and International Penal Law, Freiburg.

Wright, M., & Galaway, B. (Eds.) (1989). *Mediation and Criminal Justice. Victims, Offenders and Community*. London: Sage Publications.

The Impact of Professional Roles on Subjective Explanations of Juvenile Delinquency

Mechthild Averbeck and Friedrich Lösel[1]

There is a broad range of scientific explanations and theories on what causes juvenile delinquency and crime. A lot of them can as well be found in common explanations of lays or professionals who work in contact with offenders. Studies on those subjective theories of crime showed aspects or dimensions such as social, economic and individual causation (Carroll, Perkowitz, Lurigio, & Weaver, 1987) or defective education, mentally unstable, temptation, excitement, alienation and parents' impacts (Furnham, & Henderson, 1983). The underlying structure found in the studies depends on the number and differentiation of items as well as the groups of persons studied. However, it has been shown repeatedly that respondents often differ greatly in the importance that they attach to different components (Averbeck, & Lösel, 1992, 1994; Dienstein, 1960; Kennedy, & Homant, 1986; Ortet-Fabregat, & Pérez, 1992; Reuterman, & Cartwright, 1976; Saulnier, & Perlman, 1981).

To explain differences in subjective theories of crime a number of variables have been used. An obvious set of variables to look for sources of differences are demographic variables, especially gender and age. Whereas some studies have reported a strong impact of respondents' gender on subjective theories of crime (Cann, Calhoun, & Selby, 1980; Furnham & Henderson, 1983), in others it was only moderate (Hollin & Howells, 1987; Lillyquist, 1980; Ollenburger, 1986) or even had no impact at all (Banks, Maloney, & Willcock, 1975; Hawkins, 1981; Silverman, Smith, Nelson, & Dembo, 1984). With some exceptions (Hawkins, 1981; Silverman et al., 1984), most studies have reported a significant impact of respondents' age on everyday psychological ideas about delinquency. For example, Flanagan (1987) and Carroll et al. (1987) have found that older probation officers rate drugs to be a more significant causal factor in crime than younger probation officers. Banks et al. (1975) have found that older persons tend to refer to the loss of authority in parents and teachers as well as the decline in religiousness. These findings are also found – alongside other age effects – in Furnham and

[1] The present study was funded by the Bavarian Ministry of Justice. We wish to thank Jonathan Harrow, University of Bielefeld, for his help in translating this paper from German into English.

Henderson (1983) and Hollin and Howells (1987). Nevertheless, age is only a surface variable. There is a need for further explanations on underlying meanings.

One set of variables related to age are attitudes, for example conservatism, that has been investigated in some studies on lay explanations. Whereas Bottenberg and Gareis (1987) were unable to find effects of the attitude variable conservatism, Furnham and Henderson (1983) found that conservative versus liberal political attitudes (based on choices of political parties) have a particularly strong effect on ratings of the importance of social explanations of crime. Some studies on adjudication have also shown clear relationships between attributions and various scales addressing the goals and purpose of sanctions (Carroll et al., 1987; Cullen, Clark, Cullen, & Mathers, 1985; Oswald, 1992).

It has been tried to subsume the impact of attitude variables under somewhat wider variables like personality traits – until yet with little success. So Lillyquist (1980) has reported that personality traits do not relate to internal versus external attributions of responsibility. Likewise, Bottenberg and Gareis (1987) have found no relations between everyday psychological ideas and neuroticism or extraversion. Gudjonsson (1984) has also found no effects of extraversion, but he does report relationships between causal attributions and scores on psychoticism, neuroticism, and depression scales.

Finally, the respondents' experiences with or their relationship to the problem area of crime were identified as an important source of differences in explanations. Thus groups working in the field of justice make more internal attributions (Fielding & Fielding, 1991) that have been interpreted as agent-observer "error" when compared to the more external attributions of prisoners (Averbeck & Lösel, 1992, 1994, in prep.; Saulnier & Perlman, 1981). Goldstein (1990) and Henderson and Hewstone (1984) have also found strong evidence for external causal attributions in prisoners. However, also the various professional groups do differ greatly in their subjective theories of crime. This is frequently explained in terms of role-specific socialization (Averbeck & Lösel, 1992, 1994, in prep.; Dienstein, 1960; Fielding & Fielding, 1991; Kennedy & Homant, 1986; Lentz, 1969; Melvin, Gramling, & Gardner, 1985; Reuterman & Cartwright, 1976). For example, Ortet-Fabregat and Pérez (1992) have found that police officers give higher ratings to genetic and other individual causes than, in particular, prison rehabilitation services (psychologists, social workers, prison teachers). In contrast, legal experts (judges, public prosecutors, lawyers) place more emphasis on social, economic, and environmental influences than police officers.

The present paper studies the subjective explanations of personally concerned persons, that is prisoners, and of different groups working in the justice system applying the same methods. The analysis tries to estimate moderations of age and attitude variables, but focuses on the role-specific group membership or socialization in the legal system; a variable that is not only highly relevant from experiences of everyday prison life but also empirically. For example, Jurik (1985) has applied findings from industrial psychology (e.g., Miller, 1980) showing that working conditions, work surroundings, and professional role expectations overshadow the effects of individual attributes in the perspectives and behavior of employees in order to study a group of prison officers. He has found that both individual and organizational aspects have roughly equally large effects on the attitude toward prisoners. However, in this study, role-specific socialization was only one subcategory among the organizational variables. Despite the fact that only prison officers were studied, its relative importance was very high. Studies on attitudes and perceptions of professional roles in various groups involved with prisons indicate that role-specific socialization may well be a greater source of the variability in everyday psychological ideas about crime (Lösel & Bliesener, 1989; Lösel, Mey, & Molitor, 1988).

Method

The most important groups involved in juvenile detention were surveyed in 112 interviews at the Bavarian reformatories Ebrach, Laufen-Lebenau, and Niederschönenfeld, and, when necessary, outside them. Respondents belonged to the following five groups: legal experts (juvenile judges and juvenile reformatory governors combined; N=14, age in years: M=49.0); prison officers (N=33, age in years: M=43.0); professional services (social workers, psychologists, and reformatory teachers; N=18, age in years: M=40.2); probation officers (N=19, age in years: M=36.3); and prisoners (N=28, age in years: M=21.1). For some parts of the survey, the first four groups were aggregated as "experts". All prisoners were male; and the majority of experts were also men (70 men, 14 women). The youngest group was – quasi per definitionem – the juvenile prisoners. However, the various expert groups also differed significantly in age. Unfortunately, the sample was too small to ascertain how far these age differences corresponded to population characteristics. Nonetheless, they seemed fairly plausible: Whereas the population of probation officers may well also include persons at the beginning of their careers, this is hardly likely in the case of, for example, reformatory governors.

Subjective theories of crime were assessed with semistructured interviews and questionnaires. Answers to open questions about the causes of crime were not used in the present analyses (see Averbeck & Lösel, 1994). Alongside everyday psychological ideas about crime, the interview also asked about the respondents' attitudes toward the reformatory. Their attitudes about current practice at juvenile reformatories were rated on a 5-point scale with the poles *negative* (1) and *positive* (5). Their attitude toward the juvenile prisoners were also rated on a 5-point scale with the poles *disapproving, distrustful* (1) and *benevolent, supportive* (5).

Subjective theories of crime were assessed with two questionnaires. In the *Fragebogen zu Kriminalitätserklärungen*, respondents had to rate the significance for crime of 52 items on 7-point scales. The items were formulated on the basis of well-known theories of crime (e.g., Amelang, 1986; Lamnek, 1990; Lösel, 1993).

Table 1: Description of factors

Factors	Summarized description of items loading on the factor
C1 Immature personality	– Uncontrolled, scarcely planned, dependent, childish behavior – No successful development (as yet) into a personally responsible, morally based coping with problems – Crime simply 'happens' in the momentary situation, impulsive
C2 Labeling	– Self-rating and external rating as 'professional' criminal – Frequently in the society of criminals, shares their views
C3 Rational choice	– Cost-utility considerations: greater material wealth achieved more rapidly through crime; chance of being caught or receiving severe punishment low – Justification through own rules for life
C4 Rebellion against social disadvantage	– Less favorable living conditions and opportunities than others – Competence in dealing with penal control institutions – Self-responsible activity for revenge of protest – Disagrees with social norms and values
C5 Relative deprivation	– Unemployment and real financial problems – Boredom, few opportunities to meaningfully design leisure time
C6 Lower-class culture	– Aggression – Low social class – Talked into things by friends – Involvement of alcohol in committing crimes
C7 Sensation seeking	– Desire for adventure, search for sensation – Fascination with wrong-doing, favorable opportunities – Criminal models
R1 Early signs of antisocial development	– Predelinquent behaviors such as truancy, running away from home – Disturbances and problems in training and work – Borderline psychological problems – Disturbances and problems in parents
R2 Lack of motivation and volition	– No desire and motivation to change life-style – Does not accept the social system of norms and achievement – Irritable, insincere – Lack of response to educational measures
R3 Unemployment – low income	– Unemployed, low income, living on welfare, high debts
R4 Long history of deviance	– Delinquent at early age, high number of prior offenses – Criminal parents – Alcohol/drug problems, personality disorders and other psychological disorders
R5 Lack of social support	– Disturbed or nonexistent partnerships and family relationships – Little support from other reference persons either – Alcohol/drug abuse and effects on social relationships
R6 Lack of improvement during imprisonment	– Few excursions/vacation, no remission – Negative ratings from professionals – Judged to be a habitual criminal
R7 Inability to make commitments	– Inability to make commitments – Unfavorable childrearing style: spoiling, privations, hard punishment – Disturbances in partnership/marriage, large age difference bw. partners
R8 Differential associations	– Positive evaluation of deviant behavior – Majority of contacts with criminal friends – Lack of (other) leisure-time interests

The second questionnaire, the *Fragebogen zu Rückfallkorrelaten*, contained 89 items based on risk factors collected from empirical studies of recidivism. Respondents had to estimate the size of the relationship between each item and actual recidivism.

Answers to the questionnaires were subjected to factor analysis. This produced seven Crime (C) factors (Fragebogen zu Kriminalitätserklärungen) and eight Recidivism (R) factors (Fragebogen zu Rückfallkorrelaten) that explained 48% and 51% of the variance respectively. These factor analyses (principal-component analyses) are reported in detail in Averbeck (1993) and Averbeck & Lösel (in prep.). Table 1 illustrates the factors with either items or clear descriptions.

Table2: Analyses of Variance

Factors	Total	Group/Role[c]	Age[d]	Evaluation[a,d]	Attitude[b,d]
C1 Immature personality	**	(PRO≥PS≥PO≥L>PR≥)	(+)		
C2 Labeling	*	* PR≥PS≥PRO≥PO≥L			
C3 Rational choice	***	***PO>PR>PS≥L≥PRO			
C4 Rebellion against social disadv.	*	(*) PR>PO≥PRO≥PS≥L			(*) +
C5 Relative deprivation	*		(*) –		(*) –
C6 Lower-class culture				(*) –	
C7 Sensation seeking	(*)	* PR≥PS≥L≥PRO≥PO			
R1 Early signs of antisocial devel.	*				* –
R2 Lack of motivation and volition	(*)	* PO≥PRO≥L≥PS≥PR			
R3 Unemployment – low income	**	(PR>PO≥L≥PS≥PRO)	(*) –		
R4 Long history of deviance	*	(*) PS≥PR≥PRO≥L≥PO	** –		
R5 Lack of social support	(*)	(*) L≥PRO≥PS≥PO>PR			
R6 Lack of imp. during imprisonm.	***	(PR>PS≥PRO≥PO≥L)	(–)		* +
R7 Inability to make commitments	**	** PS≥PRO≥PR≥L≥PO	** +		
R8 Differential associations		(*) PS≥PRO≥PO≥PR≥L			

Note: Analyses of variance with simultaneous inclusion of main effect and covariates.

[a] Negative (lower scores) to positive (higher scores) evaluation of the current practice of juvenile reformatories.

[b] Disapproving, distrustful (lower scores) to benevolent, supportive (higher scores) attitude toward juvenile prisoners.

[c] As main effect: individual comparisons (t-tests). L: legal experts (reformatory governors, juvenile judges); PO: Prison officers; PS: Professional services (social workers, psychologists, teachers); PRO: Probation officers; PR: Prisoners. >: Significant higher scores (p<.1). ≥: Nonsignificant higher scores.

[d] As covariate: +: positive correlations; –: negative correlations: (*): p<.1; *: p<. 05; **: p<.01; ***: p<.001.

The evaluation of the current practice at juvenile reformatories had hardly any impact on the ratings of the importance of individual factors. Only for Factor C6 was there a trend indicating that respondents who gave a more positive evaluation of the reformatory tended to attribute little importance to lower-class culture.

However, as this trend was the only effect and there was no total effect for this factor, it may well have been a Type 1 error.

The second attitude variable, the attitude toward juvenile prisoners, showed significant relationships to the subjective theories of crime. The more benevolent and supportive the attitude of the respondents, the less they considered early signs of antisocial development (R1) to be important and the more they emphasized lack of improvement during imprisonment (R6). In addition, there was a trend toward greater emphasis on social disadvantage (C4) and less emphasis on relative deprivation (C5) among those with a benevolent and supportive attitude. Results were similar when the other variables were not partialled out in advance, that is, when viewing the simple correlations (see Averbeck, 1993).

The third covariate was age. There were highly significant relationships to Factors R4 and R7. Compared to younger respondents, older respondents placed less importance on the prior criminal history, but considered an inability to make social commitments to be more decisive. Unemployment and related aspects (C5, R3) tended to be emphasized more strongly by younger respondents. It was conceivable that these trends were only due to the much lower age of prisoners, and that – after weighting the values in the role-specific groups – they would disappear or even invert when only experts were considered. However, this was not confirmed by an analysis of variance (with simultaneous observation of the main effect and covariates) across expert groups alone. In contrast, the effect of age – in the same direction – tended to increase ($p<.05$).

Most effects (and trends) were found for the role-specific group distribution (C2, C3, C7, R2, R7; trends for C4, R4, R5, R8). Looked at individually, prison officers particularly emphasized the lack of motivation to change one's life-style. They also considered – even more than the prisoners – that crime was an economically based, rational decision. Alongside monetary reasons, the prisoners also placed more emphasis on social disadvantage than the other groups, whereas they considered a lack of support from reference persons to be less important. These groups can be discriminated clearly from the others in individual comparisons, whereas the contrasts are not so clear for other factors. The experts, particularly legal experts and prison officers, considered identification with the criminal role to be less important. Sensation-seeking received similar ratings; prison officers particularly rejected it. The two social-science-oriented groups of professional services and probation officers, but also the prisoners themselves, emphasized the prior criminal history. The social-science-oriented groups likewise placed more emphasis on inability to make social commitments and living in a criminal subculture.

So far, we have reported on differences in subjective theories of crime that can be traced back to specific variables. Table 2 also shows some overall effects that could not be classified clearly with the analyses of variance (C1, R3, R6). Removing the attitude variables from the analyses confirmed the suspicion that age effects were confounded with effects of role-specific group membership here. The role contrasts clarified that, in each case, the group of prisoners differed from the other groups. The negative direction (positive direction for C1) of the correlation with age might well have been due to the fact that the prisoners were by far the youngest group.

Closer observation and analysis revealed that differences in the ratings of the factor immature personality (C1) were due to its markedly lower importance for prisoners compared to experts. Thus, an analysis of variance without the prisoners showed neither significant main effects nor effects of group membership and age. How far differences between prisoners and experts were due to group membership or age (or a combination of the two) could not be ascertained in this study. Results were similar for R6: Prisoners considered lack of improvement during imprisonment to be highly important, whereas the experts assigned it less importance. For R3 – unemployment, low income – it was already confirmed above in an analysis of variance across the expert groups that there was a trend toward a negative relationship with age. The following observation showed that an additional effect of the role-specific group was also plausible. The (simple) correlation between the importance ratings of experts and their age was not particularly high at –.15. However, if the group was taken into account when computing this correlation, that is, the mean of the correlations within the four expert groups was used, it was much higher at –.25. This indicated an additional effect of group membership, at least for the various expert groups.

Clusters of Subjective Theories of Crime

To combine the subjective theories of crime into groups, a cluster analysis (agglomerative hierarchical clustering, Ward's method with squared Euclidean distances) was computed across the factor scores. Six clusters were selected on the basis of the heterogeneity curves (sum of squared error) and according to parsimony and internal consistence. The results are presented in Table 3.

The factor scores in Table 3 are scaled in terms of the total sample (M=0, SD=1). However, the six clusters did not just differ in the importance assigned to individual factors, but also in the mean importance (mean importance indicates the sum of the factor scores per person divided by the number of factors). That is, the clusters differ significantly in the importance assigned to all factors together. In order not to overemphasize these differences, each cluster will be described according to its distribution of mean importance. Marker factors of the cluster are those that differ from the average mean importance of the cluster by at least two standard deviations.

Cluster 1 summarized subjective theories of crime that particularly stressed the criminal's immature personality (C1), his childlike behavior. Envy and protest against social disadvantage (C4), in contrast, were not considered to be very important.

Table 3: Clusters of Subjective Theories of Crime

		ANO-VA	Cl. 1	Cl. 2	Cl. 3	Cl. 4	Cl. 5	Cl. 6
	N		35	10	16	17	6	26
Mean importance	M	***	.16	-.26	-.12	.38	-.09	-.27
	SD		.20	.26	.24	.24	.38	.20
Factors		M (according to cluster)						
C1 Immature personality		***	.80	-.37	-.86	-.13	.11	-.35
C2 Labeling		**	.01	.62	-.05	.55	-.46	-.48
C3 Rational choice		***	.14	-.68	-.42	.36	1.47	-.24
C4 Rebellion against social disadvantage		***	-.40	-.34	.63	.69	.41	-.26
C5 Relative deprivation		***	.42	-1.48	1.03	.02	-.90	-.44
C6 Lower-class culture		***	-.15	.46	-.23	1.12	-.22	-.51
C7 Sensation seeking		***	-.15	.46	-.23	1.12	-.22	-.51
R1 Early signs of antisocial development		***	.38	-.87	-.08	.03	.84	-.35
R2 Lack of motivation and volition		***	.38	-.87	-.08	.03	.84	-.35
R3 Unemployment – low income		***	.00	-1.12	.53	.87	-1.47	-.12
R4 Long history of deviance		(*)	.25	-.01	-.68	.10	.22	-.02
R5 Lack of social support		***	.21	-.21	-.67	.47	-1.43	.23
R6 Lack of improvement during imprisonment		***	-.23	.43	.17	1.13	.16	-.73
R7 Inability to make commitments		**	.27	.35	.42	-.09	-.76	-.53
R8 Differential associations		**	.36	.71	-.50	-.25	.00	-.28

ANOVA: Univariate analyses of variance without covariates.
Cl.: Cluster. (*) p<.1; * p<.05; ** p<.01; *** p<.001

Cluster 2 summarized everyday psychological ideas that particularly emphasized differential associations (R8) and identification with the role of the criminal (C2). This was accompanied by the explanation that crime resulted frequently from the "lure of the forbidden" and sensation-seeking (C7). Lack of improvement during imprisonment (R6) also played a fairly important role in these subjective theories of crime. In addition, a trend toward deficits in the ability to make and maintain relationships (R7) was emphasized. On the other hand, aspects of relative deprivation (C5), in particular, unemployment and low income (R3) were hardly ever offered as explanations. Predelinquent behavior and other signs of antisocial development (R1) as well as a lack of motivation for a legal life-style (R2) were likewise more in the background.

Cluster 3 contained subjective theories of crime that strongly emphasized explanations through actual social disadvantage including unemployment as well as insufficient money for leisure-time pursuits (C5, R3). This was accompanied by the idea that criminals may use these disadvantages as an excuse and express their envy or protest through criminal means (C4). Attention was also focused on signs of a trend toward an inability to make social commitments (R7). Far less emphasis was placed on immature personality (C1), prior criminal record (R4), and lack of social support from others (R5).

The subjective theories of crime in Cluster 4 emphasized not only the unfavorable behavior of the prisoner in the reformatory (R6) but also the function of crime in permitting adventure and testing limits (C7) – a more adolescent motive. Other frequent elements of explanation were high juvenile unemployment and low income (R3). Living in differential associations (R8) or immature personality (C1) were rarely used as explanations.

Cluster 5 summarized subjective theories of crime that focused strongly on personal decisions to commit crime based on cost-utility considerations (C3) as well as low motivation to adjust and strive toward legal life-styles (R2). Earlier delinquent behavior was also stressed (R1). In contrast, lack of social support (R5) or deprivation through unemployment or low income (C5, R3) were considered to play hardly any role in explaining juvenile delinquency.

The subjective theories of crime summarized in Cluster 6 emphasized explanations based on class-specific influences (C6); a social environment in which the criminal also received little social support from the family or other relationships (R5). Less importance was assigned to lack of improvement during imprisonment (R6).

Table 4: Groups of Respondents Per Cluster in the Six-cluster Solution

		L	PO	PS	PRO	PR	Sum
Cl. 1	Number	6	13	7	8	1	35
	% column	17.1	37.1	20.0	22.9	2.9	
	% row	46.2	39.4	41.2	42.1	3.6	31.8
Cl. 2	Number			5	4	1	10
	% column			50.0	40.0	10.0	
	% row			29.4	21.1	3.6	9.1
Cl. 3	Number	1	3		2	10	16
	% column	5.9	17.6	11.8		64.7	
	% row	7.7	9.1		10.5	35.7	14.5
Cl. 4	Number	1	3	2		11	17
	% column	5.9	17.6	11.8		64.7	
	% row	7.7	9.1	11.8		39.3	15.5
Cl. 5	Number		5			1	6
	% column		83.3			16.7	
	% row		15.2			3.6	5.5
Cl. 6	Number	5	9	3	5	4	26
	% column	19.2	34.6	11.5	19.2	15.4	
	% row	38.5	27.3	17.6	26.3	14.3	23.6
Sum	Number	13	33	17	19	28	110
	% row	11.8	30.0	15.5	17.3	25.5	

L: Legal experts (reformatory governors, juvenile judges); PO: Prison officers; PS: Professional services (social workers, psychologists, teachers); PRO: Probation officers; PR: Prisoners. Cl.: Cluster.

Analyses of variance across cluster memberships with the simultaneous covariates age, evaluation, and attitudes (as in Table 2, though with cluster membership instead of role as main effect) showed a similar pattern to that in Table 2 (apart from the more frequent and stronger significances of cluster membership due to methodological artifacts). This raised the question regarding how far clustering and role interrelated, that is, how the role-specific groups were distributed across the clusters (see Table 4).

Table 4 shows that most of the prisoners (three quarters) held the subjective theories of crime summarized in Clusters 3 and 4, that is, ideas that offenders are frequently disadvantaged but not immature or mentally disturbed or that they seek sensation and do not improve during imprisonment. Experts mostly had other subjective theories that were hardly ever found among prisoners. This separation between prisoners and experts was confirmed when the dendogram of the cluster analysis was followed further: The next steps summarized Clusters 3 and 4 on one side and the remaining clusters, 1, 2, 5, and 6 on the other side. A good four fifths of the experts reported explanatory patterns in the latter cluster combination. Alongside the prisoners, only a notable portion of the prison officers were represented in the combination of Clusters 3 and 4.

The various expert groups could not be separated from one another as clearly as the separation between prisoners and experts (see Table 4). Cluster 5 – mostly explanations through cost-utility considerations and lack of motivation – was made up almost exclusively of prison officers. Subjective theories of crime in Cluster 2, that is, emphasis on a criminal subculture and identification with it, was represented mostly by members of the social-science-oriented groups. Explanatory patterns in Cluster 6 focusing on an unfavorable milieu and family relationships were reported most frequently by legal experts, but also prison officers and probation officers. Finally, the idea of an immature offender or one with a disturbed personality (Cluster 1) was found in almost equal proportions in all expert groups.

Discussion

This study investigates possible sources of the variability in subjective theories of crime. It shows that there are no significant relationships between positive or negative evaluation of the current practice in juvenile reformatories and respondents' ideas on the origins and persistence of juvenile delinquency. In contrast, the attitude toward juvenile delinquents has some effects on the type of everyday psychological explanation. Stigmatization of offenders and social disadvantages are emphasized by respondents who have a benevolent and supportive attitude toward the prisoners. A more disapproving, distrustful attitude is accompanied by emphasis on the labor market situation as well as prior delinquency, mental problems, and antisocial behavior in the offender. Carroll et al. (1987) have also found relations between authoritarian attitudes and internal, individual causal attributions.

Furnham and Henderson's (1983) finding that conservative voters consider failed education and socialization to be more significant than liberal and socialist voters do, whereas socialist voters place more emphasis on the consequences of an unjust society, also shows similarities with our findings.

Respondent's age is also studied. Older respondents place more emphasis on the young prisoner's inability to make commitments and immature personality. Younger respondents place much more emphasis on the possible prior history of crime as well as financial problems, unemployment, and restricted leisure-time opportunities. Other studies have produced similar findings (Flanagan, 1987; Furnham & Henderson, 1983; Hollin & Howells, 1987) indicating that older persons emphasize aspects of emotional instability or a lack of basic values whereas younger persons emphasize unemployment and related problems.

In the present study, role-specific socialization has the greatest impact on subjective theories of crime. On the one hand, we can confirm that prisoners tend to make external causal attributions (see Goldstein, 1990; Henderson & Hewstone, 1984), whereas experts tend toward internal attributions (Saulnier & Perlman, 1981). On the other hand, we also find large differences between the various groups of experts. Prison officers' ideas are closest to those of the prisoners. They emphasize rational and economic considerations that lead to a decision in favor of crime. Likewise, they place more emphasis than other expert groups on the prisoners' insufficient motivation to adopt a legal life-style. Legal experts, that is, prison governors and juvenile judges, consider a lack of family support and sensation-seeking to be important aspects. The social-science-oriented groups of professional services and probation officers place more emphasis than other experts on a possible identification with the criminal role and living in a subculture that places a positive value on deviant behavior as well as on the inability to make commitments. Other studies have revealed similar findings (Ortet-Fabregat & Pérez, 1992; Reuterman & Cartwright, 1976). For example, Reuterman and Cartwright (1976) have reported that persons working in the justice system more frequently mention a lack of parental supervision as a cause of crime than respondents in schools and welfare and mental health institutions. The latter more frequently emphasize emotional and mental problems.

The particular aspects emphasized indicate that group membership measures something like role-specific socialization. The groups emphasize those aspects that they would choose – within their respective roles – in order to induce a change in the situation. Thus, prisoners are more interested in having external conditions changed than in changing themselves, whereas the expert groups focus more on the individual offender. In this respect, each of the various expert groups emphasizes aspects that are central to their daily work, their occupational task. For example, the social-science-oriented groups, whose tasks lie in the social, psychological, and educational field, emphasize social and psychological factors. In contrast, prison officers emphasize cost-utility considerations and the prisoners' insufficient willingness to adapt and make an effort. This corresponds to, for example, the function of their power of incarceration, which represents the socially imposed disadvantages of criminal activities, that is, the restrictions linked to the adjudication as well as the requirements to integrate into given structures, in this case, the reformatory.

It is not just analyses of variance that show the most effects for role-specific group membership; the clustering of subjective explanations according to their degree of similarity also reveals the great importance of these variables. The clusters mostly reflect the role-specific group distribution. (It can also be shown – by discriminant analysis – that the variability in the subjective theories of crime can be better represented by role-specific group membership than by the computational clustering; Averbeck, 1993). Future studies on subjective theories of crime should therefore focus on each respondent's relationship to the problem area of crime, their role-specific socialization. As, in the present study, age effects and role effects cannot always be separated clearly, a new inspection of the impact of age is just as necessary as an analysis of its intrinsic meaning, that is, whether the variable represents, for example, cohort effects or a certain progress in personal development.

The practical importance of subjective theories of crime has been discussed frequently. Furnham and Henderson (1983) have concluded that attitudes in the general public play a role in determining the acceptance of rehabilitation programs. Only programs that focus on aspects that the general public considers to be important are regarded as meaningful. Likewise, success and, in particular, the mutual support and cooperation of professional employees working on such intervention programs depends on their beliefs and the level of agreement between their ideas (Reuterman & Cartwright, 1976). When there are large differences between various professional groups, as repeatedly found, there is a lack of a common frame of reference for cooperative, integrated work. Thus, in the implementation of intervention measures, it is necessary to anticipate difficulties and even reciprocal hindrances (see, already, Dienstein, 1960; Lentz, 1969).

As in other organizations, a degree of consensus on central attitudes and perspectives is also important in reformatories if organizational goals are to be met. Thus, it would be worthwhile for all persons involved to first get to know the subjective theories of crime of their colleagues. In view of the great importance of role-specific socialization, care should be taken that possible role stereotypes are not reinforced when evaluating one's self as well as others, and especially in evaluating the other's anticipations of one's own role (see, also, Lösel & Bliesener, 1989; Lösel, Mey, & Molitor, 1988). After getting to know each individual and group-specific subjective theory of crime, a consensus on ideas should be worked out in order to actually implement measures.

References

Adelson, J., & Gallatin, J. (1983). The adolescent view of crime and justice. In D. S. Laufer & M. J. Day (Eds.), *Personality theory, moral development and criminal behavior* (pp. 373-384). Lexington, MA: Lexington Books.

Amelang, M. (1986). *Sozial abweichendes Verhalten: Entstehung – Verbreitung – Verhinderung.* Berlin: Springer.

Averbeck, M. (1993). *Subjektive Kriminalitätstheorien im Kontext des Jugendstrafvollzugs.* Unpublished doctoral dissertation, Friedrich-Alexander-Universität, Erlangen-Nürnberg.

Averbeck, M. & Lösel, F. (in prep.). *Subjektive Kriminalitätstheorien im Kontext des Jugendstrafvollzugs: Eine Fragebogenerhebung.*

Averbeck, M., & Lösel, F. (1994). Subjektive Theorien über Jugendkriminalität: Eine Interviewstudie im Justizsystem. In M. Steller, K.-P. Dahle, & M. Basqué (Eds.), *Straftäterbehandlung – Argumente für eine Revitalisierung in Forschung und Praxis* (pp. 213-226). Pfaffenweiler: Centaurus.

Averbeck, M., & Lösel, F. (1992). Subjective crime theories of young offenders and criminal justice officials. *International Journal of Psychology, 27* (3/4), 446.

Banks, C., Maloney, E., & Willcock, H. D. (1975). Public attitudes to crime and the penal system. *British Journal of Criminology, 15*, 228-240.

Bottenberg, E. H., & Gareis, B. (1987). Rückfall-Prognosen von Voll-zugsbediensteten im Jugendstrafvollzug – Von welchen Anzeichen gehen sie aus? *Zeitschrift für Strafvollzug und Straffälligenhilfe, 36*, 75-78.

Cann, A., Calhoun, L.G., & Selby, W. (1980). Attributions for delinquent behaviour: Impact of consensus and consistency information. *British Journal of Social and Clinical Psychology, 19*, 33-44.

Carroll, J. S., Perkowitz, W. T., Lurigio, A. J., & Weaver, F. M. (1987). Sentencing goals, causal attributions, ideology, and personality. *Journal of Personality and Social Psychology, 38*, 575-630.

Cullen, F. T., Clark, G. A., Cullen, J. B., & Mathers, R. A. (1985). Attribution, salience, and attitudes toward criminal sanctioning. *Criminal Justice and Behavior, 12*, 305-331.

Dienstein, W. (1960). Inter-professional differences in beliefs about the etiology of juvenile delinquency. *Journal of Criminal Law, Criminology, and Police Sciences, 51*, 79-80.

Fielding, N. G., & Fielding, J. (1991). Police Attitudes to crime and punishment: Certainties and dilemmas. *British Journal of Criminology, 31*, 39-53.

Flanagan, T. J. (1987). Change and influence in popular criminology: Public attributions of crime causation. *Journal of Criminal Justice, 15*, 231-243.

Furnham, A., & Henderson, M. (1983). Lay theories of delinquency. *European Journal of Social Psychology, 13*, 107-120.

Goldstein, A. P. (1990). *Delinquents on delinquency.* Campaign, IL: Research Press.

Gudjonsson, G. H. (1984). Attribution of blame for criminal acts and its relationship with personality. *Personality and Individual Differences, 5*, 53-58.

Hawkins, D. F. (1981). Causal attribution and the punishment for crime. *Deviant Behavior, 2*, 207-230.

Henderson, M., & Hewstone, M. (1984). Prison inmates' explanations for interpersonal violence: Accounts and attributions. *Journal of Consulting and Clinical Psychology, 52*, 789-794.

Hollin, C. R., & Howells, K. (1987). Lay explanations of delinquency: Global or offence-specific? *British Journal of Social Psychology, 26*, 203-210.

Jurik, N. C. (1985). Individual and organizational determinants of correctional officer attitudes toward inmates. *Criminology, 23*, 523-539.

Kennedy, D. B., & Homant, R. J. (1986). Security managers' attitudes toward locus of responsibility for crime. *Psychological Reports, 59*, 199-205.

Lamnek, S. (1990). *Theorien abweichenden Verhaltens* (4th ed.). München: Fink.

Lentz, W. R. (1969). Research note: Attitudinal barriers to delinquency control. *Criminologica, 7*, 68-75.

Lillyquist, M. J. (1980). *Understanding and changing criminal behavior.* Englewood Cliffs, NJ: Prentice-Hall.

Lösel, F. (1993). Kriminalitätstheorien, psychologische. In G. Kaiser, H.-J. Kerner, F. Sack, & H. Schellhoss (Eds.), *Kleines kriminologisches Wörterbuch* (3th ed., pp. 253-267). Heidelberg: Müller.

Lösel, F., & Bliesener, T. (1989). Psychology in prison: Role assessment and testing of an organizational model. In H. Wegener, F. Lösel, & J. Haisch (Eds.). *Criminal behavior in the justice system: Psychological perspectives* (pp. 419-439). New York: Springer.

Lösel, F., Mey, H.-G., & Molitor, A. (1988). Selbst- und Fremdwahrnehmung der Berufsrolle beim Strafvollzugspersonal. Untersuchungen zum Problem der Stereotypisierung. In G. Kaiser, H. Kury, & H.-J. Albrecht (Eds.), *Kriminologische Forschung in den 80er Jahren. Projektberichte aus der Bundesrepublik Deutschland* (Vol. 1, pp. 389-418). Freiburg: Max-Planck-Institut.

Melvin, K. B., Gramling, L. K., & Gardner, W.M. (1985). A scale to measure attitudes toward prisoners. *Criminal Justice and Behavior, 12*, 241-253.

Miller, J. (1980). Individual and occupational determinants of job satisfaction. *Work and Occupation, 7*, 337-366.

Ollenburger, J. C. (1986). Panel members' attitudes towards justice. *British Journal of Criminology, 26*, 372-384.

Ortet-Fabregat, G., & Pérez, J. (1992). An assessment of the attitudes towards crime among professionals in the criminal justice system. *British Journal of Criminology, 32*, 193-207.

Oswald, M. E. (1992). Justification and goals of punishment and the attribution of responsibility in judges. In F. Lösel, D. Bender, & T. Bliesener (Eds.), *Psychology and Law: International Perspectives*. Berlin, New York: Walter de Gruyter.

Reuterman, N. A., & Cartwright, D. S. (1976). Practitioners' views of delinquency causation – A consideration in comprehensive juvenile justice planning. *Criminal Justice and Behavior, 3*, 67-84.

Saulnier, K., & Perlman, D. (1981). The actor-observer bias is alive and well in Prison: A sequel to wells. *Personality and Social Psychology Bulletin, 7*, 559-564.

Silverman, M., Smith, L. G., Nelson, C., & Dembo, R. (1984). The perception of the elderly criminal when compared to adult and juvenile offenders. *Journal of Applied Gerontology, 3*, 97-104.

Turning Heroes into Villains: The Role of Unconscious Transference in Media Crime Reporting

Peter B. Ainsworth

Cases of mistaken identity and wrongful conviction are understandably worrying both for the Criminal Justice System and for society at large. Psychologists in both Europe and the U.S.A. have spent a great deal of time examining how and why these occur. (See for example Shepherd et al 1982; Loftus, 1979; Wells & Loftus, 1984; Wagenaar, 1988; Ross et al., 1994.) Many reasons for such cases have been found ranging from witness expectations, prompts, time delays, incorrect procedures, etc.

However there are some cases where incorrect identifications have resulted from the process of *unconscious transference*. This is the phenomenon in which a face is remembered as being familiar, but is incorrectly remembered as the face of the suspect. Through this process of unconscious transference an innocent bystander at the scene of a crime may thus be wrongly identified as the perpetrator. The witness correctly remembers that the face is familiar, associates it with the scene of the crime, but incorrectly recalls it as the face of the perpetrator.

The process was neatly illustrated in a case cited by Houts (1963). A railway booking clerk was held up at gunpoint and was later asked to attend an identity parade. He there picked out the suspect who was a local man. However, the accused was then able to provide a cast-iron alibi which the police accepted. When trying to explain the incorrect identification, the booking clerk claimed that the suspect's face looked familiar, and that was why he had picked him out. It later came to light that the suspect (a sailor from a local camp) had bought tickets from the clerk on a number of previous occasions. The clerk had thus recognised the person as familiar, but had then misclassified the face as that of the robber. Other examples have been provided by Loftus (1976), Brown Deffenbacher & Sturgill (1977) and Gudjonsson (1992) among others. However as Ross et al have noted recently:

> To date there are only a handful of studies on unconscious transference and the findings are mixed, providing weak and inconsistent support for the existence of unconscious transference. (Ross, Ceci, Dunning, & Toglia, 1994, p. 81.)

Whilst cases of unconscious transference only occasionally come to light, there is no objective way of knowing whether it is a more common occurrence. Some suspects who were wrongly identified but could not provide an alibi may at this moment be languishing in prison. It would be naive to presume that all miscarriages of justice are later rectified.

There are undoubtedly pressures on a witness to pick out *someone* from an identity parade. Despite the introduction of a caution, warning the witness that the "person who you saw may or may not be on the parade", the witness may understandably believe that the police would not bother to bring them to the police station unless they were pretty sure that they had the right suspect. If the witness is particularly nervous, this may also interfere with memory retrieval processes. (See Ainsworth & King, 1988.) Thus if the witness scans the parade and sees 10 faces, nine of which are unfamiliar and one which is familiar, they may well pick out the face that appears familiar. Perhaps this is not unlike the everyday memory problem where we recognise a face as familiar but cannot for the moment "place" it. This process often occurs where we see a person out of the usual context. A local television presenter may be recognised instantly when she appears on screen at her usual time-slot but identification would be much more difficult if she was encountered filling up her car at the local garage.

One way in which unconscious transference may occur is where the media show photofits or artists' impressions of suspects, or where crime reconstructions are staged using actors. The purpose of such reconstructions (such as those featured in Britain on *Crimewatch U.K.*) is said to be to "jog people's memories" and to provide new leads for the police to pursue. One potential problem with such reconstructions is that viewers may well remember the face of the actor who played the suspect, but may not remember the photofit picture of the real suspect. Alternatively features of the "new" face (i.e. of the actor) may well interfere with the original memory or lead to a new memory which blends together some features of the old face with some features of the new one. (See Ross et al., 1994.) There remains an interesting piece of research to be carried out to discover the number of occasions on which actors who play the part of suspects on Crimewatch U.K. are later identified as the real suspect by both members of the public, and police officers.

There may be similar problems of interference or unconscious transference when newspapers carry portraits of suspects alongside or near to pictures of non-suspects. This is the subject examined in this paper. It stems from a report in the *Manchester Metro News* dated March 12 1993. The story is titled "Sex Fiends Hunted" and describes a number of sex attacks in the Manchester area. The story also contains two pictures. The first of these is a photofit of a suspect (labelled "Sex Monster: Face of a Fiend"). The second is an actual photograph of a local man who rescued one female who was being attacked, and who may well have prevented serious injury to the victim. This photograph is labelled with the name of the man and the caption "Foiled Attacker".

This caption may in itself be interesting as it could have been interpreted in one of two different ways – he was an attacker who was himself foiled or he was someone who foiled an attack by someone else. It was the latter which was intended and this was made abundantly clear in the text.

Method

63 British students were recruited to take part in this study. 59 were Undergraduates and four Postgraduates. Over 90% of the subjects were non-psychology specialists. All subjects were told that they were to take part in a simple memory test. When subjects entered the experiment they were asked to read the article from the *Manchester Metro News*, and were told that they would later be asked a number of questions about the contents of the article. Each subject was given 5 minutes in which to study the material. At this stage, subjects were not informed that they would later be asked to try to identify the suspect whose face was shown in the article. At the end of the 5 minute learning period, subjects were given a distracter task for 1 minute and were then given a simple 10 part questionnaire asking about factual information which had appeared in the article. They were not at this stage asked any questions about the facial appearance of either the suspect or the intervener (hereinafter referred to as the "Good Samaritan").

One week later subjects were asked to view a photospread of 6 pictures and to say whether the suspect whose face had appeared in the original article was present. As would be the case with real-life identification attempts, subjects were warned that, "the person who you saw earlier may or may not be in the array and you should only make an identification if you are certain".

Subjects in the experiment were in fact randomly assigned to one of three groups:

Group A were shown an array of six photographs which had been cut from the *Manchester Metro News* but which did *not* contain the original suspect's picture nor that of the "Good Samaritan".

Group B were shown an array of six pictures which contained the real suspects's picture along with 5 foils.

Group C were shown an array of 6 pictures which contained 5 foils and the picture of the "Good Samaritan" which had appeared in the original article. The array did not contain the picture of the actual suspect.

Results

For the purposes of this paper only the results relating to identification accuracy are presented.

Table 1: Numbers in each group who failed to identify/identified suspect, foils and "Good Samaritan"

		Failed to pick out anyone	Picked out suspect	Picked out foil	Picked out "Good Samaritan"
Group A	N=21	14	n/a	7	n/a
Group B	N=21	8	8	5	n/a
Group C	N=21	7	n/a	4	10

Table 2: Number of subjects who picked from array x familiar/unfamiliar face presentation

	Unknown face presented (Group A)(N=21)	Familiar face presented (Groups B+C) (N=42)
Pick made	7	27
No pick made	14	15

Table 3: Number of subjects who picked/failed to pick when presented with suspect v. "Good Samaritan"

	"Good Samaritan" presented	Real suspect presented
Pick made	10	8
No pick made	11	13

Discussion

The results of this study provide a number of interesting findings. Firstly one third of Group A (who were shown an array which contained neither the suspect nor the "Good Samaritan") picked out a foil as the suspect. Although numbers were small, there did not appear to be a tendency to pick out any one particular foil, subjects choosing four of the six foils present.

Within Group B (who were shown an array which contained the suspect plus five foils, but not the "Good Samaritan") only eight (38%) correctly identified the real suspect. A further eight failed to pick out anyone while five (24%) picked out one of the foils in the array.

Within Group C (which contained the "Good Samaritan" plus 5 foils, but not the real suspect) seven subjects (33%) failed to identify anyone. A further 4 (19%) picked out one of the foils. However the most interesting finding is that 10 subjects (48%) picked out the "Good Samaritan" and identified him as the suspect in the case. This finding offers some support for the existence of unconscious transference in this case.

As can be seen from Table 2, the probability of a face being picked is much higher when one of the faces is familiar as opposed to when there is no familiar face. This difference was statistically significant. ($p<.05$)

Furthermore the probability of detecting a familiar face as the suspect is no different whether that familiar face is that of the actual suspect or that of the "Good Samaritan". ($p>.05$ i.e. there is no statistically significant difference between these two groups.)

In other words, and crucially, familiar faces tend to be chosen, but the familiar face of the real suspect is chosen no more often than the face of the previously presented "Good Samaritan" in this study.

Analysis of the data presented here is still at a preliminary stage, but the results give some cause for concern. Here, a man whose actions saved a victim from injury, was incorrectly identified as a suspect by almost 50% of subjects who were shown his photograph. This provides strong evidence for the existence of unconscious transference. In the absence of the real suspect, almost half of the subjects appeared to be picking out the person whose photograph was familiar, and incorrectly thinking of it as the picture of the suspect. Whilst this research was based on a newspaper article, the results are worrying for other cases. Suppose for example that the police arrested (and put on an I.D. parade) the wrong suspect, but one whose face was familiar in some way. If the results of this research are generalizable, then there is an increased chance that the (innocent) suspect would be picked out simply because of the familiarity of his face.

It must be acknowledged that the results of this study may in part be due to the particular conditions encountered. The fact that subjects were not warned in advance that they would be asked to identify someone, and that identification was attempted one week after viewing, may have contributed to the subjects' tendency to pick out the wrong person. However such conditions are not dissimilar to many real-life cases where witnesses are not warned in advance, and are called to an I.D. parade a week or more later. There are however certain other factors in this case which may have contributed to a high level of incorrect identifications. The fact that the article was headlined "Sex Fiends Hunted" and then contained two pictures, may have contributed to the confusion. As was noted earlier, the caption below one of the photographs ("Foiled Attacker") may have added to the confusion. Perhaps newspapers should be warned of the possible consequences of such reporting. In this case their desire to portray the bystander as a hero may in fact have branded him as a suspect in this case. Having identified that there are unique conditions in this study the findings are very much in line with the more traditional laboratory based studies described by Ross et al (1994).

Future research in this area will need to establish other circumstances in which unconscious transference may occur. Planned future variations of the current study will involve showing one group of subjects arrays which contain both the real suspect and the "Good Samaritan". This may reduce the number of incorrect identifications, and will test whether unconscious transference might still occur when the real target is also present. It would also be interesting to carry out what might be called the "reverse" unconscious transference experiment where subjects are asked to identify the "Good Samaritan" but are shown an array containing only the suspect's picture and 5 foils.

References

Ainsworth, P. B. & King, E. (1988). Witnesses perceptions of identification parades. In M. M. Gruneberg, P. E. Morris, & R. N. *Sykes, Practical Aspects of Memory: Current research and Issues.* Chichester: Wiley.

Brown, E., Deffenbacher, K., & Sturgill, W. (1977). Memory for faces and the circumstances of encounter. *Journal of Applied Psychology, 62*, 311-318.

Gudjonsson, G. (1992). *The Psychology of Interrogations, Confessions and Testimony.* Chichester: Wiley.

Houts, M (1963). *From Evidence to Guilt.* Springfield IL: Charles C Thomas.

Loftus, E.F. (1976). Unconscious transference. *Law & Psychology Review, 2*, 93-98.

Loftus, E.F. (1979). *Eyewitness Testimony*. Cambridge MA: Harvard University Press.

Ross, D. F., Ceci, S. J., Dunning, D., & Toglia, M. P. (1994). Unconscious transference and lineup identification: toward a memory blending approach. In D. F. Ross, J. D. Read, & M. P. Toglia (Eds.), *Adult Eyewitness Testimony*. Cambridge: Cambridge University Press.

Shepherd, J. W., Ellis, H. D., & Davies, G. M. (1982). *Identification Evidence: a Psychological Evaluation.* Aberdeen: Aberdeen University Press.

Wagenaar, W. (1988). *Identifying Ivan*. Hemel Hempstead: Harvester Wheatsheaf.

Wells, G. L. & Loftus, E. F. *Eyewitness Testimony: Psychological Perspectives*. Cambridge: Cambridge University Press.

Part 7
History and Perspectives of Law and Psychology

Comparing Legal Cultures: Difficulties in the Cross-Cultural Applicability of Psychological Research Results

Johannes F. Nijboer

Professional background

The concise statements in this paper must be viewed in the context of my professional background. As a lawyer through education, I have been working in the area of criminal law and other relevant fields for about twenty years now. At the moment I teach criminal law, criminal procedure, evidence, and comparative law in Leyden. Apart from that I serve as a judge in the Court of Appeal of Amsterdam (criminal section).

Purpose of the paper

This paper is meant as some sort of "warning" about the general applicability of psychological findings to the legal system. Modern psychological expertise, including forensic psychological expertise, is widely known within the Western world. Its scholars are used to working on an international level. The academic forum is internationally composed and in a certain way "globally" oriented.[1] As advisors, consultants, witnesses and theorists the forensic psychologist contributes to very different legal systems. In my experience they are often not aware of the limitations of what they are saying; sometimes it can not be applied outside the legal and/or professional province in which they usually work. This paper does not mean to discourage psychologists from working in the legal arena; on the contrary: it should serve as an incentive for close collaboration across national and disciplinary borders.

Summarised: Four general remarks which apply to most of the research in the field of law and psychology:

1. Psychological research is often related to 'single locus'-problems in the legal system;

---

1 This conference is a fine example.

2. It often focuses on individual behaviour, and individual tasks, rather than collective (group) behaviour and tasks;[2]
3. The researchers in this field often have a too restricted concept of the law in their minds;
4. 100 years of comparative legal studies has made legal scholars and practitioners cautious: the enormous differences between legal systems stand in the way of easy generalisations and direct applications.

Explanation

My argument consists of a combination of some general statements and a few examples, which demonstrate my point. I have chosen examples from criminal law.

Ad 1: Psychological research applied to legal problems usually means that it is applied to just one kind of problem. This is especially the case when we discuss experimental psychological research. "Rules" for a proper use of techniques of witness identification are only relevant for the very small group of cases where these cause problems. For the average case such rules are completely irrelevant.[3] Another example: During this conference we listen to statements about the impact of victimisation and the role of victims, after which conclusions are drawn in general terms about "crimes" or "the crime". Be careful: there are lots of (even very serious) crimes without victims![4] Recommendations that are based on the position or role of the victim are totally irrelevant in this area.

Basically there are three areas in the criminal law which are subject to involvement of psychologists. The kind of problems and the kind of questions the psychologist is asked are relatively characteristic. In the substantive law we can look for regularities in specific offences and specific offenders: typology of behaviour, typology of personality are the relevant issues. Modern forms are crime analysis and offender profiling – which lie close to classical criminological research. In the adjective or procedural law we can think of techniques (insights)

2 This applies to micro level (group crime, group decision making); meso level (organised crime, the court system) and macro level (criminality as a social phenomenon, the legal system).

3 Interestingly enough, psychologists who work in this area adopt their 'rules' as legal rules. However, there are too many of these rules for a comprehensive adoption. Imagine how a Code of Criminal Procedure would look like, if, for every technique in every field out of the over 100 fields of forensic expertise, each related to numbers of single locus-problems, the 'rules of good practice' were to be adopted! Apart from this: the various legal rules of evidence in the various jurisdictions serve as a methodological minimum rather than a methodological maximum.

4 Examples of such serious crimes: intentionally or through negligence causing high risks/dangers for the lives and security of people.

that can help develop better tools for investigation, improvement of proof taking and theories of proof (e.g. Wagenaar, 1993). Finally, in the area of sanctions and treatment we find the "original" forensic psychologist, who advises about the possibilities and perspectives of penalties or therapies for one accused.

Ad 2: A lot of research is based upon knowledge of individual characteristics and predispositions. This is interesting for the explanation of individual behaviour. However, criminality often exists as group behaviour or as interactions between people. To what degree is this taken into account? Another example: the individual decision making in evidentiary matters by a jury. How relevant is research of individual behaviour to the group process of decision making?

Ad 3: In some legal cultures lawyers only discuss black letter law and abstract normative concepts. This is different in most Common Law countries where the law in action is also included in the concept of law. Most psycho-logically educated scholars in this area take only one level of the law into account and are not aware of the discrepancy between what they perceive as the law and what lawyers perceive as the law. Psychologists, for instance, can come up with the thesis that the presumption of innocence is not observed by the police when they investigate a case, and they express their surprise. Lawyers are not surprised, except about what they see as the stupidity of these psychologists. Still, you might say these psychologists have a point as long as they are unaware of the deep rooted differences between normative and factual reasoning the lawyers are brought up with. The presumption of innocence to lawyers means no more than that definitive measures or sanctions can not be applied as long as the suspect has not been proven guilty as required by the law. More generally said: modern legal analysis of the law, especially the adjective law, distinguishes between three different levels (black letter law/law in the books; court approved variations/law made by the courts;[5] legal practice/law in action). Statements which are valid on one level are not necessarily valid on another. The presumption of innocence is not a valid descriptive statement on the level of legal practice.

Ad 4: The differences between legal systems, in structure and in culture, are numerous and substantial. Comparatists are aware of this after over 100 years of struggling within the field. They know how soon non-comparatists compare apples to pears. They know that you almost never find equivalents, but mostly just look-alikes. Some examples: the system of remedies in France is totally different from that of in England. The role of the expert witness in America is very much different from the role of an expert (not expert witness) in Germany. Some doctrines that are well known in continental systems cannot even be expressed in

---

5 In earlier times the Germans had typical "Professo-renrecht" (dogmatics) apart from court made law.

legal English (such as "concursus").[6] In comparative legal scholarship there have been many attempts to develop tools for comparison (families, models, systems). It is a difficult area and lawyers are often not aware of this. The same applies for psychologists. For psychiatrists it's even worse: in the USA there is a strong tendency to prevent psychiatrists giving an opinion as an expert witness about the "ultimate issues" (e. g. "guilty or not"). As a result, American forensic psychiatrists have developed different kinds of syndromes of which the "battered woman syndrome" is the best known. Legal systems are still national, forensic psychiatry is not: the syndromes are exported worldwide as concepts, also to jurisdictions where there is no need at all to resort to such complex concepts to avoid the barriers within the legal system there. The poor psychiatrists don't know...

Final remark

As said in the beginning, this paper does not aim to stop interdisciplinary work and exchange. The purpose of it is just to warn.

References

Crombag, H. F. M., et al. (1994). *Dubieuze zaken* (2nd ed.). Amsterdam.

Lösel, F., Bender, D, & Bliesener T. (1992). *Psychology and Law*. Berlin, New York: Walter de Gruyter.

Nijboer, J. F. (1994). *Een verkenning in het vergelijkend straf- en strafprocesrecht.* Arnhem.

Nijboer, J. F. (1995). *Strafrechtelijk bewijsrecht* (2nd ed.). Nijmegen.

Pradel, J. (1995). *Droit pénal comparé.* Paris.

Twining, W. L., & Stein, A. (1992). *Evidence and proof.* Aldershot.

Wagenaar, W. A., et al. (1993). *Anchored narratives*. Hemel Hempstead.

6 Recent example. My Ph.D. student Caroline Pelser asked a native English speaker who is also a Dutch lawyer to translate her summary on the decision of qualification of the proven fact. This subject (related to i.a. the 'concursus-doctrine') is important in French, Belgian, and Dutch law. The person who was asked to translate could not comply with the request; it was impossible to translate. However it turned out to be an easy task to translate it into legal French.

Recent Changes of the Hungarian Legal System and Their Psychological Impact

Endre Bócz

I have the complimentary task of informing you about the recent changes in the Hungarian legal system and their impact. It is obvious that this is a topic too complicated to be discussed in this paper, therefore I have to concentrate on those phenomena that I consider to be the most decisive. As a result, the following is only a subjective outline of the subject matter. You also have to bear in mind that: I am a public prosecutor; a lawyer, not a psychologist. Consequently, there might be some points in my reasoning where the psychological considerations are somewhat neglected.

1. *The changes in our legal system are the result of the changes that have occurred in the economic and political system of this country.*

The erosion of the economic system of "really existing socialism", – an economic system based on "socialist property" owned by the state or cooperatives and operated by centralised planning – had a long history in Hungary. Nevertheless, it was no sooner than 1989-1990 that the shift to the basis of private property, free enterprise, and market economy was declared.

It is obvious, there is a significant difference between *declaring* the establishment of a market-economy and *really establishing* one; the former had been done, the latter had only begun, but its completion will take many years.

The most important steps toward market economy were: the repeal of state-monopoly in foreign trade, the prohibitions and limitations that prevented or hindered individuals in establishing trading companies by owning means of production and by employing workers, the prescriptions for price-calculation and discontinuing the nearly unlimited financial support of state-owned enterprises. Simultaneously, the shift from one-party dictatorship to the democratic system with many parties and the "Rule of Law" was also declared; it implied the adoption of a number of fundamental legal acts on constitutional matters, the enactment of human rights into the Constitution and amending some Acts so that they be in accordance with the Constitution from a human rights point of view.

As a result the real processes of a developing market economy got to work in a wider extent and with them the shortages of the legal system as well as the effects and side-effects of the said processes became more and more obvious.

a) Due to the economic transformation many of the former state-owned enterprises and the cooperatives went bankrupt; hundreds of thousands of people lost their job. At the same time the governing principles of *labour l*aw had been changed; while in the former regime they gave preference to the employee protection, provided the trade unions with dominant influence in labour law cases and limited the rights of employers to discharge employees, the legal positions nowadays are much more balanced, or the opposite of the past.

b) In *civil law* the new legislation represents a shift in approach as well. Under "socialist civil law" the starting point was: the debtor, the tenant, or in civil litigation, the defendant – who were supposed to be "poor" – enjoyed increased protection against the creditor, the owner or the plaintiff, who were regarded "rich". These suppositions once might have some real basis but they had already lost it even by the 1960's.

c) Legal regulation concerning the *trade, commerce and banking*, etc. – otherwise underdeveloped during the old system – lost its object. The new set of respective acts was made in a hurry, mainly by adopting laws of other, more developed countries, without any experience. Due to the method, the urgency and the consequent hurry, there are a lot of shortages, contradictions and the lack of consistency seems to be characteristic.

d) When speaking of *public law* legislation of the transition, one has to keep in mind that the matters concerned have – as a rule – stronger political charge. That is why the enactment of European version of human rights into the Constitution was accompanied with heavy attacks on the limitations and confinements that had been applied on that rights by the old regime, without – or in stead of – discussing the limitations and restrictions that are necessary and therefore should be applied on them. Consequently many people had the impression that in the new democracy there would be no restriction at all.

In the years 1989-1990 a great amount of information was published and discussed in detail concerning the frame-up trials and other abuses under the old regime. As it is well known, many of them had resulted the victim's death. No wonder, in this atmosphere the Constitutional Court declared the death penalty unconstitutional. In the same period some offences and penal measures – which had been tightly, though not always correctly, connected to the old regime, like "publicly dangerous work-shyness", all the political offences, the indefinite term incarceration for certain groups of repeated recidivists etc. – were abolished. On the other hand series of new criminal offences were created to protect the new constitutional system and to regulate activity in the new economic environment.

e) The new system called for legislative changes also in *criminal procedural law*. The Code on Criminal Procedure was amended in order to strengthen the rights of defence. Some of the new rules of this sort – due to political atmosphere referred to concerning the constitutional legislation – provided the defence more rights than it has in any Western country, e.g. defence counsel was entitled to participate in police questioning of all witnesses. The rights of Police were cut down significantly. The use of secret informants, wire-tapping and other "secret service methods" had been prohibited for years even in criminal investigations, it was finally restituted only by the Act on Police of 1994.

In a nutshell, these were the most important legislative events of the transition period that – in my opinion – attracted public attention.

2. *It is necessary to take into consideration two further traits of the transition period before we examine the reactions.*

a) One of them is the question of crime and public security. By now it is commonplace in criminology that higher crime is the price to be paid by democratic societies for their freedom.

The number of criminal offences, reported to Police in this country used to be about 120 000 in the 1960's and had grown to 130 000 by the 1970's and to 180 000 by the 1980's; it was over 400 000 in 1992 and the following years. Though the majority of the offences were petty ones, there was a marked rise during the late 70's in the number of burglaries and robberies, which carried serious danger to public security. Later on, in the late 80's we were faced with organised gangs of burglars, car-thieves and now we have also racketeering and even kidnapping cases not to mention phenomena of gang-warfare.

There are two statements, both of them true: first, the crime in Hungary has significantly risen and the public security has markedly worsened. The second: the crime in Hungary has remained lower and public security is better than in Western countries of comparable size and character.

b) The other question that I think necessary to consider is the way the press deals with matters concerning crime, investigations, Police activity including cases of alleged Police abuses.

Under the old regime the press used to be a mouthpiece of the authorities. They published what the authorities wanted to be published and refrained from criticizing authorities even in cases when it was obvious there was wide room for critique. During the old system Policemen were subject to military jurisdiction in criminal proceedings and the disciplinary proceedings in Police forces had been qualified "official secret". No statistical data of this sort had ever been published. That is why the public did not know anything of the numbers and results of such proceedings; it was a widespread belief policemen were seldom – if ever – called to account for misbehaviour or even abuse.

At the very beginning of the transition – back in 1988 – there were two cases of police abuse that were widely discussed by the media; not only the complaints were published but the police officers involved as well as their superiors and military prosecutors were repeatedly interviewed by reporters. This made the impression – a false one, in my opinion – that it was the media alone that enforced criminal prosecution of the policemen involved. The media celebrated itself but those who were more familiar with the relationships within the Police knew well: cases like those ones had always been similarly handled; the only difference was the extreme severity of the sentences meted out in the cases in question. Anyway, police abuses since then had become favourite topic of newsmen and one may say any alleged police abuse-case will get wide publicity. This change in their publicity made the impression that their number or frequency would have grown.

3. *What was the reaction to these changes like?* I think we should not speak of a uniform and consequent reaction. The overwhelming majority in this country was convinced that marked changes in the economic and political system were necessary. Elements of the legislation we spoke of were overt signs of these changes and that was why people were happy to have political freedom, e.g. to have an Act on Companies that made legal to form, say, limited companies which they thought to be the first step towards wealth.

It is well known that the overwhelming majority of the Hungarian population had no practical experience with the market economy. Many of Hungarians had visited Western countries and so they had some shallow impressions; many of them had relatives or friends in Western countries and they knew that they were well-to-do compared with Hungarian living standards; many of them had information of the wages and salaries paid to employees of their occupation, trade or profession. Considering this sort of knowledge plus the rhetorics applied in the election campaign one can easily imagine what sort of expectations my fellow countrymen had fostered regarding the new system, and what shocking effects they had to endure.

Let us take some examples. Under the old system there was a permanent shortage of goods but all the state-owned enterprises were supported by the State itself (by the budget). As a result in a deal between an individual and an enterprise the consumer who paid an advance must – sooner or later – get either the goods purchased or the money he/she paid in advance; it was incomprehensible to get none of them on the grounds that the firm went bankrupt.

Now the private limited companies entered into the commerce but without state-backing. As it is well known, the idea behind limited companies is to make it possible for the contractor to separate that part of his/her fortune that he/she intends to risk and save the rest in case the business would not be successful.

We had a number of cases in the early 90's when hundreds and even thousands of consumers had entered business life establishing limited companies. In most cases the capital stock of these companies was only about HUF 1 million, whereas consumers had paid about HUF 500-800 thousand in advance to buy a car, only to learn later that the company went bankrupt and their money was lost. Quite often these "companies" were not even registered, or their way of doing business indicated that any deal with them carried enormous risk. In many cases the victims could have avoided material loss by taking a simple precaution like checking the company's legal existence or financial position, or (e.g. in case of pyramid-schemes) by thinking over the reality of the promised proceeds etc. Due to their blind trust in sign-boards, signatures and stamps tens of thousands of Hungarian citizens became easy pray for the predators who were at home in the labyrinth of commercial law. From the victims' point of view there is no use even in the offenders' eventual conviction; they have no hope of recovering their damages.

While the labyrinth of commercial law deprives some victims of the possibility of recovering their damages, it makes it possible to get millions at the expense of the state budget just by reclaiming the Value Added Tax.. There are some criminal cases that clearly show: this is a real possibility, there are rumours of further events that has not even been investigated and being aware of the weakness in capacity of the Taxation Office one has to admit: if the cases already cleared up and the ones that are only a matter of hearsay are put together, they will make up only a minor part of the offences that have already been committed.

Banking had been a branch of economy during the old regime which had its traditional and – when compared with that in modern market economy – simple techniques and methods. With the beginnings of market economy it found itself in a situation of great hunger for credits and shortage in money. No wonder that soon rumours of widespread corruption were heard, and though one can hardly find a handful of cases where bribery had been established I am inclined to believe that the convictions show only the tip of the iceberg.

To establish a market economy on the basis of private property requires the privatisation of the state owned enterprises; it is a task nobody has ever faced with in Hungary.

It is easy to understand that to sell a factory is a complicated deal even in a balanced situation; it should be much more complicated in a period of economic crisis in a country where there is no capital and where dozens of the same owner's factories are in sale. One has to consider also that the whole privatisation scheme from the very beginning, was looked at with political hostilities. People without proper models, skills or experience got to do a work which is very difficult in itself even from a purely professional point of view, in a situation, when – while being under the cross-fire of hostile political forces – they were expected to take into account besides the usual economic considerations the ones of economic and social policy. No wonder, in privatisation process nearly all the more significant contracts could be – and really were – questioned. To tell the truth one could find nearly in each of them blunders or at least occurrences that were suspicious: there had been something underhand and hostile political forces were quick to show suspicions that the whole of privatisation was imbued with corruption.

I am not going to say that all manifestations of market economy in Hungary are nothing but fraud, corruption and bribery. Of course, there are private enterprises that work properly, companies that do business honestly, credit operations that can not be questioned; I would say, the greater part of the business life is honest. The deals in privatisation – due to the complexity of the necessary considerations – may be the best possible ones even in case they seem to be reprehensible from one or two points of view. The problem is that on the surface there is no difference between a correct and an incorrect deal; some deals that apparently had been correct, turned out to be incorrect, and one can find people at any moment who feel hurt by the actual outcome and try to make capital by dropping hints of corruption.

The public is unfamiliar with the general mechanism of the system and feels disappointed in the results of the change when comparing them to their expectations. People are ready to believe these sort of rumours. I am convinced that it would not be a great help if each case involved was investigated in details – which is, in fact, impossible. In this atmosphere of general doubt the best possible result would be: “OK – in these cases there were nothing underhand. But there are other cases that we have not even thought of...”

Another feature of the shift to democracy was the opening of the frontiers. At the same period the socialist system had collapsed in the surrounding countries and what followed was the well known confusion in the former Soviet Ukraine, Soviet Russia and civil war in the former Yugoslavia. As a result large masses of refugees from Croatia, Serbia, and Bosnia appeared in Hungary together with the representatives of the so called “Russian Mafia”, “Ukrainian Mafia” and several groups dealing in illicit arms trafficking. None of them are fastidious in choosing methods to settle accounts – as we had already had opportunity to learn it.

The majority of the population was bewildered. They had experienced the collapse of the world around them that they were familiar with; they witnessed institutions that they had regarded firm and powerful go to nothing; values, they had respected turned out to be worthless; skills and knowledge they had believed reliable lost sense, points of orientation that used to serve for planning the whole of one’s life disappeared. Many of my fellow countrymen feel exposed to the effects of unidentified processes and powers without having possibility to influence his/her own future; they do not know how things work in this new world and cope with changes by the method of “trial and error”.

a) Among people in this situation the anguish, the fear of unidentified evil, is quite obvious. People in anguish are even unconsciously trying to find something they could regard as the source of the threatening danger.

In Hungary such an evil at hand is the crime. Crime has risen significantly. Quite new forms of crime have appeared. Besides, detailed accounts of criminal offences can be found in papers or seen on TV every day. The more bloody, the more hideous, cruel or unusual the offence is, the more the media focuses on it, exaggerating by this the sense of the fear induced by the offence itself.

This is an explanation, given by professor László Korinek, as a result of extensive research for the phenomenon, that the sense of public order and security in Hungarian population is markedly worse than it is justified by the extent and character of crime. In my view this explanation is correct.

b) Inadequate channelling of anguish leads to further consequences like intolerance in criminal law matters. Many people attributes the rise in crime to the abolishment of death penalty which they demand to be restored. It is a matter of common knowledge that the marginal deterrent effect of death penalty has never been demonstrated – not to mention international law obligations which make its eventual restoration in Hungary very expensive from a moral point of view.

c) Sentencing practice is also under constant criticism in spite of the fact that it is – when compared with sentencing practice of the surrounding and other European countries – not at all lenient.

4. *How these legislative changes were received by the staffs of the authorities involved?* I have already mentioned the number of offences known to the Police used to be about 120 thousand per year in the 1960's. All the authorities dealing with administration of criminal law – the Police, the prosecution service and the Court – had been designed to such crime, and they hardly adapted themselves by size to the increased scope of crime even in the 80's. The leadership of the socialist state had adhered to the Marxist theory crime and state withering away along with the development of socialism. The increase of crime was considered provisional only. In addition to this the public administration in wide meaning of the word – administration of justice included – was considered an "unproductive sector" where salaries were low, the technical equipment of the offices was out-of-date and no one cared about developing it.

As a result, by the middle of the 1980's the workload in Police, prosecution service and Courts were enormous, the prestige of these professions was very low and the replacement of staffs was nearly impossible. At the Budapest Prosecutor's Office we needed 30 young lawyers and there were 5-6 applicants. At the same time full-fledged prosecutors left the service for much higher salaries that they could easily get for less – and less responsible – work at state-owned enterprises and cooperatives. The same holds true for the judiciary, not to mention Police forces.

On the Eve of the transition period these processes increased partly as a result of the politically motivated rhetorics I referred to concerning the constitutional legislation; it had invited on an everyday level a behaviour to give the authorities a "political" kick even in cases of most common criminal offences.

However, the independence of Courts and judiciary was a leading slogan of that times; that's why Courts and judges as a rule, were left alone, but policemen and prosecutors were turned into scapegoats. Any convicted felon might claim having been innocent but brutalised by the Police, enforced by the torture to confess and framed up by a "Stalinist" prosecutor. Letters of this sort were readily published by papers and magazines without any reservation or doubt and the eventual official answers were published with comments like "dog doesn't eat dog".

Easy to understand that the overburdened, underpaid, poorly equipped and ceaselessly criticised machinery of the administration of criminal justice – first of all the police and the prosecution service – was provisionally demoralised. My young colleagues could hardly understand why they were called "Stalinist" and blamed of "framing up an innocent individual" for pickpocketing as they were born after Stalin's death, never had heard, told or even thought anything good of him and the actual defendant was a well-known pickpocket with a long record, who had been caught in act.

The problem was significantly relieved by self-organisation. At the Police Forces they organised the Independent Trade Union of Policemen, at the prosecution service the Association of Hungarian Prosecutors. According to the latter's statute no prosecutor of higher rank is eligible to any elected office in the Association. Allegations of the sort I referred to were investigated by an "ad hoc" commission of the Association whose answers were accepted.

At the Police there was an event which contributed to calming the waves: in early days of 1990 the former opposition was given access to proofs of abusive data collection about their political activities by the state security forces. These forces had been a separate branch of the Police. As a result of the scandal – the criminal and the uniformed branches of the Police Forces, which had always been pushed into the background by the State Security Branch, publicly condemned the action and by doing so, they had earned some sympathy: many people told "they are not working for the political establishment!"

Anyway, by the spring of 1990 it was clear that the former opposition would win at the elections and they realized they would need the loyalty of – among others – the machinery of administration of criminal justice. This country had learned bitter lessons of "revolutionary" changes in the 1940's and 1950's. The communist take-over of power was followed by discharging a large number of judges, prosecutors, officials of public administration – including police officers and detectives. Those discharged were replaced by untrained or poorly trained people who were considered talented and to be "the right men in the right place". For replacement discharged judges an prosecutors people without law degree and often high school education were appointed after completion a short special law course ("Judicial and Prosecutorial Academy"). These people were already in charge when the cases of 1956 were tried, but the lack of professional education of the appointees of the late 1940's and 1950's had been heavily criticised also in general. On the other hand it was obvious, there was no second set of professionals to replace those actually in charge, consequently replacement of all the judges, prosecutors and/or policemen by properly trained ones was beyond comprehension and by untrained ones was out of question.

So the attitude towards the actual personnel of authorities had changed. First the independence of the courts was praised for the judges' ability to make the best of their independence; even the past activity of the individual judges was not mentioned, and finally the Minister of Justice on behalf of the new government declared: they unreservedly trust in the Judiciary. The same trust in the Police was expressed by the new Minister of the Interior.

The prosecution service was to some extent a different story due to its constitutional position. Under the Constitution the Prosecutor's Office of the Hungarian Republic was independent of the government and subjected – via the Prosecutor General – to the Parliament alone. The said independence had been challenged by a Draft Constitution in 1988 and this idea was heavily attacked by prosecutors for fear of direct political influence. Anyway, the new government might feel: "This is not my Prosecutor's Office". However, by electing a Prosecutor General the new Parliament expressed some trust in this organisation as well.

By the middle of 1992 in all the organisations we speak of the revision of the chiefs of all levels had been completed; some of the chiefs, appointed during the old regime, were replaced by "new faces", others were confirmed in their positions and with this one of the causes, that had worried the officials, ceased to exist.

However, a number of reasons for policemen, prosecutors and judges to feel uneasy when facing with their tasks, still remained. One has to accept this worry when discovering how many legal rules have been made, changed or modified in the last 5 years, while a different approach to problems was also expected.

Police is still overburdened, underpaid, in short of personnel, first of all well-trained officers. Those on the service are exhausted and frustrated because of the frequently unjust criticism they are exposed to.

The international relations of Hungarian Police have significantly increased. Many police officers of different rank and level got opportunity to study the activity of Police Forces in other countries. As a result they have learned something about the interpretation of some rules governing Police behaviour in democratic societies and they feel their hands too tightly bound by the effective Hungarian regulations. On the other hand they experience the new forms of crime and the new style of criminals; the increase of violence, the increasing frequency of the use of firearms by felons, their own backwardness in technical level if compared with their Western colleagues, not to mention the criminals at home. Taking these circumstances – and the results they achieve – into consideration they expect more appreciation. The clearance rates and other indexes of effectiveness are – in international comparison – satisfactory or even good. But for reasons we have already discussed they are not appraised neither by the general public nor by the press, even in spite of the professional explanations that point out the merits and real values of Police-work. As a consequence, due to disappointment, low salaries, quantity of overtime work and the poor prospects of significant improvements in the near future there is a rather high rate of fluctuation.

Prosecutors and judges were equally poorly paid but in 1991 a new system of remuneration and promotion was enacted by the Parliament for them; this was an effective remedy – at least temporarily – to stop fluctuation and make these professions more appealing. Recently this effect of the system is in danger as the inflation was not compensated for in this year.

Members of judiciary as well as prosecutors and policemen are often uncertain in deciding legal questions that rise in connection with market economy processes. The greater half of judges and prosecutors as well as that of policemen are young people and everything I have told of lack of experience regarding the market-operations etc. holds true to them. Given the inconsistency of the legal rules and lack of experience regarding the practical processes that should be measured against these legal rules, the hesitation and the tendency to evade decision-making is quite obvious. The big case-load, the lack of experience and the shortage in well-trained specialists lead also to defects in investigations and to poorly prepared trials. As a result trials are often adjourned.

One has to mention: postponements and adjournments are also often necessary due to the fact that parties and witnesses frequently miss appearances before the court. This can be regarded as a sign of diminished respect to courts, or, in general, authorities.

Besides, those who commit "white collar crimes" are skilled in evading those rules of law, application of which is a hard problem for the officials. The more skilled the offender is, the harder problem will be the offender's – the defendant's – insisting he/she is well aware of the "business-practice" of "developed countries" and claiming, the method in question is not at all illegal; it is "everyday practice" in those countries; and officials here – who are going to stop him – are but stupid troublemakers, bureaucrats, who try to restore communism, etc.

Though allegations of this sort are not accepted at face value anymore, there's a doublefold problem. First, "a man from afar says what he wants to" – as the saying goes; the policeman, prosecutor or judge for lack of direct and personal experience does not know what to believe. In the background of any legal regulation there is always a system of written and unwritten rules of behaviour which either supports or weakens the effectiveness of the legal regulation and the knowledge of this system may help in interpretation of and finding one's way in it. But this system of norms does not yet exist in Hungary and officials don't know the existing systems of other countries. Second, to solve the problem by interpretation of law is not at all a simple task when one does not know all about the factual circumstances, including the motives, reasons and considerations behind the actions of the parties involved – that is: the work of the economic system. And further: some ways and methods that may be usual in a developed market economy in this country – where market economy structures and institutions are hardly present – may serve as a pure camouflage for corruption or any sort of property offences. However, to recognise which of the two the case is requires thorough knowledge of the relationships in real life and the reasons behind the legal rules; to obtain all the knowledge necessary needs time and practice; just what we are short of.

In some cases the officials feel uncertain in front of the parties because of lack of practical knowledge concerning the relevant real processes and they try to evade deciding. As a result the proceeding takes longer; but there are other cases which will get tried later because of the continuation of the postponed trial, and so on, and so on. And so the backlog grows. The official feels guilty for prolonging proceedings; and for having a bad conscience, he/she does not take severe measure against participants of proceedings who fail to appear or to act in proper time and by doing so they hinder the procedure. This practice have led to further erosion of the respect to authorities – including courts – in general. The length of proceedings in civil litigation is in a period of high – about 30% – inflation hardly bearable for someone who wants to make money by means of the money claimed. That is why cases of fist-law occur more frequently, promoting again the further erosion of respect to authorities and – eventually – increasing the number of untried criminal cases, and we are at the backlog again. And with this the circle is closed.

The knowledge of the backlog and the implications listed here are felt oppressive by officials involved and this has its impact on their work and even on their behaviour; that is an other case.

Surely, my home country is in a very delicate and difficult situation which has a special projection when examined from the point of view of crime and criminal justice; and further on, the problems arising here are differently reflected by the public in general, by the participants of the proceedings and by the officials. Anyway, the last ones – as I see it – are over of the most troublesome period of the transition. They are not demoralised any longer; they are step-by-step getting used to being criticised by the media. There are efforts made to cope with the backlog and projects to relieve case-load to a normal level. The theoretical understanding of the new system's work improves every day along with the experience that accumulates by each solved case. So I hope one day we can experience in this country what is a policeman's, a prosecutor's or a judge's normal state of mind while doing his/her normal, everyday job. And – partly as a result of that state of affairs – perhaps we shall find remedy for the anguish of the public as well.

The Effects of the Guarantee System of Human Rights and Legality on the Delinquents

György Vókó

Execution of penal law measurements taken in the course of impeachment of the criminal procedure in its broadest sense, and the connected tasks, make up part of the fight against criminality.

Penal impeachment is implemented for offences implying the greatest danger for the society, therefore issues of efficiency and of legality are raised in the sharpest way in this field. For the sake of other people, and of the whole society, delinquents have to be impeached, however penal sanctions inflicted upon them by the court, and also enforcement actions against them should be carried out in a lawful manner, which satisfies the requirement of the society.

We are speaking about strictly connected stages of the criminal proceedings, neglect the role of any – including that of penalty execution –, as well as the loosening their connection, may prejudice the efficiency of other stages and the whole procedure. What use is a successful and quick investigation, a correct trial and a fair sentence, if the inflicted punishment is not administered correctly and the condemned gains no positive influence from serving his sentence, and is not aided in adapting himself to the society?

Efficiency of a punishment, or that of a penal measurement, depends on the quality of the law enforcement agencies' activities, including their ability to implement the newest scientific results – among them the newest psychological methods and means – under the prevailing statutory conditions. There may be a contradiction between the actual legal prescriptions and the applied new scientific attainments, which has to be resolved through an approach from both sides. The legal environment is changing slowly due to its nature. Development has always been breaking its limits, changing it, such that it could serve again the development. During this progression it is necessary to consider the conventions on human rights, the recommendations supporting their implementation, and the individual decisions of the international organisations' competent organs.

Basic principles of the criminal jurisprudence's branches, such as the penalty enforcement law, and the theory of criminal psychology, agree, that a greater attention must be paid to the delinquent, instead of to the crime itself in the enforcement stage of the penal impeachment. Though, when analysing the actual penalty and its enforcement, differences are increasingly emphasised. In consideration of the fact, that it goes about limitation of basic rights – even if enforced by the state itself, based on the statute – an extensive protection against eventual abuse is to be ensured. Increased importance of the personal rights and generally speaking that of the human rights demands it. This has also conveyed the requirement to reassess judgement of the delinquent.

Changes coming up in the legal status of the subject through his conviction – that is through the lawful limitation of his civil rights by a sentence of the court – are not of absolute character, the convicted does not become a wholly outlawed person; he is not an object, but a subject of the penal enforcement, vested with certain rights and obligations while serving his sentence. legal status of the sentenced expresses the substance of the whole penal enforcement system. Acknowledging the rights of the prisoner is a sine qua non precondition. The starting point of all actions is to try to reintegrate him into the society. A perfect harmony between the provisions concerning legal status of the sentenced reflect substantial characteristics of the penalty enforcement system. The intention of punishment may only be established through ensuring rights of the sentenced and steadily insisting upon fulfilling of his obligations which are imposed in a sensitive way and measured to the requirements of efficiency. One of the prerequisites of the punishment's efficiency consists of excluding or reducing all negative effects pertaining to the punishment. Therefore, civil rights may only be limited to the indispensable extent, and this abridgement may not go over the boundaries necessarily required for a righteous enforcement of the sentence. For example, the following provision introduced by the Act XXXII. of the year 1993 may be cited from the prevailing Hungarian law: "Human dignity of the sentenced has to be respected; it is not allowed... to try on him medical experiment or scientific research or test without his agreement." [Penal Code, Article 21, paragraph (1)]. This prohibition also includes psychological experiments.

Those serving their sentences are only restricted in exercising certain rights, that is they do have rights, which are no favours.

The only way of the future is to respect in a human not only the individual, but also our fellow-creature. Protection and respect of the human – both as delinquent and offended – should be in the centre of the conception and structure of the penalty enforcement, allowing the deduction of his freedom's limits. Anyone may exercise his freedom and require respect from others to the same extent, as long as he does not offend the same and equally respectable freedom and rights of his fellow-creatures.

The intentions of punishment are to be formulated under consideration of man – both as individual and social entity. It is not to be tolerated, that infringement of rules remain without consequences, and limits of freedom and protection spheres upset by this action are to be re-established quickly and publicly for the sake of efficiency. Besides justice (as measure and instrument of establishing and maintaining safety and peace among humans having equal dignity and liberty), the punishment should have both short term and long term purposes.

Act XXXII. of the year 1993, modifying the legal regulation of law enforcement in Hungary, reflects the increased value of freedom – also confirmed by our socio-psychological assessment report of the year 1989 – manifested in the requirement, that only factual loss of liberty should constitute the true sense of confinement, as the form of punishment having a central role both within the law and penalty enforcement system and within the field of interest of domestic and foreign researchers. [After prolonged research, many experts have already supposed – on the base of the social costs of criminality (salaries of policemen etc., prisons, damages caused to the victim, costs of prevention, justice, dread of the society etc.) – that investments in prisons would be less expensive for the society. Prisons have as much accommodation possibilities – when equipped with all facilities allowing humane treatment, including psychological means – for the delinquents deserving it – as the amount of damages caused by them to the society and the costs of the prevention.] The European model can be adapted in consideration of the national properties by the use of cost saving but effective methods.

According to our recent assessments, increasing trend of recidivism is produced by habitual delinquents. Effective means for handling this "hard core" should be elaborated. Disadvantageous social conditions, erroneous socialization, personality disorders, and low education are well-known factors.

Special categories exist within the enforcement of imprisonment punishments: juveniles, young adults (aged between 18 and 25), women, therapeutic-educational groups, transitory groups before release, and foreigners. They are regulated by special, lightened prescriptions, partly motivated by the personality of the convicted of these categories, partly for serving a more effective re-socialisation.

There are allowances and aggravations with respect to humanism, which can be obtained during imprisonment. Application of lenient enforcement rules does not mean commutation to a lower degree of penalty, but it is an allowance within the given degree. As it was demonstrated from the practice, it was a mistake to neglect definition of the earliest possible date of application in the statute.

Demand for ensuring civil and human rights is the most accentuated in the fields where the state can restrict these rights in the strongest way during enforcement of the penal sanctions. Protection of the society from the delinquents must be taken into consideration, however the delinquent must also be protected against the rage of society, and against eventual arbitrary procedures of some swerved members of the authorities. Unlawful enforcement activities do not generate respect for the statue of the state, and of course, they do not suit the requirements of a constitutional state. The most important of the expectations towards the activity of the jurisdictional and penalty enforcement authorities, and also the highest value of their activity, is the observance of legality. Countries with sometimes quite different legal and institutional systems, established during their history, are equal in their striving to legality. Infringement of law may obstruct assertion of the state's penalty claim and, at the same time, they can inflict disadvantages beyond the purpose of the punishment to the person under the effect of enforcement.

This was the reason in most countries of the world the particular institution of the Prosecution's supervision of legality developed. Its value was recognized throughout several centuries. This institution contributes to the protection and assertion of the rights of the prisoners and other persons suffering legal restrictions inflicted by a penal decision through exercising controls, inquiries, and other supervisory powers, ensuring maintenance of the state's retributive power within the legal frames.

In Hungary in 1989 during the time of change of regime, it had been included in the constitutional provisions, that the supervision of legality belongs to the competency of the prosecution, this being one of the most important guarantees of a constitutional state.

The basic principle accepted in 1978 by the UN, and recommended by the European Council of 1987, concerning imprisonment regulations, determined that the supervision of legality of the prisoners should be relegated to a legal authority, independent from the prison management. Also the 1990 resolution of the UN Criminal Prevention and Control Commission during its 11th session in Vienna prescribed that prosecutors should have an active role in the execution and supervision of the decision of the court; they should pay great attention to any abuse of authority or grave violation of the human rights.

Supervision of the legality of penalty enforcement requires regular controls, inquiries, and authority over legal procedures. For example, in Hungary the prosecutor may order to any law enforcement agency to immediately stop an unlawful condition, and the law enforcement agency is bound to fulfil this order, and has the right to submit an appeal to the higher prosecutor, and no power to delay the actions. It also requires the authority to make propositions to any criminal investigation, jurisdictional, executive, or judicial administrative authority. This differs basically from an internal control or a legal remedy authority in itself, The latter may and should be a court which is able to judge only the grievances of the prisoner (if he had possibility to protest) to the court, (unable to make more, as site inspections, inquiries, and investigations are incompatible with a judge's functions) and is not in the position to monitor or discover other violations because of its constitutional status.

Consequently, the prosecution's supervision of the legality of penalty enforcement – which is slightly different from the other prosecution functions, but at the same time allows the maintenance of strict co-operation – constitutes protection of the rights of subjects and prisoners. At the same time it also means the assertion of the state's punitive claims of protection of the society, and of the other subject, and of enforcing governmental and other organizations and persons to fulfil their obligations. Additionally it is a guarantee of the elimination any abuse of rights on both sides. Its aim consists in supporting the execution of penal decisions in a lawful way, but also in assisting – through discovering and preventing violations of law – the given punishment or penal measure fulfils its intended purpose. It also has a duty to co-ordinate and standardise practice of the organizations participating in the law enforcement, and belonging to different institutional and hierarchical systems under control of different ministries. Taking into consideration the above, its strengthening is highly justified in a constitutional state.

The prosecutor is present in every stage of the penal procedure, he may answer questions of the prisoners concerning any stage of the procedure and give them information about state of their affair, which may have a reassuring effect. In my experience, 80% of the claims and complaints of the prisoners are connected with the penal proceedings initiated against them. If the private interview between those responsible for supervision and the prisoners – allowing them to make complaints, petitions, declarations – is not held at least once a month or as necessary, a tension could be produced among prisoners.

The work of this external legal authority, independent from the executive organ, will continue to be indispensable and is supported by the international expectations. Both the criminal psychologist and the pedagogue examine the individual under penal impeachment through a procedure which constitutes the whole social, psychological, interconnecting system. Their expertise is also required by the legal supervisor, both in penalty enforcement issues and during investigation.

Besides the Prosecution's supervision of legality and the potential to appeal to the court, there is also a social control, and the right of the convicted – just like of any other human – to appeal to the ombudsman, and other international organisations. Obviously, the social control can not immediately solve serious legal issues connected with the penal or enforcement procedure or violations of law, but it has the possibility to forward the problems to the competent authorities. Its role mainly consists of strengthening the relation between the penitentiary institute, its neighbourhood, and in supporting integration of the convicted.

The court takes decisions in the affairs belonging to its realm of authority. In such affairs, any subject including the convicted may appeal to the court. Moreover, the convicted has the right to appeal directly to a judge experienced in law enforcement questions, expressly in the case of law enforcement problems itemised by the statute. The judge, schooled in law enforcement questions, decides about degree and duration of the detention, which is made indispensable, to ensure the appellate his rights against the decision. Hungary belong to those European countries, where the judge competent in law enforcement questions has a wide range of authority.

The ombudsman also constitutes an authority for receiving complaints in regards human rights, but exclusively in individual questions; he may examine such problems, but only if it is brought to his notice by the convicted. Should the procedure be in course, he has to wait till legal remedy possibilities are exhausted. He carries out control only as necessary, what constitutes no more than a supervision, and has only a slight preventive force, as he may only examine the individual injuries. Otherwise he may propose an inquiry or a legal remedy to the competent authority. The ombudsman may not – and in lack of special professional knowledge, methods and means can not – carry out comprehensive preventive, disclosing examinations. He does not frequently visit the examined organ, can not comprehend the whole of its function, and he is not present in the penal impeachment procedure. Still the overwhelming majority of the injuries may be derived from the penal impeachment procedure. Therefore the role of the ombudsman does not constitute a supervision of legality, but he serves as a forum for human rights. His role is usually considered as "intermediary", the legal protection offered by him as "additional" or "substitute" legal protection. His procedures do not have any legal consequences, rather are only of formal importance.

Summing up we may conclude that the ideal solution is: if the system of guarantees and controls surrounding the whole penal impeachment and penalty enforcement are as ample and varied as possible, then of these possibilities may contribute – from different standpoints, having different experiences, knowledge, competence and proceeding authorities – to the fulfilment of the requirement of constitutionality, legality, efficiency, and either of them may replace or substitute the other one. Without them both, the convicted and the law enforcement system would be more isolated from the society, and it would be impossible to ensure their lawful and efficient functioning.

Legal Psychology in Europe: Results of a Survey

Helmut Kury

Introduction

Legal psychology is considered one of the oldest disciplines of applied psychology – its origins can be traced back to the end of the last century. Earliest publications dealing with questions pertaining to the psychological background of crimes even date back to the late 18th century – at that time there did not yet exist a discipline such as academic psychology (cf. e.g. v. Eckartshausen, 1791; Schaumann, 1792; Muench, 1799; cf. also Gross, 1898). The importance of legal psychology has experienced ups and downs during its more than 100-year old history, but it has definitely increased within the last years – at least in several western countries. Legal psychology has boomed in particular during the last 20 years. This applies to the USA as well as to a number of Western European countries. Before 1973 only a few psychological institutes offered as much as one course in legal psychology, whereas by 1982, merely nine years later, one fourth of the graduate programs in psychology offered at least one such course. Meanwhile, numerous programs have started offering advanced courses. "Yet this short period of less than 20 years has been a dramatic level of activity" (Diamond, 1992, p. V). According to Weiner and Hess (1987, p. XI), "forensic psychology has become a rapidly emerging professional specialty". Bartol and Bartol (1987, p. 17) even speak of a "literature and research explosion in all areas of Forensic Psychology".

Reference to this explosion of activities is generally made with respect to the USA and, regarding Europe, with respect to England, the Netherlands and Germany. Particularly in Germany, at least in the former FRG, the importance of legal psychology has experienced a noticeable increase in the last years both in the fields of research and practical application (Lösel, 1989). Groups of psychologists concerned with expert opinions in penal and family court matters (credibility as well as child custody and the right of access, respectively) have been existing for years (cf. Arntzen, 1994; Fabian and Wetzels, 1991). Particularly, changes in the divorce laws contributed to the distinct increase in the practical application of legal psychology in the domain of family legislation (the welfare of the child as the decisive criterion of child custody and the right of access).

In spite of the positive development in legal psychology, we ought not to forget that this science still constitutes a borderland of psychology – its position has become more firm within the last years, though. As mentioned above, reference to the increased importance of this science is generally made with respect to few Western European countries and particularly to the USA. We know little or in fact even nothing of the situation of legal psychology in France, Spain or Italy, a fact resulting from language barriers. We have still less information on its situation in the Eastern European countries (in this context cf. Lösel et al., 1992). On this background we decided to conduct a survey on the situation of legal psychology in a number of European countries, focusing in particular on the Eastern European countries.

Survey on the situation of legal psychology in Europe

On the basis of a fully standardized questionnaire we conducted the first survey on the situation of legal psychology in individual European countries early in 1994. Early in 1995, prompted by questions raised by the results of this survey, we decided to carry out a second poll again based on a standardized inventory. While planning this study, we were aware of the considerable difficulties it might raise. To begin with, we had difficulties in finding well-informed legal psychologists in the individual countries – in particular in Eastern Europe. The study was conducted on the basis of a fully standardized questionnaire in English. In order to rule out possible misunderstandings on the part of the respondents due to a lacking knowledge of English, we had to check up on a number of answers. A number of respondents gave their answers in their native languages. Owing to the fact that the Max Planck Institute of Foreign and International Criminal Law employs scientists who are conversant with the language of the country they specialize in and the presence of guests from the individual countries – particularly from Eastern Europe – we were able to examine the data and take them into account in our study.

We also ought to bear in mind that the individual countries differ with respect to their legal systems, a fact rendering extremely difficult an international comparison. On this background, our two studies, which we intend to continue, can give but a first impression of the situation of legal psychology in Europe. 14 Western European (Austria, Belgium, Cyprus, Finland, France, Germany, Greece, Ireland, Italy, Luxemburg, Portugal, Spain, Switzerland and Turkey) and 9 Eastern European countries (Bulgaria, Croatia, the Czech Republic, Estonia, Hungary, Lithuania, Poland, the Slovakian Republic and Slovenia) participated in the investigations. In the following we shall report a number of first results, focusing particularly on the second survey conducted early in 1995 which furnished more differentiated and up-to-date results and contains also the essential data derived from the first survey.

Essential results of both surveys

Considerable differences in training in legal psychology were found to exist between the individual countries, in particular between the countries of Eastern and Western Europe (cf. Tables 1a, 1b and 2). In France, a number of universities offer courses in legal psychology, which, however, are for physicians only as a rule. There is an increasing need for training in legal psychology, particularly on the part of psychologists, jurists and social workers. Austria offers training in legal psychology on a comparatively low level. At the university level, only a few courses in this discipline are offered in this country. In the meantime, an additional training program offered by the professional association has been discontinued. In Portugal, training in legal psychology has existed since 1991, at least plans for courses in this discipline exist on paper so far. A number of universities have apparently announced the introduction of training courses, which, has not yet been realized. In Finland, courses in legal psychology are offered only irregularly. Additional training in criminal psychology is only accessible to the 21 prison psychologists.

Denmark, Finland, Austria and Sweden take a rather sceptical view of the prospects for the situation of legal psychology. It is estimated to remain as it is at best, on the currently prevailing low level. Experts in France, the Netherlands, Portugal, Norway, Spain and also Germany, in contrast, predict a more or less clear increase for their countries.

Estimations regarding the current situation of research are rather sceptical as well. The central domains of research in legal psychology differ considerably. In Finland, e.g., research in this field is currently focussed on aggression within the family, imprisonment and victimology. As expected, clinical legal psychology constitutes the current focal concern of research in France. Projects are currently being conducted on the topics such as “Juveniles within the system of criminal law”, “Prognosis”, “Violence within the family”, “The police”.

In Germany, no less than 18 psychological university institutes, approximately one third of all institutes, offer courses in legal psychology. Simultaneously they offer to draw up legal-psychological expert reports for the courts. 63% of the German university institutes of psychology are engaged in research in legal psychology. The general trend in legal psychology is clearly positive, at least as far as the West German universities are concerned. On the whole, university students are reported to be highly interested in training in legal psychology (cf. Kury 1994).

In Eastern Europe, in contrast, the situation is partly clearly different (cf. Table 2). We ought to bear in mind, however, that the disparities should not on any account be overinterpreted, as the case numbers are partly rather small. The results hence ought to be regarded as first indications only. Whereas legal psychologists in Western Europe are mainly trained at the universities, this is the case with only about one fifth of the Eastern European countries. In Eastern Europe training courses in legal psychology are apparently held in public institutions such as the prisons, and police facilities.

Table 1a: Legal Psychology, 2. Survey (beginning 1995)

	Tests[1]	Who orders the work of forensic psychologists (F.P.)[2]	Training: UT=university training; FT=further training programs	Main fields of activity[3]	F.P. N total (full-time, part-time, casual)	Organizations: official professional federation for psych.; N members of section; year of foundation	research: existing; financing; institutions; changes[4]
Western Europe							
Austria	I; IQ; NEU; PT; PROJ	J; PL; CD; L; $=	UT: only some seminars; FT: BÖP: stopped	P; PENL; FAML; RES; TR	170 (50, 70, 50)	yes, yes; 17-50, 1994	yes; public; yes;=
Belgium	I; IQ; NEU; PT; PROJ	J; (PROS); (PL); CD; L; $=	UT	PENL; FAML		yes, no	yes; public+ private; yes; +
Finland	I; (IQ); (NEU); PT; PROJ	J; (P); (PL); CD; (L); $=(+)	UT: special courses at university; FT: only for P. in prison	P; RES; TR	23 (21, –, 1-2)	yes; no: in planning	yes; project funding + individual grants; yes =
France	I; IQ; NEU; PT; PROJ	J; PROS; (PL); (CD); (L); $ — (penal —, civil ++)	UT; FT	(P); PENL; FAML	(-, 350, –)	yes; yes …; 1992-1993	yes; no specific programs; yes; +
Germany	I; IQ; (NEU); PT; PROJ; (PHYS)	J; PROS; (PL); (CD); L; $=(+)	UT; FT	P; PENL; FAML; RES; TR	1.500 (100, 400, 1.000)	yes; yes; 900 (BDP), 70 (DGPS); refounded 1978	yes; public; yes; +
Great Britain	I; IQ; NEU; PT	J; P; PROS; (PL); (CD); L; $=(+)	UT; FT	P; RES; TR; psychiatric hospitals	400	yes; yes; 400; 1978	yes; public + private
Greece	I; IQ; NEU; PHYS	J; P; PROS; L; $	UT	P		no	yes; public; …; +
Ireland	I; IQ; NEU; PT;	J; CD; L; $ +	UT; FT	P; PENL; FAML; RES	34 (9, –, 25)	yes; no	yes; public; yes;=
Italy	I; IQ; PROJ	J; CD; L; $=	UT	P; PENL; FAML; RES; TR		yes; yes	yes; public; yes
Luxemburg	I; IQ; NEU; PT; PROJ	J; PROS; CD; (L); $ ++		P; PENL; FAML	10 (3, –, 7)	yes; no	no; no; no;=
Portugal	I; IQ; PT; PROJ	J; PROS; PL; L; $=	UT	P; PENL; FAML; RES; TR	300 (300, –, –)	yes; yes; 70; 1989	yes; public; yes; +
Spain	I; IQ; PT; PROJ; PHYS	J; PROS; L; $=			40	yes; yes; 120 in Catalonia; 1988	yes; public; …; +
Switzerland	P[5]	$=		P[6]	40	yes; yes; 23; 1991	no; no; no;=
Turkey	I; IQ; NEU; PT; PROJ	J; P; PROS; PL; CD; L; $=	FT	P; PENL; TR	45 (45, –, –)	yes; yes; 40-50; 1972	yes; private; yes; +

Table 1b: Legal Psychology, 2. Survey (continued from Table 1a)

Eastern Europe							
Bulgaria	I; IQ; NEU; PT; PROJ; PHYS; LD	J; P; PROS; CD; L; $ +	UT; FT	P; PENL; FAML; RES; TR (police p., criminal investigation training)	80 (60, 20, –)	yes; no	yes; ...; +
Croatia	I; IQ; PT	J; PROS; $=		P; FAML; RES; TR; juvenile delinquency	45-50	yes; (no: sec. of penal P. till 1991);15-20 penal P.	yes; public; yes; –
Czech Republic	I; IQ; PT; PROJ	J; P; PROS; CD; $ +	FT		120 (80, –, –)	yes; yes; 120 (assoc.); 1993 (assoc.) 1968 (div.)	yes; public (very minor); yes; +
Estonia	I; IQ; PT; PROJ; PHYS	J; PROS; CD; L; $=	FT	P; PENL; RES; TR	7-8 (2, 2, 3-4)	yes; no	yes; public; yes; +
Hungary	I; IQ; (NEU); PT; PROJ; PHYS; LD only police	J; P; L; $=	FT	P; PENL; FAML; RES; TR	86 (15, –, 80)	yes; yes; 34; 1972	yes; public; yes;=
Lithua-nia	I; IQ; PT; PROJ	J; P; $ +		P; PENL; RES; TR	12 (10, –, 2)	yes; yes; 15; 1988	yes; ...; yes; +
Poland	I; IQ; NEU; PT; PROJ; (PHYS)	J; P; PROS; (PL, CD, L only by mediation of J); $ prisons ++, others		P; PENL; FAML; RES; TR	730 (530, 100, 100)	yes; yes; 250; 1990	yes; public + private; yes; + –
Russia					500		
Slovakia	I; IQ; NEU; PT; PROJ	J; P; PROS; L; $ –	UT; FT	P; PENL; FAML	120 (35, –, –)	yes; yes; 160; 1968	yes; ...; no; +
Slovenia	I; IQ; NEU; PT; PROJ	J; P; PROS; PL; CD; L; $ +		PENL; FAML; RES; TR	very small	yes; no (F.P. is included. in sec.of clinical P. which covers forensic issues)	yes; public; yes; +

[1] 1=interview/anamneses; IQ=IQ-tests; NEU=neuropsych. tests; PT=standardized personality tests; PROJ=projective personality tests; PHYS=physiological tests; LD=lie detection.

[2] J=judges; P=police; PROS=public prosecutors; PL=plaintiffs; CD=counsels for the defense; L=lawyers/solicitors; $=payment/fee in comparison to other psychologists;=means equally, + slightly better, ++ much better, – slightly worse, – much worse

[3] P=prisons; PENL=expert reports/penal law; FAML=expert reports/family law, civil law; RES=criminological/forensic-psych. research; TR=criminological/ forensic-psychological training.

[4] Changes in the past years concerning practice, training, research in forensic psychology;=means no changes, + increase, – decrease.

[5] When P. are involved within expert reports then only within psychometric tests, in addition to the expert report written by the psychiatrist in charge.

Table 2: Legal Psychology, 2. Survey – An Overview

		Western Europe	Eastern Europe
Training	university training	71%	22%
	further training programs	50%	56%
Main fields of activity	prisons	92%	88%
	expert reports: penal law	69%	88%
	expert reports: family law, civil law	62%	75%
	criminological/forensic-psychological research	54%	88%
	criminological/forensic-psychological training	54%	88%
Tests	interviews/anamneses	100%	100%
	IQ- tests	100%	100%
	neuropsy tests	77%	56%
	standardised personality tests	85%	100%
	projective personality tests	77%	89%
	psychological tests	31%	44%
	lie detection	0%	22%
Who orders the work of forensic psychologists	judges	100%	100%
	police	31%	78%
	public prosecutors	69%	78%
	plaintiffs	62%	11%
	counsels for the defense	77%	44%
	lawyers/solicitors	100%	56%
Payment/fee in comparison to other psychologists	equal	71%	44%
	slightly better	7%	44%
	much better	7%	
	slightly worse	7%	
	much worse	7%	11%
N.F.P. with inf.	about full-time, part-time, casual jobs=100%	~2450	~1040
	– with full- time jobs	~22%	~70%
	– with part- time jobs	~34%	~12%
	– with casual jobs	~44%	~18%
Official federation for psychologists		74%	100%
Section for F.P.		69%	55%
Existing research		80%	100%
Institutions of research		77%	89%

With respect to the main fields of activity we found that legal psychologists in Eastern Europe obviously focus on the domain of expert reports in penal law as well as on research and training in criminology and forensic psychology. Regarding the testing instruments employed in the drawing-up of expert reports, we found that neuropsychological test procedures are applied even less in Eastern Europe – obviously the considerable progress in this field of research has been adopted only rudimentarily so far –, whereas the psychological testing procedures used are mostly "classical" ones, partially including even lie detection, a procedure definitely not found in Western European countries. In all countries interviews, anamnesis, and intelligence tests constitute the standard inventory of legal-psychological examinations.

Additionally, the commissioning of legal psychologists was found to vary clearly from one country to another. As expected, legal psychologists in both Eastern and Western Europe act on behalf of the judges and frequently also on behalf of the public prosecutors. Whereas in the Eastern European countries the police frequently commission examinations from legal psychologists, this is rarely the case in Western Europe. In the West, on the other hand, legal psychologists are commissioned by the plaintiffs, the counsels for the defence or the lawyers/solicitors more often than in Eastern Europe. In approximately one half of the Eastern European countries legal psychologists are estimated to be paid more in comparison with psychologists on the whole, whereas three fourths of the Western European countries show no difference. The Eastern and Western European countries also differ with respect to the status of employment: whereas more than two thirds of the legal psychologists in Eastern Europe are employed on a full-time basis, the corresponding proportion equals approximately one fifth in Western Europe. In the West the majority of legal psychologists apparently work in this field on a part-time basis, only casually and without being permanently engaged as a rule. Approximately one half of the relevant professional associations in Eastern Europe have a special section of legal psychology, in contrast with approximately two thirds in Western Europe. In Eastern Europe the existence of research in the field of legal psychology and of relevant institutions is judged more favorably than in the West.

Discussion and summary

Our analysis furnishes a first and still very cursory survey of the situation of legal psychology in Europe. As expected, not all the countries exhibit the same – recurrently ascertained – positive trend in this discipline. Particularly in a number of Eastern European countries and also in several Western countries the course of development has stagnated or even taken a retrogressive turn. The situation in the Eastern countries is understandably connected with the political and economic developments which have taken place in the last years. Legal psychology, and in particular the branch of forensic psychology, also depend on the advancement and humanization of the law. In Germany, for example, reforms of the provisions governing criminal responsibility (§§ 20, 21 German Penal Code) and revisions of the divorce laws as a part of the family laws (the introduction of the term "welfare of the child" in connection with decisions pertaining to child custody and the right of access) have necessarily led to an increasing inclusion of psychological expert opinions in judicial decisions (Böttger et al., 1988; Kury, 1991). In a number of Eastern European countries this development in the field of law is still in its infancy.

Psychology for its part ought to become more aware of the broad spectrum of legal-psychological issues. Now as before, the relevant research focuses merely on few legal-psychological issues such as imprisonment and forensic expert reports.

Legal psychology as an essential part of applied psychology, requires a problem-oriented integration of findings and experiences furnished by all disciplines of basic psychological research. In many countries the number of psychologists occupied with legal psychology is on the rise and rightly so. Psychology is capable of making more fruitful contributions to a great deal more issues in the field of law and law applications, as well as criminology as is currently the case.

References

Arntzen, F. (1994). *Das Bochumer Institut für Gerichtspsychologie*. Unpublished manuscript. Bochum.

Bartol, C. R., & Bartol, A. M. (1987). History of forensic psychology. In J. B. Weiner, & A. K. Hess (Eds.), *Handbook of forensic psychology* (pp. 3-21). New York: Wiley.

Böttger, A., Kury, H., Kuznik, R., & Mertens, R. (1988). Kriterien der gutachterlichen Schuldfähigkeitsbeurteilung und ihr Einfluß auf die richterliche Entscheidung. In G. Kaiser, H. Kury, & H.-J. Albrecht (Eds.), *Kriminologische Forschung in den 80er Jahren* (pp. 323-373). Freiburg, 2 vols.

Diamond, S. S. (1992). Foreword. In D. K. Kagehiro, & W. S. Laufer (Eds.), *Handbook of psychology and law* (pp. V-IX). New York: Springer.

v. Eckartshausen, K. (1791). *Über die Notwendigkeit psychologischer Kenntnisse bey Beurtheilung der Verbrechen.* München.

Fabian, Th., & Wetzels, P. (1991). Zur gegenwärtigen Praxis von forensischen Psychologen und Psychologinnen: Ergebnisse einer Befragung. *Praxis der Forensischen Psychologie, 1*, 10-17.

Gross, H. (1898). *Criminalpsychologie.* Graz: Leuschner & Lubensky's.

Kury, H. (1991). Zur Begutachtung der Schuldfähigkeit: Ausgewählte Ergebnisse eines empirischen Forschungsprojektes. In R. Egg (Ed.), *Brennpunkte der Rechtspsychologie.* Polizei – Justiz – Drogen (pp. 331-350). Bonn: Forum.

Kury, H. (1994). *Zur Situation der Rechtspsychologie in den deutschsprachigen Ländern.* Unpubl. Manuscr. Freiburg.

Lösel, F. (1989). Zur neueren Enwicklung der Rechtspsychologie: Versuch einer Standortbestimmung. In W. Schönpflug (Ed.), *Bericht über den 36. Kongreß der Deutschen Gesellschaft für Psychologie in Berlin. Vol.2* (pp. 291-306). Göttingen.

Lösel, F., Bender, D., & Bliesener, T. (1992). International perspectives on psychology and law: An introduction. In F. Lösel, D. Bender, & T. Bliesener (Eds.), *Psychology and Law: International Perspectives* (pp. VII-XVII). Berlin, New York: Walter de Gruyter.

Muench, J. G. (1799). *Über den Einfluß der Criminalpsychologie auf ein System des Criminal-Rechts, auf menschliche Gesetze und Cultur der Verbrecher.* Nürnberg: Steinische Buchhandlung.

Schaumann, J. G. (1792). *Ideen einer Kriminalpsychologie.* Halle.

Weiner, J. B., & Hess, A. K. (Eds.) (1987). *Handbook of forensic psychology.* New York: Wiley.

Difficulties Experienced in Conducting Research in Forensic Psychology

Janet Clare Wilson and Elizabeth Noon

Introduction

From the first eyewitness memory researchers (Binet, 1900; Whipple, 1918). there has been criticism about making the eyewitness research directly applicable to the courtroom where it professes relevance (Wigmore, 1909). More recently, this issue has been termed "ecologically valid" research. However, the more ecologically valid research in child witness issues has become, the more the research has been conducted outside the laboratory. This may result in little control over most variables and the prospect that the results obtained will be only applicable to the time period and cultural group targeted by the experimenters. For example, Ebbinghaus conducted his memory tasks in 1885 yet his findings could be easily replicated today, the eyewitness research conducted by Stern (1939). was partially replicated fifty years later by Bringmann, Tyler, McAhren & Bringmann (1989), yet it is unlikely that recent courtroom research conducted on child witnesses will be easily replicated in the future (Davies & Noon, 1991: Goodman, Taub, Jones, England, Port, Ruby & Prado, 1992; Davies, Wilson, Mitchell & Milsom, 1995). The latter group of studies are subject to caveats in their conclusions due to difficulties in obtaining the data and generalisation of the findings may, at times, be difficult due to the specific nature of the legal system in the judiciary under examination, and due to the political climate under which the research was conducted.

This paper will describe some of the difficulties experienced when conducting research with child witness and liaising with police, social workers, and the legal profession. It will also briefly discuss the issue of experimental design, validity, reliability, and questionnaire and rating scale designs.

Experimental designs

When conducting research with the general public numerous problems in experimental design frequently arise. The main focus will be on non random sampling, low frequencies and questionnaire design.

Non random sampling Randomization of subjects ensures a representativeness of the population sample. However, it is rare for the researcher to have a totally random access to their sample population. For instance in the allocation of questionnaires – even if every person receives a questionnaire, response rates vary and those that do respond may present a biased view from the general population sampled. For example, in the research project conducted by Davies, Wilson, Mitchell & Milsom (1995). approximately 1,000 surveys were sent out to British social workers asking their opinions on the Criminal Justice Act (1991). yet only 117 were returned. The original mailing sample may not have been representative – and this non-representativeness would be amplified by the few returns. Furthermore, around the same time period, the National Society for the Prevention of Cruelty to Children (NSPCC). conducted a similar survey at their national conference and their results differed significantly from those of Davies et al. The NSPCC sample contained the opinions of 65 social workers with a response rate of approximately 56% (Westcott, 1994). This conference also had a very clear political agenda. It is therefore very difficult to decide if either surveys, or both, should be weighted too heavily.

A further problem causing the non-representativeness of the sample is also related to the co-operation of various bodies in aiding the research. Research on any criminal justice system requires the co-operation of numerous professional groups. For example, the judiciary and the law professions. Often the government departments responsible will not give unlimited access to such people, but instead will give the researcher a list of names of people who may be contacted for their opinion. These people are invariably pro the status quo or the government guidelines and thus may give another highly biased finding.

Questionnaire development

When asked a question (either verbally or in written form), the respondent has three options: to give an answer (that is, the respondent understands the question and therefore answers it), to give a response (that is, the respondent does not understand the question but answers it anyway), or to give no response. Open-ended questions allow the respondent to give any answer he or she would like (a task young children often find daunting). It also can limit the respondent as s/he does not know or understand exactly what it is that the interviewer is asking. Such question types can also be problematic to code as it requires the experimenter to develop elaborate coding of responses. For example, 10–20% of respondents may mention an issue which most feel strongly about, but because most failed to spontaneously mention it, the issue is attributed as being less relevant. Most questionnaires attempt to initially gauge what type of issues are important to the relevant study and then to include these in a closed question survey using either multiple choice or rating scales. It is commonplace for likert type rating scales to be used when rating witnesses behaviour in court (Goodman et al, 1992; Davies et al, 1995), yet such scales can be of limited usefulness. For example, rating anxiety as a seven point likert scale with "very relaxed" as one anchor and "very anxious" as the other can be problematic in courtroom ratings – nearly all witnesses are either anxious or highly anxious, thus skewing responses to one end of the scale. This skewing results in an inability to correlate extreme anxiety with any other factor. This dramatically reduces the usefulness of such a rating.

Low frequencies

When actual eyewitnesses are being tracked through the legal system, a long time period is required. Due to the related financial support required for such research, often sample sizes are small. For example, in the Davies et al, (1995). project there were 470 trials involving children and videotapes during the time period of the data collection (18 months). However, resources allowed the researchers to attend only 93 of those trials. This involved 150 children. If the general category of "all cases involving children" is used as the limiting factor, then there are numerous ways a child may be involved with a case (e.g., witness to murder, robber, witness to abuse, the victim of multiple types of abuse, one of multiple children, custody dispute, the defendant), yet the frequency of any one of these cases is likely to be low. However, the impact on the child of the court procedure is likely to differ depending on the type of case he or she is involved with. Thus, any analysis which puts all children together may well gloss over these differences and give a result which may not be indicative of any child's experience in court, yet treating them all as separate groups allows for little meaningful analysis due to very small group sizes.

Liaising with different professional groups

Often to get meaningful results one must obtain the co-operation of various professional groups. Each professional group operates in totally different than any other professional groups. For example in the UK there are 43 police forces, all police forces have a clear hierarchy associated with them and usually by contacting "middle management" they will help to conduct the research if they approve of it, there are 107 social work authorities in the UK, none of which map onto any police force area. Furthermore, social work, by its nature is non hierarchical and contacting team managers may help, but the system operates more at the individual level. Thus, in one given city, there may be one police force and five social services authorities to co-ordinate. The police force may agree to the research but only three local Social Services authorities.

This does not include the multitude of other professional groups, for example, one (or more). crown courts, multiple listings officers, a variety of judges and barristers, as well as the local pressure groups associated with the issue being examined. For example, in the area of children appearing in court the pressure groups in the UK include, NSPCC, BASPCAN, Victim Support, and Child Link.

The witnesses

It is a very sensitive issue contacting a child once he or she has appeared in court, as often the child (and family). do not wish to be reminded of their experience. A personal contact may not be appropriate and a questionnaire may seem impersonal, yet the view of the court user is necessary in any assessment of new legislation. In a recent survey conducted by the National Children's Homes (1994). they interviewed 200 children involved with the legal process, yet were unable to interview any more than two children who had actually appeared in court, due to the unwillingness of such children to come forward.

Conclusions

Although research is conducted into actual child witnesses attending court, it is fraught with difficulties. Balancing the interests (and validity) of the research with that of the justice system and the child can be extremely difficult. Furthermore, prejudicial issues, such as the representativeness of minority groups or children with disabilities, cannot be examined without larger samples and detailed analysis of the justice system. Even if large sample sizes could be obtained, the results may be applicable only to the country and time where they were collected.

References

Binet, A. (1900). *La Suggestibilite*. Paris: Schleicher.

Bringmann, M. W., Tyler, K. E., McAhren, P. E., & Bringmann, W. G. (1989). A successful and unsuccessful replication of William Stern's eyewitness research. *Perceptual and Motor Skills, 69*, 619-625.

Ebbinghaus, H. (1885/1964). *Memory: A contribution to experimental psychology.* New York: Dover.

Davies, G. M., & Noon, E. (1991). *An Evaluation of the Live Link for Child Witnesses.* London: Home Office.

Davies, G. M., Wilson, J. C., Mitchell, R., & Milsom, J. (1995). *Videotaping Children's Evidence: An Evaluation.* London: HMSO.

Goodman, G. S., Taub, E. P., Jones, D. P. H., England, P., Port, L. K., Rudy, L. & Prado, L. (1992). Testifying in criminal court: Emotional effects on child sexual assault victims. *Monographs of the Society for Research in Child Development, 57*, 5.

National Children's Homes (1994). *Messages from children: Children's evaluations of the professional response to child sexual abuse.* London: NCH Action for Children.

Stern, L. W. (1939). The psychology of testimony. *Journal of Abnormal and Social Psychology 34*, 3-20.

Westcott, H. (1994). *One year on: Concerns about the Memorandum of Good Practice.* London: NSPCC.

Whipple, G. M. (1918). The obtaining of information: Psychology of observation and report. *Psychological Bulletin, 15*, 217-248.

Wigmore, J. H.(1909). Professor Munsterberg and the psychology of testimony: being a report of the case of Cokestone v. Munsterberg. *Illinois Law Review, 3*, 399-445.

The Development of Hungarian Forensic Psychology

Márton Szegedi

The development of Hungarian legal psychology is inseparable from the general history of the country and the region. To understand this development we have to go back to the middle decades of the previous century. In 1848–49 Hungary made an attempt to gain independence from the Austrian Habsburg monarchy. The War of Independence was put down and 18 years of retaliation and hate followed before the Compromise of 1867 was achieved. It was only after this that the formerly rebellious Hungarians could focus their attention on building their own state, and capitalist development began. It has to be viewed in this context that Paul Ranschburg appeared on the scene at the end of the last century.

Paul Ranschburg graduated from the Medical University in 1894. While seeking his carrier he had been directed to the outstanding researchers of neurology of his time: Professor Laufenauer and Charles Schaffer. In the beginning he focused on the more strict scientific direction derived from the physiological basis created by Kraepelin, Ziehen, Wundt and Sommer. He achieved international success when he made his instrumental measures more accurate by using values measured on children and healthy adults. At the same time he introduced new psychometric statistical procedures. Although basically he was interested in mental phenomena and not in neurophysiology, he started brand-new research projects in Hungary, by applying new methods. This signalled the birth of Hungarian Psychology in 1899. The 29 year old psychiatrist/neurologist created an intellectual workshop which, in its structure and by the nature of research tasks, was an experimental psychological laboratory.

During the first years of this activity he was received with passive benevolence. At first his work in the field of psychology had not attracted the attention of leading intellectuals in Hungary. However, by the turn of the century Ranschburg began receiving invitations from renowned institutions and his findings relative to psychiatric patients attracted the attention of Hungarian and international specialists. Naturally, Ranschburg had been influenced by the scientific community of Europe: his psychiatric mentality had been affected by the French school, Charcot and Janet, while his psychopathological approach was presumably affected by the German scientists of his age.

On December 6, 1902 his laboratory was attached to the system of state-administered remedial institutions, thanks to the efforts of remedial educator Artúr

Sarbó and head of the section for remedial education at the Ministry of Religious and Public Education Dr Sándor Náray Szabó. To understand this decision one has to have an insight into the historical developments of his age. In our days it is easy to detect all the consequences and implications this decision had on the development of psychology in Hungary. From 1903 up to 1928 Ranschburg was the director of the Royal Hungarian Laboratory for Remedial Psychology and a full-time lecturer at the State Remedial Teachers' Training College. By the turn of the century the system of social institutions had been established, and the integration of his laboratory into this system determined both his personal fate and the future development of Hungarian psychology, and within that the development of criminal psychology. As you can see, Hungarian psychology was given birth within the realms of pedagogy and remedial education.

"Ranschburg found an atmosphere in almost every stratum of Hungarian scientific culture that evaluated him according to his merits and import thus offering him appreciation and support." wrote his first proponent Dr János Schnell in 1928, who later became his successor as the director of his laboratory. "After this decision his educational activity points to pedagogy as this field appears to be open to the problems of psychology. Remedial education, apart from demonstrating receptivity to psychology, also needed to expand the insight into its subject matter in order to meet the requirements of society – and this is where Ranschburg made a meaningful contribution."

In his decision one can detect elements of the existing social structure that I consider to be crucially important for the development of criminal psychology. Obviously, this is supposed to mean that this decision amounts to a paradigm in the interrelation of society and psychology. What are the elements in question?

(1) Elementary public education;

(2) Development, differentiation and expansion of pedagogy: remedial education (talent enhancement);

(3) The system of social institutions related to pedagogy: (a) pedagogical societies, (b) spontaneous organisations focusing on children, (c) children-specific social institutions (child protection, court of guardians, juvenile court, penalty execution, correction system).

(1) The bill on *comprehensive public education* was submitted to parliament by baron József Eötvös in 1868, one year after the Compromise with Austria. The resulting law opened the way for a general system of education and the establishment of a network of state-owned elementary schools. The standardisation of public primary education widened the scope of behavioural attitudes governed by society. Through the mediation of educators the state established a contact with some layers in the society that had remained previously untouched by societal influences prior to their adulthood. As a result, the introduction of public education led to the restructuring of society. It is easy to see the validity of this statement. Let us take an example. The school as an institution keeps track of all

the stages of the development of the personality of children. The mere requirement of daily attendance gave rise to a previously unknown phenomenon: *truancy*. This form of behaviour has more to it than mere misdemeanour – all the more so as the law to punish parents for not sending children to school was enacted only in 1921 – among others it draws the attention to the problems of personality development of children.

(2) *Compulsory public education*, with the standardisation of the curriculum and requirements, inevitably leads to a differentiation among children based on their skills. This differentiation is not the invention of pedagogy, i.e. schooling, but a characteristic of self-fulfilment. The process of self-fulfilment may take place in either social or antisocial, normal or abnormal conditions and draws the attention to a layer of child population that needs treatment to ensure their development. Thus, alongside elementary education there emerge *the institutions of remedial education*. Right from the beginning the task of educating the so-called morally retarded, as a correctional pedagogical task, was delegated to the remedial network. At the turn of the century two terms were used in this connection: moral *mental retardation* and *moral desertedness*, though their diagnosis was later to be refined with the advent of public education. Both of these conditions were originally brought under control of the social functions of pedagogy without sanctioning the parents responsibility, although present legal regulations do not ignore implications of such cases on parents either. The status of moral mental retardation is the last of the remains of the distorted personality development concept of the 19th century when any antisocial or asocial behavioural attitudes were put down as forms of the moral mental retardation of the child. In this state the development of the moral mentality and that of social sympathy is impeded to such an extent that the individual is rendered incapable of complying with social rules. This concept is based upon the assumption that criminal behaviour in such cases is basically determined by internal inclinations. Moral desertedness is a condition in which a child is denied even the minimum education needed to get to the specific phases of natural self-restraint and moral development. Classification into any of the two categories is accomplished through diagnostic methods and envisages differing treatment procedures of education. One can easily detect the psychological needs of remedial education here.

(3) The standardisation of public elementary education and the numerical increase of educators resulted in the establishment and consolidation of the *pedagogical community*. Through its self-organisation, scientific and social functions and due to its numerical strength alone, this community became one of the most important professional strata of Hungarian society. The setting up of the Jewish *National Association of Teachers* marks the beginning of the process of self-organisation, well before the drafting of the Eötvös bill. The legal status of state-financed educators, teachers and university lecturers became systematically regulated in 1927, thanks to the functioning of professional associations. The pan-denominational Alliance of Teacher Associations was brought about only later in the late

twenties. The first Pedagogical Society was organised in 1878, and the first entry in its programme quoted the promotion of psychology as one of its prime objectives. On its termination the Hungarian Pedagogical Society was founded in 1891 to enhance the cultivation of pedagogy and related scientific research in the Hungarian language, first of all by giving a theoretical and scientific overview of instructional and educational activity in Hungary. The society published a periodical under the title *Magyar Paedagógia* (Hungarian Pedagogy). The society also had a department concentrating on criminal pedagogy.

It was also in this same period that the legal and social institutions for child and youth care brought into existence. Child care was shaping amongst national peculiarities that definitely made the child protection movement more colourful but this fact also weakened its influence. Up to 1892 child protection was considered to be a local duty, it was in this year that the state took over some of these duties, as in the case of abandoned and found children. This commenced the creation of the child protection network. In 1901 the right of abandoned children to state protection under the age of fifteen was granted by law. Up to 1919 this task had been assigned to the Ministry of the Interior, later it was delegated to the Ministry of Welfare and Labour.

The Act of 1925 already differentiated between *material and moral desertedness*. Moral desertedness is stated if the child under the age of fifteen is exposed to the danger of moral deterioration as a result of neglecting education or the detrimental influence of the environment with the exception of cases when there is a reformatory court ruling against the child in question.

The state of desertedness is proclaimed by the *Orphans' Court*. The preconditions of assigning a child to a reformatory home is officially regulated, the society at large, however, has a wide range of competence to initiate such an action. The Orphans' Court is an independent administrative body brought about during the course of legal development in Hungary, and has the mission to give all kind of protection and care to underage children and children under guardianship. The Orphans' Court is also assigned the task of guardians' court. In most countries these duties are delegated to the court of law. In Hungary the situation is different inasmuch as the Orphans' Court is an administrative unit, although not without the characteristics of a legal court. Each county and city had an Orphans' Court of its own, this network was abolished only after World War II. The Orphans' Court closely cooperated with the school network.

In the beginning the *Court of Guardians* comprised a number of institutions. These were administrative units at state and local government level with supervisory and executive roles regarding underage children and children under guardianship. Related duties could be partially addressed in each settlement throughout the country via the notary's office or the so-called village principle, this was to become a standardised authority only later.

It would be a futile effort to try to understand the social and legal development of this period without taking into account the role of Hungarian pedology (child study). In Hungary it was László Nagy who gave dynamism to this movement. As is known pedology focuses on the complex knowledge about the nature and development of children. Its primary interest is the child's personality and its development. Ranschburg was attracted to the movement quite early. His reset drew him even closer to child study, as a matter of fact the Hungarian Society for Child Study elected him chairman of its Experimental Section. Pedology played a crucial role in the development of Hungarian psychology on two accounts. Ranschburg was to be the first factor and Mérei the other one. Although with his book *Gyermektanulmány* (Child Study) Ferenc Mérei promoted the concept of pedology to the status of a fundamental principle for pedagogical psychology, in 1949, at the time of the personality cult, pedology was labelled 'class alien' approach, and this was the ideological reasoning for the elimination of psychological research in Hungary.

Western legal patterns undoubtedly had a role in shaping the legal practice and regulation of children and juvenile courts and their correctional system but we cannot ignore the role of Hungarian development either which, through its scientific attitudes and postures, significantly influenced both the process of legislation and execution. The *Büntető Novella*, published in 1908, defined the penal age content of childhood and juvenile age. Childhood is up to the age of 12, juvenile age is between 12 and 18, after 18 one is considers to be an adult from legal point of view (one notable exception was that death penalty was not to be passed on individuals under 20).

The *Büntető Novella* stated that personality traits of juvenile and adult offenders did not significantly differ. In the case of juvenile offenders, however, decent environment and moral education could counterbalance the effects of rough living conditions, bad examples, budding instincts thus hampering their criminal inclinations. The *Büntető Novella* defined the set of applicable penalties: reprimand, probation, reformatory education, minimum security incarceration.

Another stage of progress, as far as underage offenders are considered, began in 1913 with the establishment of *juvenile courts*. These courts dealt not only with offences committed by children and juvenile offenders but also acted as supervisory bodies in cases of anti-juvenile behaviour. The protection of the interests of juvenile offenders was decreed by law. It prescribed collecting information on the personality, mental and moral level, living conditions of the juvenile offender, together with a report from a medical expert. The need for a psychological report is not yet mentioned but this is hardly a surprise considering the lack of psychological experts. The involvement of remedial educators in drawing up expert reports is sporadic. In most cases juveniles are assigned to reformatory homes by court decrees. It is the remedial educators that are trained to work at these reformatory homes. Interest in psychology emerges in the appropriate sections of the scientific circles of psychology-related sciences.

The first exception is the Ranschburg laboratory. Ranschburg recruited people from various fields into his laboratory. Two of his subordinates showed a lasting interest in the problems of criminal psychology, they are Margit Révész and Júlia György. Júlia György's book is an integral part of contemporary psychological literature.

In his research project on "the criminal psychology of the mentally retarded", prior to 1904, Ranschburg examined the psychological problems of giving testimony. He studied the proportion of false statements, difference in reactions according to sex, the number of hesitant answers, the problems of suggestibility. At the request of courts he and his two colleagues he made a somatic and psychiatric examination of a great number of deserted juveniles and underage offenders before World War I. Relying on his experience thus accumulated, the then minister of the interior asked him to set up the guidelines for a professional examination and observation of such children. The product of his work was given out to doctors at child protection institutions with the practical result of the introduction of a standardised registration sheet and an observation sheet. Ranschburg reflected on his experiences in a lecture delivered at the *International Congress on Correction*, which was held in Budapest in 1905. He emphasised the need for a somatic and psychiatric examination of juveniles prior to their placement in reformatory homes and that teachers at such institutions should have appropriate remedial education and pedagogical training, or they should at least do a special course on psychopathological issues related to children. Mentally retarded and psychopathic juvenile offenders should be accommodated in institutions led by psychiatrists. The congress approved his suggestions.

By the beginning of the 1910s based on a vast amount of experiments and empirical experience Ranschburg initiates a typology of juvenile offenders and sets up two categories for them: the psychically normal and abnormal categories. He comes to the conclusion that many of the children with criminal inclinations come from good family background and in about half of these cases criminality is generated on an inner constitutional basis. He arranges pathological cases into the following fundamental groups: 1) offenders with psychopathic inclinations, 2) mentally challenged offenders, mostly morally retarded, 3) mentally ill offenders. He emphasises that all forms of desertedness and abandonment tend to push every child and juvenile, even if they are originally normal, into the state of acquired mental and physical degeneration, but this can be cured through proper remedial education.

In 1914 he published *The psychological basics of the pathology and remedial education of abandoned juveniles*, which in actual fact was an edited collection of his lectures delivered for judges at juvenile courts. Together with Margit Révész he gave an analysis of a specified range of mental faculties of the morally retarded, with special regard to their memory skills, arithmetic performance, etc. His research included matters related to their manageability as well, and he expounded that new approaches were needed in cases where intervention ameliorated the prospects for improvement. He also gave an account of some cases when he worked with neurosurgeon Lobmayer, in particular of a treatment applied to a 15 year old vagrant.

Ranschburg was of the supporters and proponents of the Hungarian Psychological Society. The founding meeting of this society took place on February 24, 1928. Its constitution defined three basic courses of action: (1) *from the angle of universal science* – cultivate all fields of both pure (theoretical) psychological research and its applied branches together with the bordering and overlapping areas adjoining other branches of sciences; (2) *from the angle of Hungarian science* – (a) enhance Hungarian psychology, (b) maintain diverse and systematic research, (c) promote the standardisation of psychological terminology in Hungarian literature; (3) *from the angle of practical life and general culture* – (a) put into practice as widely as possible all the justified theorems of psychology, (b) intensify links with other countries.

In 1932 the Society, being dissatisfied with its results in the implementation of its objectives, submitted an *Elaboratum* to the leaders of the Ministry of Culture and in fact to many key figures and institutions of the Hungarian political and cultural life. The *Elaboratum*, apart from giving emphasis to the role of psychology in the protection of the nation, gives an account of the major areas where "a practical implementation of the findings of psychology" are desirable, making specific references as to the applicability of criminal psychology. The document elaborates on the practical possibilities for the application of psychology and makes a number of recommendations, among others to set up psychological sections at the arts faculties of universities; to enhance psychological training for educators and school doctors; to integrate psychology into the curriculum of medical, engineering and legal training; to establish university faculties of psychology and to set up a central institute of psychology. The Society operated a department for criminal psychology, and later in 1938 the department for practical psychology also included the cultivation of certain problems of criminal psychology into its programme of action.

At this time practical activity was carried out by the Laboratory for Remedial Psychology (under the direction of Dr János Schnell and later Lipót Szondi) and by the State Remedial Carrier and Education Advice Centre. In fact the Advice Centre was the only official institution where juridical experts operated. Its constitution was approved in 1933. The advisory activity was done by a team of 24 doctors, psychologists, educators with psychological and mental hygienic training. One of their three areas of activity was giving expert advice for courts and orphans' courts in cases of divorce and penal proceedings, alongside juvenile courts. Some non-official advice centres were also involved in similar activities, such as the Charite Poliklinik, the Buda Ambulatorium, the Apponyi Poliklinik, the National Association for Private Employees, the advisory centre of the National Association for Family Protection, the Workers' Association for Child Protection. As far as structural matters are concerned no changes took place quite up to the end of World War II. Tasks related to giving expert reports on psychiatric and mental matters in the case of adult offenders were completed by psychiatrists, sometimes with the help of psychologists.

Juridical psychology was shaped through publications on practical experience, lectures and printed articles. This area of psychology brought no unified theoretical concepts or new methods up to the appearance of Dr Lipót Szondi's fate-analytical geno-test. His activity marked a major contribution to the development of criminal psychology. When he took the leadership of the Laboratory he set up a research team of famous Hungarian psychologists. This research group remained active even after they were dispersed following the emigration of Szondi. *Fate analysis* is a mutation of psychoanalytical depth psychology, which introduced the concept of the family unconscious alongside the individual and collective unconscious. Its line of thought was determined by a combination of biology and psychology. According to this theory human behaviour is a series of decisions, in other words choices. Human behaviour is based on several possibilities and is characteristics are predominantly shaped by the subconscious and not by the environment. The subconscious is driven by instincts that are inherited from the two parents. Inheritance is present in two forms shaping the phenotype and the genotype of the individual. Dominant genes determine the phenotype, the personality traits, while latent genes determine the choices. Szondi's theory calls this choice tropism. Thus our major choices are influences by the latent genes, in such crucial areas of life as choosing friends, love, profession, choices of psychic anomaly. He did an extensive family research to verify his propositions. He examined the personality traits of married couples in crisis by studying their family trees to gain information about the ascending line of both the husband and the wife. He found the results astonishing: characteristics that were non-manifest in the couples appeared to be significantly frequent in their families. Szondi considered the presence of these personality traits in the ascending line to be genotypical. The genotypical traits were not manifest in the characteristics of the couple in crisis but influenced their choice of partners. He focused the psychological essence of this phenomenon on *manifestations of sympathy*, he explored the latent instincts by showing photos and sympathy preference tests. He chose photos of 48 mentally ill people, who underwent thorough psychiatric analysis with reliable documentation and mostly with materials published in case studies. He looked at mental illnesses as manifestations of shaping fate that in phenotypical cases explore the inherent tendencies in the manifest and latent instincts of the person under examination. Using the syndromes and illness categories of psychopathology and attaching them to the practical evaluation of the test, Szondi drew up a new system of personality. Quite unusually for his time he used a vast amount of samples and worked out a psycho-diagnostic evaluation system, comprising all problems starting from job aptitude to an attempt to have a deeper understand of criminality. The test in question is still one of the most widespread psycho-diagnostic procedures. A number of important representatives of Hungarian psychology was a colleague of Szondi, like Ferenc Mérei, István Benedek, László Noszlopy, etc. The criminal psychological indicators of the test were elaborated by István Benedek. This research was the most comprehensive project of Hungarian criminal psychology. At present it is used only for diagnostic purposes.

The psychological environment in the wider sense significantly improved in the 1930s. It was in this period of time when the Psychological Institute was established at the Pázmány Péter University of Sciences, psychological faculties were set up at other universities and, through a specialisation of the Royal Hungarian Laboratory for Remedial Psychology, there emerged the Institute for Child Psychology that played an important role in the history of psychology and later the Psychological Institute of the Hungarian Academy of Sciences.

The Society, the major contributor to Hungarian psychology, made its weight felt basically through scientific section meetings, research support and publications. Unfortunately, its scientific session planned for the end of March, 1944 was never to be convened as a result of the German occupation. Because of this event, the wartime activities on the territory of Hungary and the Russian occupation of the country at the end of the war the Society had to suspend all its functions till December 1945. Even then, the revitalisation of the Society was not to be a lasting process for in 1948, in the so-called year of change, i.e. the Communist takeover, it had to be suspended again.

Nevertheless the short period of merely two and a quarter of a year of its functioning proved to be an active period for criminal psychology, since the people's tribunal had psychiatric and psychological examinations done when investigating war crimes. A number of psychologists were drawn in, but the bulk of the work was done by psychoanalyst psychiatrists. Sorry to say, their findings were scientifically processed and published only in sporadic cases. In my opinion István Benedek did the most meticulous work, and in true compliance with the Szondi school of thought. For the sake of illustration let us analyse the descendent table he compiled for one his cases (Figure 1).

The case involves a Hungarian Nazi mass murderer, the first to be executed for war crimes, whose family tree verifiably goes back to a great grandfather who was a gendarme in the previous century. The "instinct content" of the family tree was identical to the instinct formula of a war criminal. The two sons of the gendarme were so-called 'persecutors', and as members of the law enforcement authorities their job was to catch and torture offenders. Szondi also indicated the profession of his client's descendants and in-laws on the family tree. There are a number of soldiers, gendarmes, spies – among them a high-ranking arrow-cross mass murderer. The other half of the family tree shows a line of paranoid in-laws, people with persecution complex or religious fanatics, thus we have a line of persecutors, parallelled by a line of persecuted people. According to the theorem, the dominance of the two contradictory instinct properties is determined by the actual possibilities that open up: if the persecutor is given power, he might become a mass murderer; if he is not, he might become a persecuted psychopath – a paranoid.

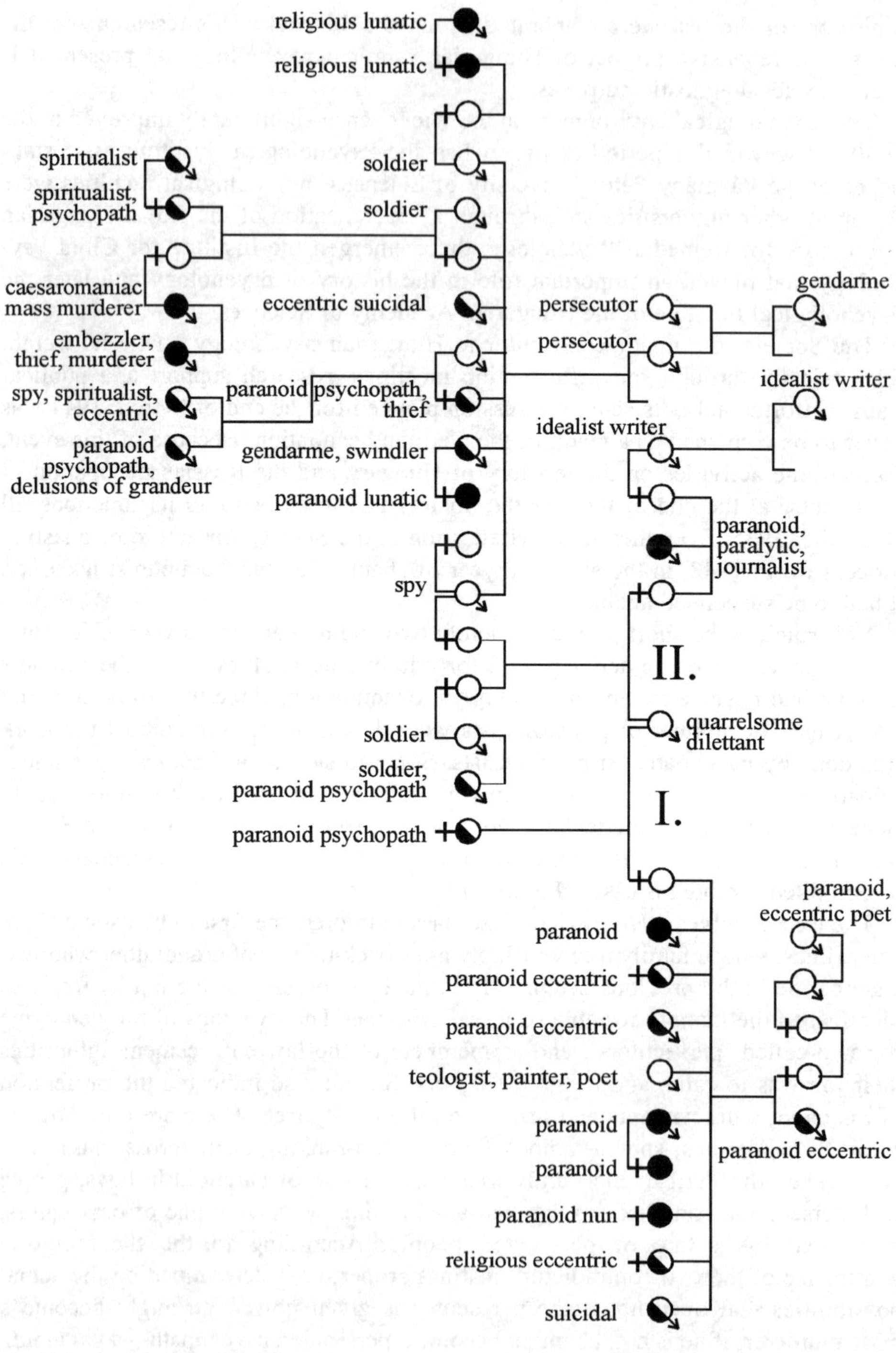

Figure 1: A paranoid family of persecutors and persecuted, creative and dilettant personalities

Within the room of manoeuvre left open by the cultural policy after 1948 the Marxist-Communist psychologists in actual fact supplied "theoretical" help for the ruling political power in deforming psychology with regard to both content and structure. This process of transformation that unilaterally focused on national traditions led to the elimination of psychology proper but later also of its transformed version. The main thrust of psychology was redirected to the child study approach, and the complex and differentiated training and research framework of the pre-1945 times was pushed back to pedagogy. But then even the new set-up was doomed to crisis due to the anti-pedology resolution of the Communist Party of the Soviet Union in 1936. At the time of the conceptual trials from 1949 Hungarian psychology as such ceased to exist, even Marxist-communist psychologists were held in house arrest. Psychology training was abolished psychology disappeared from everyday life. It was remedial education again that could offer some safe haven, under the leadership of Dr Gusztáv Bárczi. Remedial education, with its diversity of approaches remained present in society, and psychology was made presentable by getting partially infiltrated by the concept of Pavlovian nervism and thus was integrated into the curriculum of teacher trainees through the agency of the head of psychology faculty and his assistant, Lajos Kardos and Béla Radnai. This level of representation for psychology was considered inevitable even from official point of view, taking into account that the still existing institutions for child and juvenile protection remained under the aegis of remedial education. Quite up to 1956 there existed only one institution offering training in criminal psychology and field work to gain practical experience. It was appropriate faculty of the Remedial Teachers' Training College. The head of this faculty was Vera Roboz Groák and her colleague Margit Noszlopyné Vég, both one time students of Szondi. Unfortunately for criminal psychology and pedagogy both professor Roboz Groák and her assistant had to leave the country in the aftermath of the 1956 revolution. The scientific seminar meetings and consultations with them are still among my nicest memories of my studies.

After the period of personal cult the reorganisation of psychology took a start with the activity of the Psychology Committee of the Hungarian Academy of Sciences under the leadership of paediatrician professor Pál Gegesi Kiss. Before 1945 the Hungarian Psychological Society published two periodicals: the *Lélektani tanulmányok* (Studies in Psychology) and the *Magyar Pszichológiai Szemle* (Hungarian Psychological Review).

The first signs of revival are the Institute of Child Psychology and the Studies in Psychology. After 1960 the process of revival gains fresh impetus. Psychology training is resumed, for some time within a training scheme based on three major subjects, the Society is reorganised, and the Hungarian Psychological Review is restarted as a monthly periodical. Psychology is gaining weight at a rate never seen before, especially in areas such as health care, administration of justice, penalty execution, etc.

The status of the psychologist's diploma is legally regulated, new university faculties are opened, special training is started in the following categories: clinical adult psychologist, child psychologist, educational psychologist and labour psychologist.

From 1970 onwards the criminal investigation authorities, courts in general and later the courts of guardians ever more often consult psychologists. The increased demand for expert advice in juridical psychology encouraged the Ministry of Justice to regulate psychological expert activities. They set up a list of professional experts to filter out incompetence and employed psychologists at juridical medical institutions, university institutions and departments. Appropriate preparation was ensured by the psychology act of 1976 and professional training. From 1958 psychiatric institutes employed psychologists in growing numbers: remedial educators for patient treatment, psycho-diagnostics, individual and group psychotherapic activities.

The Laboratory for Clinical Psychology of the National Neurological and Mental Institute (led by Ferenc Mérei quite up to the time he went on old age pension) has played a dominant role in the development of clinical psychology since 1963. The setting up of Clinical Psychology Faculty at the Institute of Medical Further Training was a follow-up of this development.

As for the present situation of criminal psychology we also have to take into account another development of social-scientific nature, namely the founding of the Hungarian Psychiatric Society. This fact indicated the emancipation of the profession within the neurological sciences, by "peeling off" from the main body of neurology.

Through the agency of its psychotherapic section the Hungarian Psychiatric Society naturalised psychotherapic techniques within a decade. It was in the wake of this development that psychologists working at penal establishments were offered a chance to apply the latest correctional procedures along with the traditional remedial methods and educational procedures.

In spite of this rapid development the activity of juridical and criminal psychologists is still fragmented. There are two scientific-social organisations comprising in these areas: the Criminology Section of the Hungarian Psychological Society and the Psychiatric and Clinical Psychology Team within the Hungarian Scientific Association of Juridical Doctors under the aegis of the Hungarian General Practitioners' Association. The first organisation has been operational since 1978, the other one since 1985. This divergence is due to the peculiar Hungarian development. With the support of the Juridical Medical Institute of the Medical University the latter of the two organisations launched a project to work out the theory, sort out the subject matter and optimise the methods of juridical psychology. At the Clinical Psychology Team we have been organising basic and professional exam prep courses for clinical psychologists and juridical mental specialists who have to give expert opinion.

The current system of juridical criminal psychology in Hungary is as follows:

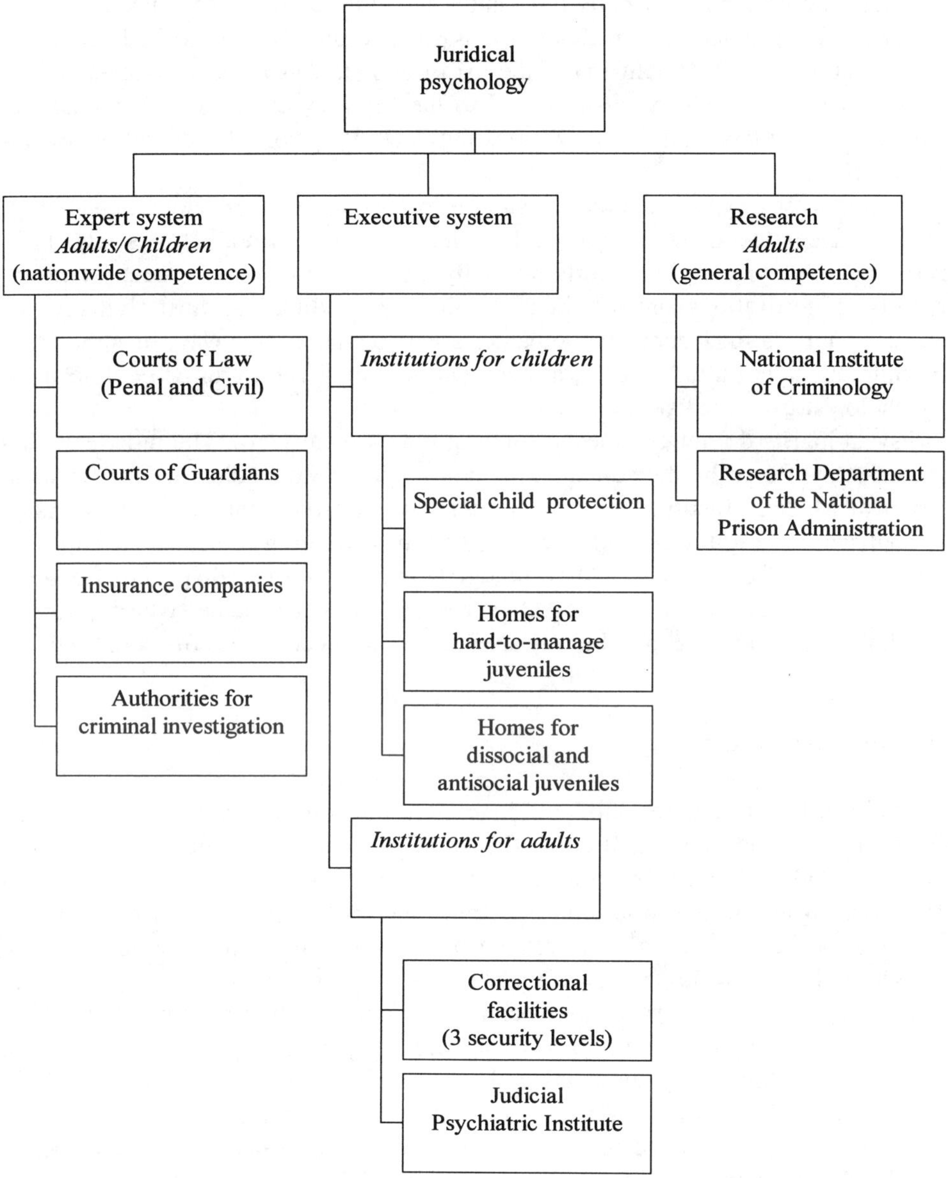

Figure 2: The institutional system of Hungarian juridical criminal psychology

I. Expert system

Juridical psychologists normally have adult and child clinical specialised training. Specialised psychologist qualification is a precondition to being rolled up on the expert list. Up to 1994 inclusion in the list of experts was decided by court chairmen, in 1995 this right was transferred to the Ministry of Justice. Previously an expert had only local authority, whereas the new regulation offered national competence.

In most cases experts operate as such in part-time, with the exception of psychologists employed by the juridical medical institutions and offices who have full-time employment. The courts normally and the police always request expert reports via institutions and offices in criminal proceedings, in most civil actions, and assignments for insurance companies are also granted this way. In some cases of child allocation after divorce, assignment may be given by directly choosing a psychologist from the list of experts.

Psychologists do not get special training for juridical work. The most essential guidance is offered by the so-called methodological letters edited by the National Juridical Medical Institute, training is done in one-week annual courses. As to specialised training the recently approved form of training indicates an improvement. Starting from next year, psychologists may get a second specialist qualification in the framework of a so-called further training scheme, where juridical psychology and criminal psychology are among the special areas offered.

II. Executive system

Specialised institutions for child and juvenile protection fall into three categories. There are (a) homes for neurotics, (b) homes for juveniles with manageability problems and (c) homes for dissocial and antisocial juveniles. Educators and psychologists working at institutions belonging the groups (b) and (c) get criminal psychological and pedagogical training as well. Normally those juveniles of 12-18 are sent to homes for juveniles with manageability problems who are exempt from school attendance because of antisocial tendencies, or they are transferred here from other reformatory institutions or they are assigned here when taken into care of the state. Homes for dissocial and antisocial juveniles accommodate those young people of 14 to 18 who clearly demonstrate dissocial and antisocial tendencies, who are referred to reformatory institutions by court decree for some crime, or whose behaviour and actions do not comply with the norms of social coexistence. These are closed institutions where legal regulations allow even isolation, up to eight days. While in such institutions, the right to parental guidance and education is suspended. Family links are regulated by special rules.

III. Research

From the early 1960s standard penal establishments and the mental observation centre also employ psychologists. In 1974, partly to coordinate psychology-related activity and partly to accomplish other tasks, the National Prison Administration set up its Research Department. It had the responsibility of preparation, organisation, coordination and financing of research in prisons, but its extensive cooperation with civil research institutions added to its scope of influence. Its main thrust of activity was to prepare prison reforms. The results of these preparation were reflected in the 1979/11 Statutory Rule on penalty execution.

In 1980s the Department conducted surveys to inspect the efficiency of the penal system, they studied prison types, the applicability of offender typology, the interaction of the effects of incarceration, possibilities for the application of psychotherapy within prison conditions. Psychologists also have the task of offering psychological assistance to the prison staff. Whilst "treatment" theory is on the wane in the western countries, it is gaining ground in Hungary, due to the upswing in psychotherapy. Currently, the prime objective of the Research Department is to promote the practical implementation of the principles propagated by the Council of Europe.

References

Benedek, I. (1987). *Az ösztönök világa* (2nd ed.). Budapest: Minerva.

Dévai, F. (1913). *A mesemódszer alkalmazása a normális és abnormis gyermek tanulmányozásában.* Budapest.

Focher, L. (1921). Kísérleti és statisztikai adatok a bűnöző fiatalkorúak psychopathiájához, különös tekintettel az értelmi fejlettségre. *Orvosi Hetilap, 32-33.*

Focher, L. (1922). Ergebnisse psychiatrischer Beobachtungen an jugendlichen Verwahrlosten und Verbrechern während der letzten zwölf Jahre. *Zentralblatt f. d. ges. Neurol. u. Psych., Vol. 31.*

Focher, L. (1925). Über enuresis nocturna bei jugendlichen Verwahrlosten. *Deutsche Zeitschrift f. Nervenheilkunde, 1-2.*

György, J. (1926). Züllöttség és neurózis. In J. Schnell (Ed.), *Psychológiai Tanulmányok* (pp. 270-289). Budapest.

György, J. (1973). *A "nehezen nevelhető" gyermek* (4th ed.). Budapest: Medicina.

Hoffmann, M. (1930). A gyermeki bűnözés és a mozi. *Néptanitók Lapja,.9-10.*

H. Révész, M. (1926). A gyermekorvosok psychológiai kiképzésének kérdése. In J. Schnell (Ed.), *Psychológiai Tanulmányok* (pp. 321-324). Budapest.

Kármán E.(1922). A gyermekek erkölcsi hibái és erkölcsi betegségei. Budapest.

K. Krausz, S. (1926). Értelmi és erkölcsi elváltozások a nagyagyvelő fiatalkori szétszórt keményedése (Schilder-féle sclerosis periaxialis diffusa) folytán. In J. Schnell (Ed.), *Psychológiai Tanulmányok* (pp. 400-423). Budapest.

Lobmayer, G. (1928). Erkölcsi gyengeelméjűségszerű psychopathiás állapotok sebészeti gyógykezeléséről. In J. Schnell (Ed.), *Psychológiai Tanulmányok* (pp. 437-451). Budapest.

Németh, P. (1931). A fiatalkori bíróságaink helyzete a gyermekvédelem nemzeti szempontjaiból. *Néptanítók Lapja, 16.*

Popper, P. (1970). *A kriminális személyiségzavar kialakulása.* Budapest: Akadémia.

Ranschburg, P. (1907). Leicht Schwachsinnige als Zeugen. Budapest: EOS.

Ranschburg, P. (1907). *A züllésnek kitett, vagy züllésnek indult gyermekek megfigyelési tervezete. Útmutató.* Budapest: M. Kir. Belügyminisztérium.

Ranschburg, P. (1911). A pathológiás alkatúak züllöttsége, a gyermekkori züllöttség psychopathiája és társadalmi higiénéje. *Magyar elmeorvosi értek. évkönyve.* Budapest.

Ranschburg, P. (1913). *A fiatalkori züllöttség lélektanának, kórtanának és gyógypedagógiájának alapjai.* Budapest: Patronázs-Egyesületek Országos. Szövetsége.

Ranschburg, P. (1924). Az érzéki, értelmi és erkölcsi fogyatékosságok megelőzése az orvostudomány és a gyógypedagógia szempontjából. *Gyógypedagógiai Könyvtár, Vol. I.*

Révész, M. (1909). Kísérleti adatok az erkölcsileg züllött gyermekek psychológiájához. *Orvosi Hetilap, 2.* (Elme és idegkórtan c. melléklet).

Révész, M. (1911). Experimentelle Beitraege zur Psychologie der moralisch verkommenen Kinder. *Zeitschrift für angew. Psychol., Vol. 63.*

Révész, M. (1913). *Az erkölcsileg züllött gyermekek élettani és lélektani szempontból.*
I. Magyar Országos Gyermektanulmányi Kongresszus Naplója. Budapest.

Révész, M. (1913). Az erkölcsi elmezavar lélektani és gyógypeadagógiai szempontból. *Klinikai Füzetek.*

Révész, M. (1916). A kriminalpaedagógia lélektani alapjai. *Kriminalpaedagógiai Intézet Kiadványa, 2.*

Révész, M. (1918). Az erkölcsileg züllött gyermek javító és gyógyító nevelésének psychológiai irányelvei. In *A gyermekmentés útja.* Budapest: M. Gyermektanulmányi Társaság.

Révész, M. (1926). *Die Kanstitutionstypen der Schwererziehbaren nach Kretschmer.*

Schnell, J. (1926). A Gyógypedagógiai Psychológiai M. Kir. Laboratórium Tudományos működése egy negyedszázad alatt. In J. Schnell (Ed.), *Psychológiai Tanulmányok* (pp. 16-104). Budapest.

Szekfű, Gy. A kiegyezés kora. In B. Homan & Gy. Szekfű (Eds.), *Magyar történet* (XIX. és XX. század), Vol. VII.

Wit, B. (1918). A középiskolás ifjúság és a bűnözés. *Magyar Közlöny.*

Subject Index

Abuse
cycles of abuse, 248- 251
sexual, 10, 18, 103-106, 108-113, 118, 217, 245, 248-253, 440
Acts, 3-5, 7, 96, 154, 214, 216, 229, 344, 413-414, 423-424, 437, 444
Affective aggression, 212-214, 218, 220
Aggression
affective/expressive, 212-214, 218, 220
instrumental, 212
Aggressive crime, 265
Anger Control Training, 213

Benchmarking, 315, 317

Capital cases, 160-163, 165, 171, 176, 178-180
the Witherspoon standard, 181
the Witt standard, 181
Capital crime, 165, 180, 185
Capital punishment, 160, 163, 187, 254, 284
Child abuse, 19, 112, 250
Child protection, 7, 248, 442, 444, 446
Child study, 444, 451
Child witness, 3, 6, 8, 10, 17-19, 32, 105, 436, 439
videotechnology, 4
Cognitive Dissonance Theory, 95
Cognitive Interview, 28, 31-32, 45, 47-73
enhanced, 11
training, 52
Context
contextual factors, 106, 112
reinstatement, 53, 58, 60-63, 65, 71
Conversational rules, 11, 16-18
Conviction rate, 114, 152, 156
Correctional treatment, 315, 318, 327-328, 330-331
Credibility, 74-81, 107, 110-114, 118, 121, 131, 138, 141-142, 144-147, 250, 428

Crime
capital crime, 165, 180, 185
crime victims, 357, 365, 372
drug abuse, 213, 221, 303, 316, 388
fear of crime, 347, 350, 352, 359-364
General Theory of Crime, 213, 221
juvenile crime, 3, 34, 210, 214-216, 222, 226-228, 293-294, 298-299, 377-380, 382, 384-385, 387, 389-390, 393-395, 397-398, 432, 442, 445-447, 451, 454
media reporting, 399
organised crime, 154, 308, 408
profiling, 95, 237-239, 241, 335, 408
rape, 74, 79-81, 104, 113-116, 118-119, 155, 369, 371, 375, 379
scene of the crime, 82, 88, 93, 115, 181, 182, 238, 240, 399
sexual crime, 33-34, 248-253, 330, 371
Crime prevention, 278, 282-283, 285, 353
Criminal court, 7, 103, 109, 111-112, 439
Criminal justice, 3-4, 43, 103, 112, 130-131, 145-150, 163-164, 171, 186-193, 214-220, 285, 301-303, 309, 342, 345, 364, 383-384, 397-399, 417-418, 421, 437
Criminal law, 119, 185, 254, 261, 277, 285, 346, 397, 407, 408, 416-417, 429-430
Custody
custodial adjustment, 297, 300
custody of children, 103, 112, 188-189, 192-193, 428, 434
custody of offenders, 142, 182-183, 269, 315, 317
parental custody, 103, 112, 188-189, 192-193, 428, 434
Cycles of abuse, 248-251

Death penalty, 111, 115, 160-167, 169-173, 176-178, 184-185, 412, 416, 445
the Witherspoon standard, 181
the Witt standard, 181

Decision rule, 146, 152-159, 168
Decision-making, 112, 114, 117, 119, 152-153, 159, 161, 172, 178, 186, 324, 378, 408-409, 419
  capital cases, 160-163, 165, 171, 178-180
  conviction rate, 114, 152, 156
  judgement by blind subjects, 122-123
  jury decision rule, 146, 152-159, 168
  the Witherspoon standard, 181
  the Witt standard, 181
Depression, 190, 198, 208, 210-211, 229, 231, 262-266, 304, 369, 372-374, 386
Deprivation, 270-272, 274-276, 283, 290, 313, 388-390, 392-393
Drug abuse, 213, 221, 303, 316, 388
Drug crime
  depenalisation, 301
Drug use, 201, 301, 308

Education, 109, 135, 140, 152, 188-189, 200, 204, 206, 222, 285, 301, 303, 305, 329, 363, 366, 385, 395, 407, 418, 424, 442-445, 447, 451, 454
Encoding Specificity Principle, 61-62, 65
Enhanced cognitive interview, 11
Errors
  Fundamental Attribution Error, 97
  in interviews, 50
  omission errors, 20, 26-27, 29-31
Evidence, 3-8, 18, 20, 26, 32, 74, 76-79, 94, 105-121, 137-142, 144-151, 153, 155, 157, 160, 164-175, 177-180, 183-184, 207, 212, 227, 249-250, 256, 299, 337, 363-364, 377, 386, 403, 407-408
  expert evidence, 149-150
  medical records, 108
  via television, 3, 4, 8, 439
Expert evidence, 149-150
Expert opinion, 256, 261, 428, 434, 452
Expressive aggression, 212

False statements, 19, 67-68, 70, 104, 446
Fear of crime, 346-347, 350, 352, 359-364
Feminist group therapy, 229
Fundamental Attribution Error, 97

General Theory of Crime, 213, 221
Group therapy, 229, 231, 234, 303

Identification
  lineup identification, 54, 57-59, 404
  profiling, 95, 237-239, 241, 335, 408

Informal status, 270-271, 273-274, 276
Instrumental aggression, 290
Interview, 4-6, 8, 10-11, 13, 16-19, 22, 25-29, 31, 47, 50, 52-60, 63-74, 96, 107-108, 133-134, 150, 215, 217, 219, 232, 234, 287-289, 387, 426, 432, 439
  cognitive, 28, 31-32, 45, 47, 49, 52-53, 55, 60-68, 71-73
  interviewing children, 19-20, 32
  investigative, 52
  police, 52, 66-67, 74, 80-81
  standard, 31, 49, 62, 64, 67-68, 71, 73
  tape recorded, 4-5
  videotaped, 4
Investigative Interviewing, 52

Judicial decision-making, 112, 114, 117, 119, 152-153, 159, 161, 172, 178, 186, 324, 378, 408-409, 419
  capital cases, 160-165, 171, 178-180
  conviction rate, 114, 152, 156
  judgement by blind subjects, 122-123
  jury decision rule, 146, 152-159, 168
  the Witherspoon standard, 181
  the Witt standard, 181
Jurors, 113-117, 119-120, 138, 152-153, 155-161, 163, 170-171, 177, 181, 185-187
Jury, 3, 6-8, 19, 110, 113-120, 122, 136, 138-141, 145, 151-160, 162-168, 171-172, 175-180, 183, 185-187, 409
  conviction rate, 114, 152, 156
  decision rule, 146, 152-159, 168
  gender homogeneous juries, 115
  judgement by blind subjects, 122-123
  jurors, 113-117, 119-120, 138, 152-153, 155-161, 163, 170-171, 177, 181, 185-187
  jury selection, 154, 163, 171
  the Witherspoon standard, 181
  the Witt standard, 181
Justice system
  criminal, 3, 4, 43, 103, 112, 130-131, 145, 149-150, 163-164, 171, 186-187, 193, 214, 217, 220, 285, 301-303, 309, 342, 345, 364, 383-384, 397-399, 417-418, 421, 437
  juvenile, 214-216, 377-378, 384, 398
Juvenile crime, 3, 34, 210, 214-216, 228, 384-385, 387, 389-390, 393-395, 397-398, 432, 442, 445-447, 451, 454
Juvenile justice system, 214-216, 377-378, 384, 398